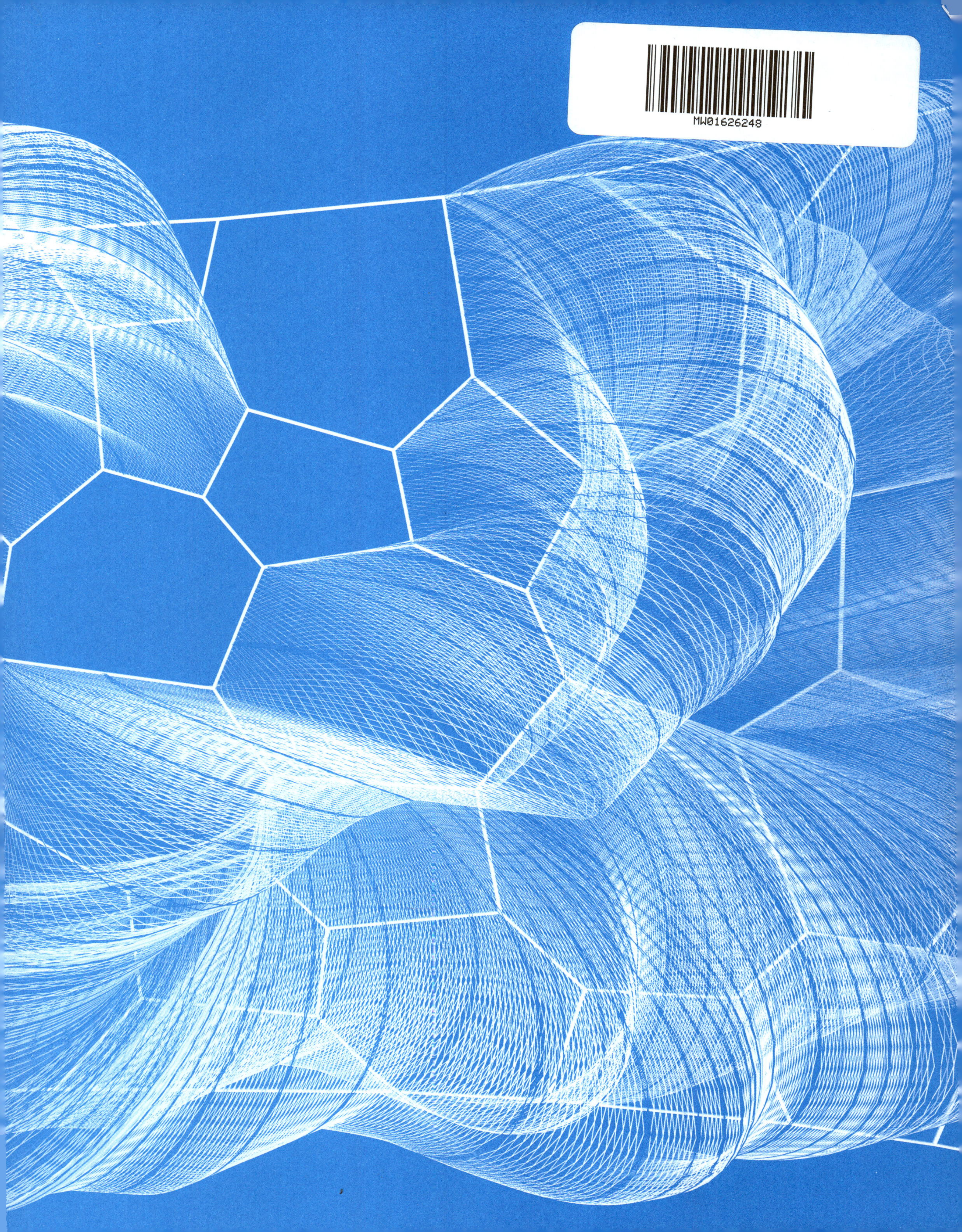

MW01626248

Radical Softness

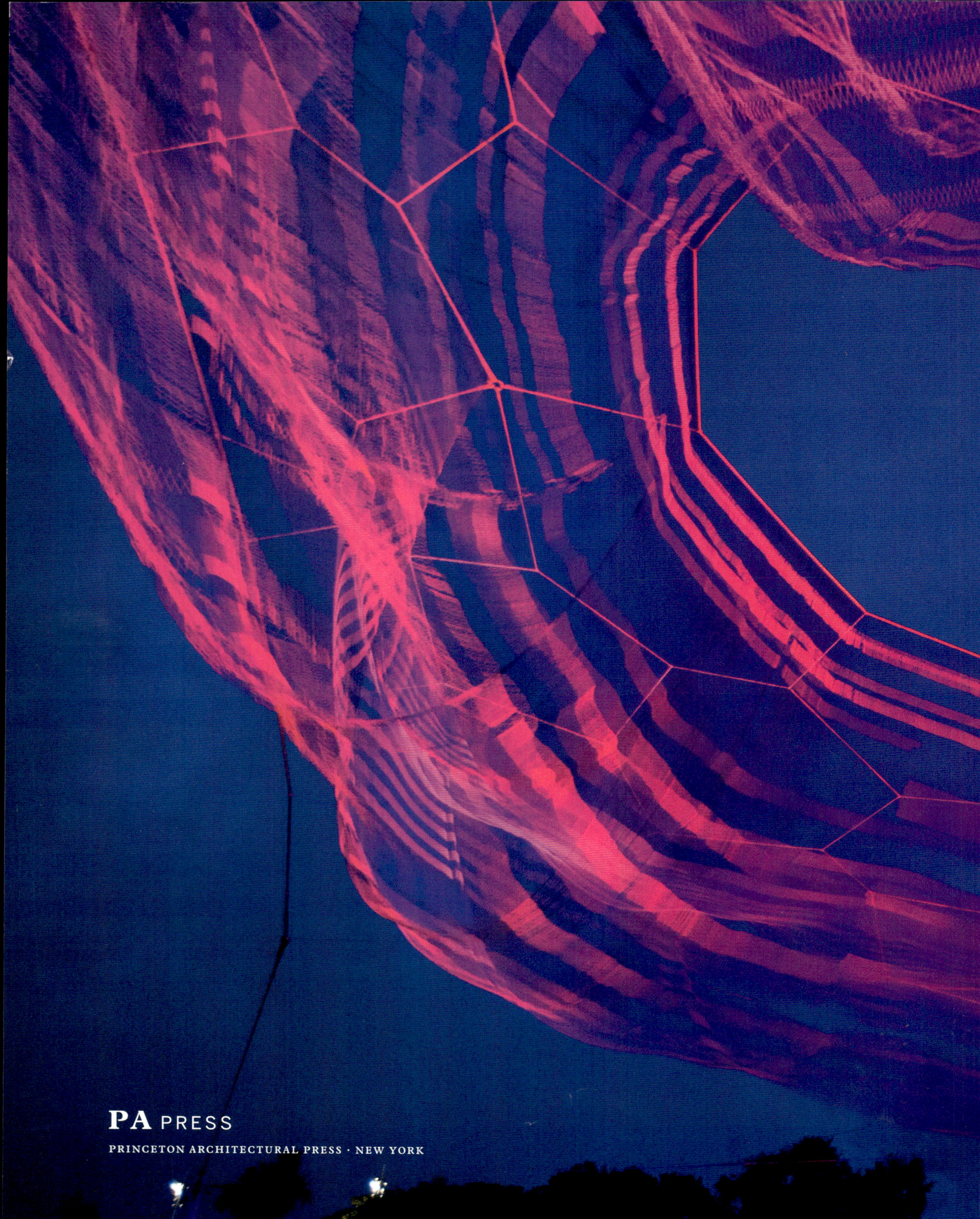
PA PRESS

PRINCETON ARCHITECTURAL PRESS · NEW YORK

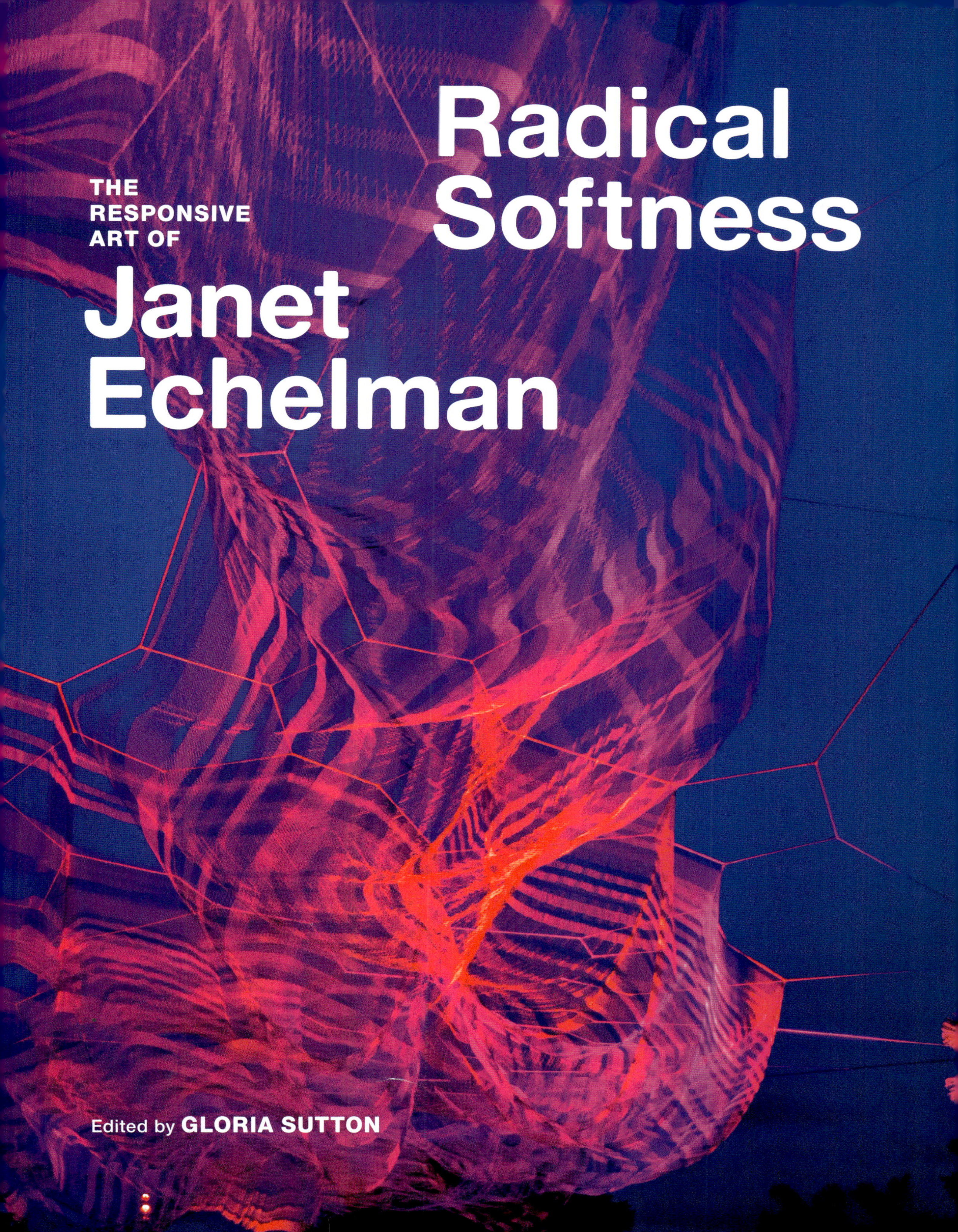

Radical Softness

THE RESPONSIVE ART OF

Janet Echelman

Edited by **GLORIA SUTTON**

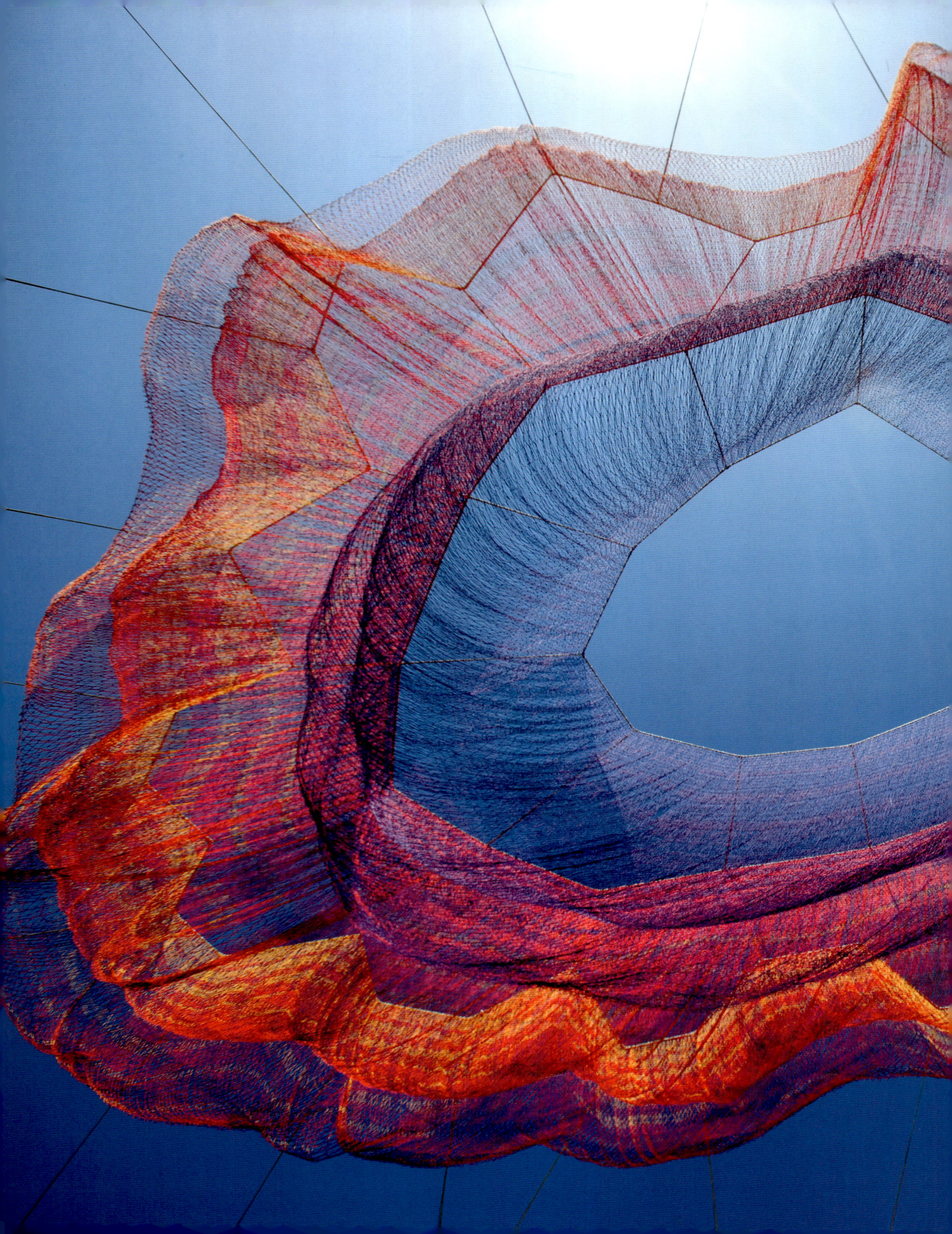

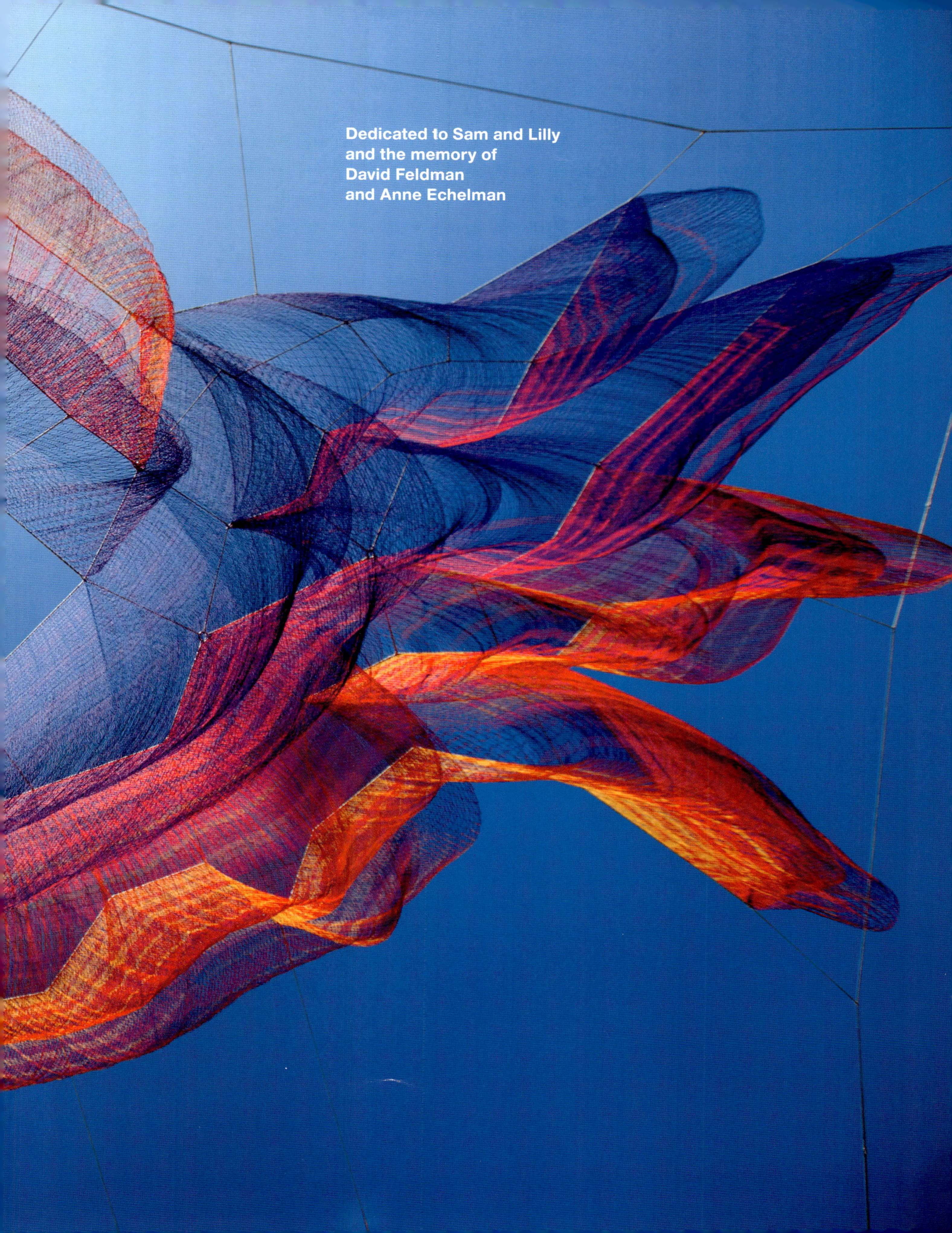

Dedicated to Sam and Lilly
and the memory of
David Feldman
and Anne Echelman

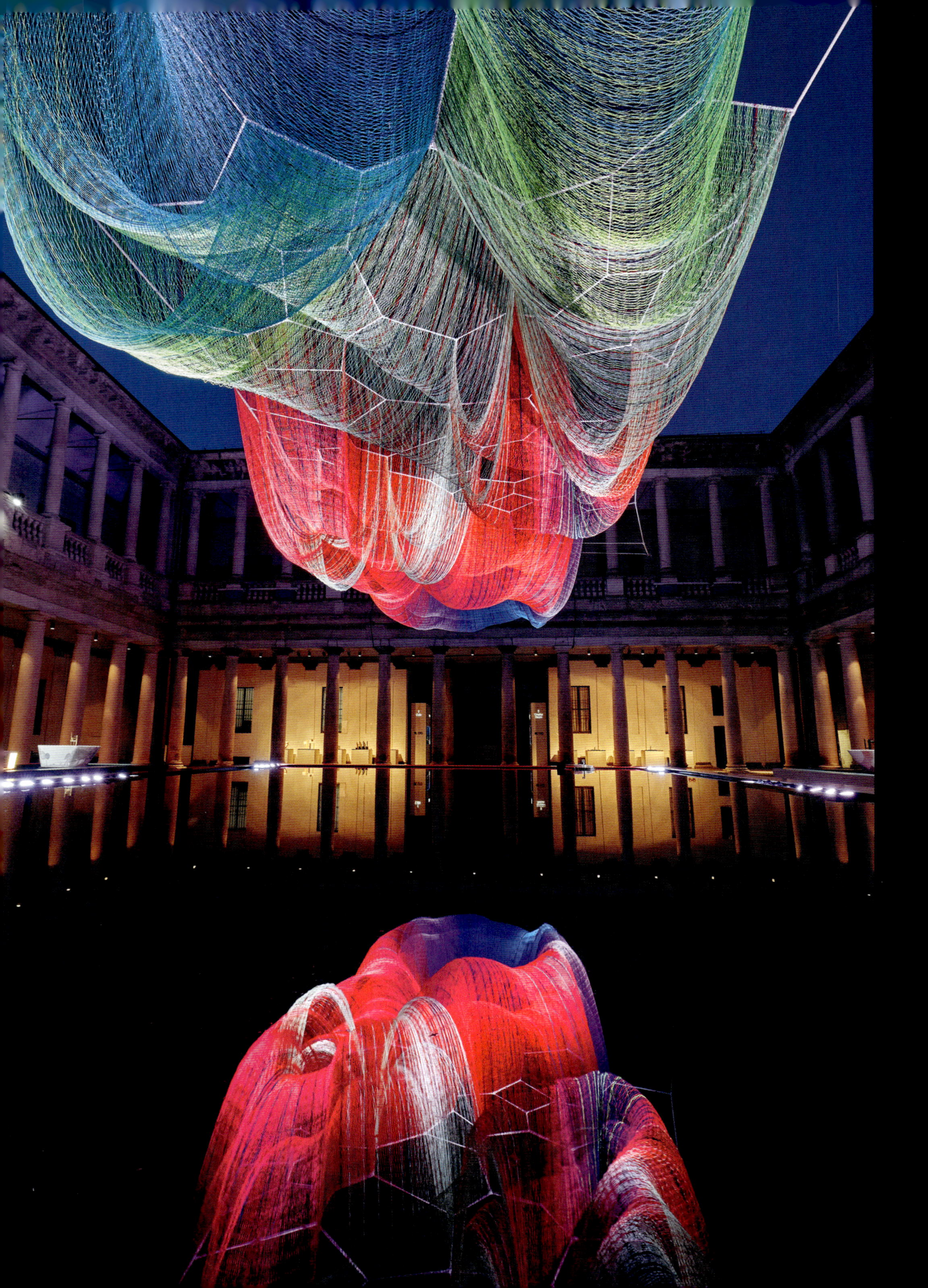

Contents

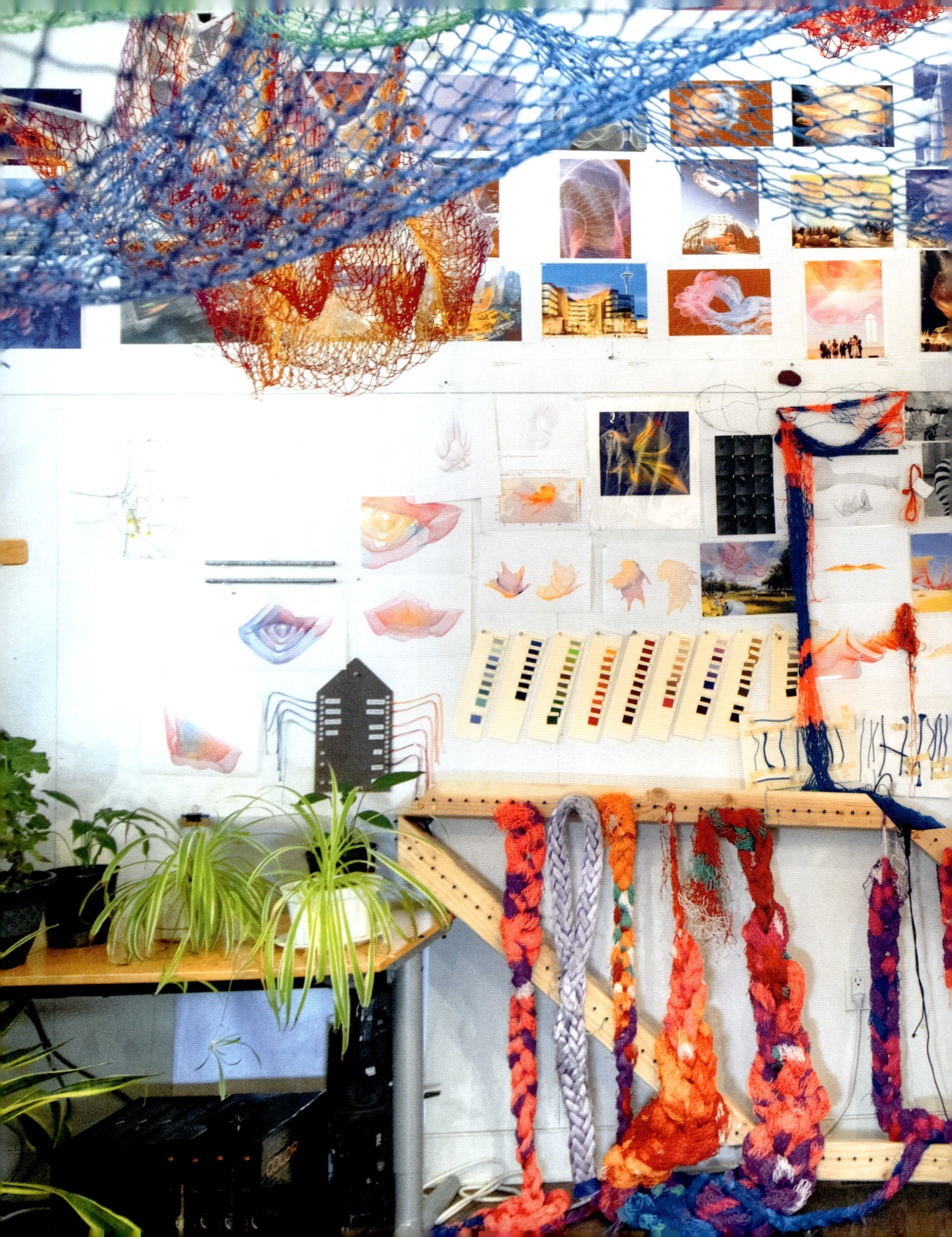

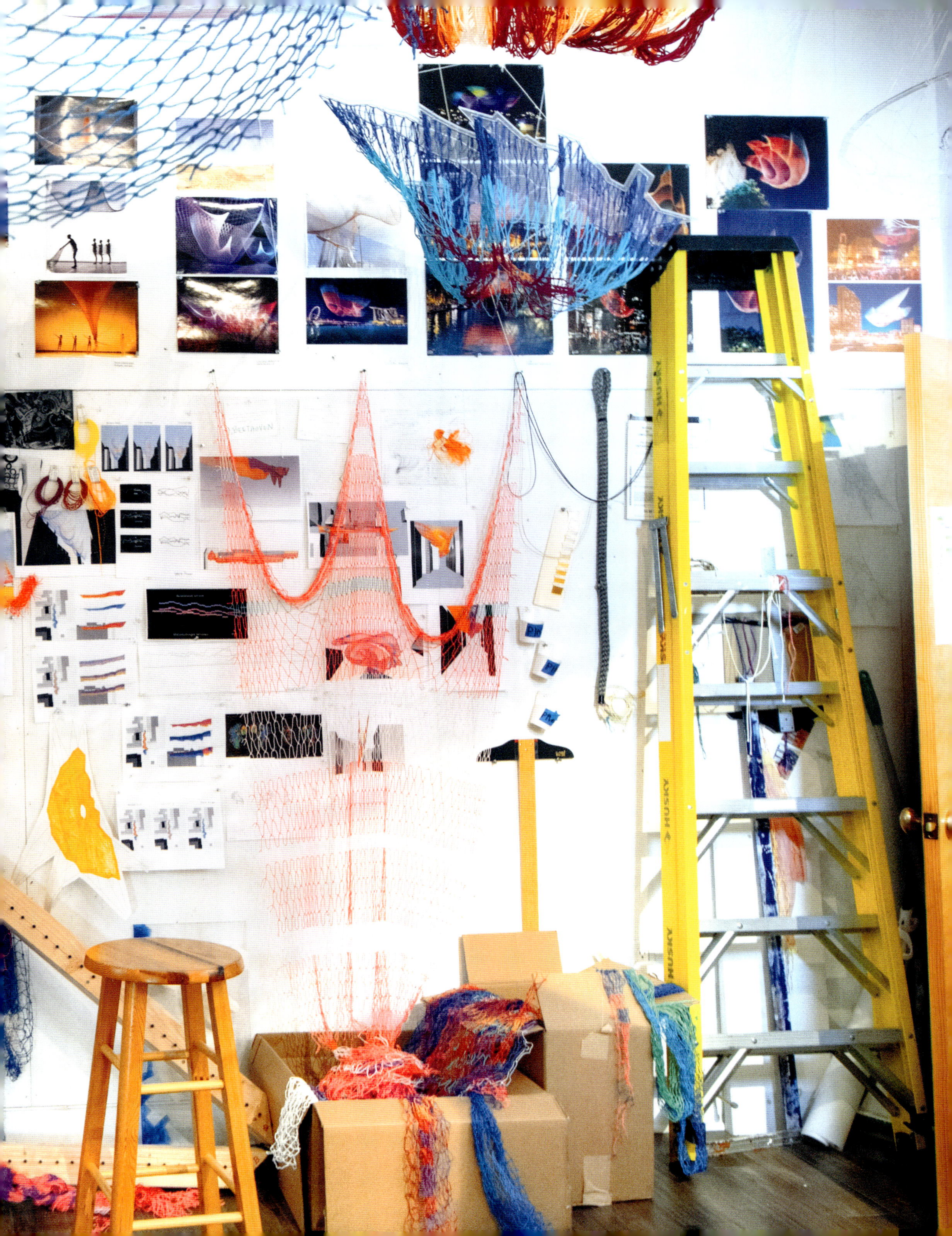
HUSKY

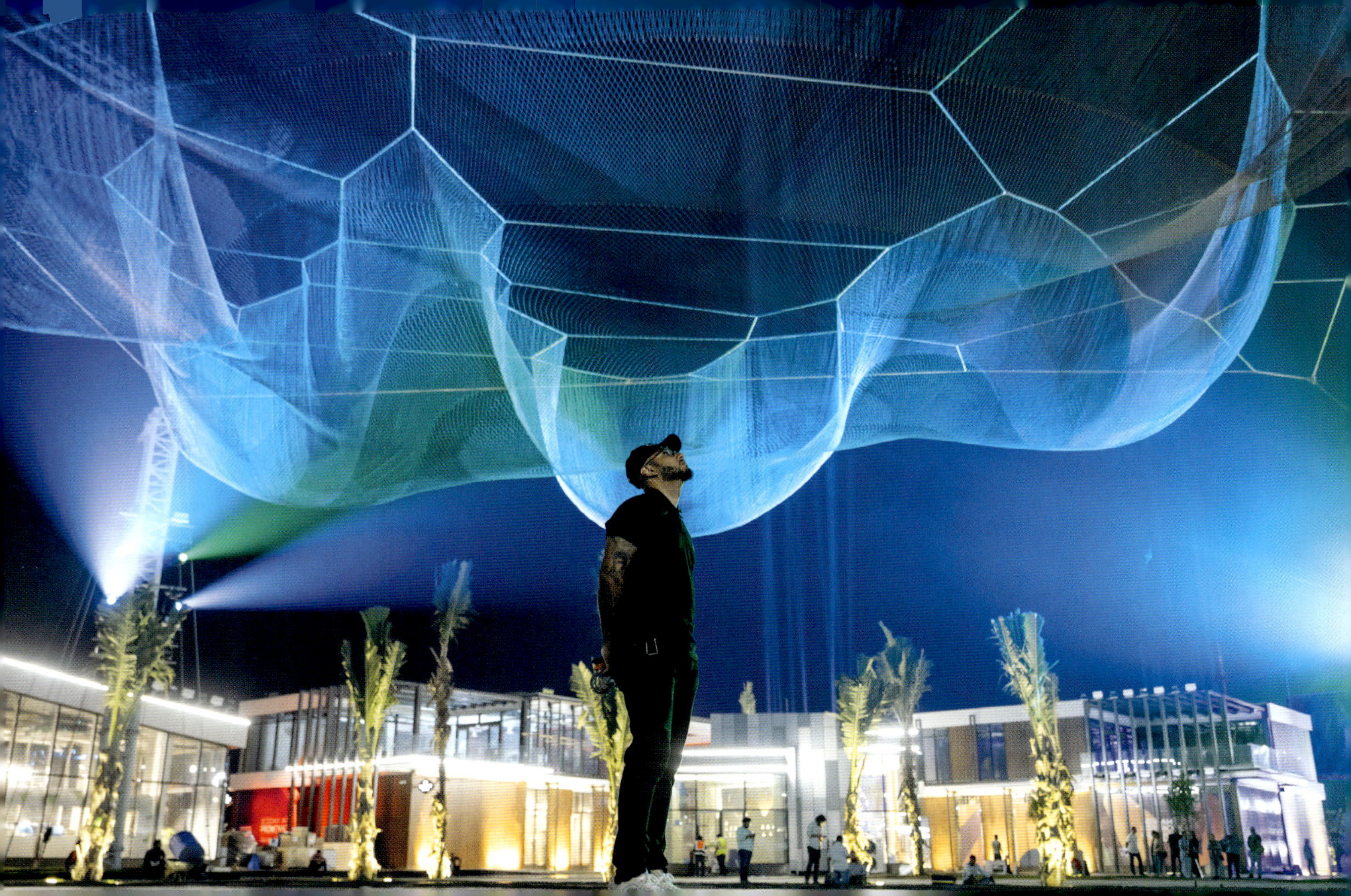

Foreword

—

Swizz Beatz

Visual art has always been in dialogue with music. Both translate the abstract ideas circulating in your brain into a sensorial experience that others can feel. That is what Janet Echelman and I have in common. We are both creatives. She is an especially gifted artist, a creative human, and I have always been a big fan of her work. So when my company, Good Intentions, was curating the Jeddah Promenade in 2021, I knew this would be a phenomenal way to introduce Echelman's powerful creative process to the Middle East and vice versa—to provide her with a new context to realize her architecturally scaled ambitions.

When I first encountered *Earthtime 1.26 Jeddah* (2021), it felt like the ocean was moving in the sky—the piece was alive. There was this softness billowing and dancing in the wind, a sense of harmony. Music and visual arts are brothers and sisters despite the fact that people like to separate them; they're both creative forms of expression. The feeling I get when making a record is the same feeling Echelman gets when making her work come to life. We are both using the creative sides of our brains, and we're leading with our passion, we're leading with our love, we're leading with our energy. At the end of the day, Echelman and I are brother and sister because we're creatives who are engaged in a global conversation about the power of women to transform culture today. One way this happens is by simply occupying space; the other is by harnessing the power of computation and science. I have seen firsthand how Echelman harnesses raw data and turns it into an energy that transforms people's experiences.
This book is a manifestation of her energy.

Swizz Beatz is a Grammy-winning rapper, DJ, cultural producer, and cofounder of the Dean Collection with his wife, Alicia Keys.

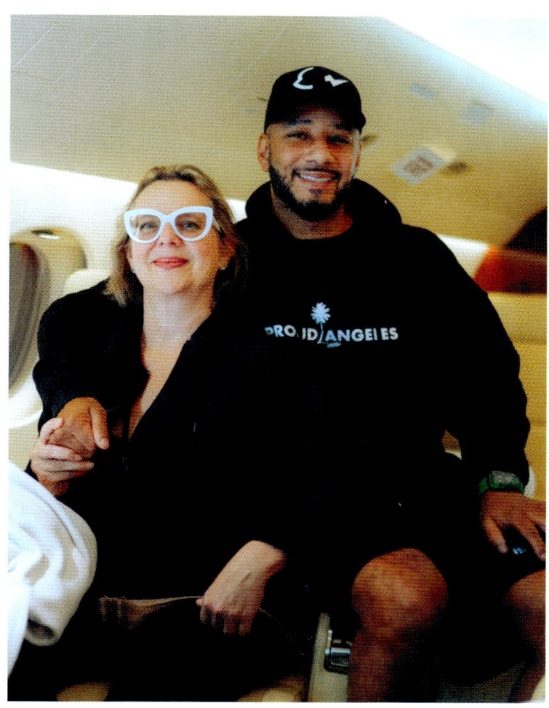

previous pages:
2–3: *Bending Arc*, 2020, St. Petersburg, Florida
4–5: *Earthtime 1.78 Beverly Hills*, 2019, California
6: *Noli Timere, Sculpture #1*, 2023, Milan, Italy
8–9: Studio wall, 2019

left: Swizz Beatz under *Earthtime 1.26 Jeddah*, 2021, Saudi Arabia
above: Janet Echelman and Swizz Beatz fly from Jeddah to Art Basel Miami Beach, 2021

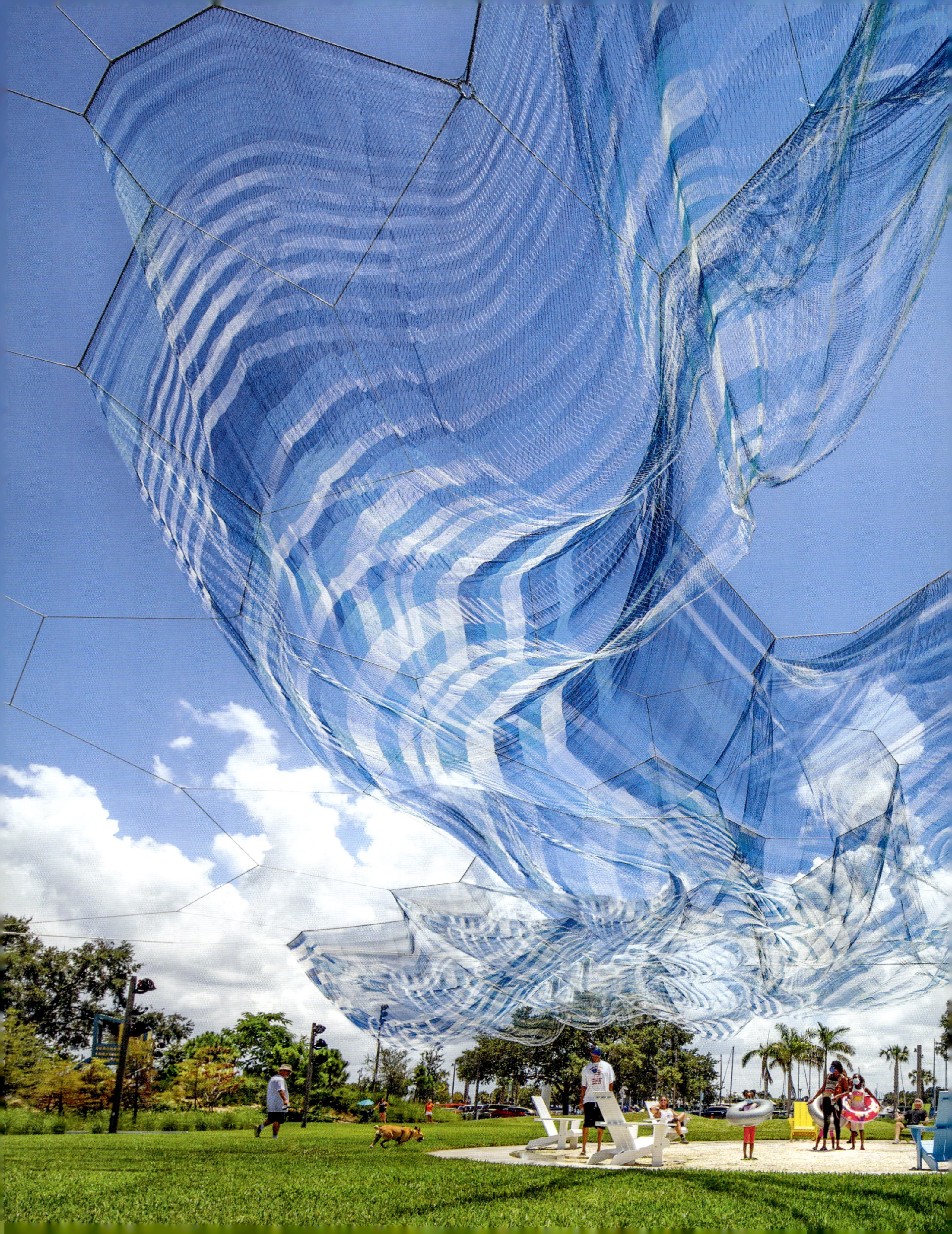

Introduction

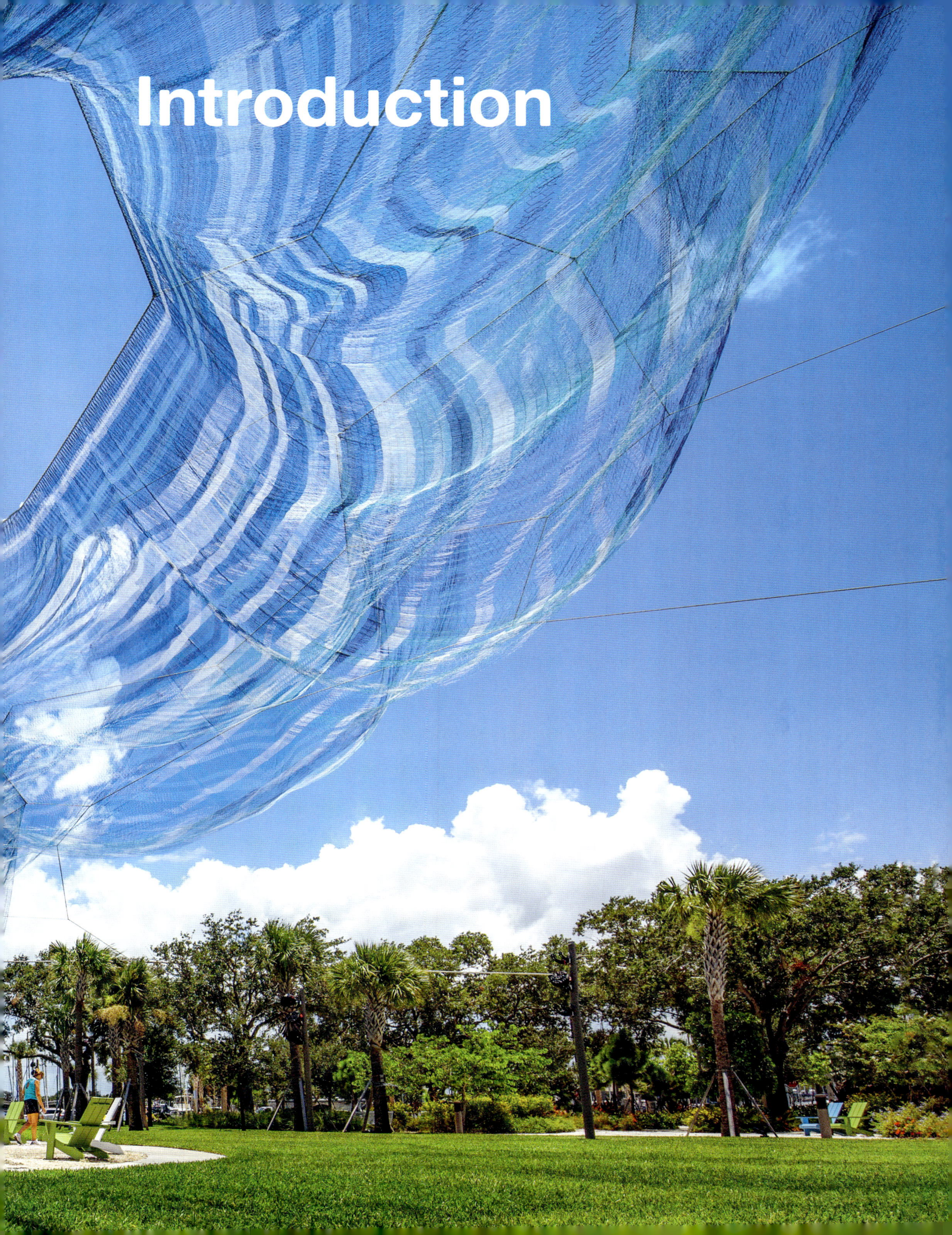

Radical Softness

—

Gloria Sutton

Radical Softness is the first sustained account of Janet Echelman's site-responsive artworks, especially her aerial net sculptures. Over the past twenty-five years, Echelman has deftly combined structural methodologies from architecture, computation, aeronautical engineering, and data visualization to form resonant sculptures that are eminently her own. In doing so, the dynamic artworks have in return recalibrated how these fields understand tensile strength, adaptive reuse of materials, and the possibilities of public art. Integrating centuries-old fishing-net knotting technology with state-of-the-art 3D modeling software designed by her Boston-based studio, Echelman generates monumentally scaled sculptures that are flexible and permeable, conveying a sense of radical softness, the artist's critical means for navigating a changing environment.

Echelman's radical softness alludes to scrims, partitions, drapes, and canopies, but also to the ways that sculptural forms might hold space and engender a sense of inclusivity in places that seem transient and seemingly inhospitable to art. For example, the hovering, cloud-like *Every Beating Second* (2011) permanently spans fifteen thousand square feet across the ceiling of Terminal 2 at San Francisco International, one of the world's busiest airports. The title comes from the acclaimed Beat poet Allen Ginsberg's invitation in his poem *Dawn* to "live in the physical world moment to moment... stop every beating second." Likewise, *She Changes* (2005) floats over a major waterfront traffic rotary in Porto, Portugal, the first permanent architecturally scaled public sculpture to use an entirely soft and flexible set of membranes moving fluidly in wind.

Echelman crafts colored gossamer fibers into massive architectonic structures that delicately sway in response to their shifting surroundings, beckoning people to pause, reflect, and revel while the world continues to swirl. Revealing the interconnectedness of networked systems—urban, environmental, human—Echelman's sculptures visualize the patterning of nature, the unrelenting force of climate change, and a feminist determination to create an inclusive space for all bodies and all ages. Established on five continents, Echelman's artworks foster imagination in the face of contingency.

Global Cross-Pollination

This comprehensive sourcebook unpacks what goes into making Echelman's rich and supple artworks come to life and her ongoing commitment to "taking imagination seriously," the title of her 2011 TED Talk, which has been translated into thirty-five languages with more than two million views and appears here in transcription. Additionally, *Radical Softness* features previously unpublished detailed project documentation, archival source materials, and an illustrated chronology narrating milestones in the artist's pathbreaking career. Contributions from a diverse range of internationally recognized scholars, engineers, designers, architects, and curators contextualize the interdisciplinary impacts of Echelman's radical softness on the fields of contemporary art, architecture, engineering, dance, and landscape architecture. Distributed across the book's five thematic sections—"Tracing Lines through Global Art History"; "Public Interfacing"; "Animating Architecture and Landscape"; "Soft Systems: Nets to Software"; and "Movement, Light, and Sound"—newly available photographs, sketches, technical spec drawings, computer renderings, and studio documentation show how her sculptures take shape. Less an anthology and more a constellation of collaborators' and colleagues' voices, the texts in this book are assembled and sequenced to foreground the global cross-pollination of discourse and dialogue that undergirds Echelman's vital practice.

Softness as a Metaphor for Resiliency

Key among these principles is the act of recuperating softness. Often used to deride or dismiss someone for lacking strength or fortitude, in Echelman's skillful handling, softness is reimagined as an advantage. The artist braids, knots, and splices fiber nets and programs custom software to generate undulating forms that can withstand hurricane-force winds. In equal measure, so-called soft skills like negotiation and compromise are key to Echelman's proven ability to maneuver through calcified layers of bureaucracy to build public works in some of the most technically challenging environments on the planet, from Vancouver's active urban waterfront to Riyadh's *wadi* desert rock formations.

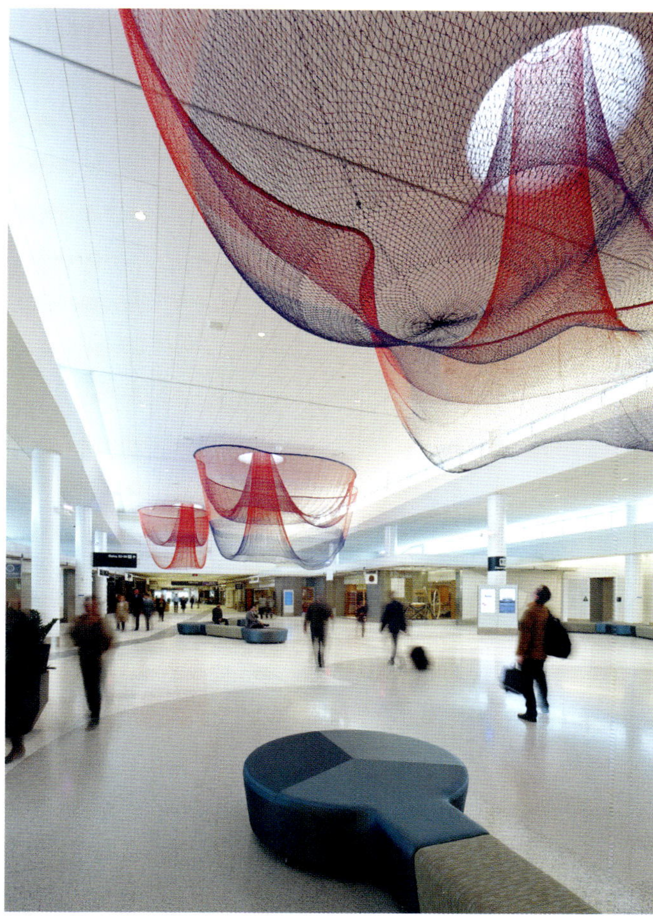

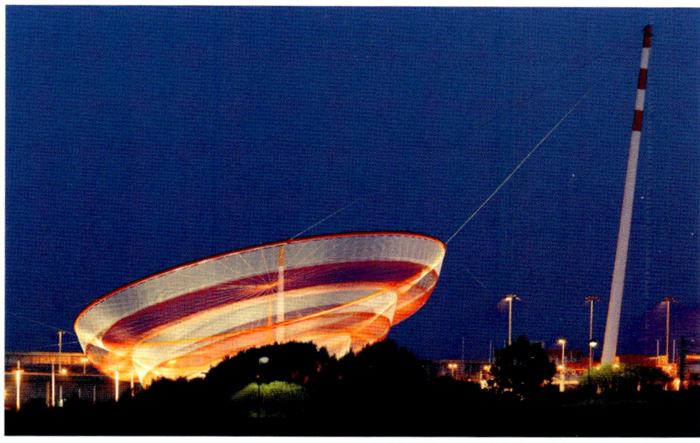

previous: *Bending Arc*, 2020, St. Petersburg, Florida
top: *Every Beating Second*, 2011, San Francisco International Airport, California
bottom: *She Changes*, 2005, Porto, Portugal

Moreover, her sculptures have been mounted in sensitive historical preservation areas, including London's Oxford Circus, Munich's Odeonsplatz, and Vienna's MuseumsQuartier, which require a soft touch to protect delicate facades and other architectural features.

Overall, Echelman's volumetric sculptures eschew blunt totality for multilayered, softly rippling mesh that evokes porosity and openness. The works gently envelop rather than occupy the spaces they float above, and seemingly embrace viewers rather than alienate them. As the artist describes, "The way that my art finds power is through its resiliency and adaptability rather than brute strength, because it lets the wind move through it rather than fighting it. I think that's a metaphor for how to live in these times."[1] By embracing the conditional and the provisional head-on, Echelman's immense sculptures adapt to their shifting ground (literally and figuratively), animating and enlivening revitalized waterfronts and landscaped parks as well as often-overlooked civic areas, transient zones, and so-called third places: interstitial spaces that encourage a sense of chance sociality such as plazas, commercial districts, and transportation hubs.

Beacons of Possibility

Equally important, Echelman's purposefully diffuse forms are designed to underscore the tendency to build over and thus erase or ignore sites of social change. A case in point is *Bending Arc* (2020). Massive in scale and ambition, *Bending Arc* permanently floats above 7,500 square feet of the bustling St. Pete Pier on Tampa Bay, Florida—the artist's hometown. The title of the billowing net sculpture refers to Martin Luther King Jr.'s 1968 statement that "the arc of the moral universe is long, but it bends toward justice," and its geographical coordinates directly connect the city's recent real estate redevelopment efforts to an earlier underexamined moment in civil rights history, illuminating and drawing attention to an area where local citizens peacefully challenged racial barricades to uphold the rights of everyone to access municipal beaches. Resilience is here *modeled* rather than *represented* in a structure engineered to withstand 150-mile-per-hour winds. Additionally, Echelman designed a blue-and-yellow lighting pattern for

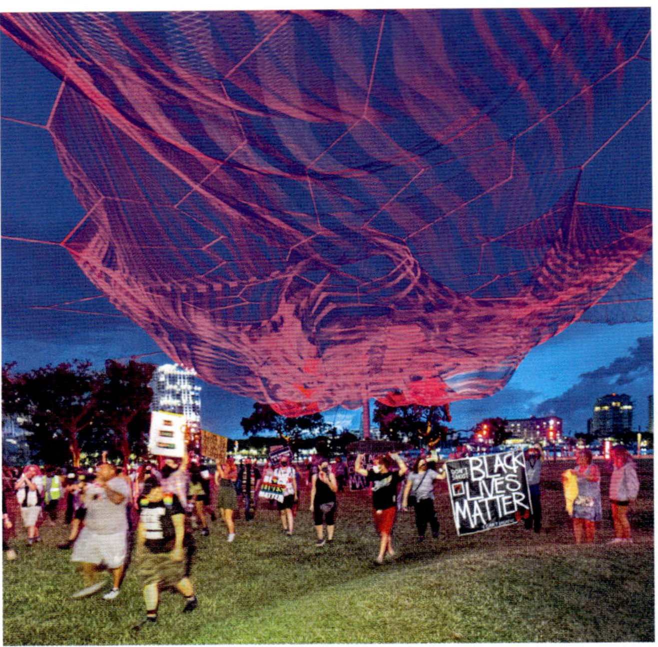

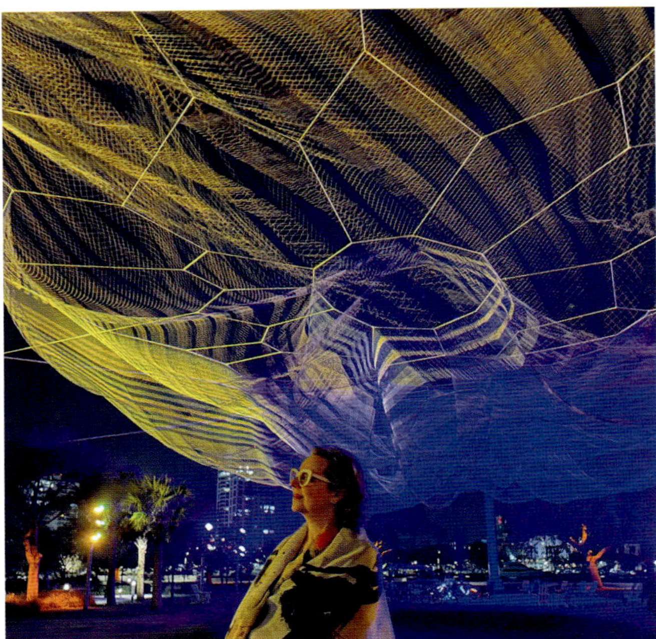

Bending Arc in solidarity with Ukraine after the Russian invasion in 2022 and a rainbow lighting program for the city's annual Pride celebration. The rope used to form its delicate shape is made of a fiber fifteen times stronger than steel by weight and was used to tether NASA's Mars rover. The net in plan covers 47,500 square feet and, together with the ropes, weighs a total of 5,330 pounds. Her site-responsive sculptures operate as both historical markers and beacons of possibility in areas that were once devoid of both.

Even Echelman's temporary structures exert enormous cultural and physical force. For example, her vision for *As If It Were Already Here* (2015) necessitated a meshwork of more than a half million knotted nodes (exerting more than one hundred tons of force) to be hoisted six hundred feet above downtown Boston through most of 2015. The work outlined three voids, recalling the city's "tri-mountain," which was razed in the eighteenth century to create the landfill that grounds the park underneath the sculpture and surrounding area. The striated colored bands evoke the six traffic lanes that once dominated the neighborhood and choked off any semblance of community until the decades-long Big Dig civic renewal project shifted the flow of traffic into tunnels, returning the surface area to pedestrian life around 2007.

left: Protest from city hall to *Bending Arc* following the death of George Floyd, St. Petersburg, Florida, 2020
right: Echelman adjusts the color of *Bending Arc*, 2020, to show solidarity with Ukraine after the Russian invasion, 2022

Form Finding

The architectural engineering technique of form finding—achieving an optimal form that delivers force equilibrium, dynamic stability, adaptability, and sustainability—allows Echelman's creativity to take shape in a world designed to maximize efficiency, find the shortest route, and avoid crowds, which often means hostility to experimentation and chance operations. Echelman's work is not simply reliant on technical feats of engineering; it also evokes perceptual powers of transformation, using the most elemental components of art making, namely the contouring of color and light in space. Despite the sense of ephemerality and ethereality evoked by her billowing forms, Echelman's sculptures are heavily grounded and require extensive technical research, testing, prototyping, and fabrication. In fact, the concrete foundations for *Butterfly Rest Stop* are forty feet wide and deep.

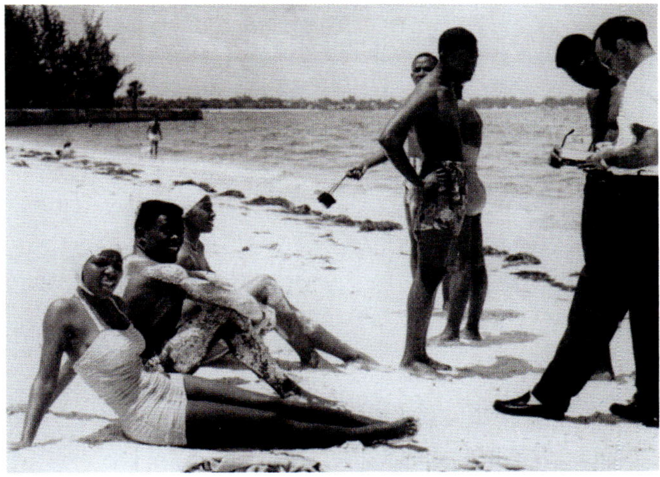

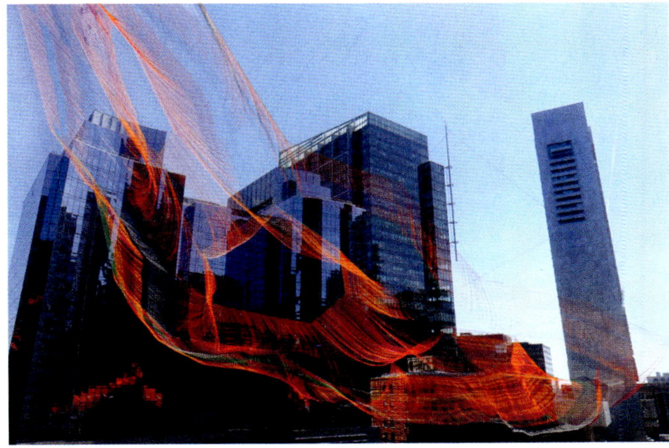

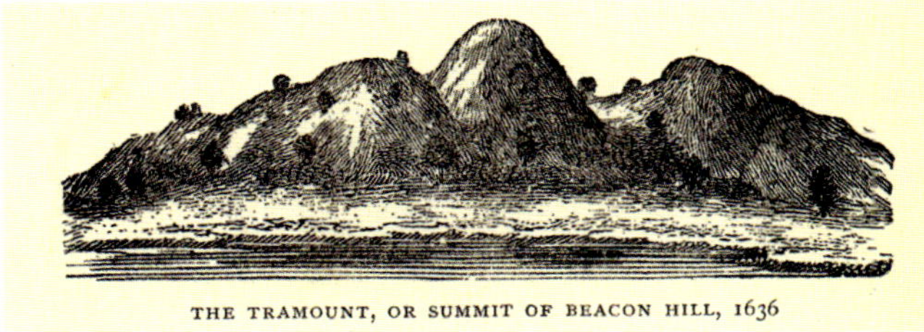

top: Swim-in protest at Spa Beach, St. Petersburg, Florida, 1958
middle: *As If It Were Already Here*, 2015, Rose Kennedy Greenway, Boston, Massachusetts
bottom: Historical drawing of the Tri-Mountain, Boston, 1636

Together with her studio team, Echelman translates forms inspired by natural phenomena and other data points into hand-loomed models, and then they experiment with different fibers. Echelman has developed a technique that makes her works far stronger than steel, yet light and lofty. Since 2001, she has been developing techniques with a family-run twine braider and net loomer in the Puget Sound region of Washington State, which has a history of serving the fishing industry.

Echelman's studio also engages deeply with a host of long-term collaborators, and her awe-inspiring feats of artistry and engineering often require navigating daunting municipal permitting and safety requirements. Since 2012, Echelman has been partnering with the international engineering and design firms Arup, Buro Happold, and Skidmore, Owings & Merrill (SOM), collectively exploring the complexities of net structures and together developing new techniques in form finding and dimensioning, and innovating splice conditions for fiber nets. The results have yielded unparalleled structural forms, including *Dream Catcher* (2017), built with SOM in West Hollywood, California, and *Impatient Optimist* (2015), created with Arup for the Bill & Melinda Gates Foundation's Seattle campus. As SOM structural engineer Alessandro Beghini notes, collaboration with the artist is a two-way street: "While Echelman was looking for input from SOM's structural engineers regarding the possible geometry of a structural net, her studio work in turn allowed us to draw connections between her ideas and research that influenced how we approached other building projects. Our ongoing collaboration with Janet is a true reflection of what art and engineering can create when woven together."[2] Echelman's use of engineering tools and shapes that demand altogether new techniques pushes the fields of engineering and architecture toward more complex, idiosyncratic, and intricate forms that literally change the profile of the built environment.

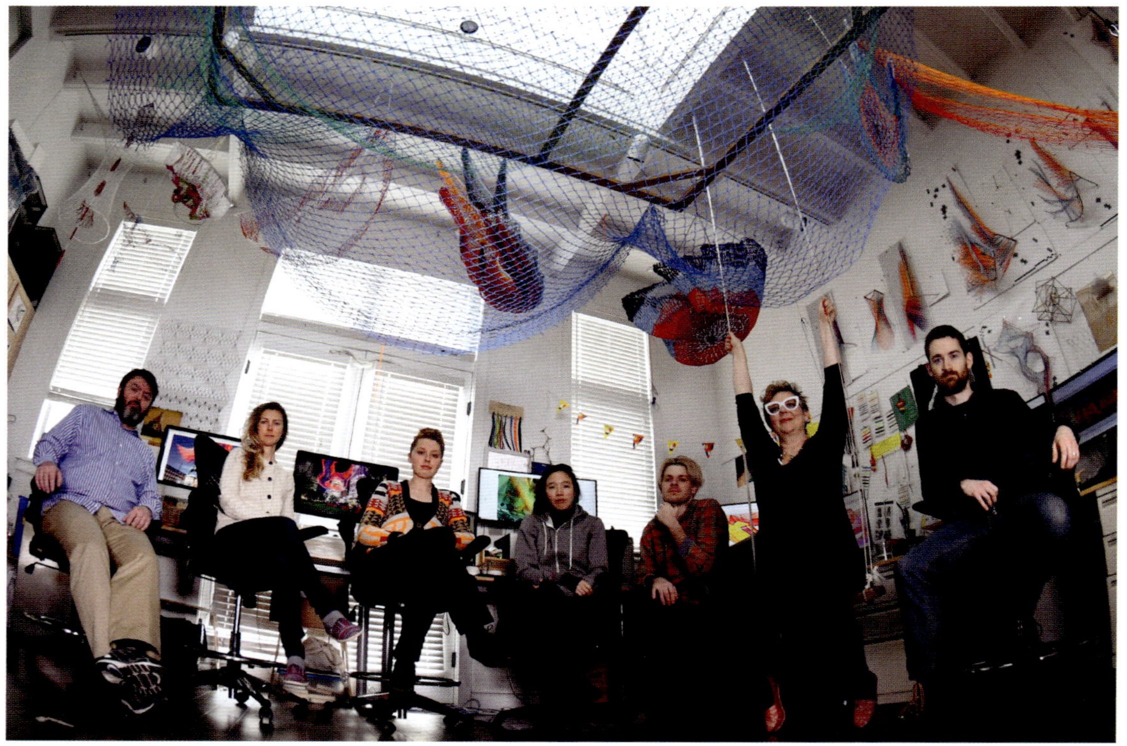

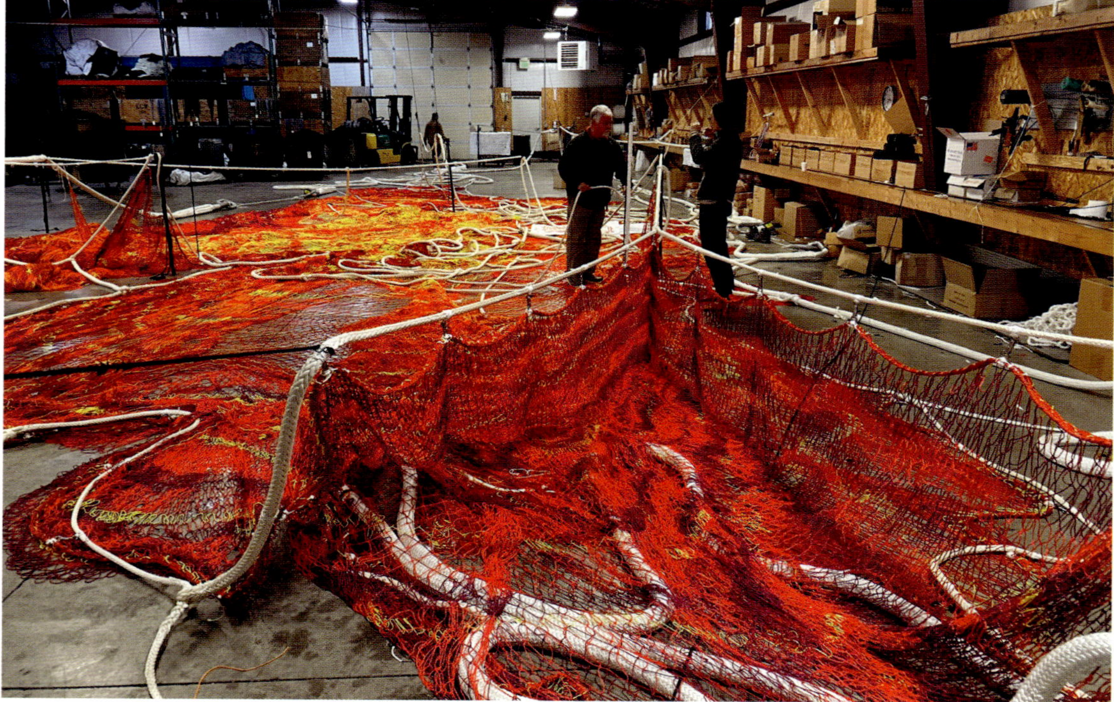

top: Studio Echelman, 2019
bottom: Fabrication of *Butterfly Rest Stop*, 2024, Frisco, Texas

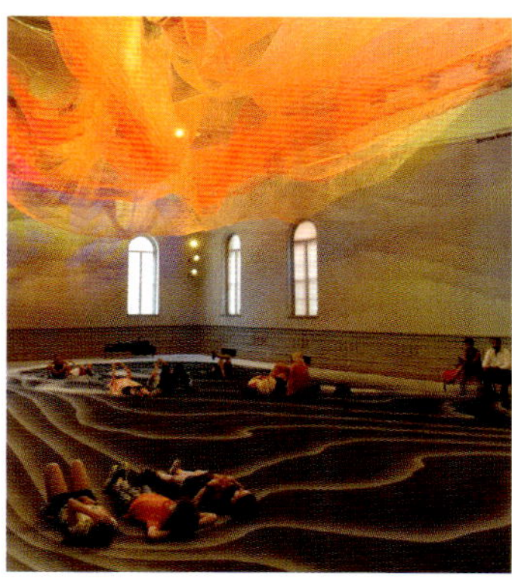
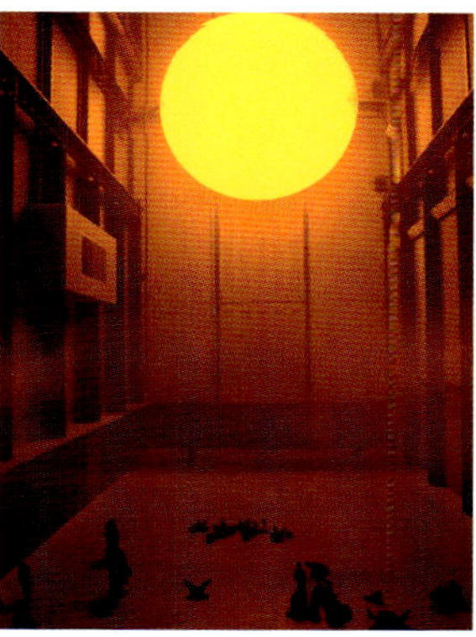
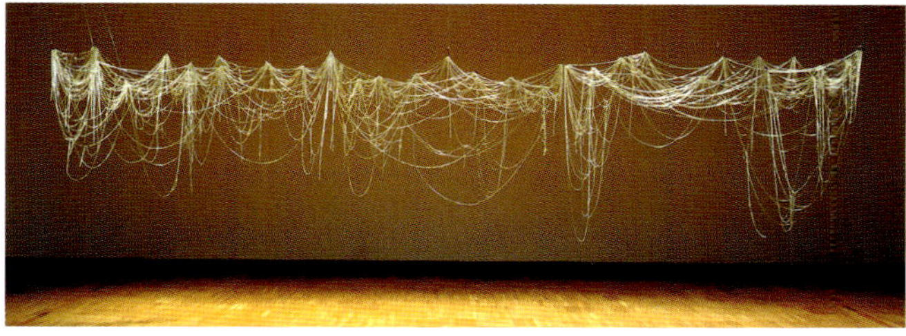
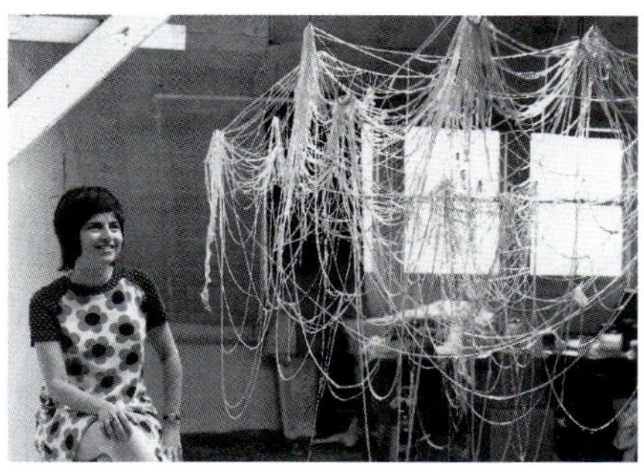
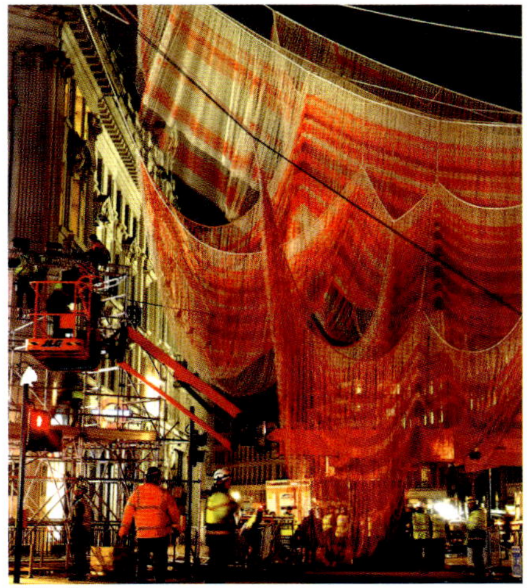

top left: *Earthtime 1.8 Renwick*, 2015, Smithsonian American Art Museum, Washington, DC
top right: Olafur Eliasson, *The Weather Project*, 2003
middle: Eva Hesse, *Right After*, 1969
middle bottom: Eva Hesse with *Right After* in her Bowery studio, ca. 1969
bottom: *Earthtime 1.8 London*, 2016, Oxford Circus

Materials and Processes

The materials and processes endemic to Echelman's work are often not exhibited or published in connection with her very public-facing sculptures, which act as a lithe rejoinder to what typically stands to commemorate, interrogate, or mark history. In this way, she joins her artist peers, an intergenerational grouping that includes Olafur Eliasson, Tomás Saraceno, and Fujiko Nakaya, who, like Echelman, create experiential works out of light, air, mist, and natural phenomena that focus our attention on the precarity of the environment and our embedded relationship to it. All of these artists visualize scientific data to convey the phenomenological aspects of liminal encounters with nature via artworks that play on reflection and tension.

Yet Echelman's artworks never strike a tone of theatricality or sleight of hand. Rather, all the elements that comprise her sculptures, including armatures, knots, and lighting sources, are exposed to the public, and viewers become integral to the dynamics of the work. This is less about the Duchampian move of an audience "completing" the work, and rather evokes what art historian Mieke Bal has termed "deictic looking,"[3] a type of encounter that turns on the linguistic markers of here/there, yesterday/today/tomorrow that Echelman often evokes in her titles or in the layering of historical reference points over the contemporary coordinates upon which her work anchors. Deictic looking is a bodily, relational experience in which the viewer is in motion—walking, rolling, strolling, shifting under and around the sculptures, which shimmer in the ever-changing light—keeping the interrelationship between viewer and artwork in a constant state of dynamism.

The works maintain seeming binaries—form and facade, organic and engineered, interior and external forces, volition and chance, intuition and data—in generative tension. In this manner, they recall Eva Hesse's string, latex, and resin works of the 1960s, which pushed the vocabulary of art beyond the binary of figuration versus abstraction to explore pliability and rigidity; they experimented with the fragility of the mechanical and the durability of the handcrafted in poignant and stirring ways.

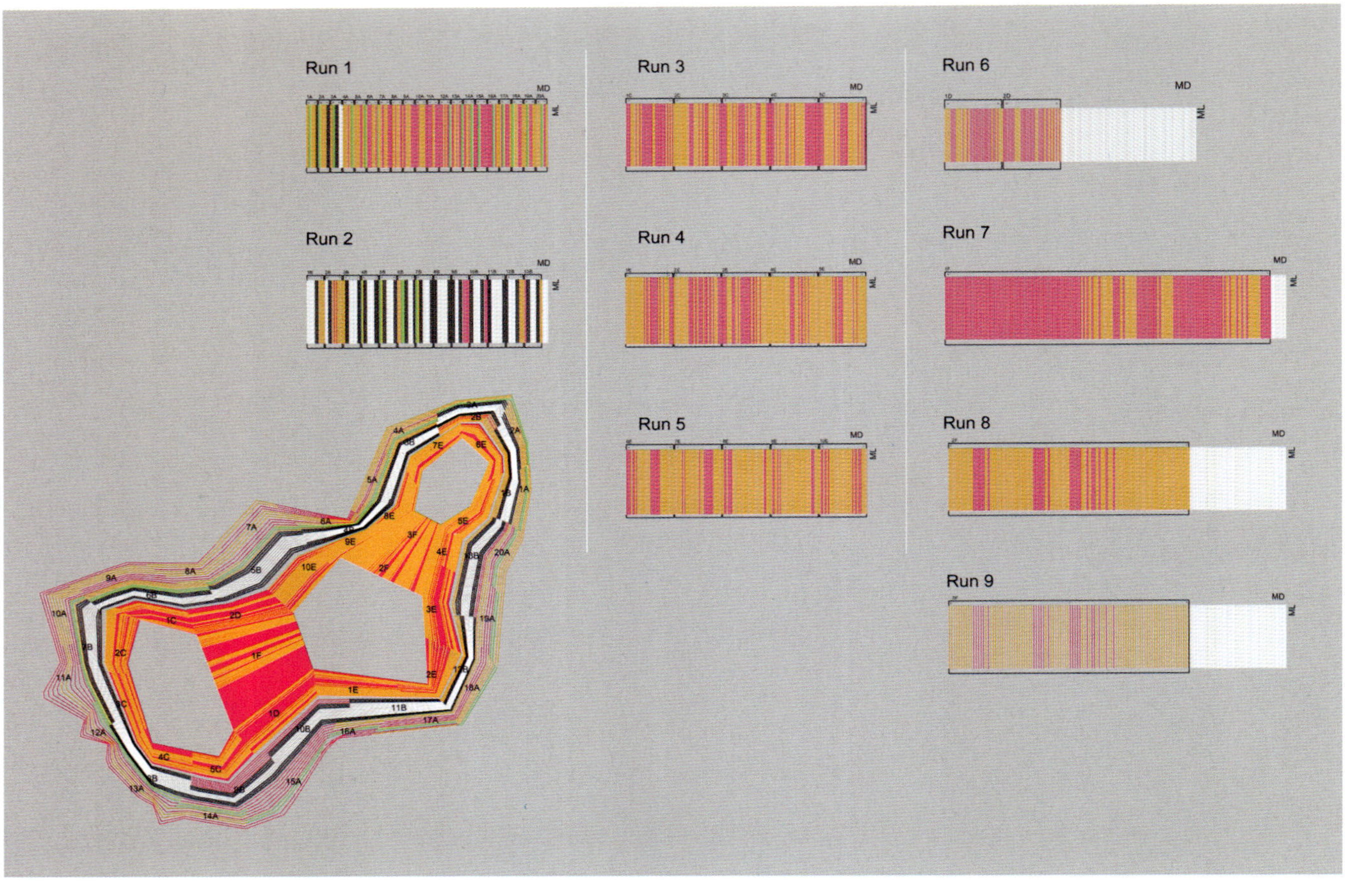

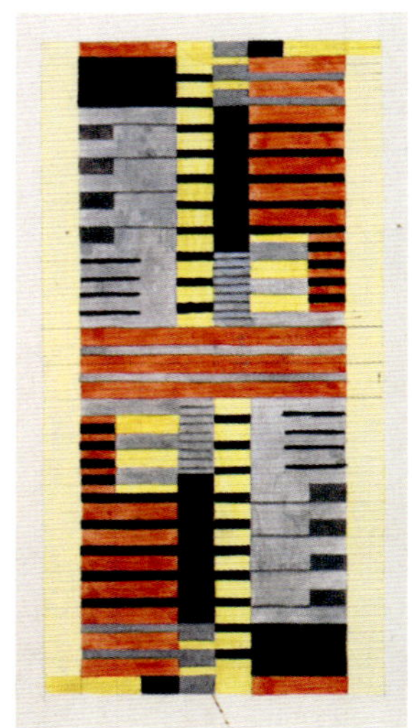

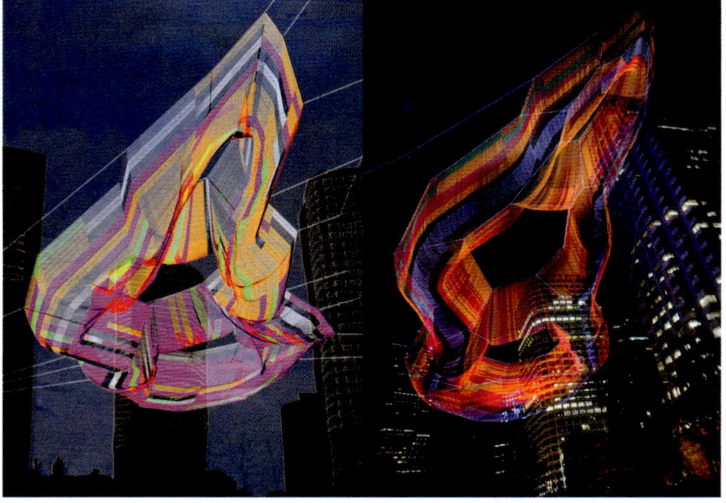

top: Looming diagram for *As If It Were Already Here*, 2015
bottom left: Anni Albers, *Design for a Silk Tapestry*, 1925
bottom right: Digital model and photograph comparison, *As If It Were Already Here*, 2015

Moreover, the depth of Echelman's work with fibers and armatures makes a tacit argument for the ways the pliable plane within architecture connects to textile weaving.

Accordingly, Echelman's sculptures evoke the pioneering design and writing of Anni Albers, whose Bauhaus and Black Mountain College teachings merged building with weaving, treating the two practices as interconnected rather than antithetical modes of cultural production. In her 1957 essay "The Pliable Plane: Textiles in Architecture," Albers identified the "character of mobility in our fabrics," outlining how textiles could be "lifted, folded, carried, stored away and exchanged easily."[4] Albers suggested that these qualities of lightness and mobility underscored the transformative powers of textiles, an approach that Echelman carries through in myriad ways. Continuing the transfer of knowledge from Black Mountain College, US artist Robert Rauschenberg directly mentored Echelman and curated her first public solo exhibition in the United States in 1989. Echelman vividly recalls their conversations about his collaborations with John Cage, Merce Cunningham, and Trisha Brown, which introduced to her the idea that even her interior gallery works might be transformed by the changing air currents within the architectural space.

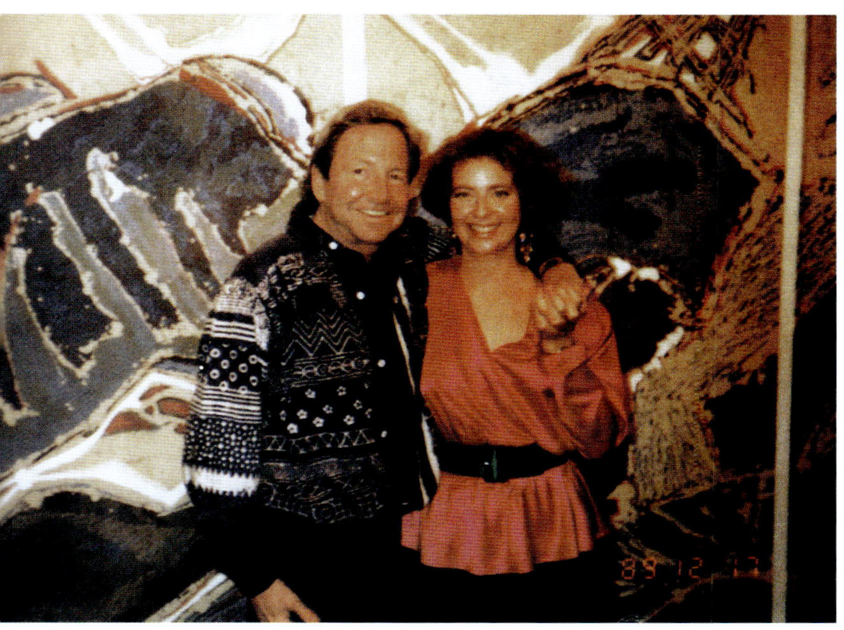

An Ethos of Empathy

For all their formal diversity, Echelman's works cohere clearly and powerfully in making a sustained argument for empathy. They carve out space and allow time for contemplation in a world that is conditioned more and more by automation and standardization. Rather than transcendent and monolithic totalities, statues that remain the same regardless of one's vantage point or position, Echelman's sculptures rely on the careful accumulation of many different parts that coalesce through an ethos of empathy. Empathy by its very definition is predicated on an acknowledgment of more than one's own self. Echelman's sculptures are not discrete, inert objects but perpetually dynamic, modeling a relational experience between self and other, inside and outside, individual and communal, thinking and feeling, seeing and sensing. There is no optimal, singular viewing position, but a constantly changing relationship to space and time that ebbs and flows against a backdrop of natural elements and human-made conditions.

These empathetic dynamics are what give Echelman's designs a choreographic sensibility, allowing their limber mesh forms to act and react in partnership with the weight and kinetic force of dancers, literally swelling, heaving, and breathing alongside their human counterparts, as when Katarzyna Kozielska of the Stuttgart Ballet enfolded Echelman's work into her 2014 staging of *A. Memory*. And recently, Echelman has been collaborating with choreographer Rebecca Lazier on a series of experimental dance and sound works that reimagine borders and boundaries through light and movement.

"Her aesthetic curiosity has encouraged her work to include experimentation.... The result is a successful worldly innocence producing surprises."

—Robert Rauschenberg, at the opening of the solo exhibition he curated of Echelman's work in 1989

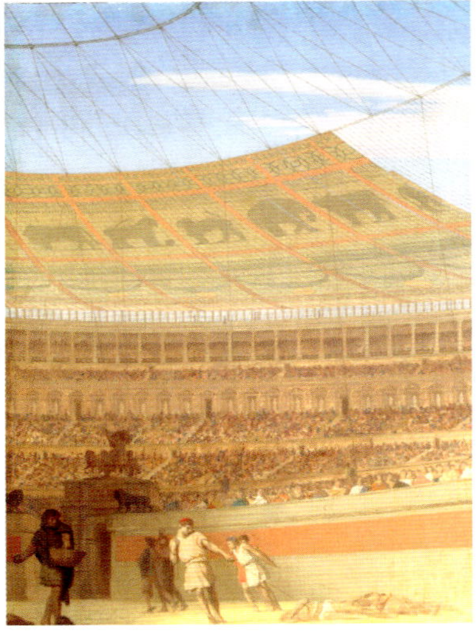

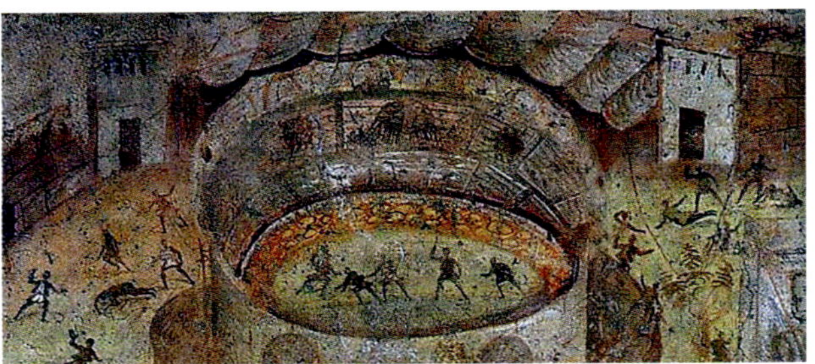

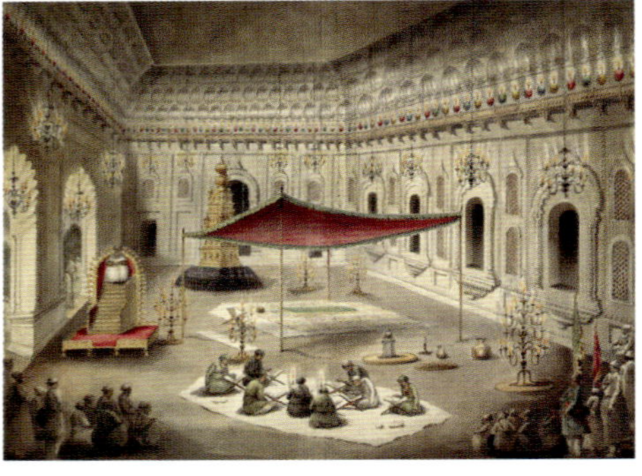

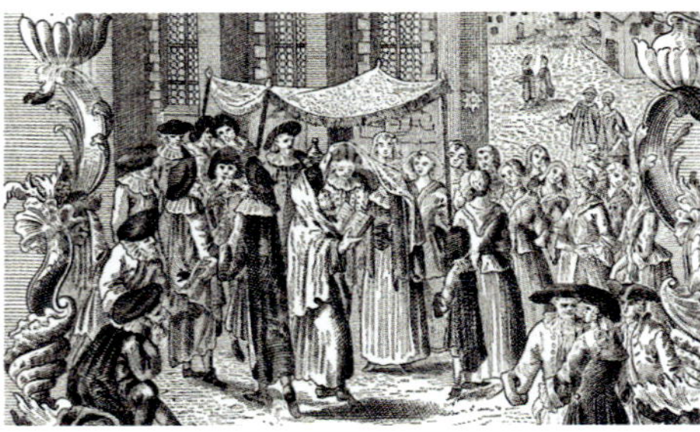

from top: Roman Colosseum velarium depicted in Jean-Léon Gérôme, *Ave Caesar Morituri te Salutant*, 1859; Pompeian mural depicting amphitheater velarium; watercolor of canopy above the grave of Asaf ud-Daula, Lucknow, India, ca. 1810; print depicting a traditional Jewish chuppah, Germany, 1748

Temenos

Another point of reference for how Echelman's works operate as placeholders for contemplation is her training as a practicing psychotherapist. Specifically, Echelman describes how she "often thought of the therapy session as a *temenos*, a container that created the boundaries needed to make it safe for powerful emotions to come out and play." In this way, her sculptures "now create a *temenos* in our communal public space, helping to hold, shelter, and even nurture us within the overwhelming chaos and isolation characteristic of our modern, secular urban life."[5] The artist also links her practice of drawing lines in space to her childhood fondness for creating play spaces: "I loved building forts, fastening sheets and blankets between furniture to create a covering we could crawl underneath and enjoy being inside. Sometimes I wonder if my sculpture springs from that same desire to have a space to crawl inside, and that playful impulse to do it with nothing more than woven threads."

Echelman also tethers her contemporary artworks to a longer historical trajectory, from the two-thousand-year-old monumental velarium, an awning that shaded spectators in the ancient Roman Colosseum, to the Hindu tradition of constructing temporary sacred textile architecture for pilgrimage and festivals, to the traditional Judaic chuppah, a temporary space for the marriage ceremony made by suspending a prayer shawl or cloth from four handheld poles—that last a practice that refers back to the biblical desert tent of Abraham and Sarah. Above all, Echelman was drawn to working with textiles because of their capacity throughout human history to hold and transfer meaning across time and place. As the artist specifies, "Whether from traditions of European trousseaus of embroidered linens, or South Asian dowries of handwoven cloth, or prayer flags in Nepal, or prayer shawls in the Middle East, textiles contain within them an enduring capacity to hold cultural meaning that is passed down generation to generation."

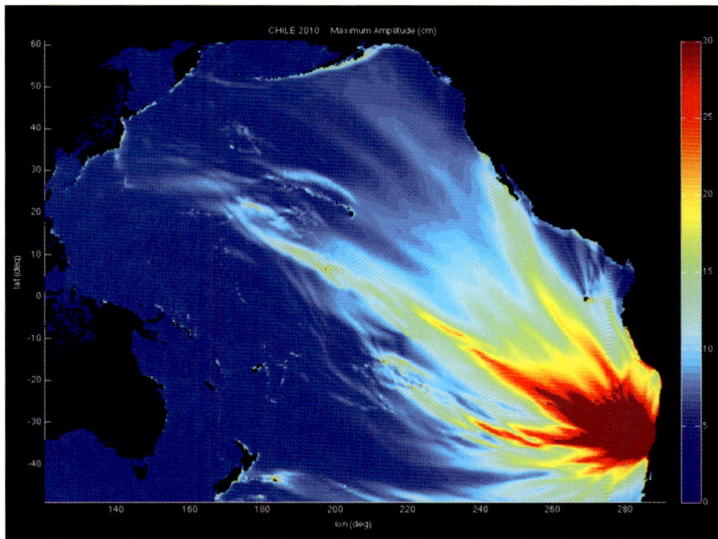

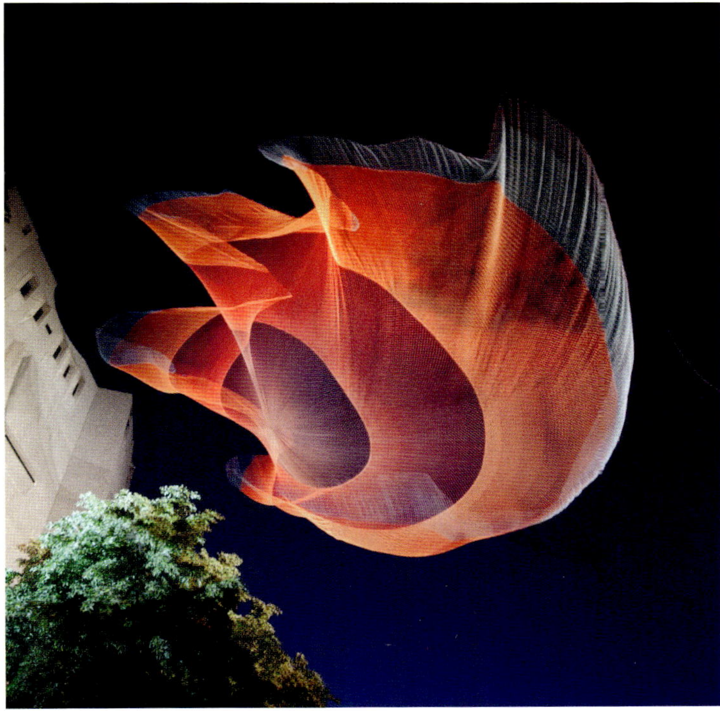

top: NOAA data set of Pacific Ocean wave heights following the 2010 Chilean earthquake
bottom: *Earthtime 1.26 Denver*, 2010, Colorado

Iteration

In both concept and form, Echelman's works are never static. The artist purposely designs her sculptures to remain iterative, responding to the conditions of each site and location. Case in point are her ongoing globally conceived artworks that explore themes of interconnectedness: *Earthtime 1.26*, *Earthtime 1.78*, and *Earthtime 1.8*. Each of the three distinct *Earthtime* artworks takes an initial set of computational data points around a geological event and successively renders new versions that respond to the architectural context of each instantiation. Each net formation is modeled after geological events that were so powerful their tremors altered the planet's rotational speed. The title for each work in the series refers to the number of microseconds shaved off the length of the Earth's day because a geological occurrence redistributed the planet's mass, followed by the city or location in which the project appears. The first was *Earthtime 1.26 Denver*, and its colored layers correspond to data from NASA's Jet Propulsion Laboratory study of a 2010 earthquake in Chile that shortened the length of the Earth's day by 1.26 microseconds. Initiated in 2010 for the Biennial of the Americas, *Earthtime 1.26* was suspended from the roof of the seven-story Denver Art Museum and floated above the downtown area's street traffic. As of 2024, *Earthtime 1.26* has been produced in sixteen cities on five continents. Each of the *Earthtime 1.26* outdoor temporary installations is composed entirely of braided ultra-high-molecular-weight-polyethylene (UHMWPE) fibers, each typically using more than fourteen hundred feet of rope and hundreds of hand-spliced connections, anchored into supporting structures and/or mounted in neighboring walls or other existing or temporarily installed architectural elements, and can be engineered to carry more than eighteen tons of force.

Earthtime 1.78 refers specifically to the 2011 earthquake off the coast of Japan and its ensuing tsunami, which slowed the rotation of the Earth's daily rotation by 1.78 microseconds. While the colorways and patterning of the netting in each instantiation of the *Earthtime 1.78* series corresponds to the geologic data from the same tsunami caused by the 2011 Tohoku earthquake, there are slight variations in the overall shape of the top net structure due to the scale of the work's expanse, which is customized to fit the surrounding architecture and site conditions at each public location. Moreover, the sequencing and hue of the lighting programs that illuminate each installation are customized to correspond to the atmospheric conditions at each locale. Often erected for weeks or months as a stand-alone cultural event, *Earthtime 1.26* and *Earthtime 1.78* have also been mounted in conjunction with art biennials, city anniversaries that sometimes include live music performances taking place under Echelman's sculpture, and other exhibition formats. In either case, at the end of its public run, the rope netting that composes the artworks (*Earthtime 1.26* spans about 117 by 102 feet, and *Earthtime 1.78* measures about 100 by 45 feet) is then carefully repacked and returned to the artist's facility to be inspected; repaired, if need be; and made ready again for future invitations in which the artist will ideate on how to present the project in response to its new environment.

In another example of Echelman's iterative practice, *Earthtime 1.8 Renwick* (2015) was the first case where Echelman devised an indoor version of *Earthtime*, which became part of the Smithsonian American Art Museum's collection. Using the same data from the 2011 Tohoku earthquake, the artist rounded up the 1.78 rotational shift, titling this version of the work *Earthtime 1.8*. The installation's hardware mechanisms had to be embedded sensitively into the ornate vaulted ceiling of the Second Empire architecture of the historically landmarked building that houses the Renwick Gallery, the Smithsonian's branch focused on contemporary art utilizing craft methods and nineteenth-century to contemporary craft and decorative arts, located next to the White House in Washington, DC. At the same time, the natural elements at play in Echelman's work, including light and wind, also had to be adapted for the indoor conditions of a heavily visited museum. So the artist developed a choreographed sequence of lighting that casts dynamically moving shadow projections in saturated colors onto the surrounding walls and a custom carpeted expanse along the floor, inviting the 1.1 million visitors who come to the Renwick each year to slow down, lie down, and look up.

In 2016 Echelman adapted *Earthtime 1.8* again to hover over London's Oxford Circus. Bands of brilliantly hued coral-orange striations interrupted the more typical mediascape of fashion ads and flashing billboards in one of the world's most crowded commercial districts, where over 125,000 people stream in and out of the tube station on a daily basis. For this iteration, *Earthtime 1.8 London*, the artist devised a mobile app that allowed the public to democratically vote on the colors of the work's lighting pattern, which calculated proportionally and projected in real time. Remarkably, city officials closed Oxford and Regent Streets to all vehicles for a day during the work's four nights, from January 14 to 17, 2016, enabling visitors to flood into the street, lie down on the asphalt, and take in the work hovering above them.

In each instance, *Earthtime* is calibrated and designed specifically to map onto an existing public structure for a certain time period, making the work more iterative than site specific. To date, *Earthtime 1.26* has been installed in sixteen cities on five continents: Denver (2010), Sydney (2011), Amsterdam (2013), Singapore (2014), Montreal (2015, 2016, 2017), Prague (2015), Durham (2015), Santiago (2016), Shanghai (2017), Chiayi (2018), Hong Kong (2018), Geneva (2020), Munich (2021), Jeddah (2021), Milan (2022), and Riyadh (2023). Iterations of *Earthtime 1.78* have been created for seven cities: Madrid (2018), Dubai (2018), Beverly Hills (2019), Borås (2021), Helsinki (2021), Vienna (2021), and Milan (2022).

Replenish

Iteration also describes how Studio Echelman designs each work to evolve as new functional capabilities are developed, taking advantage of advances in modeling software and sustainable materials. This is a practical way to contend with harsh elements such as ultraviolet light, acid rain, and high winds, but also a conceptual strategy that employs iteration to rethink the lifespan of a work. This allows the sculptures to remain renewable and sustainable as they are exposed to the elements, but also to serve as a metaphor for human existence.

In certain climate conditions, like in Phoenix where strong UV exposure and frequent dust storms or pollution that would make the works difficult and costly to clean, Echelman sometimes specifies the use of temporary recyclable fibers and the replacement of the netted components every five years. For *Where We Met* (2016) in Greensboro, North Carolina, Echelman designed a cycle of colors that changes every five years and arranged for prefabricated attic stock for the replacement pieces in advance. Echelman likens this to her approach to the roof tiles on her house: she keeps extra shingles on hand and periodically replaces them. She speaks glowingly about Felix Gonzalez-Torres and the way the common materials of his conceptual works are continually replenished, becoming an affective gesture of renewal in the face of loss, decay, and dispersion. Gonzalez-Torres's mounds of individually wrapped candies and printed stacks of broadsheets can be taken for free by members of the public, and are periodically replenished. The shapes and/or arrangements of the mounds or piles may or may not change with each installation, according to its stated guidelines. Using broadly available formats—economical construction paper, dime-store candy, strings of incandescent light bulbs—allows Gonzalez-Torres's works to be inexhaustible, and a model for how

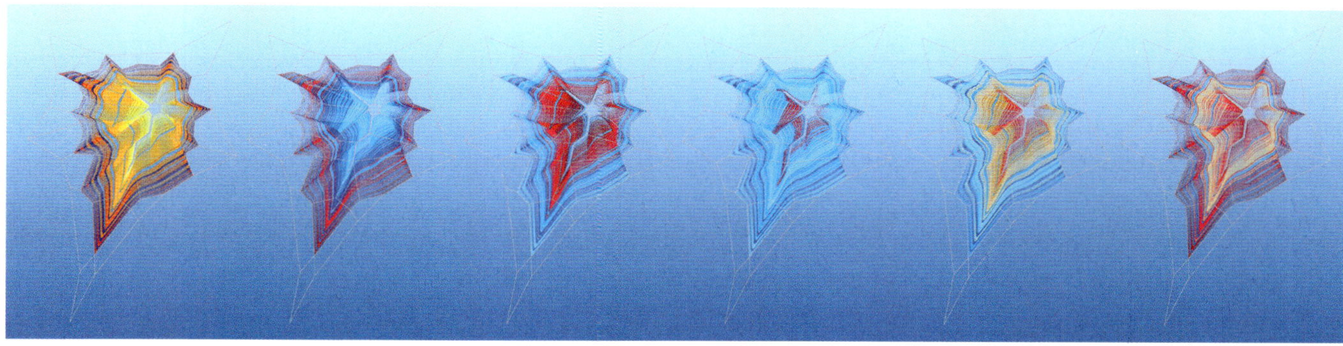

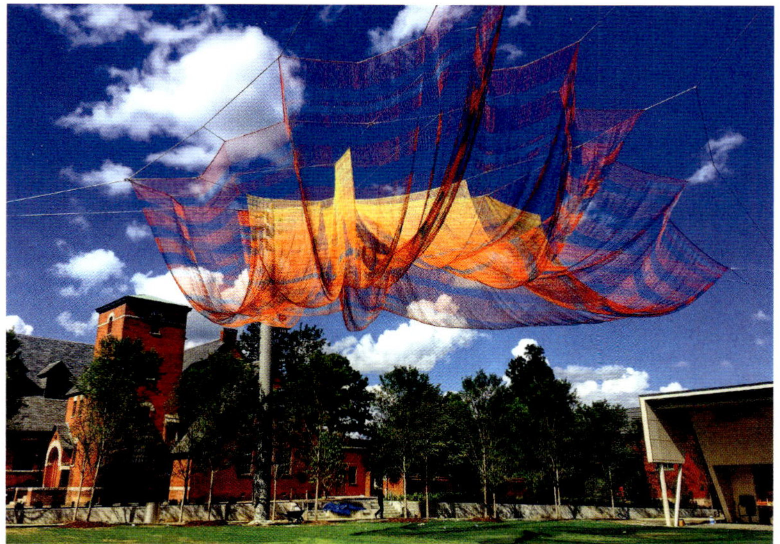

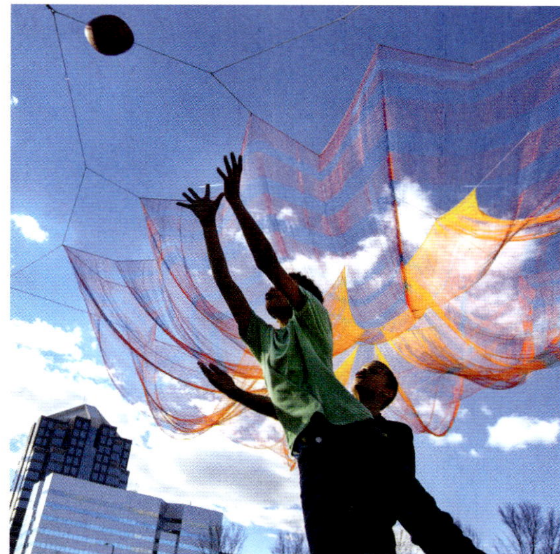

top: Cycle of color for *Where We Met*, 2016, LeBauer Park, Greensboro, North Carolina
bottom row: *Where We Met*, 2016

overleaf: *Where We Met*, 2016

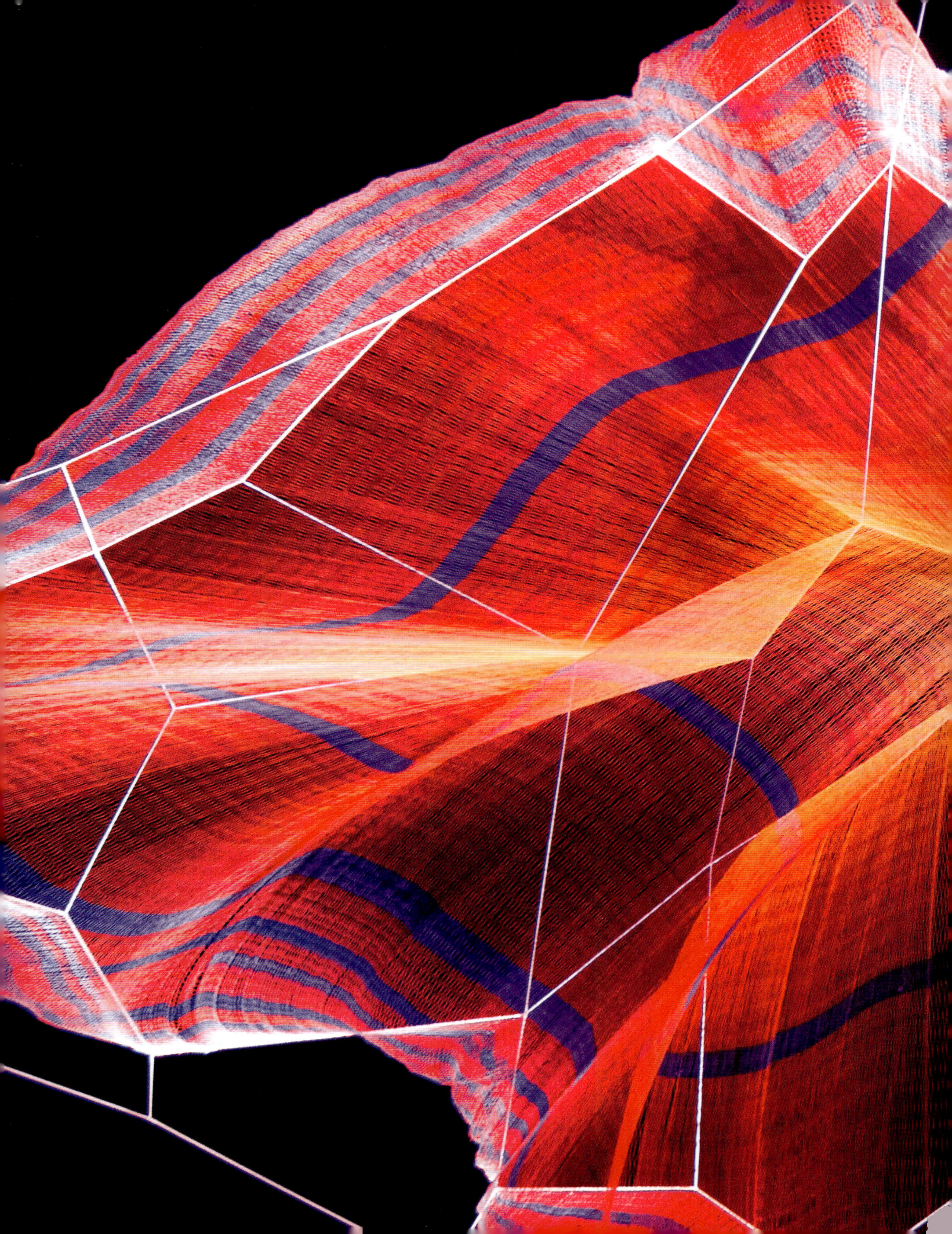

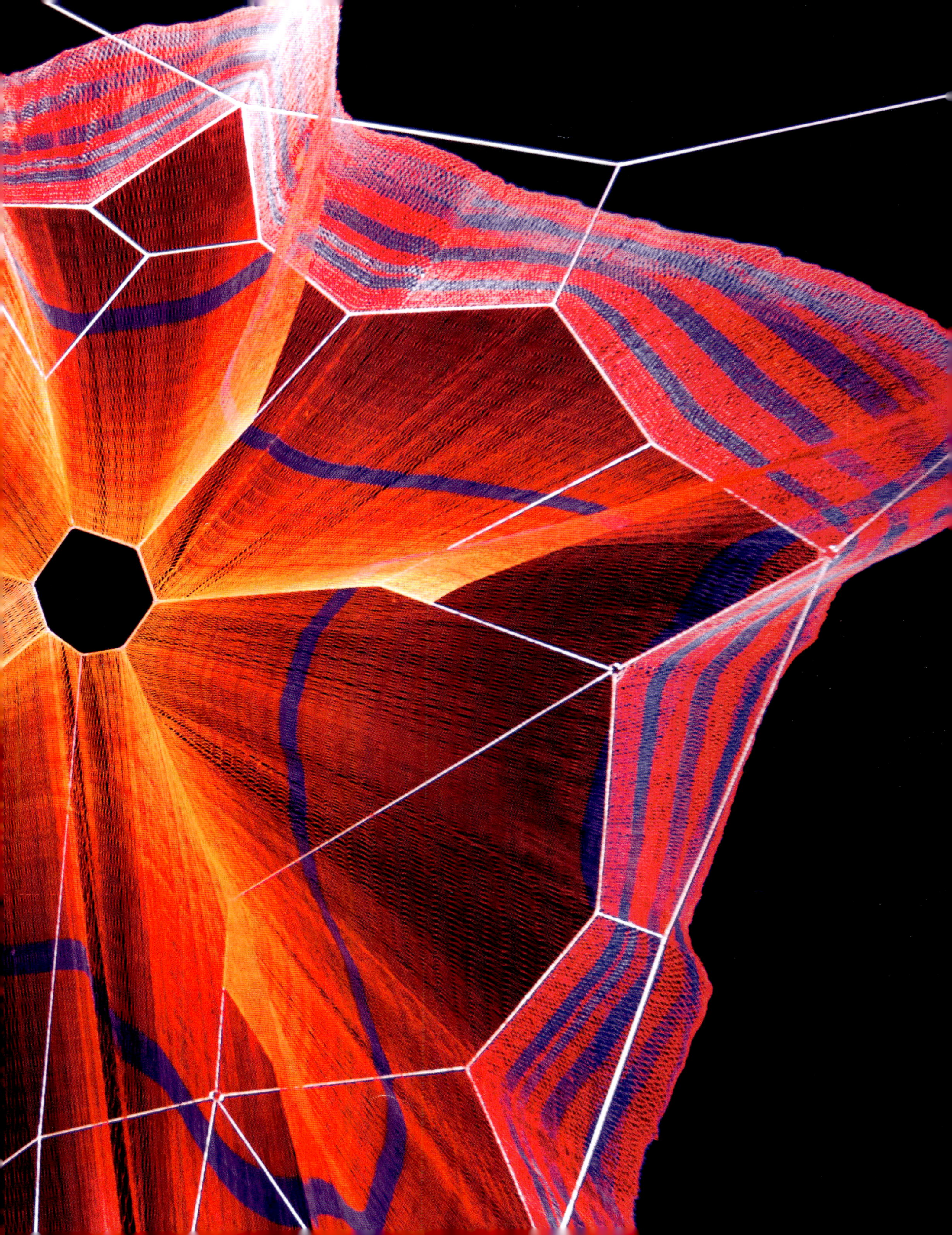

contemporary art might move beyond the aura of originality and find poetic inspiration instead in workaday materials.

Like Gonzalez-Torres, Echelman uses democratic materials in a straightforward manner to generate a natural sense of curiosity and popular appeal, inviting viewers into a position of complicity in questioning established conventions for public art and seeking to create new meanings in everyday places we often visit without paying much attention. Harnessing the power of chance operations, lived experience, and resistance to the speed of the twenty-first century, Echelman's works envelop viewers in the beauty and flexibility of a sense of radical softness.

Temporal Shifts

Collectively, Echelman's sculptures test the limits of technical feasibility while blowing open the constraints of what we expect from visual art. Designed to conduct sound, light, and kinetic elements, they prioritize interfacing with an unknown public. Sculpture in Echelman's conception remains temporal. Time unfolds as viewers explore the shadows and intervals that emerge through observable, ephemeral material changes. Colored nets visualize the rhythms and patterns of natural cycles, for instance the crepuscular moments when day shifts to night, or the gradations of blue as sea blurs into sky. Wrapping viewers with prismatic color schemes whose legibility shifts against a setting sun or becomes activated by complex lighting programs, the suspended sculptures revive visual art's core project: to engage with a universe that is constantly changing. Diaphanous and transparent, Echelman's sculptures send a message that is antimonumental and nonheroic, while spreading a shimmering glow of possibility in the face of the unfathomable.

Butterfly Rest Stop (2024), located in Frisco, Texas, just north of Dallas, is a diaphanous, monumental aerial sculpture situated along the migratory path of the monarch butterfly, inspired by milkweed, the flower species that nurtures the pollinator. Echelman's artwork includes actual milkweed planted underneath the aerial sculpture, so the art not only draws attention to the essential role of pollinators in our ecosystem, but also becomes a literal pollinator corridor that helps sustain these migrating butterflies, seasonally providing the monarchs with a place to rest and be replenished along their lengthy migration.

In this way, the works generate a mentality of transience in those who observe the materials in flux, reminding us of how we are all subject to larger systemic processes—political, biological, ecological, geological. Each twist or turn of the sculptural net suddenly seems as fragile, precious, and vulnerable as our own cellular networks of growth and decay. Public art writ large often aims to reflect democratic values of freedom and openness, but far too often the compromises necessitated by the commissioning process curtail the imagination. Echelman offers a countermeasure. Through her ongoing insistence on radical softness, she purposely threads an artistic pathway that engages the crises of living in spaces we only temporarily inhabit—this planet, and each of our own bodies.

Gloria Sutton is an associate professor of contemporary art history, Northeastern University.

opposite: *Butterfly Rest Stop*, 2024, Frisco, Texas

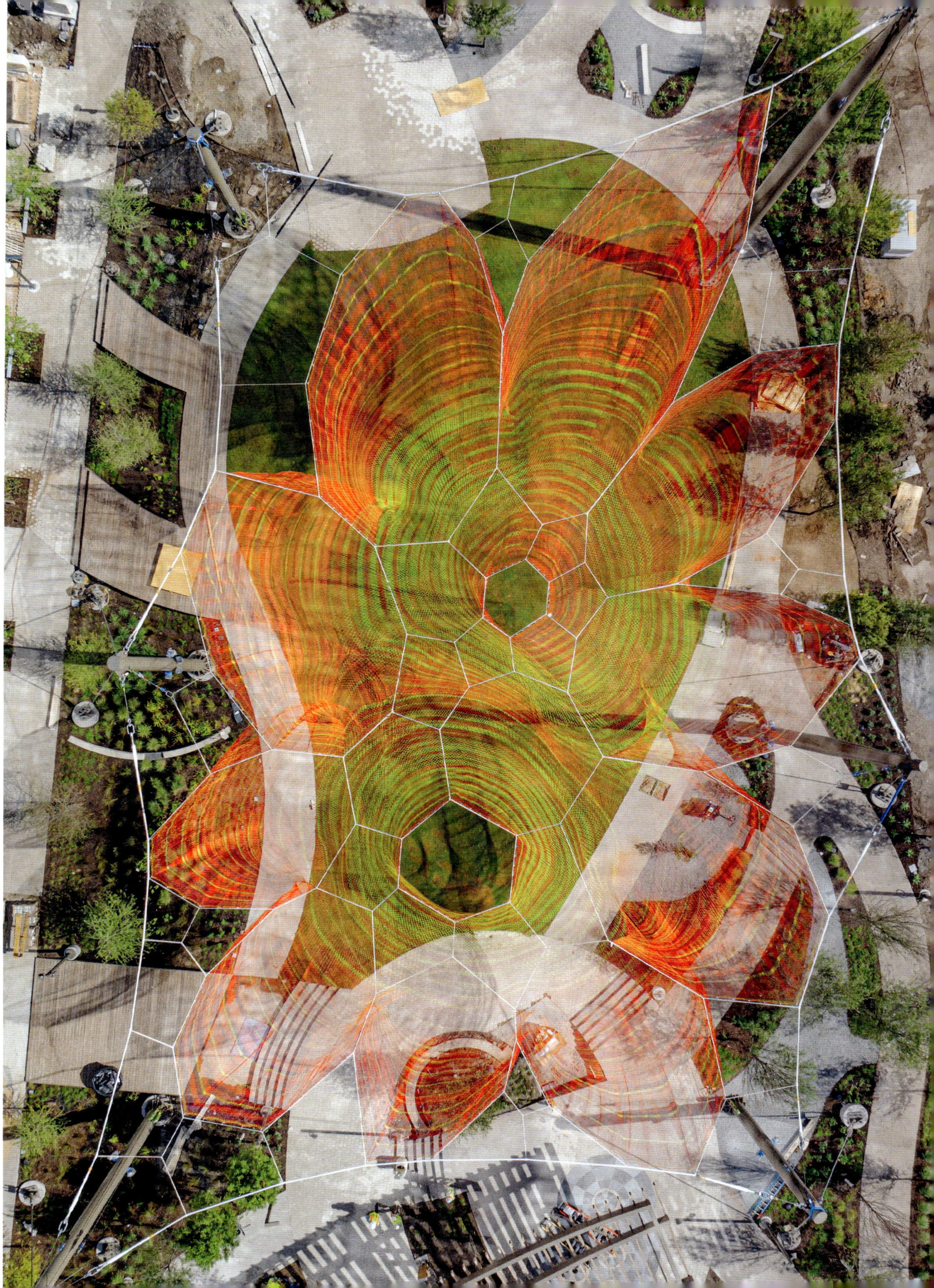

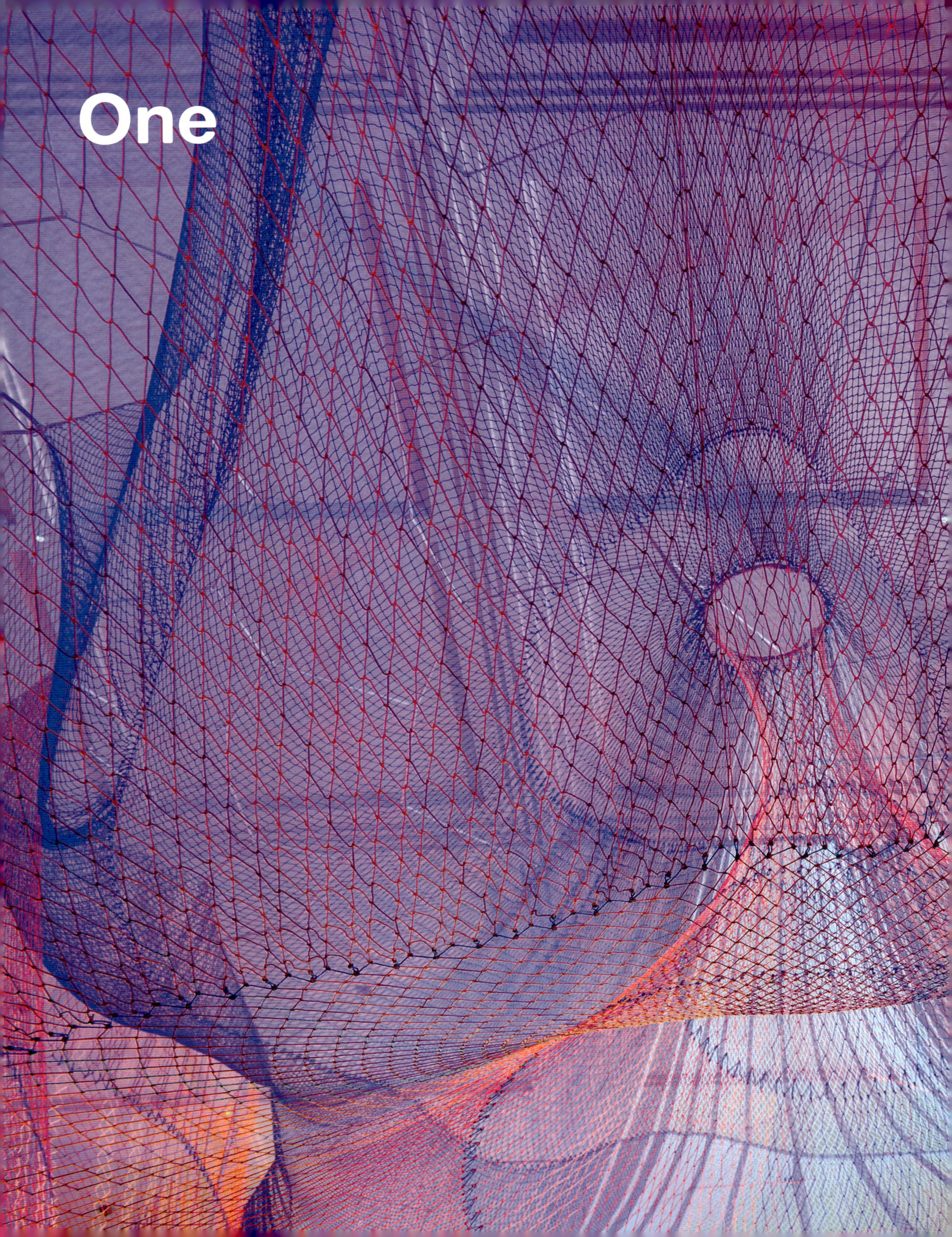

One

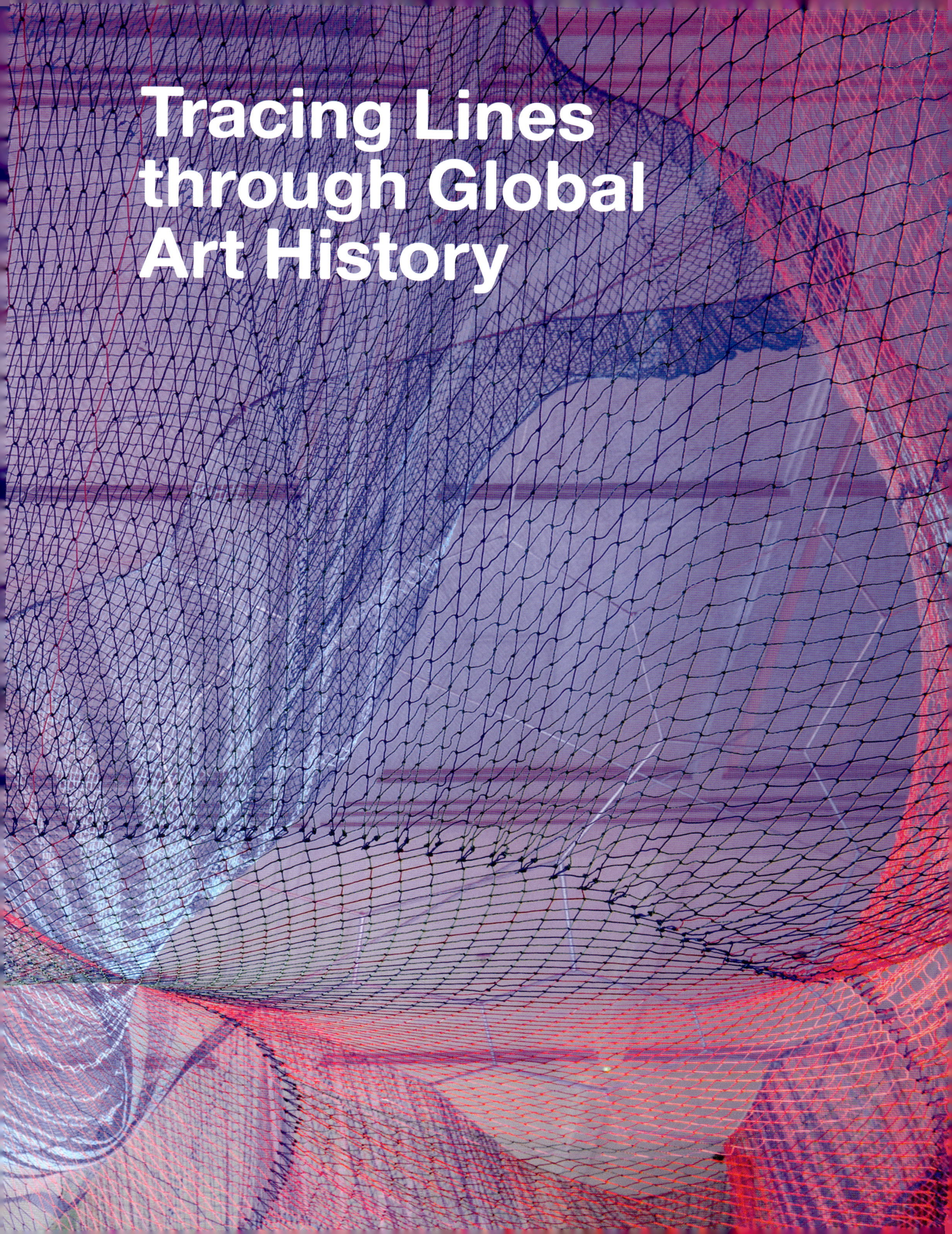
Tracing Lines
through Global
Art History

Ink, Light, and Resist

—

Michelle Lim

In a 1988 photo taken in Bali, Janet Echelman holds up a hanging line so that her larger-than-human-size paintings *Campuan I–III* (1988) can be fully unfurled against a background of bright-green *padi* fields and traditional bamboo houses. A playful nod to the painterly tradition of working *en plein air*, this charmingly incongruous display of abstract paintings in an Indonesian rice field captures the lively energy of the artist's early painting practice—an energy that enticed Robert Rauschenberg to curate Echelman's first solo show in the United States in 1989. Rauschenberg later acquired the triptych for his personal collection.

While Echelman's paintings are often steeped in the language of gestural abstraction, Asian cultural contexts have shaped her aesthetic and art practice over the years, through both serendipitous encounters while traveling and a sustained study of local art and craft techniques. As the artist reflected recently, "The beginning of my art trajectory came from the study of Chinese calligraphy and brush painting [in 1987 at the University of Hong Kong], which led to a focus on gesture, until I finally found a way to give gestural line a physical presence."[1] Chinese ink painting is as much about allusions to seemingly empty voids and in-between spaces as about the power of brushstrokes and misty washes. Throughout art history, encounters between Western artists and Asian cultures have often given rise to fascinating motifs and ideas. Famously inspired by ukiyo-e prints, Vincent van Gogh incorporated Japanese calligraphy into his oil paintings or the 1880s, and contemporary artists like Bill Viola who spent long sojourns in Japan and India likewise created bodies of work, including video installations, that reflect their deep engagement with local cultures.

Echelman creates such fluid spaces between lines and other markings in her installation works, notably in her 2000 *Kyoto Project*, where slender tubes punctuate the spaces in the garden of Hōnen-in, a quiet Buddhist temple on Kyoto's

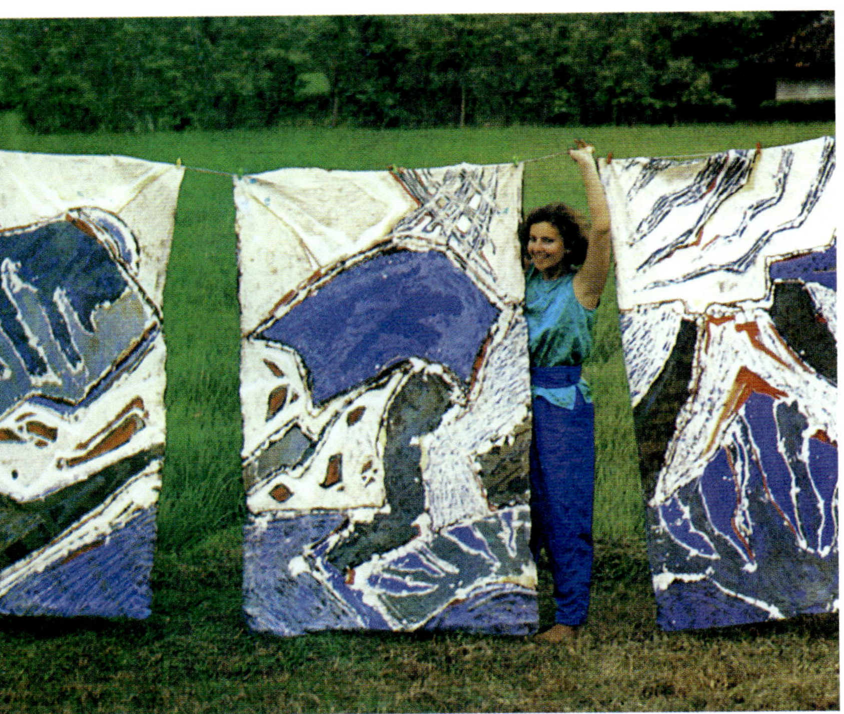

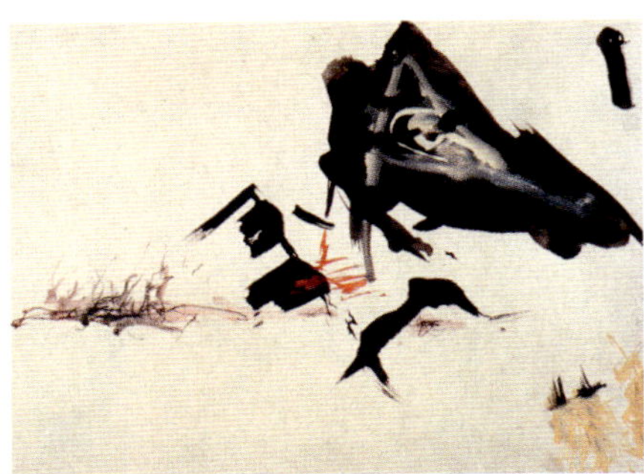

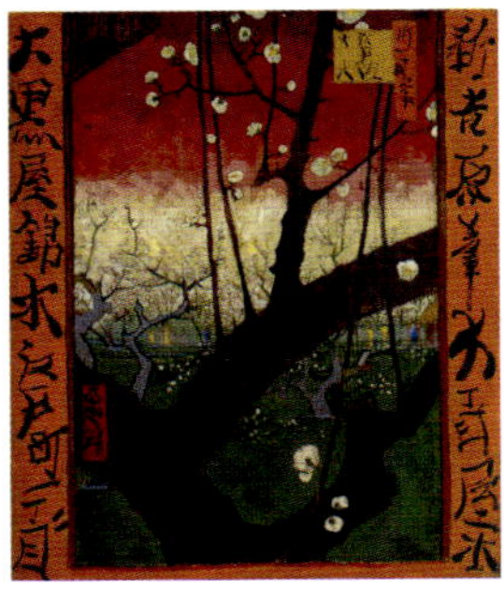

previous: *Without Beginning Middle or End*, 2020, Mumbai, India
top: Echelman with *Campuan I–III*, 1988, Bali
bottom left: *Drawing #3 Sumatra*, 1988, mixed media on paper, 11 × 15 in.
bottom right: Vincent van Gogh, *Flowering Plum Orchard (after Hiroshige)*, 1887

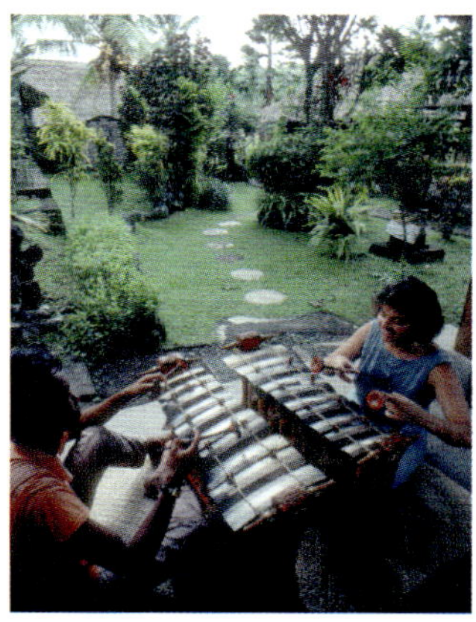

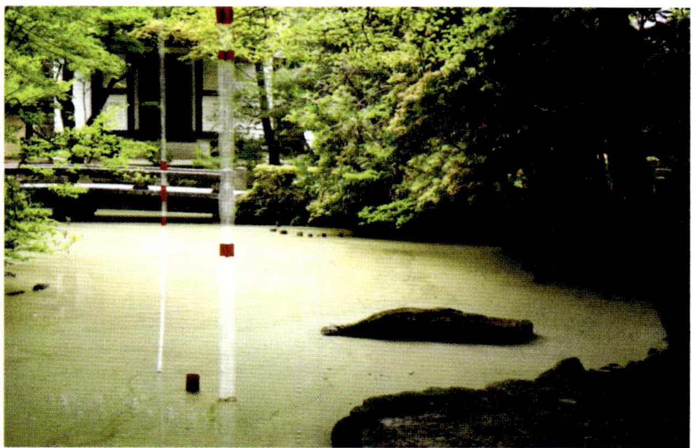

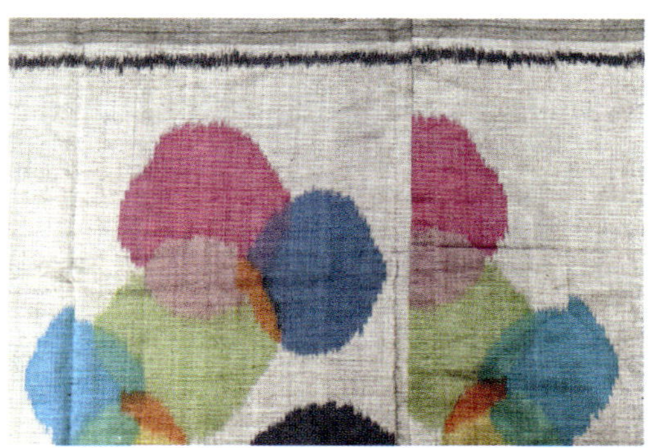

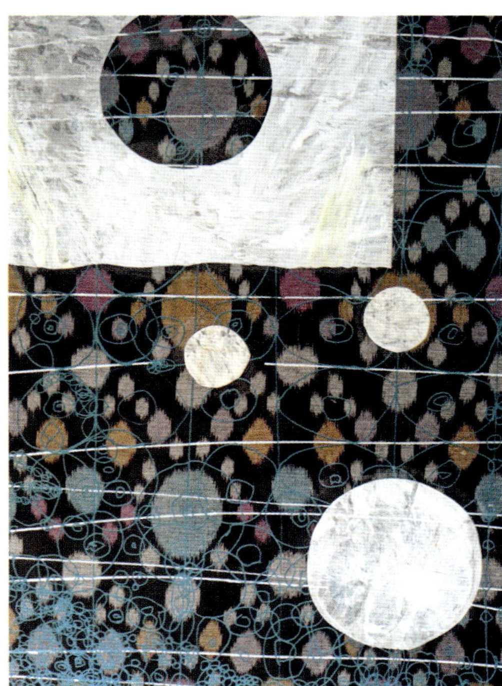

Philosopher's Path, their gentle presence evoking an ethereal bamboo grove.

Chance and destiny, two deeply ingrained spiritual concepts that permeate many cultures in Asia, have played important roles in Echelman's journey of life and art. The artist lived in Bali for almost half a decade before deciding to move back to the United States in 1992, after losing her traditional bamboo house-studio to a fire. In Bali, she had begun playing in and performing with her neighborhood gamelan orchestra, and sketched musicians and dancers engaged in ritual performances.

She soon began experimenting with craft methods, including ikat and batik, working with and learning from local collaborators about the visceral technique of creating textile patterns using hot wax and colored dyes. She later adapted these processes to paint on canvas in her studio.

The *Campuan I–III* triptych is an early example of her acrylic-batik paintings, appearing not unlike a piece of batik fabric writ large. Echelman's use of Chinese ink painting and calligraphy as a departure point for her painting practice is a mirror reversal of artist Liu Kuo-sung's 1960s reinvention of Chinese ink painting. Known as the father of modern Chinese ink painting, Liu made radical new uses of materials, themes, motifs, and installation formats,

top left: Echelman playing gamelan music in Bali, ca. 1990
top right: *Kyoto Project*, 2000, Hōnen-in temple, Japan
middle: Echelman's original ikat weaving, Bali, 1991
bottom: *Spots & Dots*, 1992, acrylic and vellum on Echelman's original ikat weaving, 36 × 24 in.

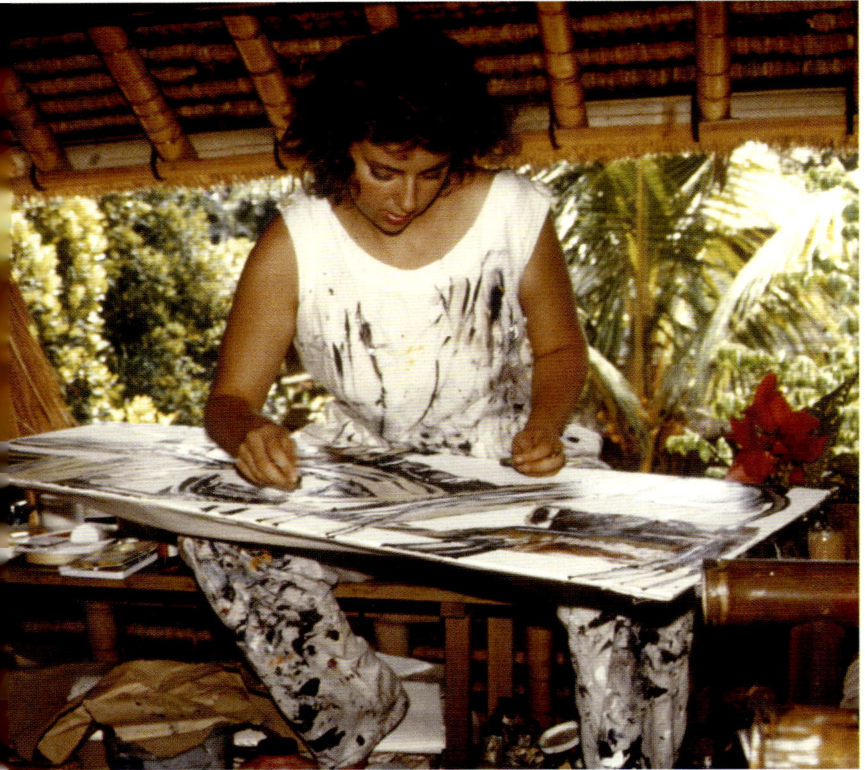

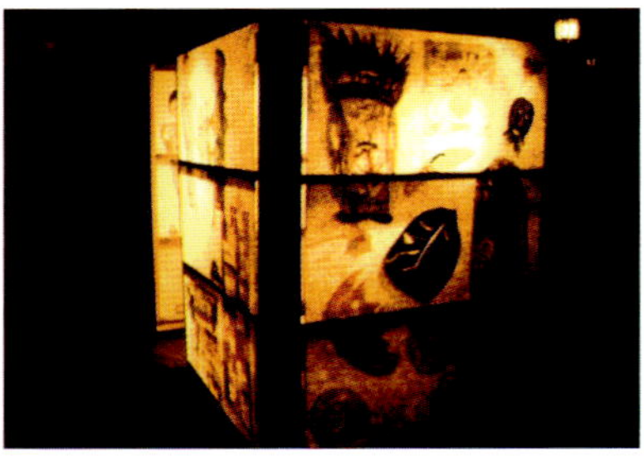

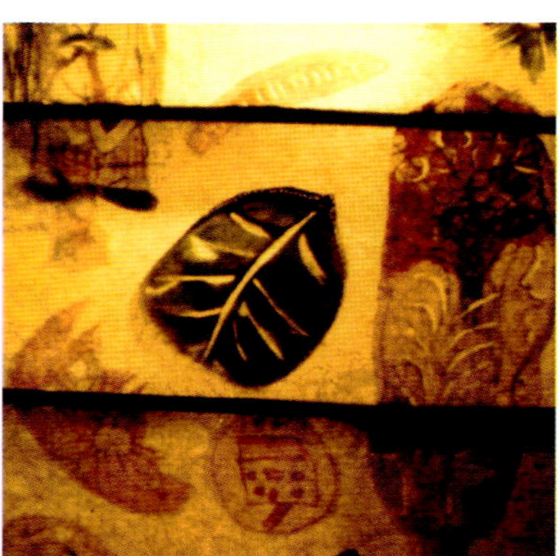

top: Echelman painting in her studio, Ubud, Bali, 1989
bottom: *Casa de Luz*, Fogg Museum, Harvard Art Museums, 1995

upturning the traditional art establishment. An early sculpture installation shown at the Harvard Art Museums, *Casa de Luz* (1995), suggests Balinese influences in the delicate drawings of leaves and figures on translucent material lit from within.

Designed as a glowing lantern structure, its play of light and shadow recalls the art of *wayang kulit* (shadow-play puppetry), a popular form of both ritual and open street performance in Indonesia, where puppeteers wittily adapt ancient stories like the Ramayana and Mahabharata to the contemporary context.

Echelman's melding of Eastern and Western influences in her architectural sculptures and installations makes for interesting conversations with works by such contemporary Chinese artists as Cai Guo-Qiang, Gu Wenda, and Xu Bing. Originally trained in traditions of ink painting and calligraphy, these artists developed their unique visual languages in spectacular installations using unusual materials like gunpowder and human hair. While Echelman's forms and materials have varied over the years, from delicate rice paper and cotton textiles to fishing nets swaying in the wind, her urban installations consistently capture the vibrant mood of Asian rituals and street festivals, with color and movement combining into brilliant visual rhythms.

Michelle Lim is a curator and assistant professor, NTU School of Art, Design and Media, Singapore.

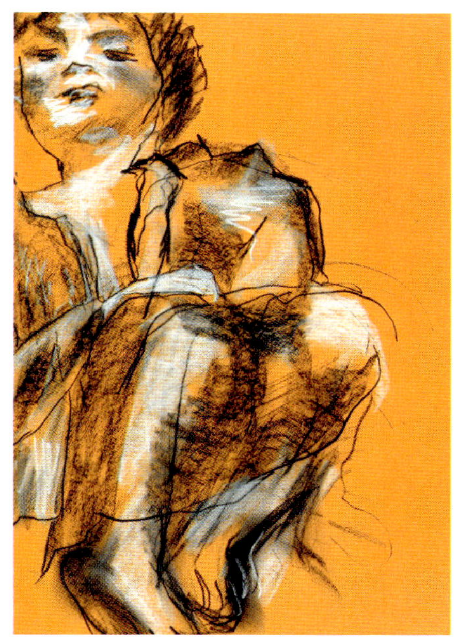
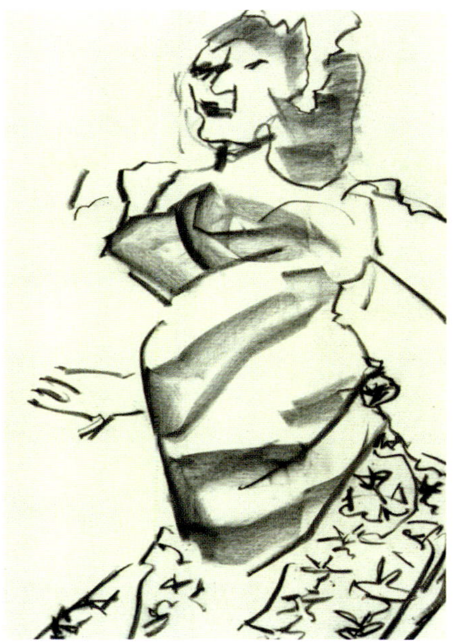
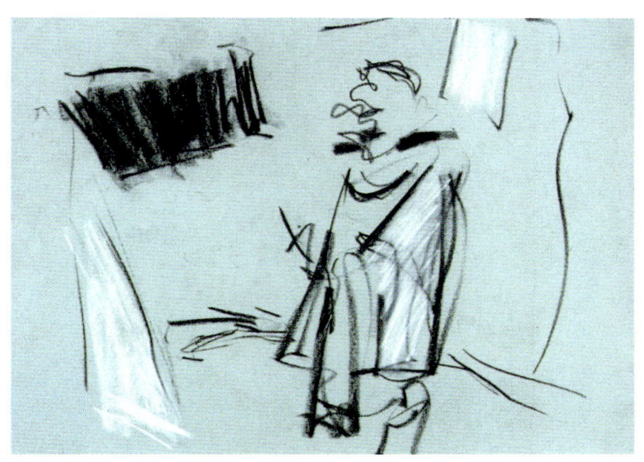
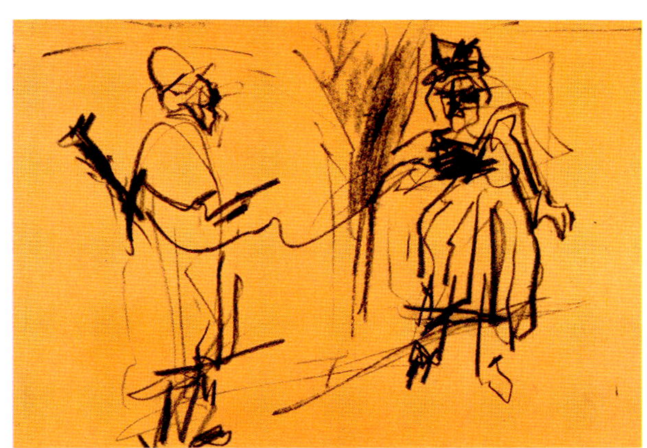
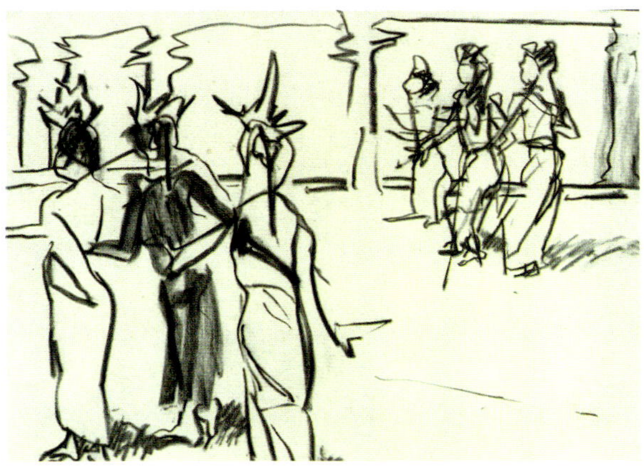
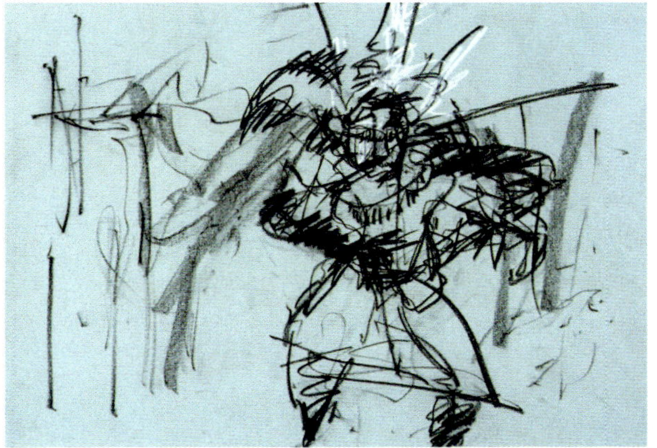

Drawings from Bali, 1988, charcoal and chalk on paper

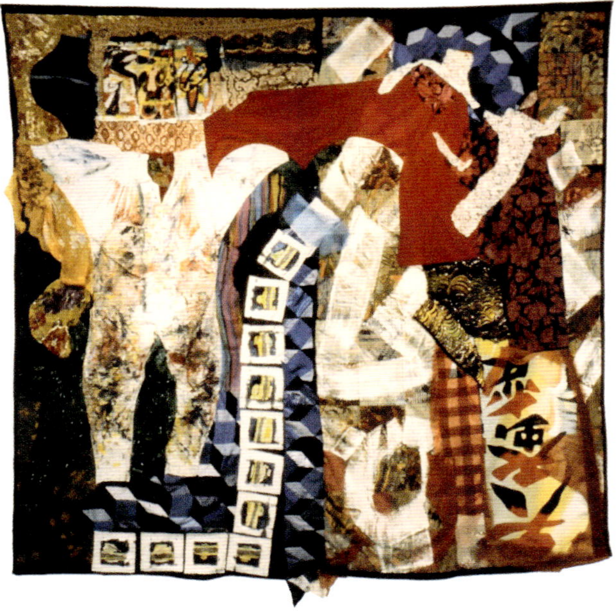

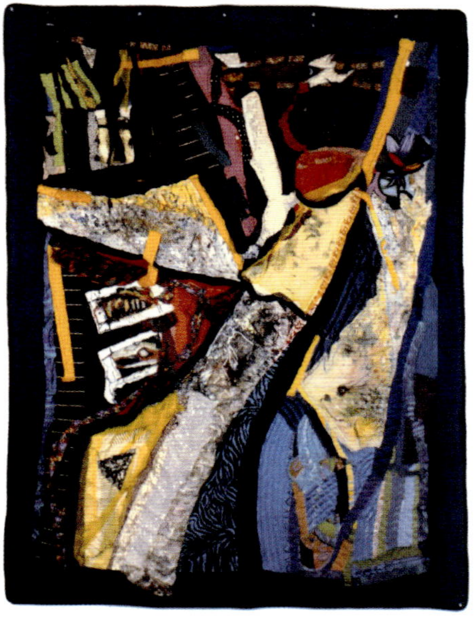

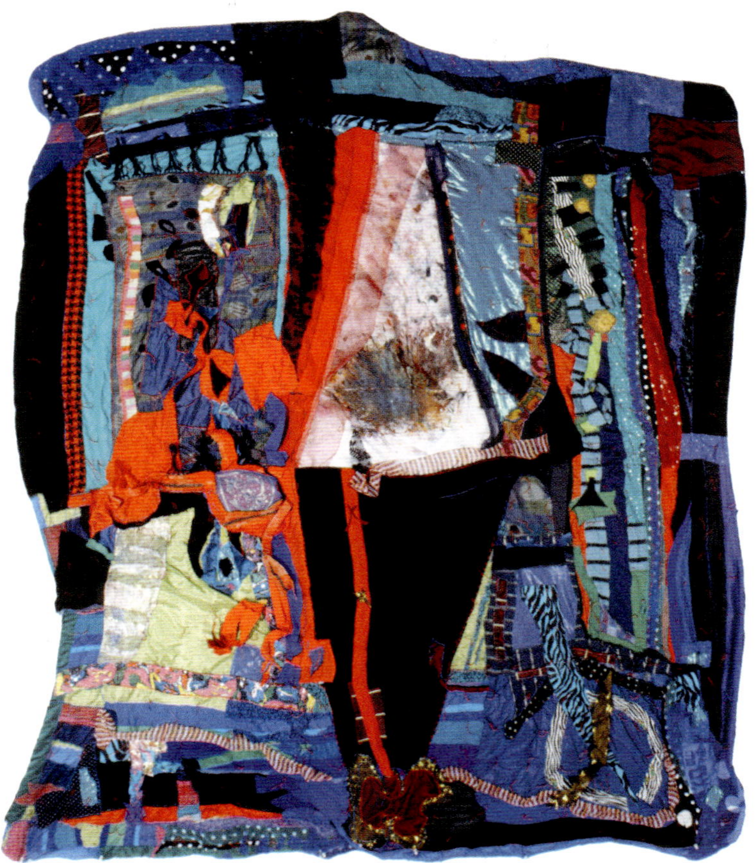

top left: *Quilt: Artist's Overalls*, 1990, acrylic on canvas sewn onto mixed fabric, movie banners, and the artist's overalls, sewn onto satin by Mary Northmore, 99⅝ × 104⅜ in.
top right: *Quilt #2*, 1991, acrylic on canvas sewn onto mixed fabric and the artist's overalls

bottom: *Quilt: Heart of Aceh*, 1992, acrylic on canvas sewn onto mixed fabric, suede, leather, sequins, embroidery, and the artist's overalls, hand-quilted by Sue Rule on batik and rayon, 96½ × 78¾ in.

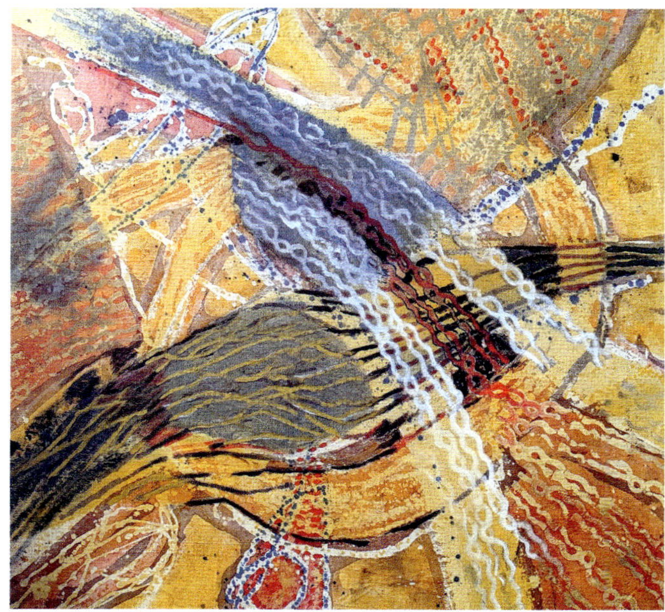

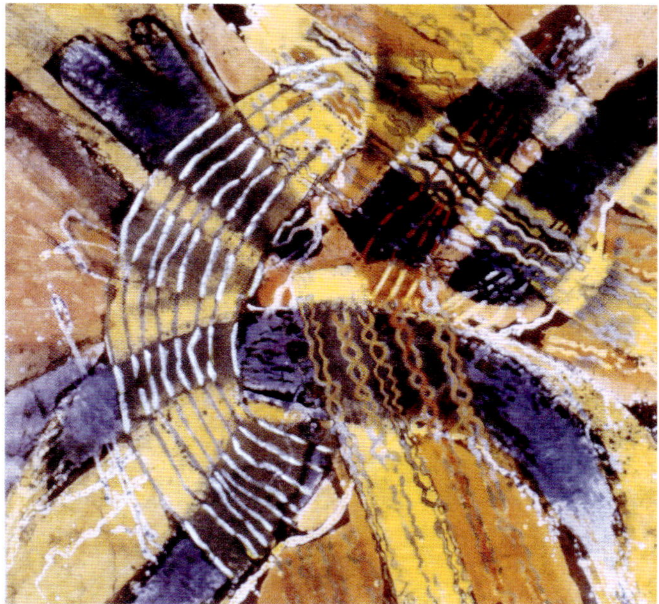

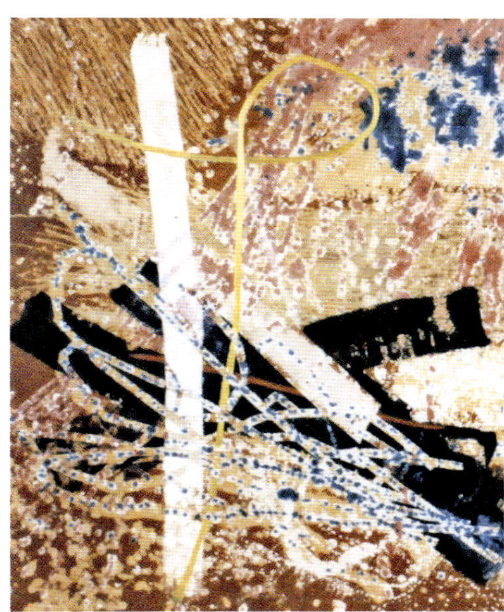

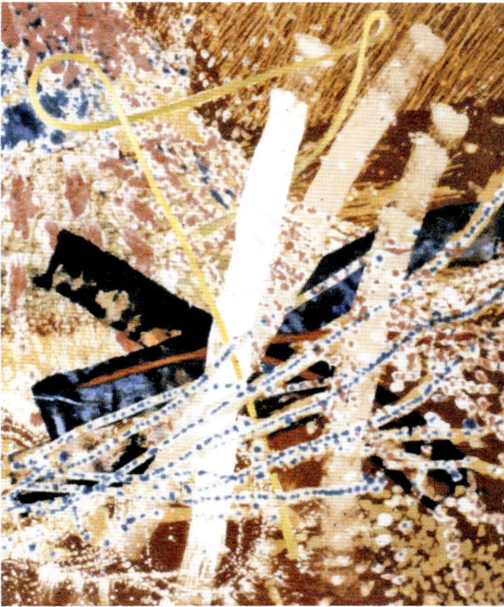

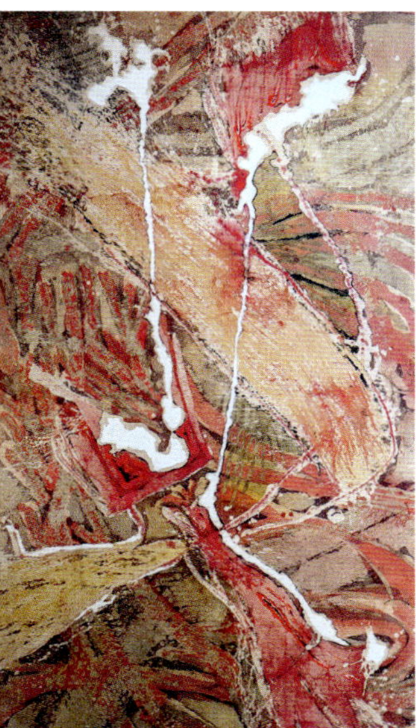

top row: *Arus #1* and *#2*, 1988, batik dye and acrylic on canvas

bottom left and center: *Supernova*, 1988, batik dye and acrylic on canvas, diptych, each 71 × 57 in.
bottom right: *Fire Flower Red*, 1988, batik dye and acrylic on canvas, 72 × 40 in.

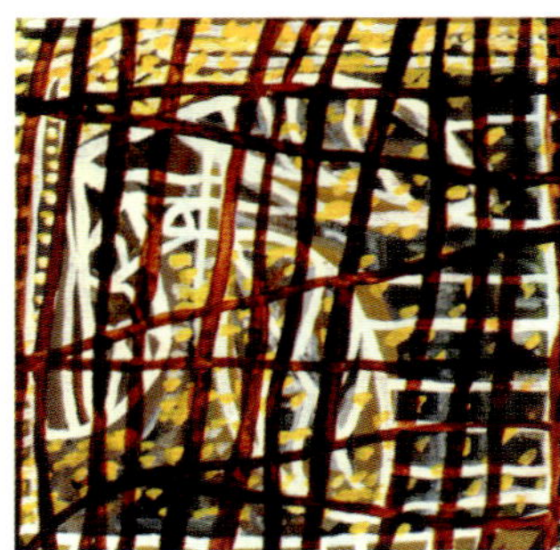
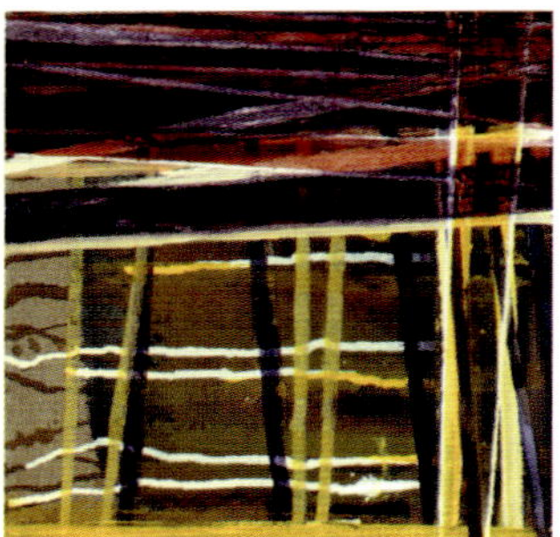
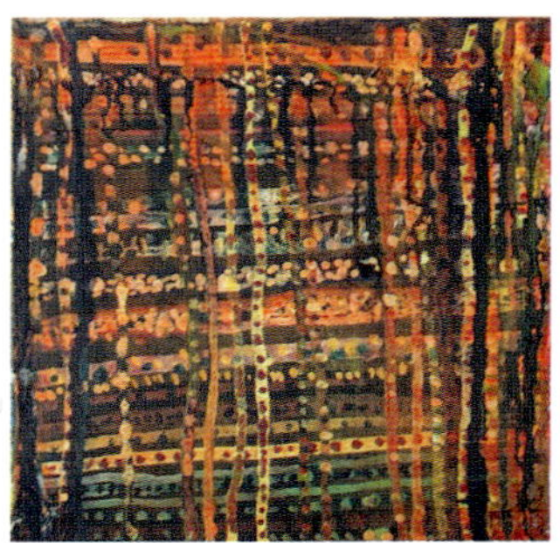
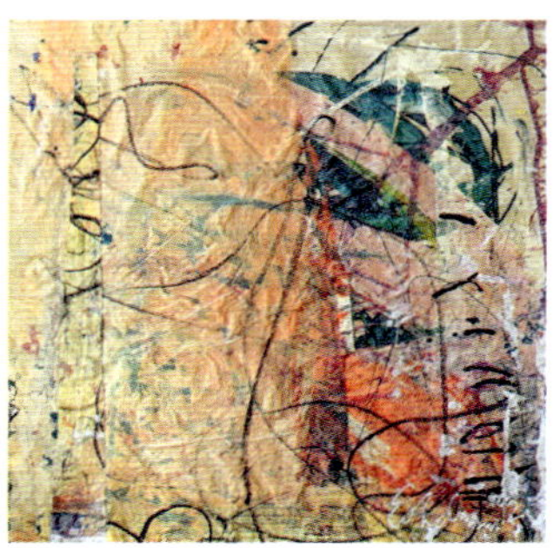
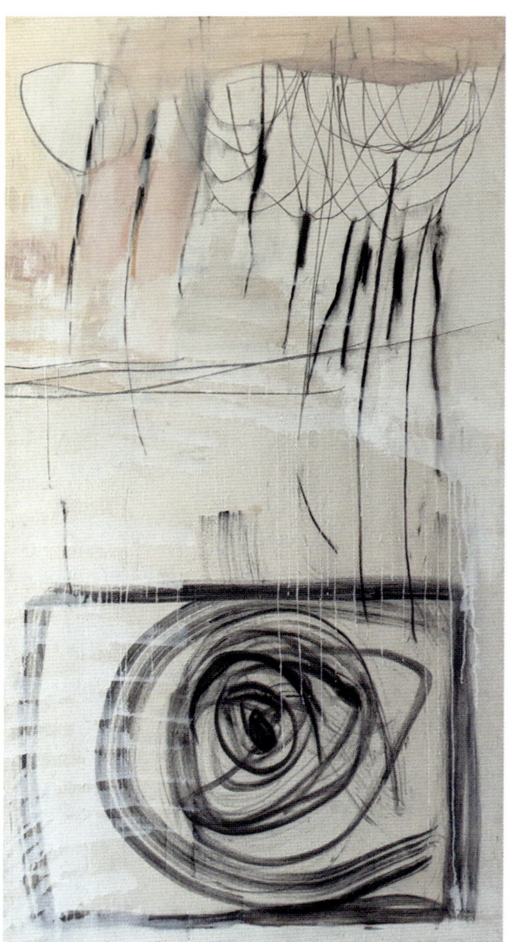
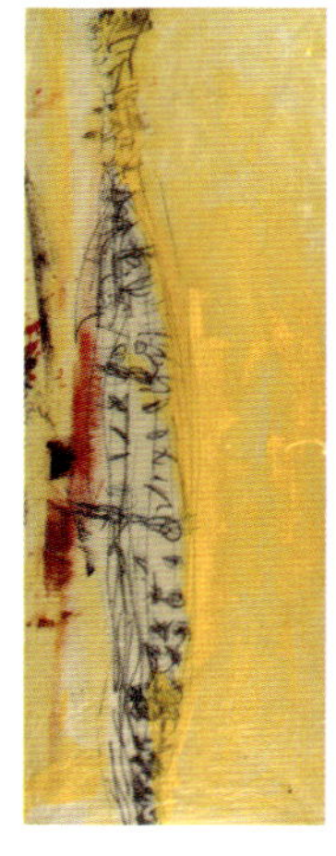
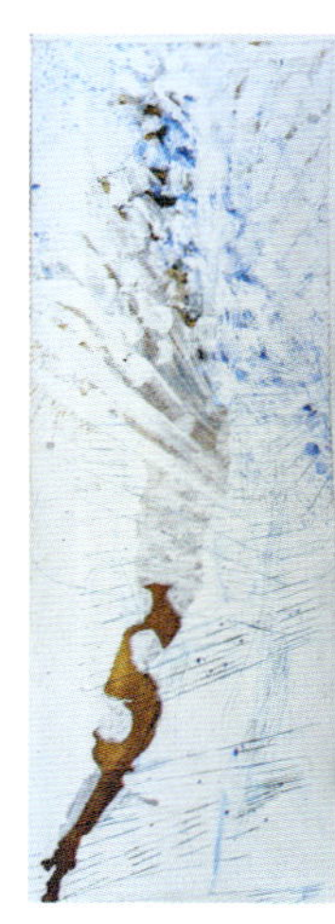
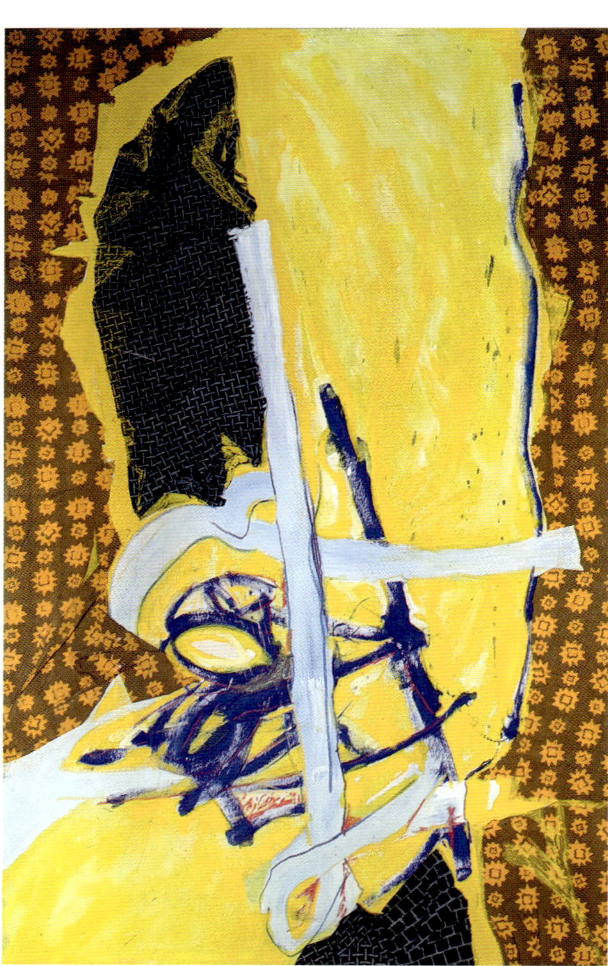

top row, left to right:
Peering Through, 1993, acrylic on canvas, 12 × 12 in.
Plaid Geyser, 1993, acrylic on linen, 12 × 12 in.
Traffic Music, 1993, acrylic on canvas, 12 × 12 in.
Gesture, 1993, ink, acrylic, and vellum on canvas

left: *Lines for Kandinsky*, 1993, burnt wood, acrylic on canvas, 65 × 36 in.
middle, top: *Trace IV (Yellow Submarine)*, 1992, acrylic and marker on trace paper, 23 × 56 in.
middle, bottom: *You Appear Calm and Collected*, 1992, airbrush acrylic, ink, and absorbent ground on canvas, 20 × 55 in.
right: *Anima*, 1989, batik fabric, acrylic, and oil crayon on canvas, 76 × 48 in.

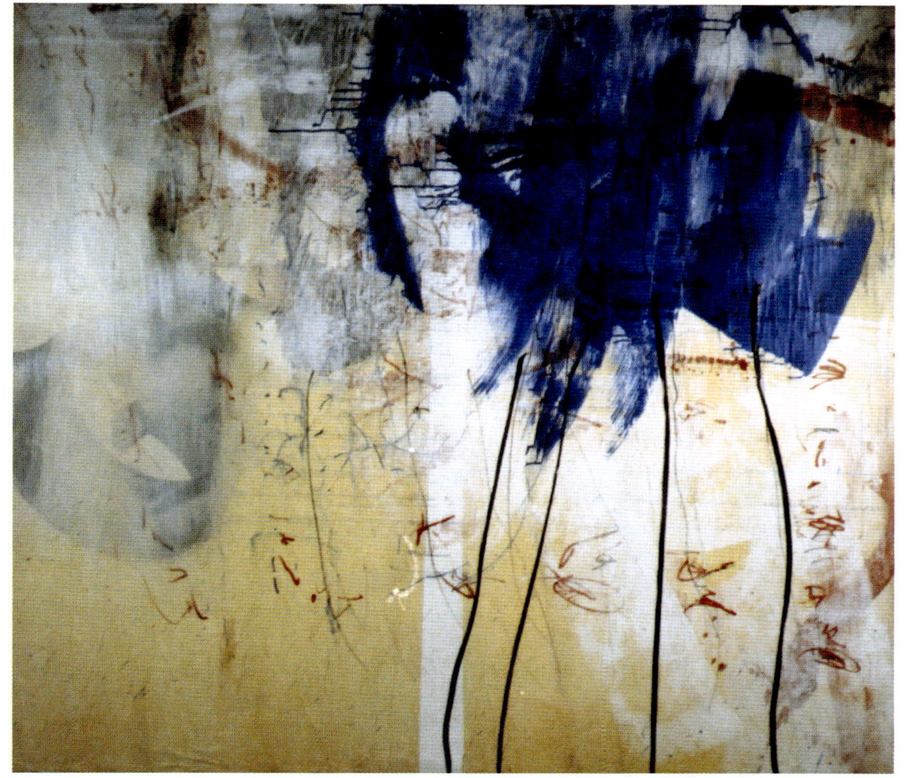

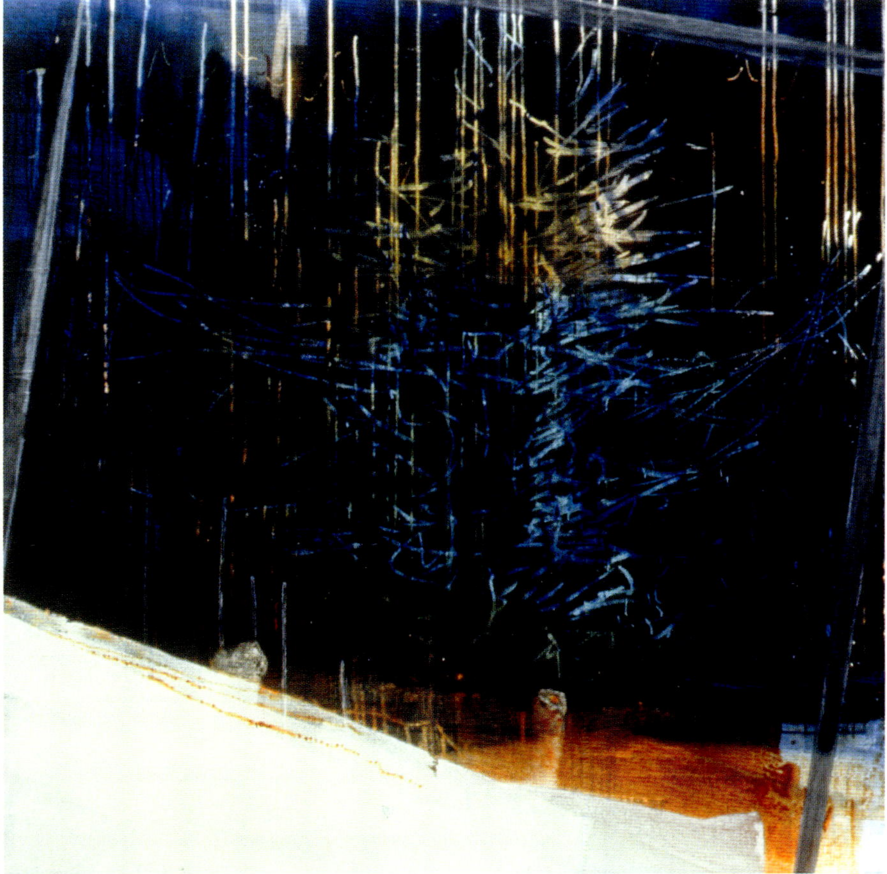

"Drips and animating repetitive strokes suggest the passage of time, while leaving us to imagine the events that might inhabit this temporal frame. Bold, gestural lines implicate the producer's body, and work, adding to the sense of past time, the awareness of corporeal action and of presence...the image, these magical, abstract signs, ask us to act and to reflect upon our own action."

—Adrian Randolph, Northwestern University, Dean of College of Arts and Sciences and Professor of Art History

top: *Mixed Metaphor*, 1993, acrylic, ink, and paper on canvas, 66 × 73 in.
bottom: *Transubstantiate*, 1993, acrylic on canvas, 59.5 × 64 in.

Without Beginning Middle or End

—

Nancy Adajania

Janet Echelman's monumental fiber sculptures soar above the horizons and public squares of cities, rippling out into the sky, burned by ice or sun, dancing with the wind, graced by the morning dew. Unseasonal rainbows by day, these works transform by night into immersive light machines glimmering in jeweled tones. Depending on the sites where they are installed, the gargantuan net sculptures are gorgeous veils or drifting shadows, cloud-sails or billowing tents. And if manifest as auroras, their auguries do not make the kind of grandiloquent claim that Percy Bysshe Shelley's *Ozymandias* (1818) does: "Look on my works, ye Mighty, and despair!"

Despite their monumentality, Echelman's works happily lack hubris—that prerogative of Greek heroes (and, I might add, many dutifully canonized male artists). The artist does not subscribe to the extractivist logic of, say, Robert Smithson and Michael Heizer, whose large-scale, site-specific interventions in nature are based on bulldozing rocks and digging long trenches into the earth, artifices premised on a relentless assault on soil and stone.

Not that Echelman is any less ambitious in playing with scale or marrying industrial processes with handmade ones. In collaboration with architects and engineers, she has developed bespoke computer software to refine her early cotton net sculptures—serendipitously inspired by the fishing nets of Mahabalipuram in southern India during the artist's period of residence there during the late 1990s—into tensile aerial sculptures. While the epic scale of her work may seem daunting, its translucency and porosity generate an inexplicable softening of edge and surface, and thus a vulnerability. The early net sculptures, made in collaboration with the fishermen of Mahabalipuram and shown at the National Institute of Design, Ahmedabad; the Birla Museum in Calcutta; and the Birla Gallery in Bombay in 1997, bore tantalizing names such as *Wide Hips* and *Playpen/Suckle Bell Buckle*. These flowing, wraparound membranes, suspended from the ceiling, alluded playfully to female sexuality. They concealed as well as exposed the body's erogenous zones. In this way, these works are suggestive of how the third eye (a broader Hindu reference to the supreme deity Shiva's supernal eye of expanded knowledge, which can destroy the world of illusion and delusion) is often associated with voluminous breasts with dark, thirsty nipples. A study in generative paradox, the concept of the third eye transposed the mythology of the all-powerful male god onto the female anatomy. The monumental breasts became carriers of an alternative life energy and knowledge. They did not explode with omnipotence, but oozed with a tender, nurturing stream of dreams and secrets harbored in the crevices and fluids of women's bodies. The third eye recalls the subversive psychologistic readings of the female subconscious long examined by such artists as Louise Bourgeois and Kiki Smith.

"The references to sagging breasts and dark thirsty nipples ring deeply true," Echelman agreed, recounting that she had "resided for five years in the island of Bali, with its Hindu culture, and was deeply influenced by the mythological character of Rangda—the queen who became a child-eating witch goddess. This is what led me to apply for the Fulbright Lectureship to teach at the National Institute of Design (NID) in India and to immerse myself more deeply in its culture and craft traditions."[2] Echelman's next collaboration in India, *Garden of Earthly Delights* in Coimbatore, contrasted her aerial billowing net forms with a trio of solid forms chiseled from local earthen bricks with Hindu temple carvers.

India gave Echelman's practice a jump start. I would situate her within a long genealogy of US artists-as-inventors who visited the National Institute of Design, established in 1961 in post-colonial India during the Cold War years with the help of the Ford Foundation and the visionary Sarabhai family, who revived the Bauhaus edict of "learning by doing." Among those who were drawn to the Sarabhai residency program were Echelman's mentor, Robert Rauschenberg, as well as Charles and Ray Eames, John Cage, David Tudor, Lynda Benglis, and numerous other avant-garde artists who experimented with sculpture, sound, exhibition design, and multimedia installation.

The legendary Frei Otto worked as an architectural consultant for the National Institute of Design in the 1970s, and his gravity-defying tensile structures of lightweight shells with hanging nets bear a formal resemblance to

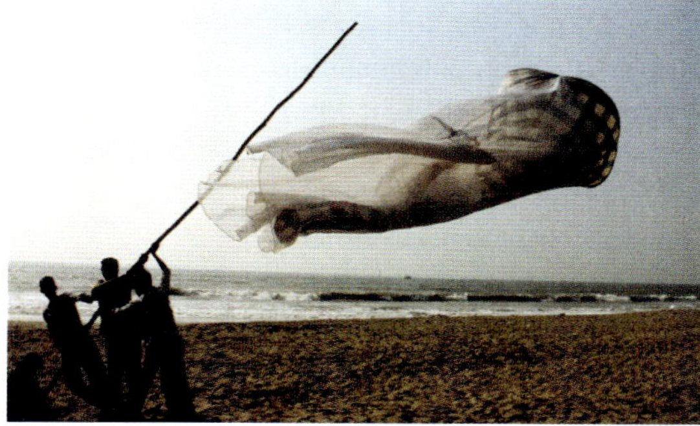

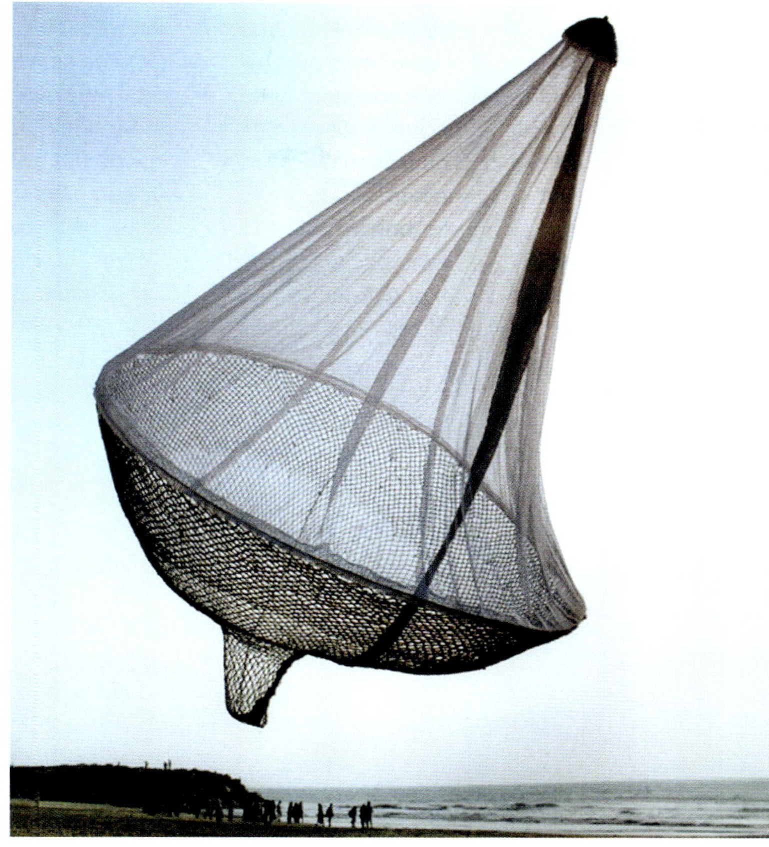

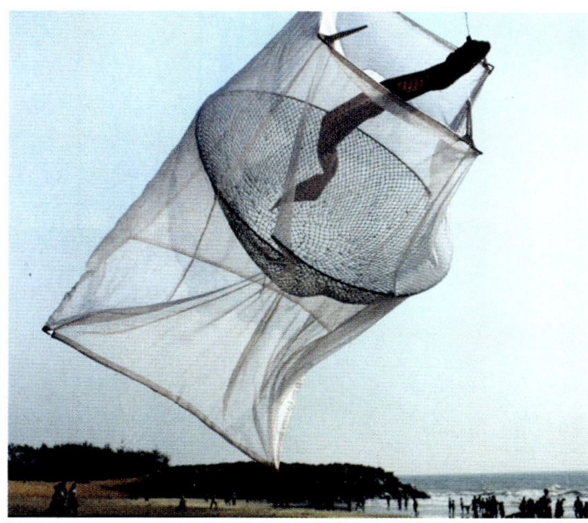

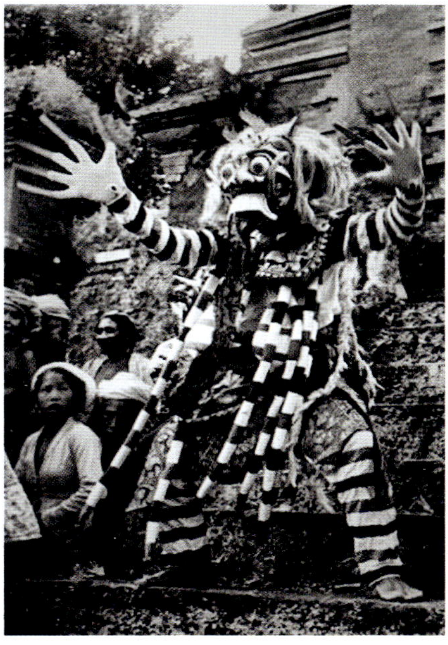

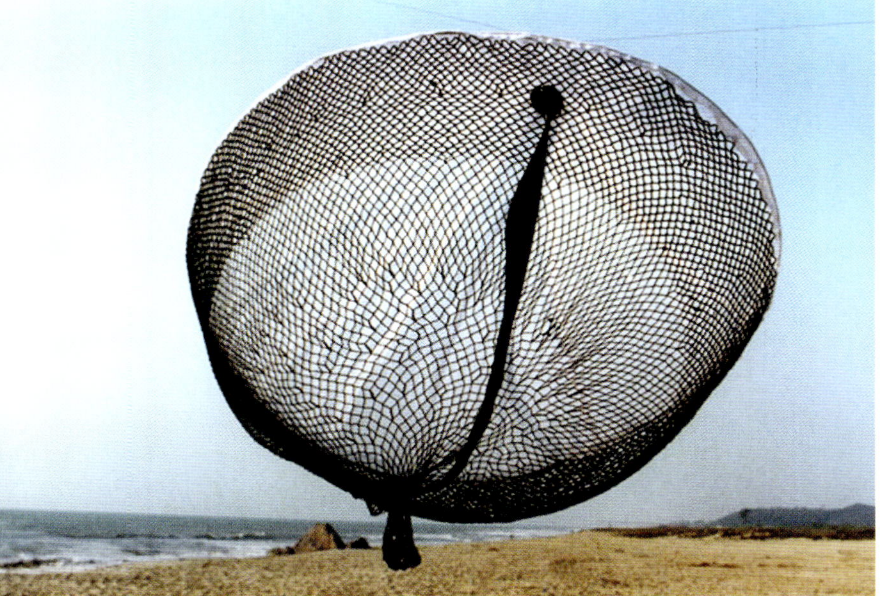

Clockwise from middle left: *Playpen / Suckle Bell Buckle*, *More Than You Can Chew*, and *Wide Hips* (side and upward views), 1997, Mahabalipuram, India
bottom left: Ritual dance of the Balinese witch goddess Rangda

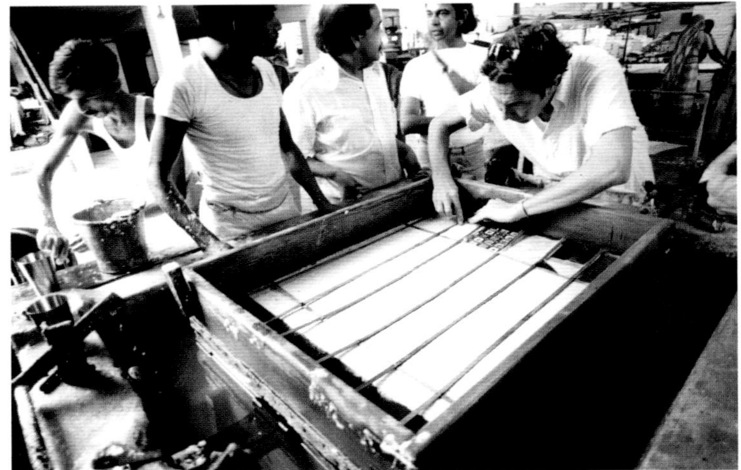

Echelman's own improvisations, made decades later. What does it mean to stand under one of Echelman's net clouds? Are we possessed by Edmund Burke's aesthetic reading of the sublime, whose ground note is terror? Something so vast and awe-inspiring that we are forced to surrender ourselves to it? Or do we experience something more intimate and softer, like the memory of the waters of the womb, or our first awareness of light or wind?

To return to India and my home city of Mumbai, I find myself standing under one of Echelman's monumental fiber sculptures, this one a work commissioned by private collectors Swati and Ajay Piramal for the interior of their sea-facing mansion, Karuna Sindhu, in 2020. *Without Beginning Middle or End* pictorially references the Earth's great rivers and the replenishing cycles of rain and evaporation.

Its genesis lies in a set of verses from the Bhagavad Gita, a key Hindu scriptural text, which have deep personal significance for Swati Piramal, and which she shared with the artist. Echelman selected verse 19: "You are without beginning, middle, or end; you touch everything with your infinite power.... Your radiance warms the entire cosmos." This verse is meant to bedazzle us with the great divinity Krishna's Vishvarupa, or universal form; his eyes hold the sun and the moon and his mouth breathes fire. It is also Krishna's device to stun Arjuna into obedience, to enter the battlefield and kill his own without any ordinary moral qualms.

This complex verse from the Gita of course requires further elaboration, but what we can safely deduce from it is the cautionary tale that the creator can so easily become the destroyer. As I look up at *Without Beginning Middle or End*, it occurs to me that it may not necessarily connote a sovereign and forbidding universal form to which we must submit ourselves. Instead, in the presence of Echelman's interpretation, I find myself thinking intuitively of another quality associated with the great divinity Krishna, one that endears him to his devotees: his capacity for *lila*, endless, childlike, cosmic play. Intriguingly, this work carries forward the ludic aspect of Echelman's bell-shaped National Institute of Design sculptures, bridging the corporeal and the sublime. It is metaphysically expansive but also tender, fluid. It feels intensely convivial and familiar. It reminds me of the twilight skies of my childhood, under which my mother and I would count the various shades of the sun as it melted into the sky: orange, cerulean, indigo, violet.

As evening falls over Karuna Sindhu, each colored knot of the sculpture shimmers like a teardrop. Our lives are far more entangled and enmeshed than the military-industrial complexes of our nations would like us to believe.

Nancy Adajania is a Mumbai-based cultural theorist and co-artistic director of the 9th Gwangju Biennale.

above: Robert Rauschenberg collaborating with Suhrid and Anand Sarabhai and paper artisans, Ahmedabad, India, 1975

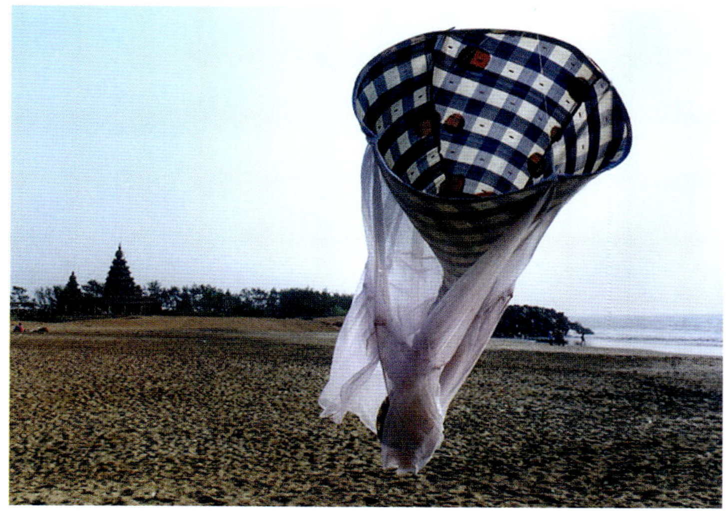

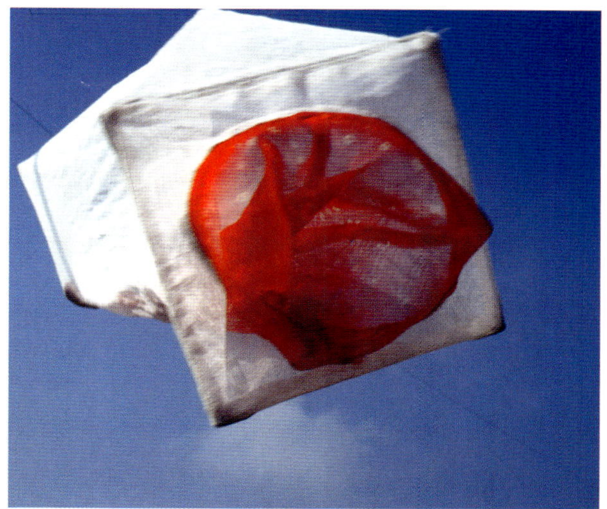

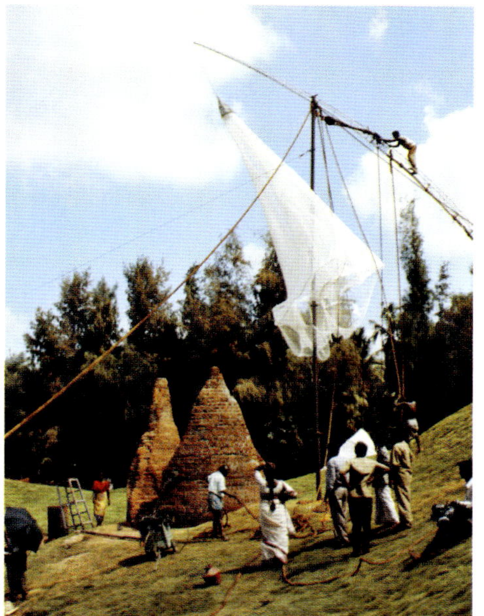

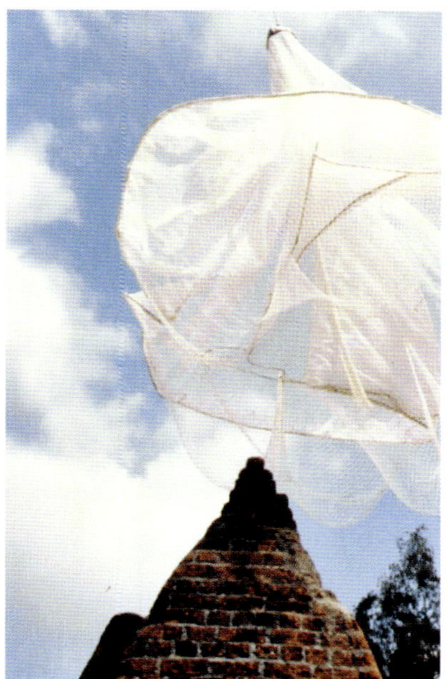

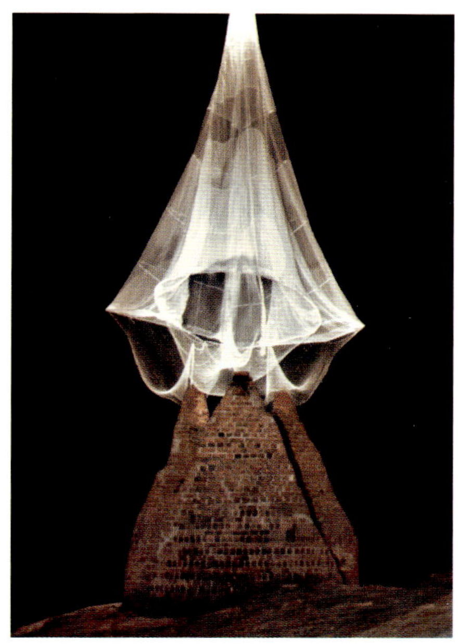

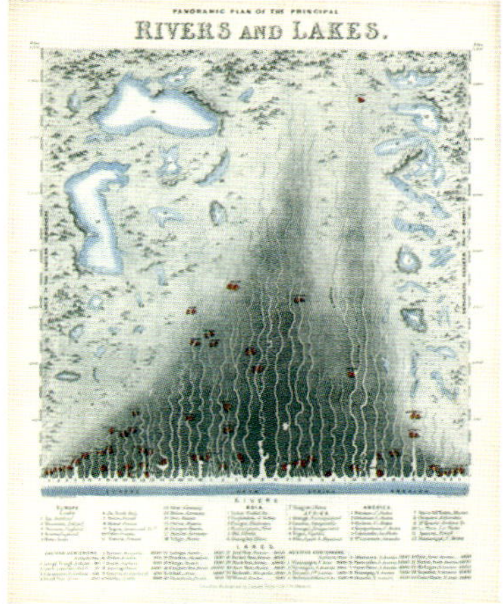

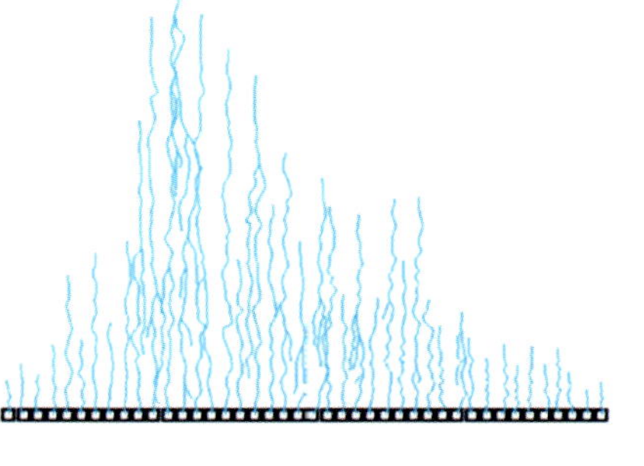

top row: *More Than You Can Chew, Red Hot Dripping*, 1997, Mahabalipuram, India
middle row: *Garden of Earthly Delights*, 1998, Coimbatore, India
bottom row: Preliminary sketch referencing major rivers of the world for *Without Beginning Middle or End*, 2020, Mumbai, India

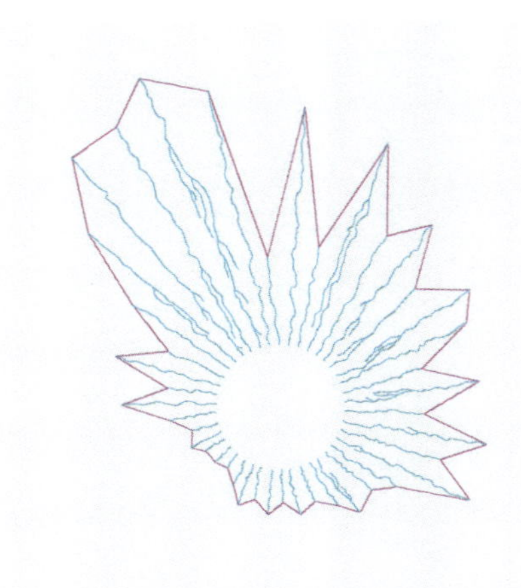

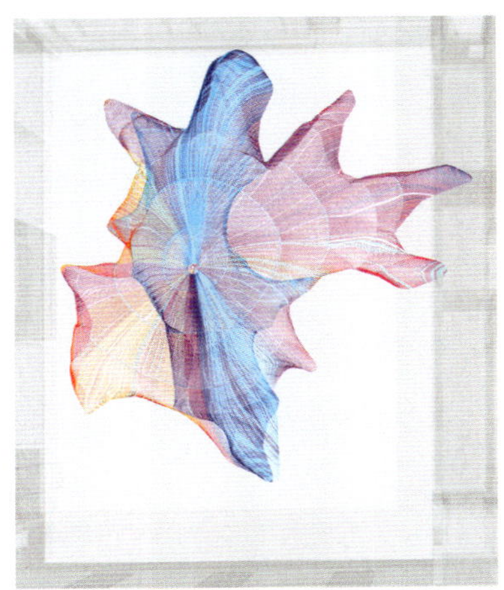

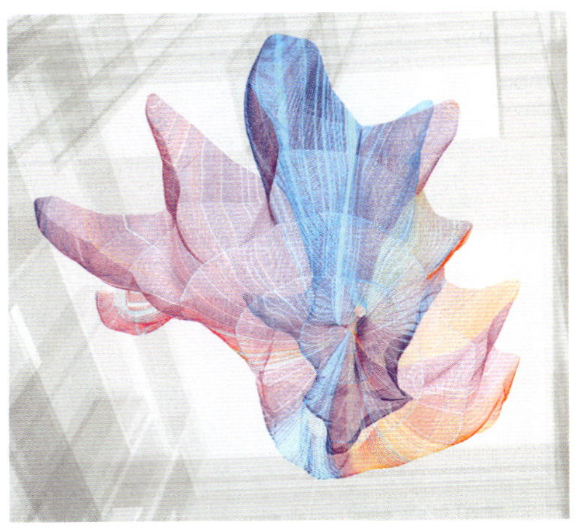

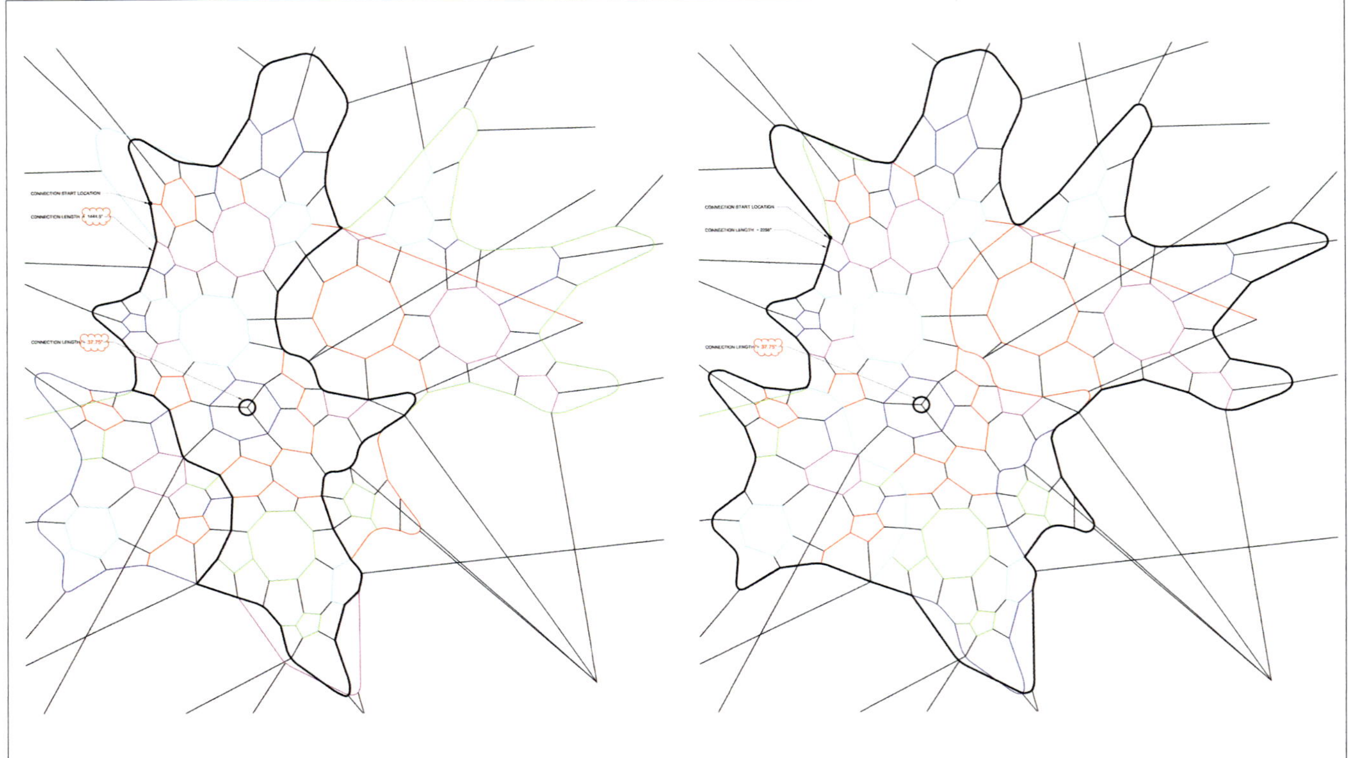

Design drawings for *Without Beginning Middle or End*, 2020

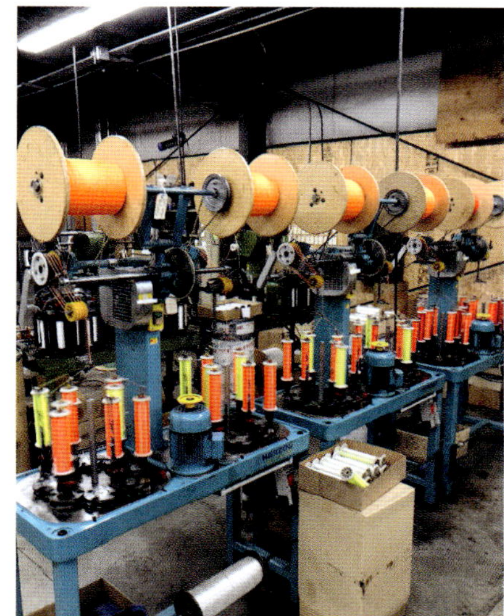

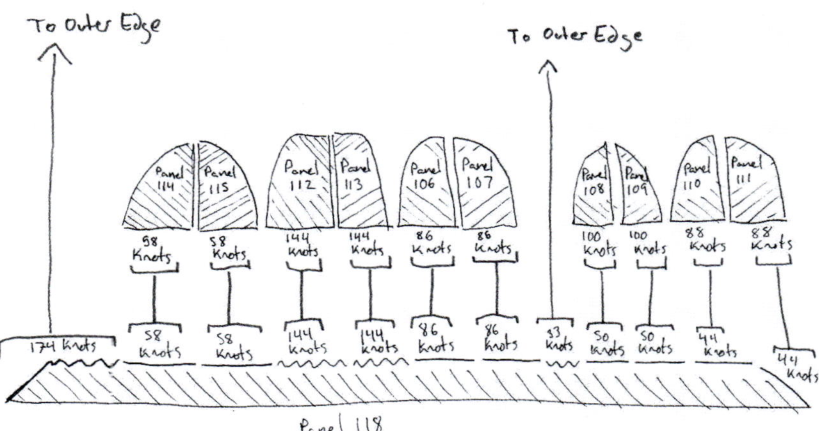

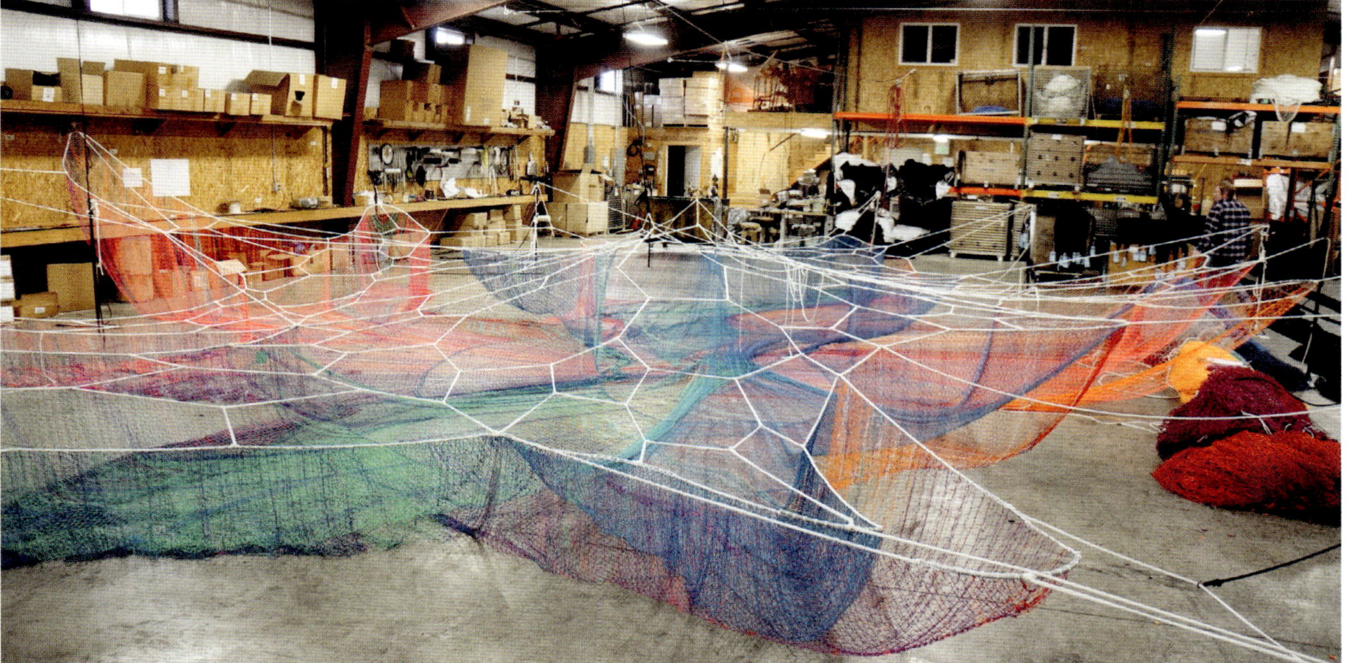

Fabrication of *Without Beginning Middle or End*, 2020

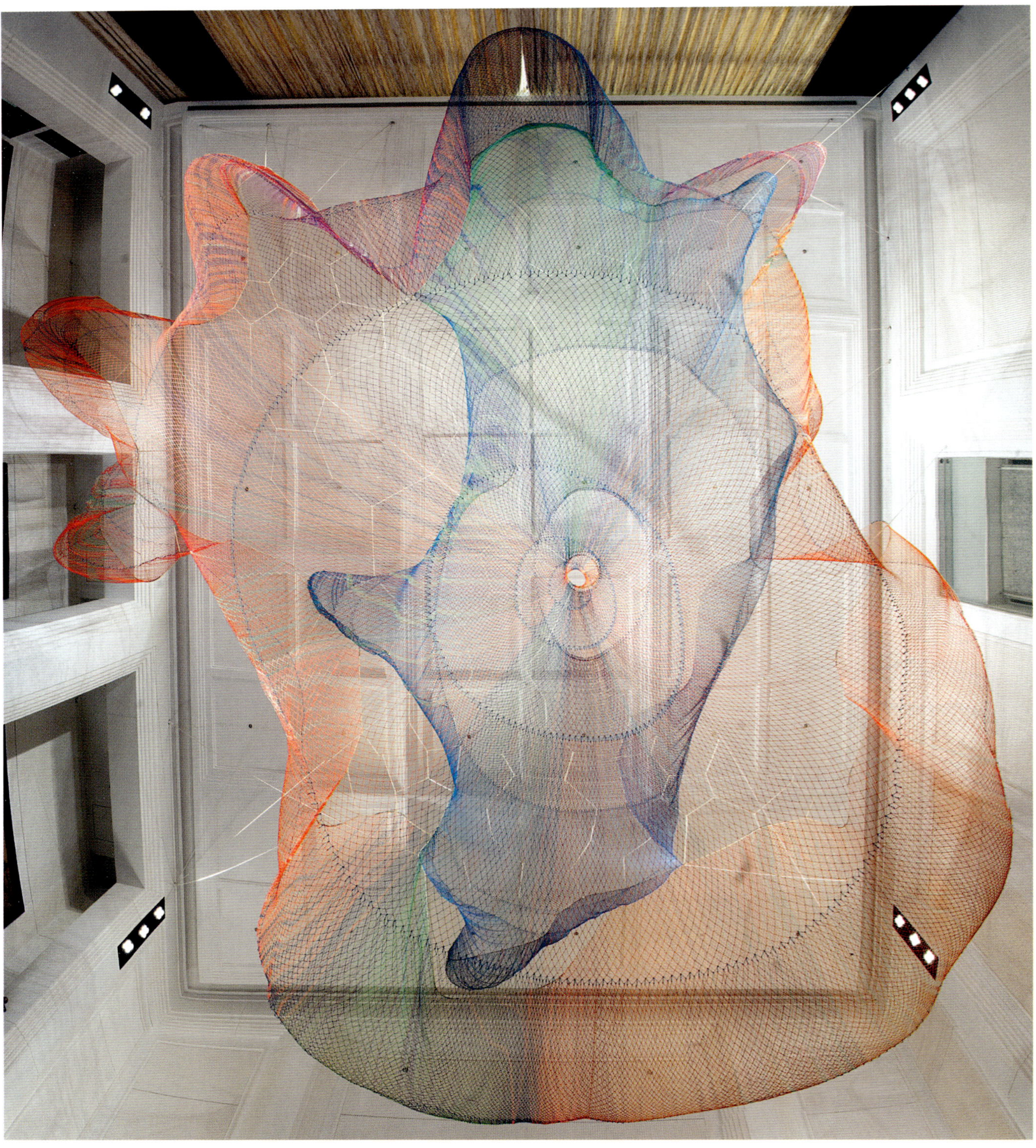

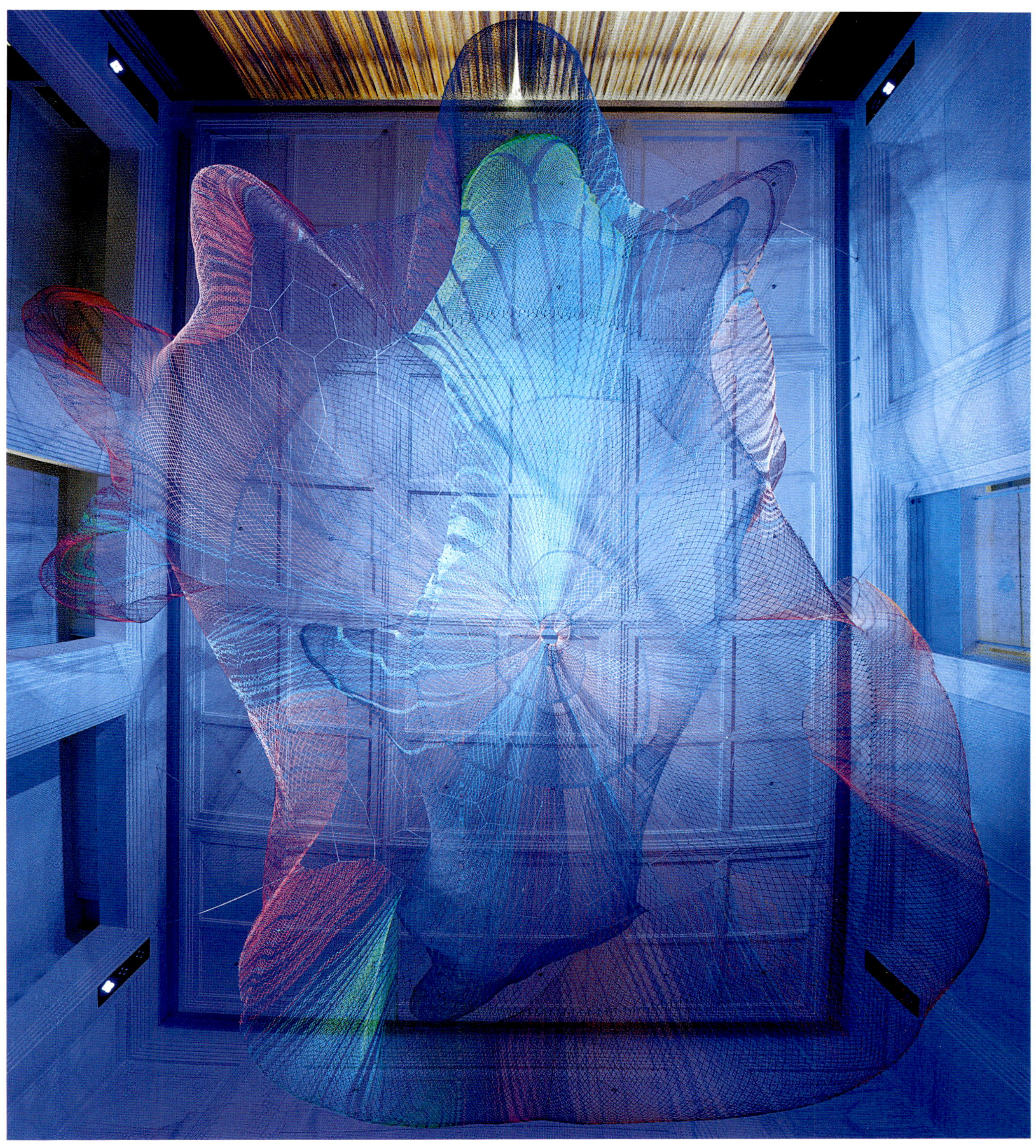

opposite and above: Upward view, day and night, of *Without Beginning Middle or End*, 2020

following pages: *Without Beginning Middle or End*, 2020, private residence Karuna Sindhu, Mumbai

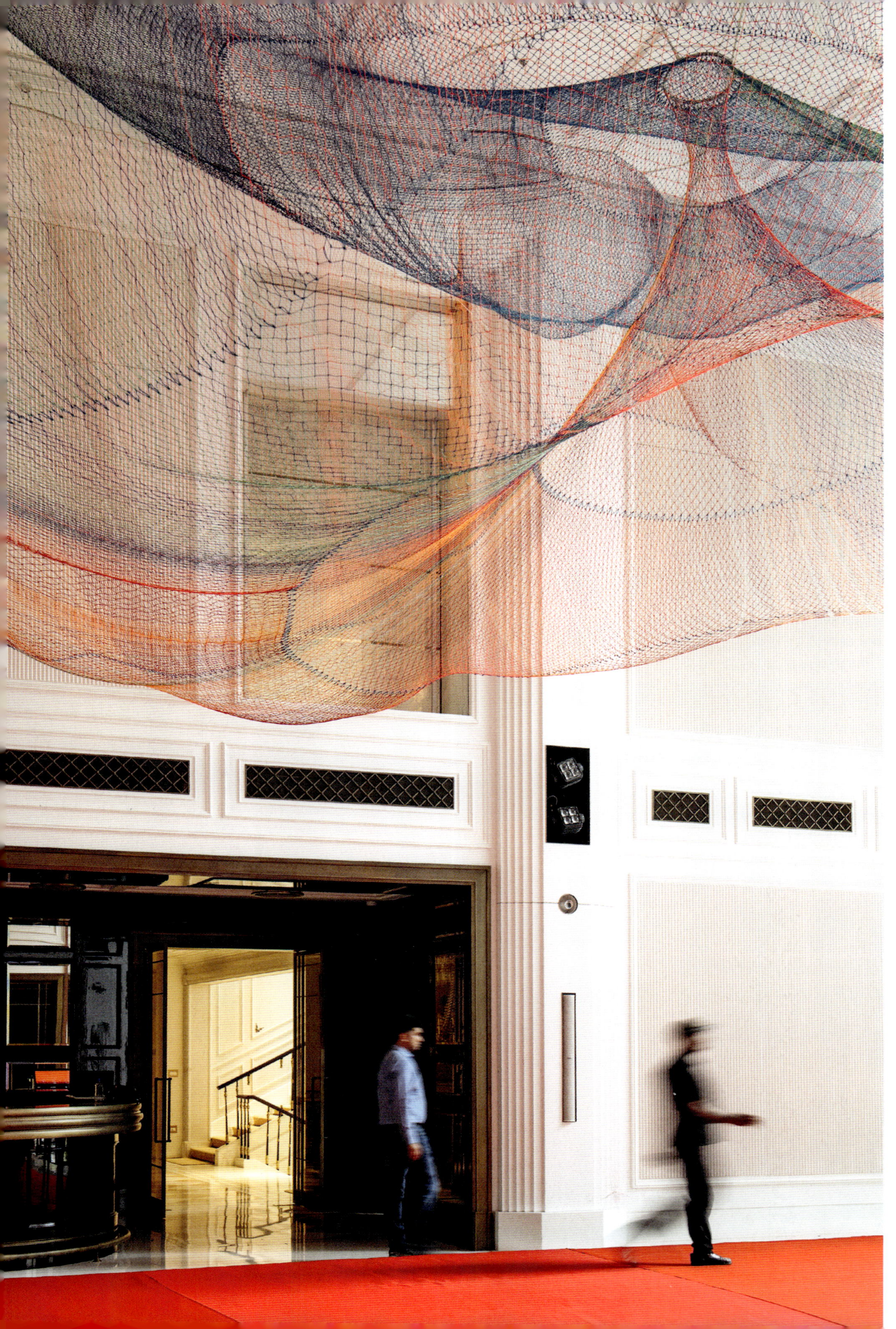

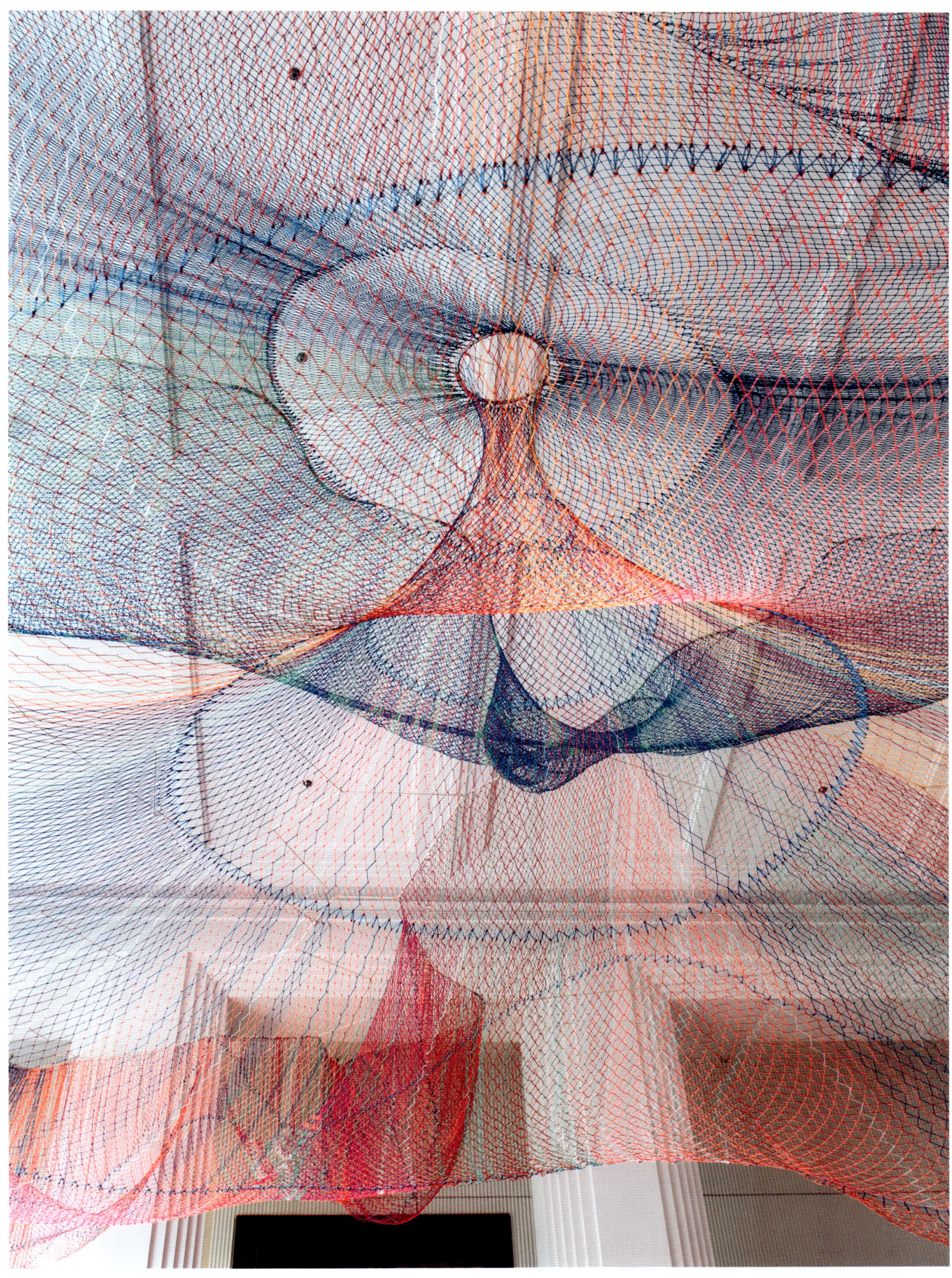

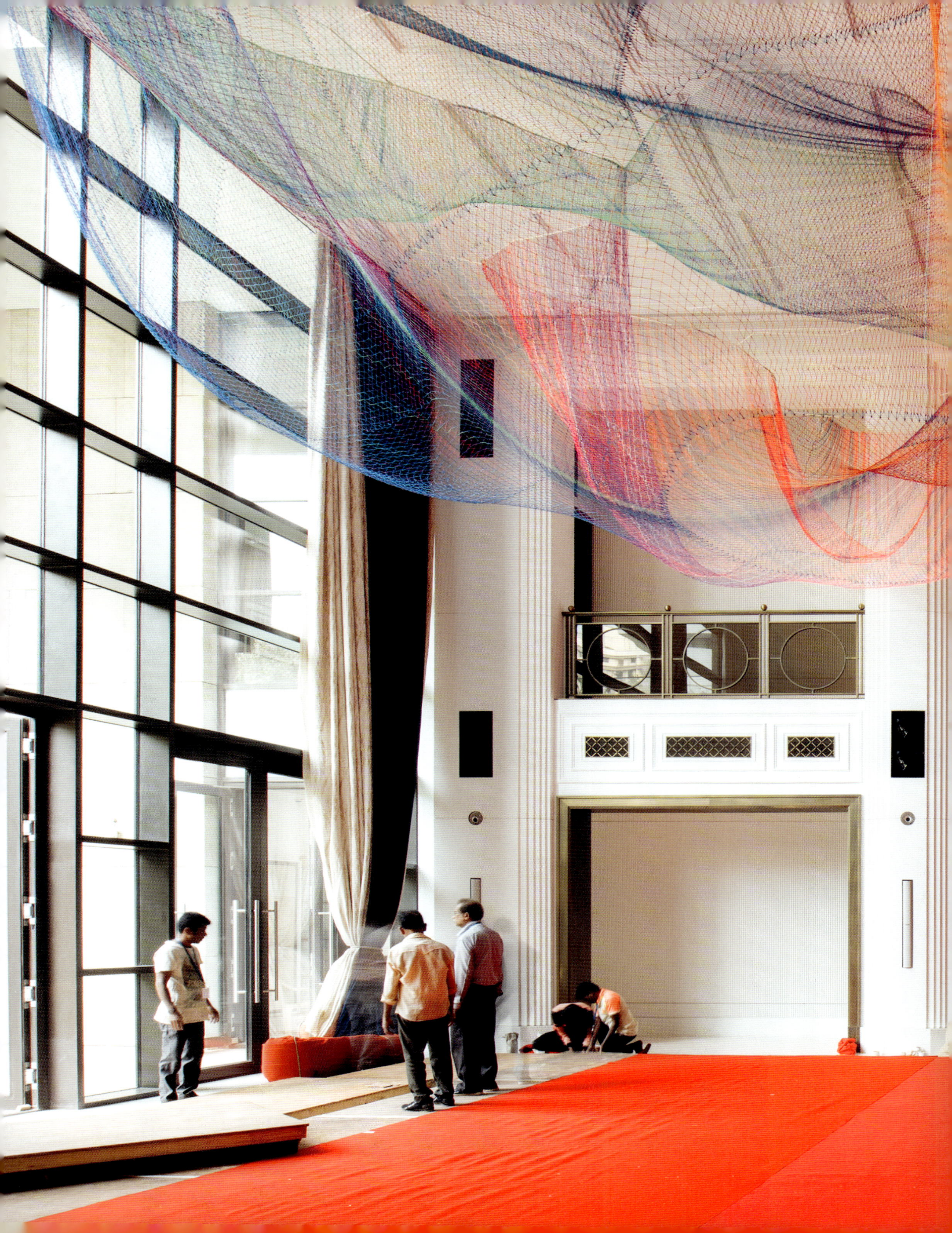

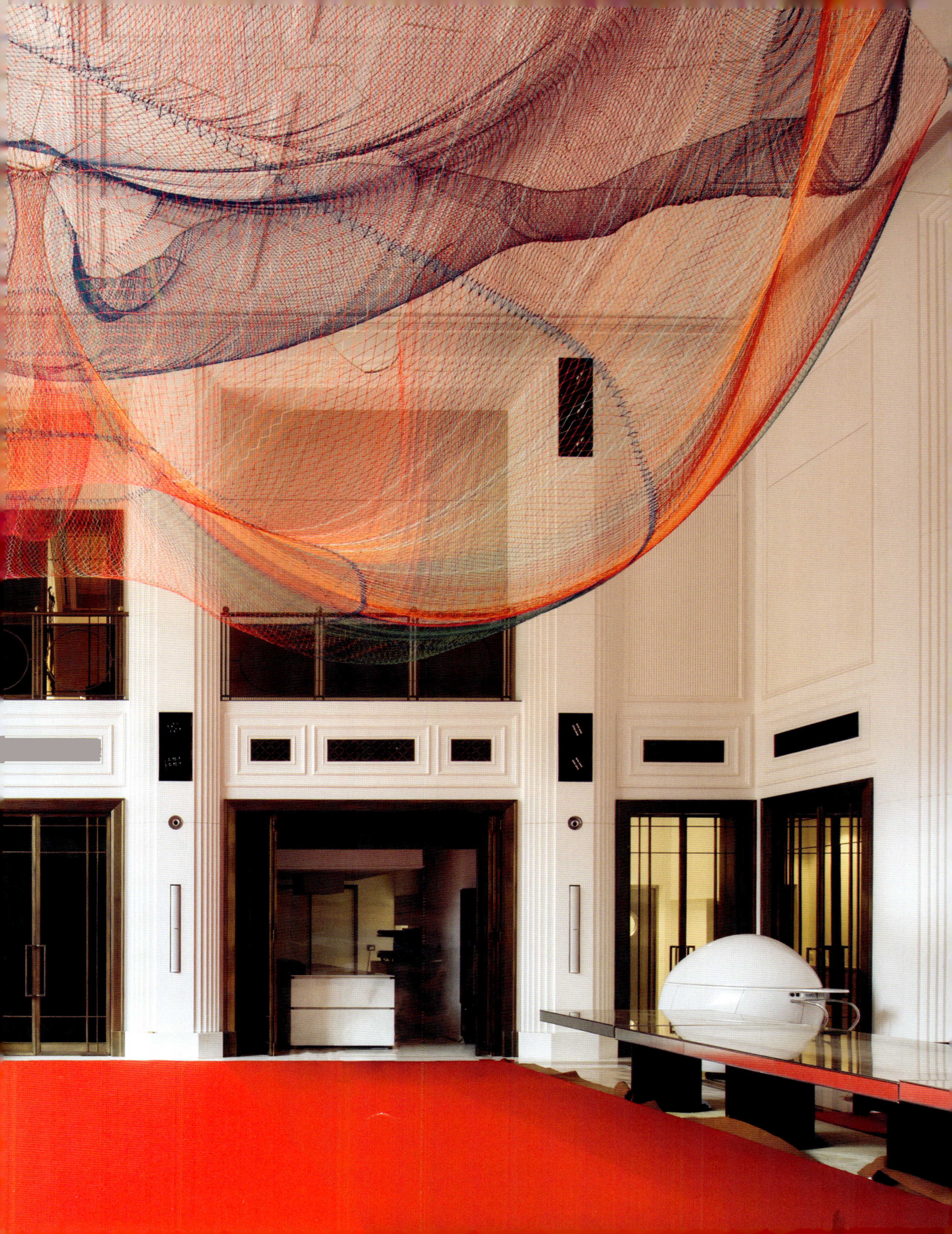

From Painting to Environment

—

Danilo Eccher

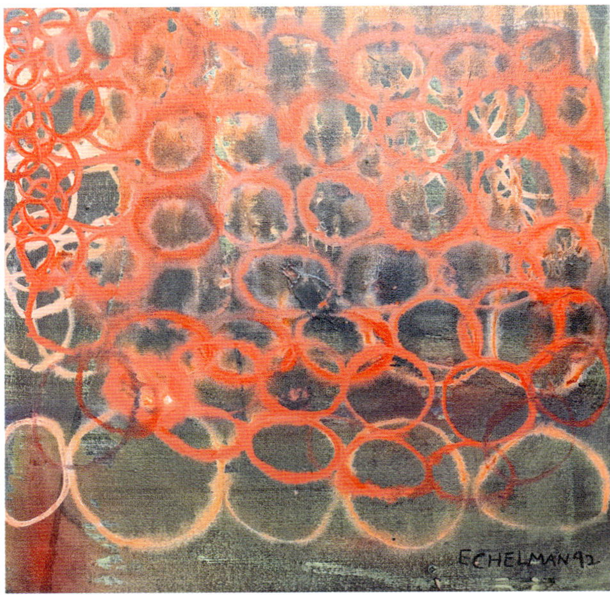

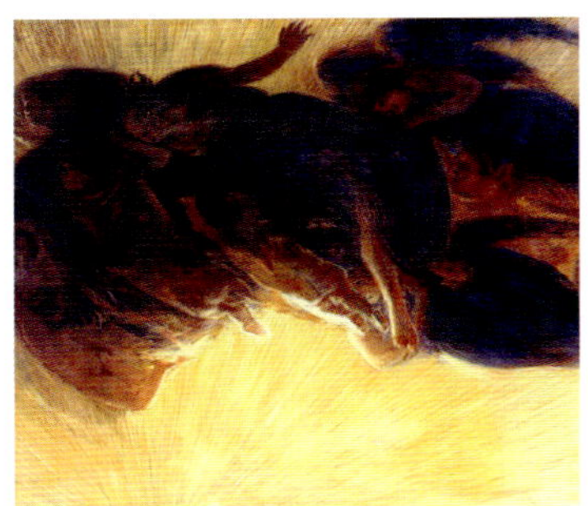

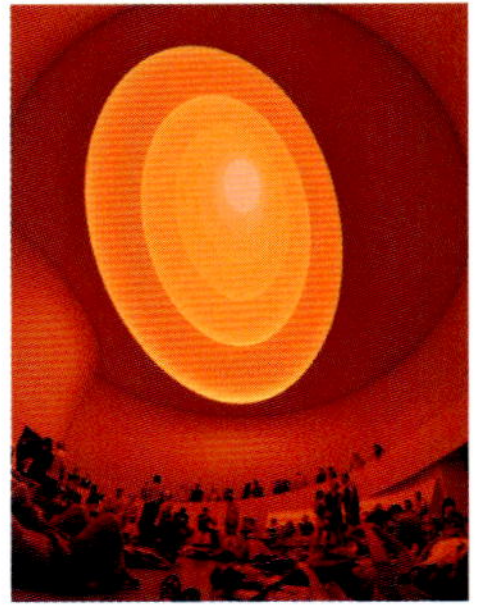

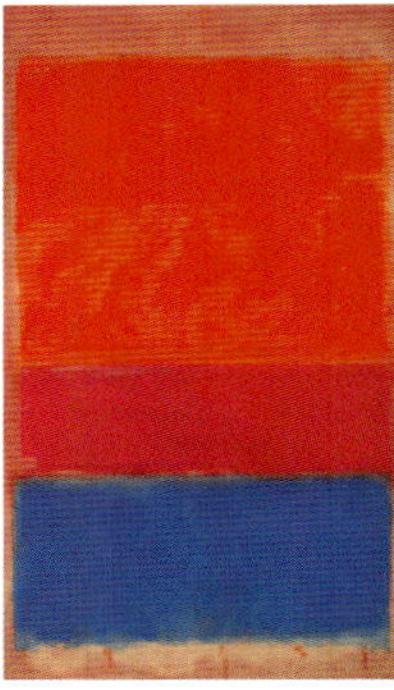

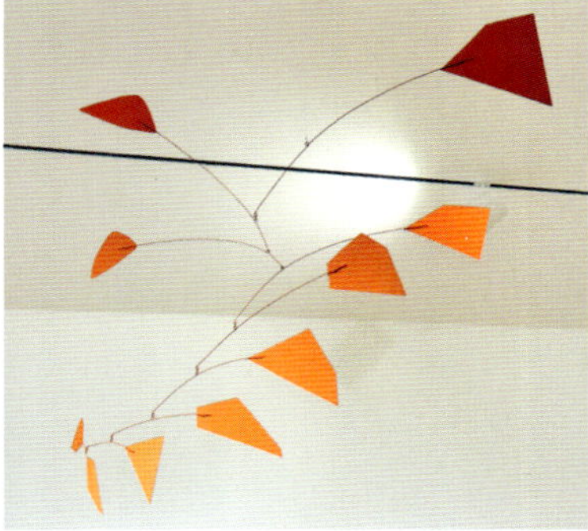

clockwise from top: Janet Echelman, *Floating Circles*, 1992, acrylic on canvas, 24 x 24 in.; James Turrell, *Aten Reign*, 2013, installation view at the Solomon R. Guggenheim Museum, New York; Alexander Calder, *Holy Red*, 1960; Mark Rothko, *No. 1 (Royal Red and Blue)*, 1954; Gaetano Previati, *The Creation of Light*, ca. 1913

Space itself is a protagonist in Echelman's ongoing research. Light, shadows, dimension, and transparency are central data points in her pictorial orientations in space, which operate in tandem with their social context: streets, squares, parks.

Tracing a critical journey through Echelman's body of work requires both analytical experimentation and an address of the complexity of the political meaning of public art. Examining her contemporary works through an art historical lens of modernist abstraction offers such a dual approach.

The dispersal of colors produced by the top-net lattice found in many of her works is suggestive of the myriad theories of painterly abstraction that emerged between the late nineteenth and early twentieth centuries in France, Switzerland, and Italy. Gaetano Previati's 1913 *The Creation of Light*, for example, depicts a chromatic cloud backlit by a brilliant yellow light. Exemplary of the emotional response sought by Symbolism, Previati's approach is similar to the way Echelman's abstract butterflies and flowers evoke a sense of silent, magical, poetic naturalism.

But Echelman escapes the romantic and decadent embrace of Symbolist painters through her scrupulous chromatic investigations, drawing on thinkers from Johannes Itten to Josef and Anni Albers and integrating color's immersive qualities and scientific laws into her works. She engages in rigorous artistic research to make works that turn on formal analysis yet do not dispense with narrative pleasure. One may perceive in them a fragile meeting point with analogous emotions in the perceptual works of artist James Turrell. But Echelman's investigations into light's chromatic principles and her activation of the viewer may be more closely aligned with the dynamic works of Venezuelan-born artist Carlos Cruz-Diez, in which rigor and fun, analysis and play, are precisely conjoined in the relationship between space and color.

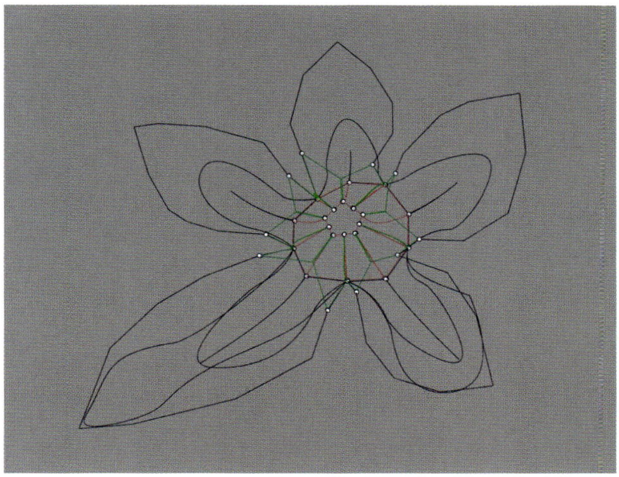

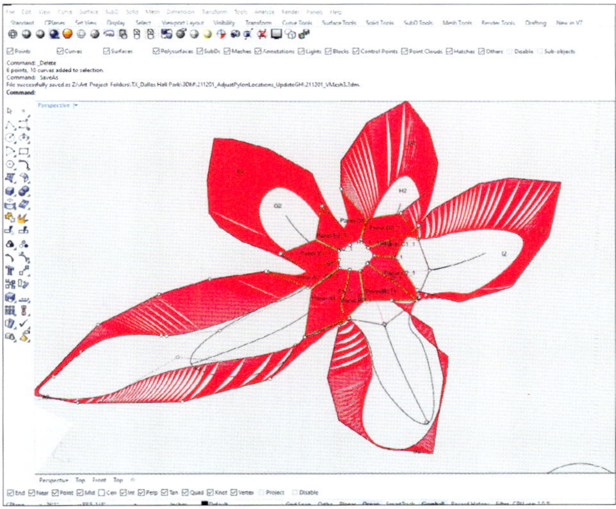

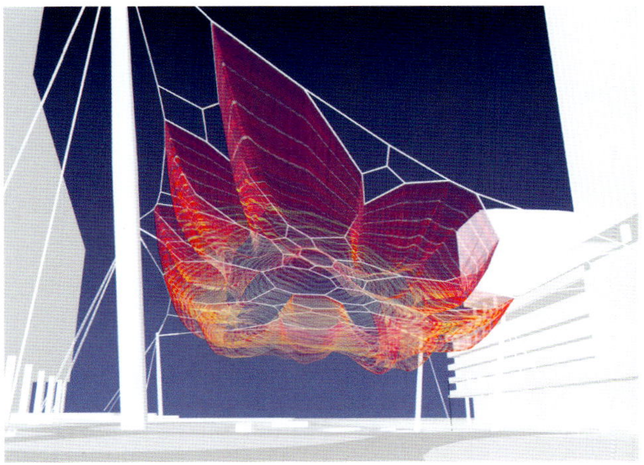

Preliminary sketches for *Butterfly Rest Stop*, 2024

This type of inventiveness is similar to the painting of two other South American artists, Julio Le Parc and Jesús-Rafael Soto, whose works, like Echelman's, transform cold psychological investigations of perception into explorations of the visual poetry of colors, plays on light, and the surprise of an elusive image. But just as she did not allow herself to be seduced by the strict palette of the Symbolists, Echelman balances the emphasis on irreverence and chance operations of these South American art practices with a more detached control of painting by drawing on a vast array of US abstract art by Mark Rothko, Ellsworth Kelly, Frank Stella, Sol LeWitt, and their ilk, and placing a small but distinct distance between herself and the work of art. Through this new pictorial awareness, one can grasp the aerial lightness of the work alongside its symbolic power. And in this way, perhaps, one can also feel the delicate breath of Alexander Calder that makes these chromatic networks vibrate, like colors in the sky.

Above all, what distinguishes Janet Echelman's body of work from these earlier modes of abstraction is her infusion of the aseptic rigor of a technical-formal language with a deeply affective experience that comes from abandoning oneself to the poetry of color. Starting from this decidedly pictorial origin point, it is possible to trace in Echelman's work a new reading of her installations' spatial dimensions and their recasting of the public sphere into a more social space.

Danilo Eccher is an art critic, curator, and former director of MACRO Museo de Arte Contemporáneo de Roma, Museo d'Arte Moderna di Bologna, and Galleria Civica d'Arte Moderne e Contemporanea di Torino.

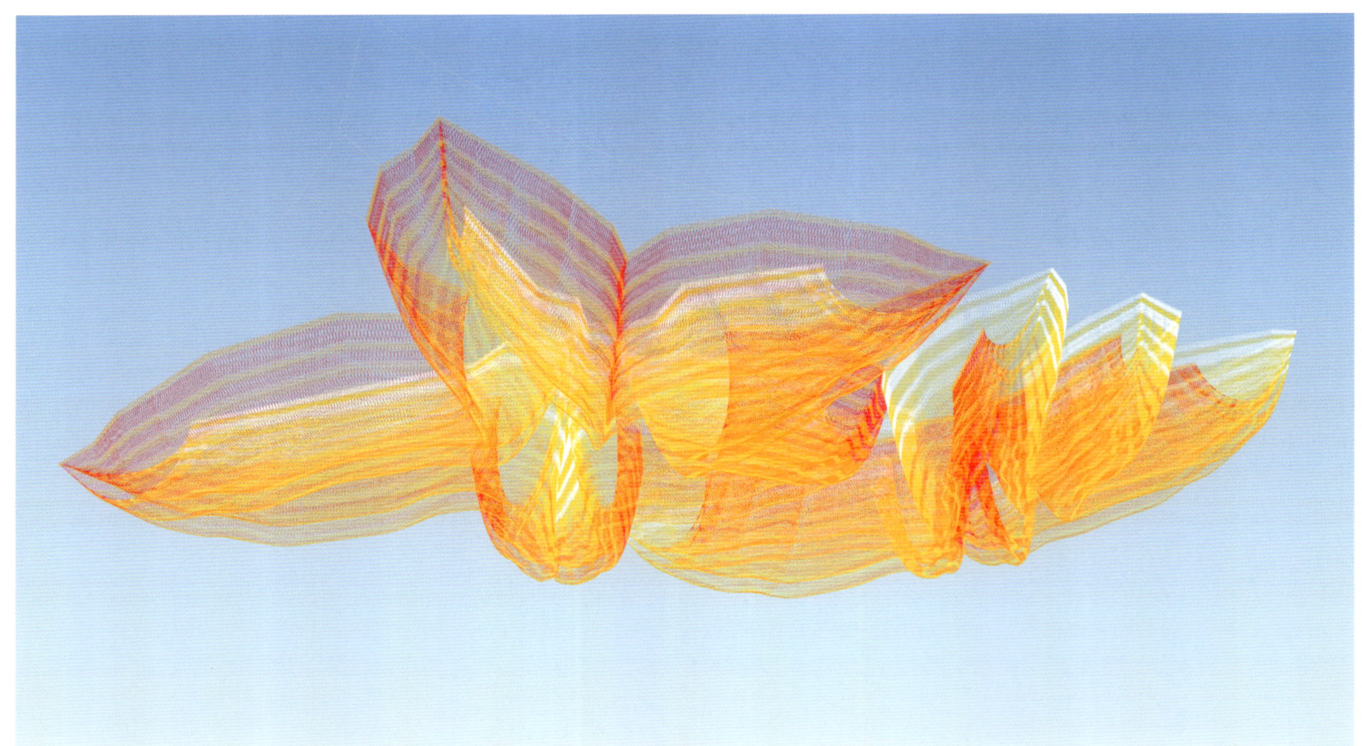

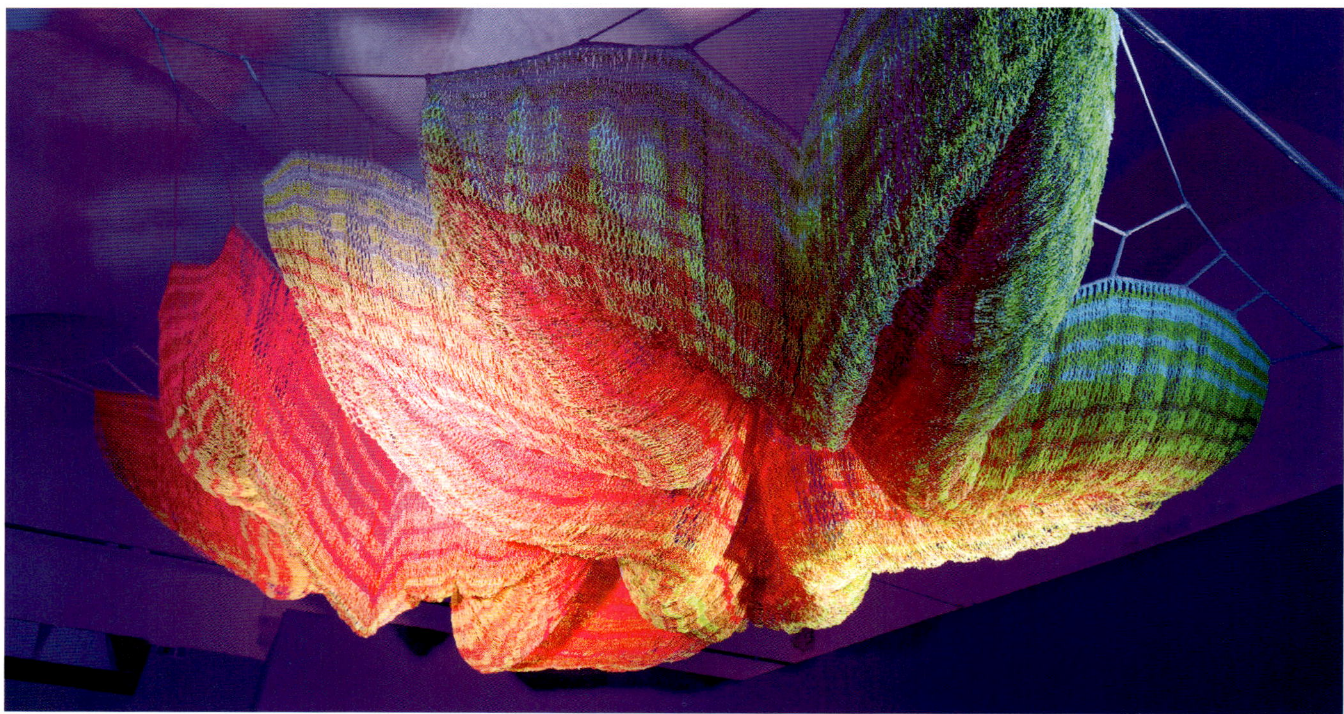

top: 3D digital model for *Study (Butterfly Rest Stop 1/9 scale)*, 2022, Rome, Italy
bottom: *Study (Butterfly Rest Stop 1/9 scale)*, 2022

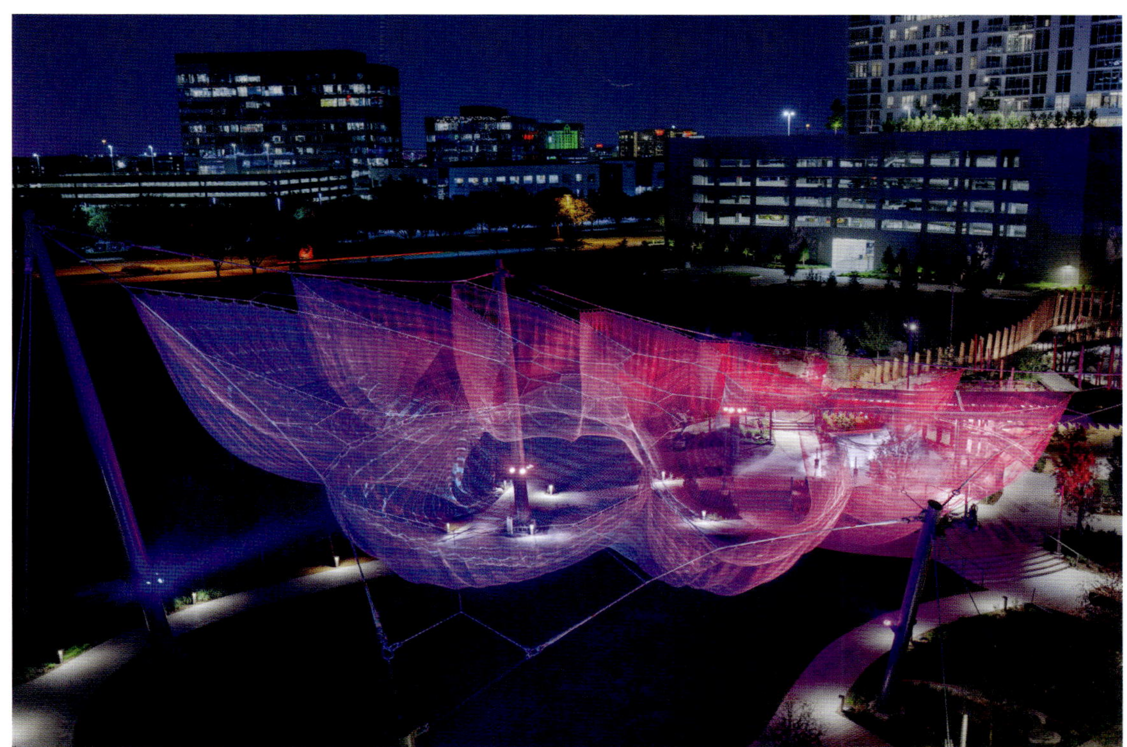

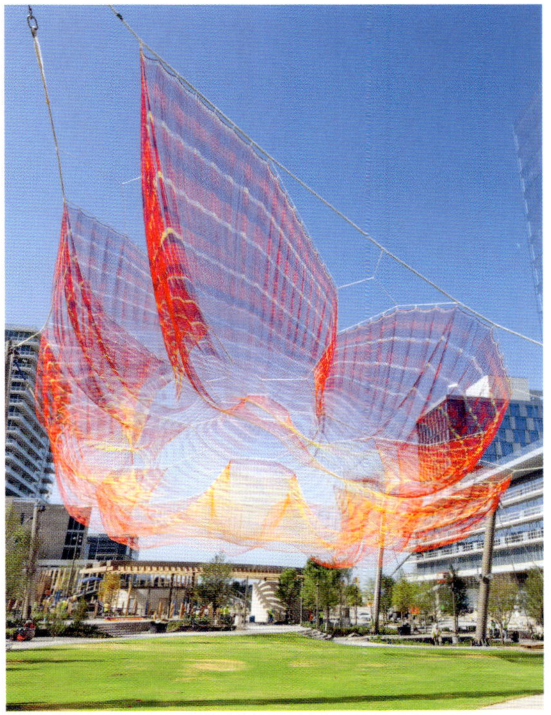

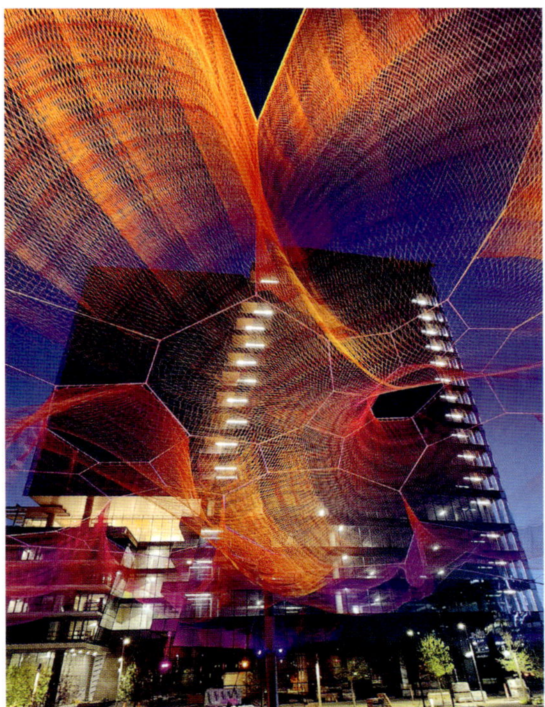

above and following pages: *Butterfly Rest Stop*, 2024, Frisco, Texas

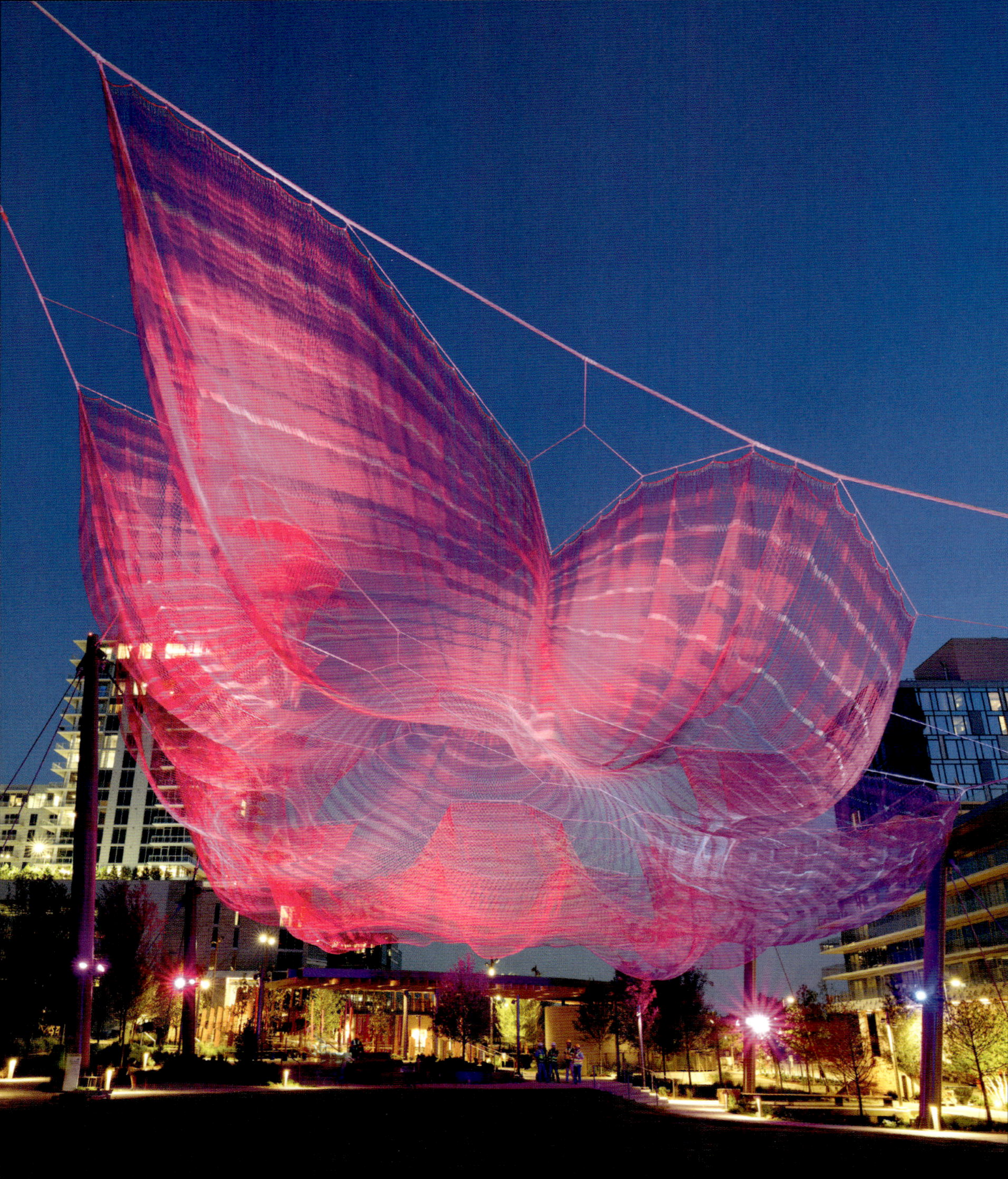

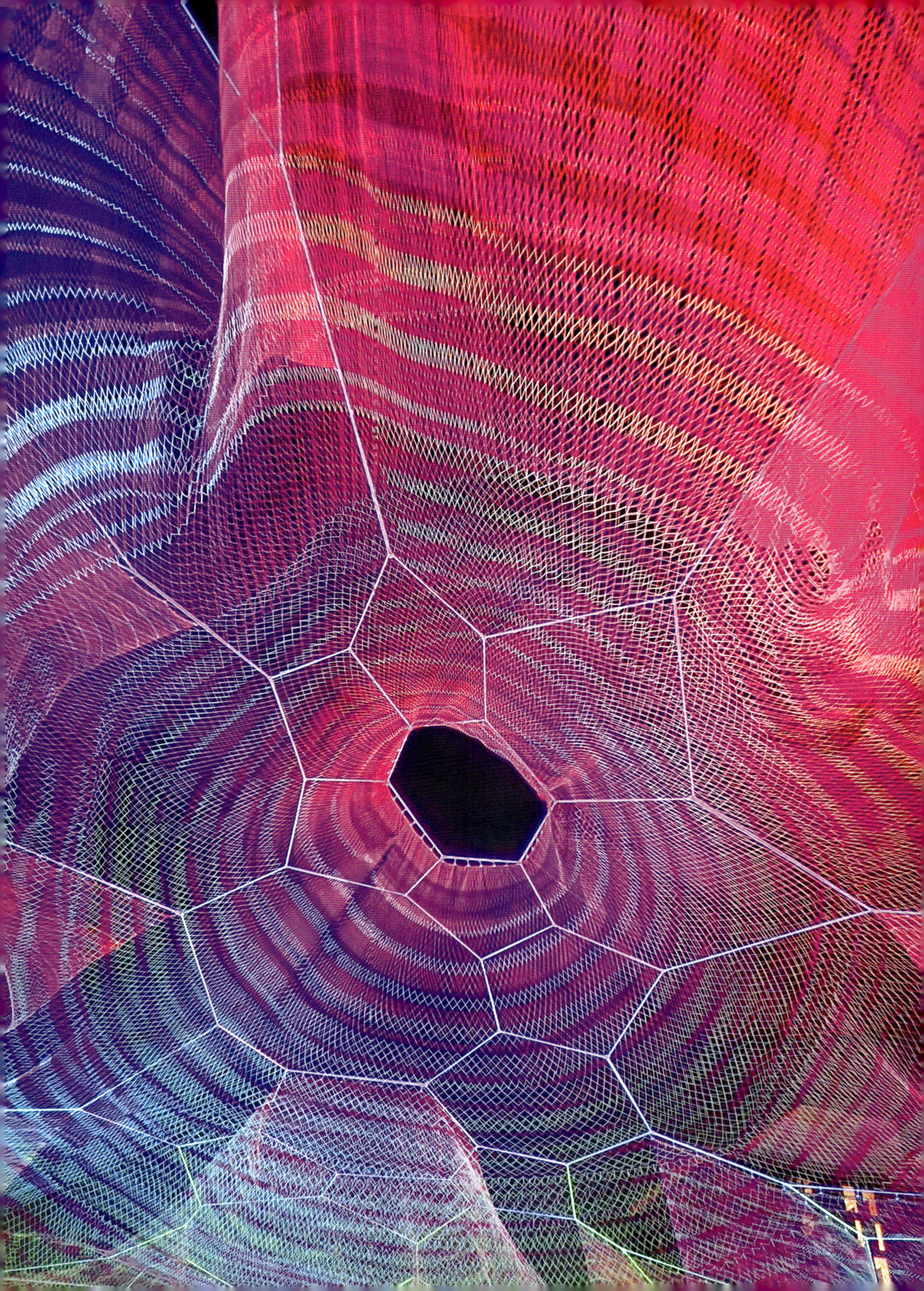

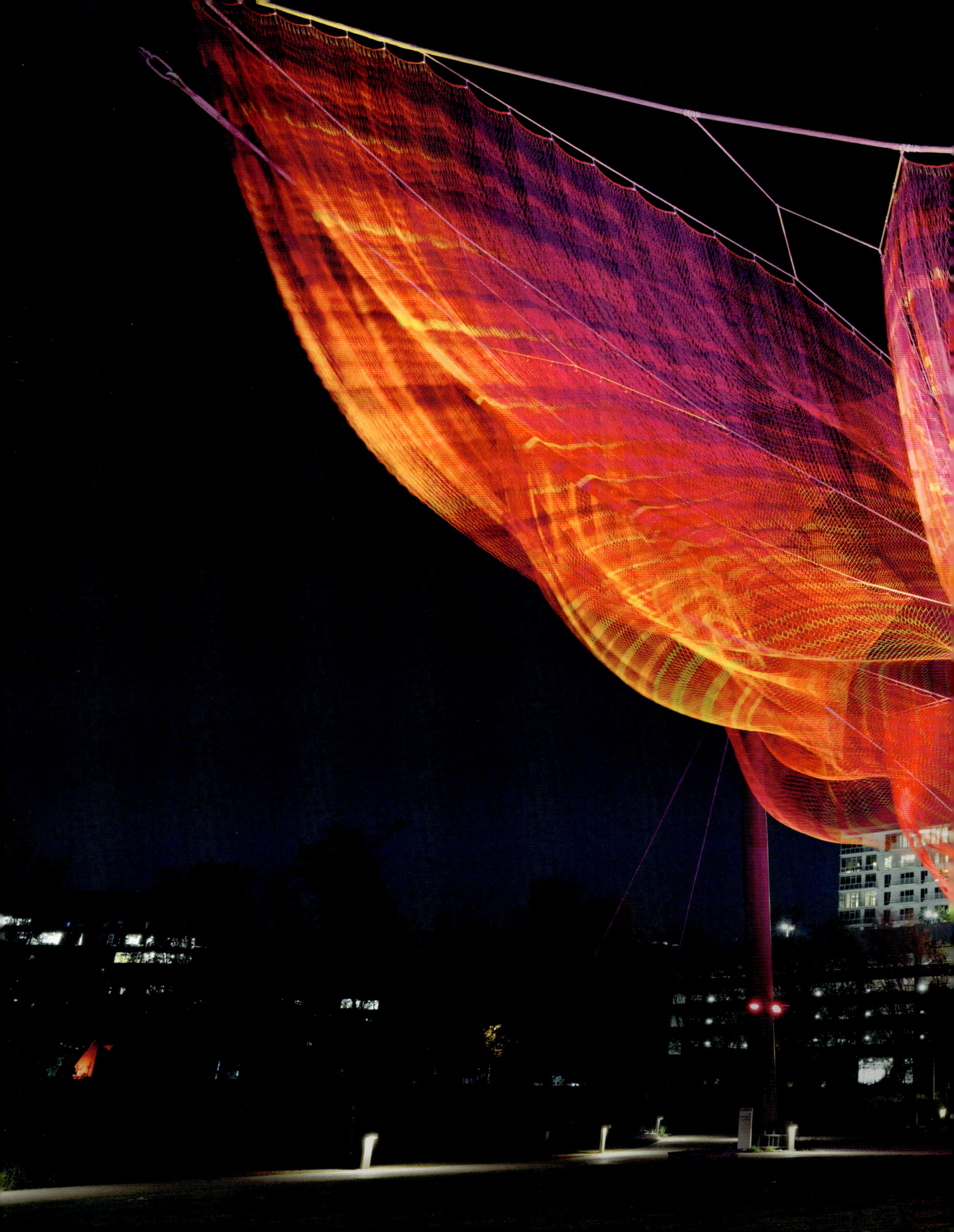

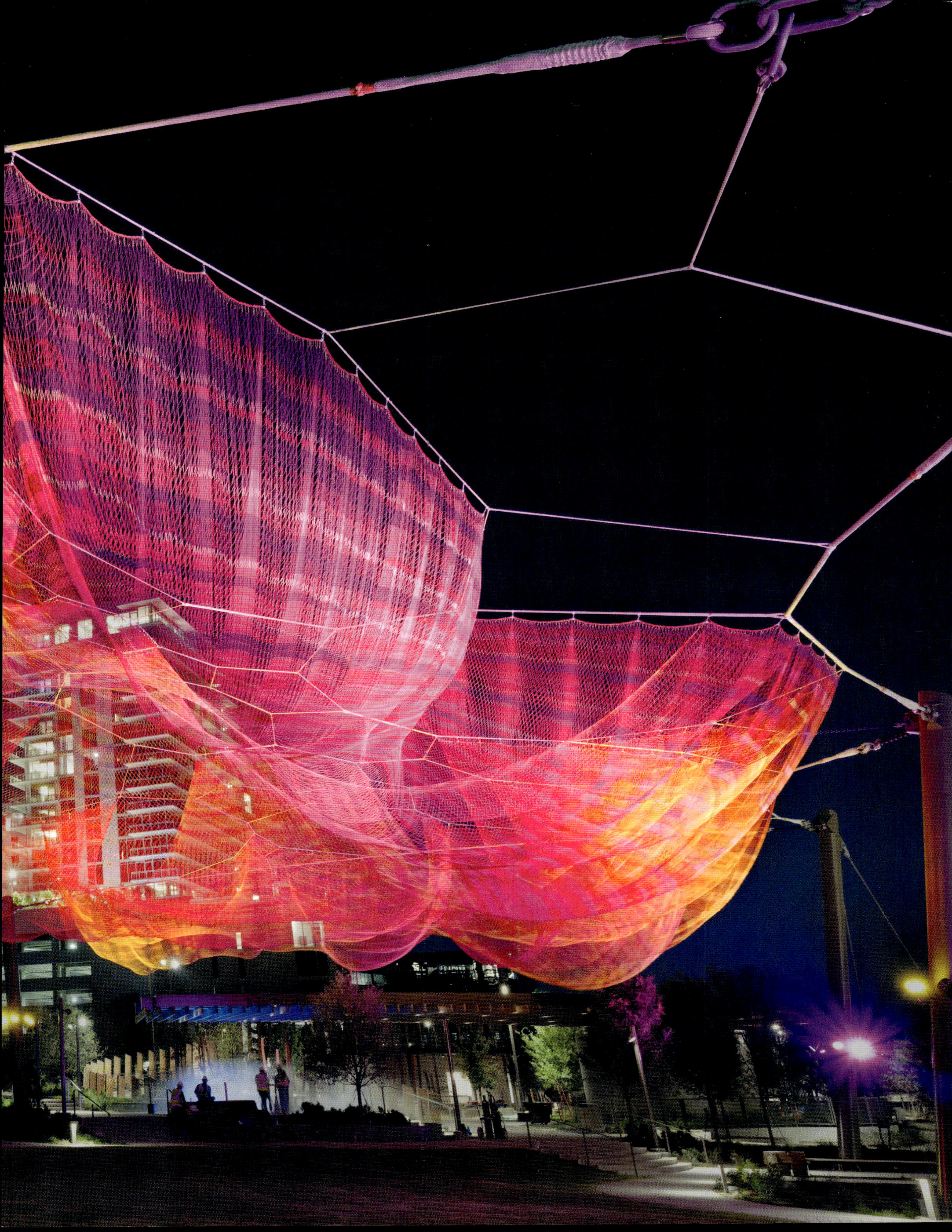

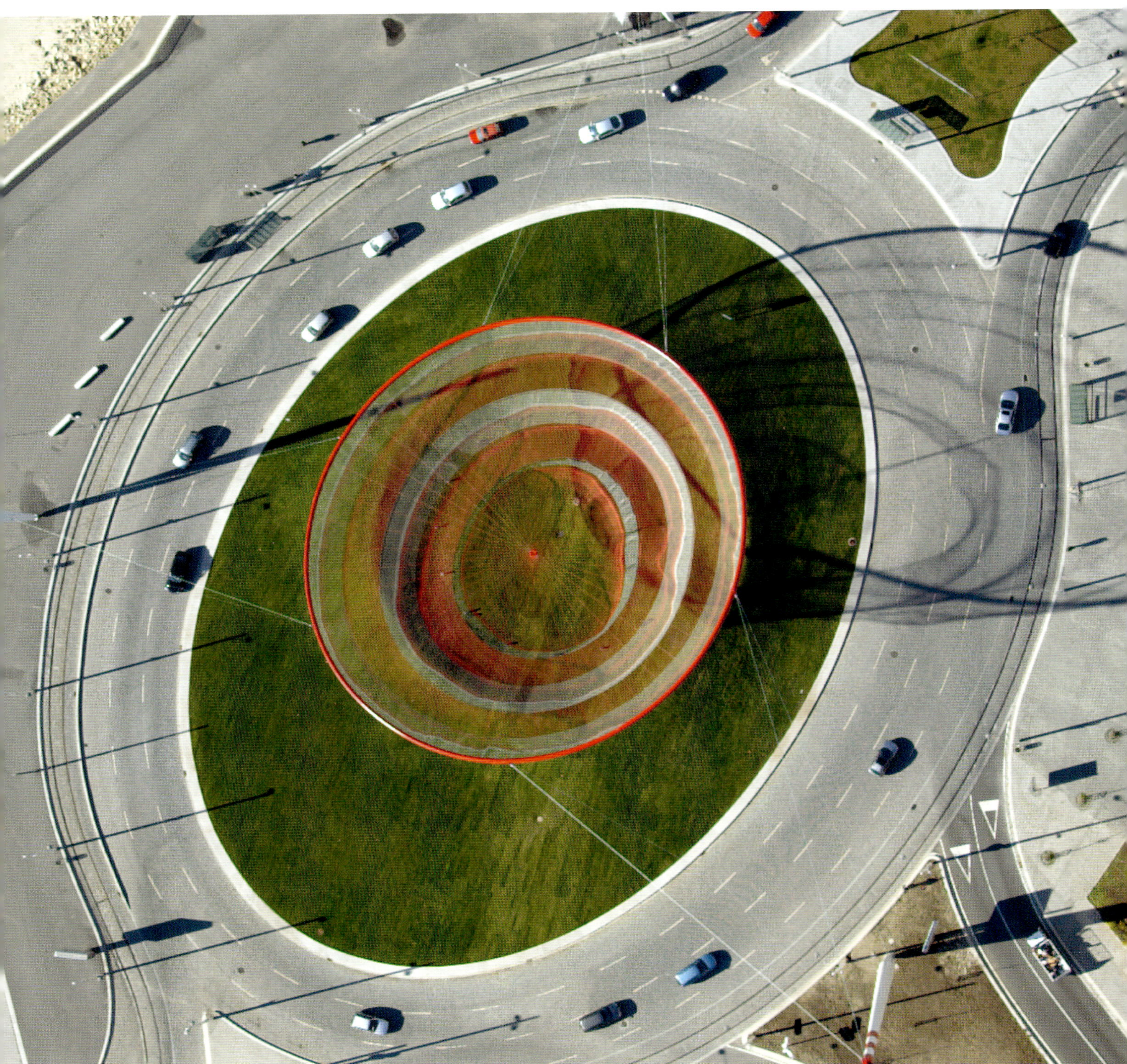

above: *She Changes*, 2005, Porto, Portugal
opposite: Installation of *Skies Painted with Unnumbered Sparks*, 2014, Vancouver, British Columbia

Urban Lace

—

Jenni Sorkin

Janet Echelman's artworks enact a dramatic arena of light-drenched biomorphic sculptures rippling and unfurling across urban plazas, harbors, public walkways, and civic redevelopment projects, where they often serve as anchors. Rarely do women artists work on the grand stage of public space—a sphere upon which Echelman has made a singular imprint. Her designs engage a wide swath of participants, from her own collaborators—the expert designers, architects, and industrial weavers with whom she regularly works to produce her feats of engineering—to members of the public who may never before have encountered her spectacular forms. The installations straddle categories, eliciting aesthetic delight while simultaneously taking up space in both the built environment and feminist art history.

The wow factor of Echelman's aerial net sculptures easily obscures the preindustrial origins of her complex constructions. In this way, her works operate as a form of "urban lace," in that they are built from a structure of entwined fibers, rooted in the open-weave textile compositions of lace making and fishing nets. Open weave is a sophisticated and complex technical patterning in which the grid is a permeable construction trapping warm air within its flexible pockets (as in a knitted scarf) rather than a tightly woven, smooth surface (as in denim or linen). Open-weave structures, related as they are to knitting and lace making, have come to be associated with "women's work," historic forms of handmade artistic production that are traditionally unsigned and uncredited, and diminished as domestic arts or craft. To this day, in many

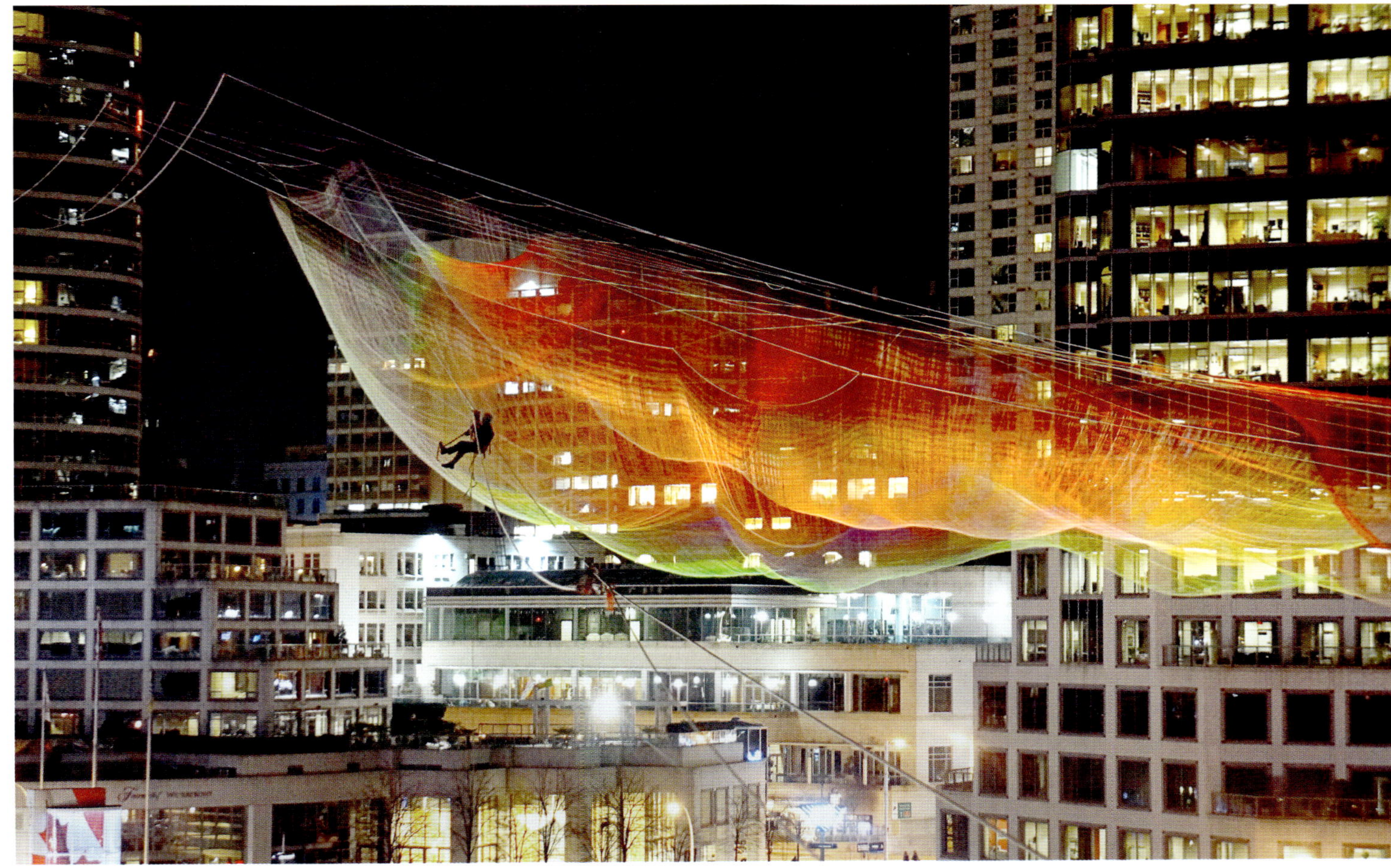

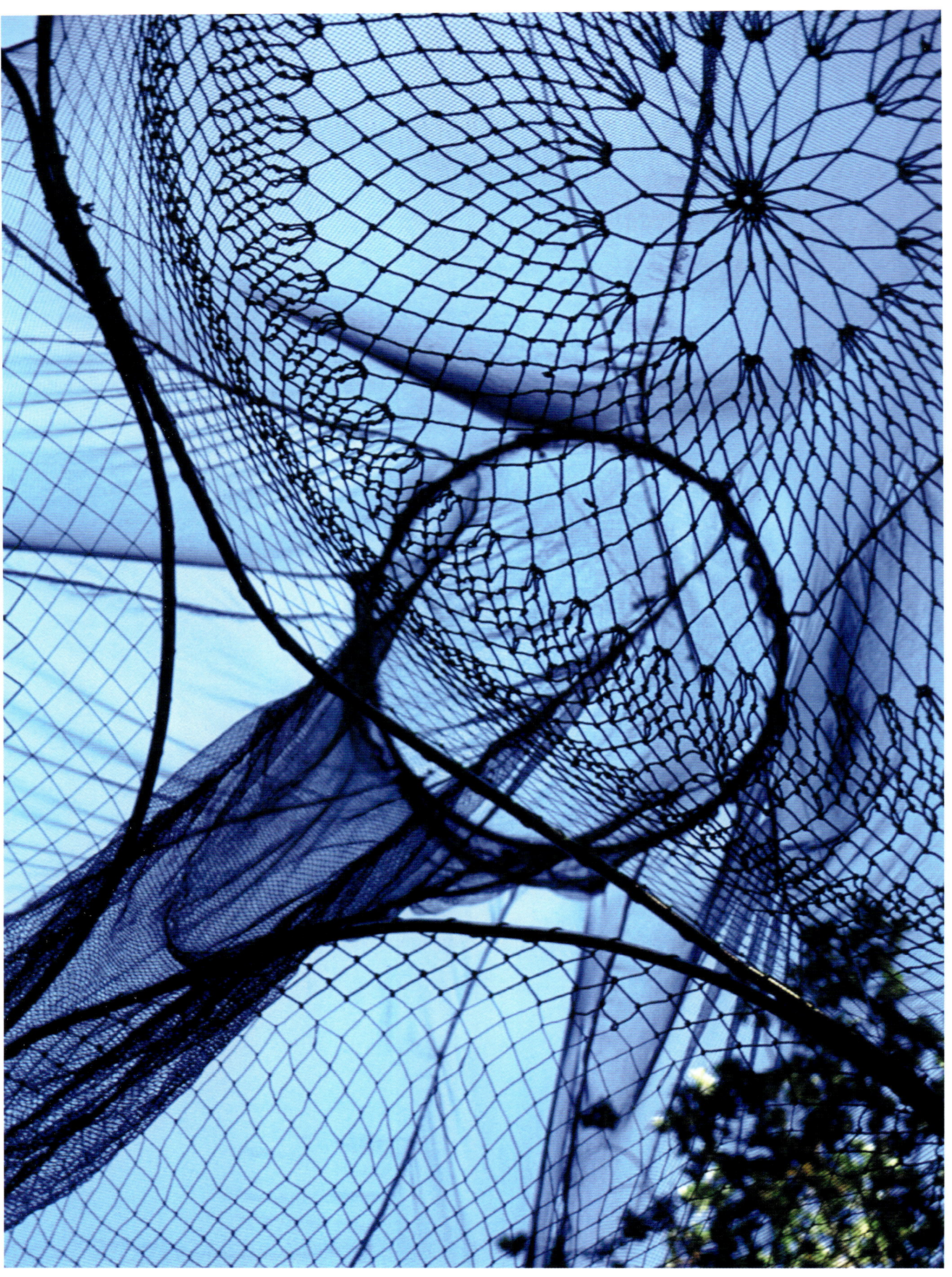

geographies and cultural contexts, homespun clothing, hand-sewn dolls, and other forms of skilled textile work are generally unpaid and unacknowledged. Throughout the developing world, it is still largely women who labor for poverty wages at their sewing machines, and workers' rights are limited or nonexistent within the global textile industry.

Prior to the Industrial Revolution, women were overlooked as skilled professionals because their work output was for personal and/or community consumption and prioritized beautification, decoration, and home decor for home and family, for instance, lace trim for domestic textiles like tablecloths, baby blankets, or Sunday-best dresses. Echelman herself apprenticed and collaborated with lace makers in 1998 while on a residency at the Open-Air Museum of the Centre of Europe in Vilnius, Lithuania, noting that the knot structures were the same as those she'd learned from Indian fishermen. In our contemporary era, the handmade is still considered an amateur form of production. Woven and knitted forms, as well as machine-made lace, are only produced in substantial yardage through the economic efficiency of industrial machinery. And these gendered associations still carry over in the terminologies, scale of production, and working methods with regard to the way that women artists are often historicized or written about, in contrast to their male peers.

Derided or dismissed within the post-1960s art historical landscape, the decorative and the domestic have remained a constant presence, hiding in plain sight but beholden to Minimalist orthodoxy. Among the best-known practitioners were Fred Sandback, who utilized nothing more than craft yarn to delineate architectonic installations, effectively creating sculptural space through the material presence of a utilitarian textile while eschewing the gendered cultural associations of fiber-based practices, and Gordon Matta-Clark, who created spatial compositions and voids by sawing through walls and floors in a dilapidated apartment building slated for demolition (*Conical Intersect* [1975]). Matta-Clark's ephemeral antimonuments or "anarchitecture" (photographed or filmed before they were leveled) reflected on domestic space and privacy, but arguably masked these concerns by forefronting the cyclical nature of speculation and gentrification, and the indisputably masculine means of power tools.

In 2000, Echelman undertook a series of experimental installations that helped form her own visual language of large-scale intervention into an existing urban milieu. For her first solo gallery exhibition in New York, she shifted the focus away from the interior of Florence Lynch Gallery and toward the building's exterior by affixing *Red Spikes on 29th Street* (2000) to three street-facing window frames, which transgressed

opposite and near right: *Trying to Hide with Your Tail in the Air*, 1998, Open-Air Museum of the Centre of Europe Europos Parkas, Vilnius, Lithuania
far right: Gordon Matta-Clark, *Conical Intersect*, 1975, Paris, France

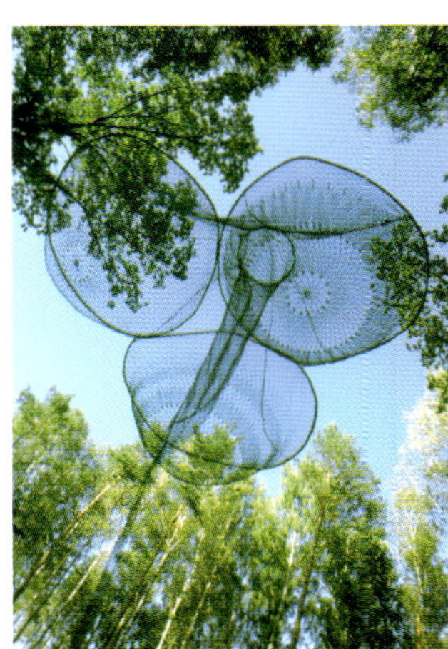

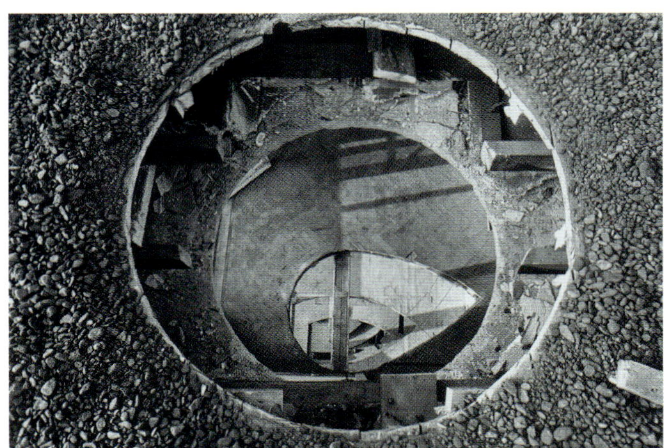

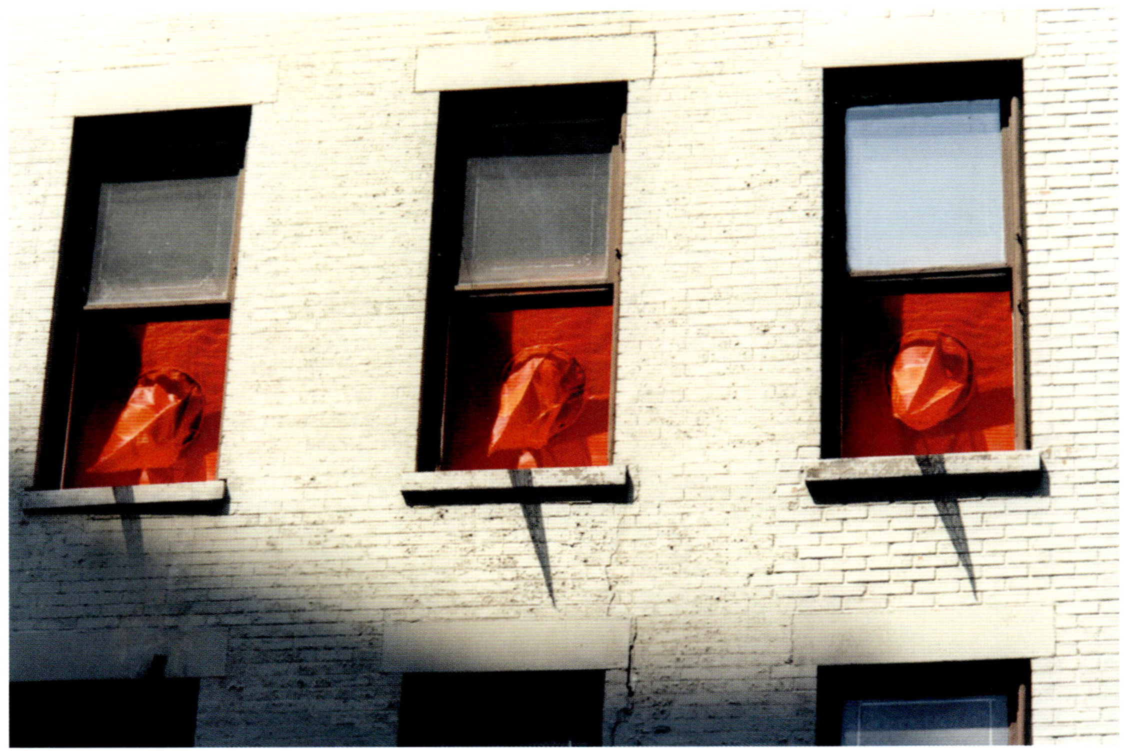

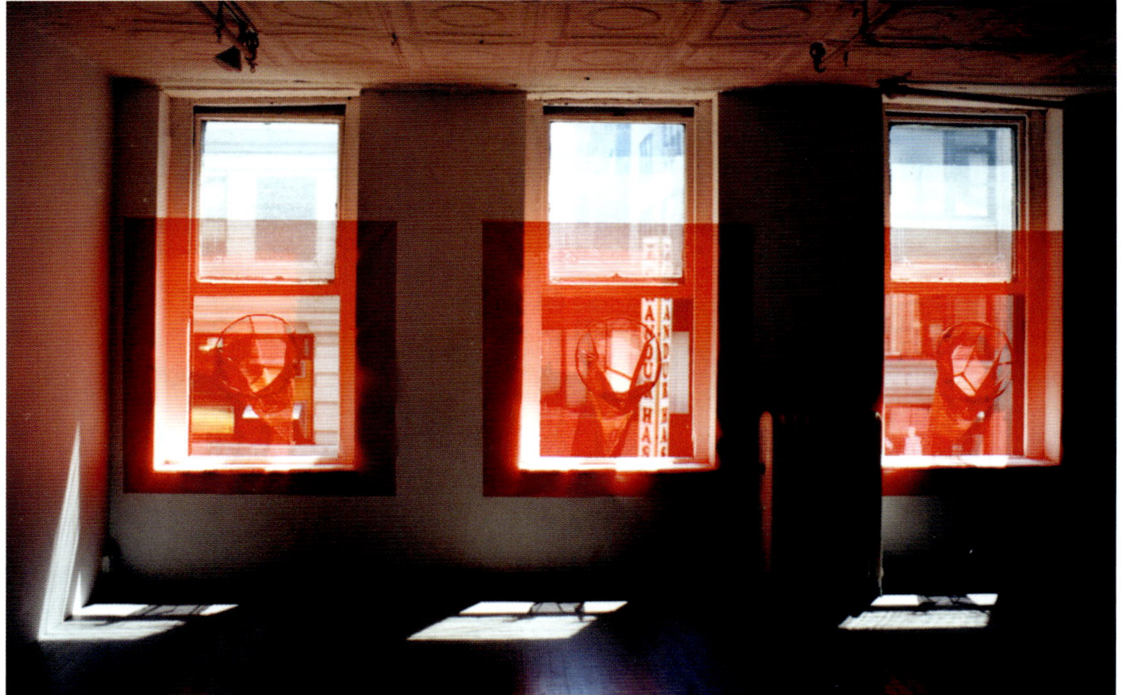

Red Spikes on 29th Street, 2000, Florence Lynch Gallery, New York City

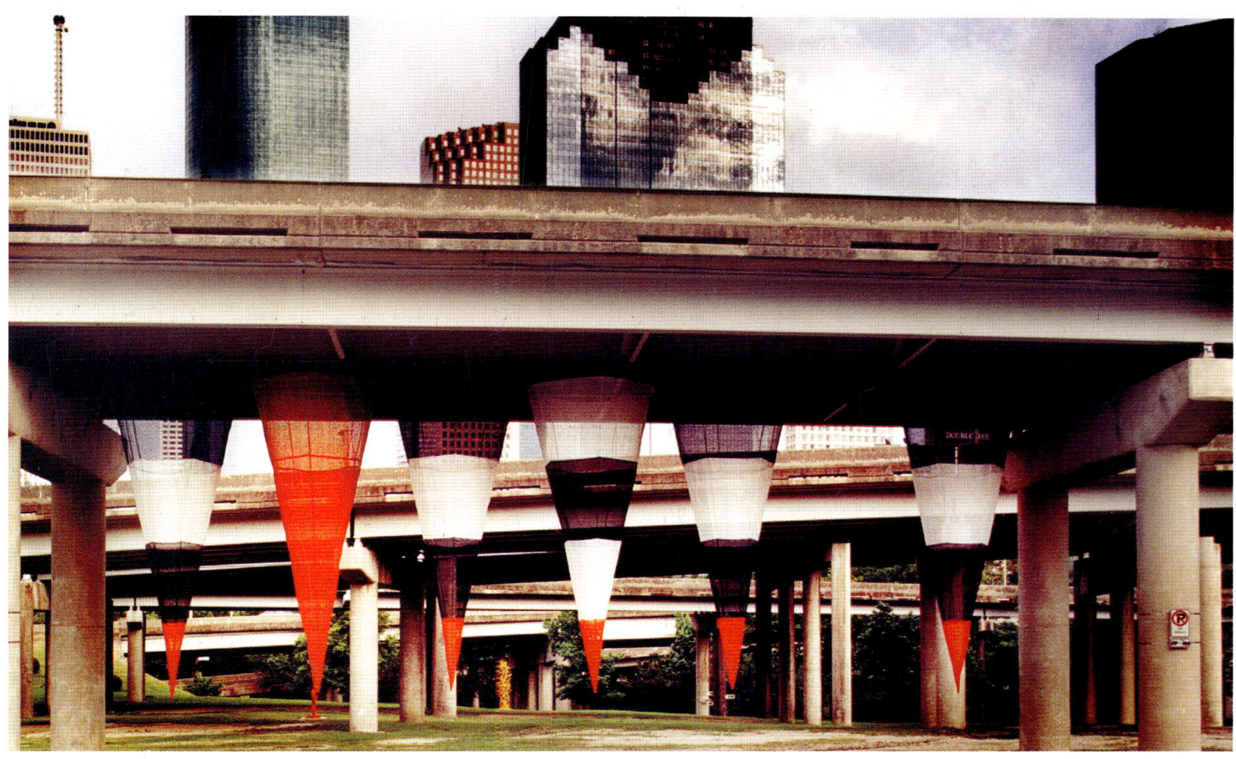

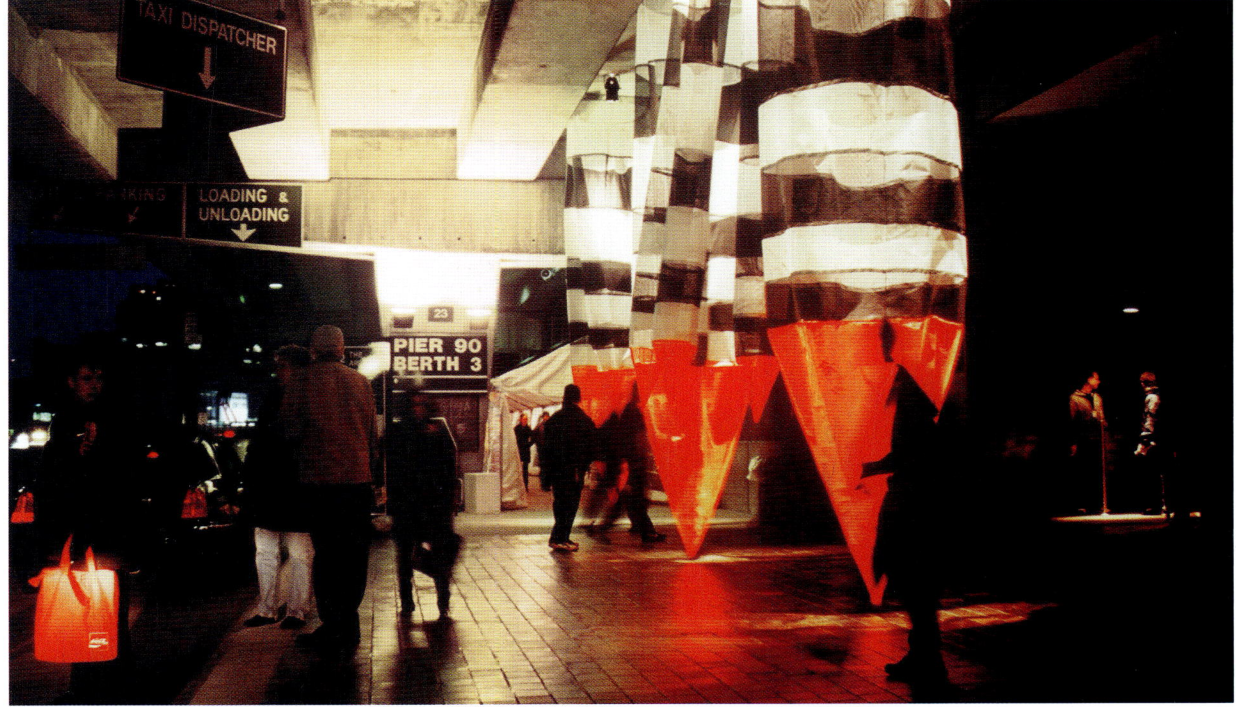

top: *Roadside Shrine I: Cone Ridge*, 2000, I-45 highway overpass, Houston , Texas
bottom: *Roadside Shrine II*, 2002, Armory Show, Pier 88, New York City

into the public realm. Vermilion vinyl-coated polyester and knitted stainless steel evoking bodily forms protruded like tongues, as though giant inflatables had filled up the space inside and had nowhere else to go. The otherwise-empty gallery was enlivened by the shadows cast by the red-hued sculptures along the walls and floor. In the four courtyard-facing windows, Echelman installed *Window Treatment with Twenty-one Tails* (2000), comprising tracts of silver ribbonlike strips, each punctuated with evenly spaced holes. Evoking ticker tape, punch cards, or conveyor belts, the strips conveyed a sense of continuous overflow. Set against the angular window casings and hard bricks, Echelman's soft forms disrupted the rectilinear geometries of the built environment.

Roadside Shrine I: Cone Ridge (2000) extended a version of these same sculptural net protrusions under Houston's I-45 highway. The artist used trucking tarp and heat-sealing methods to sculpt a hanging conical formation fifty-seven feet long by nine feet wide, recalling the visual language of roadway safety while making a playful reference to the Capitoline Wolf suckling the mythical twin founders of Rome. The fabric stalactites flashed orange, white, and black, drawing attention to the nondescript underpass and transforming an otherwise bleak running trail into a safer and more inviting pedestrian pathway. Two years later, Echelman iterated on these sculptural formations in *Roadside Shrine II* (2002), hanging a series of striped, tapered forms in front of New York's West Side Highway at Piers 88 and 90 as part of the Armory Show. Their open-weave patterning and construction recalled her earliest fishing net-inspired works. Pedestrians at ground level encountered the work as giant inverted construction cones whose brilliant orange conical tips just grazed the concrete floor, seeming to remind those entering to proceed with caution, or graze the work and watch it softly respond.

What does it mean for open-weave forms to be represented at such a vast scale, well beyond the framework of the domestic—indeed, fully immersed in a civic arena? Echelman's artworks are a bridge between preindustrial forms of handwork, modernist sculpture made by women, and the digital technologies of the twenty-first century. Initially trained as a painter, Echelman won a Fulbright lectureship in 1997 to teach contemporary painting and study textiles at the National Institute of Design in India, where she became strongly influenced by coastal fishermen knotting large fishing nets. This involved a constant cycle of amassing yardage, only to have it ripped and torn apart through use, followed by time devoted to mending and repair. Echelman transformed this methodology of amassed yardage and repair into a core element undergirding her artistic process.

One of the main characteristics of the net is its tensile strength: pulled in any direction, it is flexible and pliable due to its open-weave structure. Made of engineered fibers and knotted on industrial looms, the strands used to form Echelman's netted structures are made at a small, family-owned factory in the Pacific Northwest, based on both digital and handmade scale models that are produced in the artist's studio. At the net factory, the loomed fibers are then hand-cut and hand-knotted to form mesh structures in the same manner that nets are made for the fishing industry. The loomed net-panels are

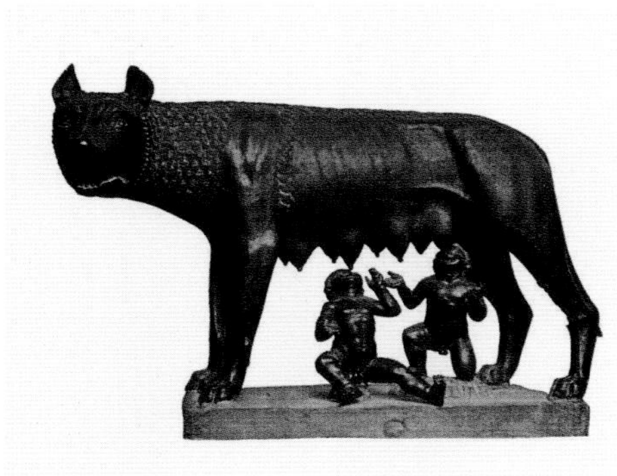

***The Capitoline Wolf Suckling Romulus and Remus*,**
late 15th–early 16th century, bronze

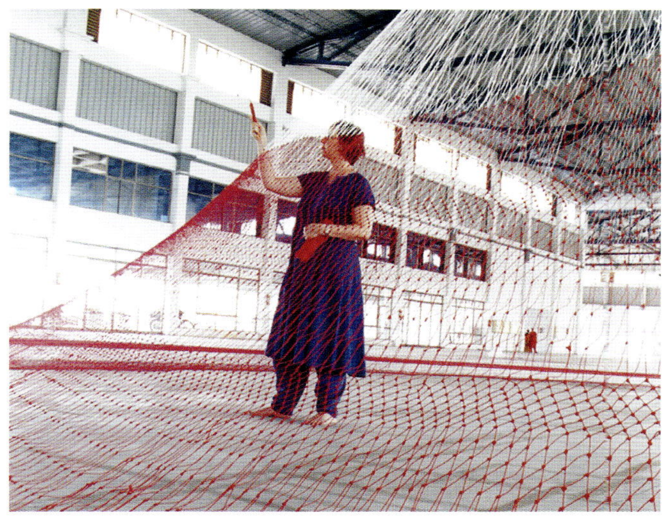

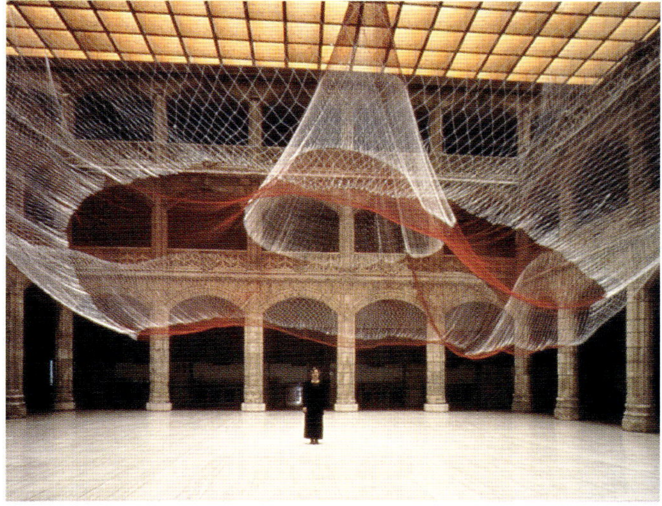

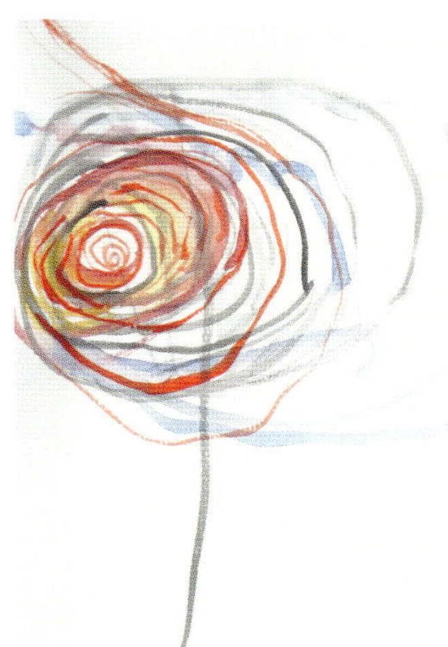

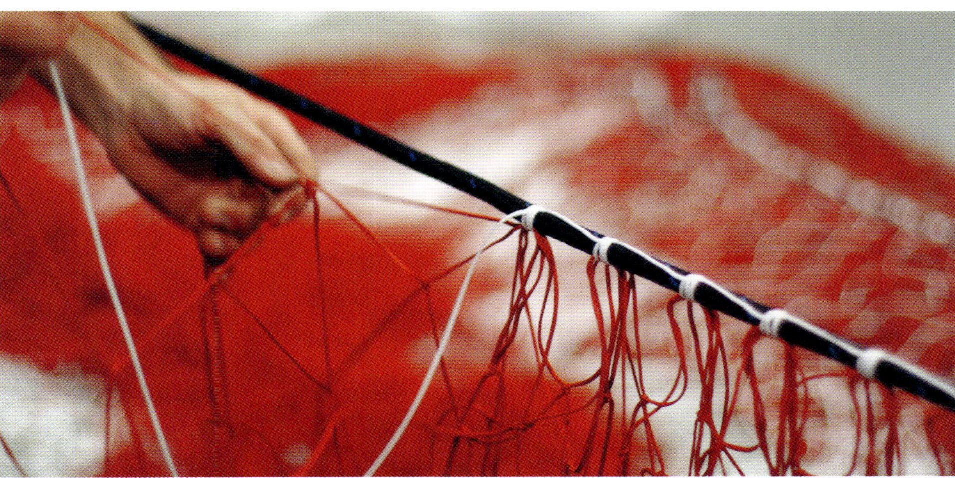

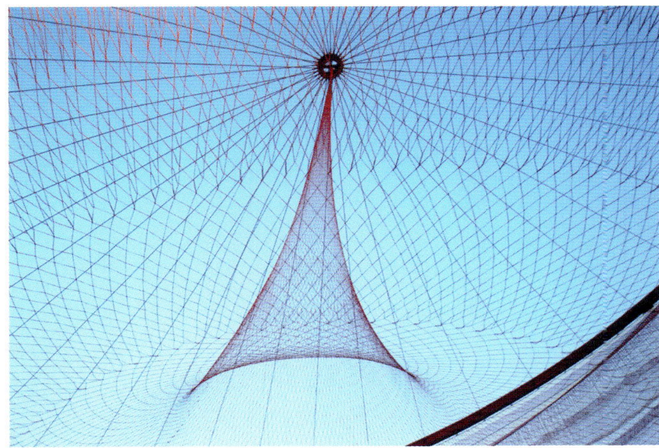

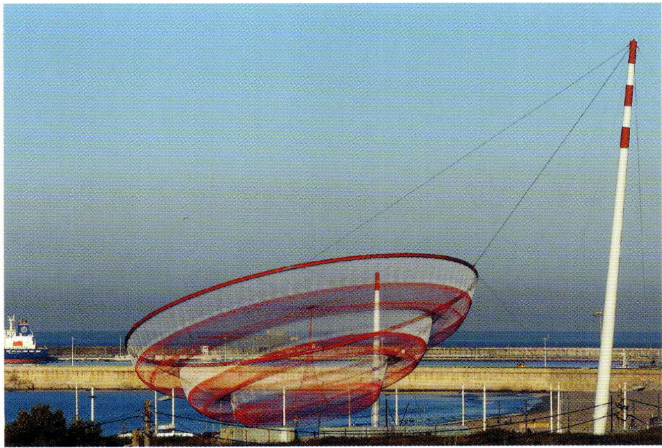

top left: Echelman knotting *Floor Target*, 2001, Coimbatore, India
top right: *Target Swooping II*, 2001, Burgos, Spain
middle left: Watercolor study, 2001
middle right: Fabrication with hand knotting for *She Changes*, 2005
bottom row: *She Changes*, 2005

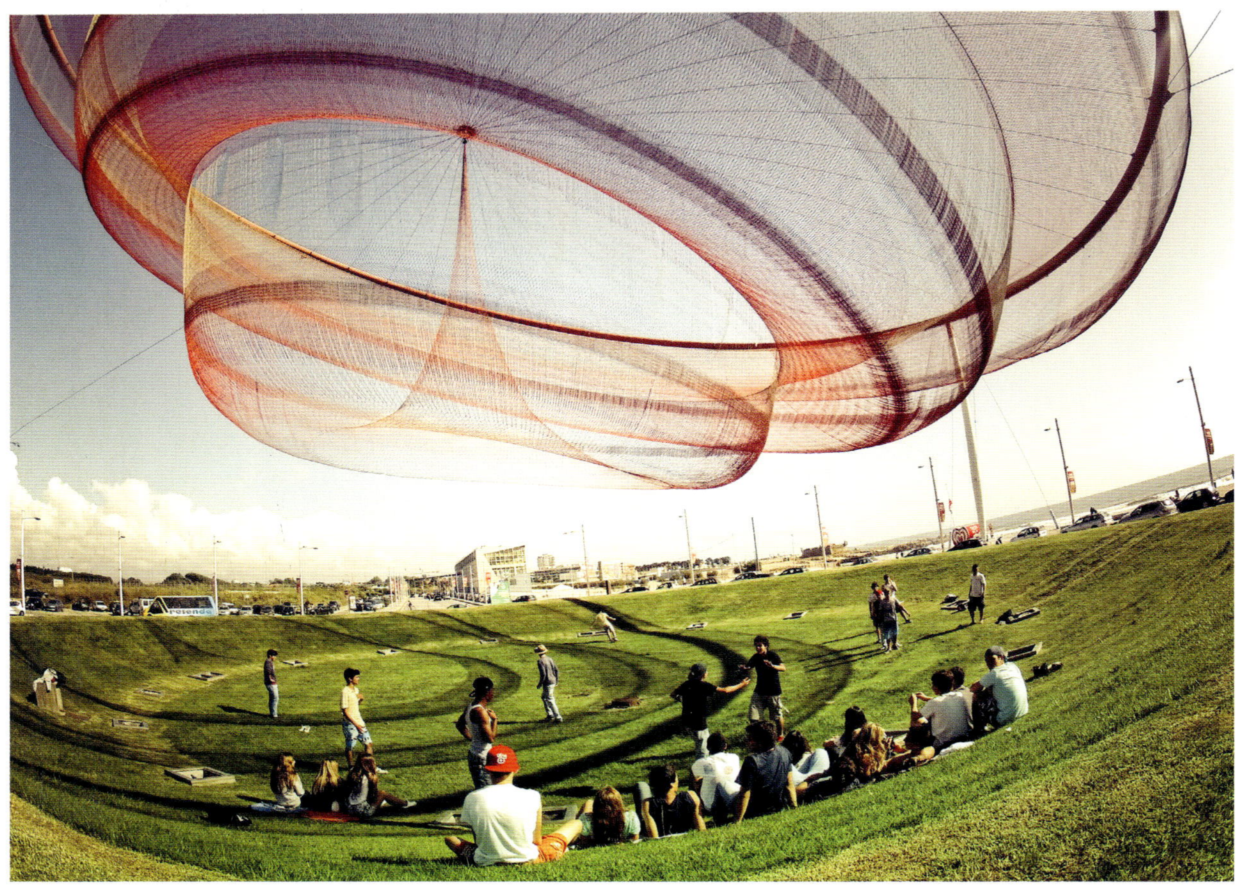

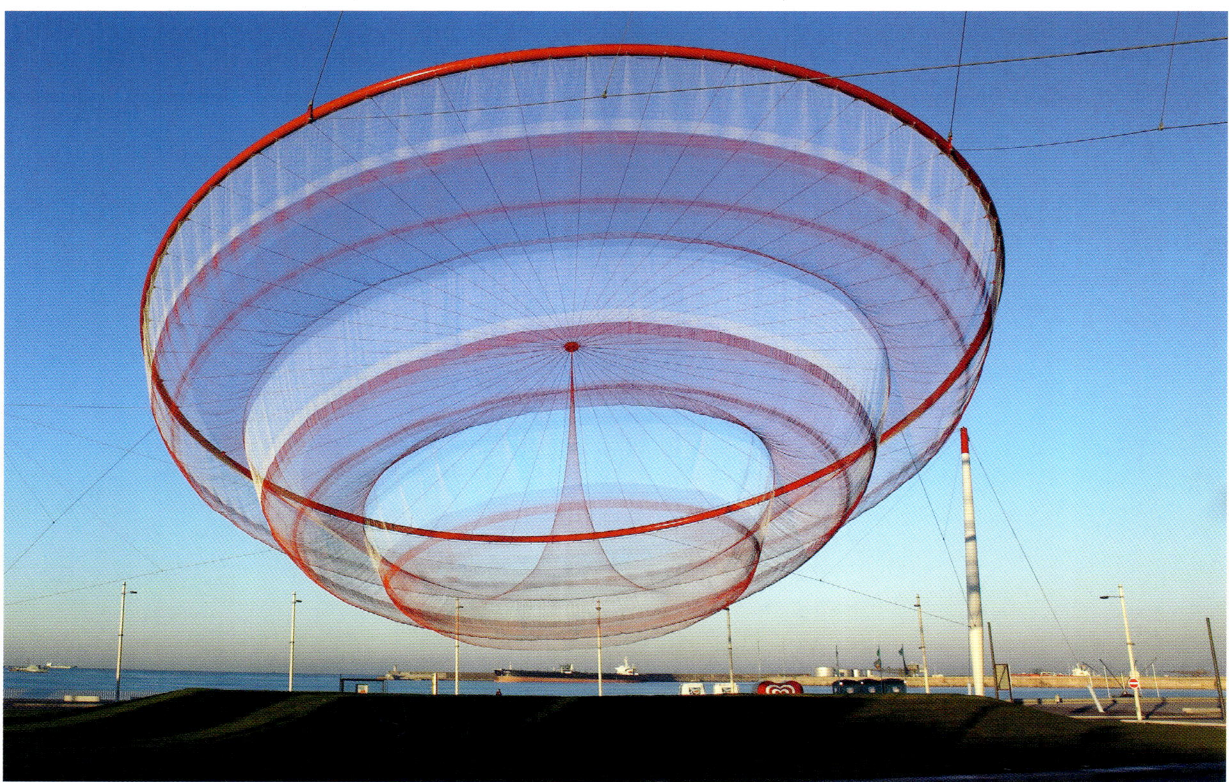

then hand-trimmed according to patterns, and then multiple panels are hand-knotted together to create complex volumetric geometric forms. Interestingly, there is a modernist precedent for Echelman's source material: the Japanese American artist Ruth Asawa famously cited Mexican basket weavers in Toluca as the inspiration for her own open looped-wire constructions, which have received renewed critical and commercial attention in the last decade as art historians have reexamined the way Asawa, working primarily in her home studio, turned utilitarian processes and materials into ethereal forms. Her hanging sculptures are accumulations of hollow, globular shapes that generate biomorphic narratives about, among many other things, the female body's relationship to the environment. Asawa's whisper-light wire forms respond to air currents and the hushed movements of viewers, with an enigmatic, floating quality that multiplies when illuminated with light from any direction.

Another art historical precedent for Echelman's net sculptures is the German-born Venezuelan sculptor Gego, who also came to art making circuitously. Trained as an engineer specializing in architecture, Gego combined the formal properties of sculpture in the round with the 2D perspectival tools of drawing, liberating the hand-drawn line from paper by rendering delicate free-form silhouettes in space using steel wire and various found materials, including chicken wire and steel mesh. Her latticed geometries illustrate her sustained examination of perspectival concepts of endless form, offering viewers the pleasures and rigors of visually tracing various permutations of the line. Her best-known artworks are collectively called *Reticulárea* (1969–76), and are composed of suspended

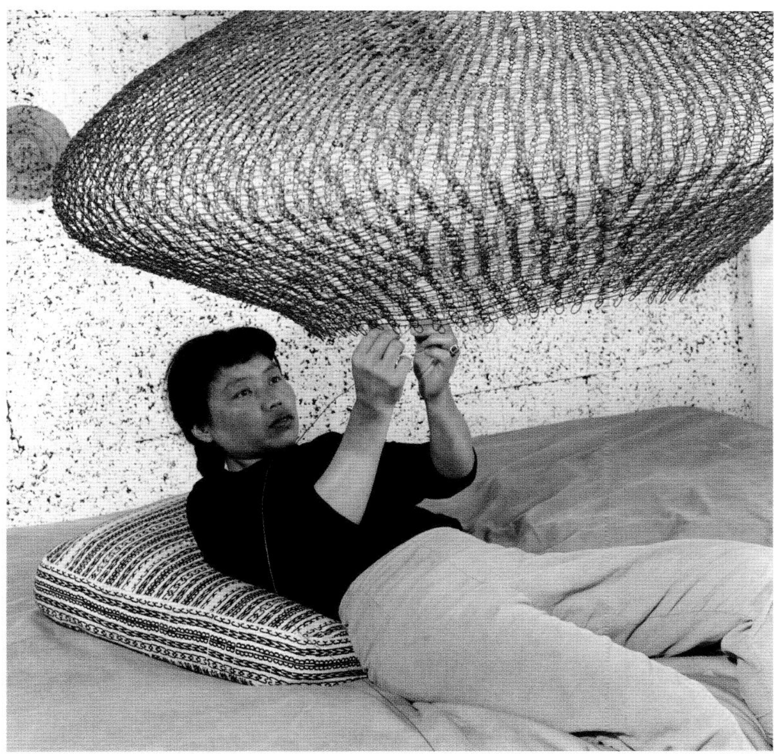

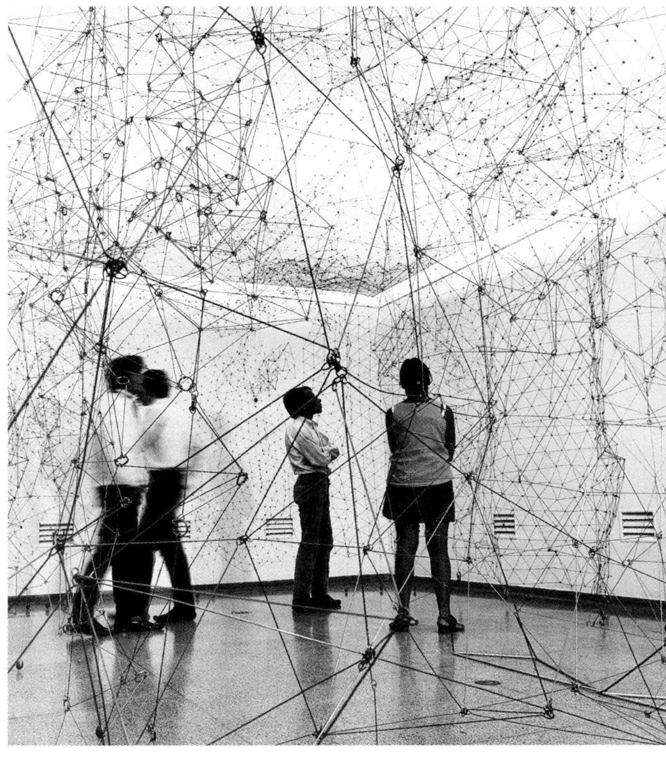

opposite: *She Changes*, 2005, Porto, Portugal

left: Imogen Cunningham, portrait of Ruth Asawa in her home studio, 1957
right: Gego, *Reticulárea*, 1969

networks of metal pieces linked using deceptively simple hook closures. The flexible, open-form grids can be described as a spatial experience of mark making. Often installed in groups, the immersive, netlike installations may encompass entire rooms. Asawa's handmade constructions and Gego's scale are crucial precedents for Echelman's drive to grow her practice beyond the indoors—whether the museum or the domestic environment of a collector's home. In their own lifetimes, neither Asawa nor Gego garnered the substantial international attention that their respective oeuvres now enjoy; both were relegated to outlier positions both domestically and abroad. The valuation of women's work is still a relatively recent phenomenon in museum collections, a response to their historic absence from public culture.

Merging handcrafted working methods with computational designs, Echelman's methodology in tensile architectural construction responds to the demands of each commission, sometimes drastically expanding in scale. Each installation is site specific. Sometimes the volumetric forms materialize abstract natural processes, such as ocean currents, and are created using scientific data sets and computer modeling systems. The *Earthtime* series (2010–), in which the sculptures undulate in outdoor plazas, are manifestations of wavelengths—tsunamis, earthquakes—that set off chain reactions across the world, felt in one part as shifting earth, and elsewhere as massive flooding. In other works, Echelman documents climate change as a form of interdependency and movement. Her textile forms are poetic and metaphorical expressions of the impossibility of remaining still, of change as a given, and of time itself as a current or wave that engulfs us, but need not overwhelm. Hence the title of the recent permanent commission *Enfold* (2022), in which more than fifty-three feet of fiber is laced seamlessly into the concrete ceiling of a residence in Montecito, California. Rising more than fourteen feet in height, the cobalt, turquoise, magenta, and crimson fibers are further heightened with colored lights that reflect in the surrounding glass enclosure, which opens onto hillside vegetation overlooking the Pacific Ocean. In this way, *Enfold* operates as a permeable inflection point between indoor and exterior landscapes.

Echelman's works are massive poetic abstractions that remain rooted in the personal and/or domestic aspects of textiles. Inspired by Sonia Delaunay's colored etchings and drawings of patterns that could be realized in loom-woven thread, Echelman extends Delaunay's experiments in creating simultaneous contrast, where tones and hues shift continuously, fully dependent upon the colors appearing next to them. This sense of simultaneity infuses Delaunay's geometric compositions with a sense of energetic movement, as in this 1924 image (opposite), in which paintings and clothing designs are enmeshed and color elicits its own sense of form, equally at home on a canvas and as worn on a woman's body. Echelman's overlapping planes of color and linear patterning reflect her own layers of expertise, offering us all the sense of comfort of pulling an open-weave blanket over one's head, and seeing a rush of color through the openings.

Jenni Sorkin is a professor of the history of art and architecture, University of California, Santa Barbara.

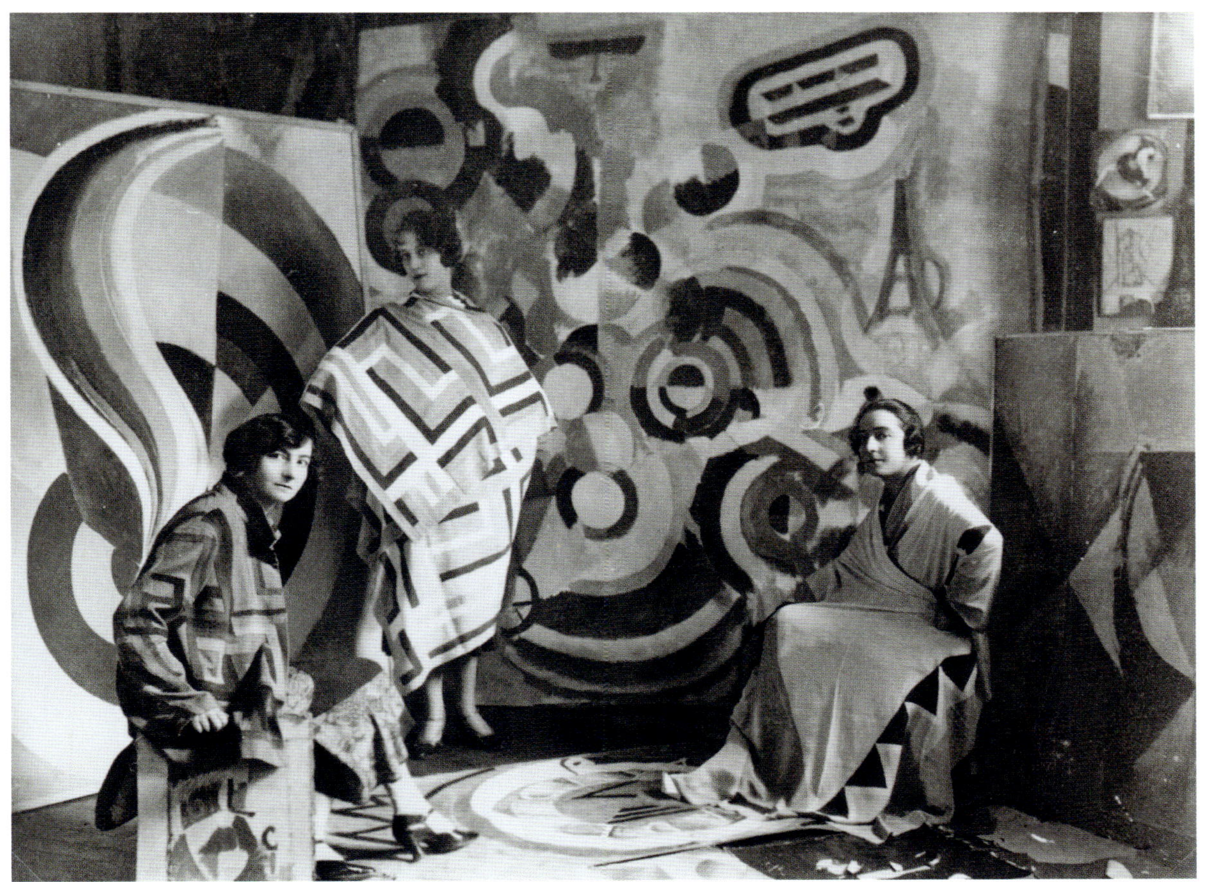

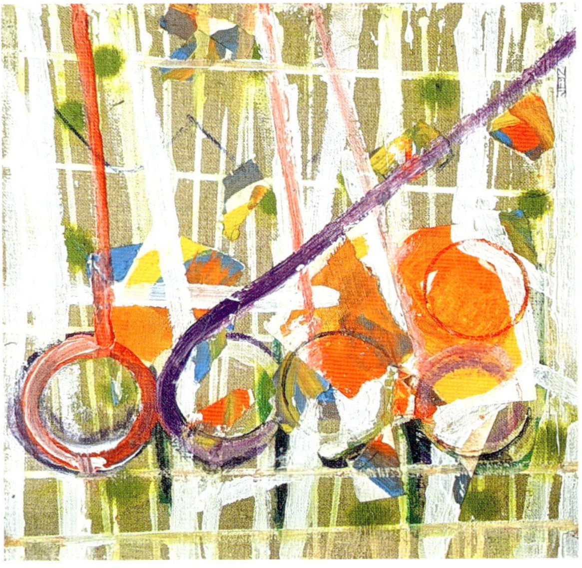

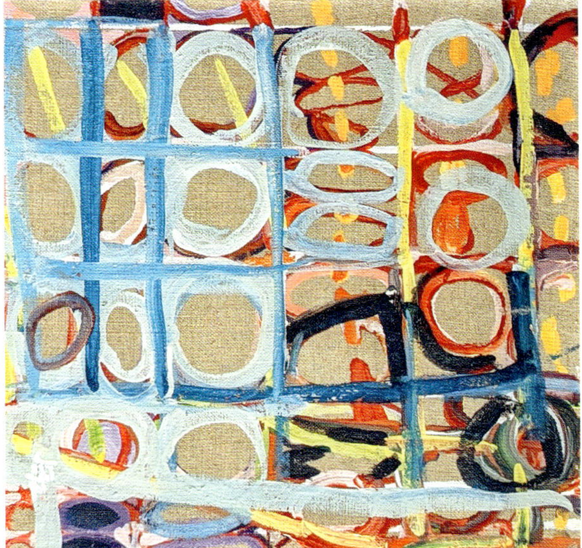

top: Sonia Delaunay with two friends, Paris, 1924
bottom: Janet Echelman, *Shifting Tracks* and *Tic Tac 0*, 1993, acrylic on linen, each 12 × 12 in.

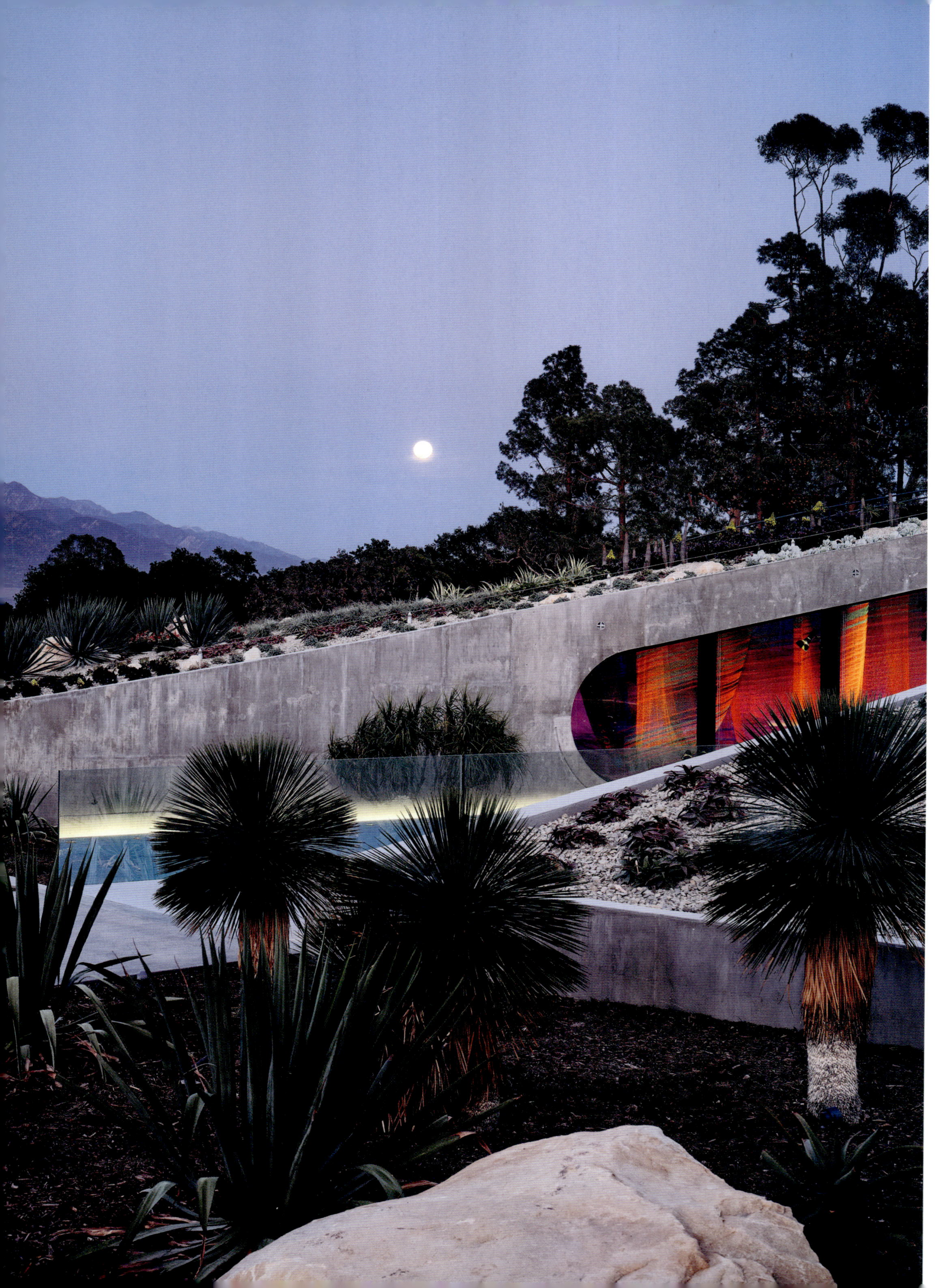

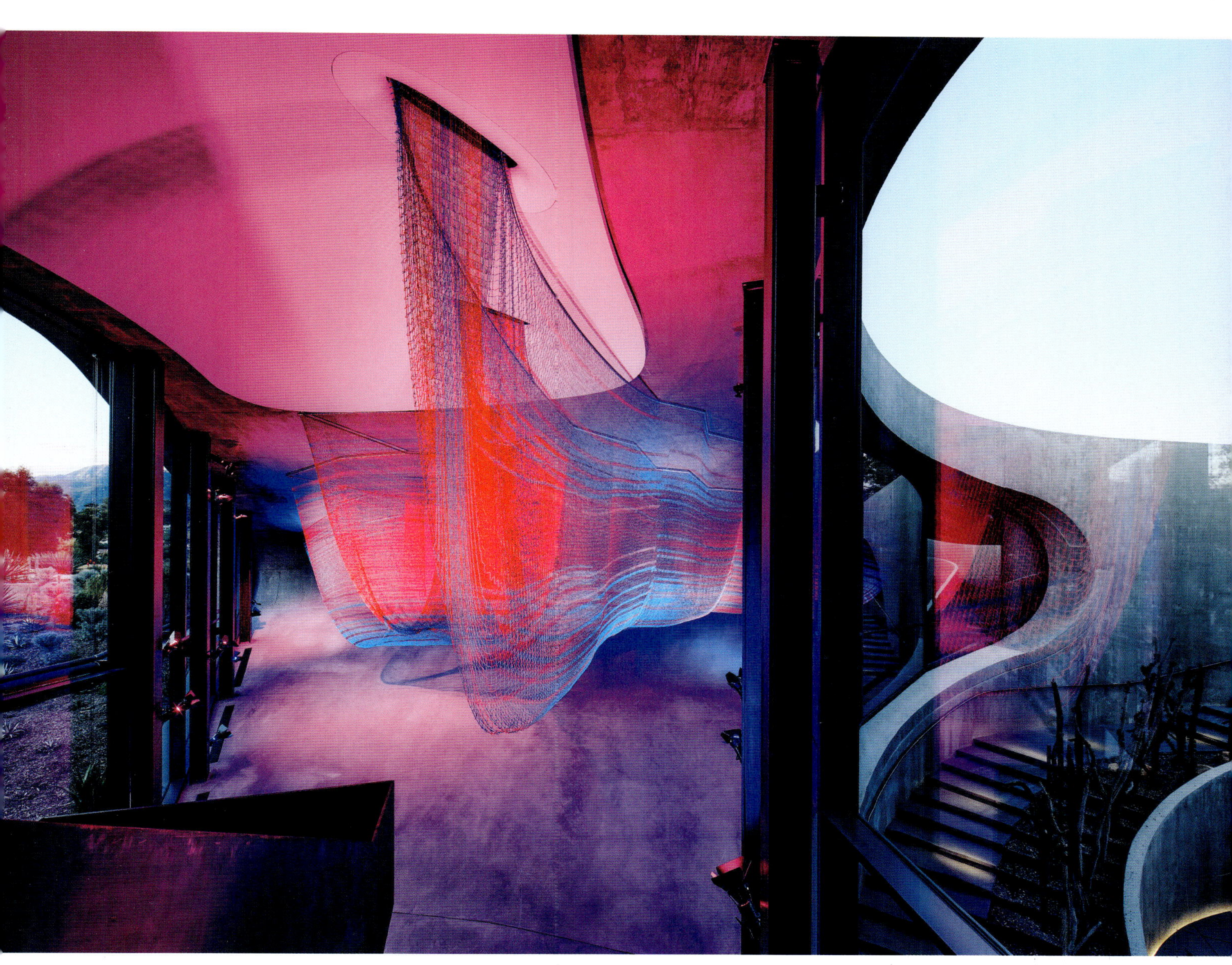

opposite and above: *Enfold*, 2022, Hill House Montecito, California

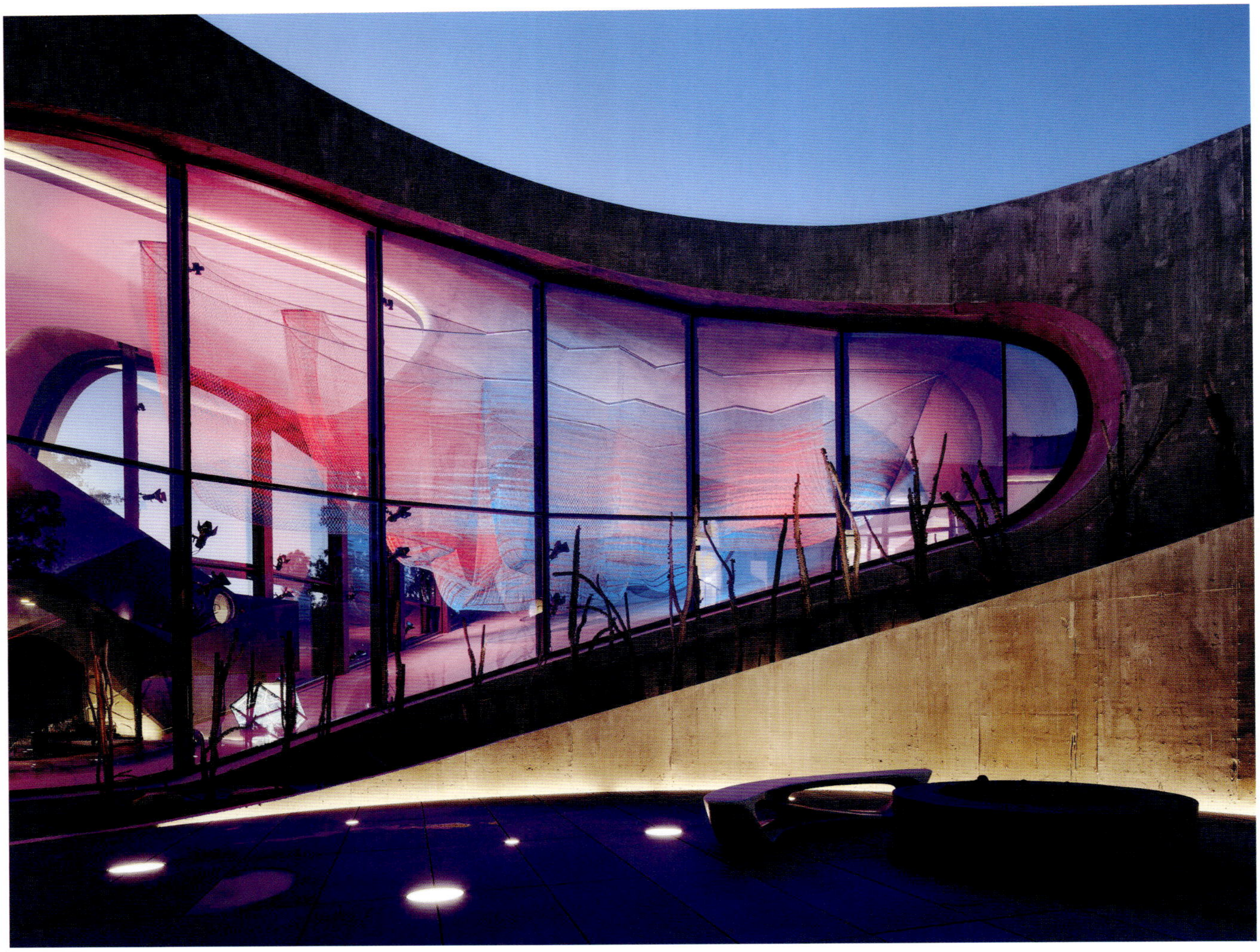

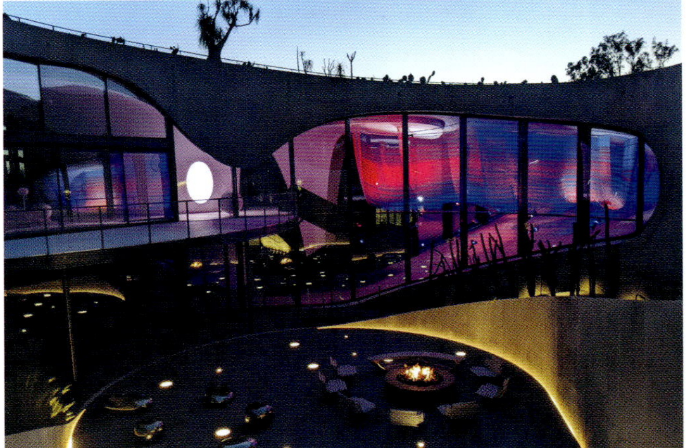

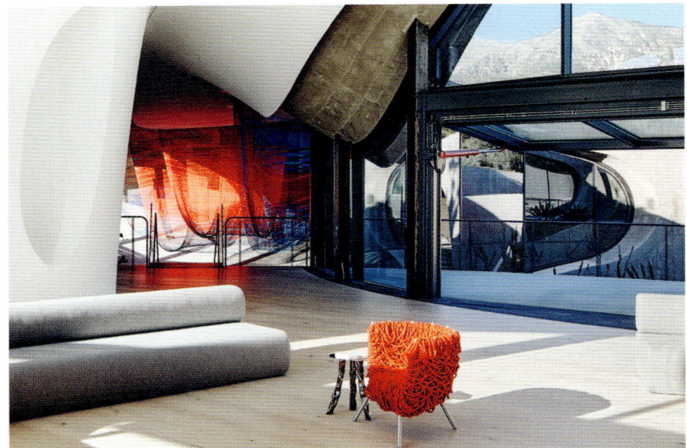

Enfold, 2022

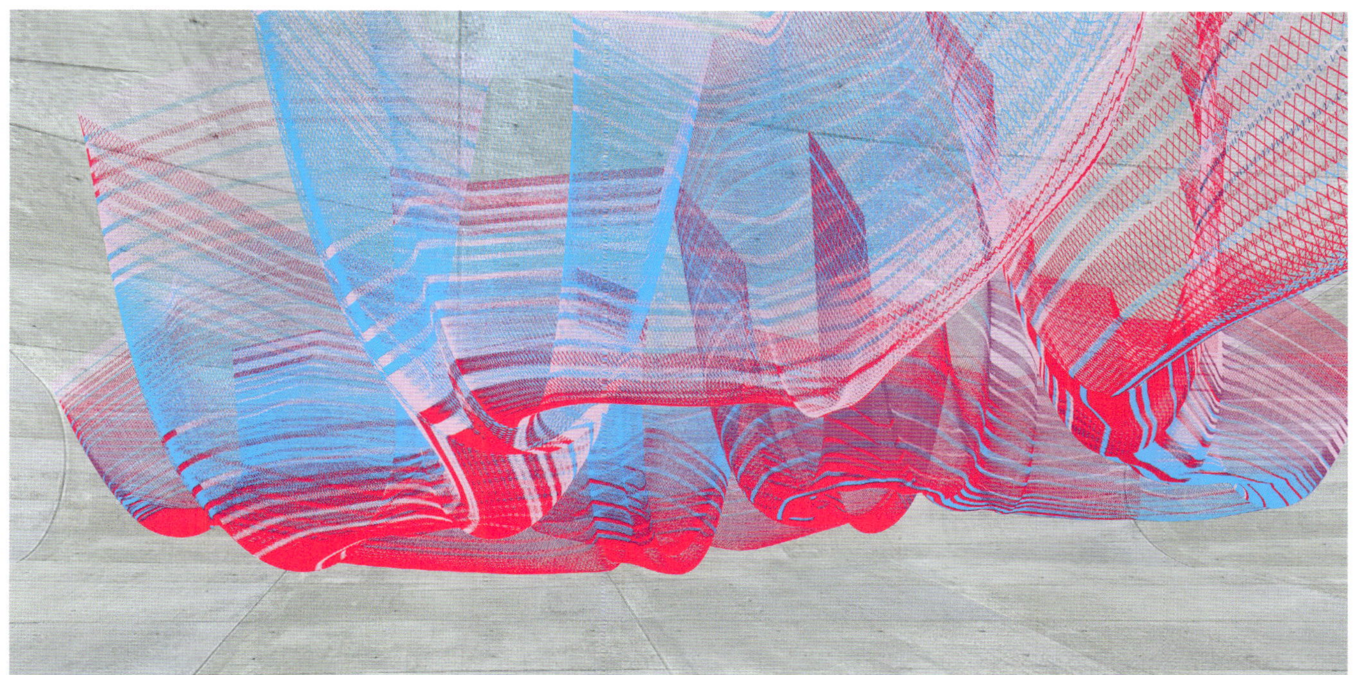

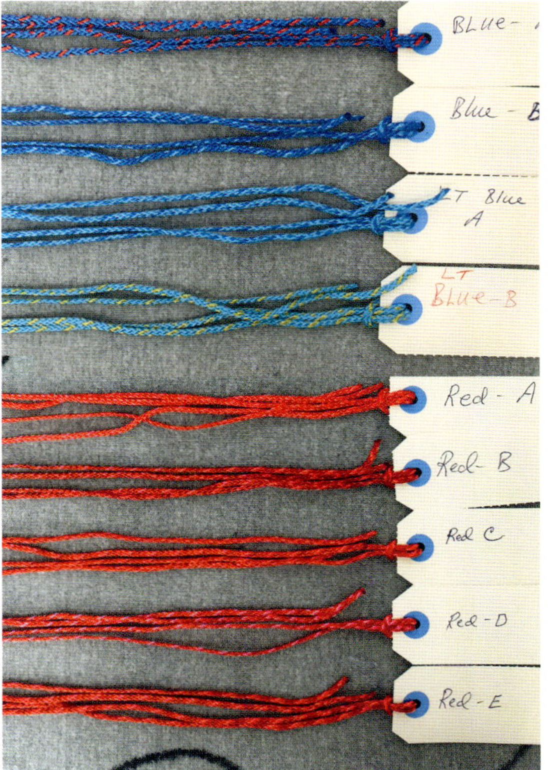

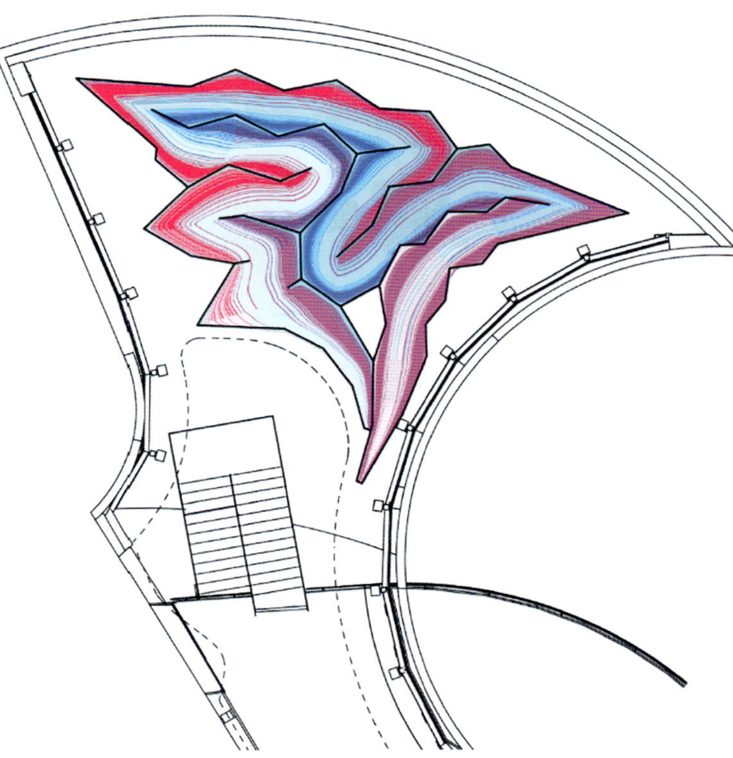

clockwise from top: 3D digital model, plan view, and twine samples for *Enfold*, 2022

following pages: Installing *Enfold*, 2022, and installation views, Hill House Montecito, California

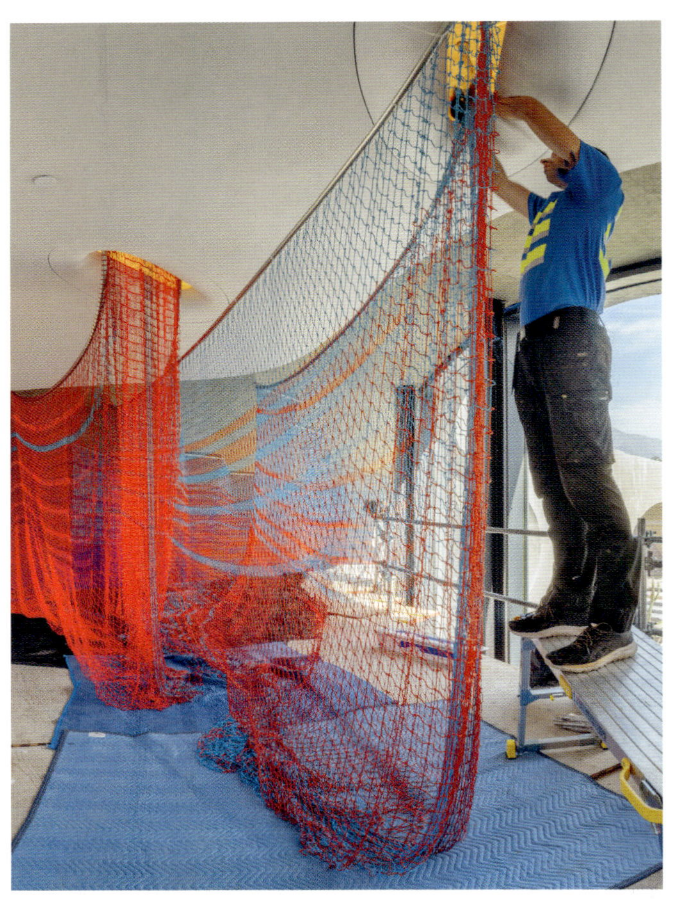

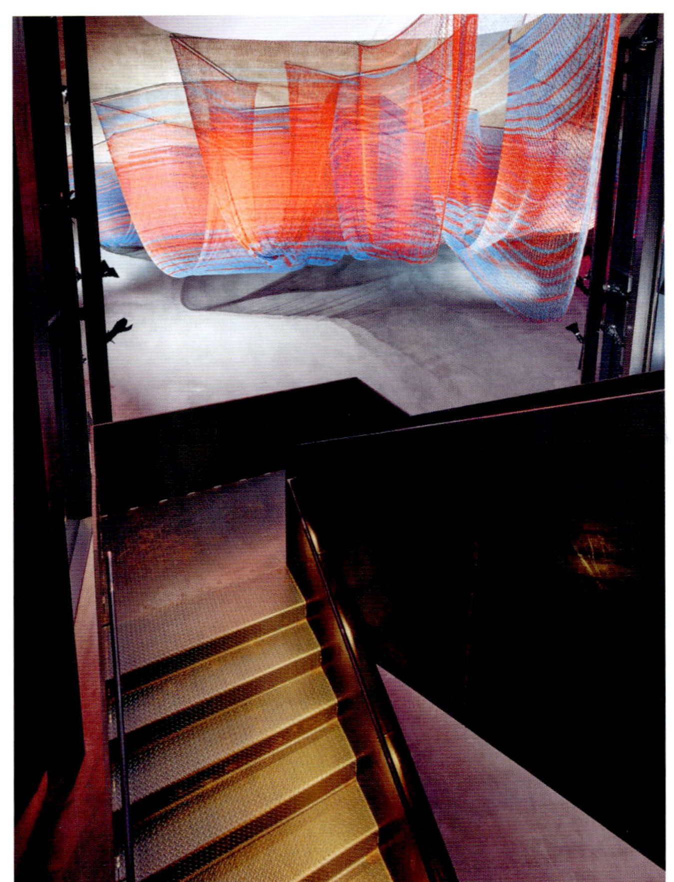

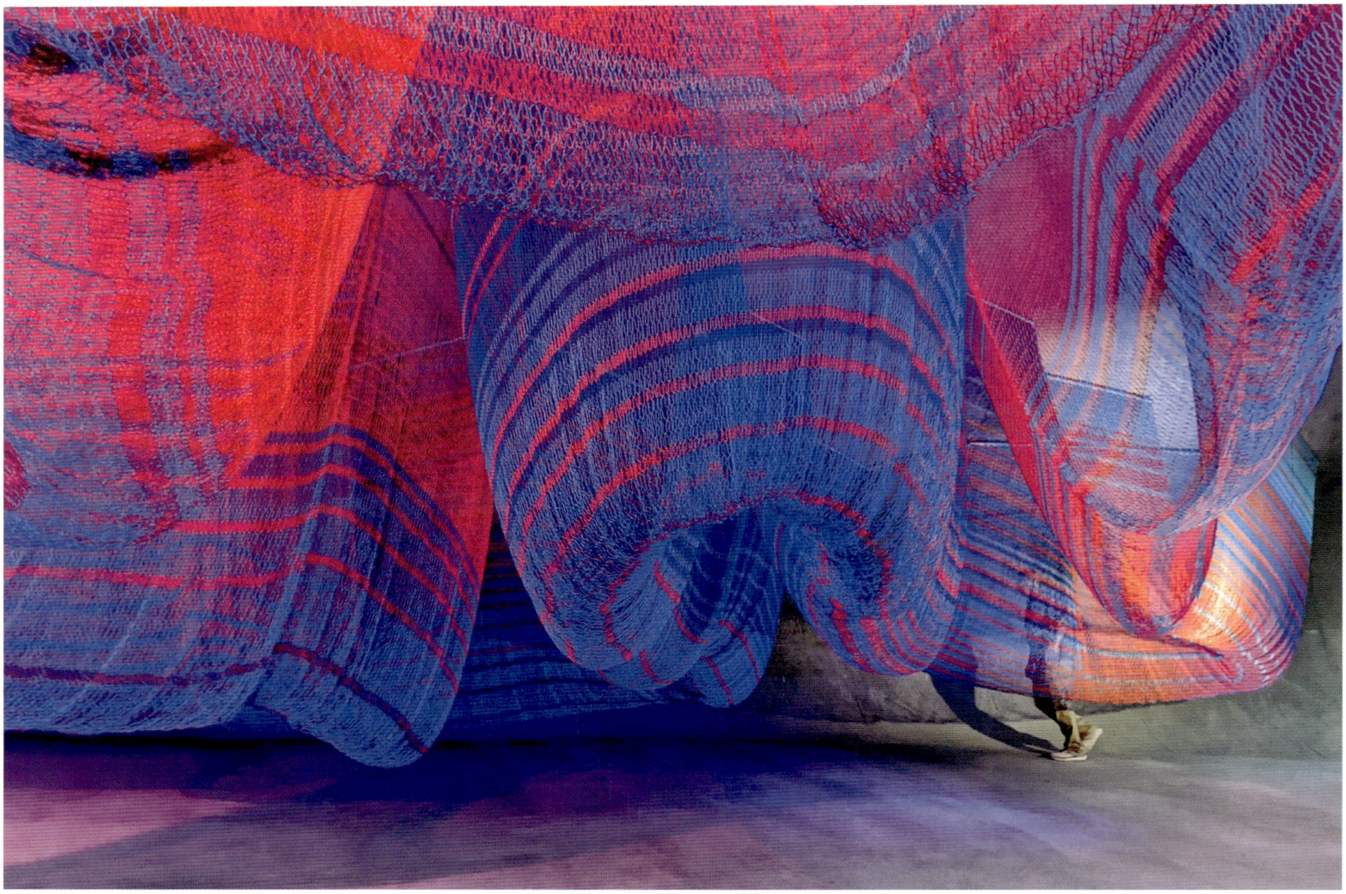

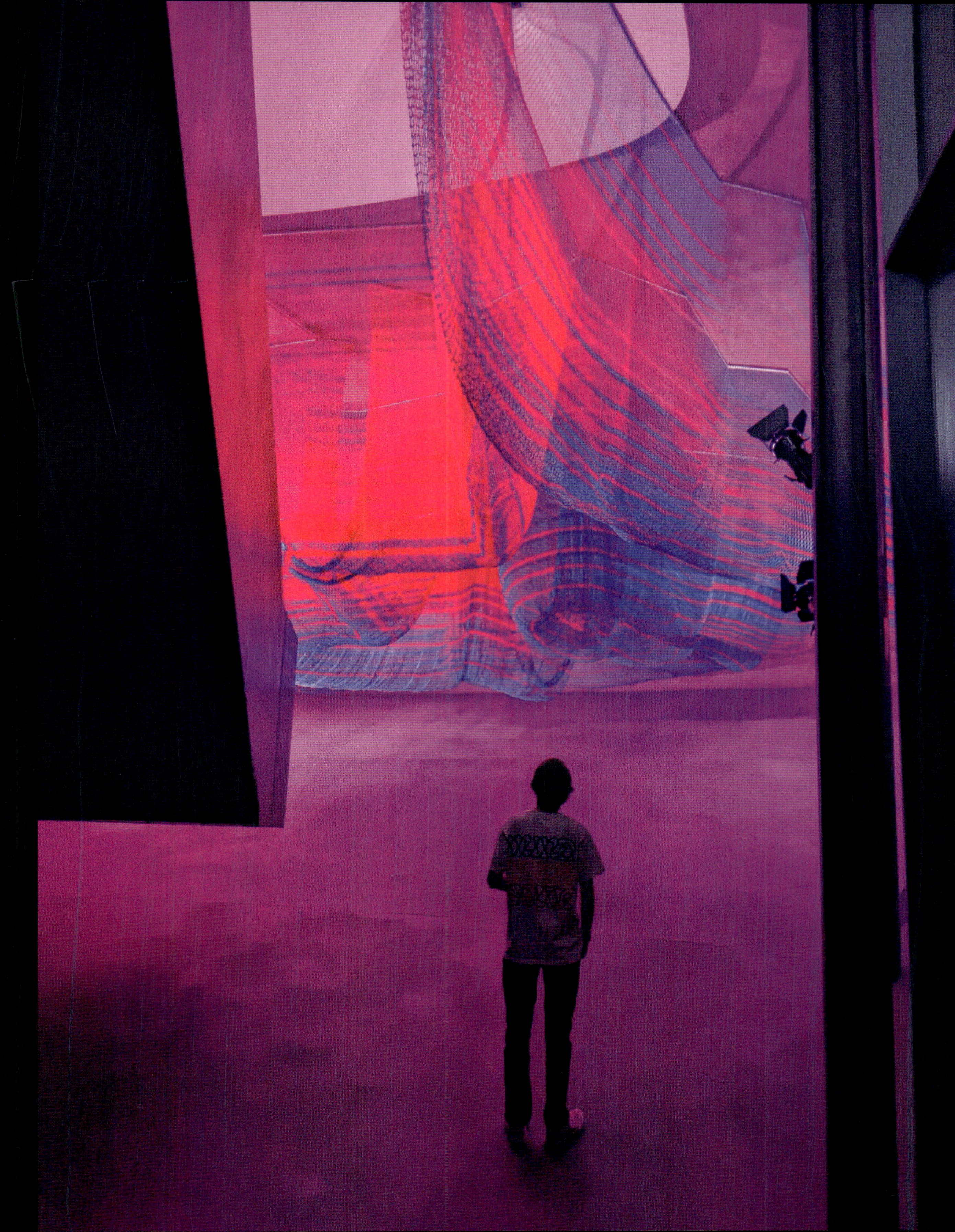

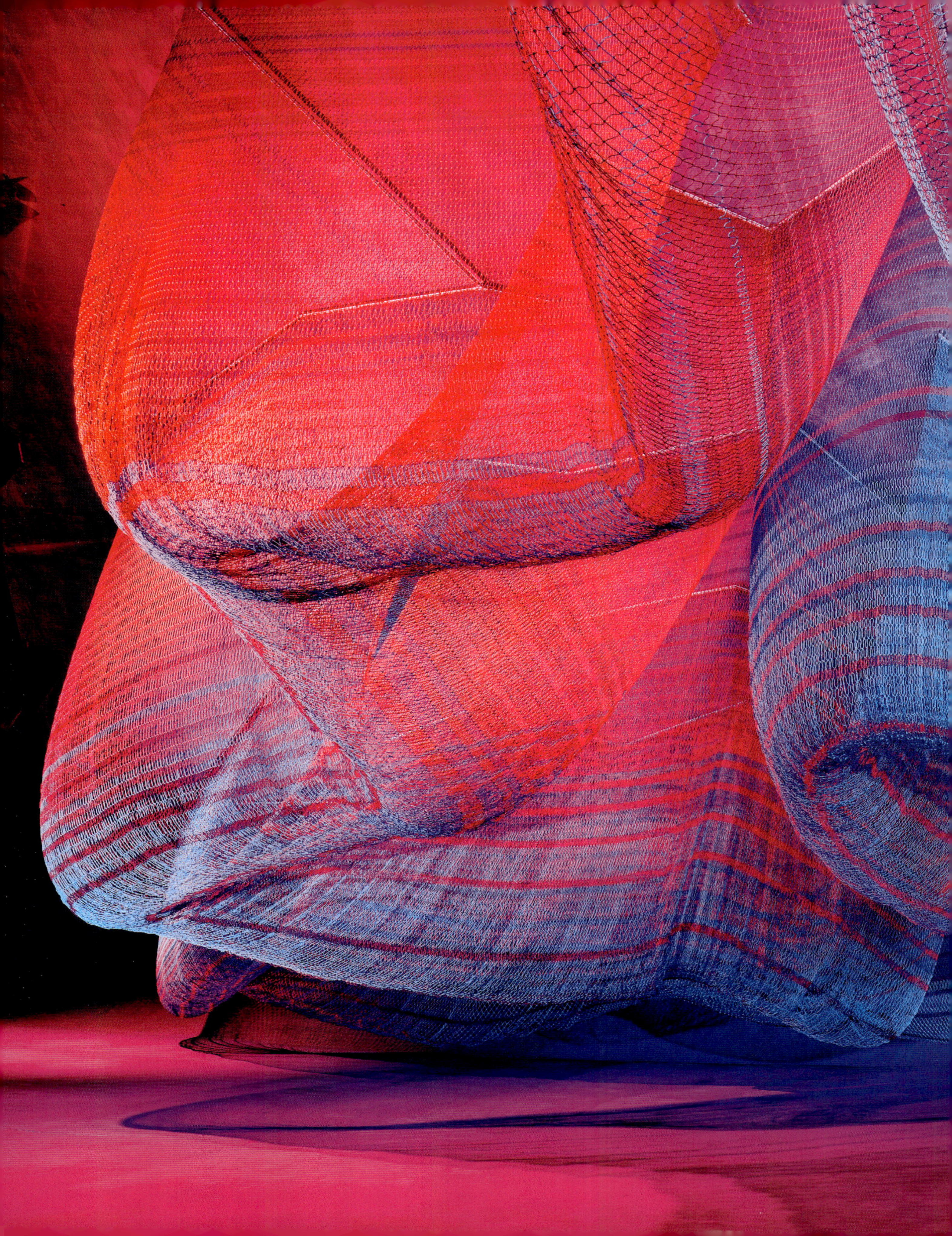

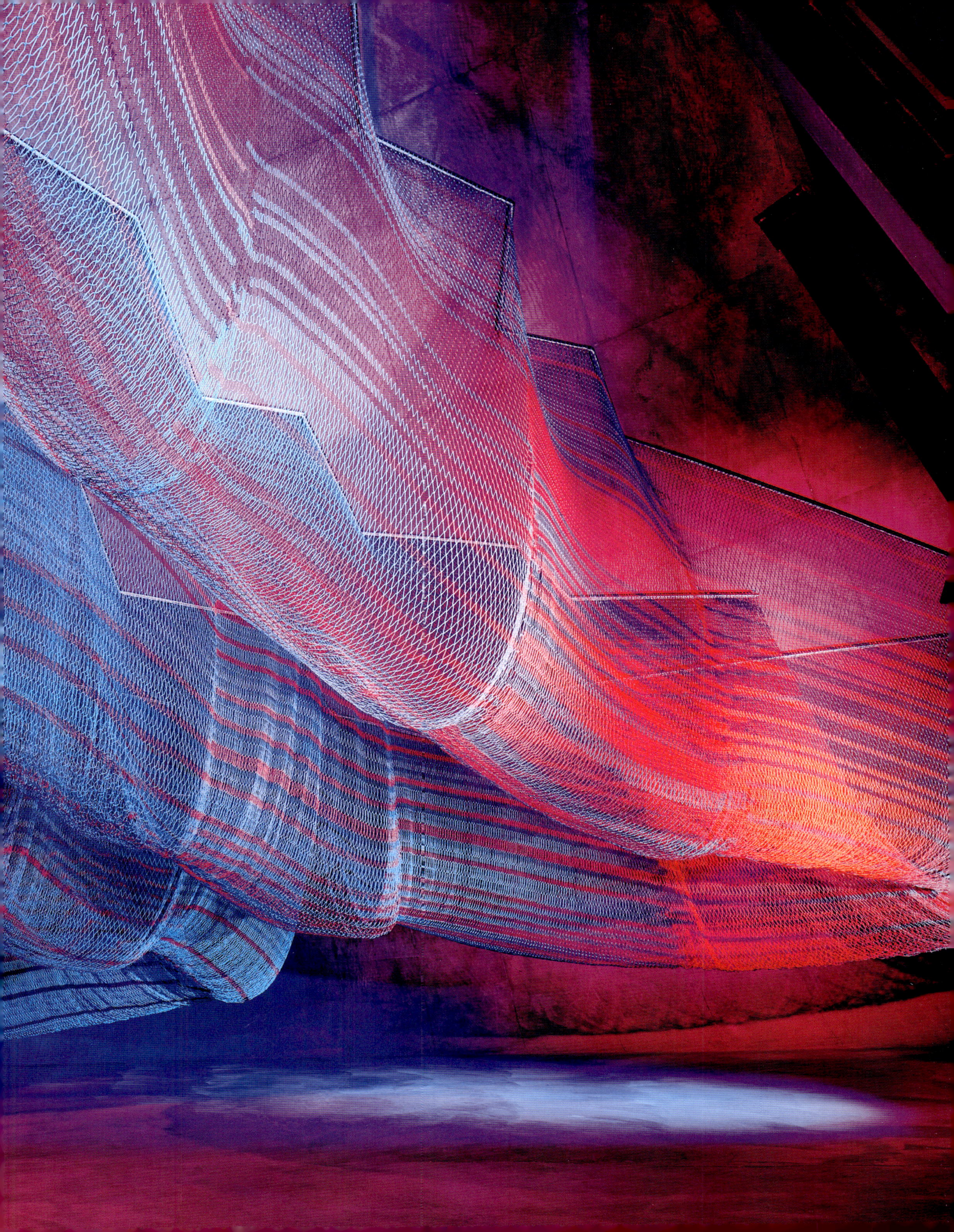

On *Current*

—

Ann Hamilton

I have had the chance to ride my bicycle under [Current]—
daytime and nighttime—to watch others look up
in awe and "find it." Oh, how very full of air and light it is,
suspended as if weightless in the sky, like a wisp
of matter gathered into a temporary constellation that
might in fact blow away.

Ann Hamilton is a visual artist who represented the United States at the 48th Venice Biennale.

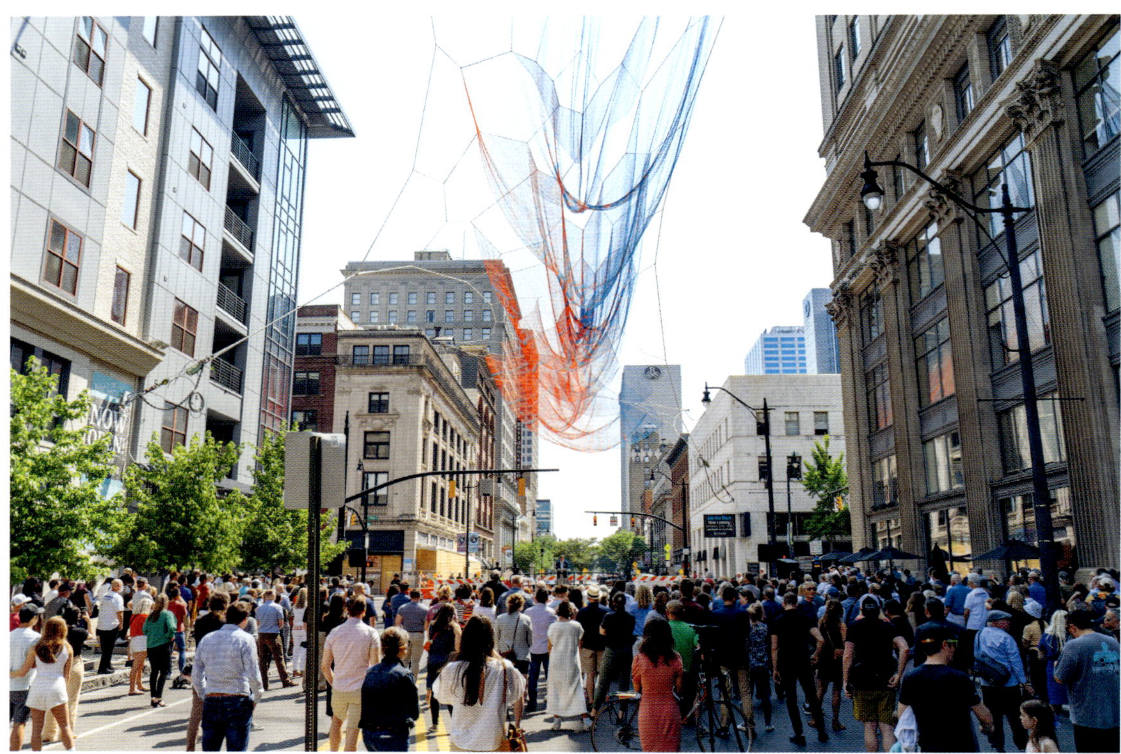

above and opposite: *Current*, 2023, Columbus, Ohio

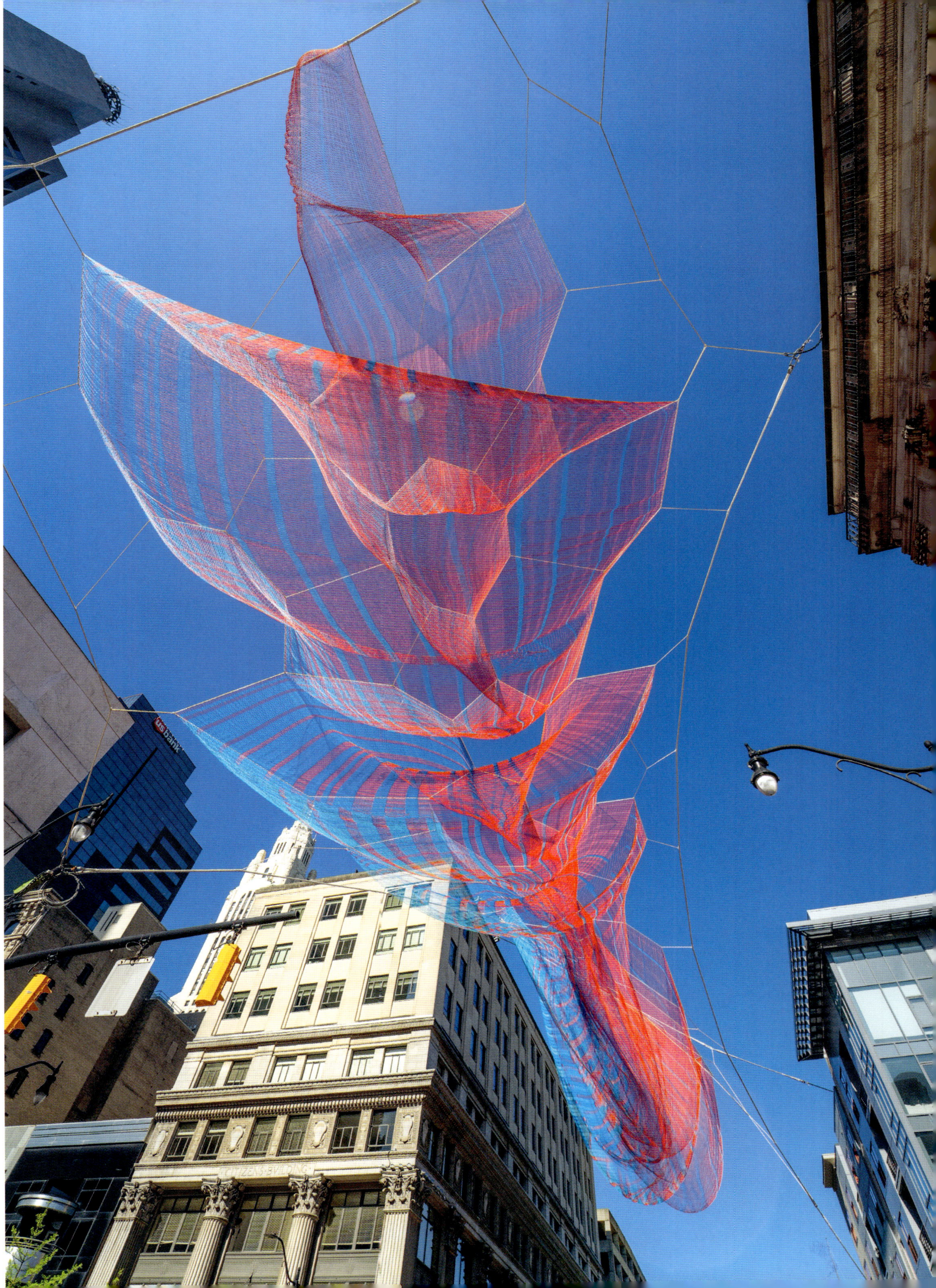
usbank
CITIZENS BUILDING

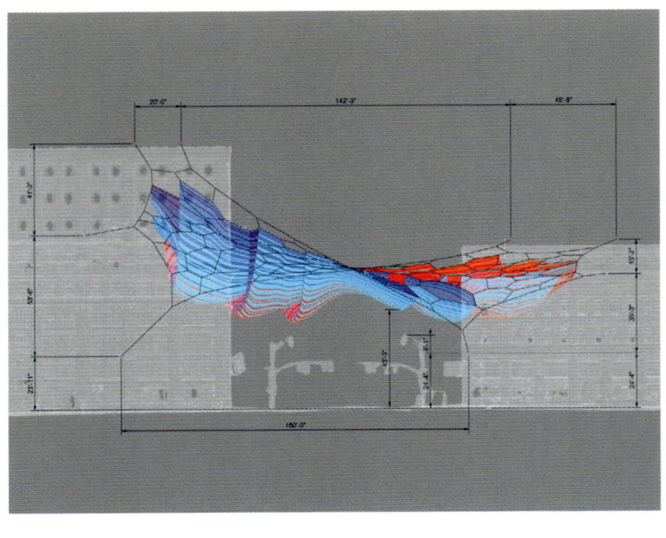

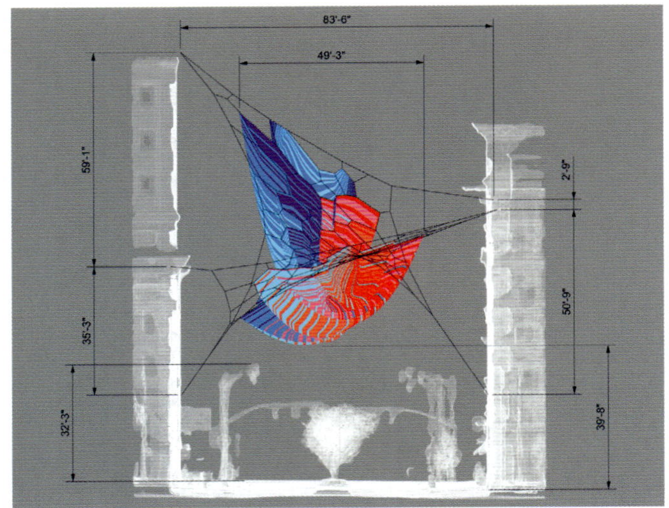

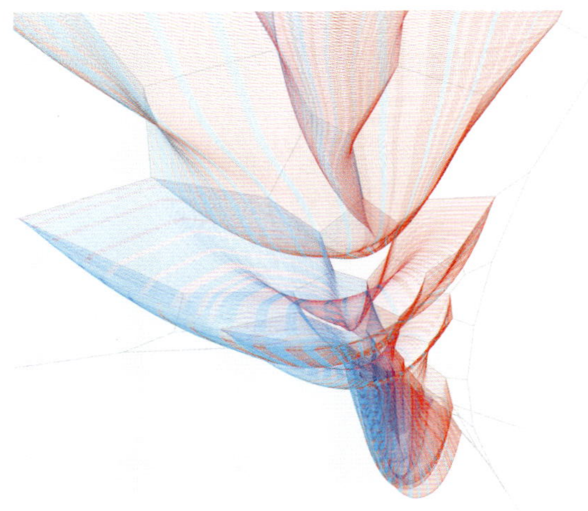

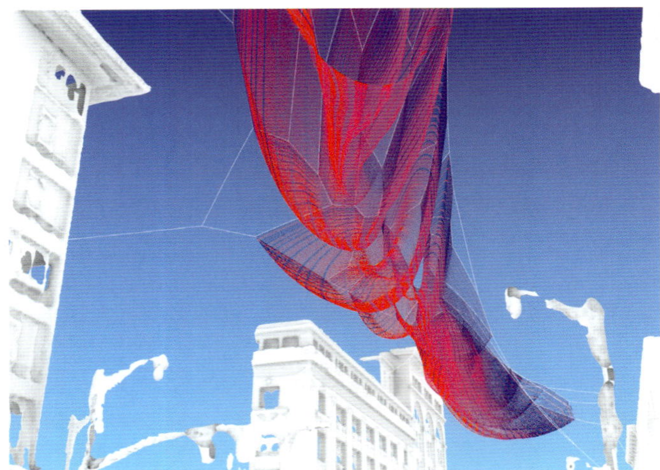

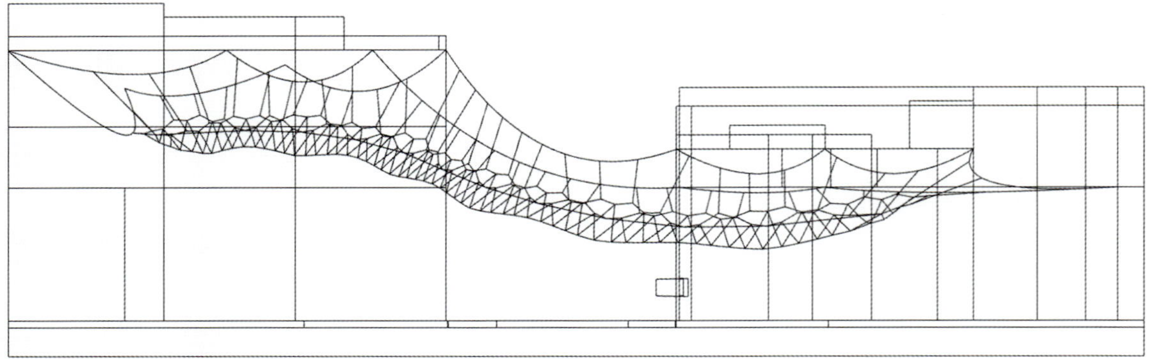

top and middle: 3D digital models of *Current*, 2023, simulated with the studio's Mango software, placed within point cloud site reconstructions

bottom: Early process drawing for *Current*, 2023

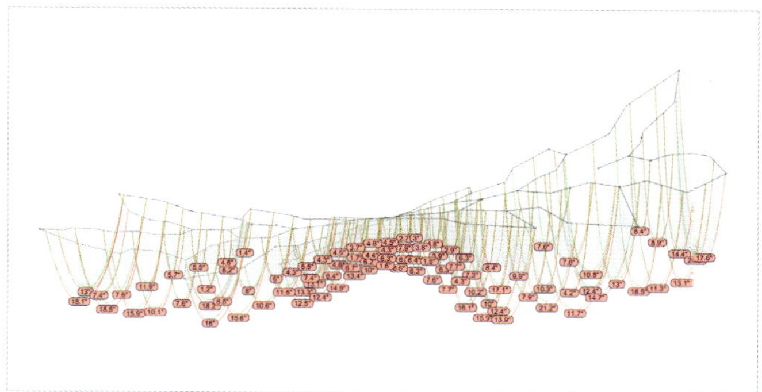

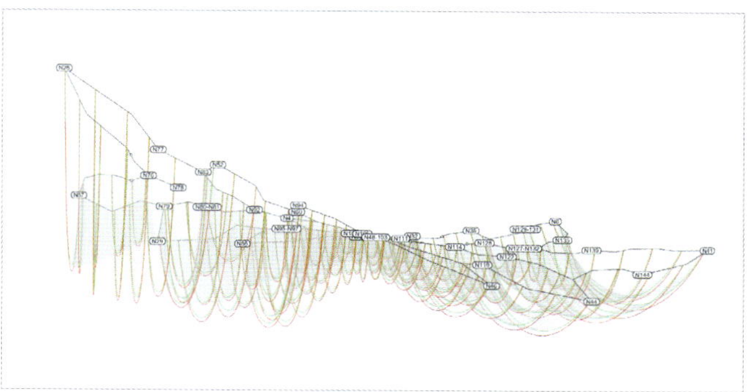

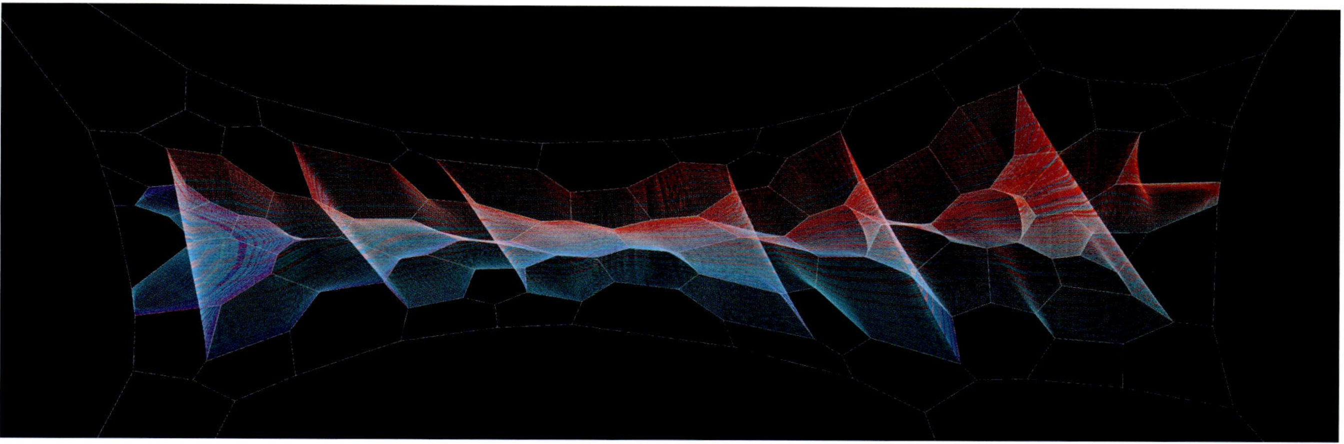

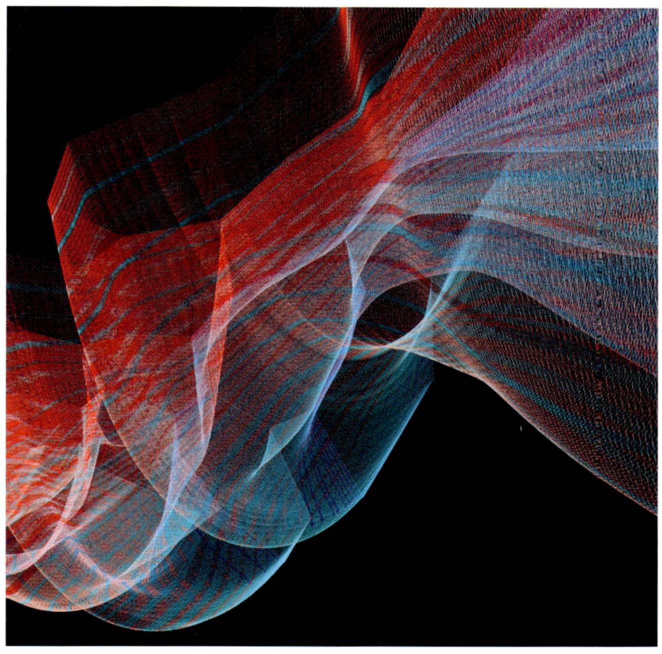

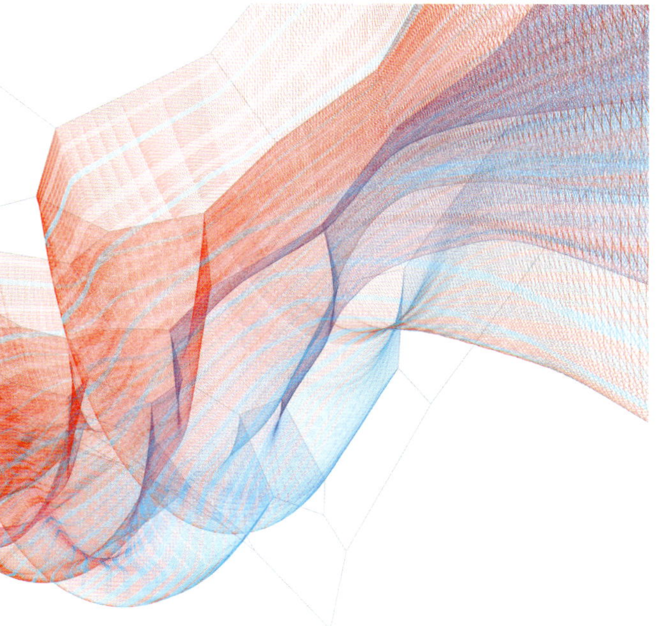

top row: Fabrication validation string models to confirm material dimensions for *Current*, 2023

middle and bottom rows: Final design renderings using the studio's Mango software for *Current*, 2023
following pages: *Current*, 2023

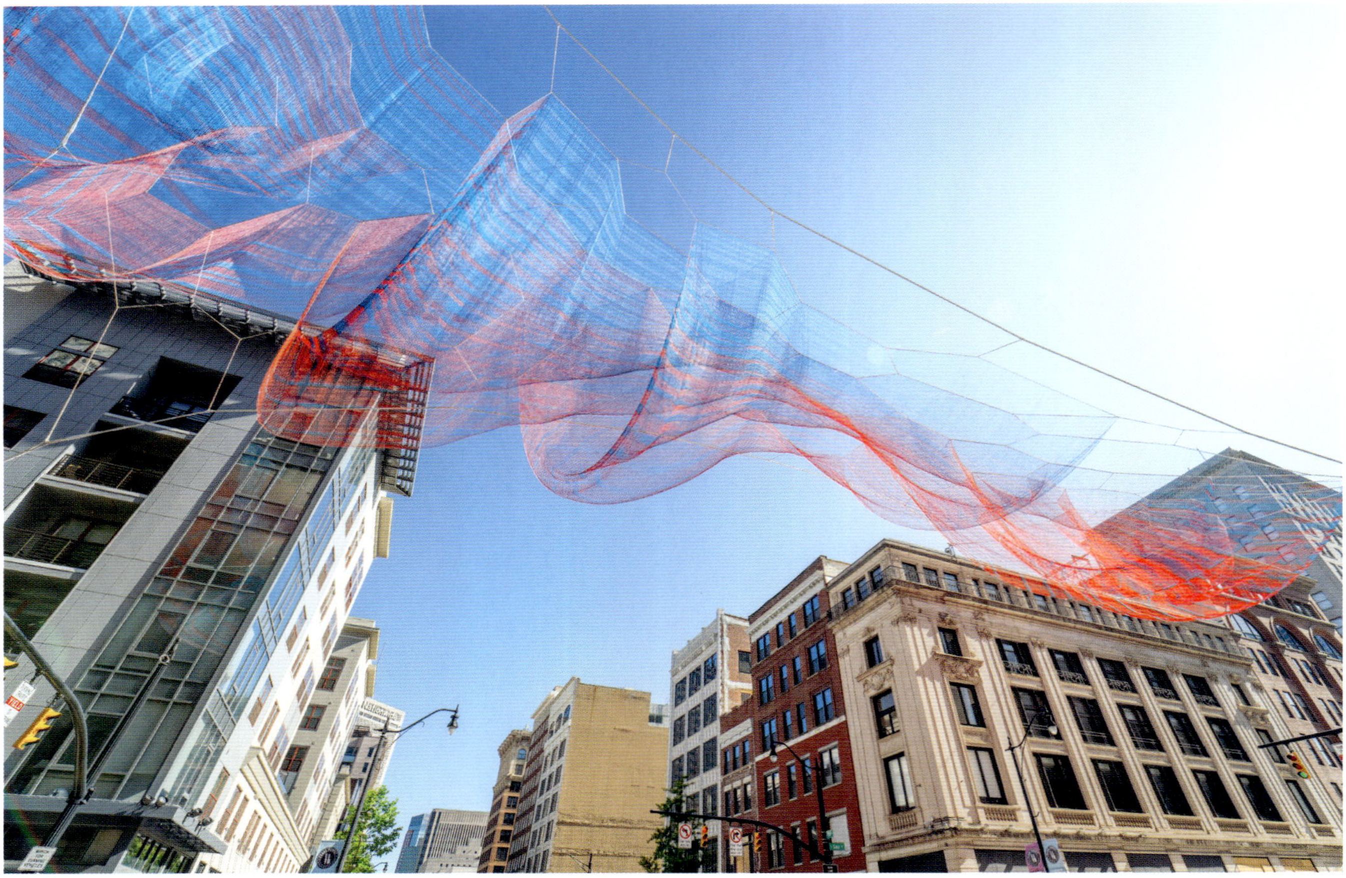

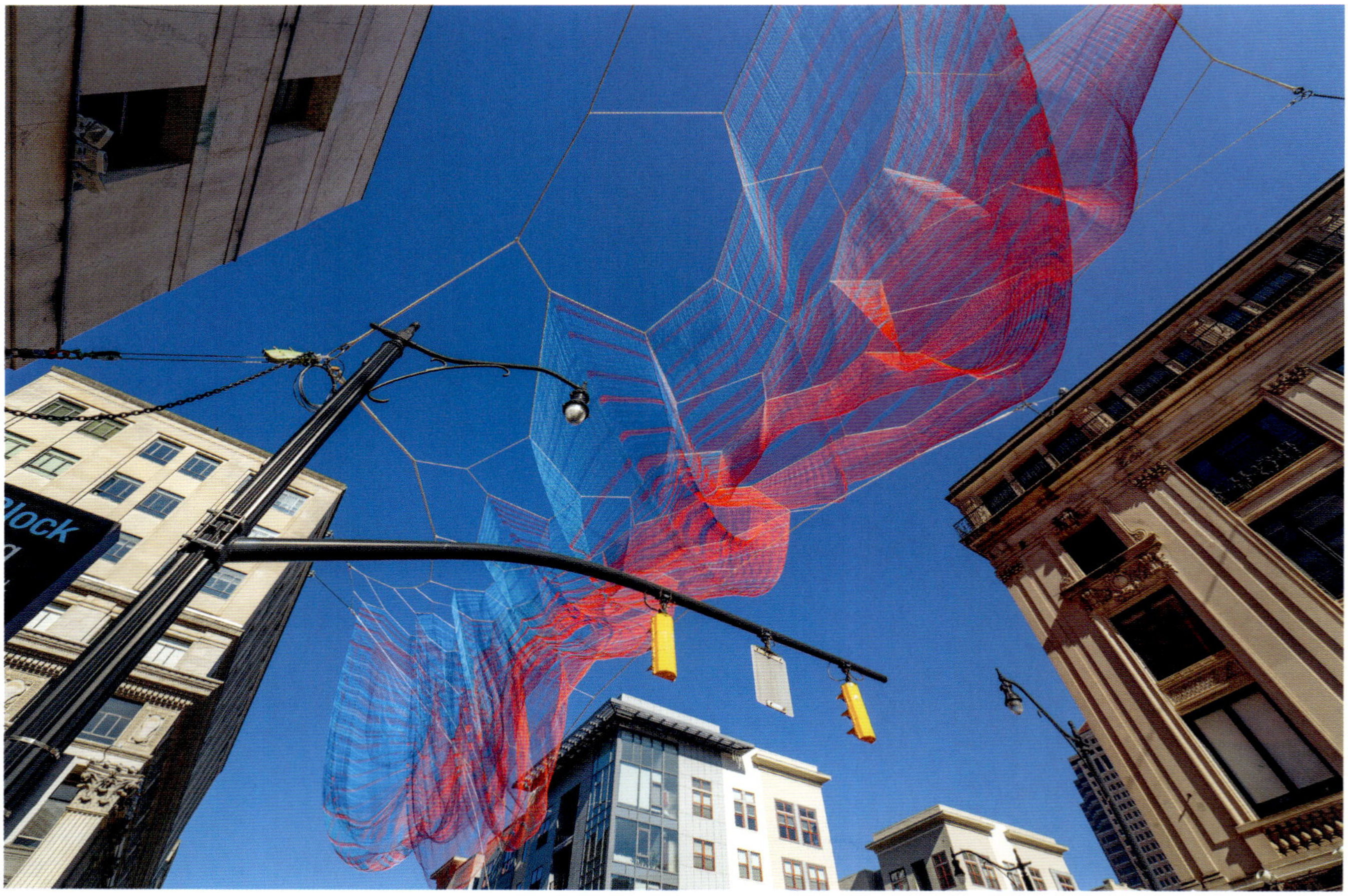

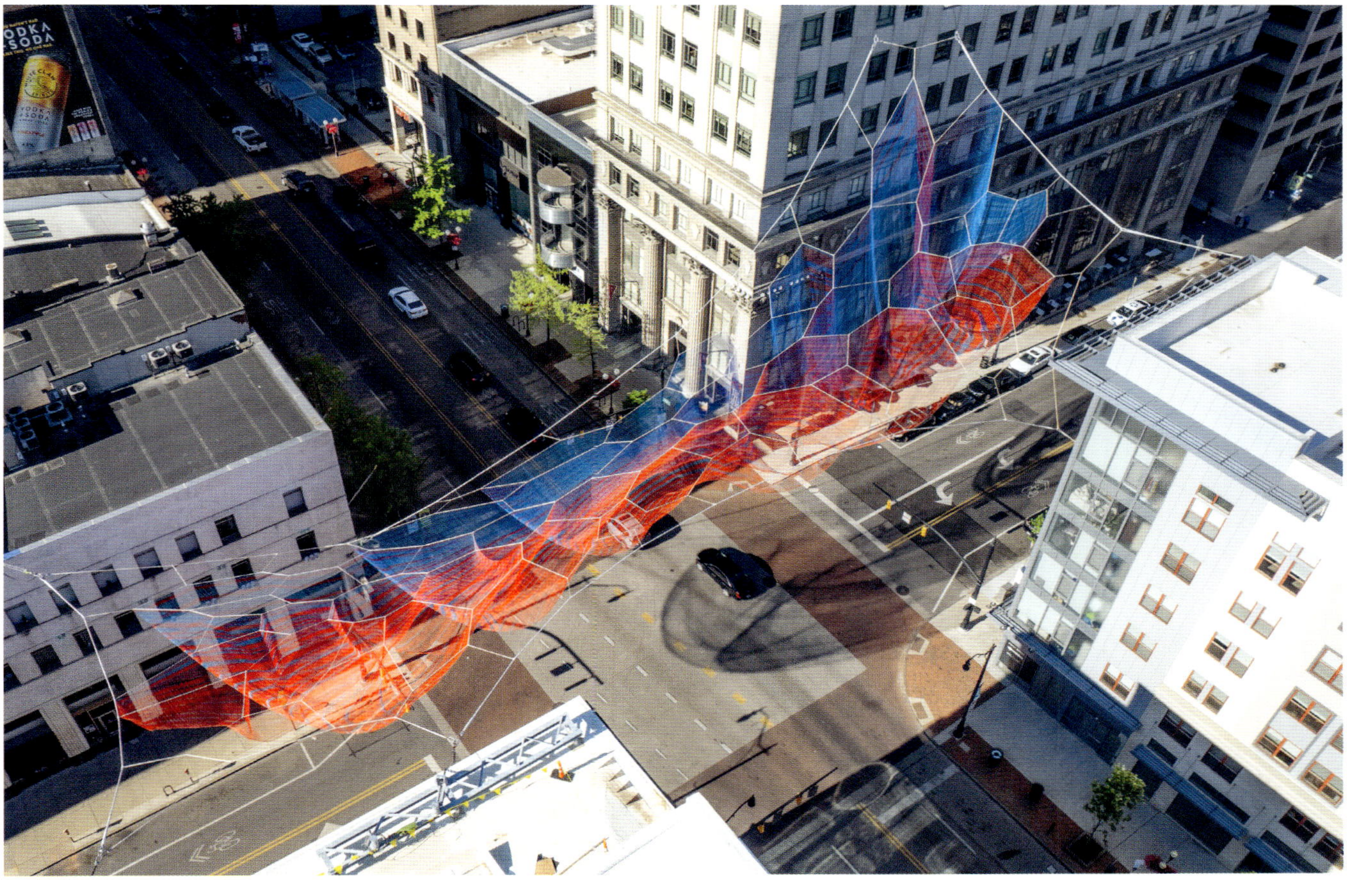

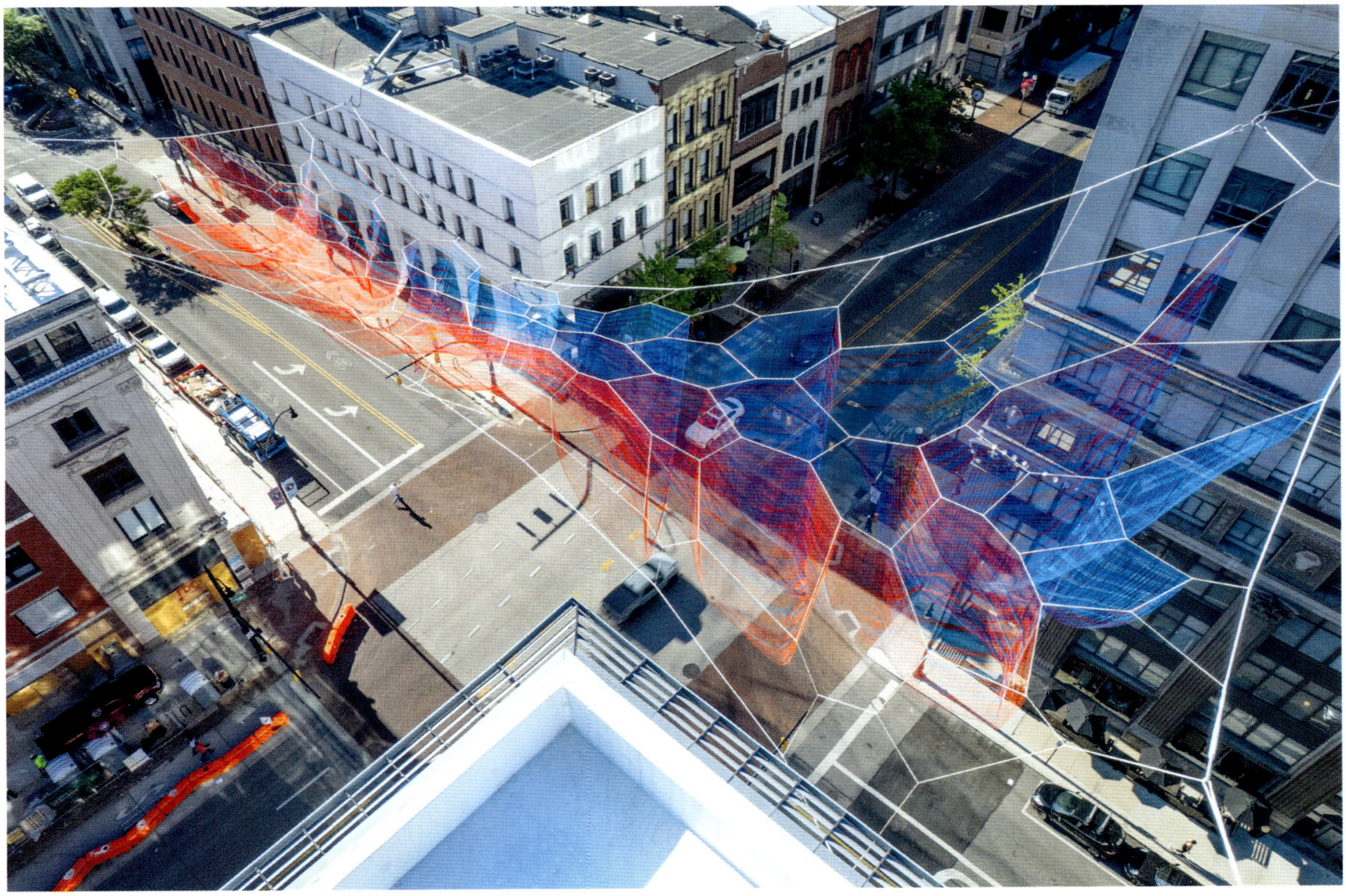

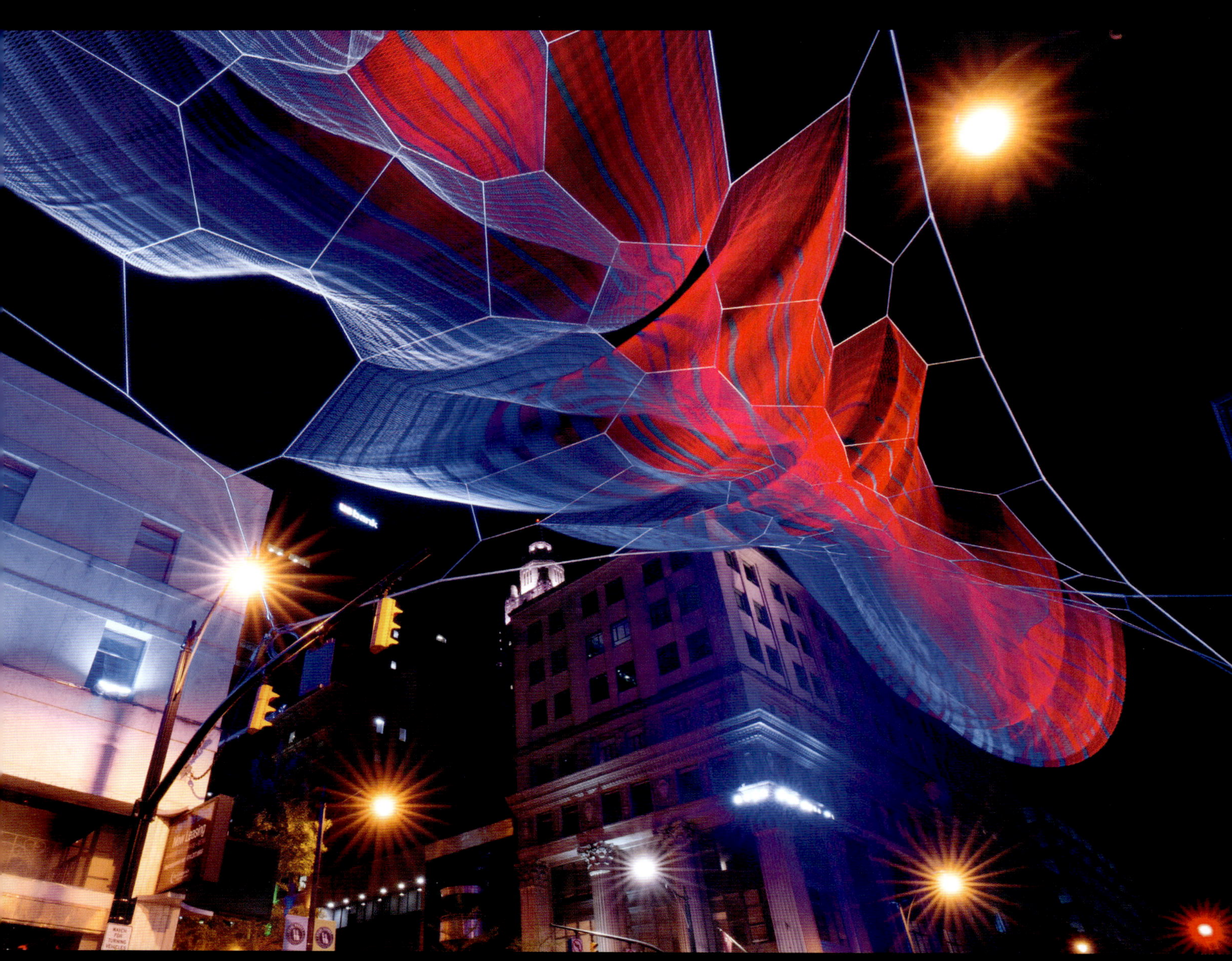

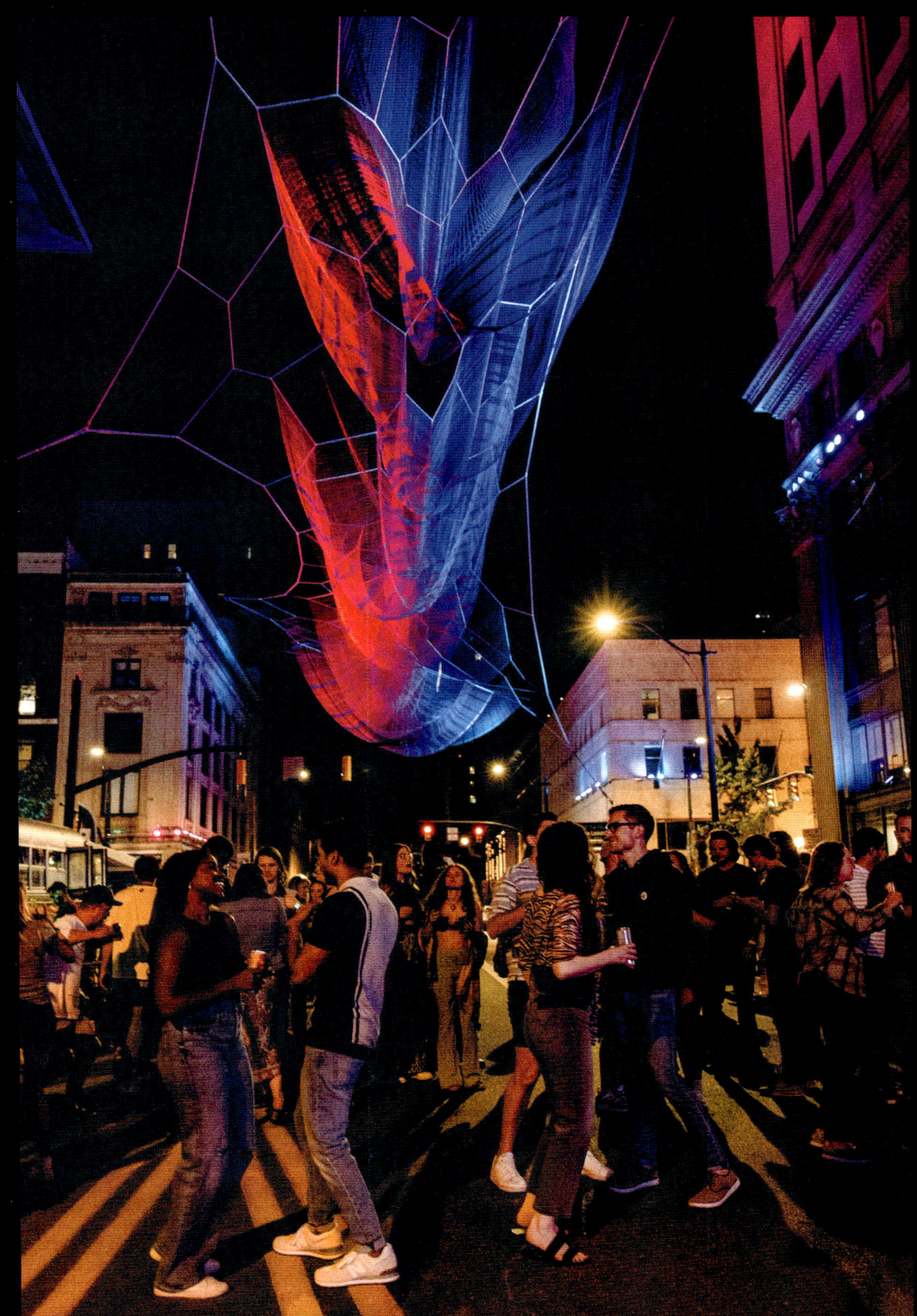

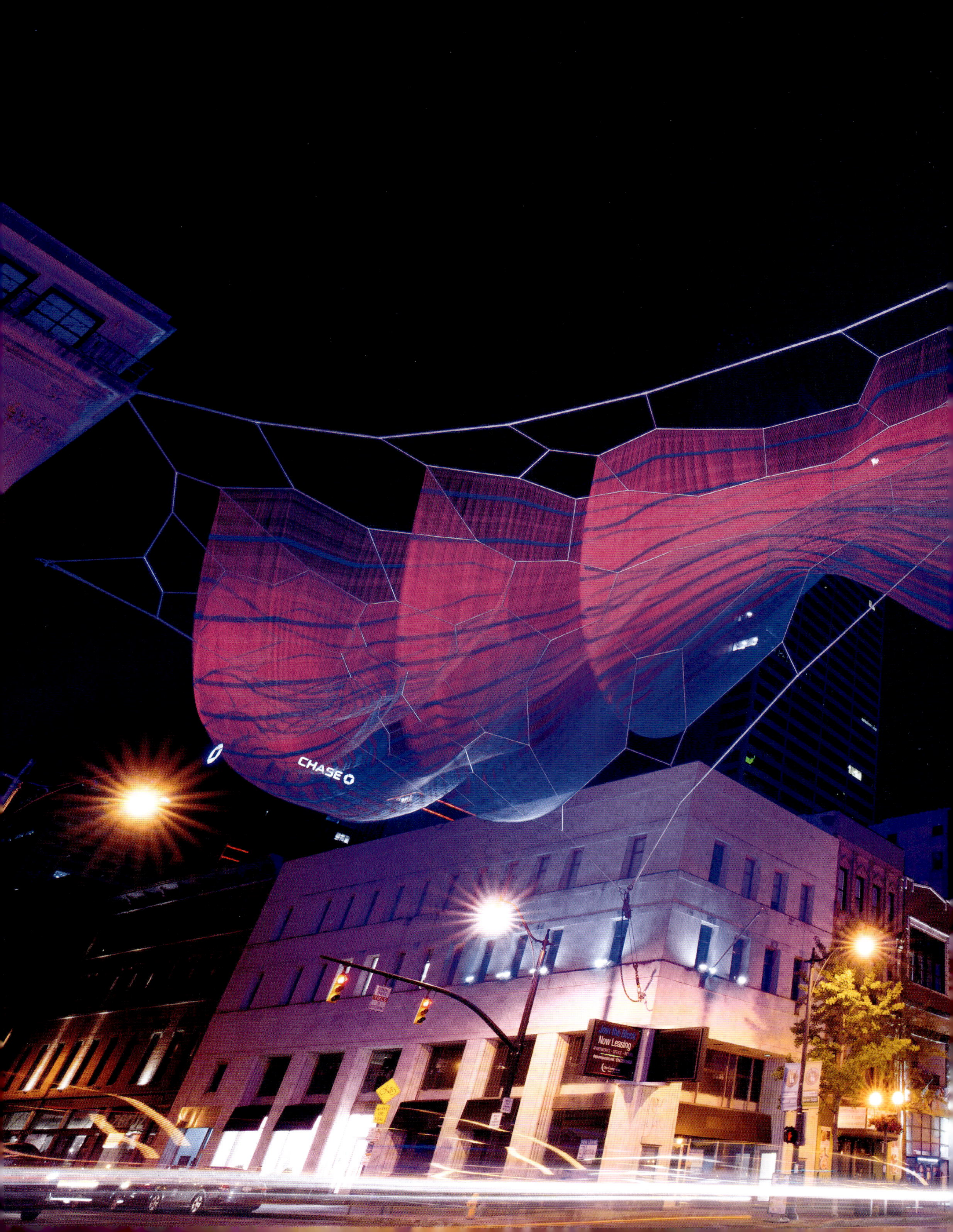
CHASE
Join the Block
Now Leasing

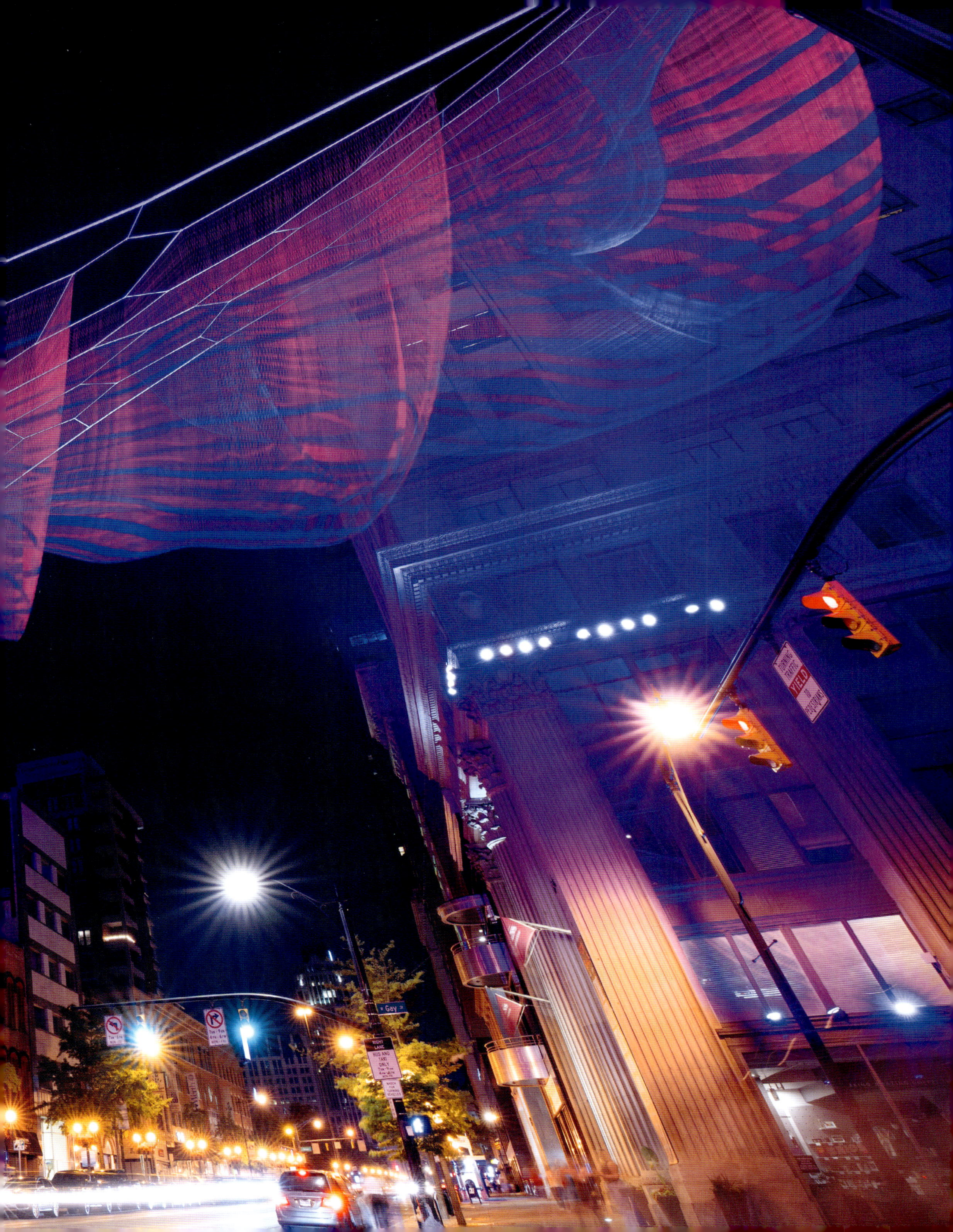
TURNING TRAFFIC
YIELD
TO PEDESTRIANS
Gay

Generative Mobility

—

Jérôme Sans

Janet Echelman is one of those artists who escape the traditional art system. Hardly destined to be hung on a wall or set on a pedestal, her works are conceived at the scale of the city, of the landscape. She is part of a history of artists who have worked on and in the landscape, from Agnes Denes, Ana Mendieta, Nancy Holt, and Maya Lin to Michael Heizer, Richard Long, Robert Smithson, and Christo and Jeanne-Claude. Her large-scale sculptures confront the real world, rather than living "outside of the world," meaning the traditional museum or contemporary art gallery or collector's domestic interior. Echelman counts among those few artists who have invented their own system to continue developing their own practice.

Working with curator Pedro Alonzo and my team, Echelman sited *Earthtime 1.26 Wadi Namar* (2023) within a vast valley surrounded by rock cliffs that is a gateway to a desert in Saudi Arabia. This positions the work in a territory that has virtually no limits, unlike an urban landscape, which is inescapably limned by buildings and thus operates in a constrained framework. Marrying the sky and the earth, the work in this context is in a state of in-between. To meander around Riyadh's Wadi Namar public park is an invitation to simultaneously encounter artworks commissioned through the Noor Festival and conjoin an everyday stroll with poetic meditation. Still urbanized in the sense that a road that passes through it, yet gradually moving away from the city, this oasis is a first step toward a total immersion in wild nature. Its site gives *Earthtime 1.26 Wadi Namar* a masterly, very particular dimension that is almost on the order of a desert mirage.

Echelman further enchanted the landscape by installing *majlis*, those low Arabic sofas that invite and incite visitors to take a moment to sit down, look up, and enjoy the work individually but also collectively. Since the *wadi* is famous for its rich sense of community, where families, friends, and loved ones sit on carpets and share food and drink, the work is situated a little further afield from the usual spaces of collectivity, operating as it does in a more open and arid context. While the sense of interconnectivity inherent to Echelman's work entirely fits within the local spirit of the place, *Earthtime 1.26 Wadi Namar* carves out new possibilities within this landscape for togetherness and contemplation.

In the context of my own curatorial work, I am fascinated by the extreme lightness of Echelman's work, as it bends to the flow of the wind, moving in space without disrupting the context. I am struck by its transparency, its fluidity, its almost generative mobility, as it never repeats the same movement twice. The work is like a living body that does not stop moving in space and time, and lives independently from any control of the hand or humanity. It is almost a work of and by nature itself.

Jérôme Sans is cofounder of Palais de Tokyo, Paris, and curator of the 5th Taipei Biennale and the 8th Lyon Biennale.

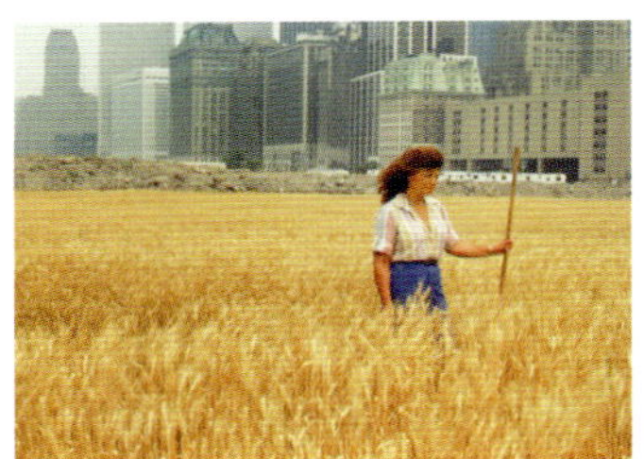
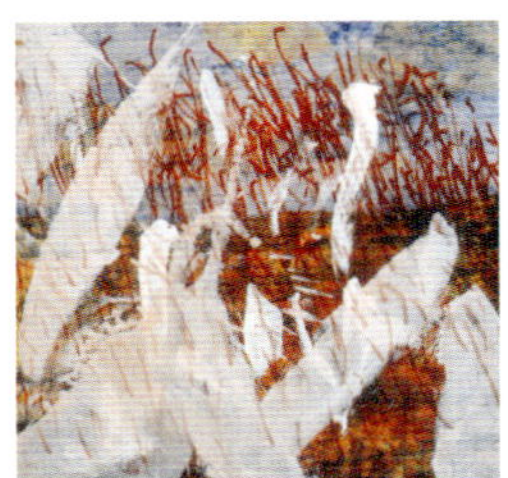
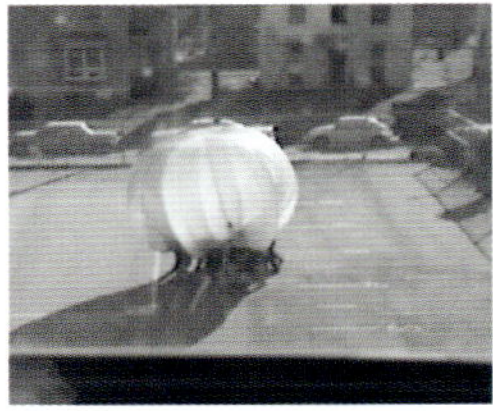
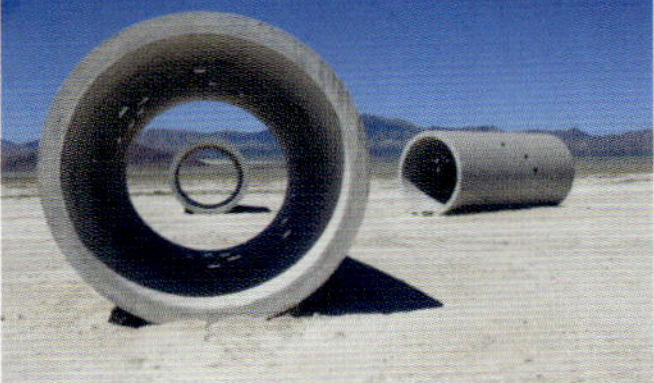
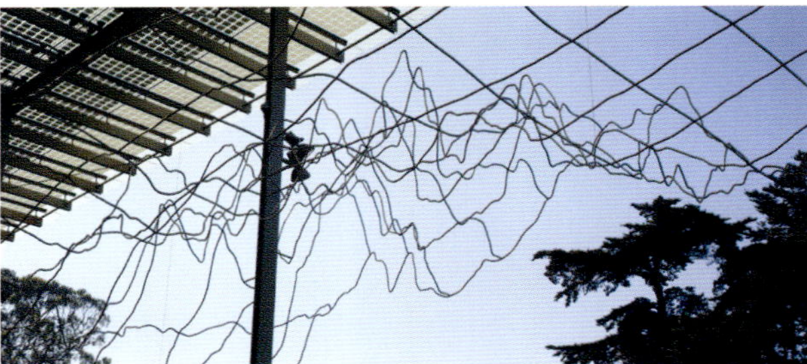

clockwise from top left: Agnes Denes, *Wheatfield—A Confrontation*, 1982; Janet Echelman, *The Occupation of a Landscape and Its Subsequent Denial (Is Wider Than Never Being Occupied at All)*, 1993, mixed media on canvas, 20 × 20 in.; Nancy Holt, *Sun Tunnels*, 1973–76; Maya Lin, *Where the Land Meets the Sea*, 2008; Ana Mendieta, still from *Parachute*, 1973

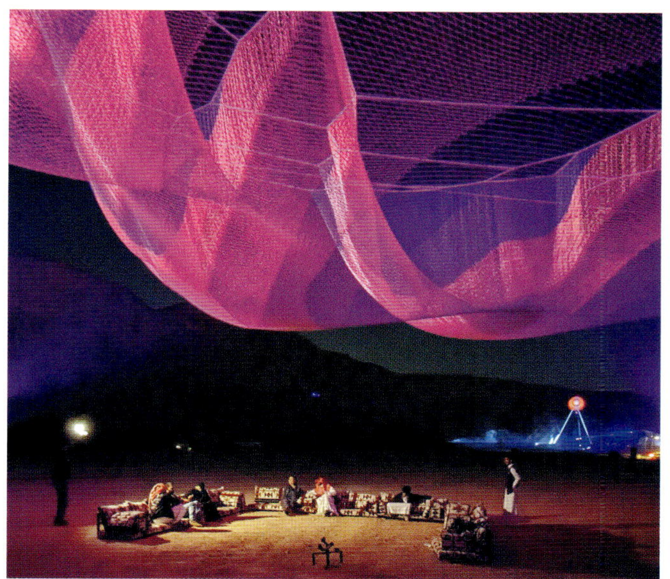

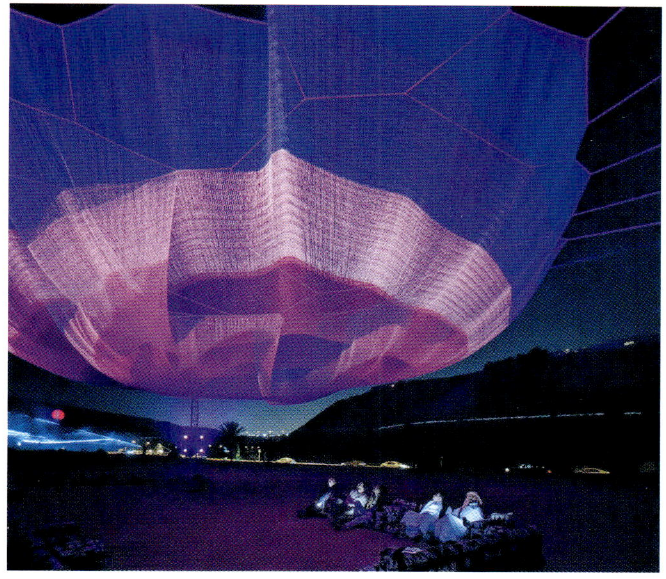

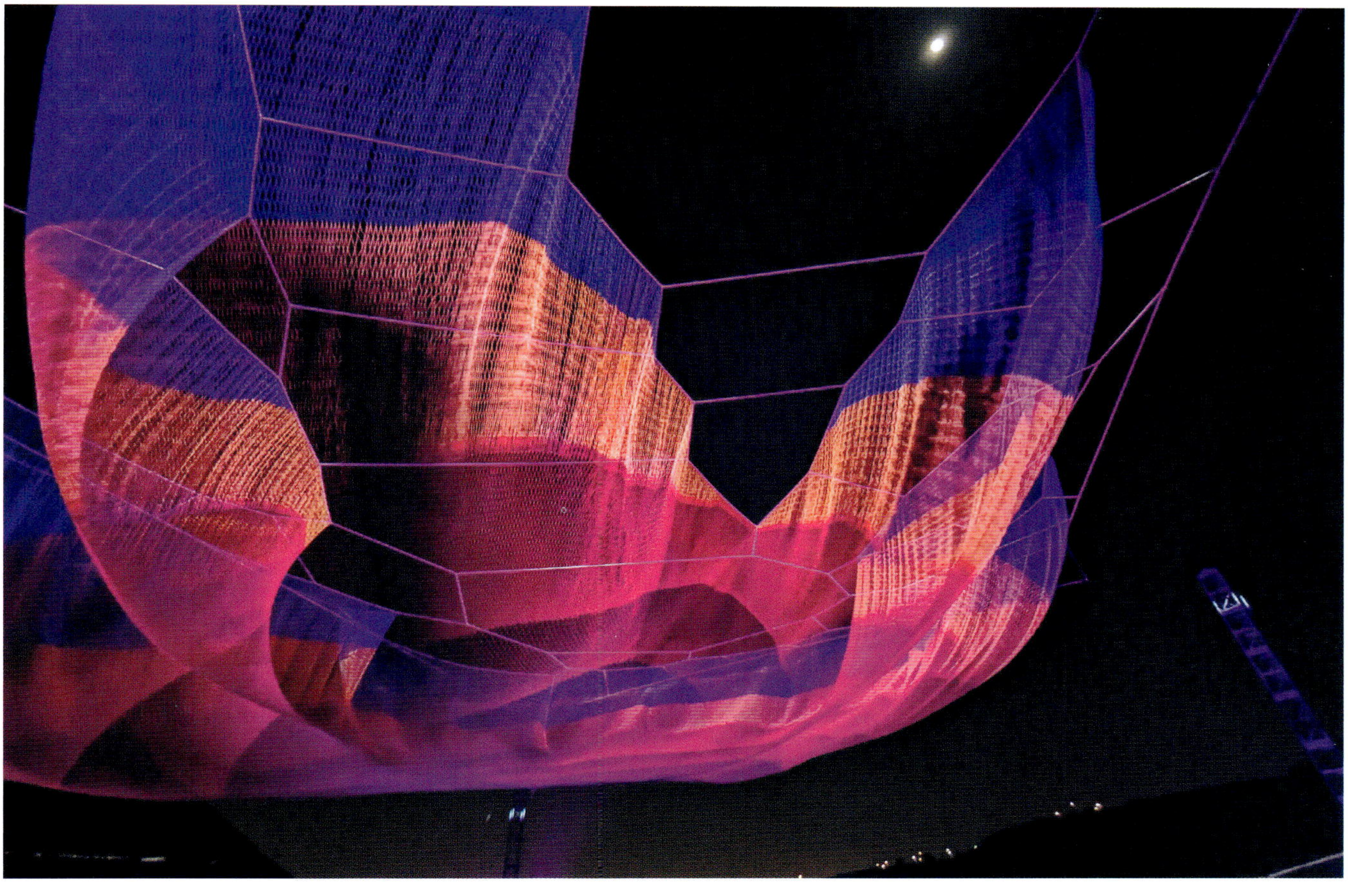

Earthtime 1.26 Wadi Namar, 2023, Riyadh, Saudi Arabia

Two

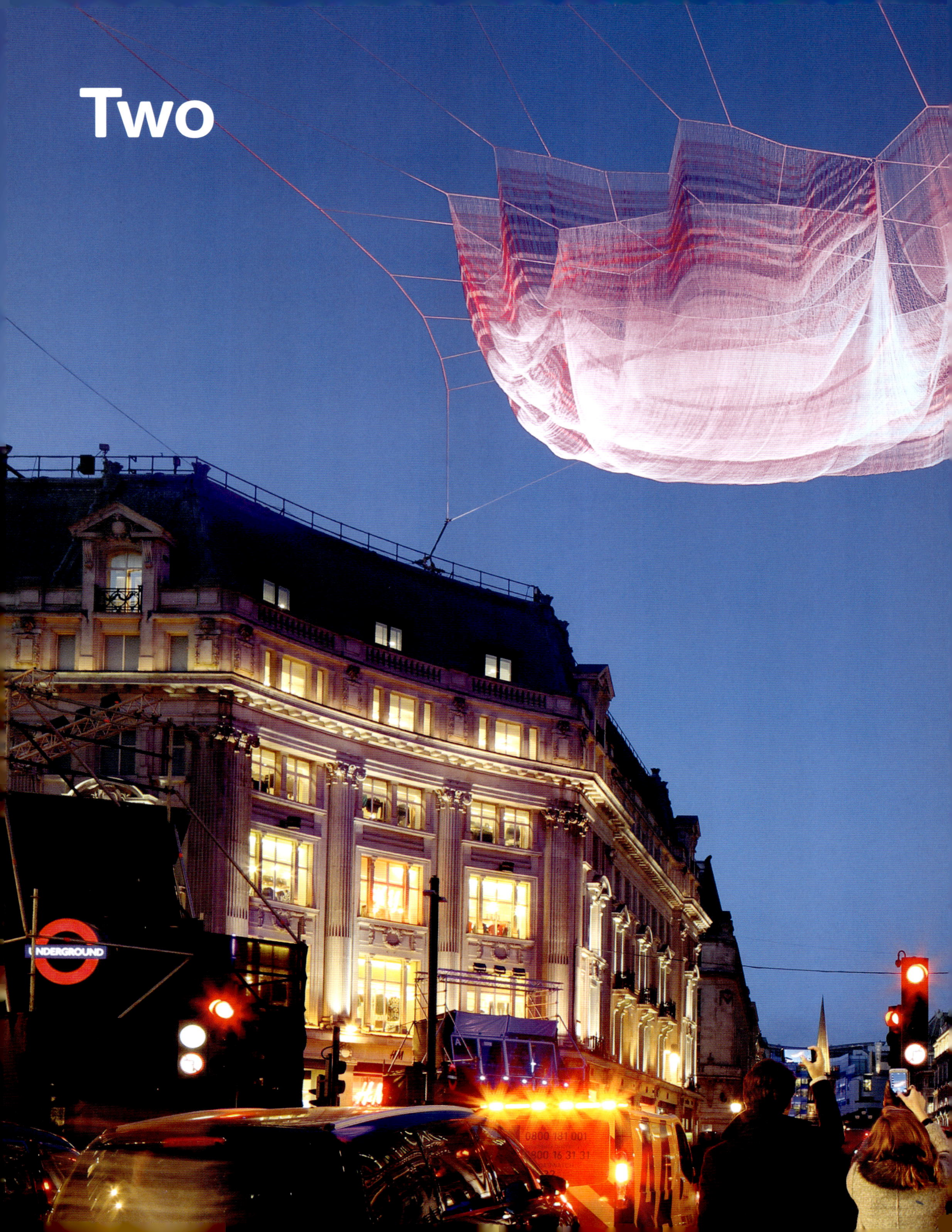

Public Interfacing

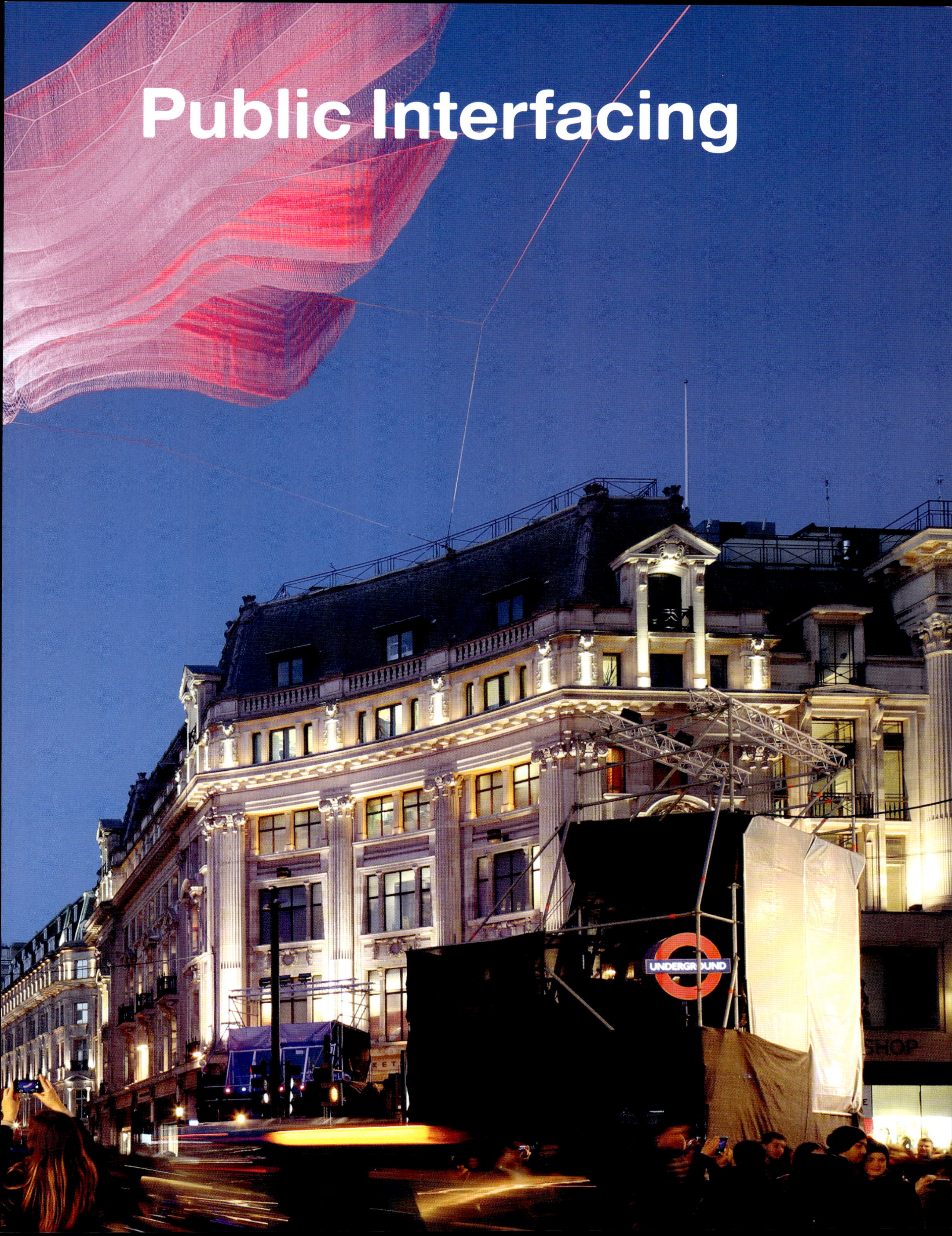

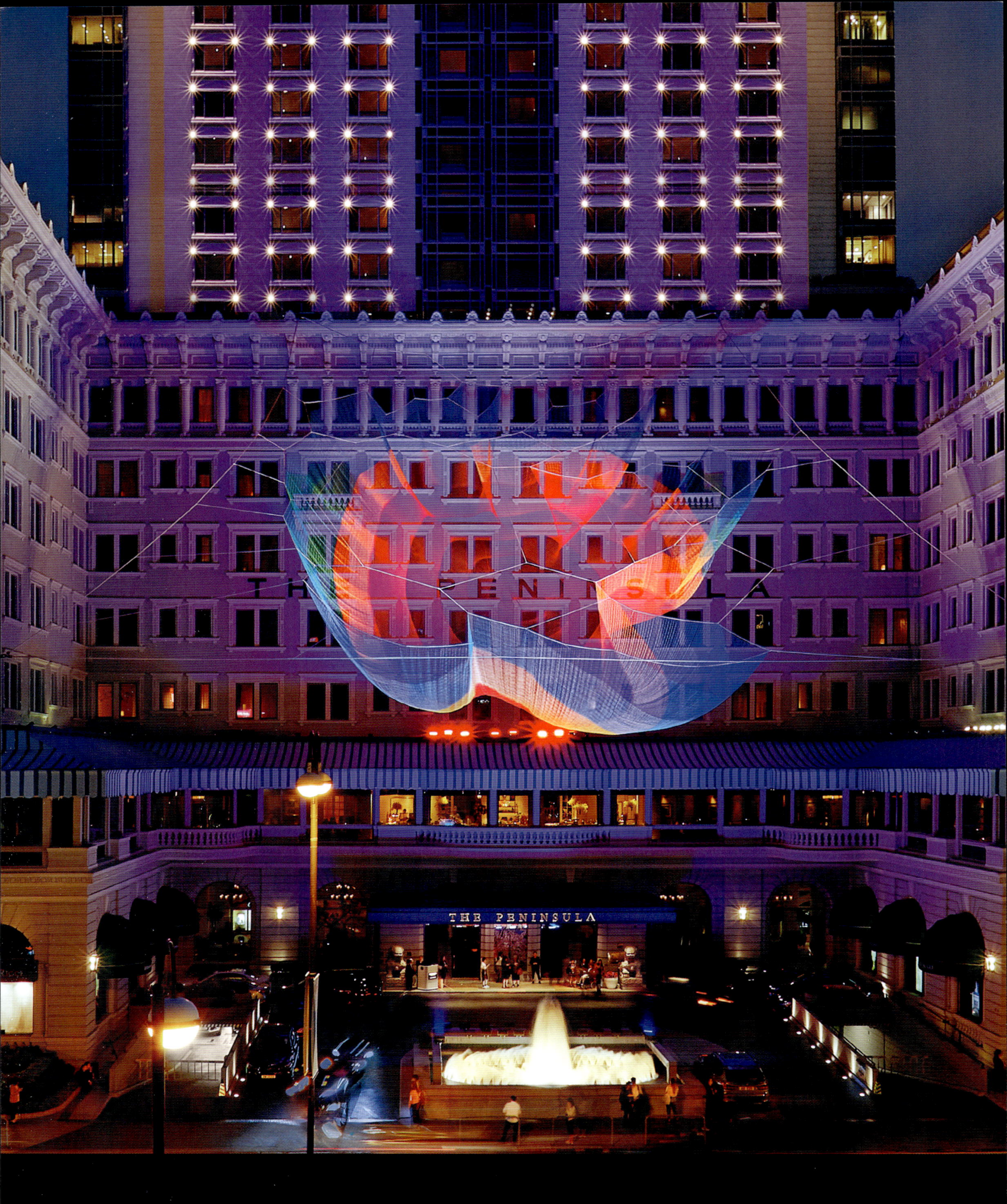
THE PENINSULA
THE PENINSULA

Earthtime 1.26 Hong Kong

—

Isolde Brielmaier

Janet Echelman's work resonates because it is engaging, experiential, and, above all, impactful. Conceptually, the nets and ropes that Echelman uses to create expansive aerial structures are grounded by their cultural ties to fishing and our relationship to the ocean and the environment. All of these elements came to bear on my decision, with co-curator Bettina Prentice, to commission *Earthtime 1.26 Hong Kong* for the city's Peninsula Hotel as part of the Global Art Program that we developed in 2019.

In many ways, *Earthtime 1.26 Hong Kong* was an open invitation. By extending to the public an inviting, pleasurable experience, it transformed the hotel into a welcoming place. Shifting light patterns across the day and night made the work both an offering and an experience. Importantly, Echelman's design process integrates and complements a space. Her works invite the public to dwell, to linger, and highlight elements that we often pass by or through every day without really taking note. In this way, her work is also performative, in that it asks one to look at and reconsider a familiar site in a totally new way. This was the iconic facade of the Peninsula Hotel, which Echelman transformed into a luminous, almost ethereal presence.

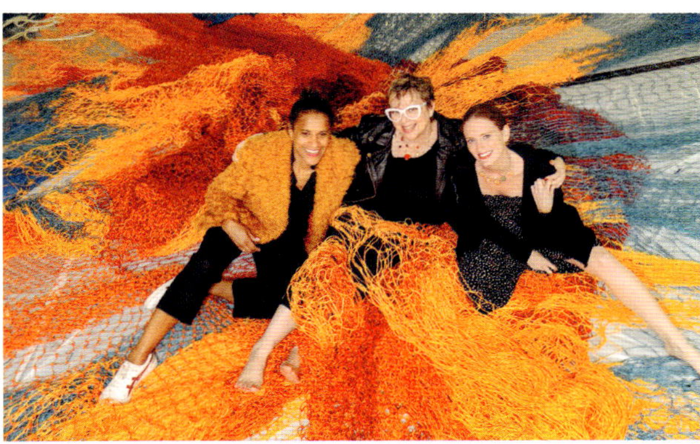

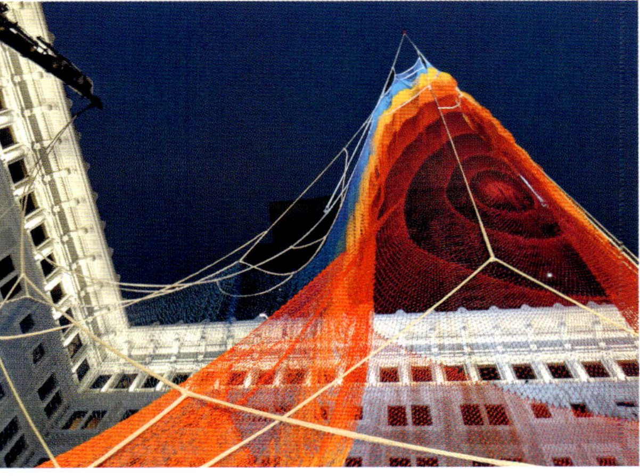

Equally, the city's remarkable nighttime skyline, with its many illuminated signs, created a unique backdrop for the work, which operates less as a static installation and more as a process that responds to its cultural context and environmental conditions. As the sun goes down, its luminosity becomes dramatically more apparent—how its shape, color, line, and overall form tune in to its space, activated by the light bouncing off or reflecting on the ropes and netting. The process of situating the work in a particular place is, for Echelman, as critical as the materials of which it is made.

Earthtime 1.26 Hong Kong was presented during Art Basel Hong Kong, which attracts a specific audience of collectors, patrons, and gallerists, many of whom were presumably already familiar with Echelman's work. At the same time, given the city's density and population, the audience also included people not necessarily expecting to encounter contemporary art when stepping off the ferry, stuck in traffic, waiting for buses, or passing by the hotel. Due to the sheer scale and enormity of *Earthtime 1.26*, viewers had to step back to take in its immensity, which is a key conceptual element to the work. The beauty of art is that it can evoke a multitude of reactions from a huge range of people. Some may recognize the fact that Echelman uses computational modeling soft-ware to render the work's distinct shape. Others who do not know this can certainly still appreciate how the lighting elements are orchestrated according to her own design, and may be equally struck by a sense of wonder and awe.

I think I most love the reaction that involves a double-take, followed by head-scratching—"What the heck is going on here? What is this?"—where normally someone would be going about

previous: *Earthtime 1.8 London*, 2016, Oxford Circus, UK
opposite: *Earthtime 1.26 Hong Kong*, 2019, China
top: Echelman with curators Isolde Brielmaier and Bettina Prentice, 2019
bottom: *Earthtime 1.26 Hong Kong*, 2019, China

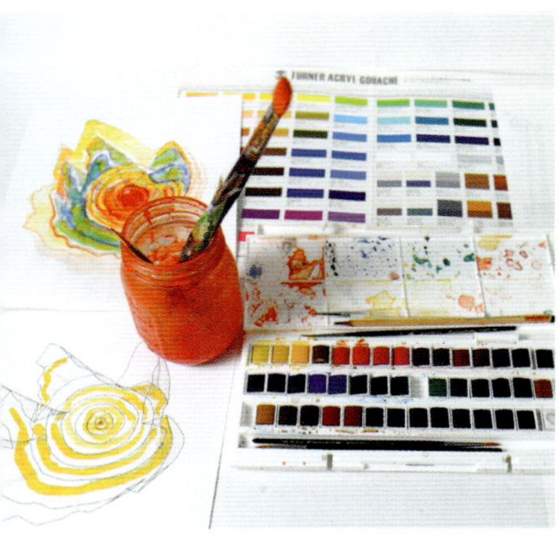

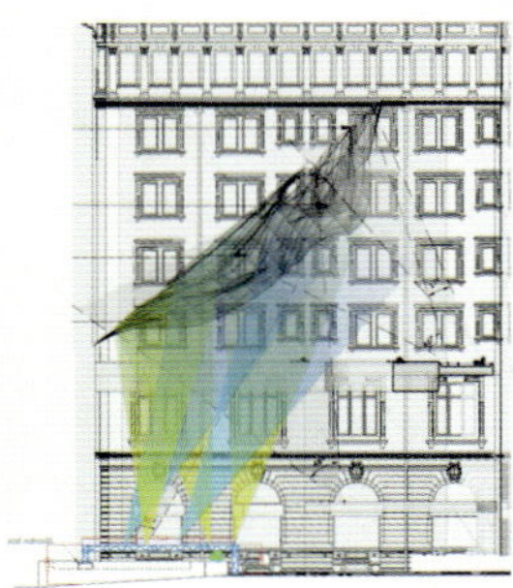

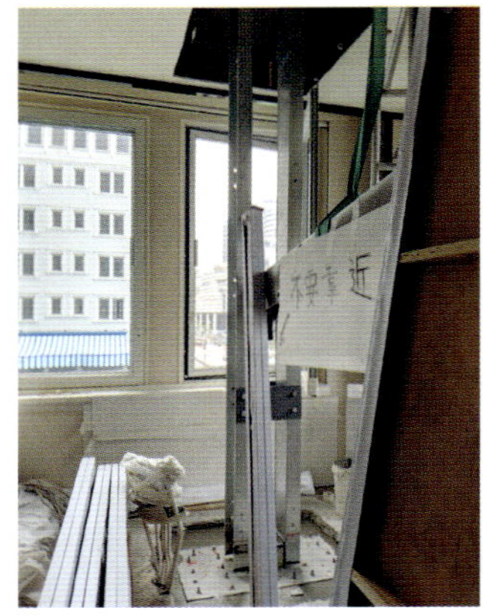

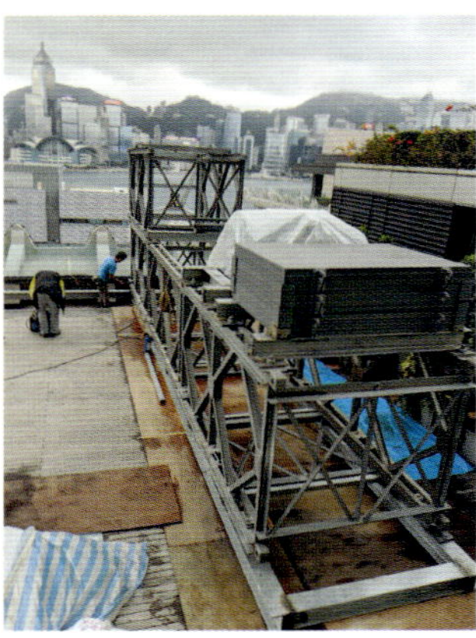

their day, meeting somebody for lunch, walking to the office, and becomes an accidental audience taken by surprise. In the best of ways, Echelman's work is disruptive.

This point extends to the field of public art more broadly, specifically large-scale public art, which, by and large, is dominated by cisgender white men. That Echelman is creating public works on this architectural scale is tremendous. My mission as a curator is to lift up and center works by women and Black and brown artists, BIPOC and LGBT artists, artists who have historically been excluded from particular conversations. When one ventures into conversations about public space, one immediately finds that public space is highly contested, not only in terms of the physical space, but also in terms of the terms we use. How we conceive of "the street" depends on where we are standing. And what do we mean by "public"? Who does that encompass? Echelman's work, not just in the particular context of Hong Kong but at large, obliterates some of those boundaries. The work makes a statement—here is the art and it is for all of you—with the understanding that every single person is going to have a different experience with it. *Earthtime 1.26 Hong Kong* literally encompassed and draped the front of one of the most iconic buildings in one of the most iconic cities in the world. This mode of working is quite different from erecting a large, freestanding sculpture in front of a particular institution. Echelman's work offers up multiple points of entry for different audiences, which by definition creates a unique kind of experience.

Importantly, Echelman's work requires you to take it in not only through your eyes, but by moving your body. When you pull back and look at all of the elements that comprise *Earthtime 1.26*, your brain asks, "What am I looking at? What is it doing? Why am I seeing all these colors?" which makes you step in a little closer to investigate, "How is it attached? Is it really floating?" which physically draws you in deeper to unpack what is happening. So while the work is visually rich, there is also a dynamic sensory element that generates a phenomenological encounter. This quality is made even more resonant by the work's own ephemerality. When it eventually comes down, the remnants become an indelible memory, a reminder of nature's own evanescence. In many ways, Echelman's projects take on the patterns of nature, going dormant at times and then reemerging, with new patterns and colors, offering a humbling beauty that pushes us to embrace change.

Isolde Brielmaier is deputy director of the New Museum, New York.

above, left to right: Watercolor studies for *Earthtime 1.26 Hong Kong*, 2019, China; lighting study for *Earthtime 1.26 Hong Kong*, 2019, China; floor-to-ceiling anchors in two corner wedding suites at the bottom of *Earthtime 1.26 Hong Kong*, 2019, China; pool deck roof truss anchoring top of *Earthtime 1.26 Hong Kong*, 2019, China

opposite: *Earthtime 1.26 Hong Kong*, 2019, China

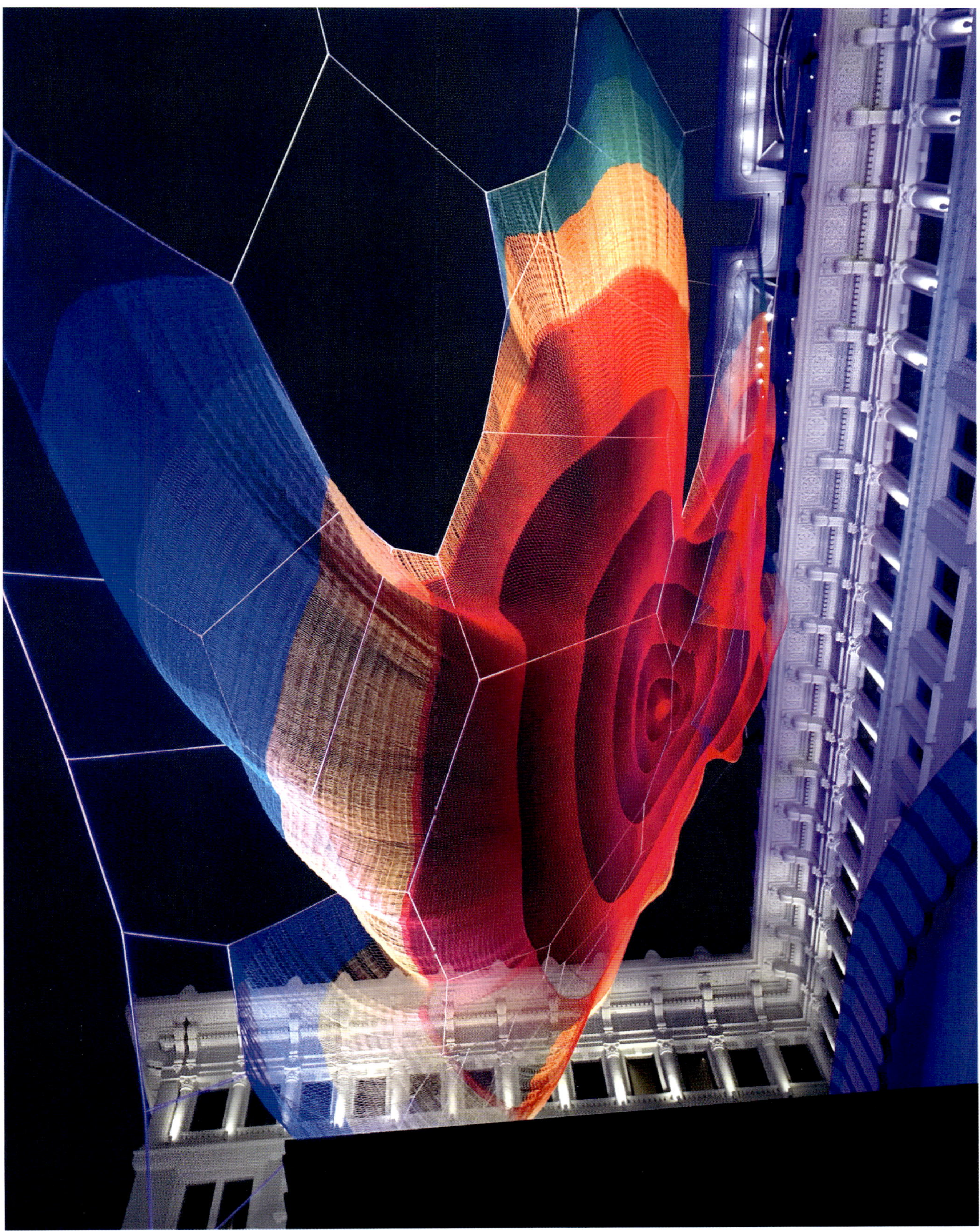

EARTHTIME 1.26 HONG KONG, CHINA

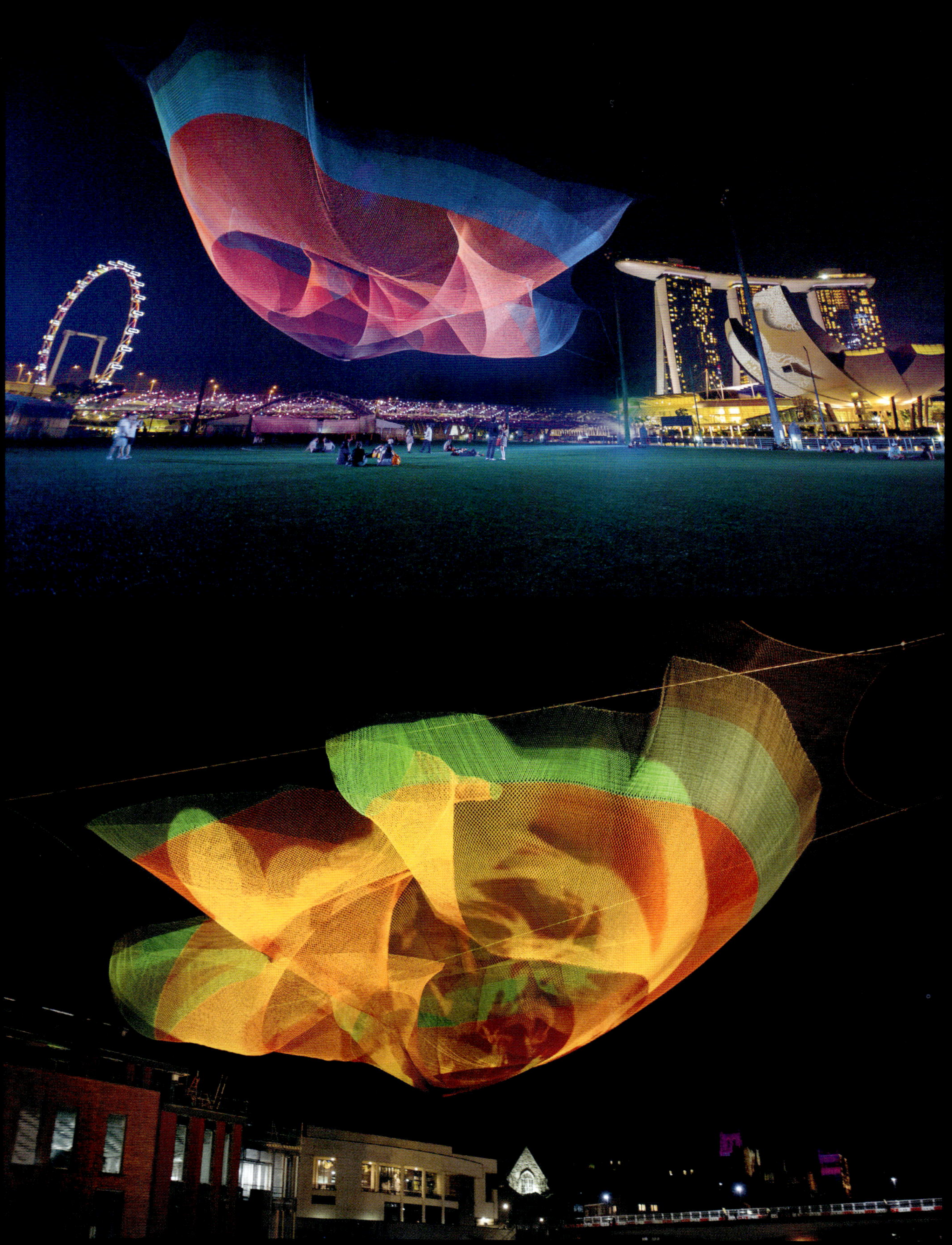

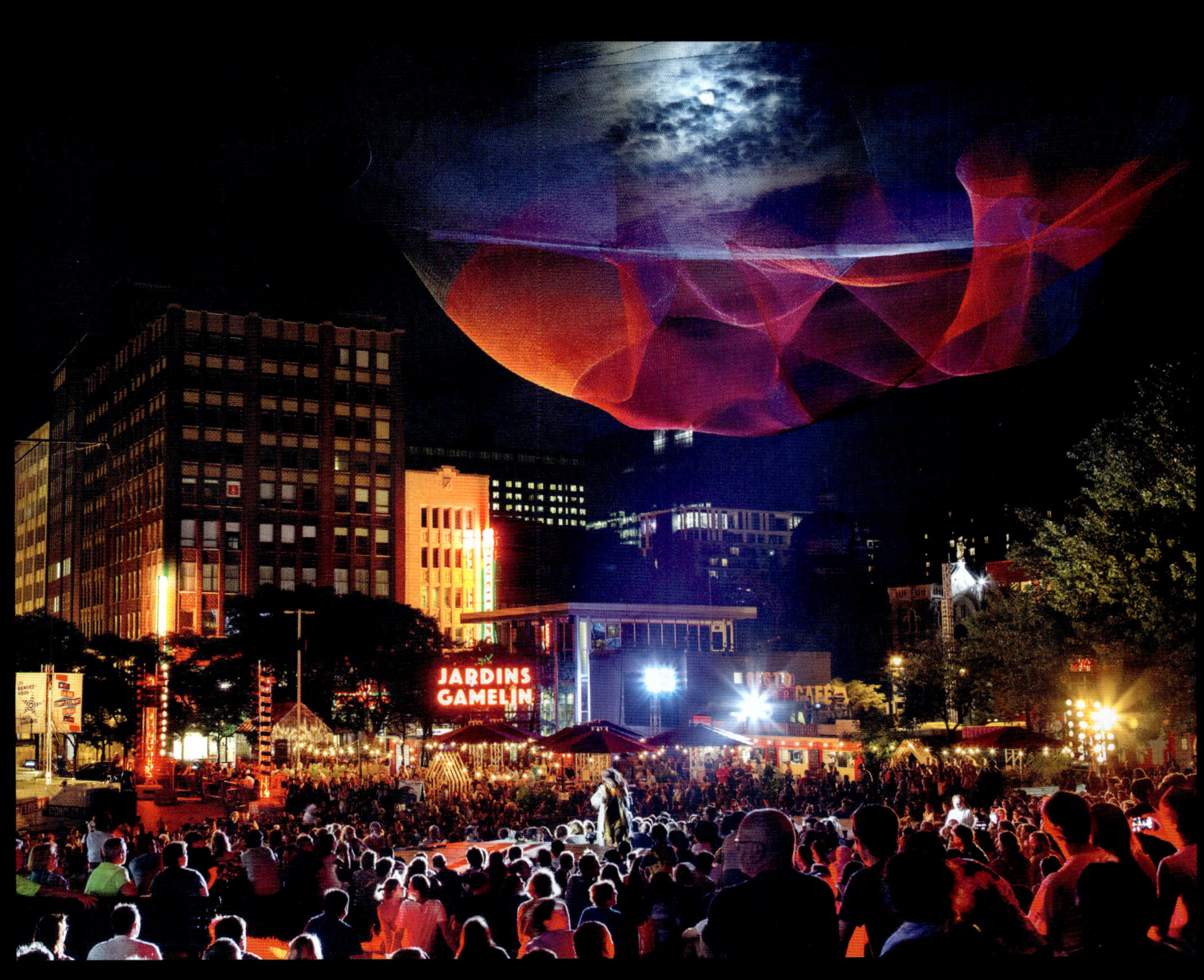

opposite, top: *Earthtime 1.26 Singapore*, 2014
opposite, bottom: *Earthtime 1.26 Durham*, 2015, England
above: *Earthtime 1.26 Montreal*, 2015–17, Canada

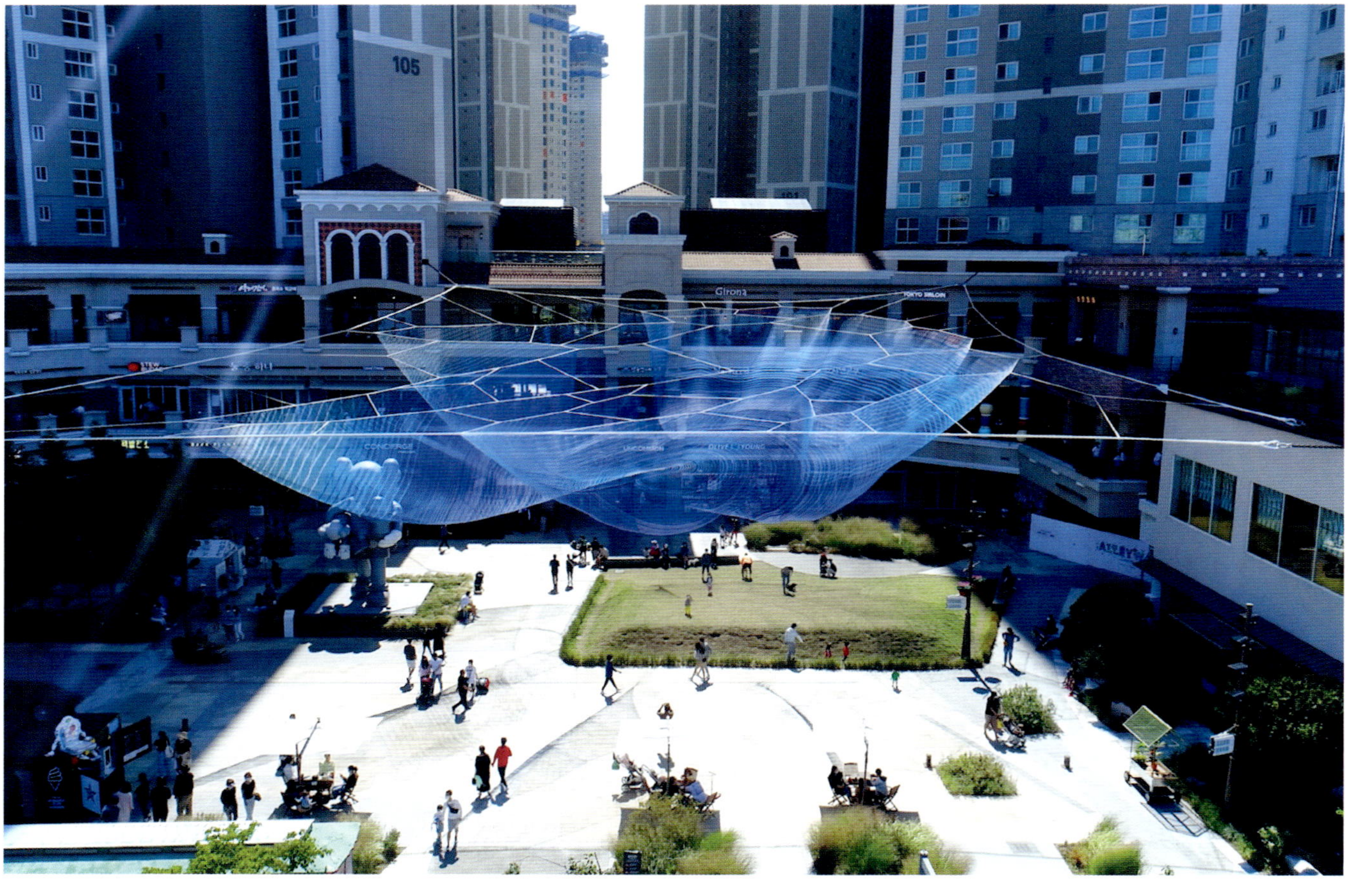

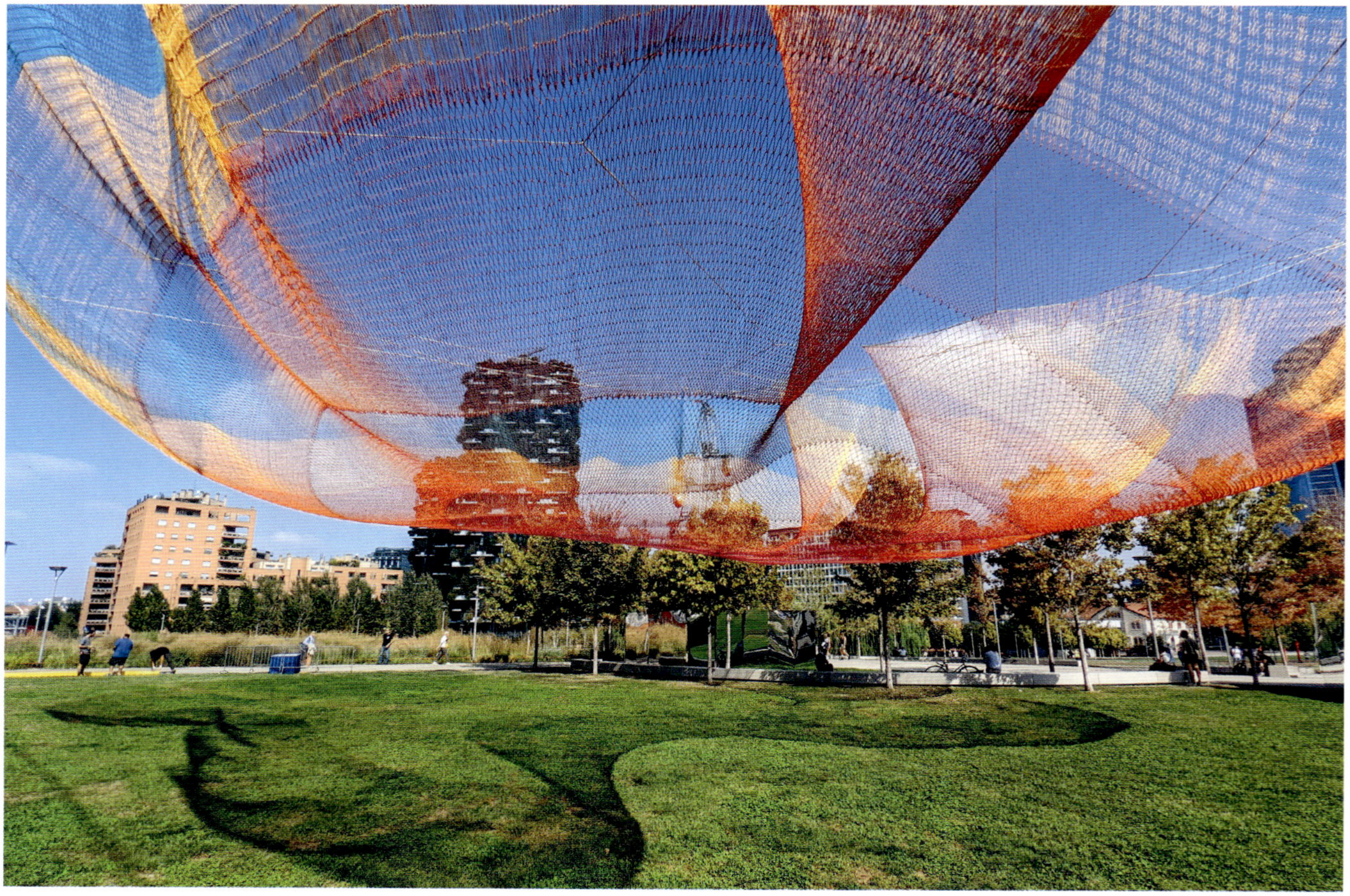

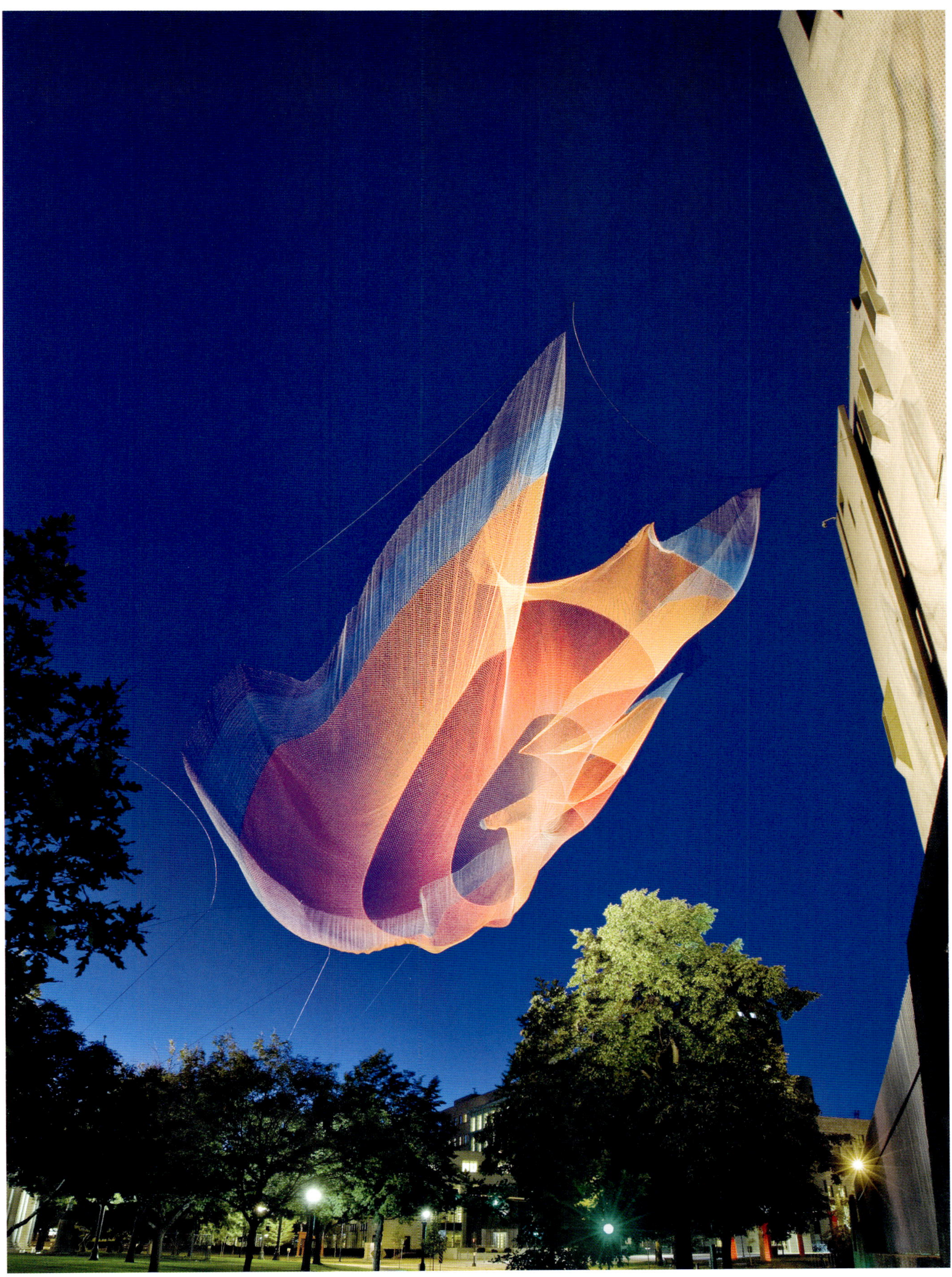

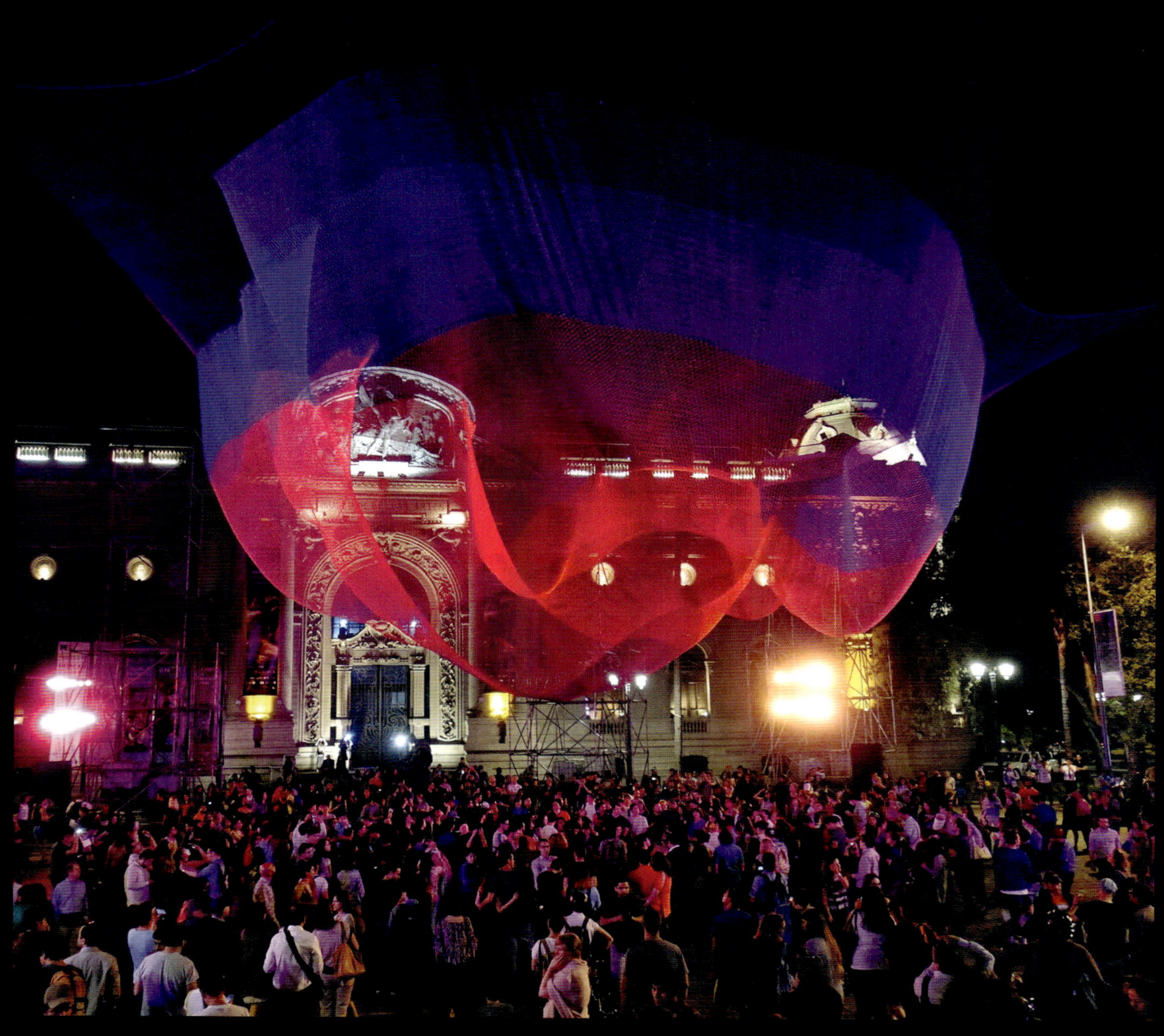

previous spread
p. 100, top: *Earthtime 1.26 Korea*, 2020, Gwanggyo, South Korea
p. 100, bottom: *Earthtime 1.26 Milan*, 2022, Italy
p. 101: *Earthtime 1.26 Denver*, 2010, Colorado

above: *Earthtime 1.26 Santiago*, 2016, Chile
opposite, top: *Earthtime 1.26 Prague*, 2015, Czech Republic
opposite, bottom: *Earthtime 1.26 Shanghai*, 2017, China

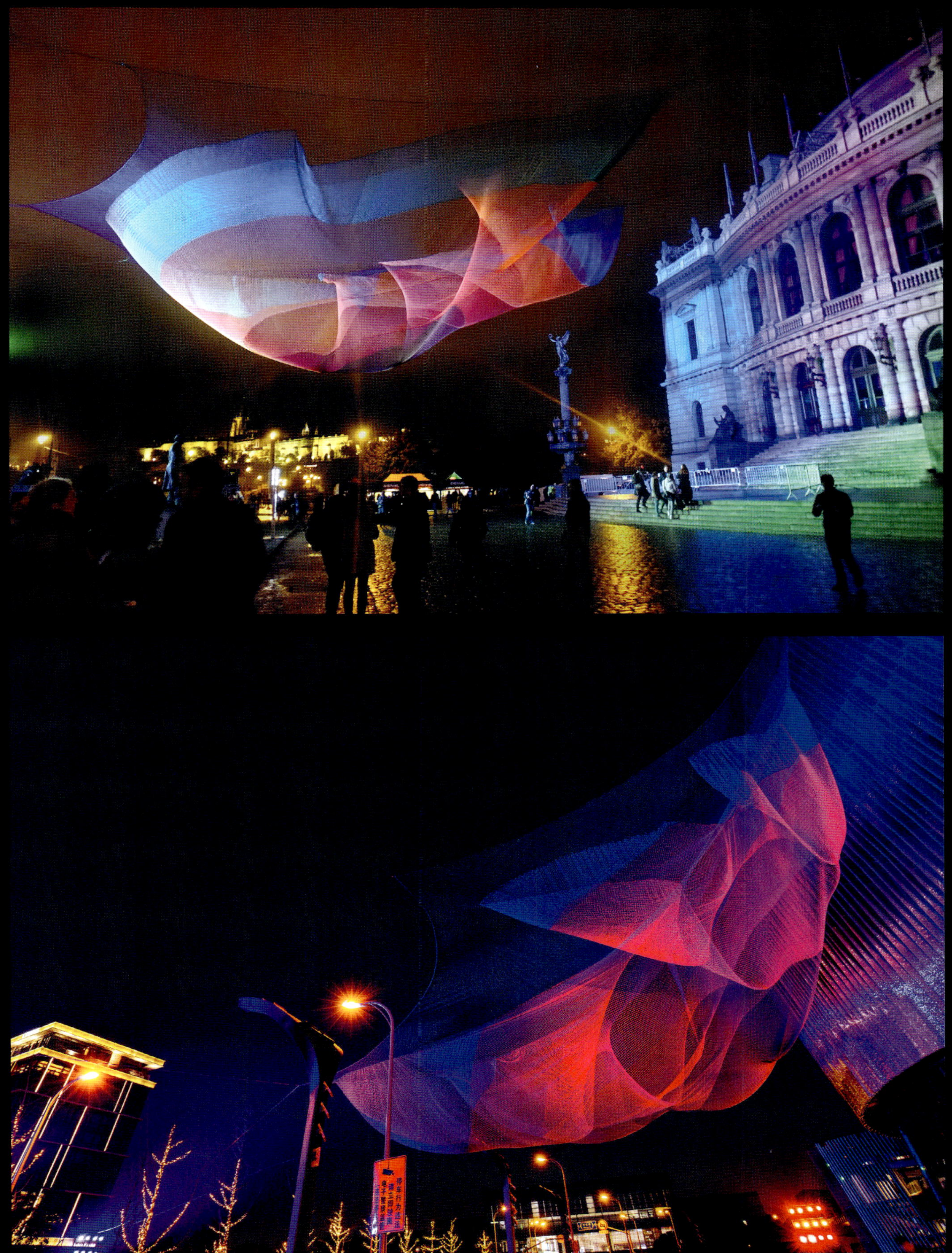

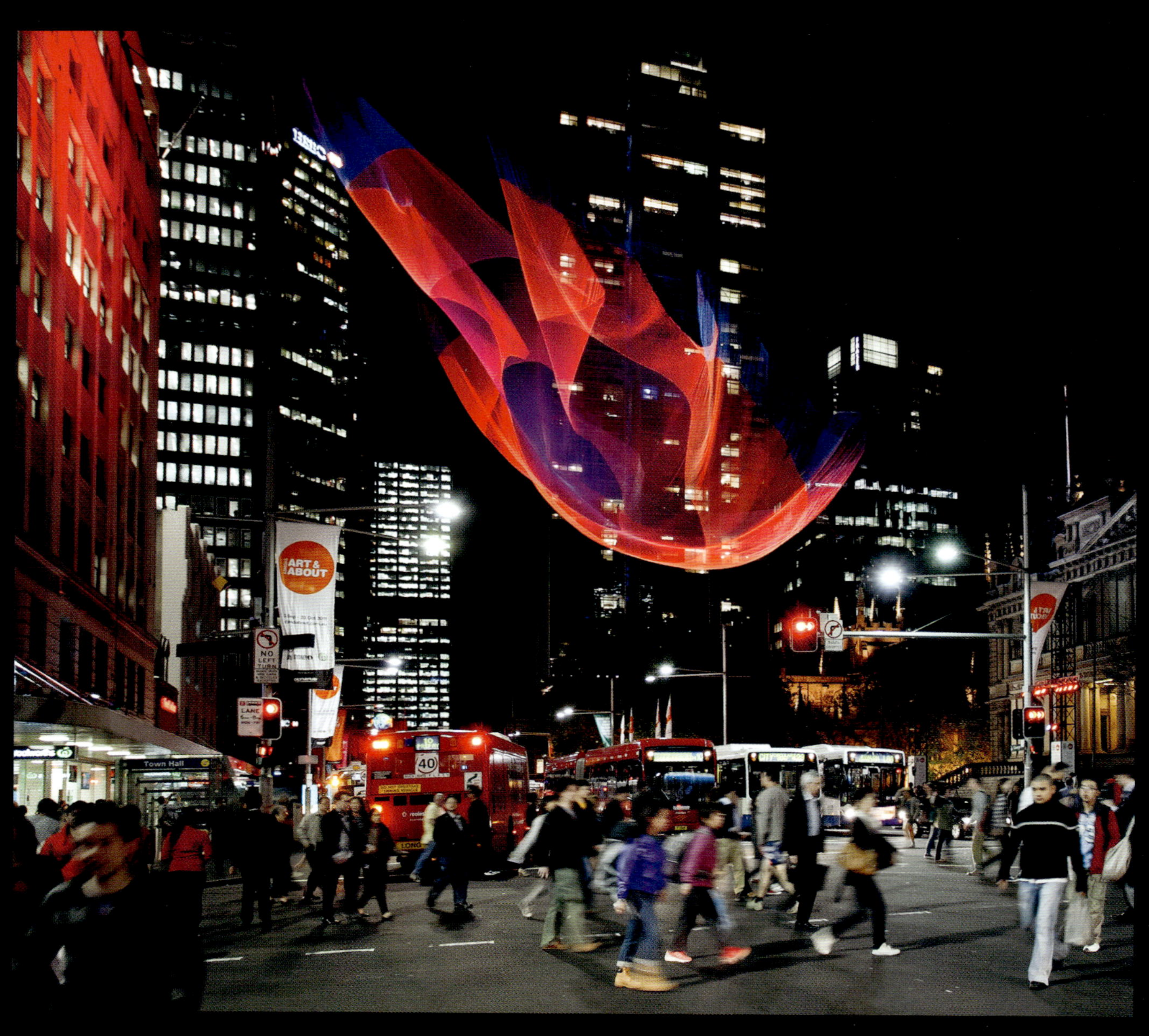

above: *Earthtime 1.26 Sydney*, 2011, Australia
opposite: *Earthtime 1.26 Amsterdam*, 2012, Netherlands

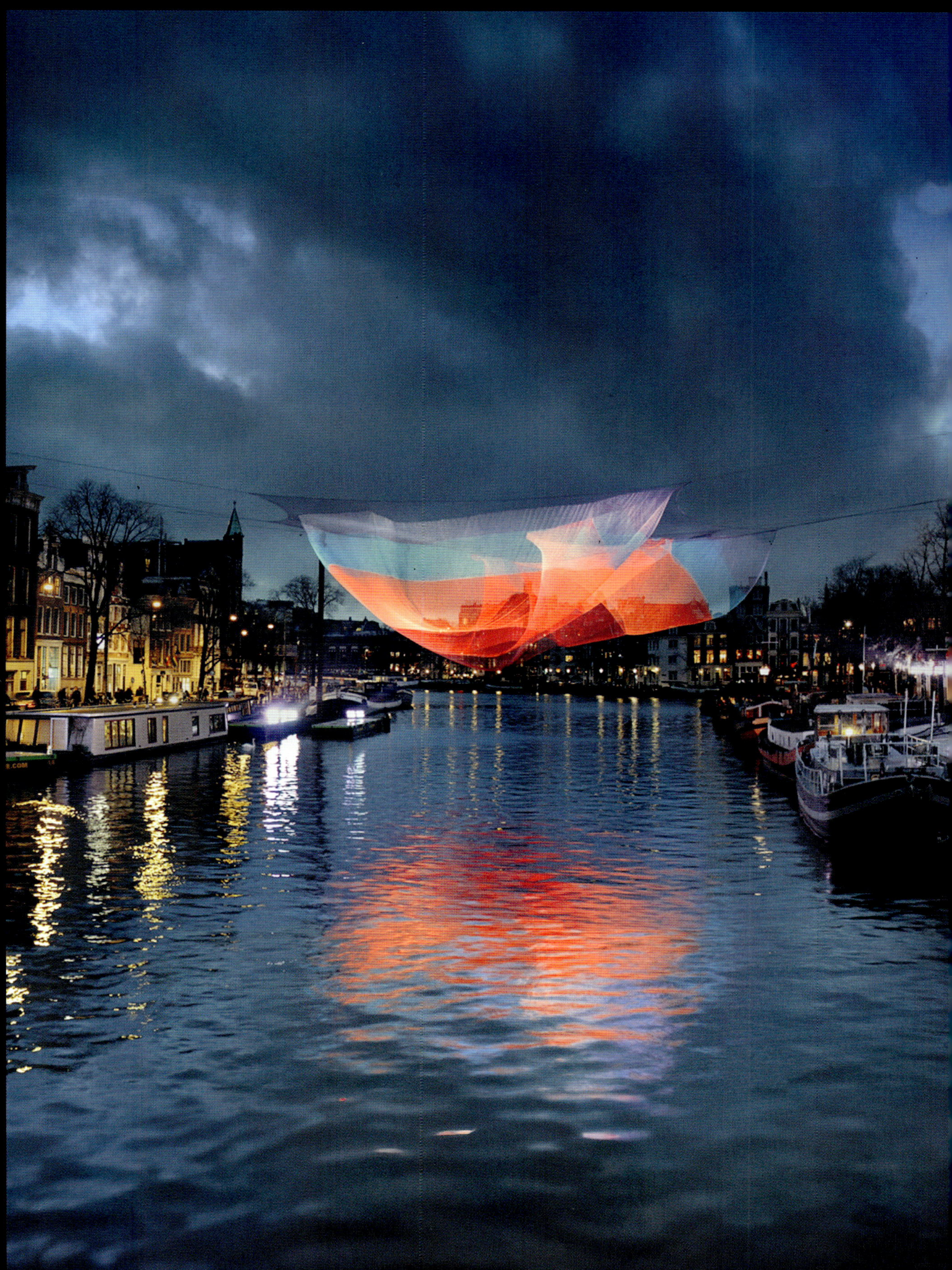

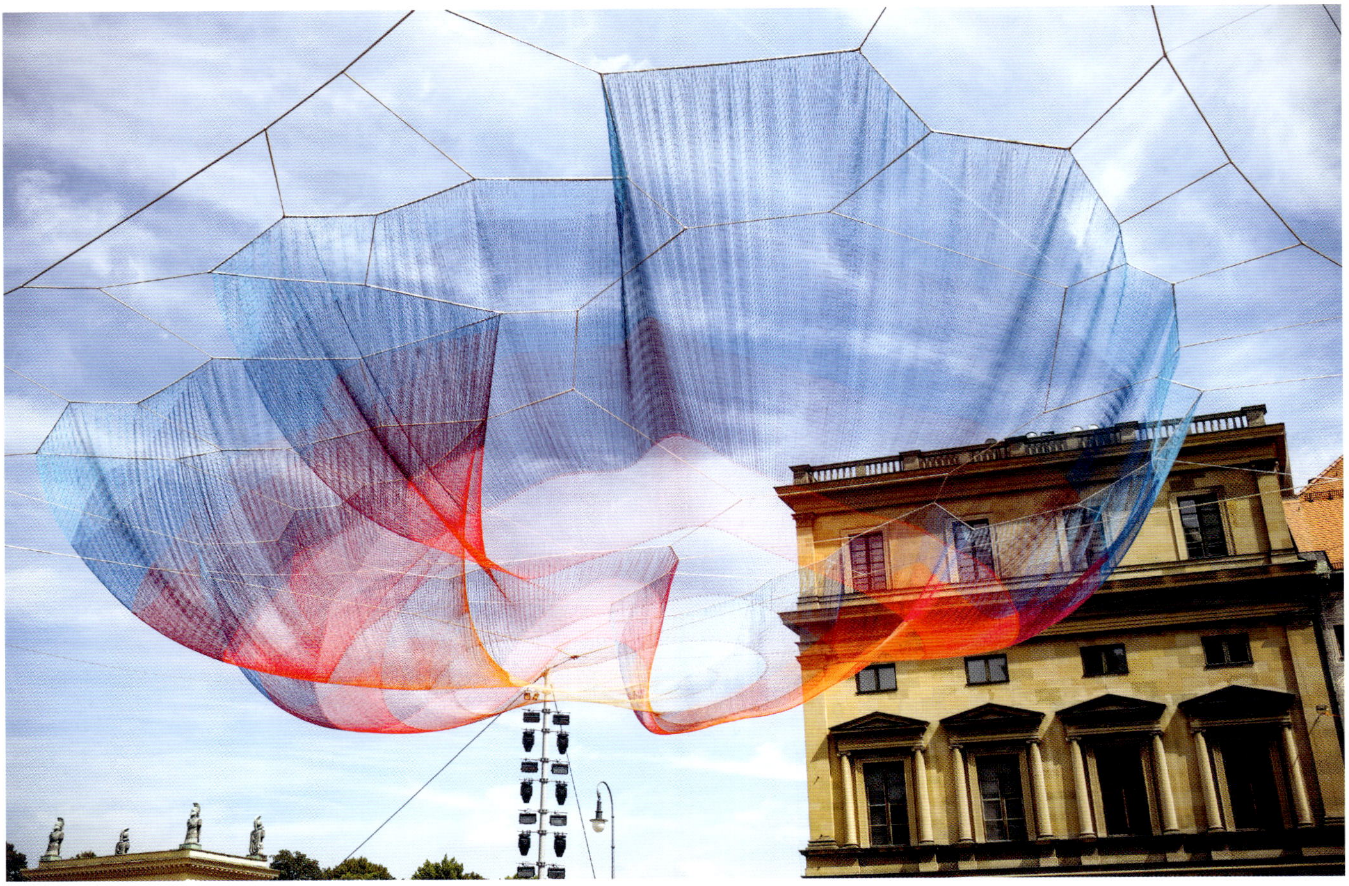

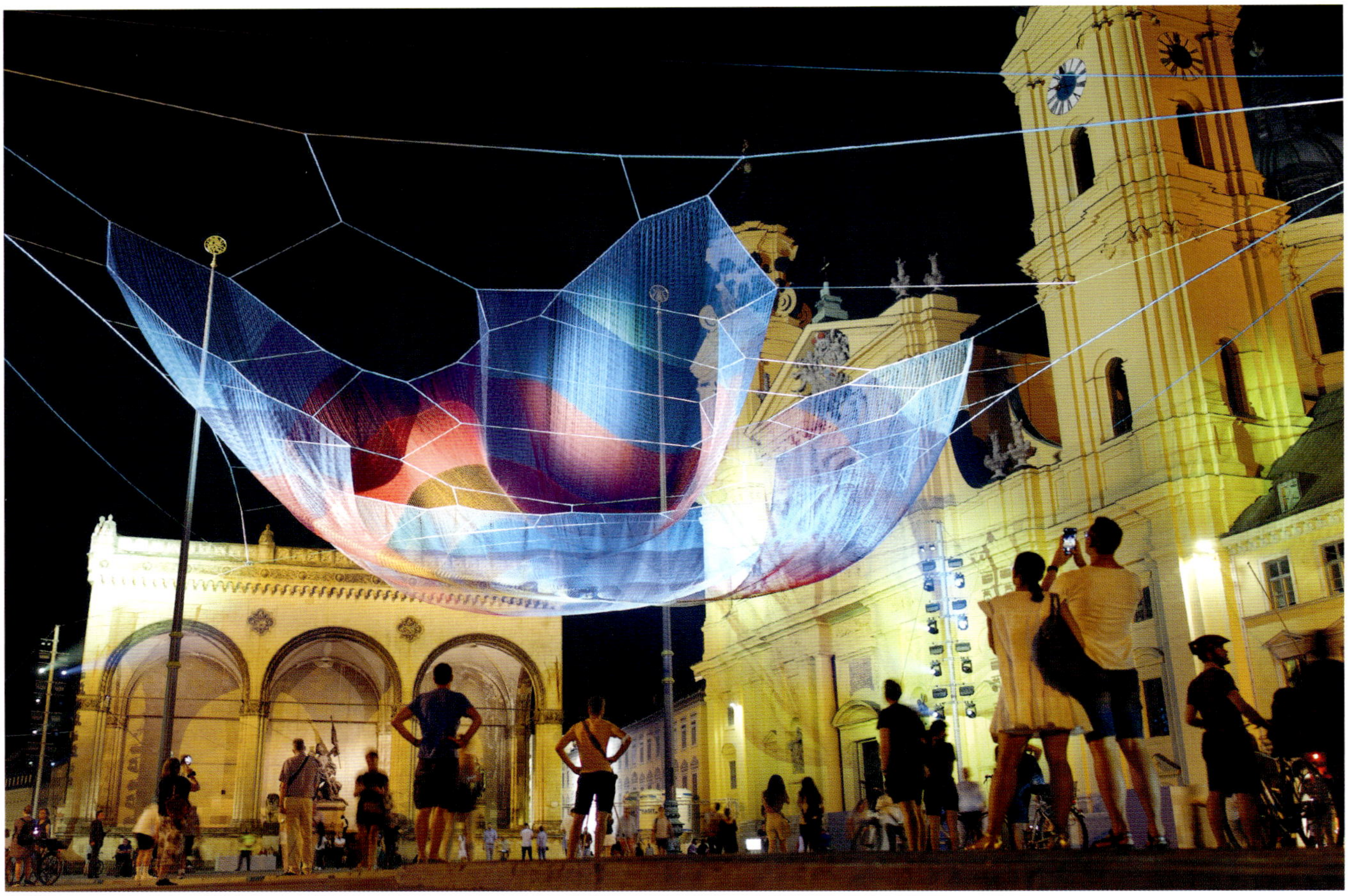

Earthtime 1.26 Munich

—

Amy Damutz

While Janet Echelman's designs make extraordinary use of fiber's material strength, they also produce specific conceptual links that tether the present to the past. In fall 2021, Echelman's *Earthtime 1.26 Munich* brought the *Earthtime* series to the cultural and civic center of Bavaria. While the work continued the artist's investigation into visualizing usually invisible relations between human, environmental, and planetary cycles, *Earthtime 1.26 Munich* took on the particular valence of the city's layered historical context.

It was mounted above the Odeonsplatz, a bustling public plaza that since the eighteenth century has been the site of public gatherings and parades (the annual opening of Munich's renowned Oktoberfest still follows a route through the Odeonsplatz) and remains an active site for civic events and demonstrations. For Echelman, whose Jewish European ancestors were among those persecuted by the Third Reich during World War II, the work hovered, meaningfully, directly above the site of the 1923 Beer Hall Putsch, the failed coup d'état that first brought Nationalsozialistische Deutsche Arbeiterpartei leader Adolf Hitler to international attention.

Almost a century after that fateful event, in the fall of 2021, Echelman's seven-hundred-pound net exuded a cloudlike lightness and comforting presence as it hovered four stories above the cobblestones that bore witness to so many pivotal political events. The 3,395-square-foot web incorporating more than 360,000 knots turned the public space from a pedestrian plaza into a living cultural experience.

During the day, the work's saturated colors—saffron, red, purple, blue—seemed translucent. Concentric circles of alternating weaves, colors, and densities emanated from its center, expanding outward to the work's irregular edges, as if reaching out to the yellow facade of the seventeenth-century Church and the Odeon concert hall that gives the square its name, which was rebuilt in 1944 after being gutted by Allied air raids.

At night, heightened drama was created through projected LED lighting. An innovative "color laundering" technique pioneered by designer Rogier van der Heide simultaneously amplified and masked hues of colored filaments embedded within each strand of threading.

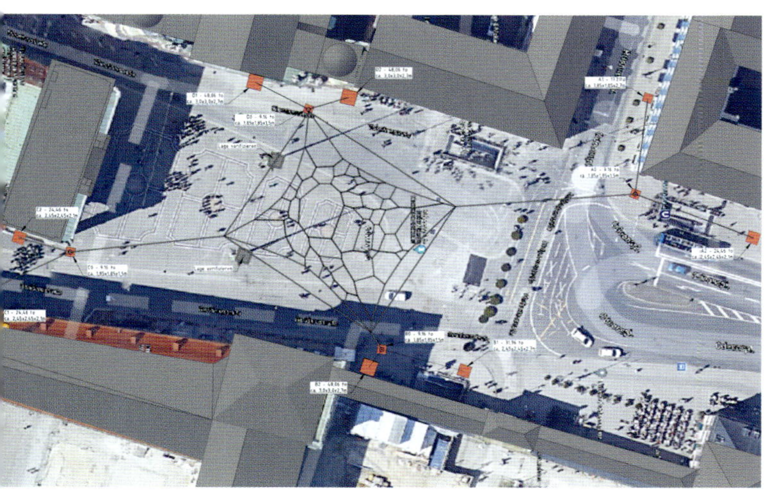

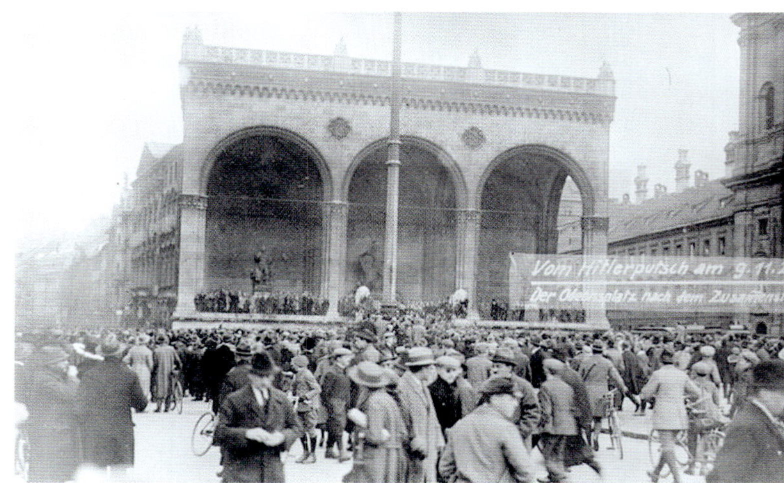

opposite: *Earthtime 1.26 Munich*, 2021, Odeonsplatz
left: Aerial plan view of *Earthtime 1.26 Munich*, 2021
right: Beer Hall Putsch, Odeonsplatz, Munich, Germany, 1923

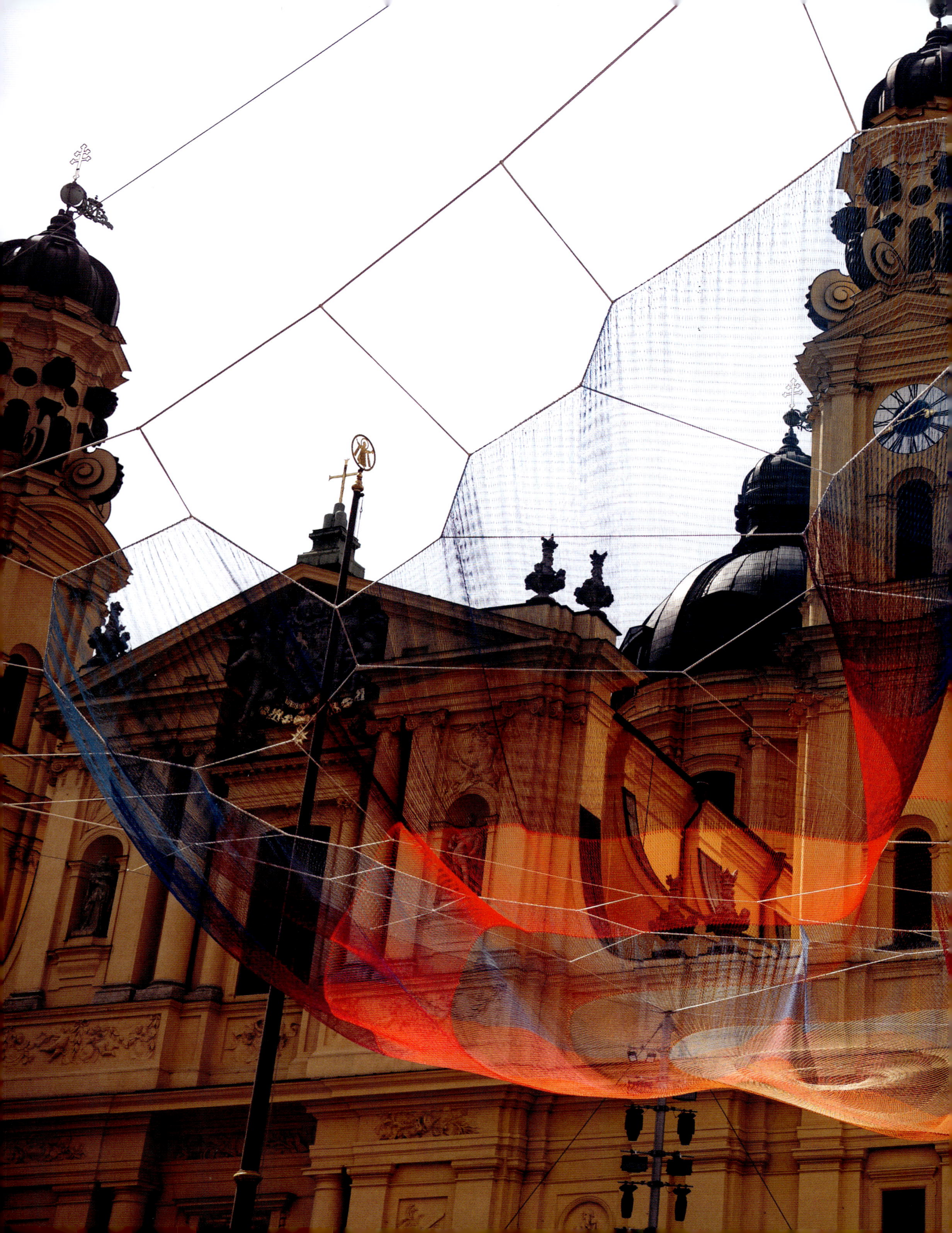

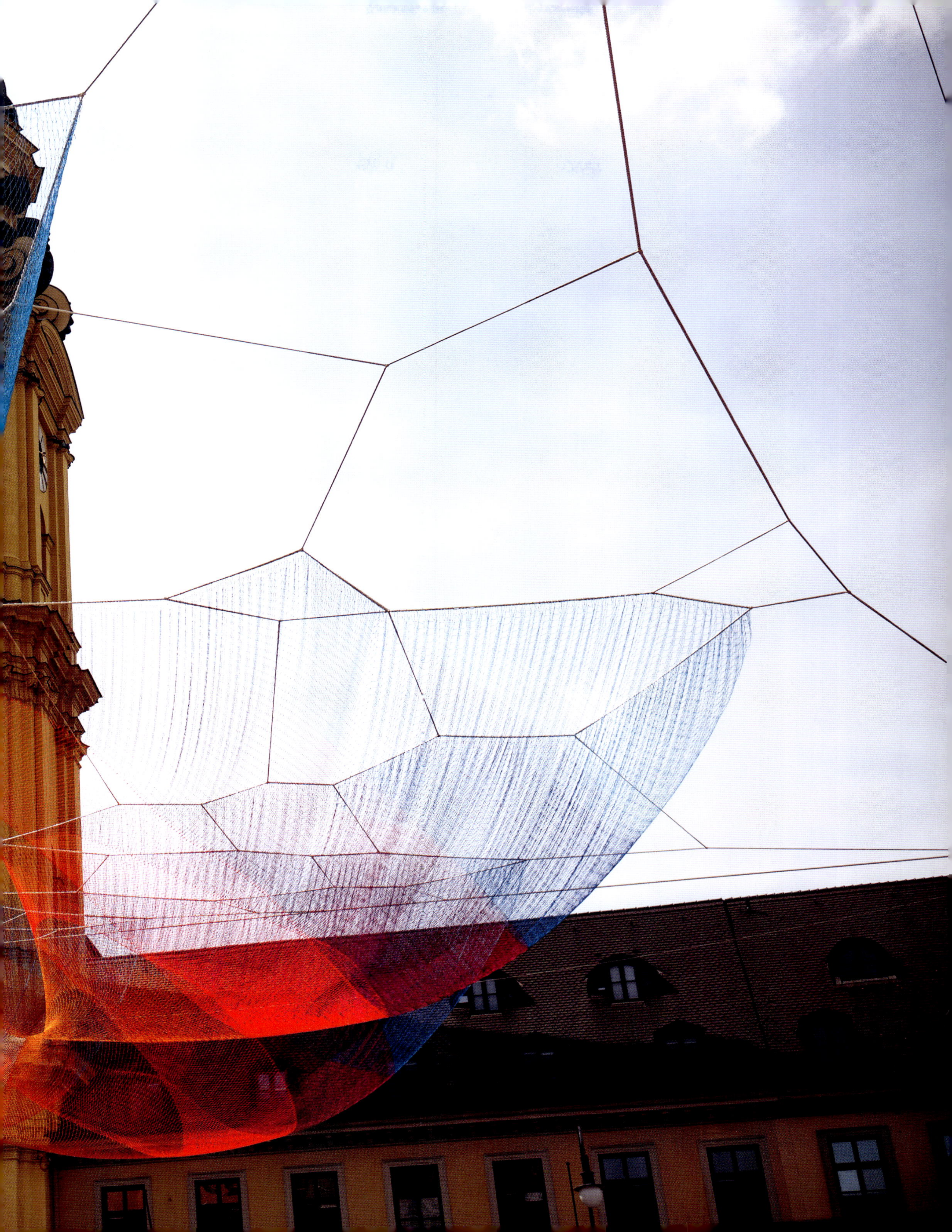

Vivid cyan, orange, red, and purple blazed in the night sky as textiles translucent in daylight became brilliant and luminescent. In the darkness below, observers looked up to see cobalt, tangerine, and violet waves unfurling across space and what Echelman calls "shadow drawings" projected onto the facades of the historic architecture.

Over its two-month exhibition, tens of thousands of pedestrians stopped in their tracks, pausing to take in the unexpected disruption of the everyday. For one week, multiple staircases were built leading up to a temporary promenade and observation deck directly under the netting as part of the Artificial Soul Festival. The design allowed observers a highly unusual intimacy with the installation. Seeing it in person, Echelman remarked, "The ground is coming up to the sculpture...allowing [observers] to step into the work and walk inside it."[1] Between August 11 and October 3, 2021, live music concerts ranged from grand piano performances from Lisa Morgenstern to more beat-focused artists including Rival Console and the Poland-based musician Hania Rani, who all performed electronic-infused compositions timed with the softly billowing structure above, its illumination responding to sound cues and dynamic surroundings—adding an additional mode for the audience to sonically enter the square.

Earthtime 1.26 Munich demonstrates how Echelman's work manages to be architecturally responsive while also speaking to the need to reexamine shifting cultural contexts. Noting the historical, political, and social significance of the maker and the site, festival curator Stefan Weil leaned over to the artist on the last night of the series during Rani's performance and whispered, "You are assisting in changing this place. We are making a new history here."

Amy Damutz is an independent scholar of public art.

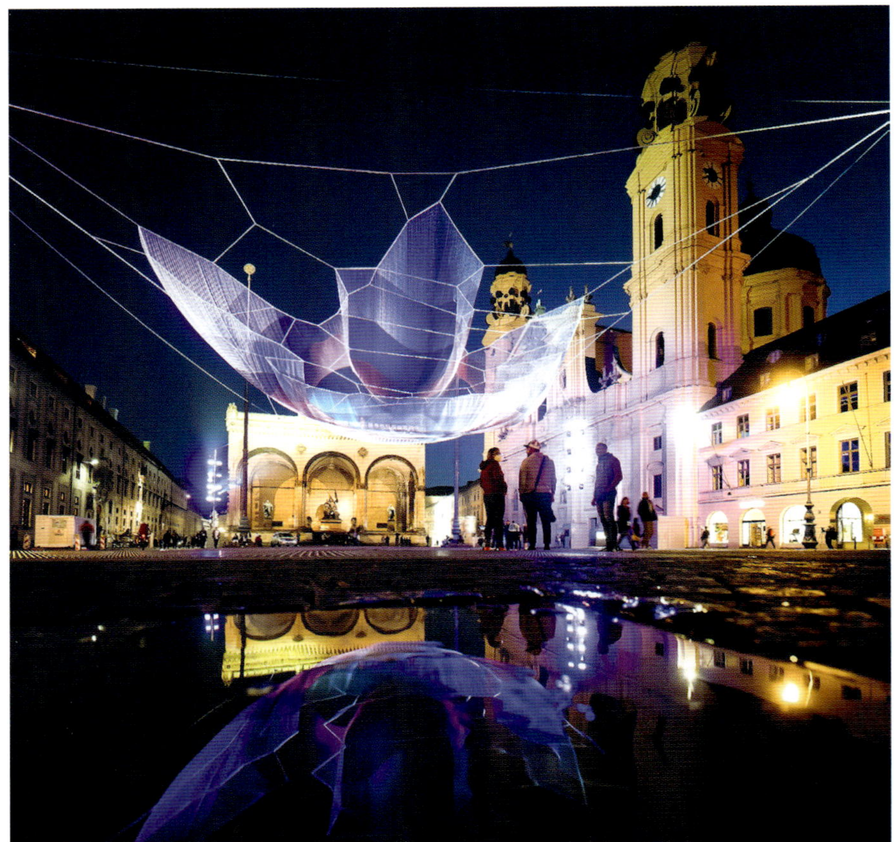

previous, right, and opposite:
Earthtime 1.26 Munich, 2021

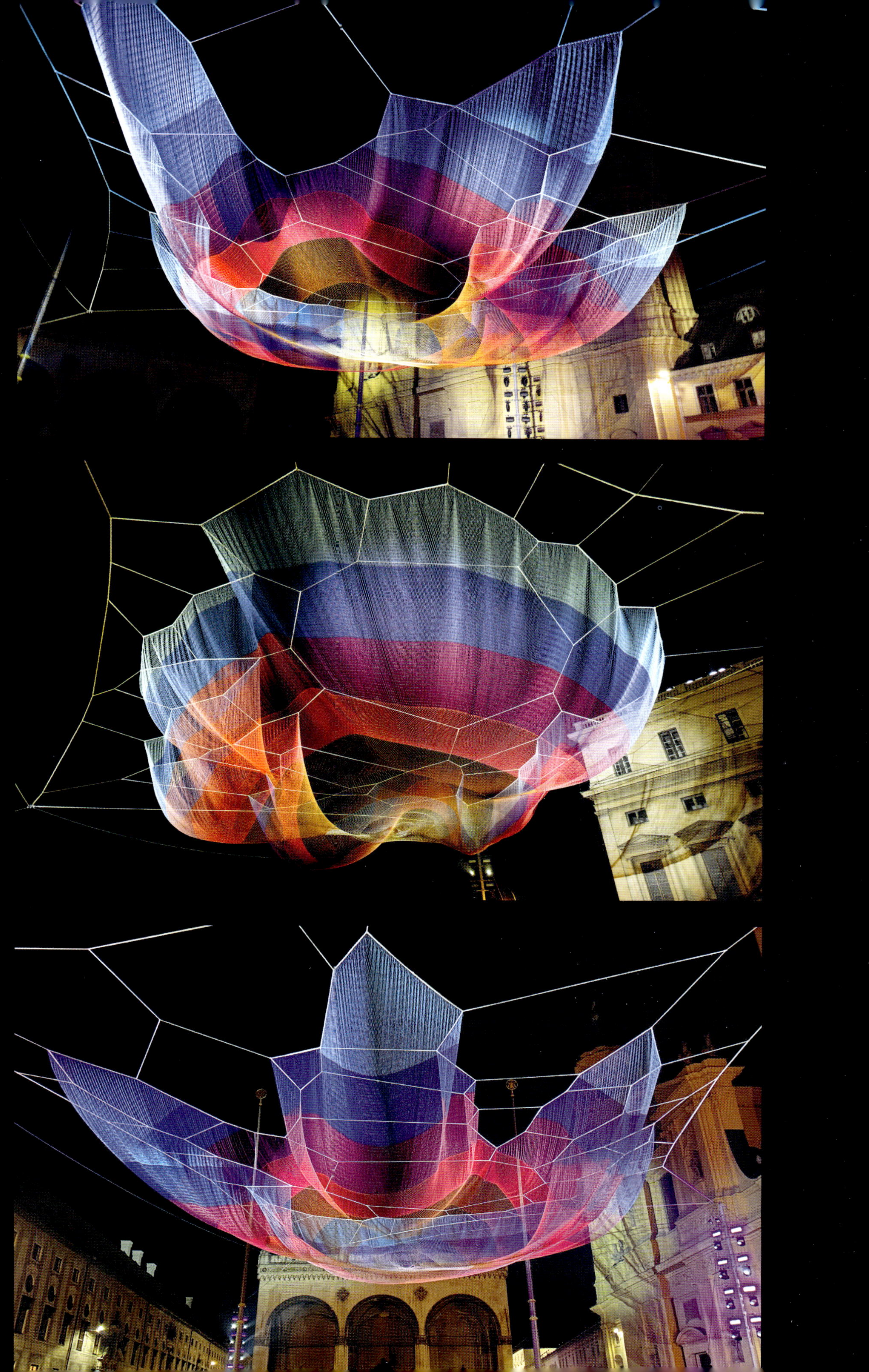

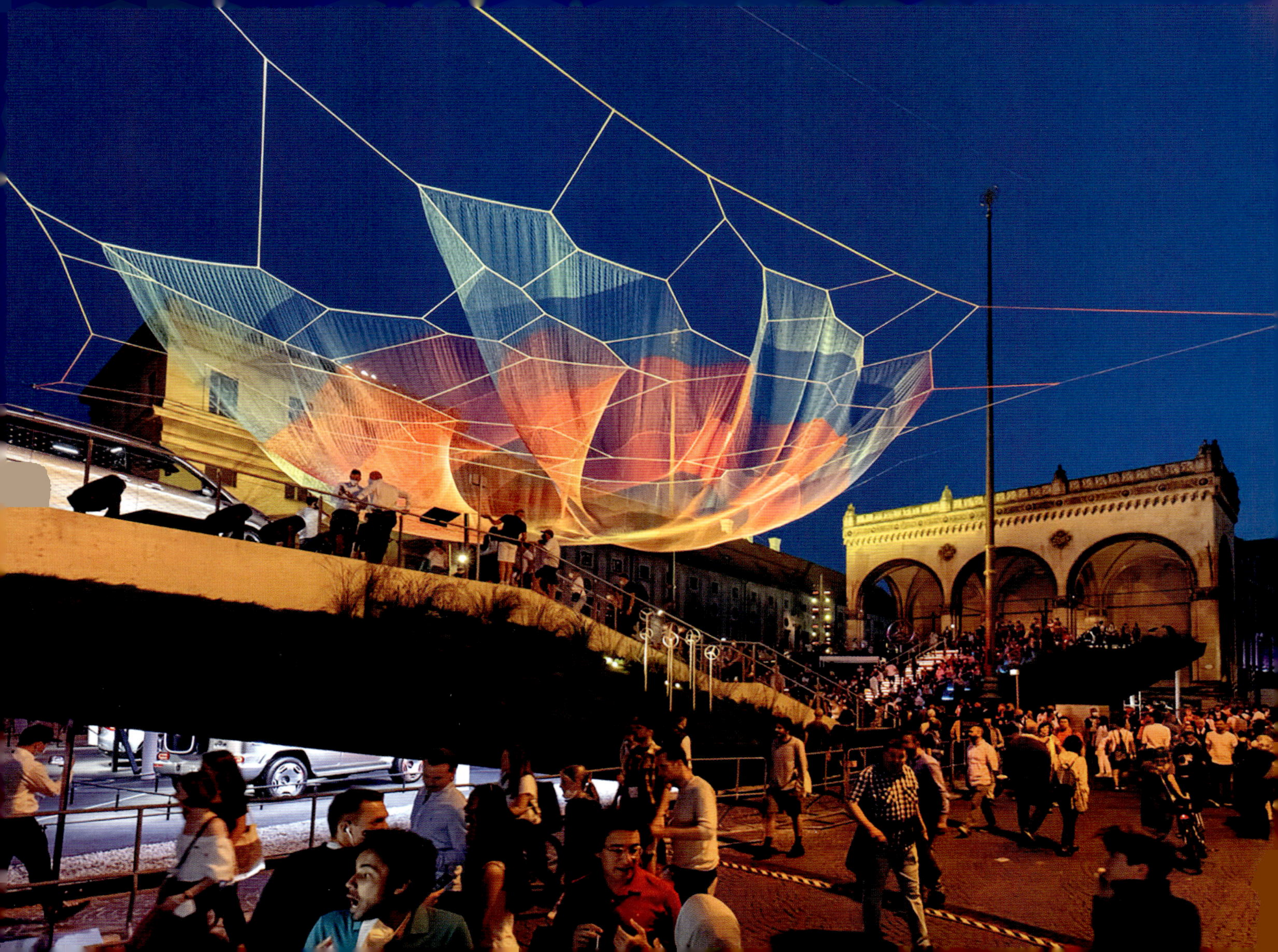

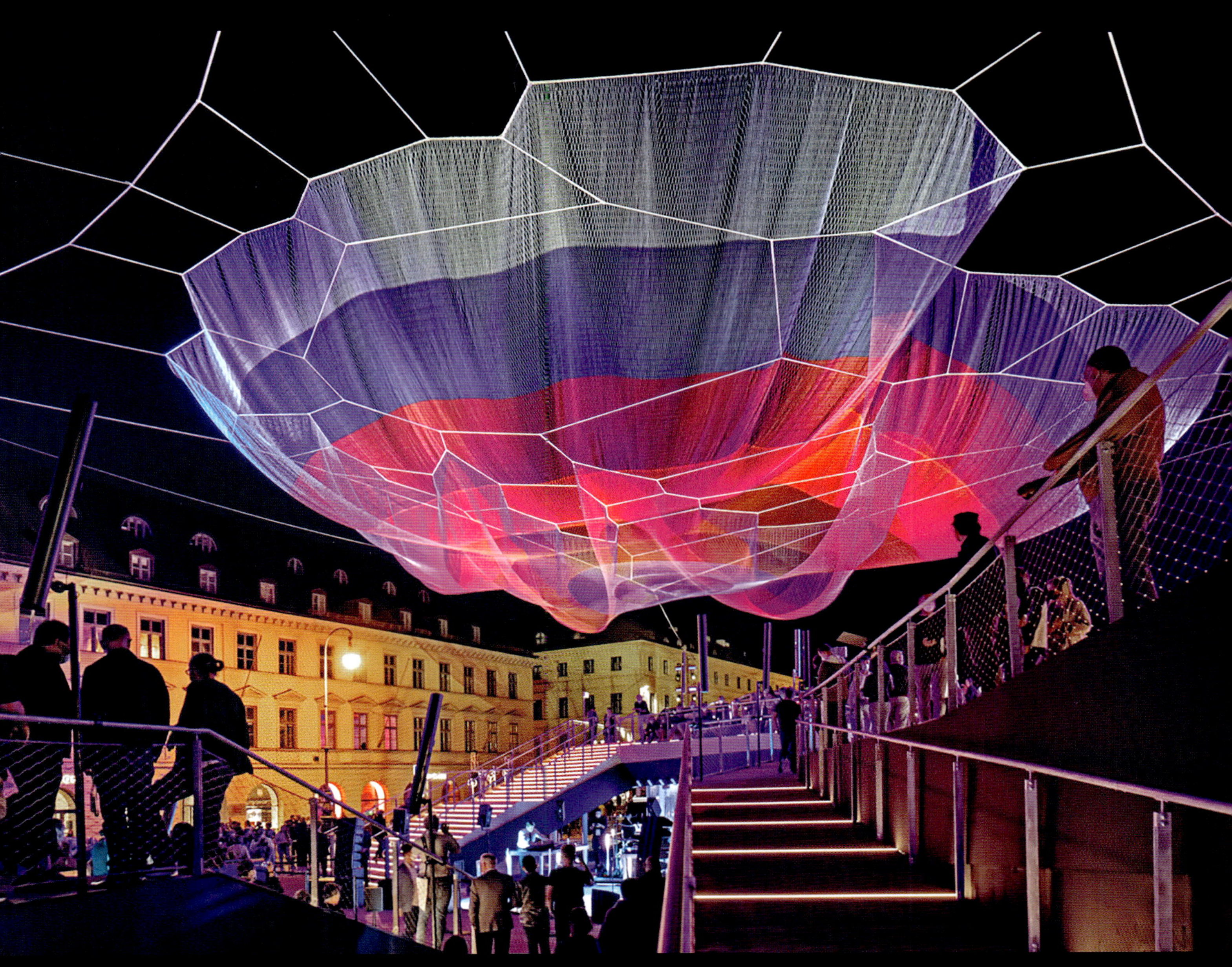

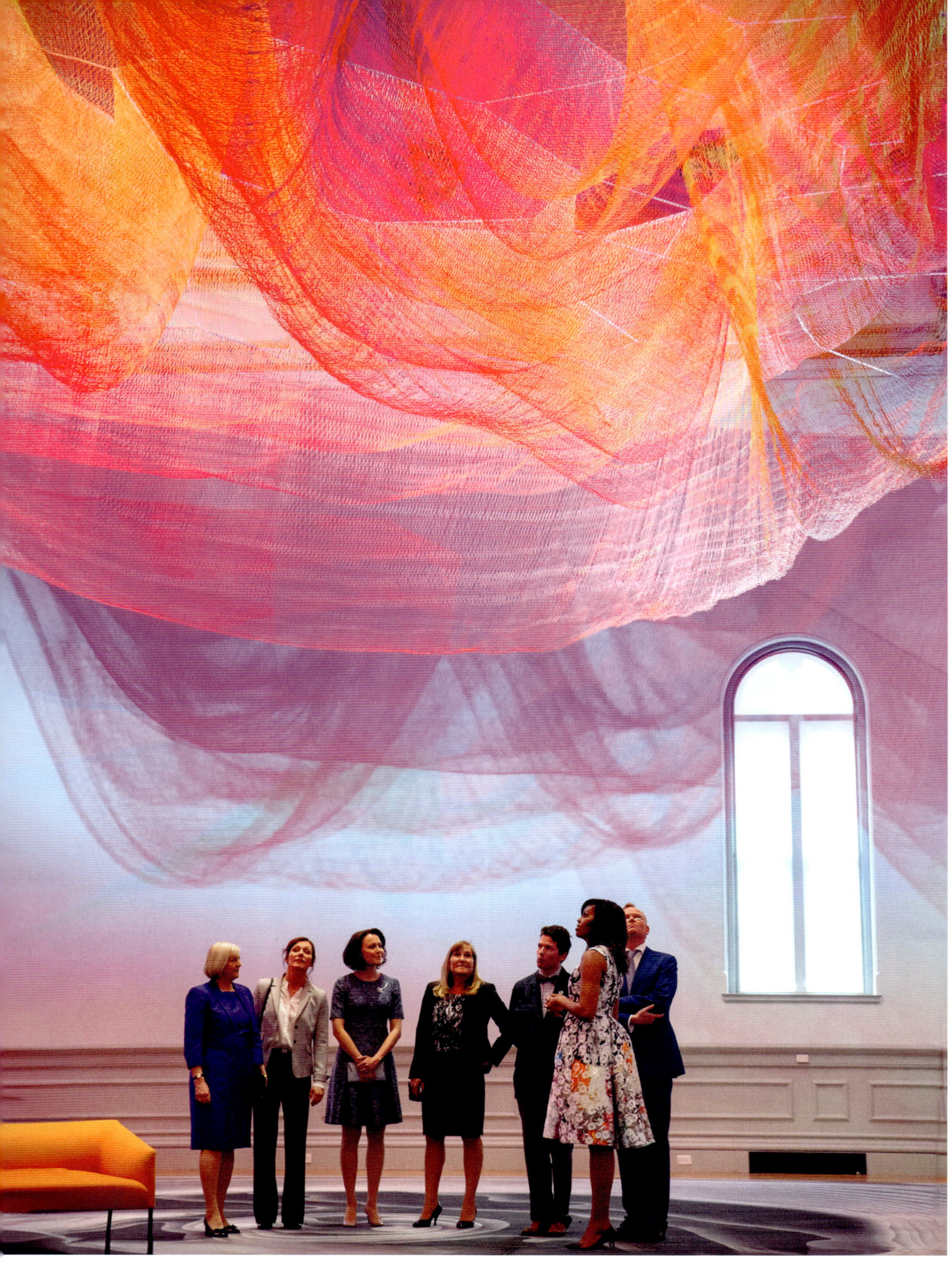

Earthtime 1.8 Renwick

—

Nora Atkinson

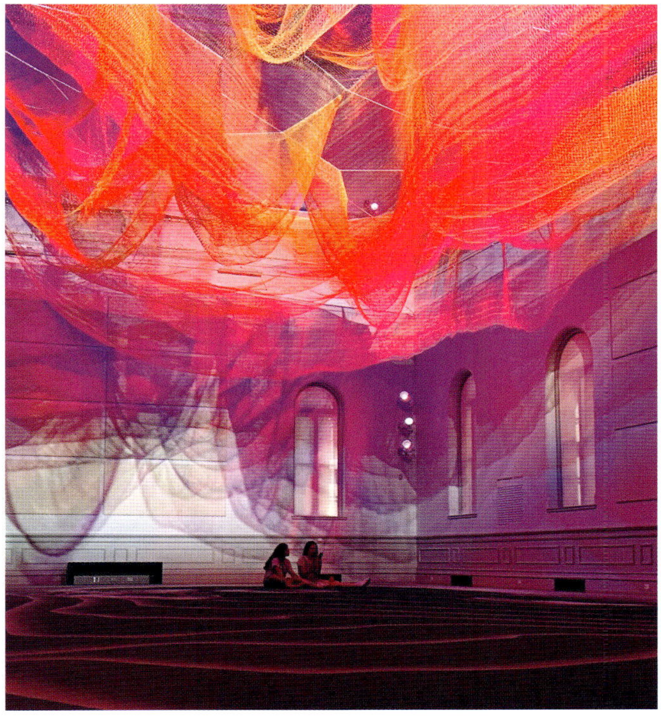

opposite: Michelle Obama introducing the Nordic delegation to *Earthtime 1.8 Renwick*, 2015, Smithsonian American Art Museum Washington, DC
above: *Earthtime 1.8 Renwick*, 2015

Janet Echelman's first permanent museum installation is suspended from the ceiling of the Renwick Gallery, home to Smithsonian American Art Museum's craft and decorative arts collection, located in the center of Washington, DC. While *Earthtime* is often erected as a temporary structure, here Echelman created a permanent installation, requiring the artist to think about how the work could remain dynamic indoors and over time. Instead of wind and the natural cycle of the sun, a carefully choreographed lighting program subtly changes the colors of the knotted layers, casting shadow drawings on the surrounding walls.

The volumetric forms of the *Earthtime* series, to me, explore a certain distrust of shadows—a wariness of sight that is baked into the very foundations of Western thought. "Bewilderments of the eyes," Plato explains in the Allegory of the Cave, "arise from two causes, either from coming out of the light or from going into the light." Whereas most museum spaces bathed in white light allow little mystery, *Earthtime 1.8 Renwick* (2015), with its embrace of shadow and color, located only steps from our nation's seat of power, offers a rare opportunity to slow down, reflect, and delight in the small joys of pure being.

Earthtime 1.8 Renwick was inspired by the Tohoku earthquake and tsunami that shook Fukushima, Japan, then developed using her studio's design translation process from data to physical manifestation. Unlike Echelman's monumental outdoor installations, which rely on wind currents for their dynamic beauty, this piece makes use of stillness, demanding we attenuate our eyes to the beauty of slowly shifting light, darkness, and color.

A brilliant flash of color through an arched doorway attracts viewers into the Rubenstein Grand Salon. Once there, the full glory of the canopy spreads out overhead in reds, oranges, and golds, while beneath their feet the pattern of the work's undulating lines is echoed in gray tones spanning the floor. As part of the building's extensive renovation, the Smithsonian invited Echelman to also rethink the flooring, and she brilliantly made it cohere as part of the work itself. The plush and inviting carpet beckons visitors to lie down and gaze upward in a state of contemplative "slow looking" we try so hard to

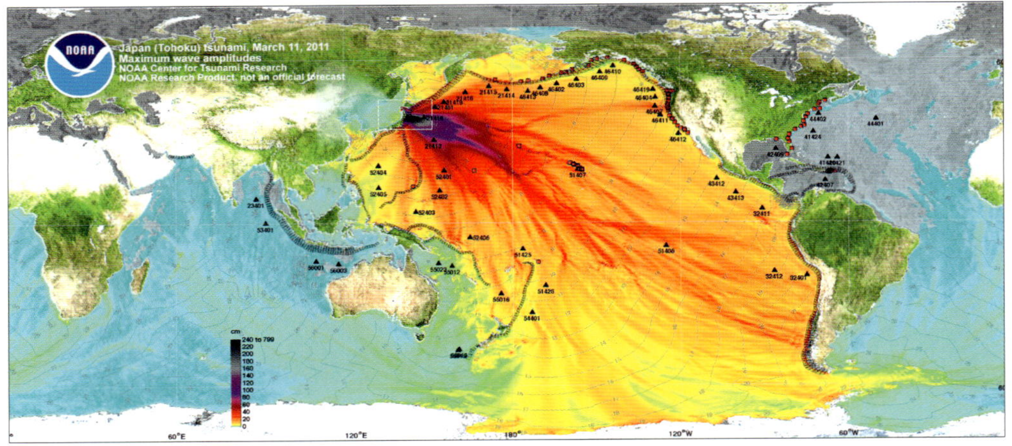

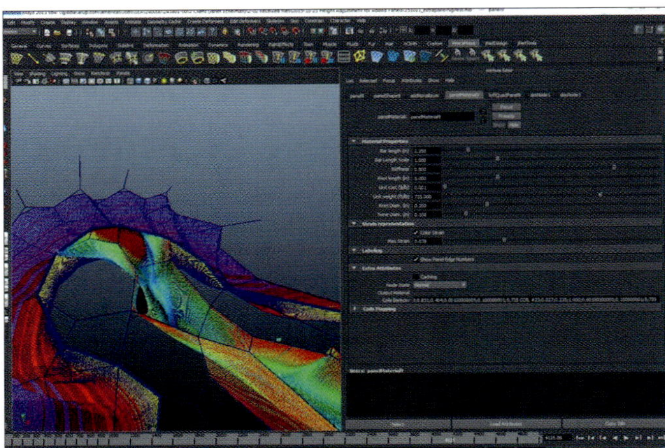

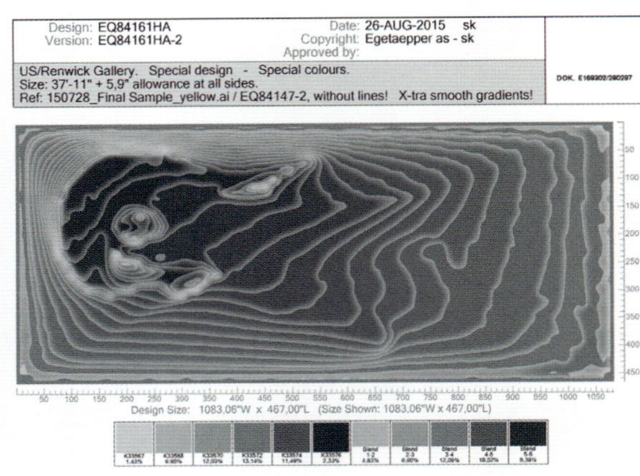

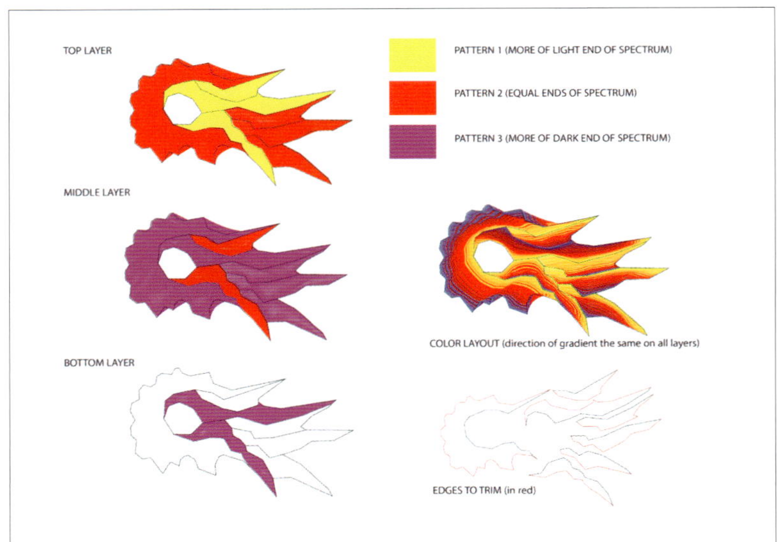

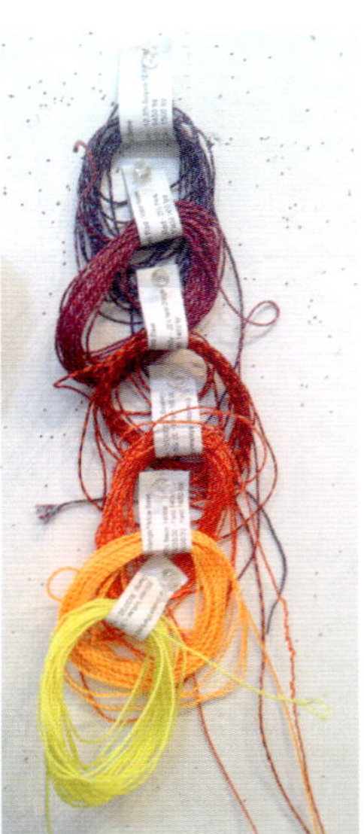

top: NOAA map of ocean wave heights following the 2011 Tohoku earthquake and tsunami that devastated the Fukushima nuclear plant in Japan
middle left: Modeling sculpture using the studio's mesh relaxation solver, JNET software
middle right: Carpet design rendering

bottom left: Schematic assembly diagram
bottom right: Fiber color samples
opposite top: Rendered mesh geometry 3D model
opposite bottom: *Earthtime 1.8 Renwick*, 2015

encourage in our galleries. One notes how the colorful netted sculpture pulls pleasingly taut in places, while draping in others. And there is more: dancing shadows, the occasional glint of gold in the postmodern cornice, the almost imperceptible shifting of colors, like a sunset, taking place over a thirty-minute cycle.

No two viewings here are the same, as the rhythms of the lighting program pair with the ever-changing atmospheric conditions to create glorious crescendos, then fade to dark, like a musical score. The ephemeral, atmospheric work taps into a sublime feminine presence, reminiscent of great fiber artist Lenore Tawney, wire artist Ruth Asawa, and artist and filmmaker Maryette Charlton, in effect if not in essence. In a letter to Charlton, Tawney cited words by the philosopher Jiddu Krishnamurti that seem resonant here: "All composite things are like a dream / A phantasm, a bubble, and a shadow / Are like a dewdrop and a flash of lightning / They are thus to be regarded."[2] So too, *Earthtime 1.8 Renwick* conjures a dream captured or evaded and, like the wonders of the natural world, just out of human reach.

Nora Atkinson is executive director of the Museum of Craft and Design, San Francisco.

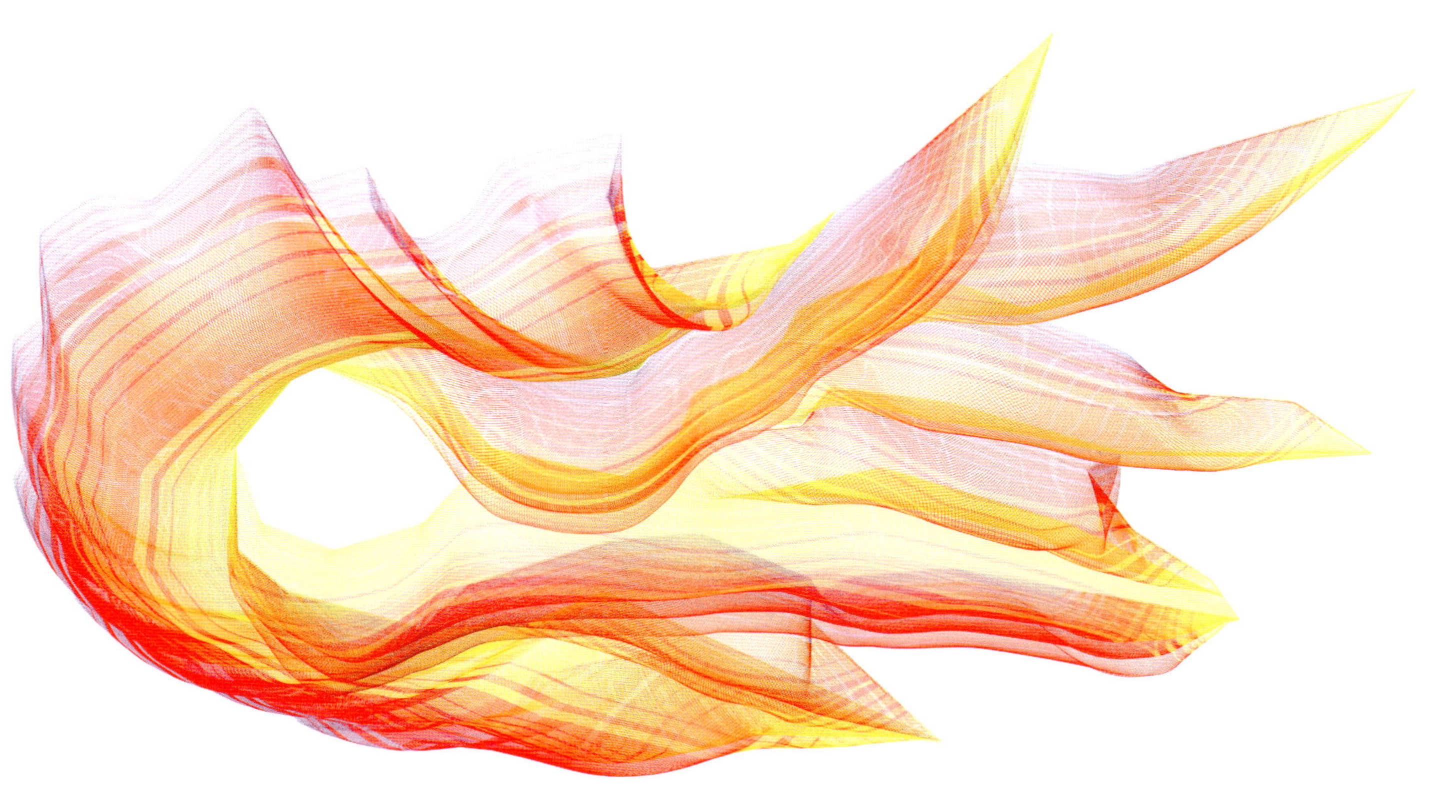

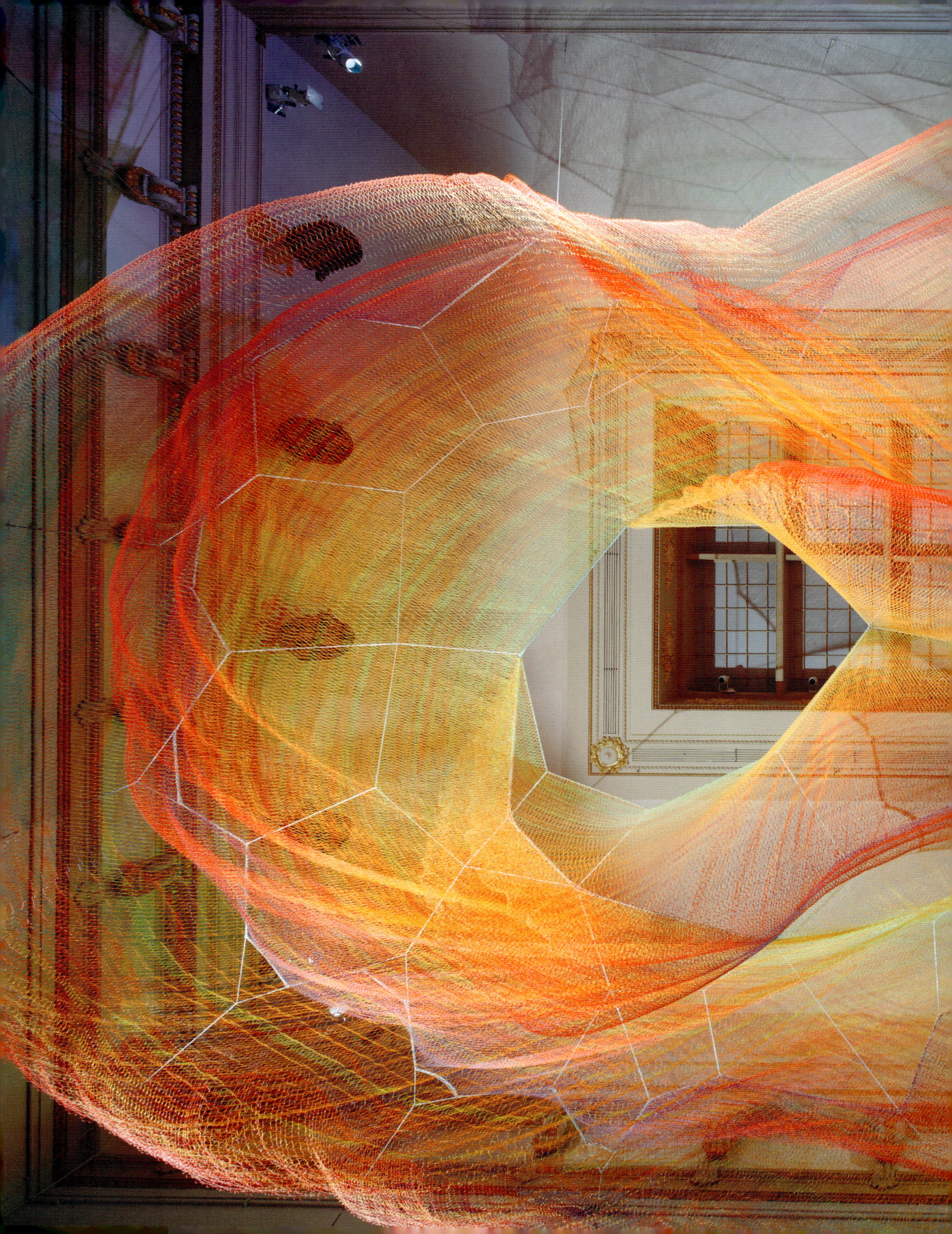

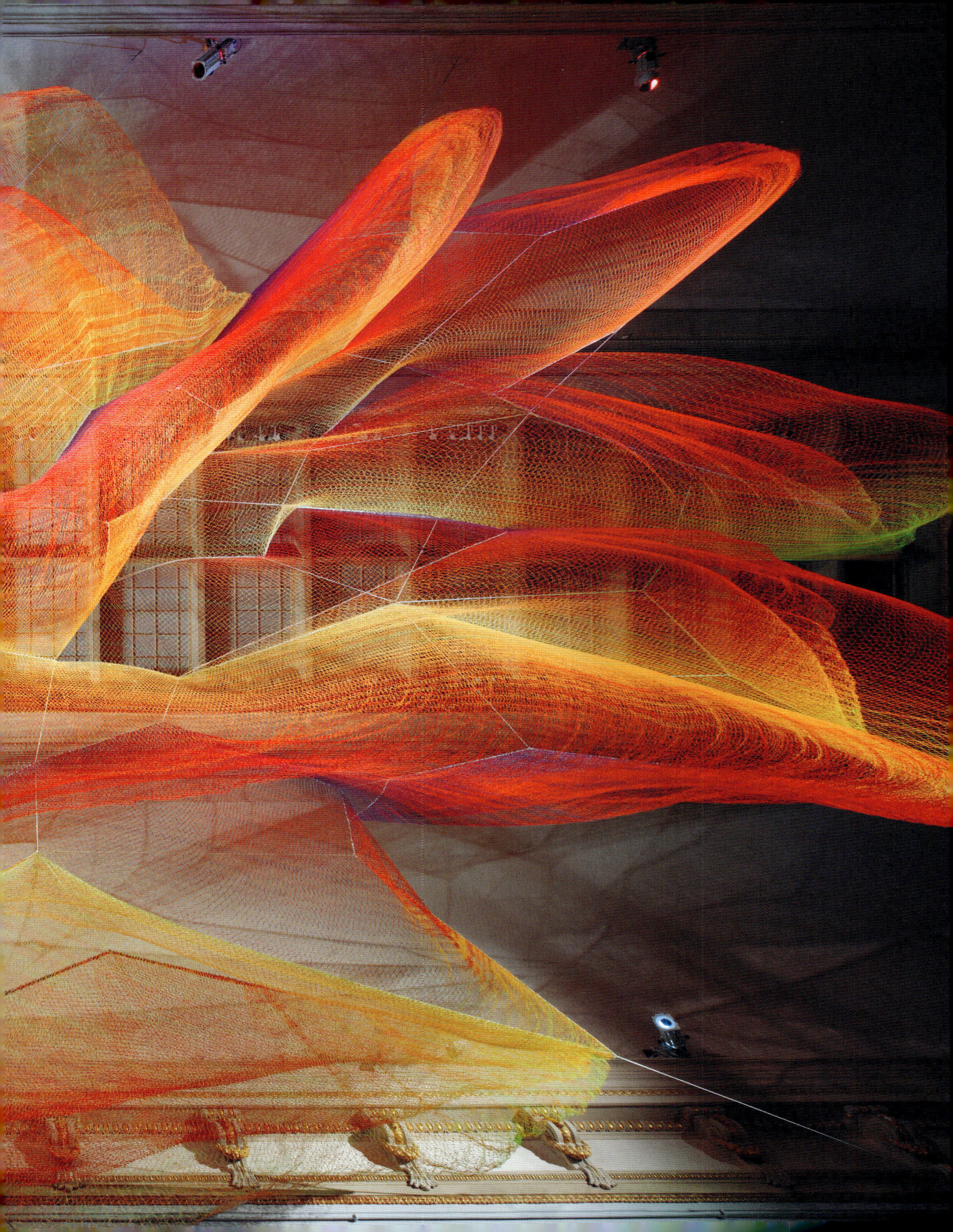

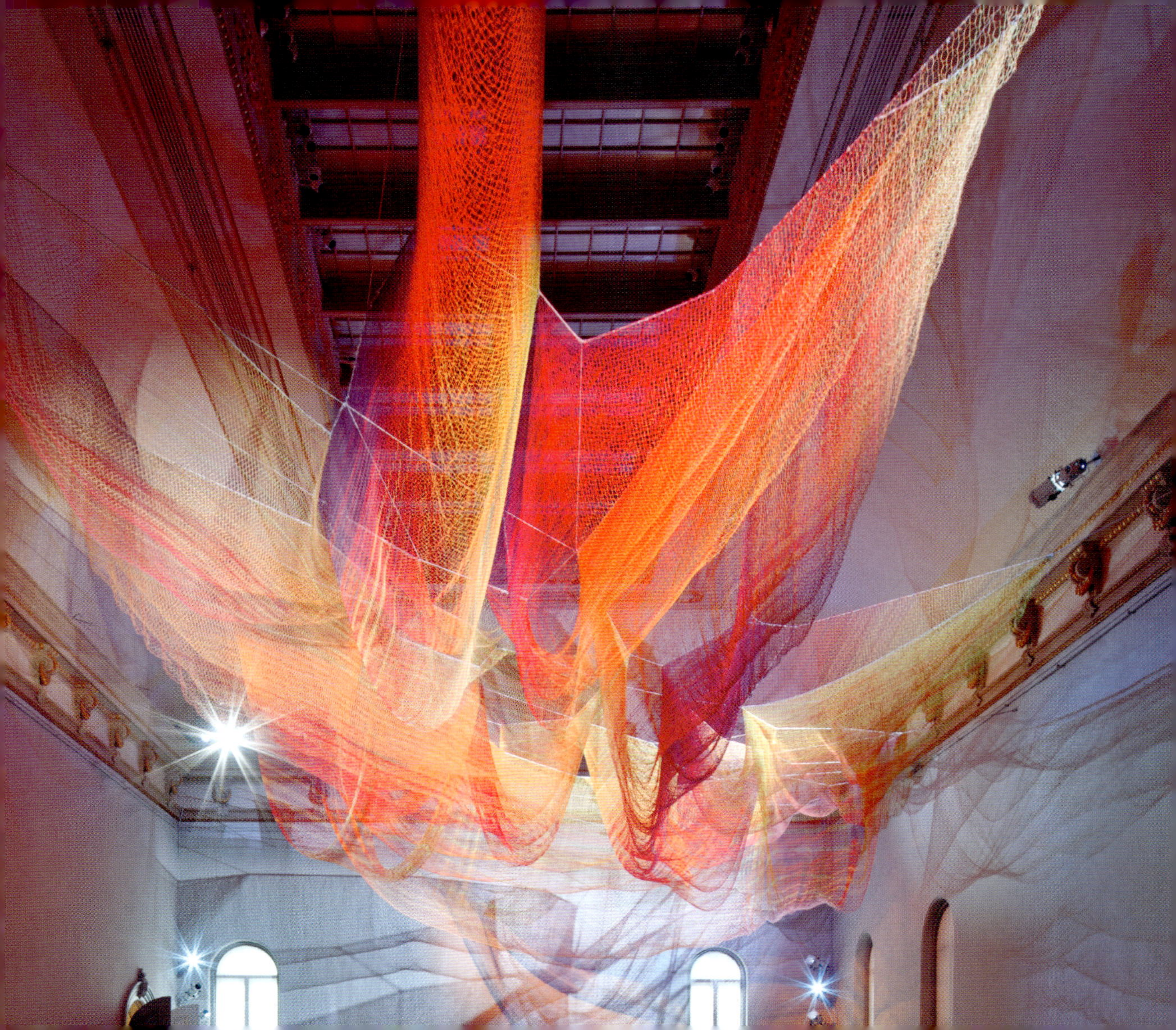

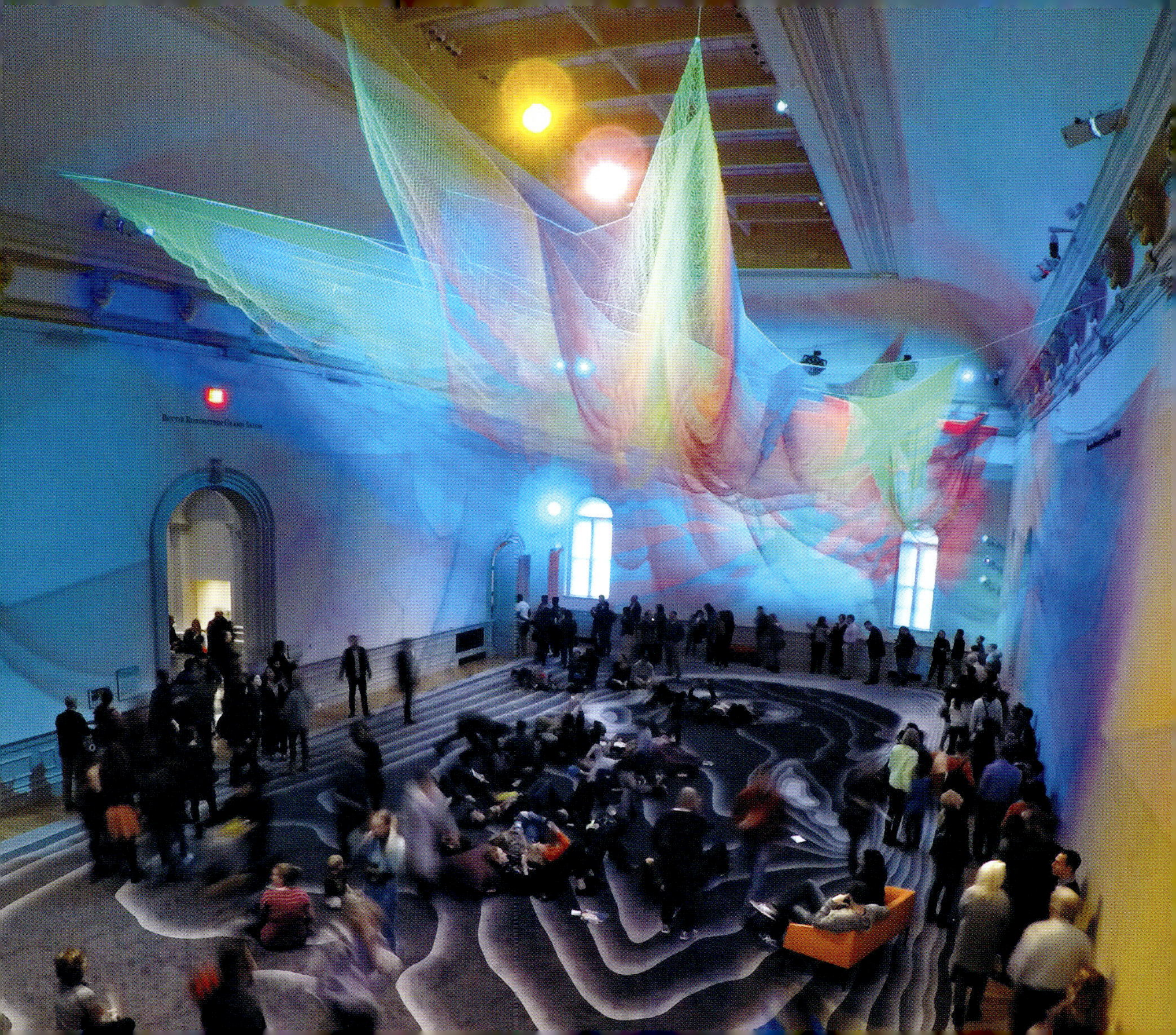

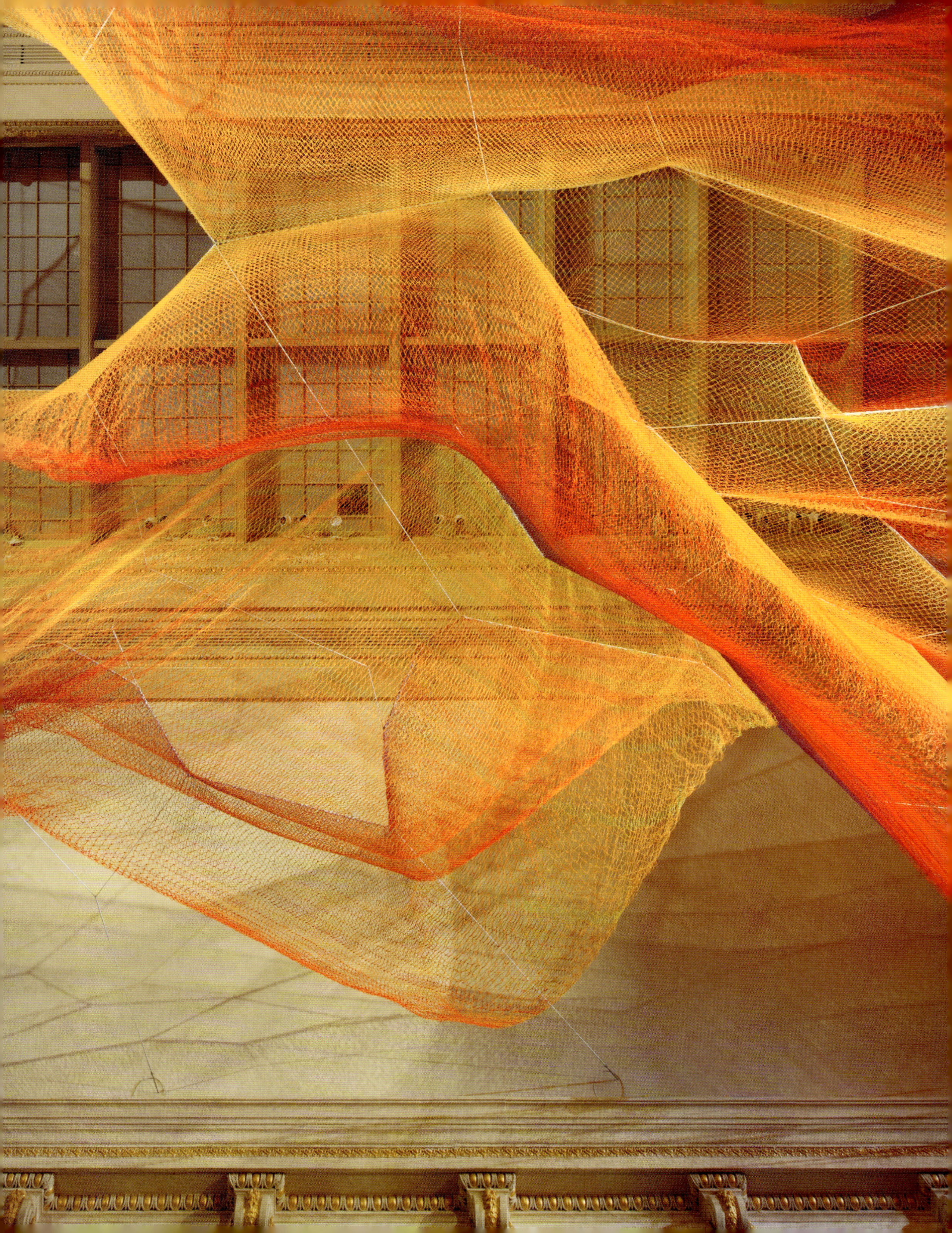

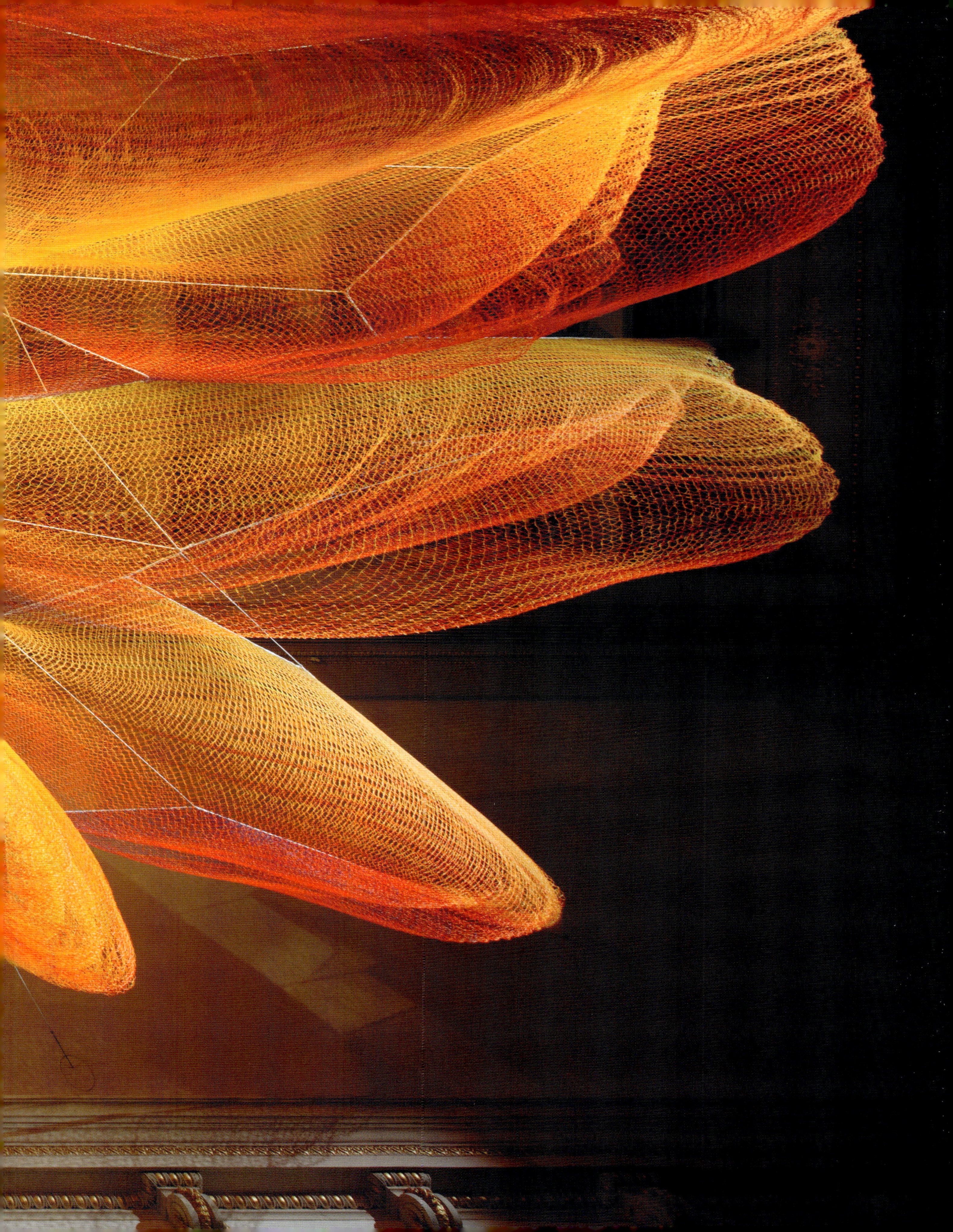

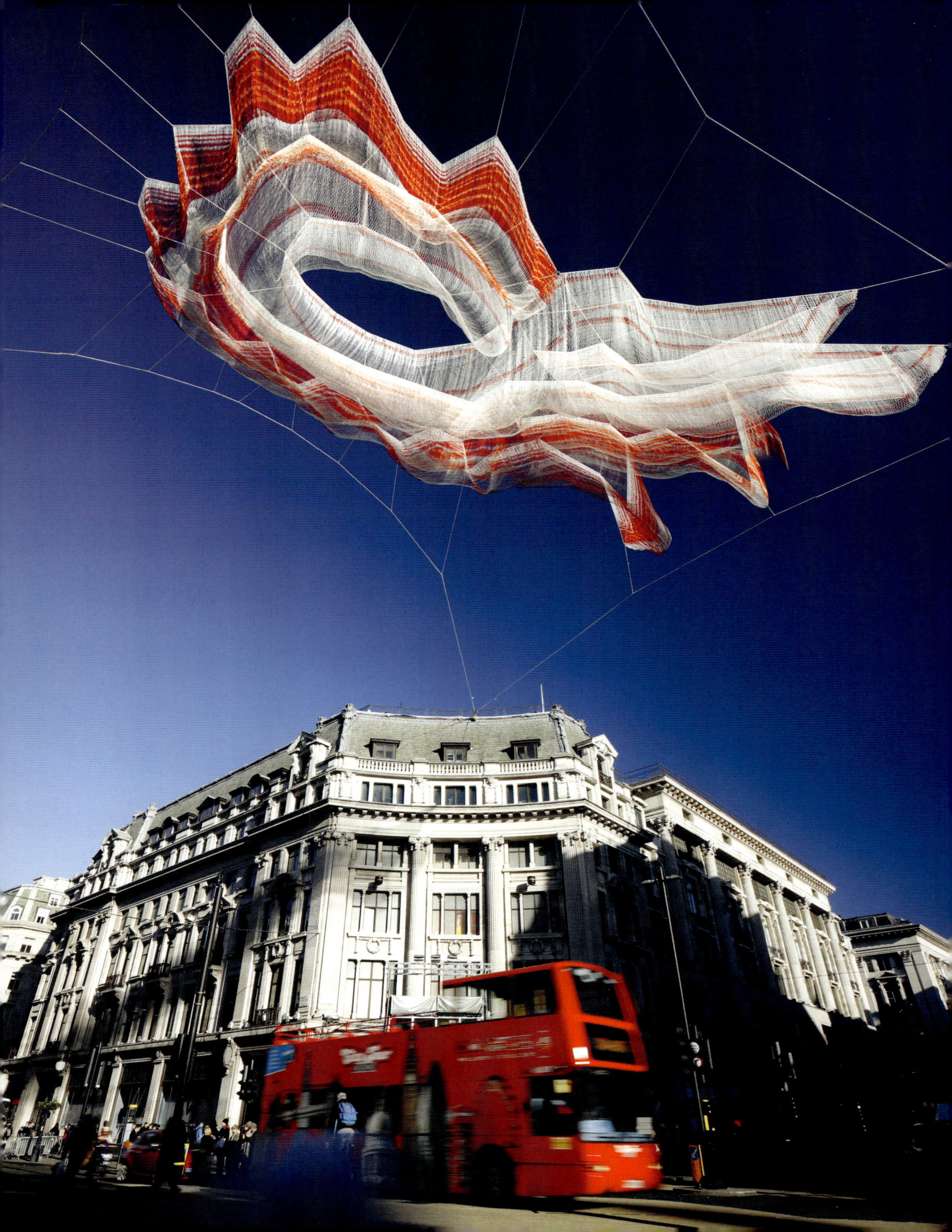

Earthtime 1.8 London

—

Gus Casely-Hayford and Janet Echelman in conversation

Janet Echelman's soft, voluminous net sculpture *Earthtime 1.8 London* surged 180 feet through the air between buildings above Oxford Circus, the busiest pedestrian area in the city. The monumental floating form is lightweight and flexible, in vibrant hues that pulse with changing wind and weather to create a choreography of undulating color. The sculpture was adapted to other cities around the world after its premiere at Lumiere London 2016, a light festival produced by Artichoke. While the custom color blends of *Earthtime 1.8 London*'s technical fibers and programmed colored lights correspond to the geological data that informs all of the instantiations of the Earthtime works, the London edition introduced a new component. The precise colors and patterns were created interactively with members of the public, who were invited to use their smartphones to select colors and tap out patterns with the touch of a finger. These patterns were projected onto the sculpture's monumental surface and interacted with one another.

The work's title refers to the length of time in microseconds that the Earth's day was shortened as a result of a single physical event, the 2011 earthquake and tsunami that originated in Japan. The sculpture's form was inspired by data sets describing the tsunami's wave heights rippling across the Pacific Ocean. The artwork alludes to our complex interdependencies with larger cycles of time and the physical world. The net structure is a physical manifestation of interconnectedness—when any one element moves, every other element is affected. *Earthtime 1.8 London* invited busy Londoners and tourists alike to pause amid the bustle and commotion of Oxford Circus, gaze skyward, and contemplate a physical manifestation of interconnectedness. The mayor of London closed Oxford and Regent Streets to all vehicles, enabling visitors to lie down on the asphalt and experience the art above. Here the artist discusses the project with Gus Casely-Hayford, director of the V&A East in London and former director of the Smithsonian National Museum of African Art in Washington, DC.

Janet Echelman: One question I am often asked is whether the fact that so many people stop to photograph *Earthtime 1.8* detracts from the art.

Gus Casely-Hayford: What's so good about this is that it's not just accessible, but actually remade, reenergized, by the people who see it.

JE: I think it's a way for people to interact right now. They understand that photographing is a creative act.

GCH: Many areas of culture, particularly digital culture, are about interactivity. The nineteenth-century idea of the gallery as a passive space in which a visitor goes and stands was more about education. We've moved on. People want to engage and feel a part of the artwork. They want to see things that make a difference to their lives and make a comment, and in my mind this really does it.

JE: I appreciate your contextualizing it in the larger view of art history and changing ideas about art's audience.

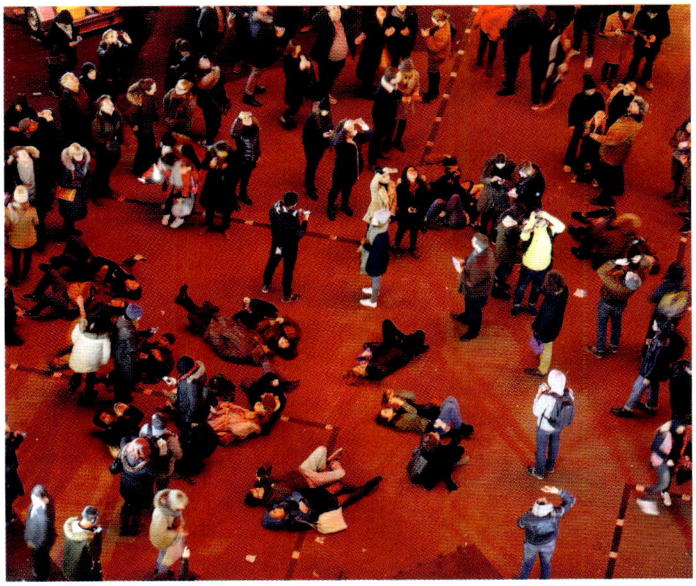

opposite: *Earthtime 1.8 London*, 2016, Oxford Circus
left: People lying on the cold asphalt to view *Earthtime 1.8 London*, 2016; the mayor of London closed Oxford and Regent Streets to vehicular traffic and made the Underground stop exit-only during the exhibition.

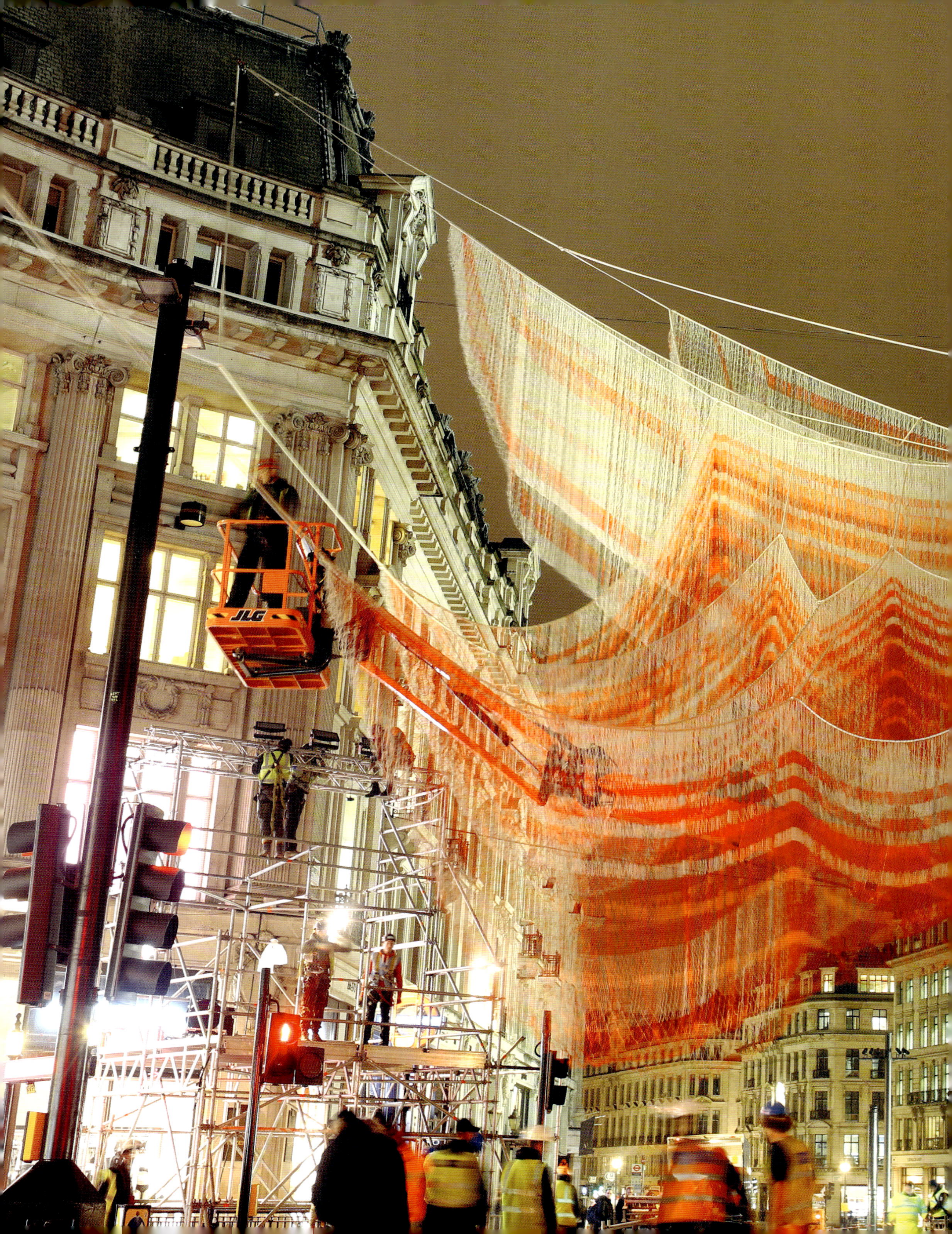
JLG

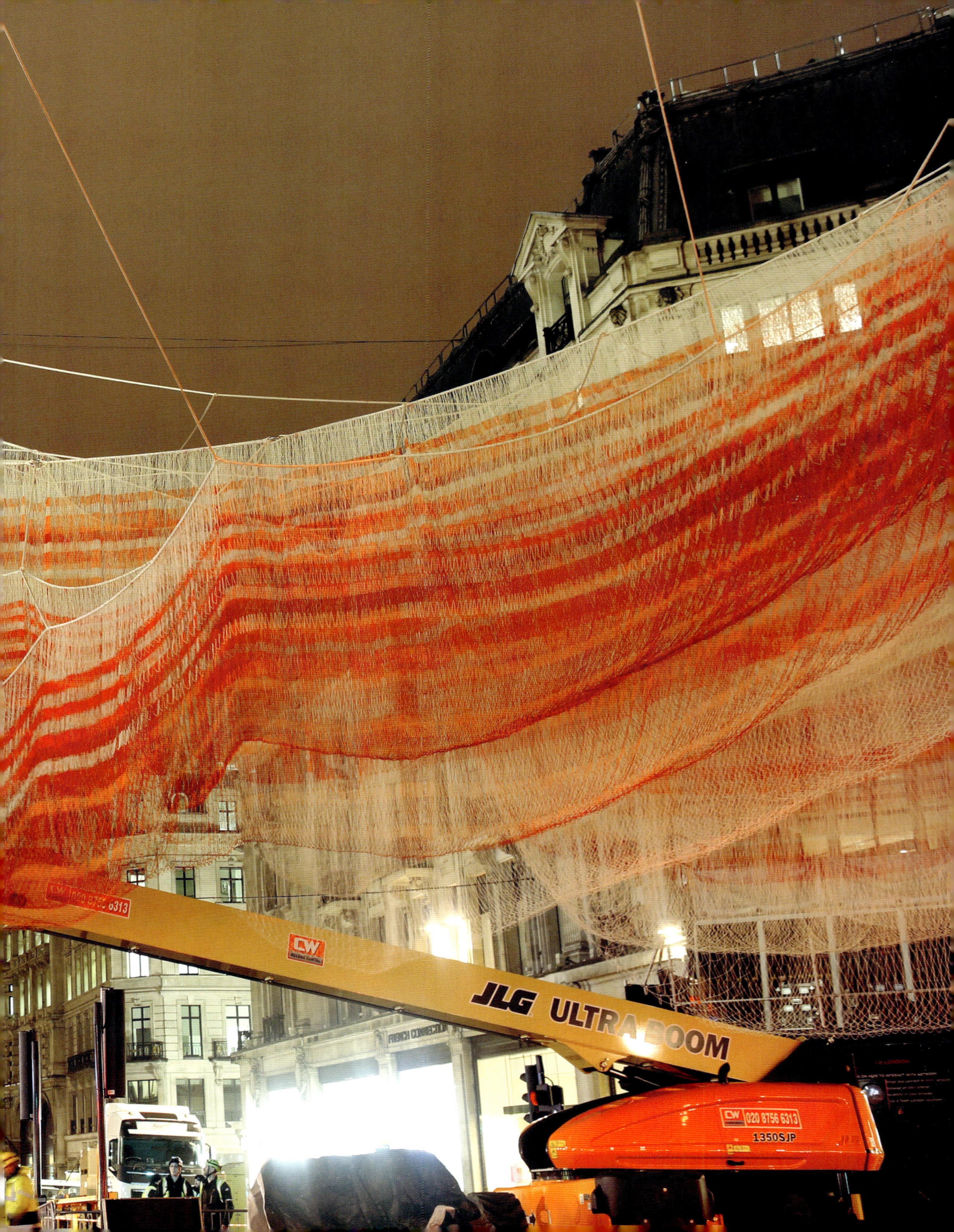
JLG ULTRA BOOM
CW
020 8756 6313
1350SJP

GCH: London is full of some of the finest museums and galleries in the world. Many of them were established around the period of the Enlightenment, and central to that was the idea of being educated in a space that is quiet, speaking only in hushed tones, passing on knowledge, and that idea of the visitor as subordinate to the agenda of the institution. Now, the viewer is not just there to be passive. They are making, remaking, the art, in a dynamic relationship with the art. It is alive. You cannot see *Earthtime 1.8* and not be impacted by it. That is the critical thing. Even by walking past this space, being here, you are helping in some way to change people's engagement with and understanding of this piece. It's changing the flow of traffic, changing the way people are walking through the space. That's what art should do: it should engage people. Even if subliminally, it should make us feel as though we are at one not just with the environment, but with other people as well. What I love about your work is that it gives us something that takes our breath away and makes us think about what it is to be human and live in this world, this changing world. To think about ecology and our responsibility to one another and also to the wider planet, in a way that is beautiful.

JE: Why is there a fear of beauty in the academic or critical art world these days?

GCH: I think there is fear of beauty because it is, or may be considered, simplistic. It's something that you feel down here, in the heart, rather than up here, in the mind. There is no easy equation for what's beautiful. Also, it's democratic. We all have a sense of what we feel is beautiful, and it's immediate. A child can come here and feel awed by something like this and articulate that it's beautiful. That kind of empowerment for ordinary people deconstructs the very need for art historians, whose job is to build some sort of interknitted structure of why art is valuable and important.

JE: Here amid life [*gestures to traffic*], I feel that it functions on all those levels at the same time. That is one of my aims.

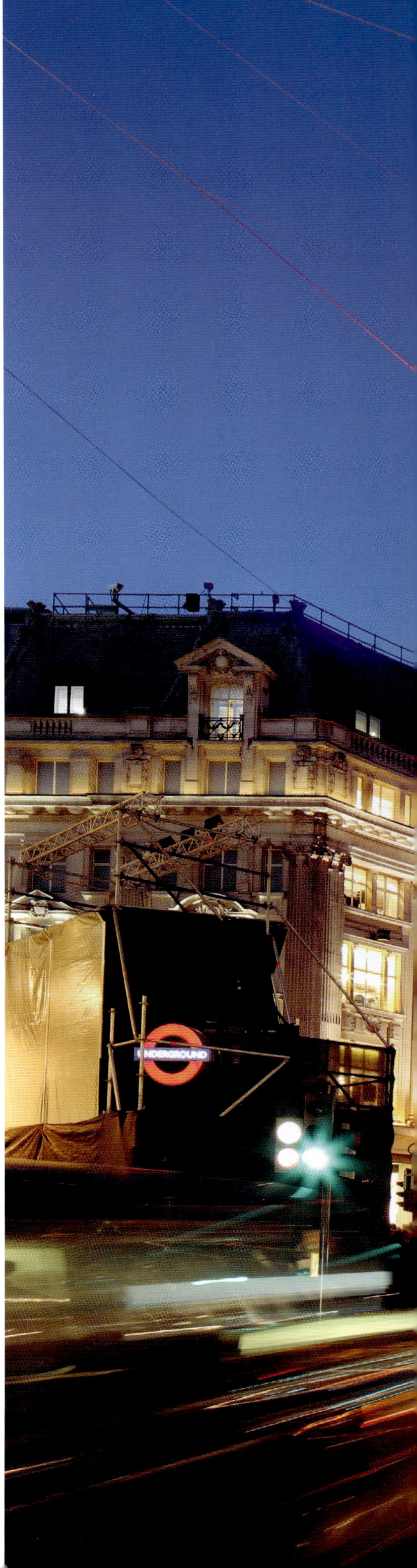

previous: Installation of *Earthtime 1.8 London*, 2016
right: *Earthtime 1.8 London*, 2016

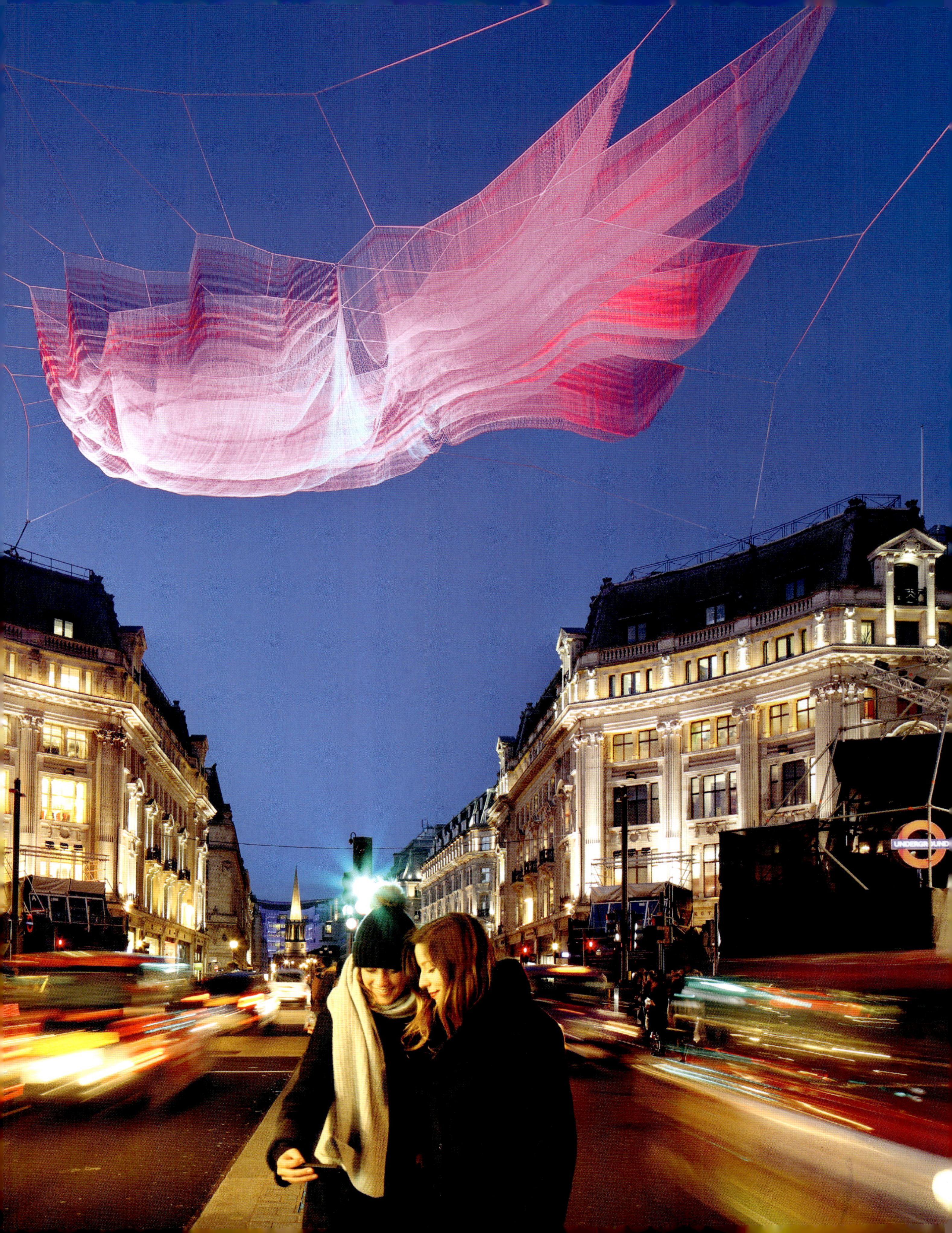
UNDERGROUND

GCH: Some people are going to stand here and engage with it. Those who use their mobile phones actually help to program it. Others who are very busy are going to passively see it out of the corner of their eye. But all of those different modes of interacting are valuable. There are so few places where we get together, come together, today. Not remotely through the internet, but physical places. And doing so around something beautiful, something affirming, allows us to think about the wider environment. That's a rare opportunity today, and something we should value.

JE: I've been observing strangers speaking to one another in response to the work.

GCH: And we don't do that! [*laughs*] It's not just a London thing, not just a metropolitan thing—it's a British thing that we don't generally interact in this way. But when terrible things happen, or when astounding things happen, we do. I think that in this case, it's about the power of beauty. Something that for a moment allows you that little bit of space in which to interact with people directly and honestly. I think it's great; it's about sharing, and about us as human beings remembering what's important. Beauty is so important.

JE: You're right about the tragedies. I lived in New York in 2001, and after 9/11 suddenly all of the barriers were stripped away. In London, other shared experiences have broken down the barriers. But there are other ways besides tragedy.

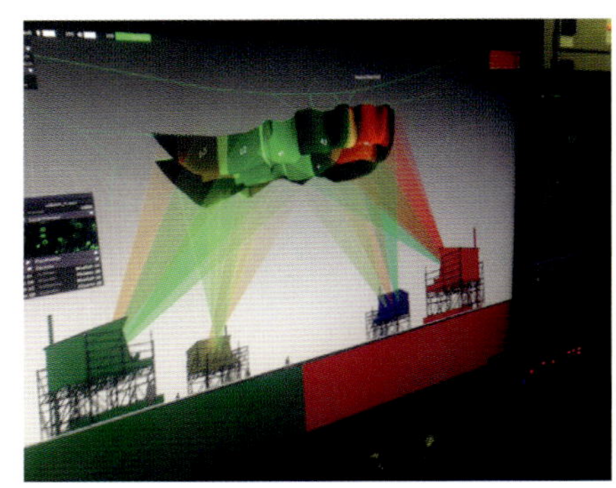

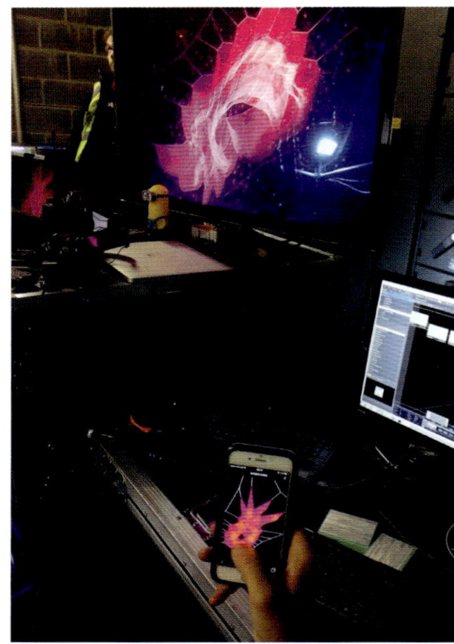

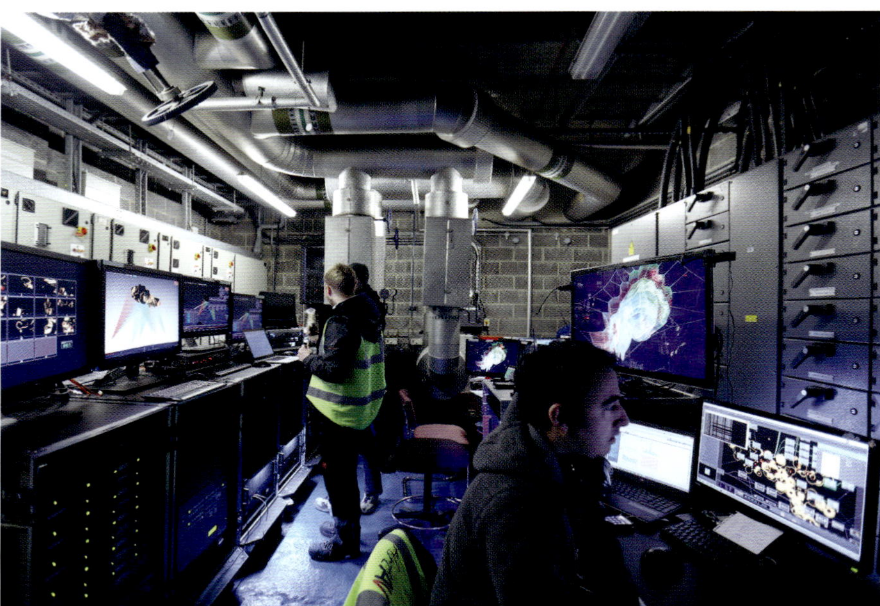

above: Lighting team on the roof at Oxford Circus, London, performing computer mapping to calculate in real time the colors selected by members of the public on their mobile phones for *Earthtime 1.8 London*, 2016

GCH: There are other ways, and we crave them so desperately. The digital age is allowing us places in which we can come together, but it is also, sadly, dividing us, such that we're usually engaging on our phones, away from public space. It's somewhat distressing. This thoroughfare is one of the most heavily utilized in the whole of Europe, which means hundreds of thousands of people are coming through this space and interacting with something beautiful. This is not about the commercial, it's about the beautiful. I think to not be forced upon it, but to stumble upon something that makes you stop for a moment and look, and engage in a different way, is so important.

JE: Would you talk about the street?

GCH: Once upon a time, when people were condemned, they would be taken along Oxford Street to the place of execution. So there would have been people lining up here clamoring for blood, shouting. This was a Roman road, and there's a history around it which is palpable. In the Georgian period it was gentrified and commercialized, but that old, savage, somewhat dangerous history is still very much here. That's a thing about London streets. It's a gorgeous city, a beautiful city, but there's always that little twist, that little bit of danger in the history, and art can remind us of that history, and how danger and beauty very often go together. We can try to cover one with the other, but neither can ever entirely obscure the other.

JE: What danger do you perceive in this work?

GCH: It reminds us of the changes in our environment. Of how small we are, but also how big our impact is when we come together. You can stand on the moon and see that the biggest intervention humans have made is in light. You see the central conurbations, the big cities and the amount of energy that we are using, and it is around light. It is around this idea of tiny little spots that together agglomerate to make something astonishing and deeply affective, and I do think that we occasionally need to think about our relationship to that. What's glorious about this is that it's not just something that as a single entity makes a statement; it's a reminder that each of its contingent parts are together forging this beautiful synthesis, and that just as we can interact with it and make a difference digitally, we likewise can with our world ecologically.

JE: That mobile phone you were talking about—I agree that it mostly brings us apart physically from one another even as we connect. So here I love that it's a tool in our hand to use however we wish. It can bring us together in a physical way. It doesn't have to be about isolation and distance.

GCH: That's the interesting tension. The digital age can isolate, but here is a fantastic demonstration of how it can bring us together and produce something that is not just aesthetically pleasing but dynamic. It's not just that there are many hundreds of people in this space, but that together we can create something which is additional.

JE: Speaking of the history of this road and this city, I was looking at the history of two thousand years ago, when this was a village along the Thames and the fishermen were splicing their ropes by hand the same way that we spliced this. There's something about linking to the origin of our survival and using technology from today at the same time. We're not separated from our past; it's all part of us.

GCH: Yes. I work a lot in Africa, and there's a place called Tassili in Algeria in the middle of the desert. If you climb up into the caves—and you have to go with a torch, because it's dark—and shine the torch up onto the roofs of those caves, you'll see that ten thousand years ago, our ancestors created beautiful paintings of the night sky, of the landscape, but it is something that you can only observe by torchlight. I think that illumination and art and the way in which you can imagine the light changing, animating those spaces, and almost making a film on the roofs of these caves—to animate and share something together is powerful, but it's not new, it's something that we've always hankered after. This idea of gazing up, seeing something beautiful, sharing it, is very powerful.

JE: What you describe makes me think of the sky as the roof of the cave. We're making this cave-like room in the city where we're sharing an experience.

GCH: I love the way you play with scale. I imagine that the view from space makes cities look a little bit like this. It's the idea of us being so powerful but also having no power. Nature ultimately has the option to destroy everything we do. We play, and we have ambitions, and we are arrogant, but ultimately it's all pretty much a folly.

JE: The softness of the fiber yields and adapts when the big forces come through.

GCH: Yes, and one hopes that that is humanity at its best. We live and learn to react to the environment rather than stand and rail against it. A part of our arrogance is that we too often stand in nature's way and refuse to work with it. One of the glorious things about this work is that it celebrates us coming together and creating, which is a very interesting, dynamic force.

JE: Would you read the artwork for me? As you would a gallery text for a nineteenth-century painting?

GCH: [*stops for several seconds to observe the sculpture*] Most of us, when we visit an artwork, are used to seeing something either two-dimensional or three-dimensional, and solid. This is both, but it is also alive, an animation of the environment it occupies, in many different ways. The wind can move it, the people around it can animate it through digital programming, the light can change the way it looks. It's ethereal; it's ongoingly changing; it is, in a way, the essence of its environment. It is utterly and completely synthetic, but also a celebration of everything natural. You have created a portal, one that is not trying to control and contain and corral people into a particular kind of engagement. You're allowing them to be, and you're allowing for the work to evolve and to be as well, and that is exciting.

JE: What might that mean for a community or a city?

GCH: Many people think that art is a bit staid and fixed, and for other people, and part of the past. So to create something interactive and evolving is to my mind analogous to this city, which is demographically and culturally evolving and changing, and that change is constantly quickening. We can either try to deny it, or we can accept and embrace how the evolution of human beings is about constantly evolving and accepting the possibility of change. I think if we do that, it allows for a dynamic possibility with our environment that is for the betterment of us all.

Gus Casely-Hayford is director of the V&A East, London, and former director of the Smithsonian National Museum of African Art, Washington, DC.

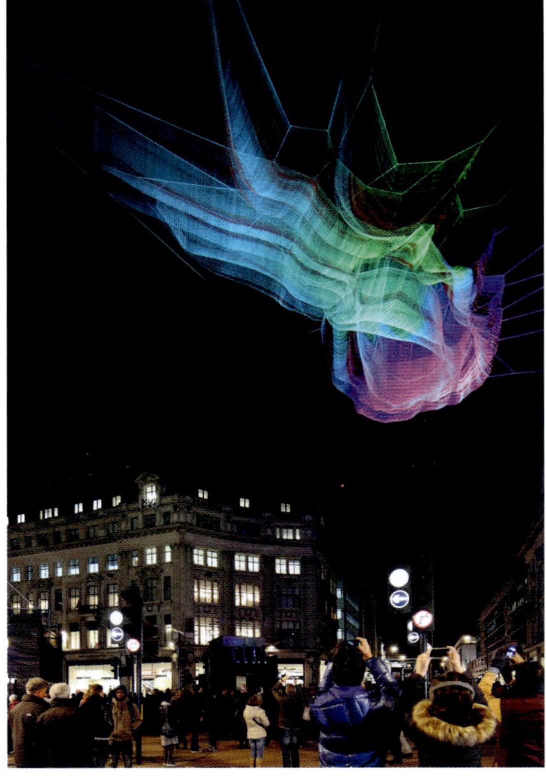

left, opposite, and overleaf:
Earthtime 1.8 London, 2016, Oxford Circus

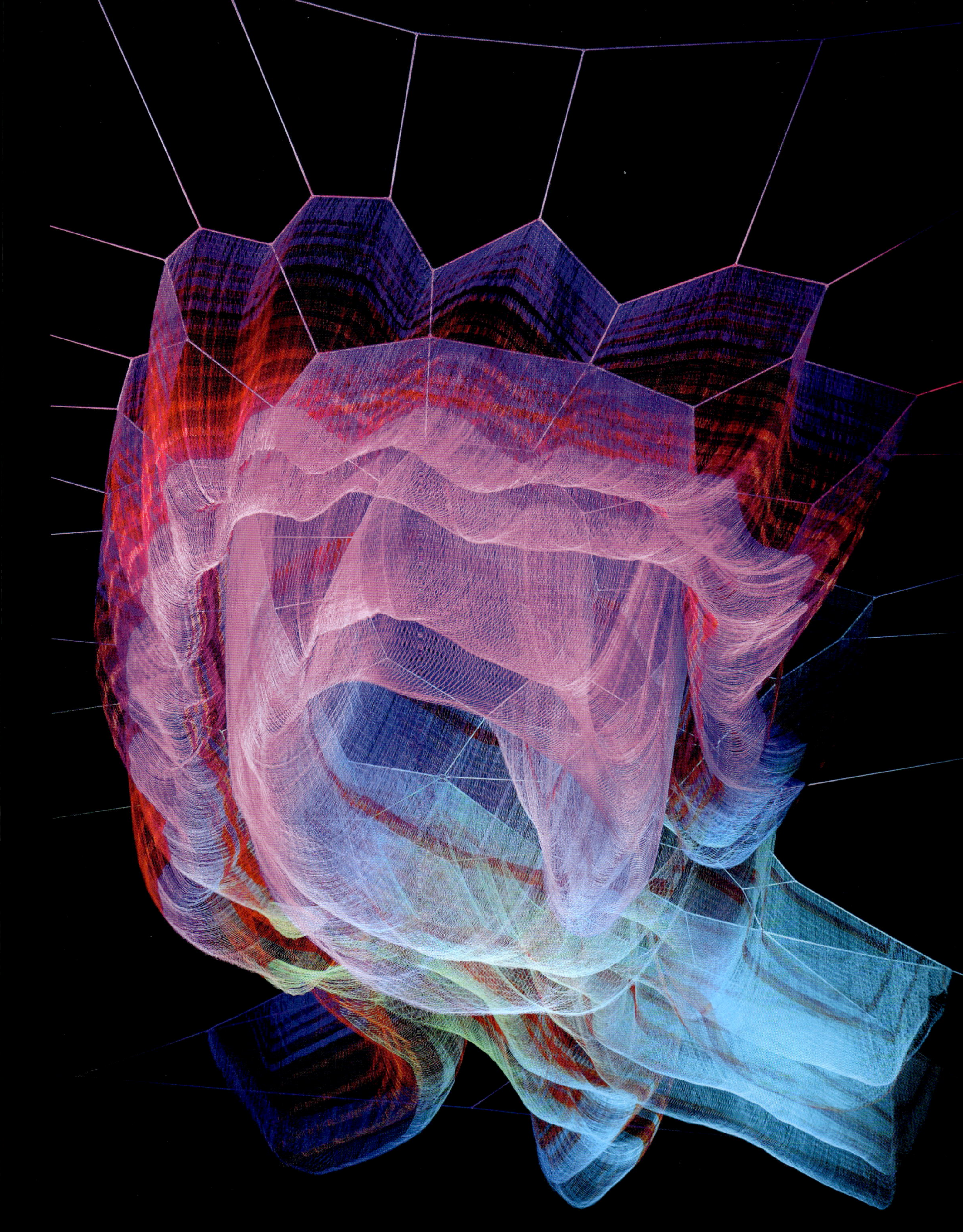

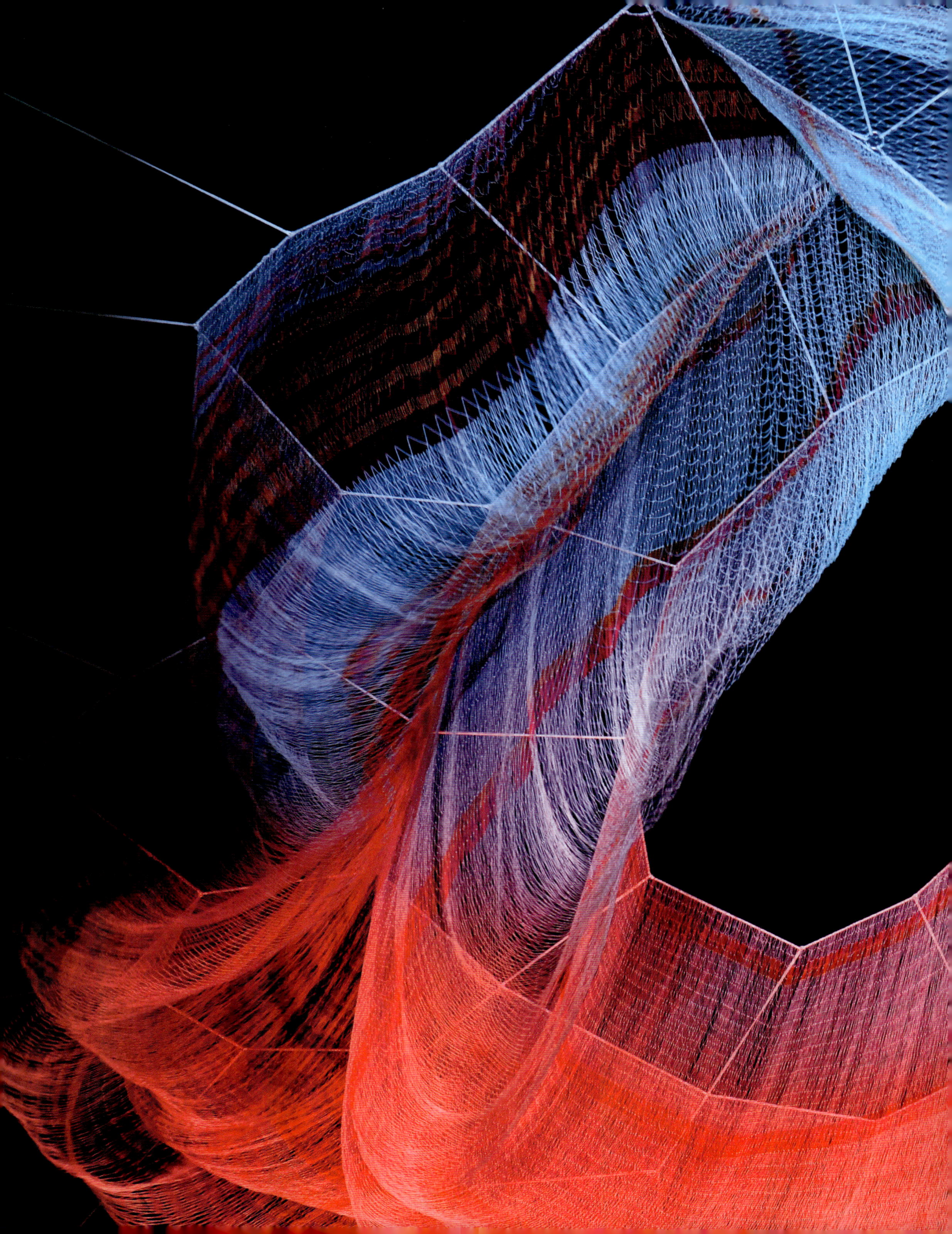

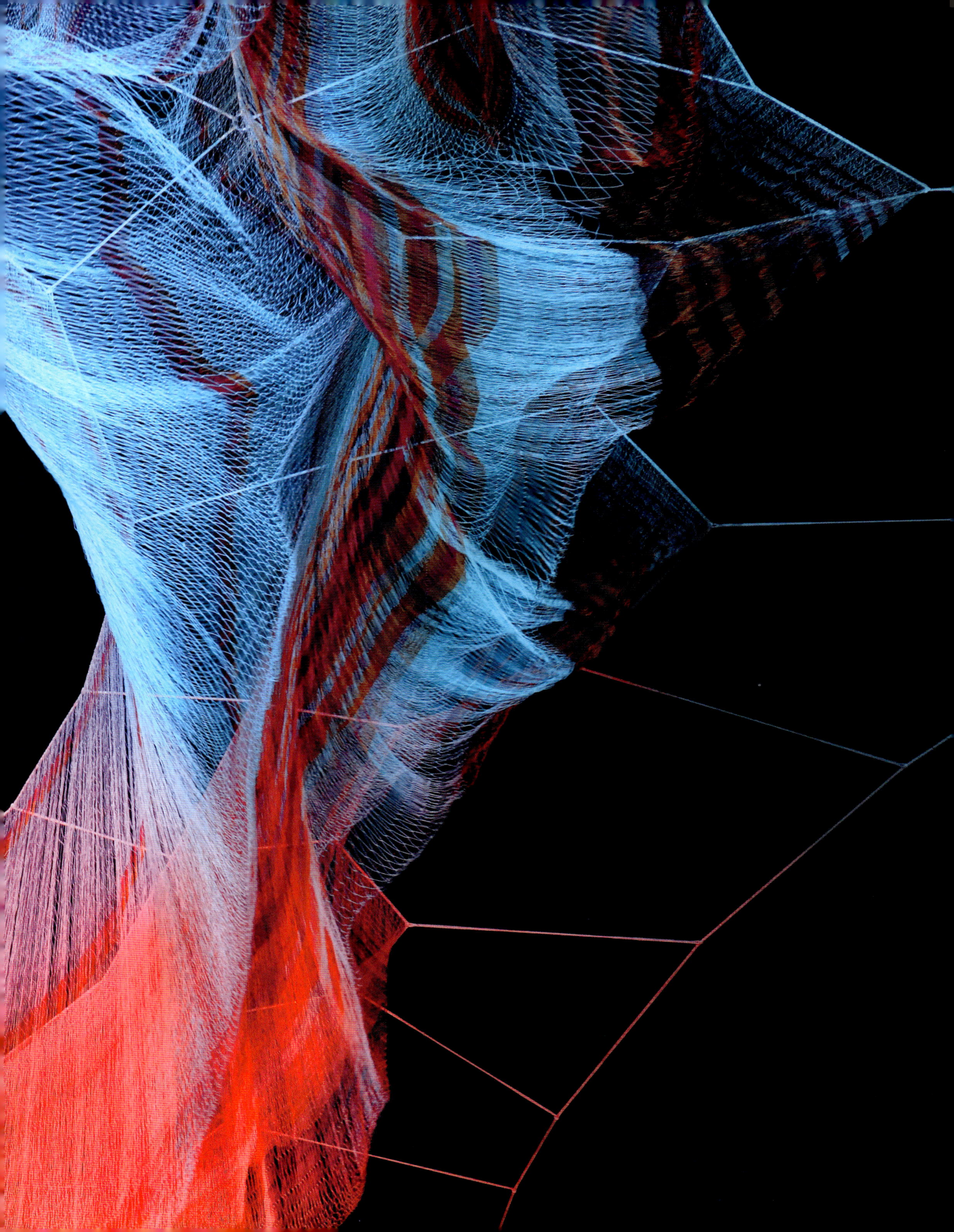

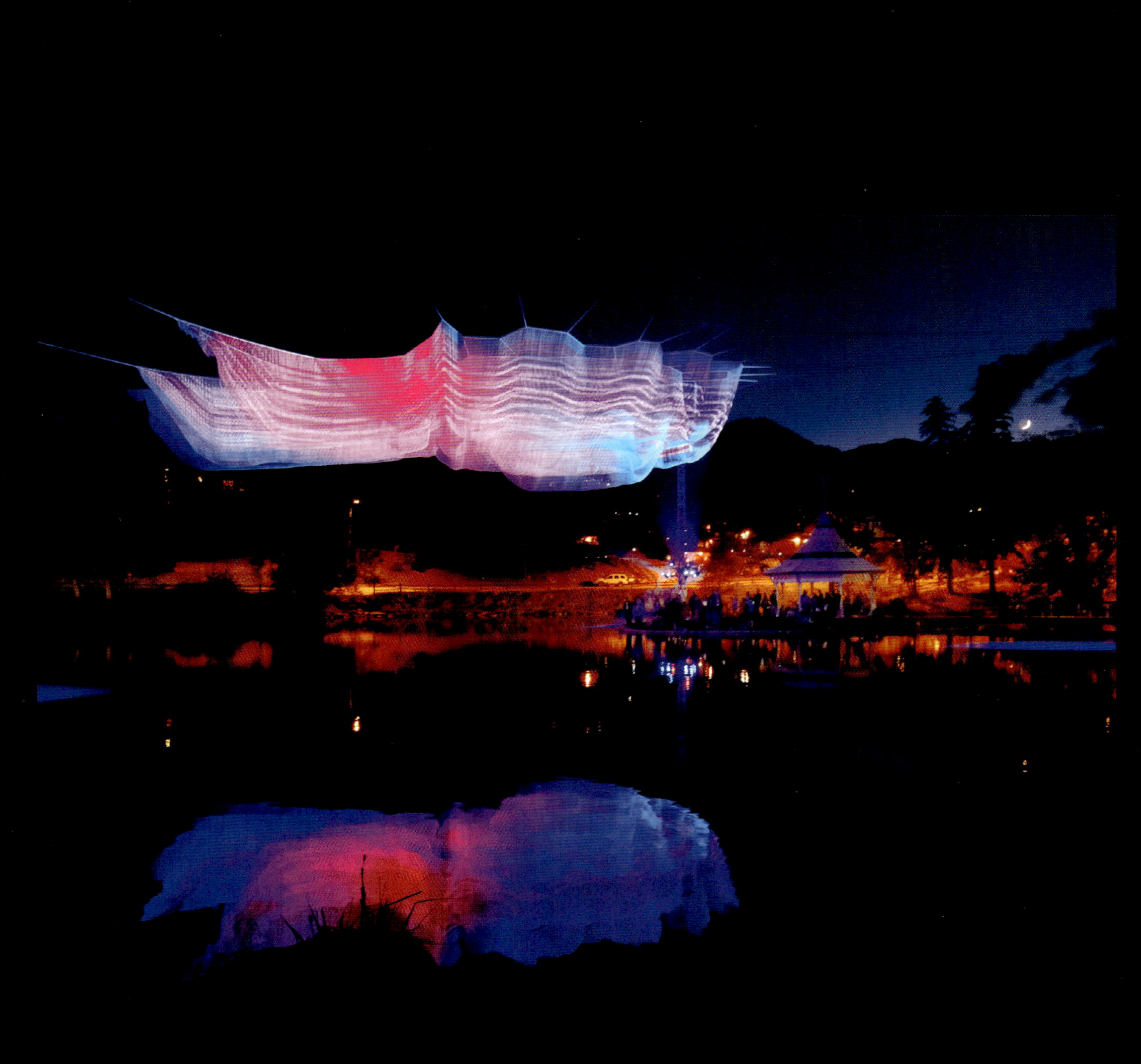

above: *Earthtime 1.8 Green Mountain Falls*, 2019, Colorado
opposite: *Earthtime 1.8 San Diego*, 2016, California

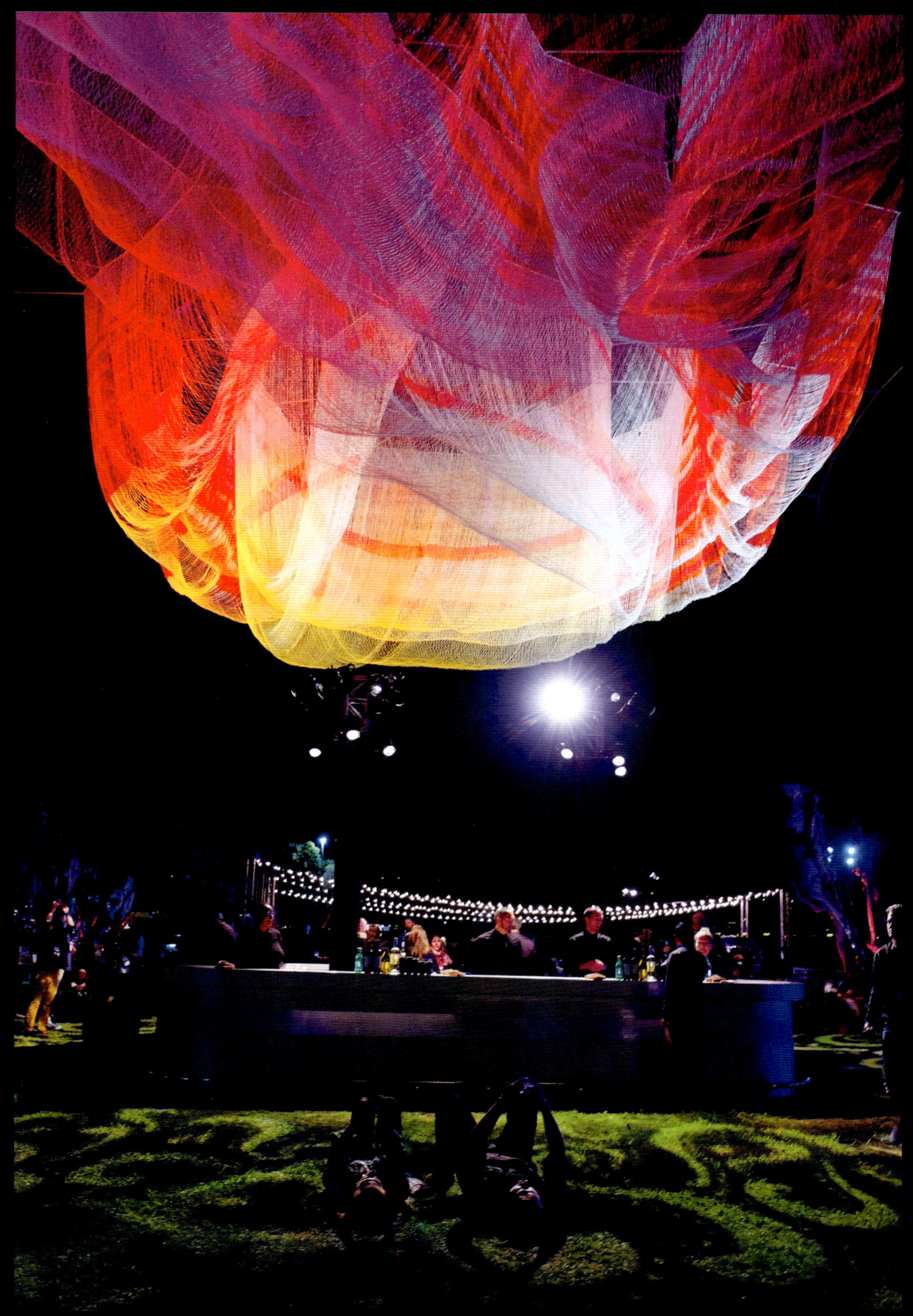

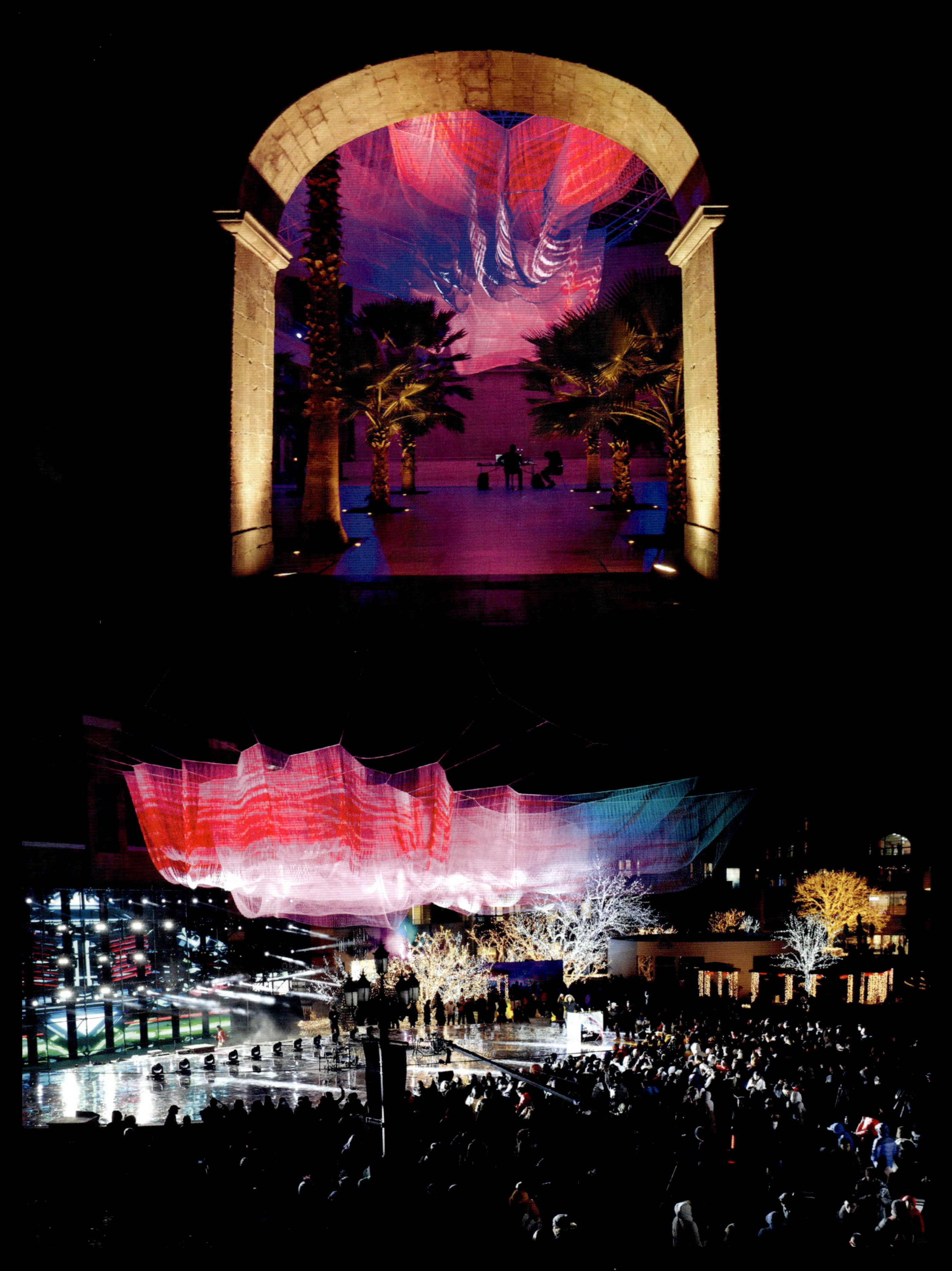

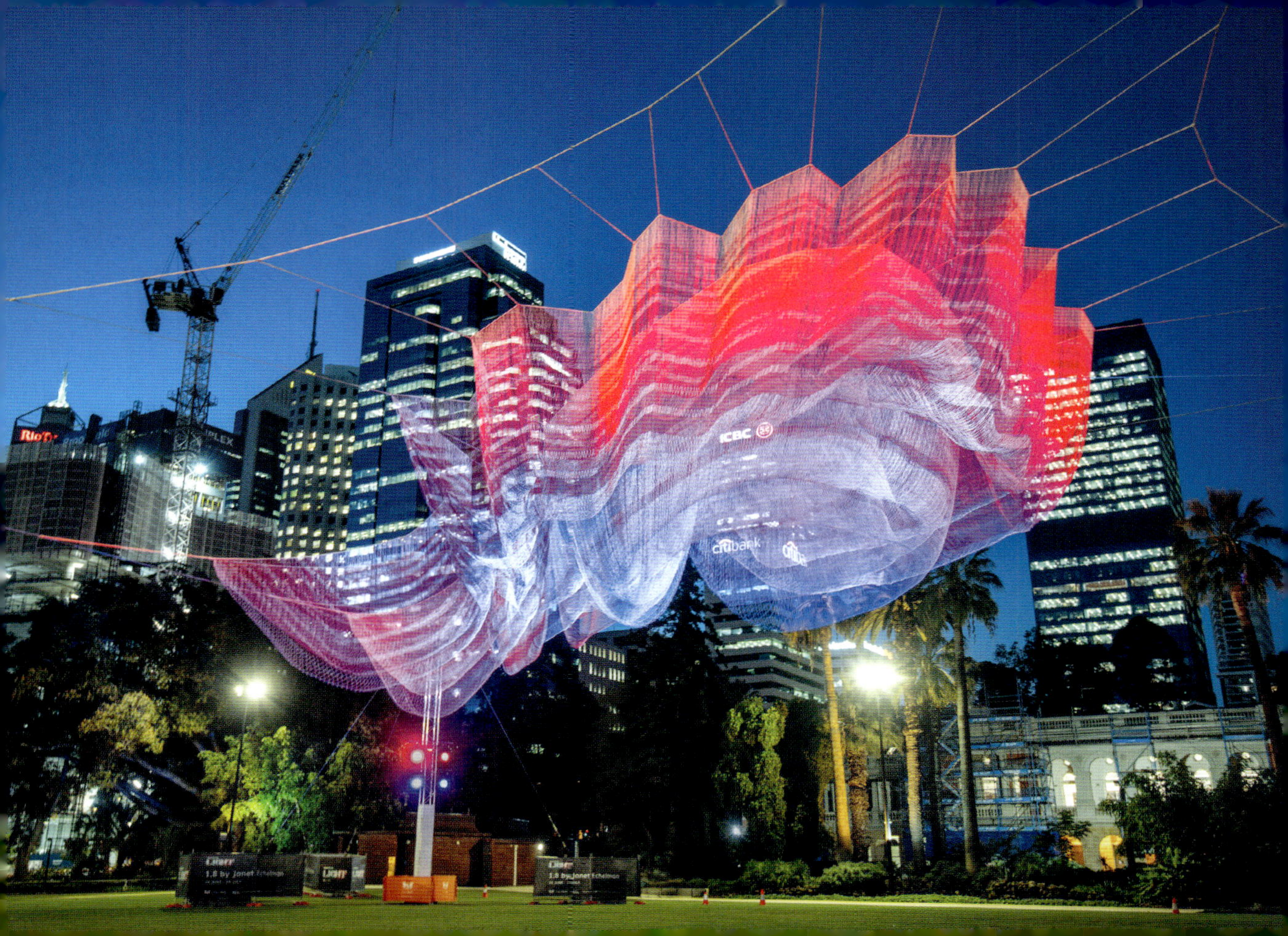
ICBC
citibank

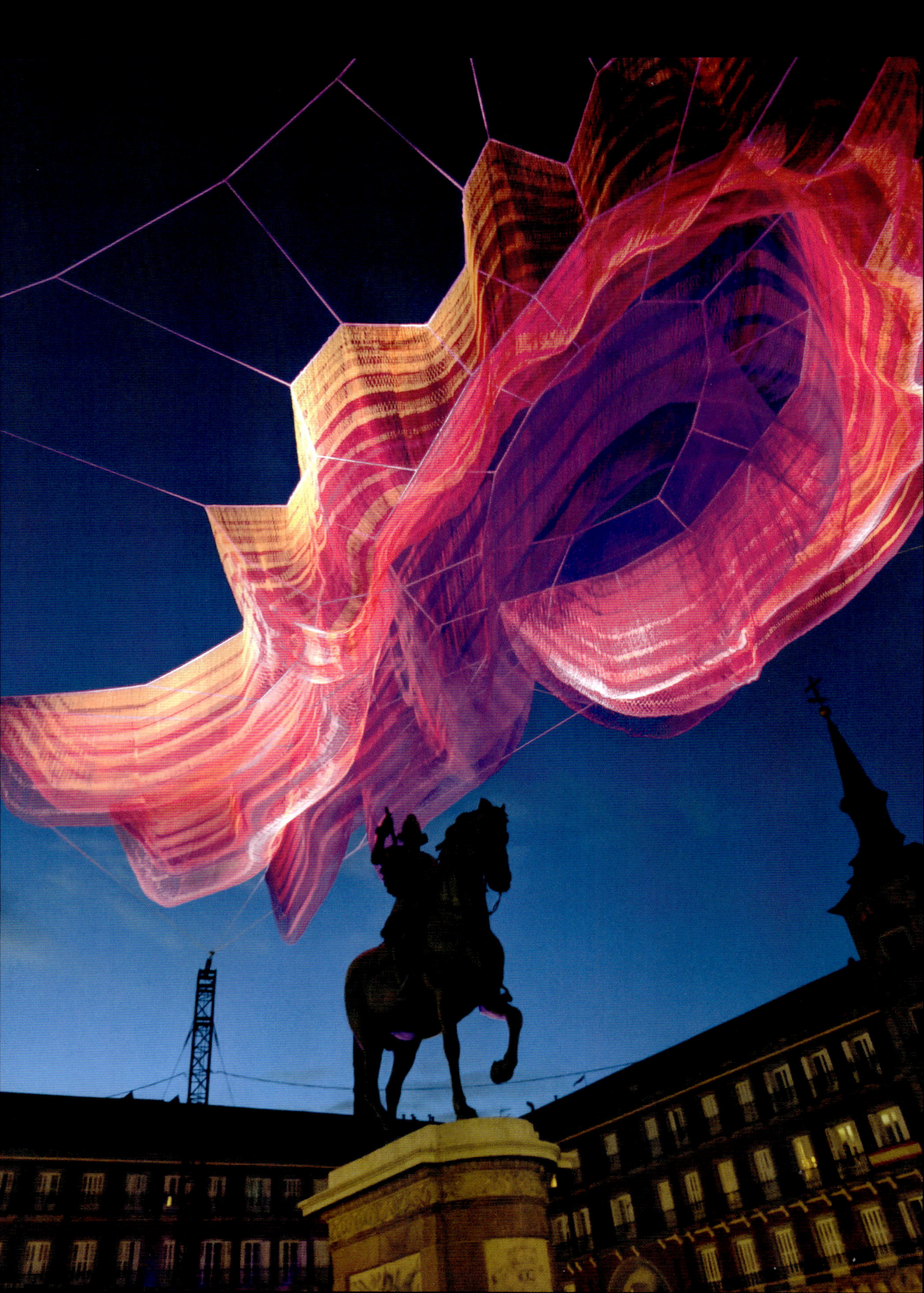

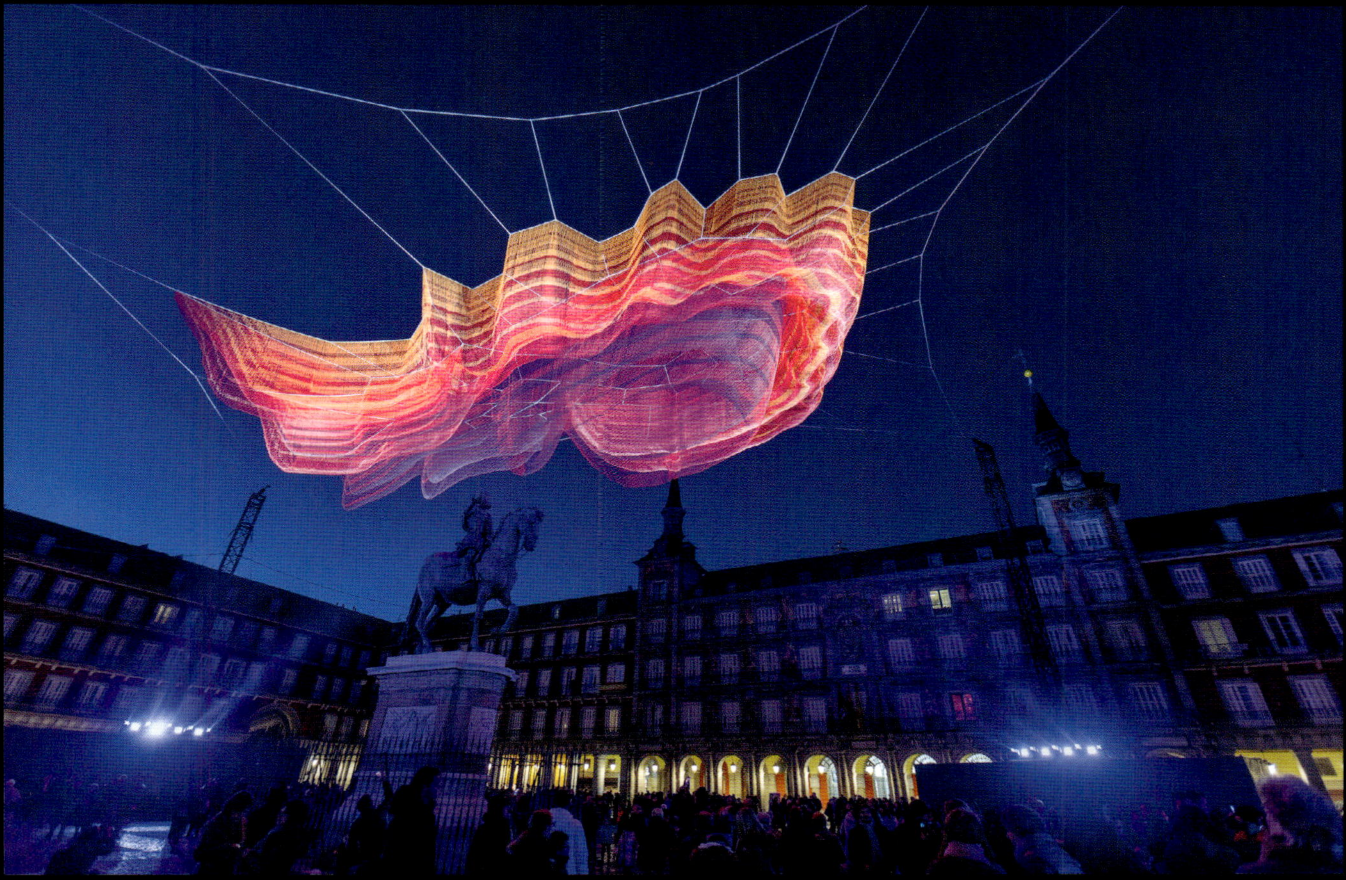

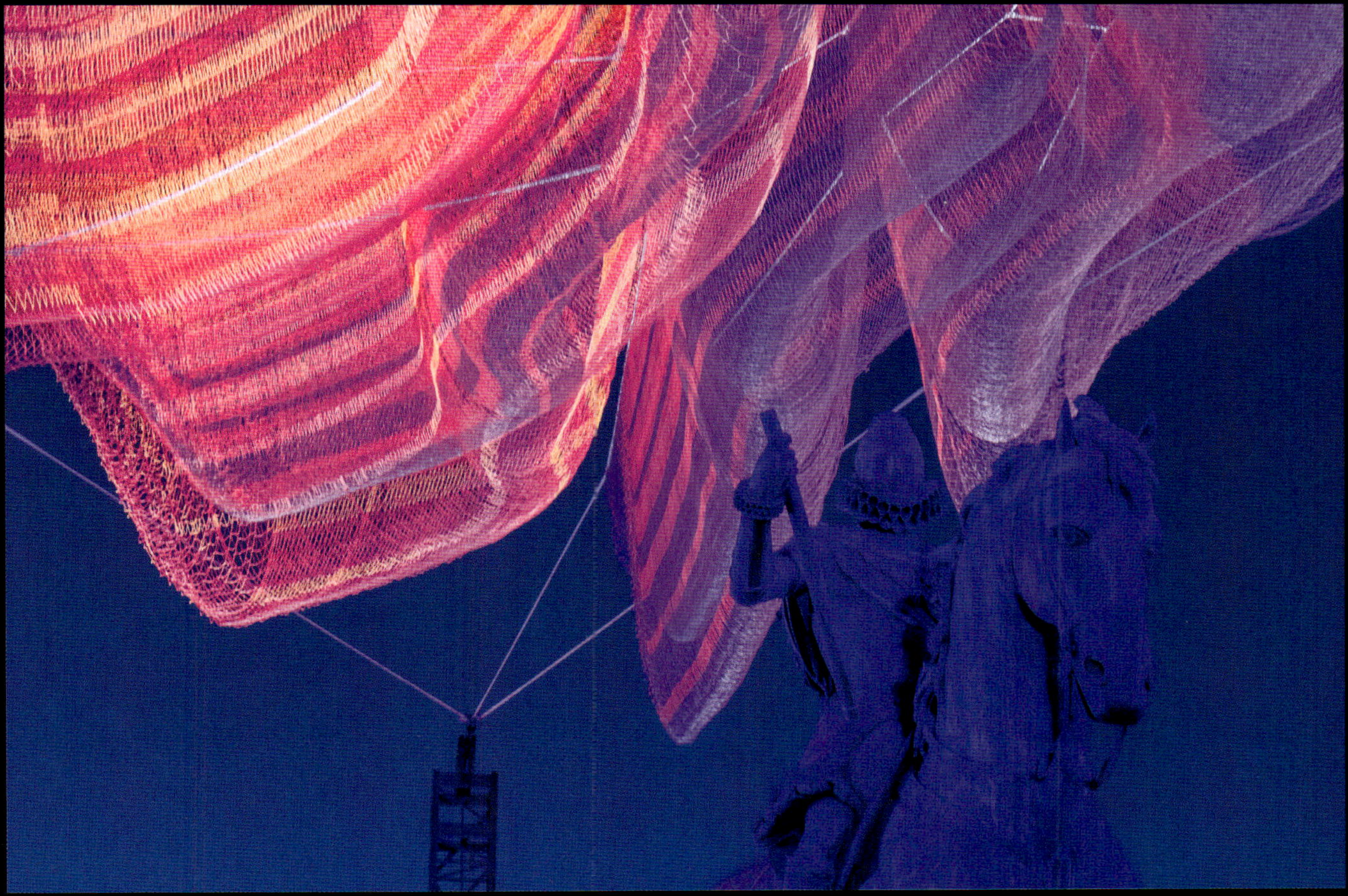

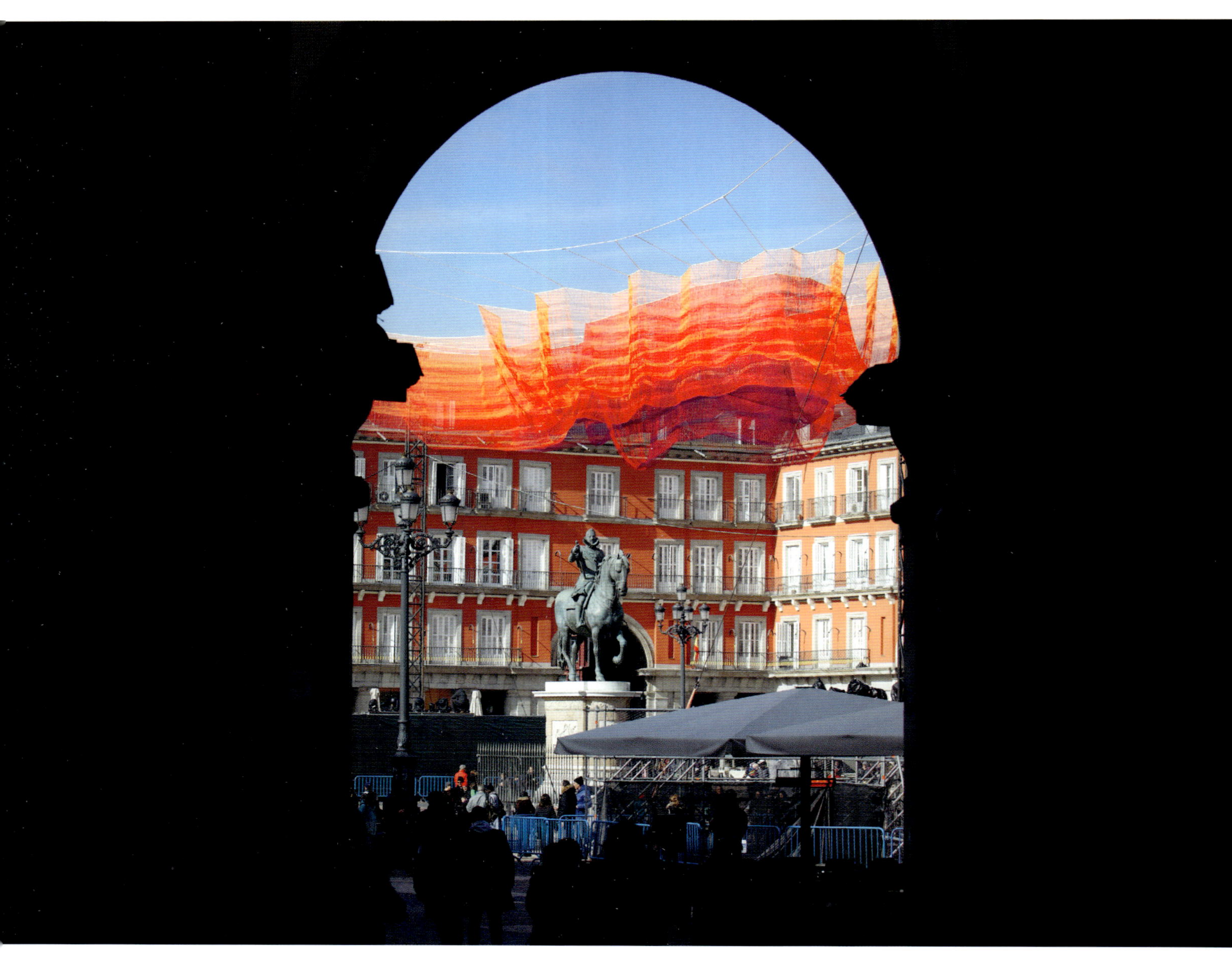

previous, above, and opposite: *Earthtime 1.78 Madrid*, 2018, Spain

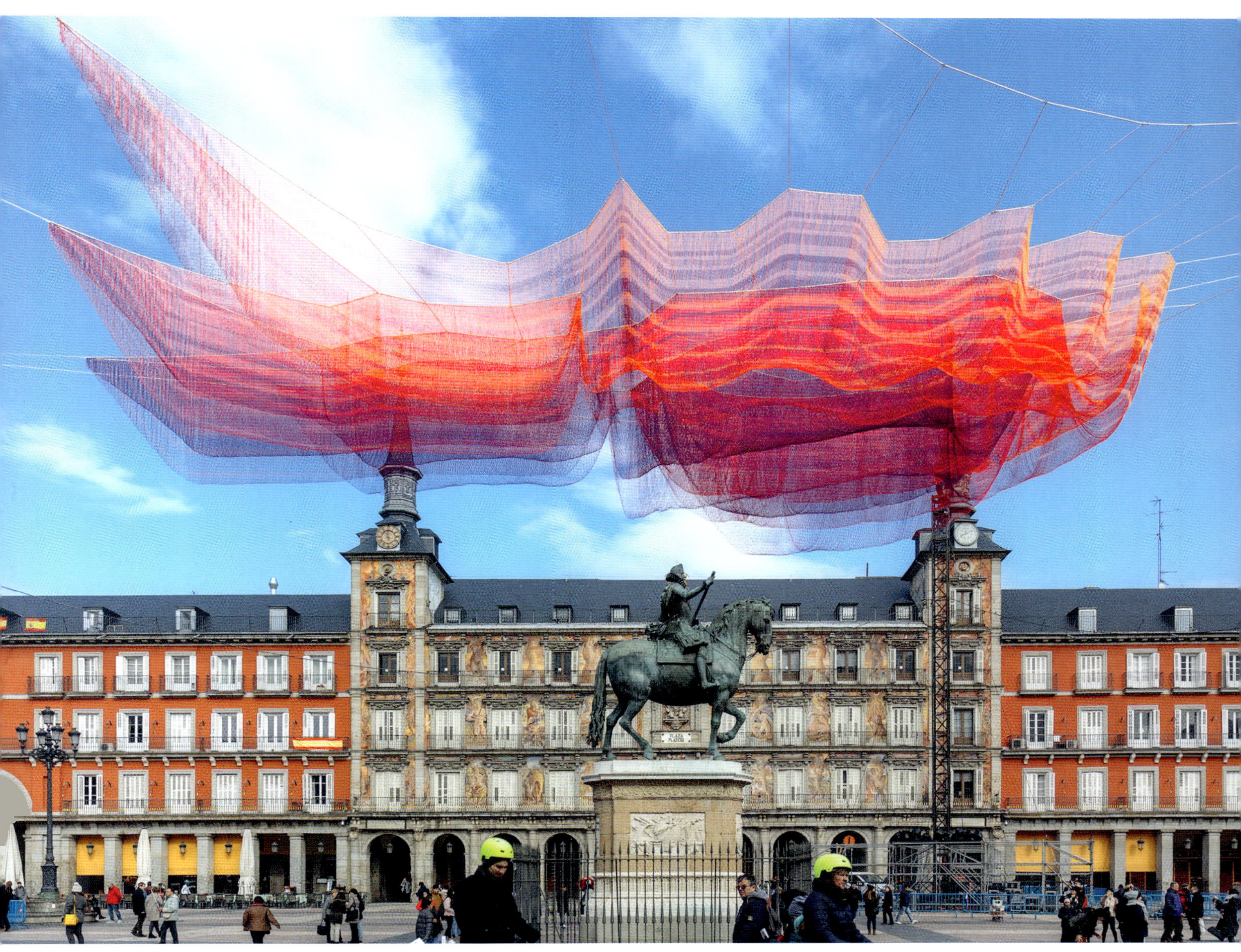

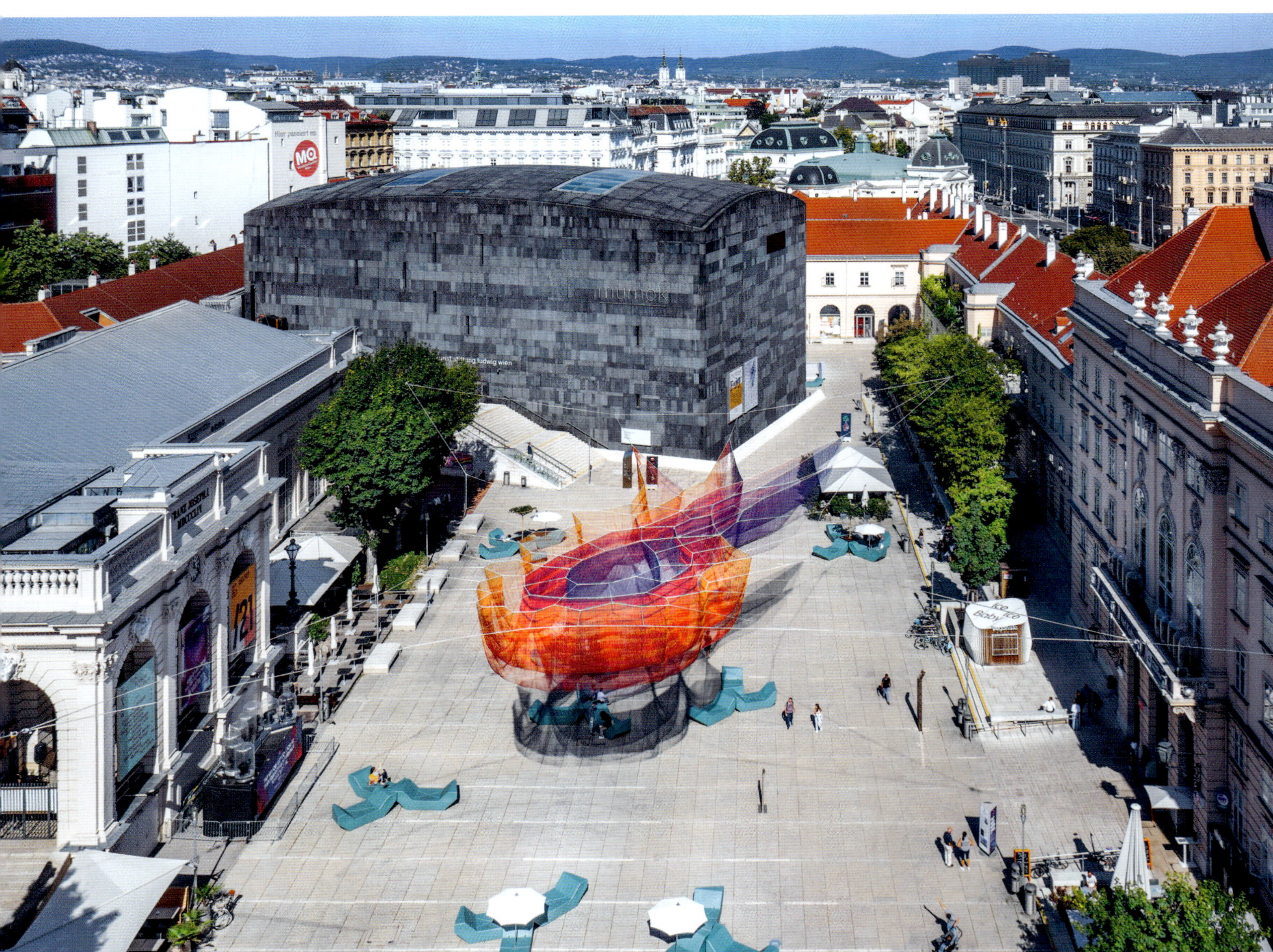

above and opposite: *Earthtime 1.78 Vienna*, 2021, Austria

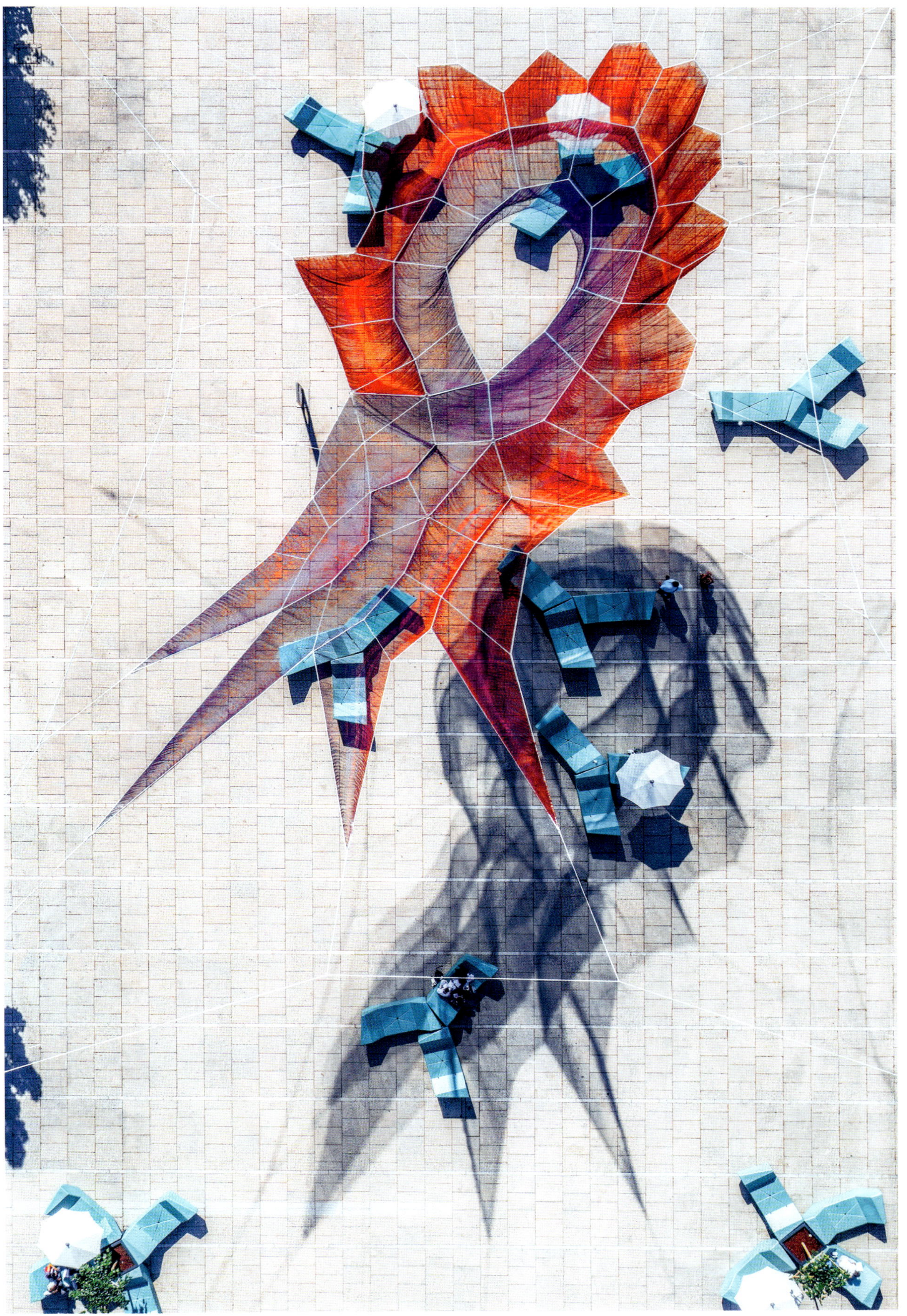

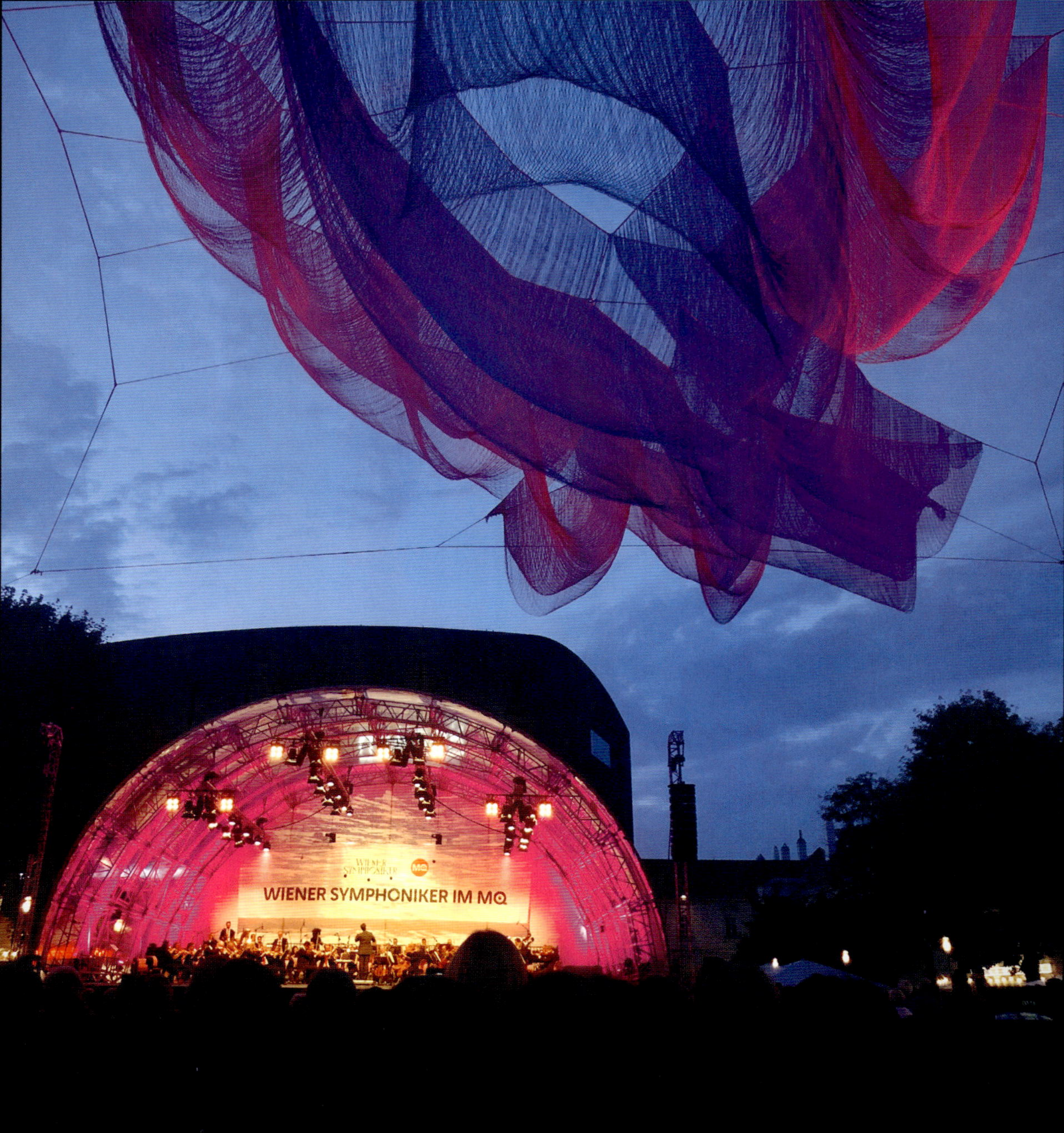

above and opposite: *Earthtime 1.78 Vienna*, 2021

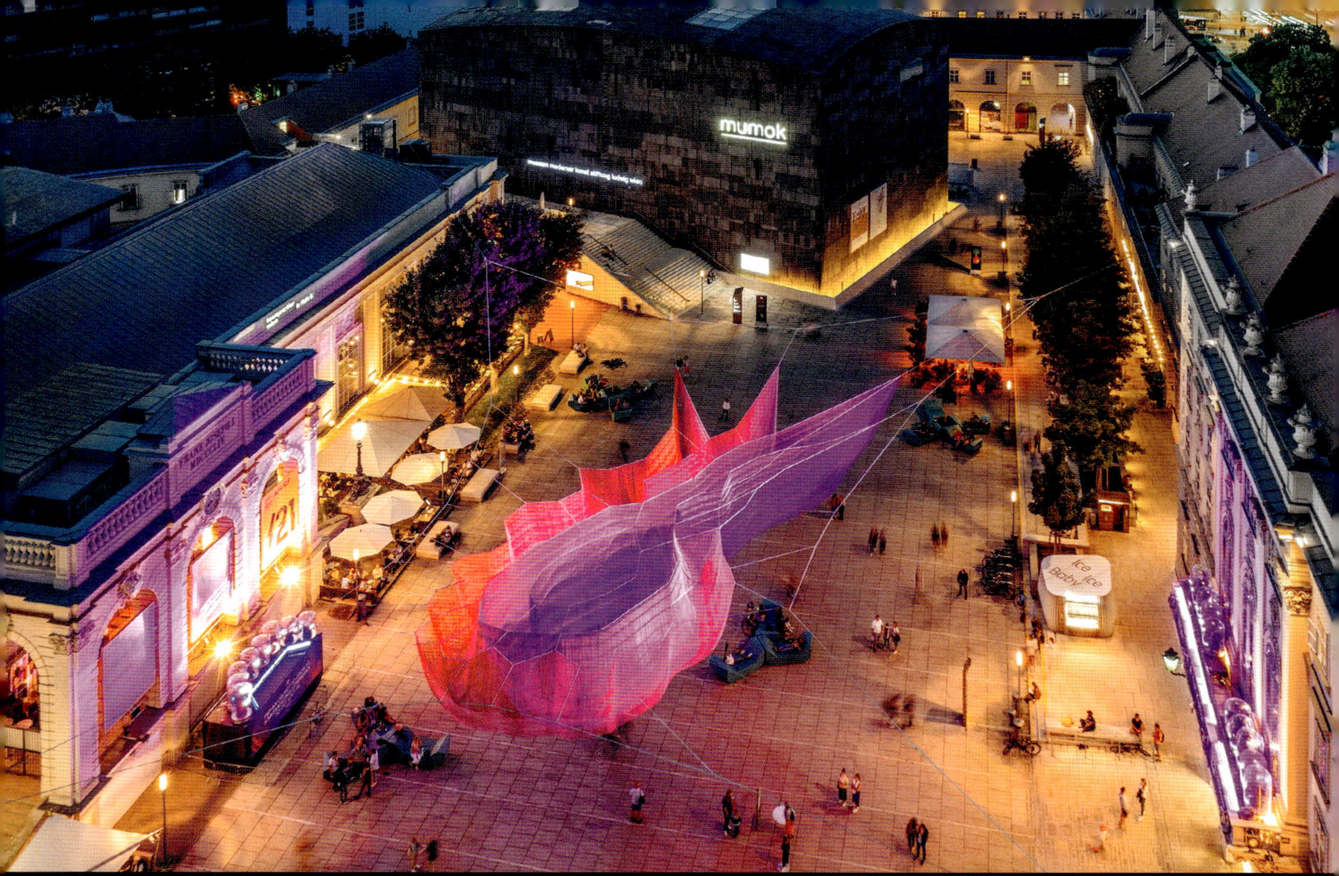

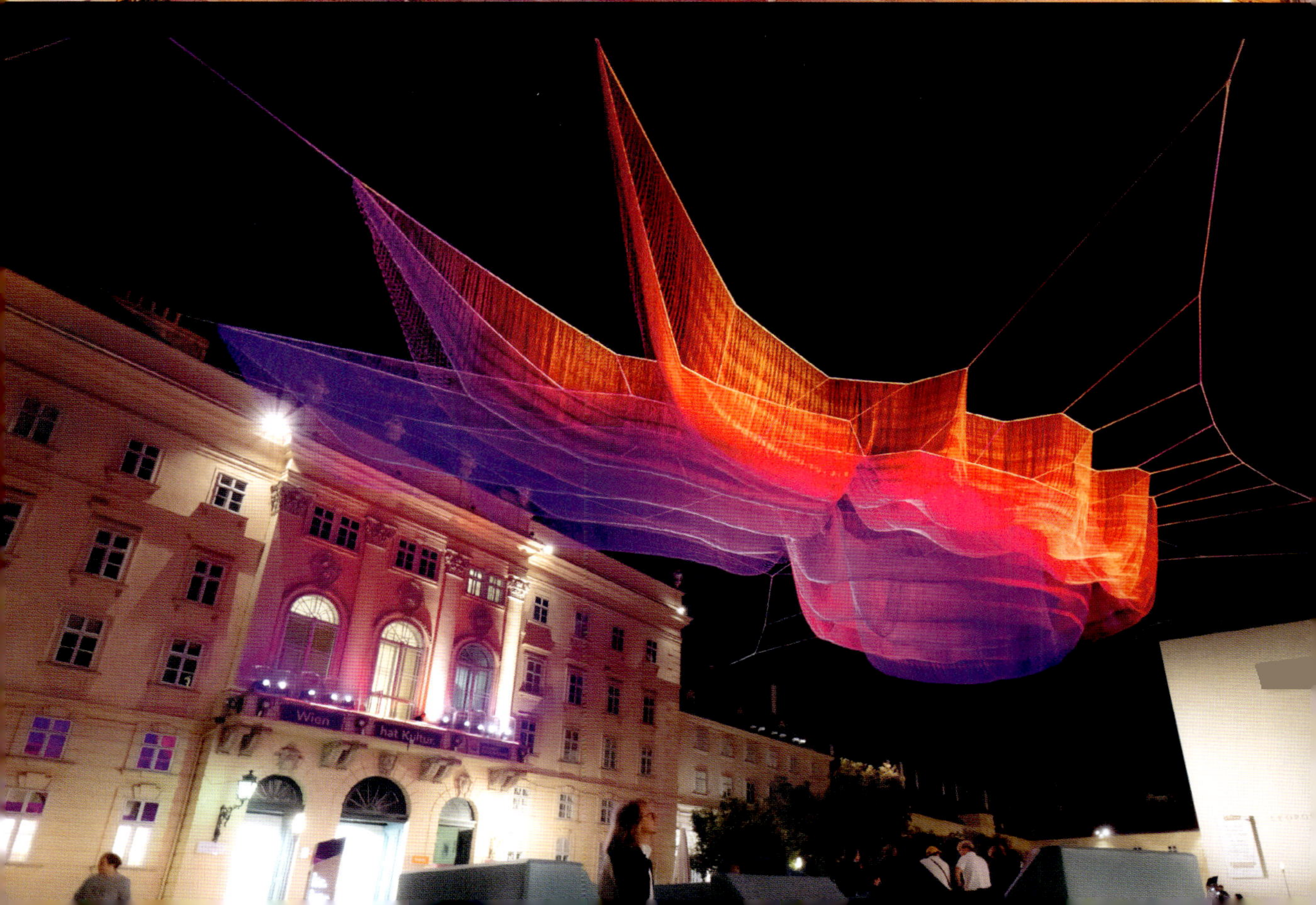

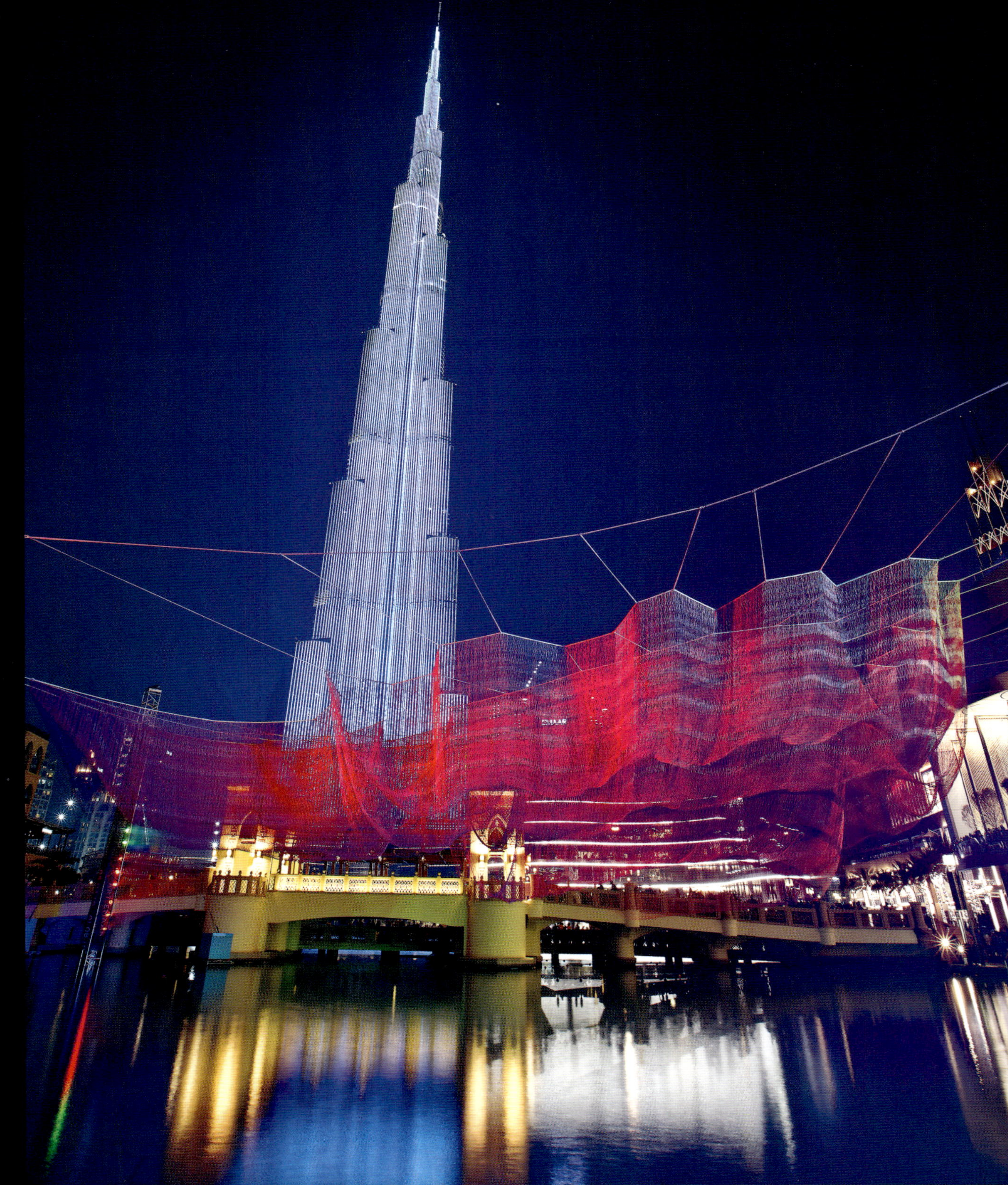

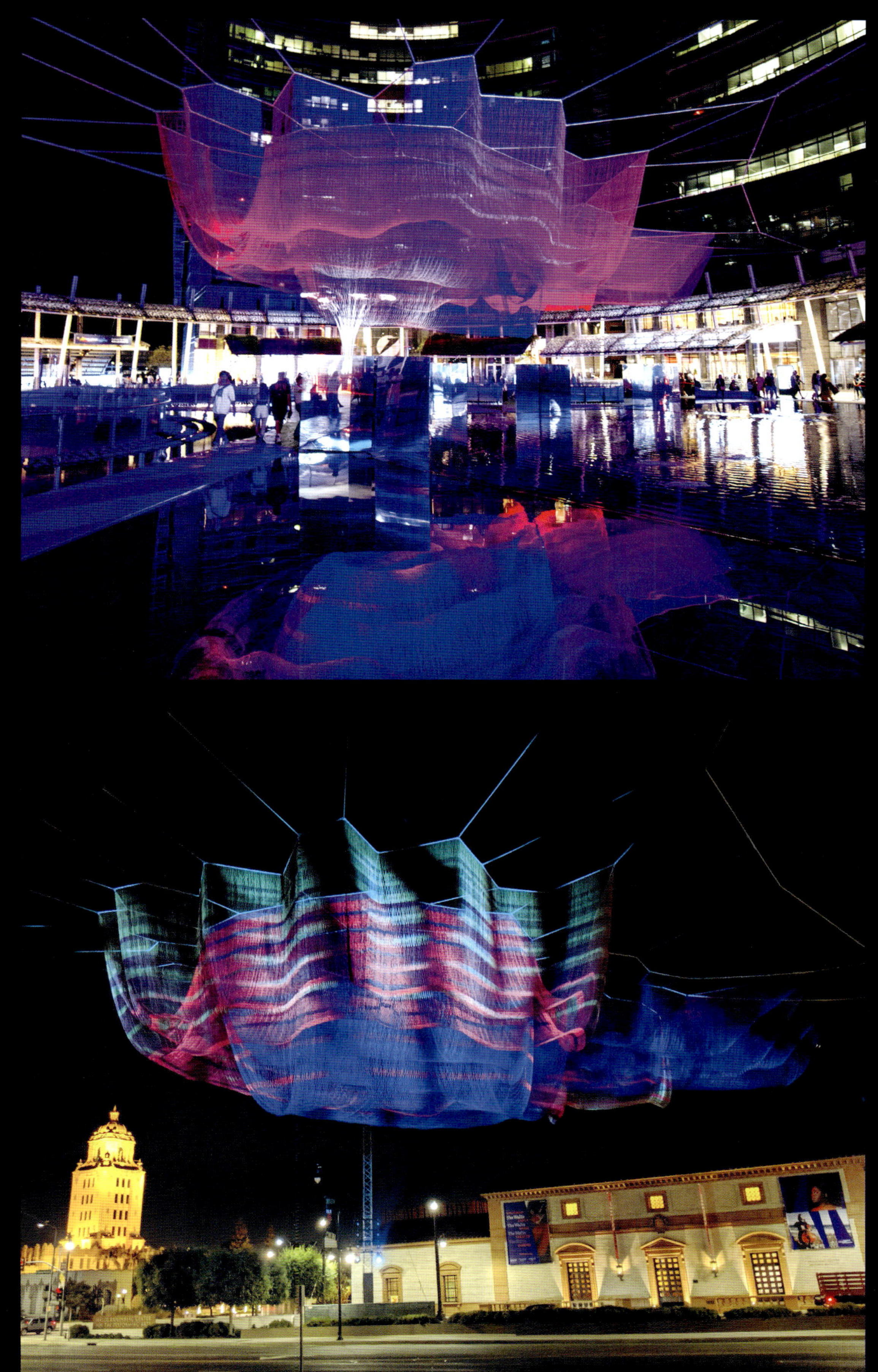
The Wallis
The Wallis
The Wallis

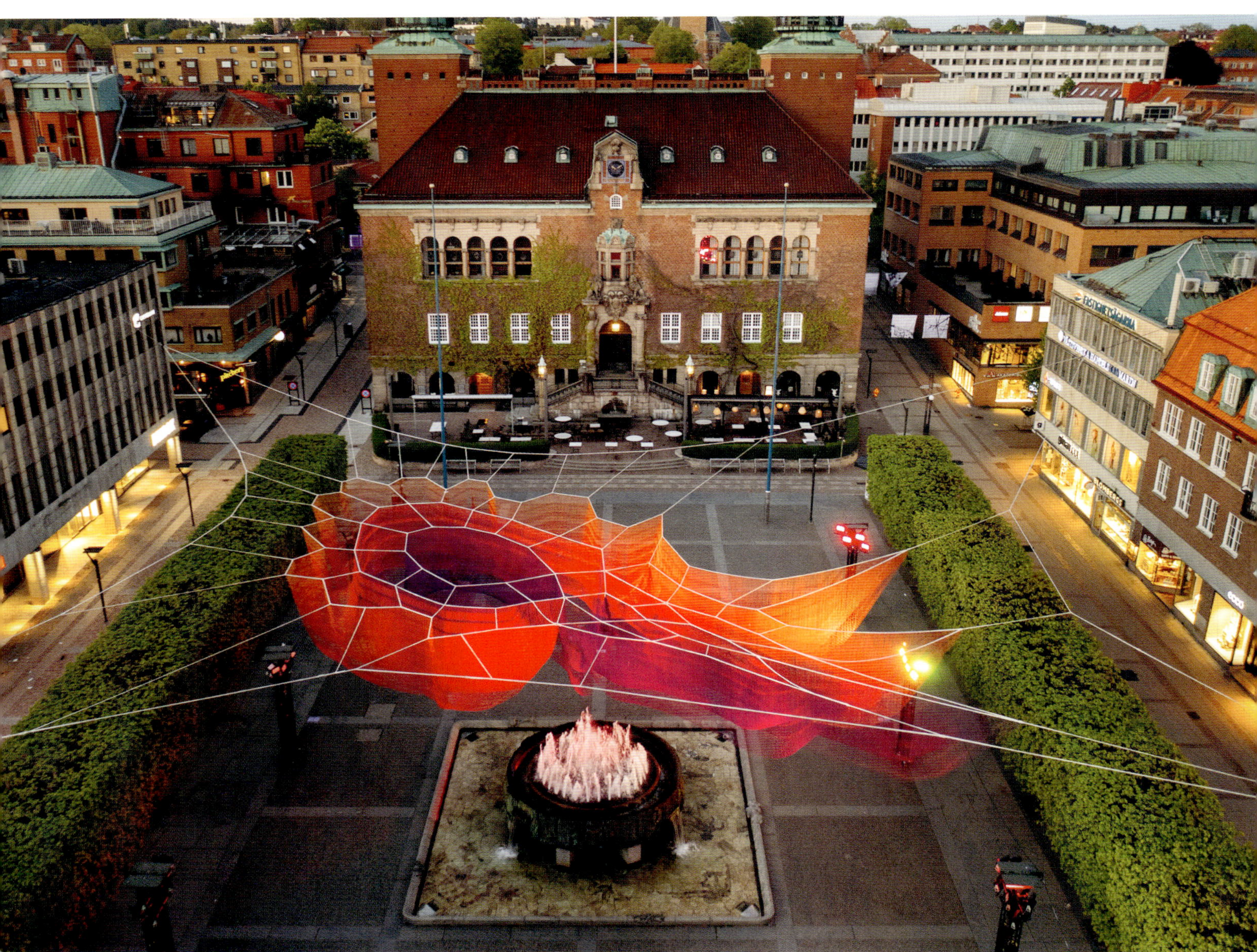

previous spread
p. 148: *Earthtime 1.78 Dubai*, 2018, UAE
p. 149, top: *Earthtime 1.78 Milan*, 2022, Italy
p. 149, bottom: *Earthtime 1.78 Beverly Hills*, 2019, California

above and opposite: *Earthtime 1.78 Borås*, 2021, Sweden

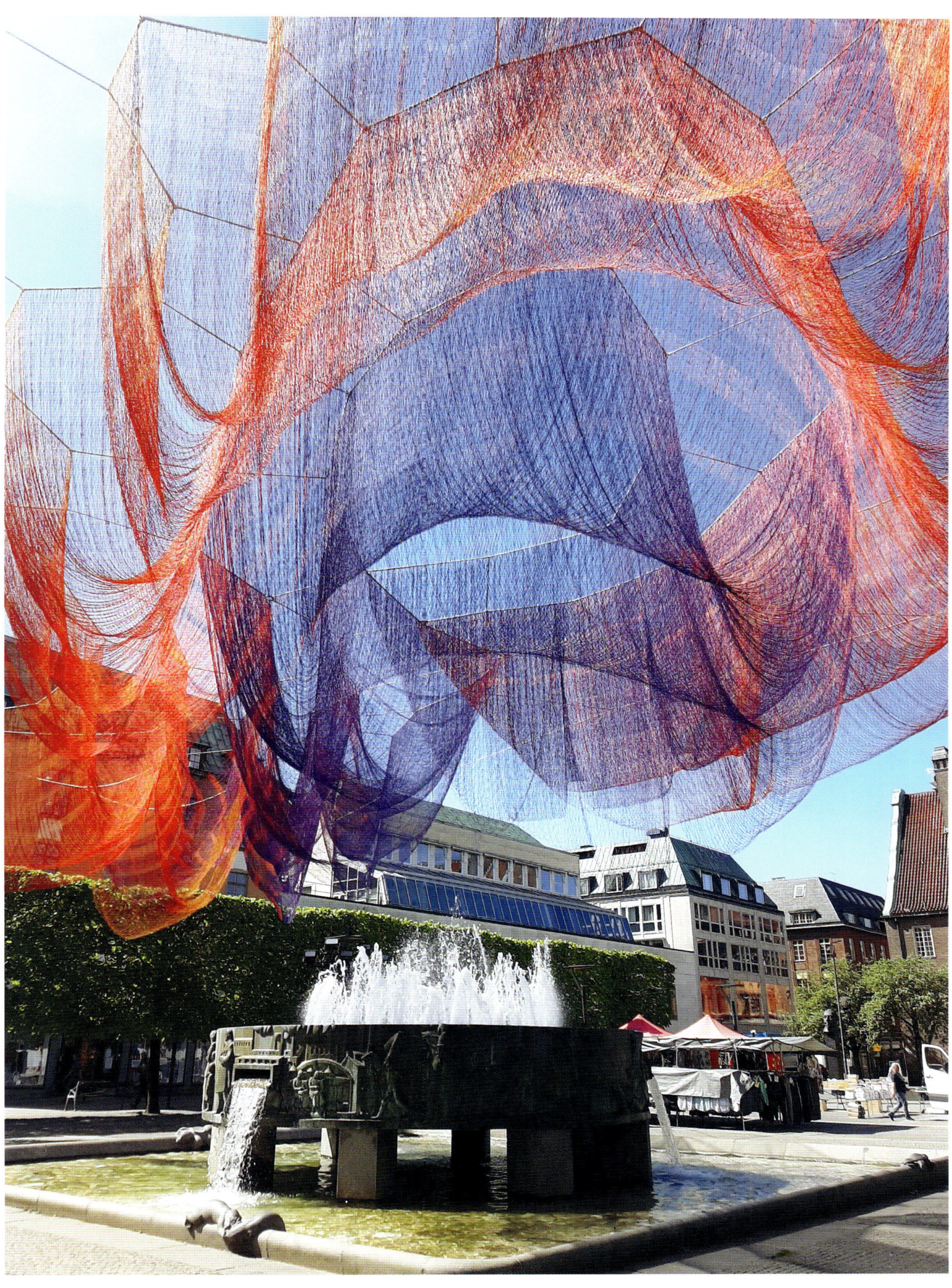

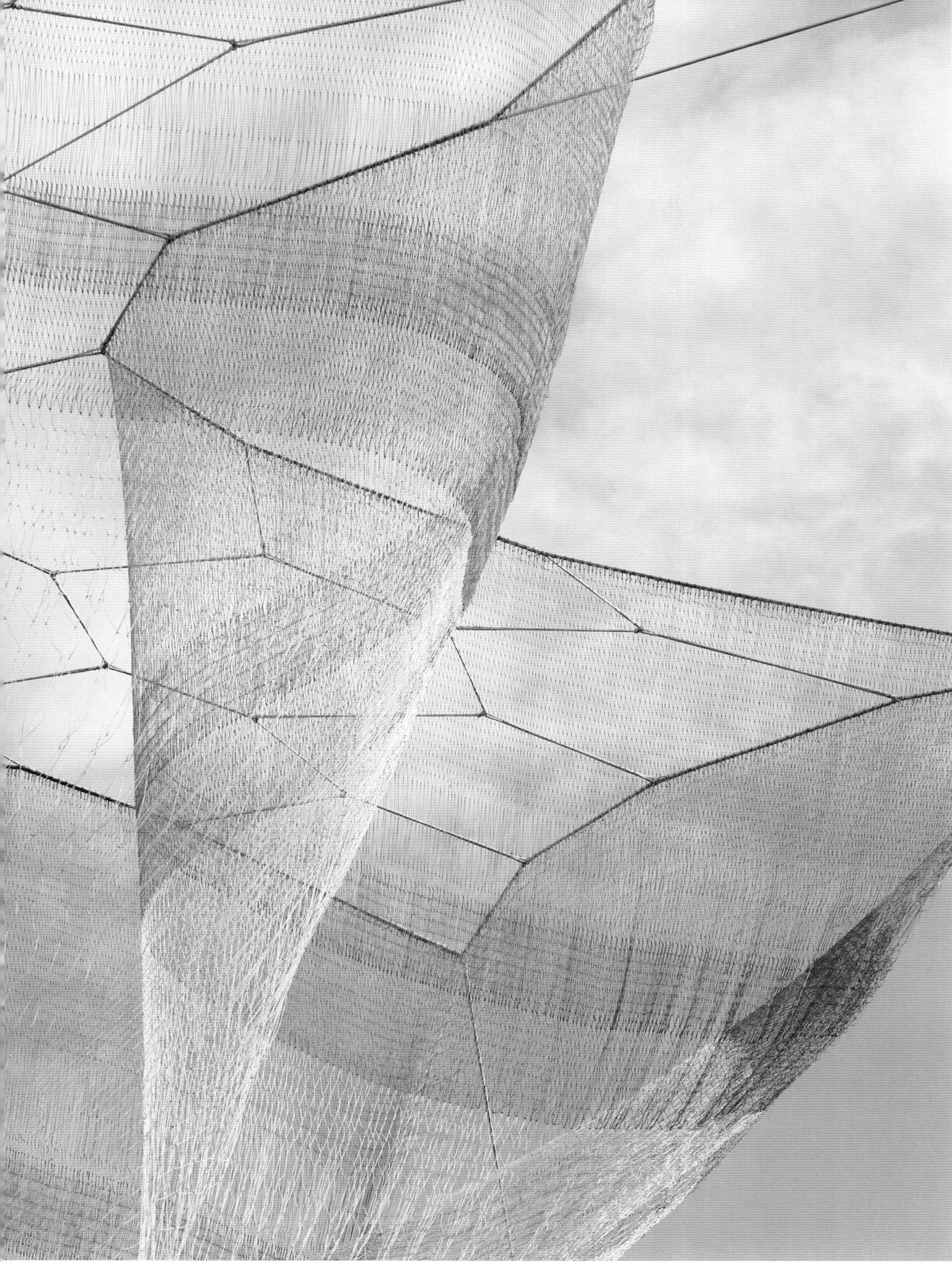

Impatient Optimist

—

Melinda Gates
and Janet Echelman
in conversation

Asked to express the spirit of the Bill & Melinda Gates Foundation's work and mission in a sculpture, and to create a heart for its twelve-acre campus in downtown Seattle, Studio Echelman created *Impatient Optimist* (2015). Composed of ultralightweight fibers that create an ephemeral presence, the piece is suspended between two buildings and is visible at all times from the campus overlook, as well as from several vantage points nearby. During the day, the sculpture's hues interplay with the changing colors of the sky. At night it becomes an illuminated beacon, as colored lighting sequences are projected in real time as the sun rises in each of the foundation's offices elsewhere around the globe. This connects the work happening on the Seattle campus to the tangible services being delivered to people around the world.

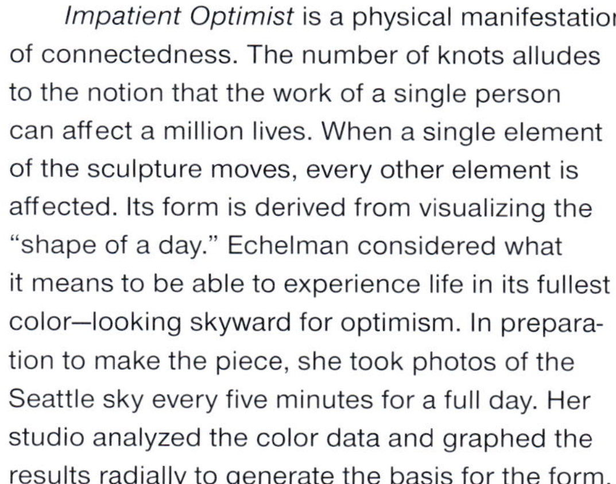

Impatient Optimist is a physical manifestation of connectedness. The number of knots alludes to the notion that the work of a single person can affect a million lives. When a single element of the sculpture moves, every other element is affected. Its form is derived from visualizing the "shape of a day." Echelman considered what it means to be able to experience life in its fullest color—looking skyward for optimism. In preparation to make the piece, she took photos of the Seattle sky every five minutes for a full day. Her studio analyzed the color data and graphed the results radially to generate the basis for the form.

Melinda Gates: The design of the Seattle campus intentionally includes art throughout. And we wanted an iconic artwork in the campus heart that celebrates the impact of foundation employees here in our Seattle home, and around the world in our global offices.

Janet Echelman: I was intimidated by the importance and ambition of the mission of this foundation, and wondered how could I give form to something so important. I kept trying to understand the mission in terms of people, and the people whose lives are impacted.

MG: Your work is visually stunning, first and foremost. This particular sculpture captures the spirit of how we try to work at the foundation. You start with an unlikely everyday material like fishing nets, use deep local knowledge of the fishermen, and build on that through intensive collaboration with structural and lighting engineers and fabricators to create something that's completely different.

JE: The sculptures I've been creating all around the world are made by hand and machine here in Washington State. So, every piece in every country happens to come from this place.

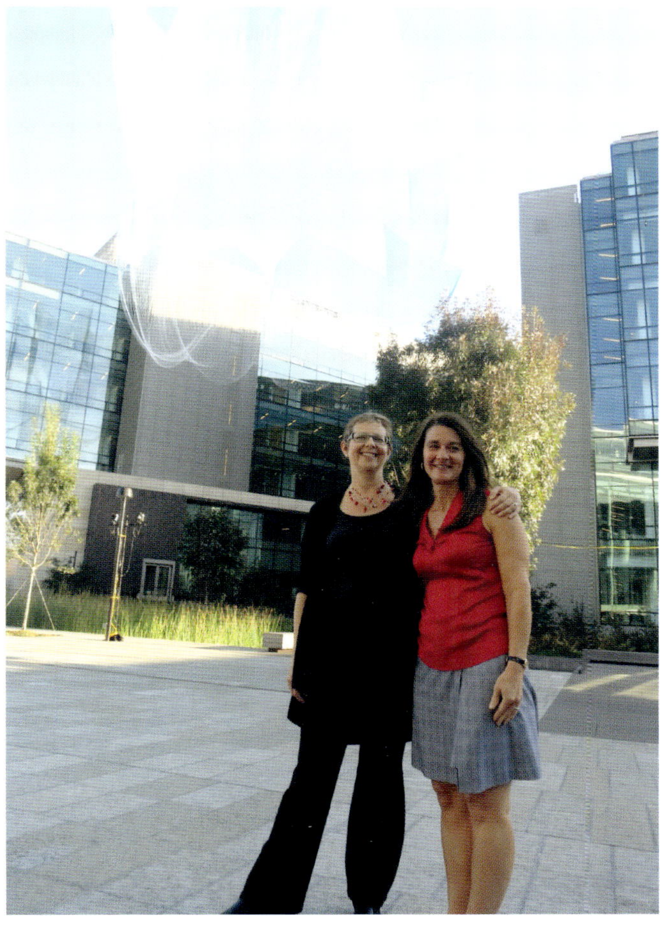

opposite: *Impatient Optimist*, 2015, Bill & Melinda Gates Foundation, Seattle, Washington
left: Echelman and Melinda Gates review a full-scale mock-up for *Impatient Optimist*, 2015

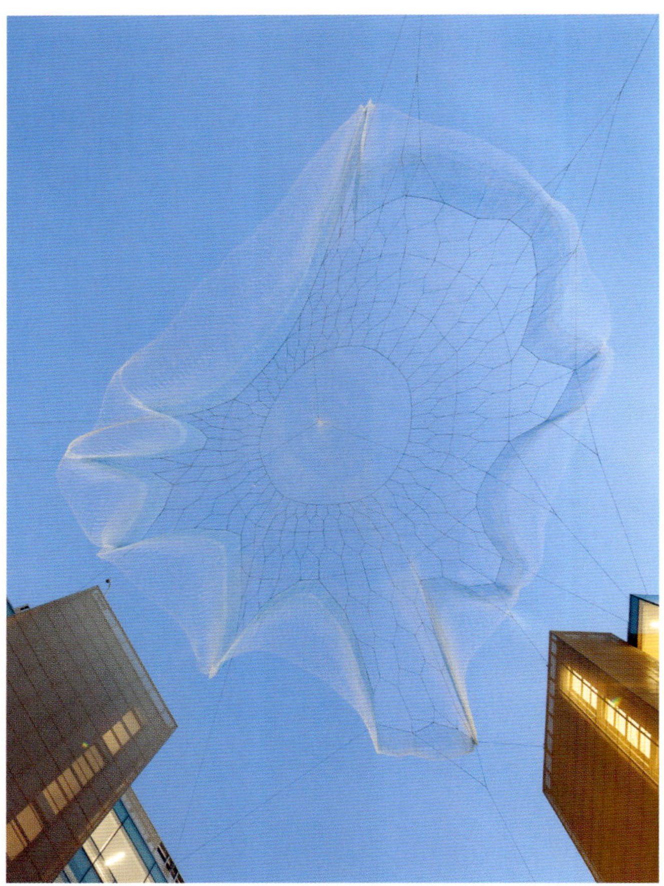

MG: This piece is a reflection of our foundation's roots here in Washington State, and our commitment to this community. And so it was really important to us that the art piece not just be viewable from inside the foundation buildings, but from many vantage points, including the Seattle Center and the neighborhoods just around it.

JE: I wanted the work to be about a sense of generosity. Everyone here is giving so much of themselves, and I wanted the sculpture to give back. Every time you look at it, I hope it's changing, and different, and like a good relationship, always unfolding. It's the first time I've been able to create a sculpture that suspends between buildings to create a structure that is incredibly light and delicate, yet immensely strong and resilient. Strength through resiliency, and the ability to change with changing conditions, is in the spirit of this place and this mission.

Melinda Gates is a philanthropist, businesswoman, and global advocate.

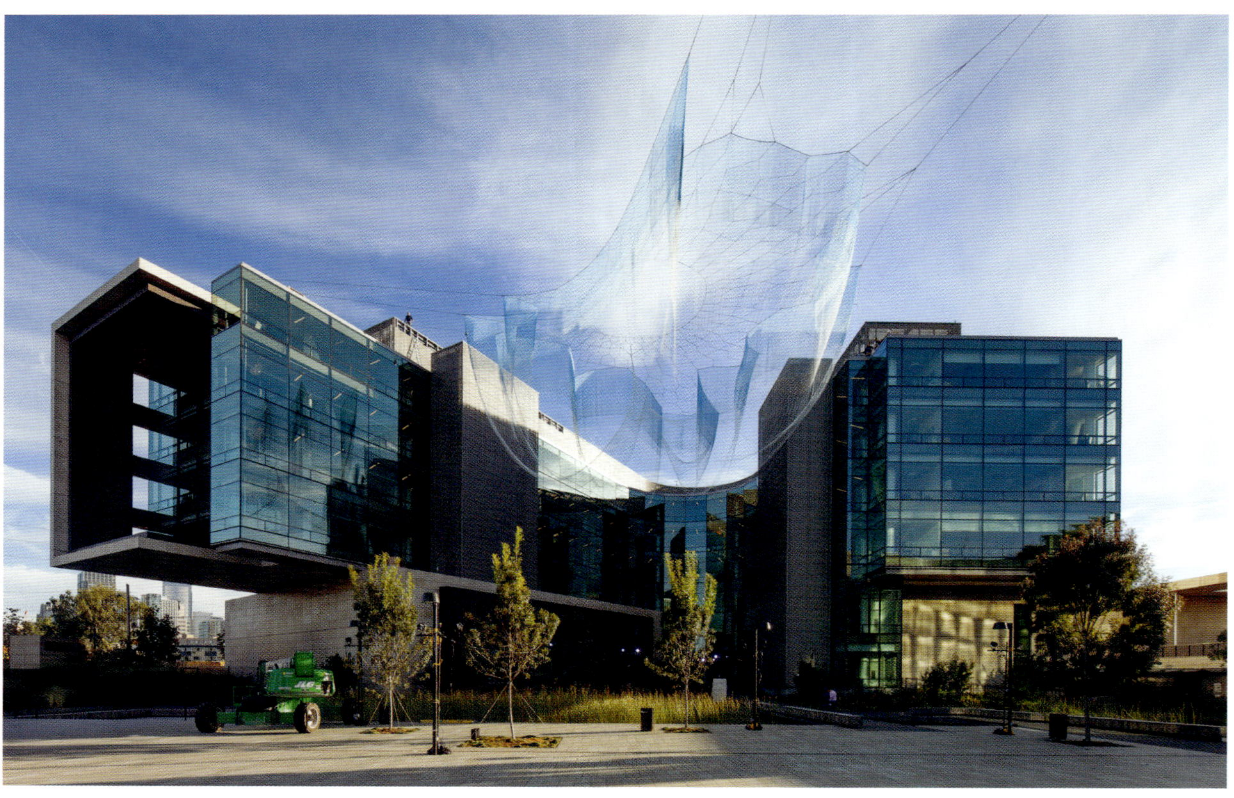

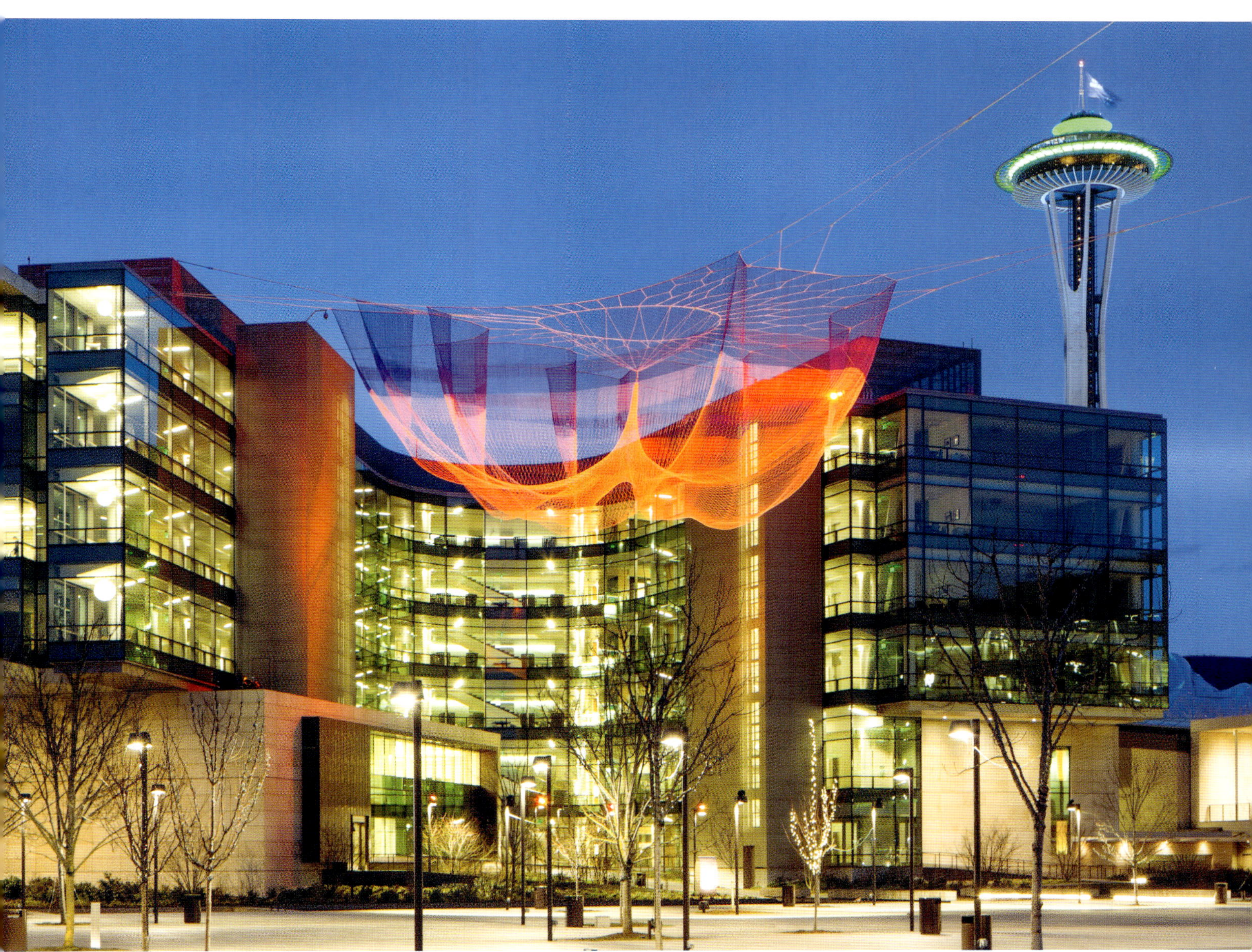

opposite and above: *Impatient Optimist*, 2015

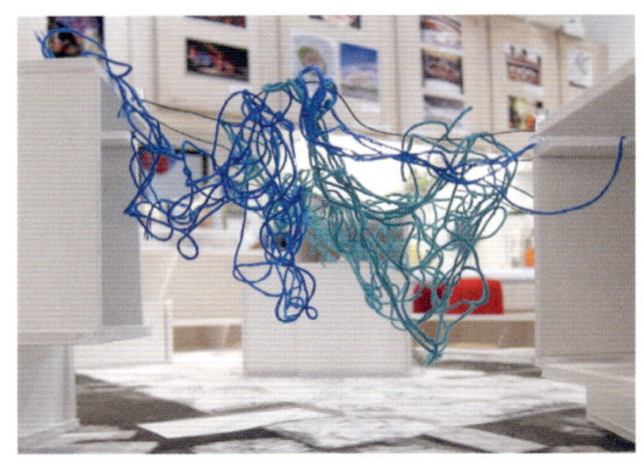

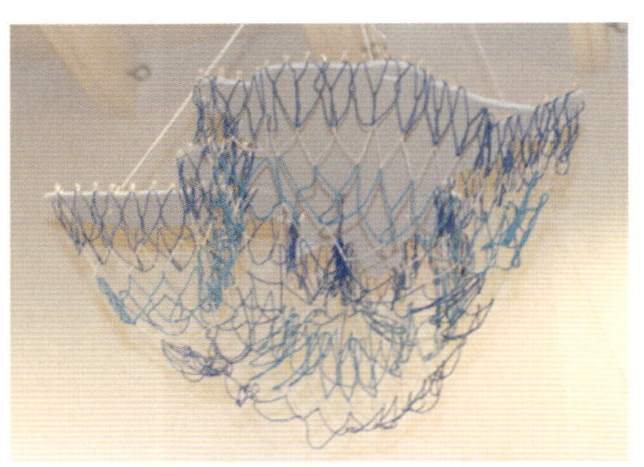

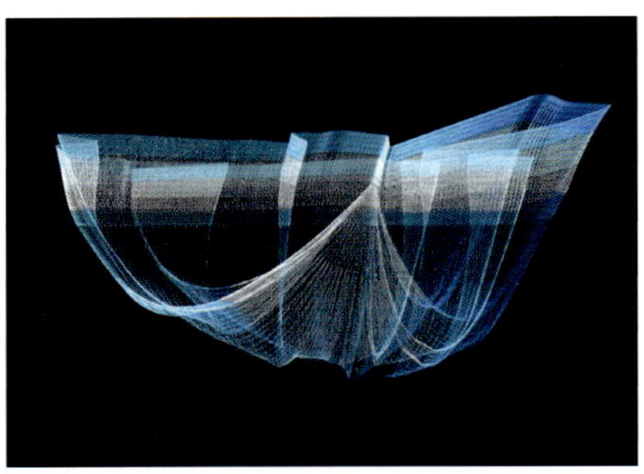

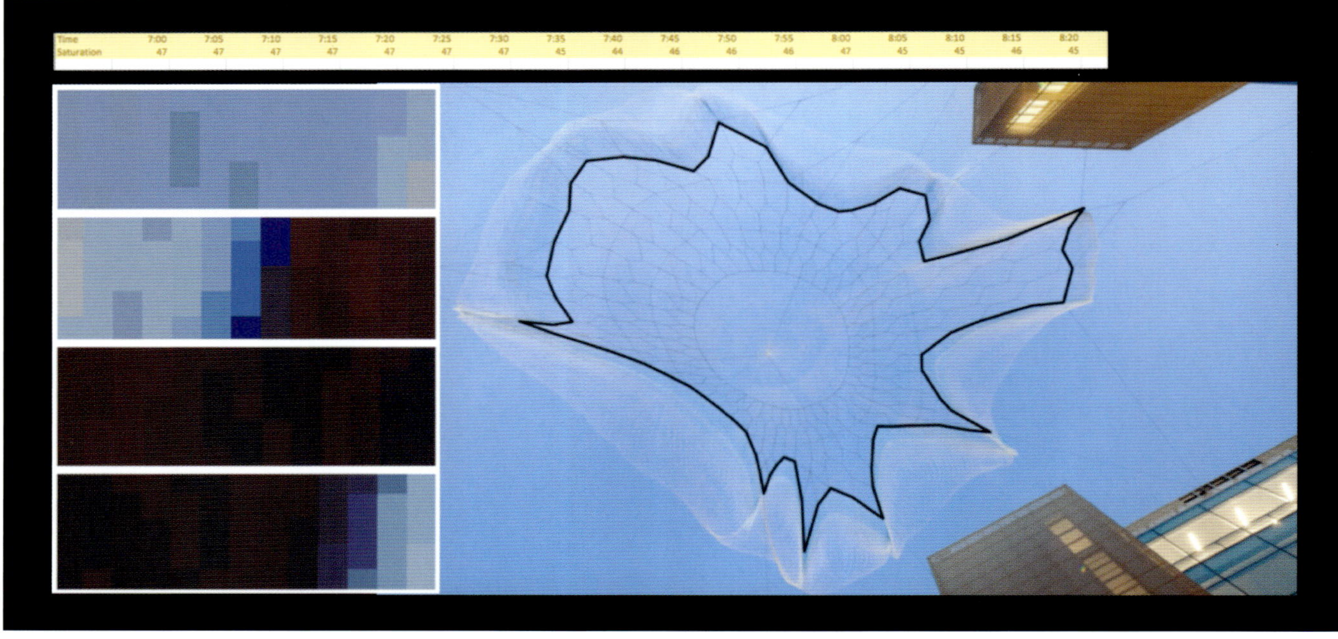

Time	7:00	7:05	7:10	7:15	7:20	7:25	7:30	7:35	7:40	7:45	7:50	7:55	8:00	8:05	8:10	8:15	8:20
Saturation	47	47	47	47	47	47	47	45	44	46	46	46	47	45	45	46	45

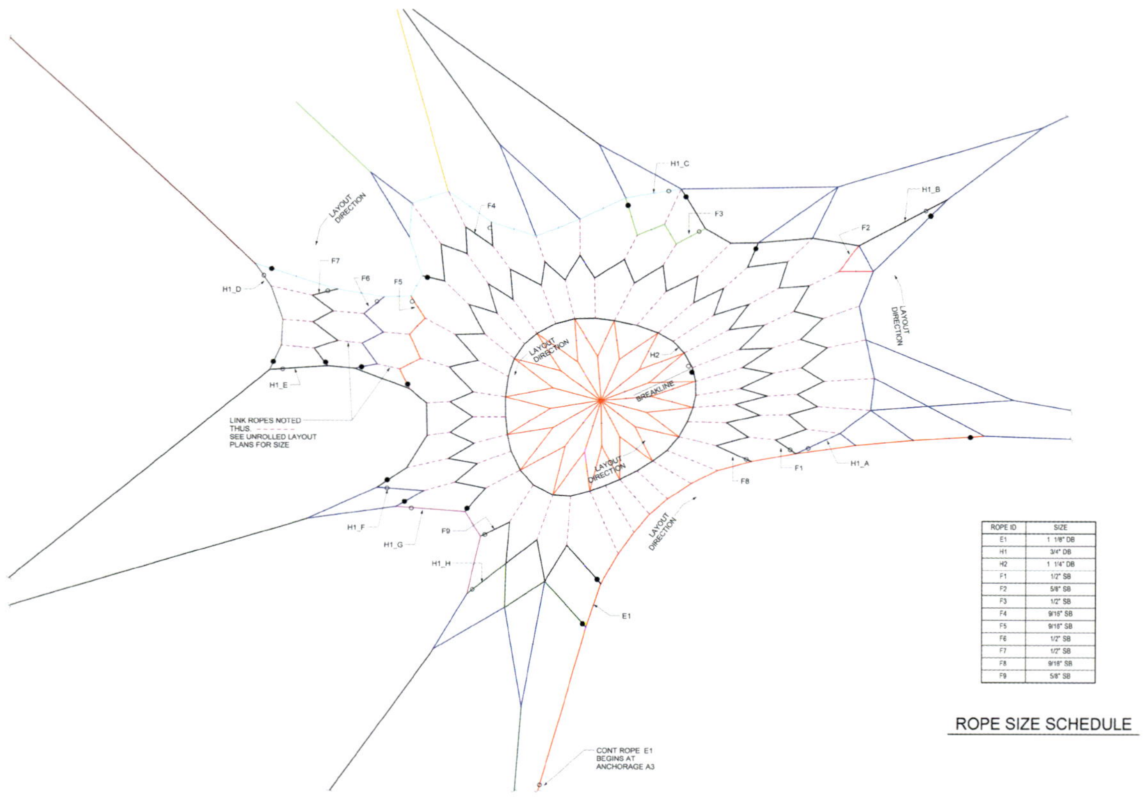

ROPE ID	SIZE
E1	1 1/8" DB
H1	3/4" DB
H2	1 1/4" DB
F1	1/2" SB
F2	5/8" SB
F3	1/2" SB
F4	9/16" SB
F5	9/16" SB
F6	1/2" SB
F7	1/2" SB
F8	9/16" SB
F9	5/8" SB

ROPE SIZE SCHEDULE

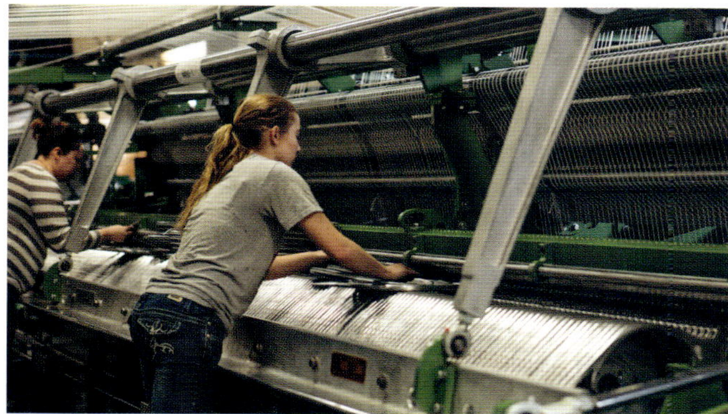
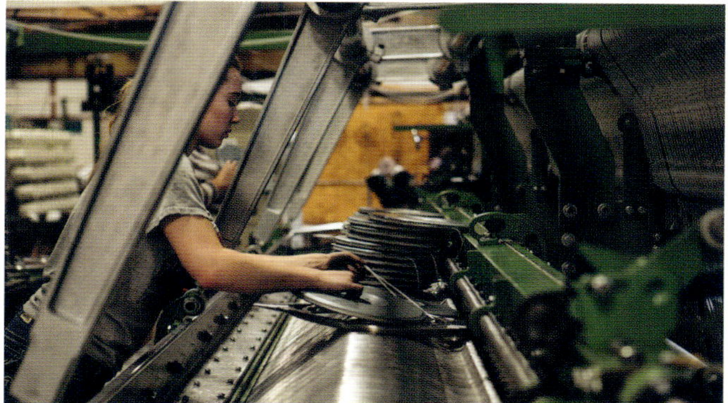
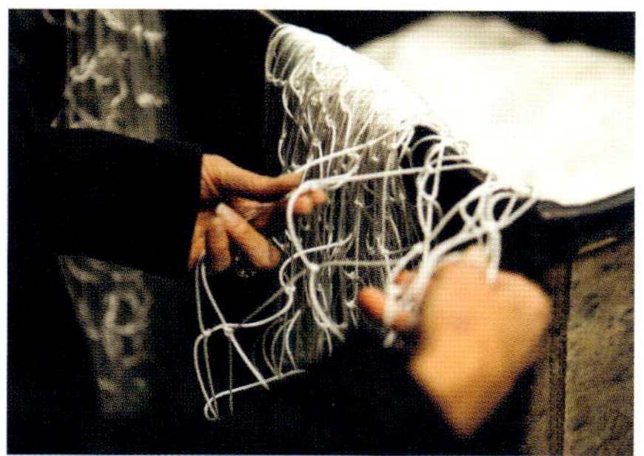
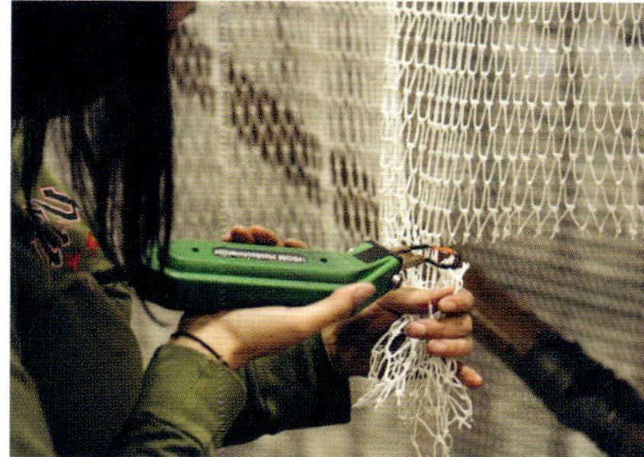
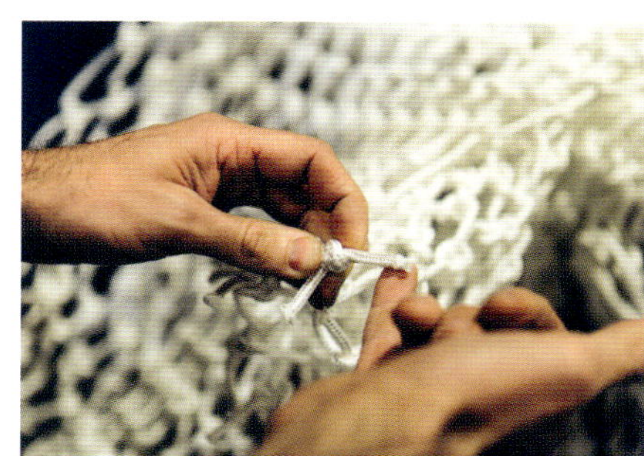
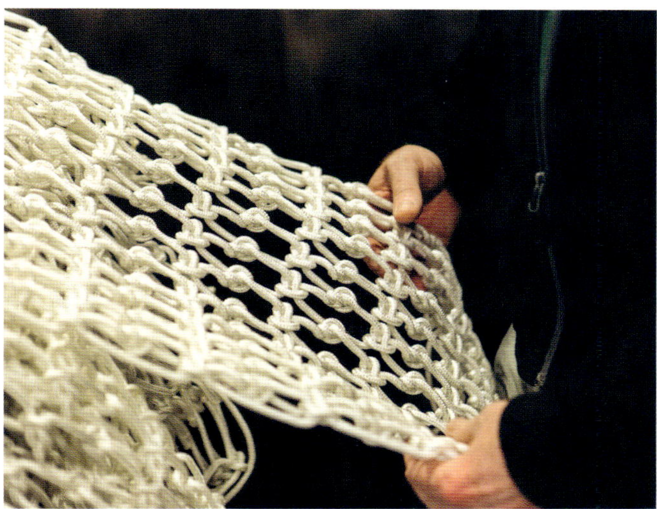
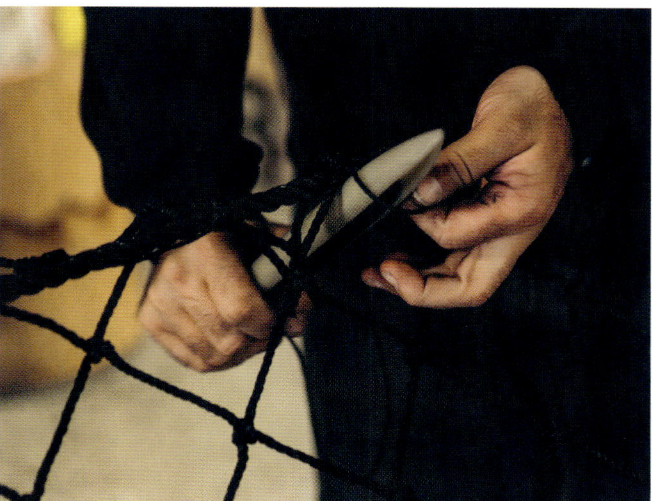

opposite, top row: Sketch model using wire and yarn; early model, hand-knotted yarn and laser-cut Plexiglas; 3D simulation using the studio's JNET software
opposite, middle: Echelman placed a camera on the Gates Foundation rooftop to photograph the sky every five minutes. Left side of image shows sky photos over a twenty-four-hour period; right side of image shows radial graphic of the RGB numeric values of the sky photos to generate a radial shape.
opposite, bottom: Engineering drawing for tensioned spliced-rope structure by Arup engineer Clayton Binkley

above: Hand and machine fabrication for *Impatient Optimist*, 2015
following pages: *Impatient Optimist*, 2015

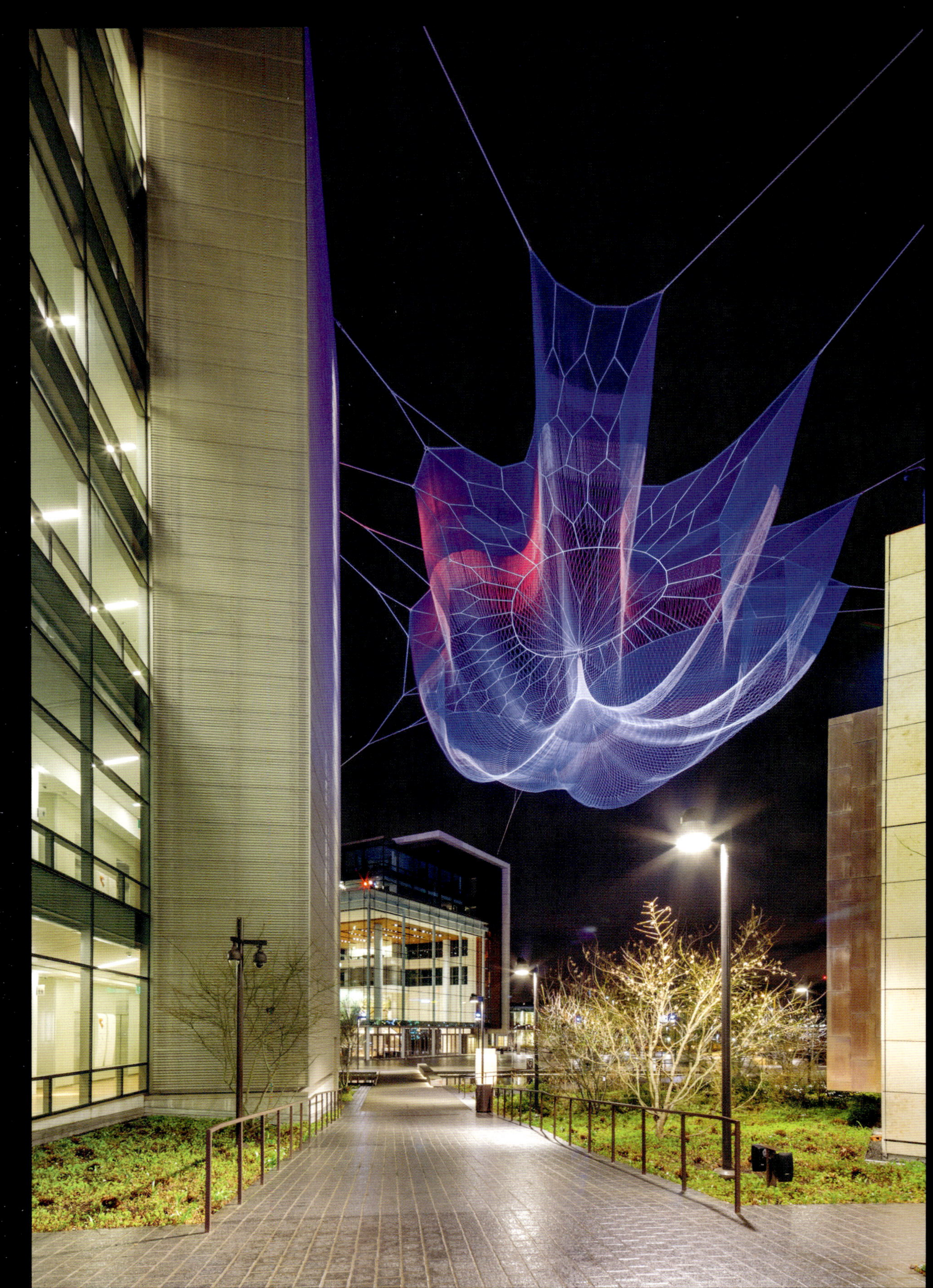

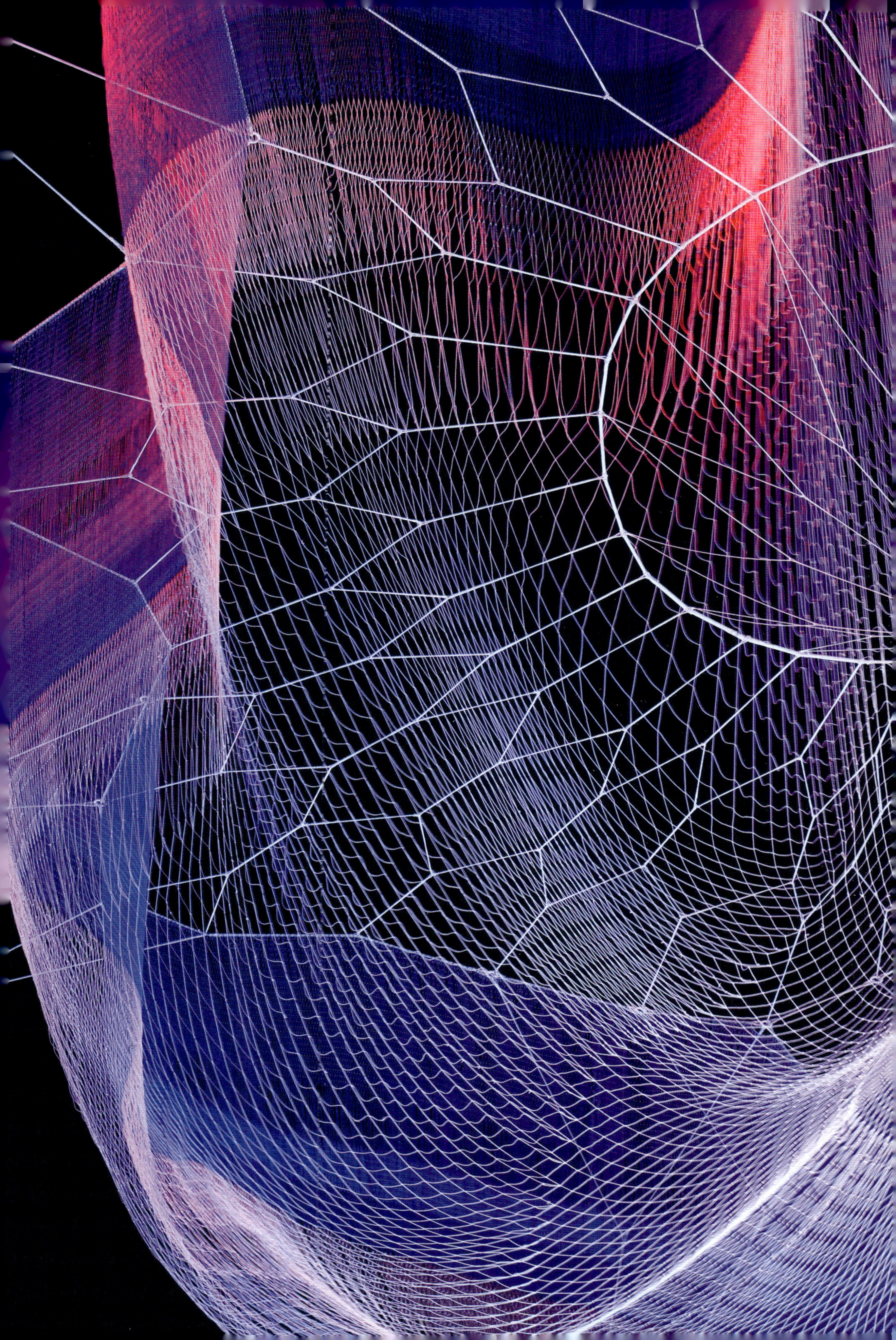

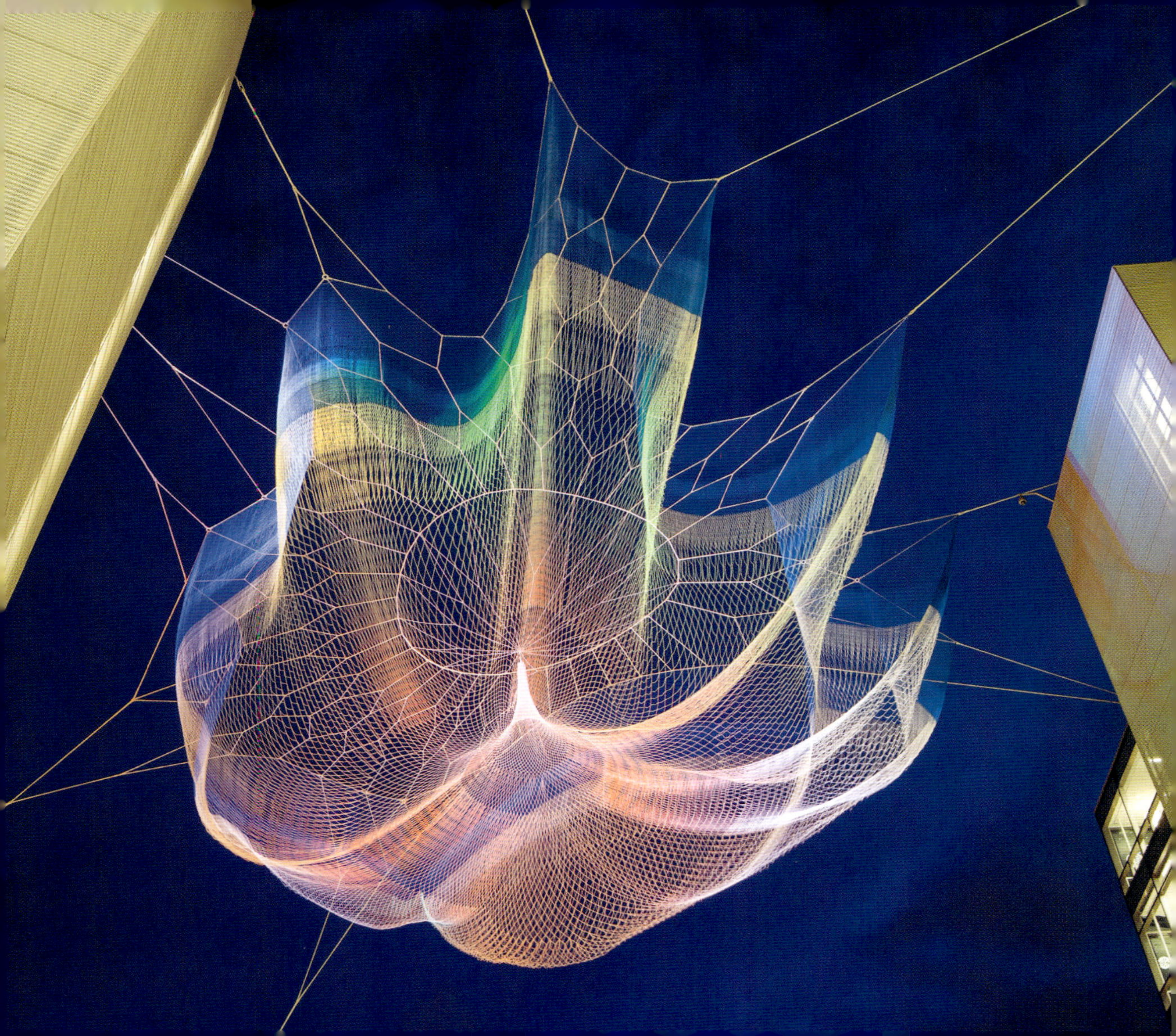

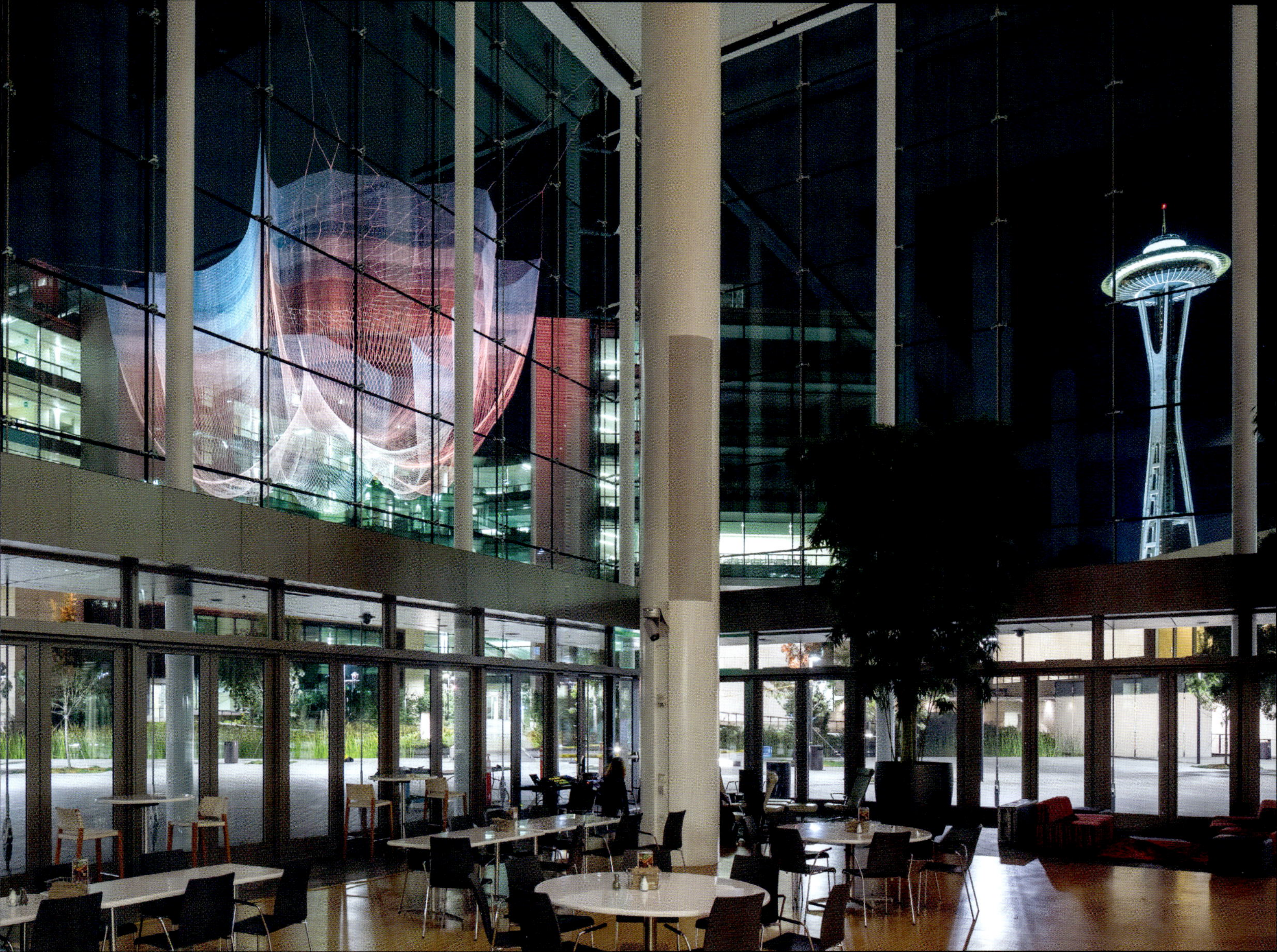

Three

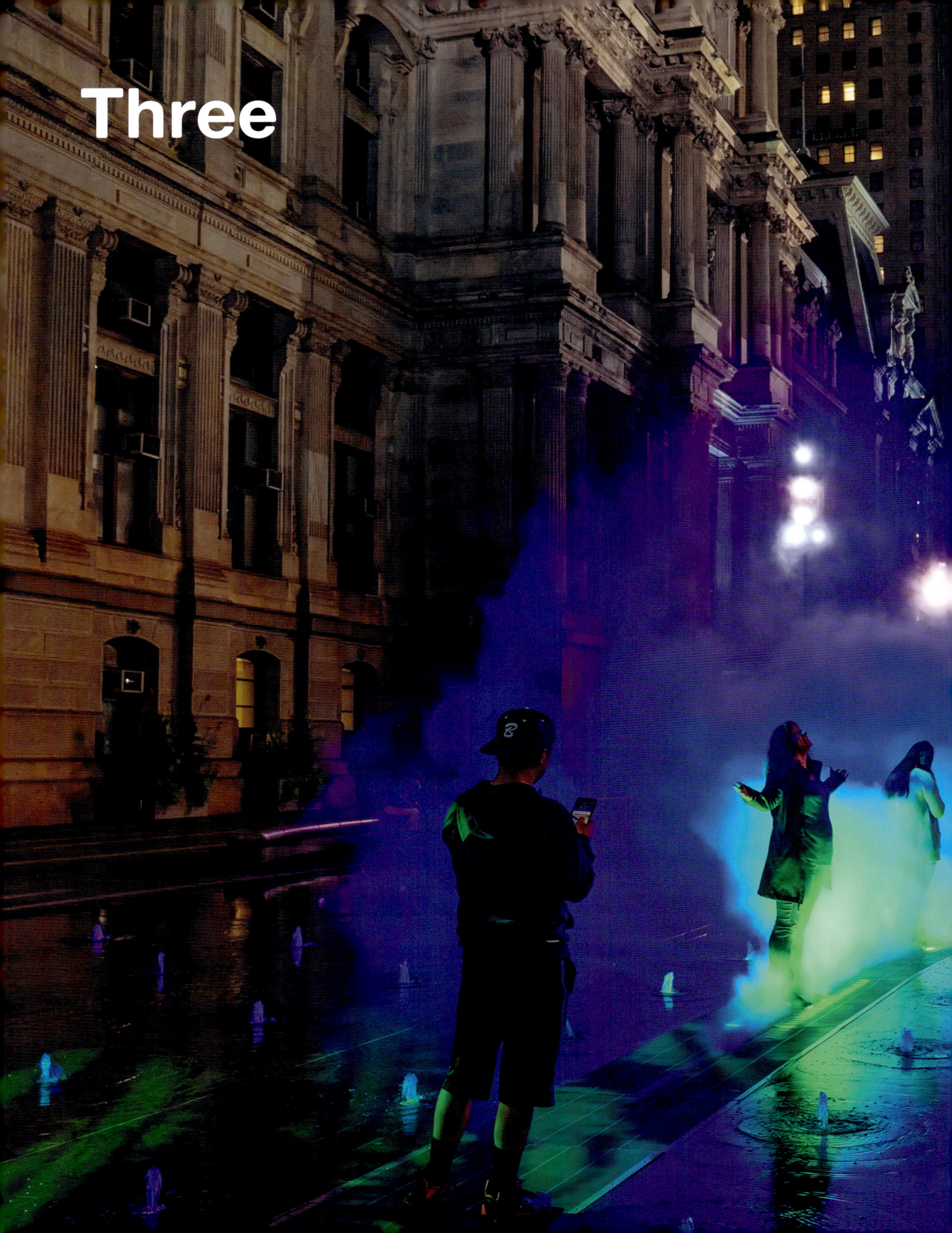

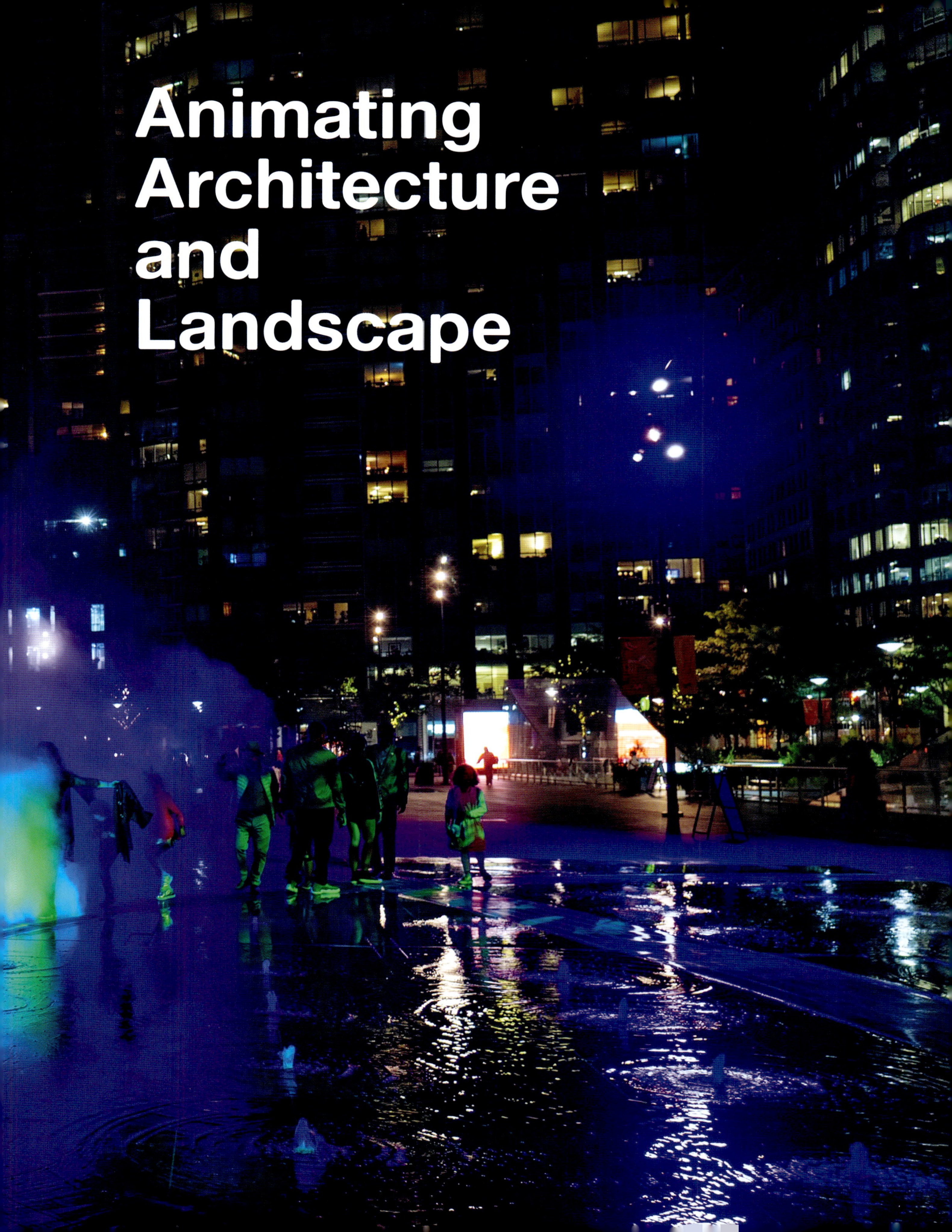
Animating
Architecture
and
Landscape

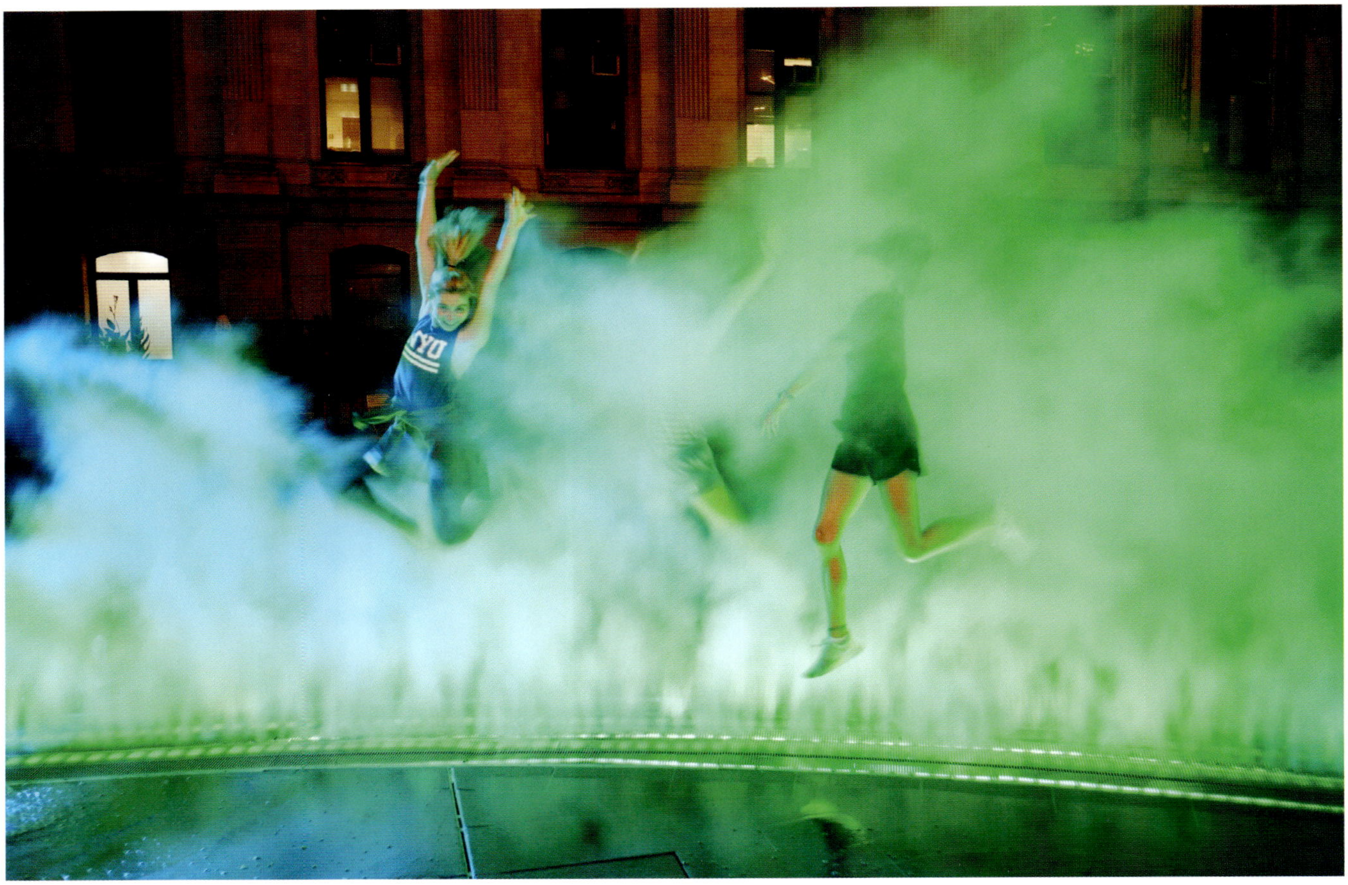

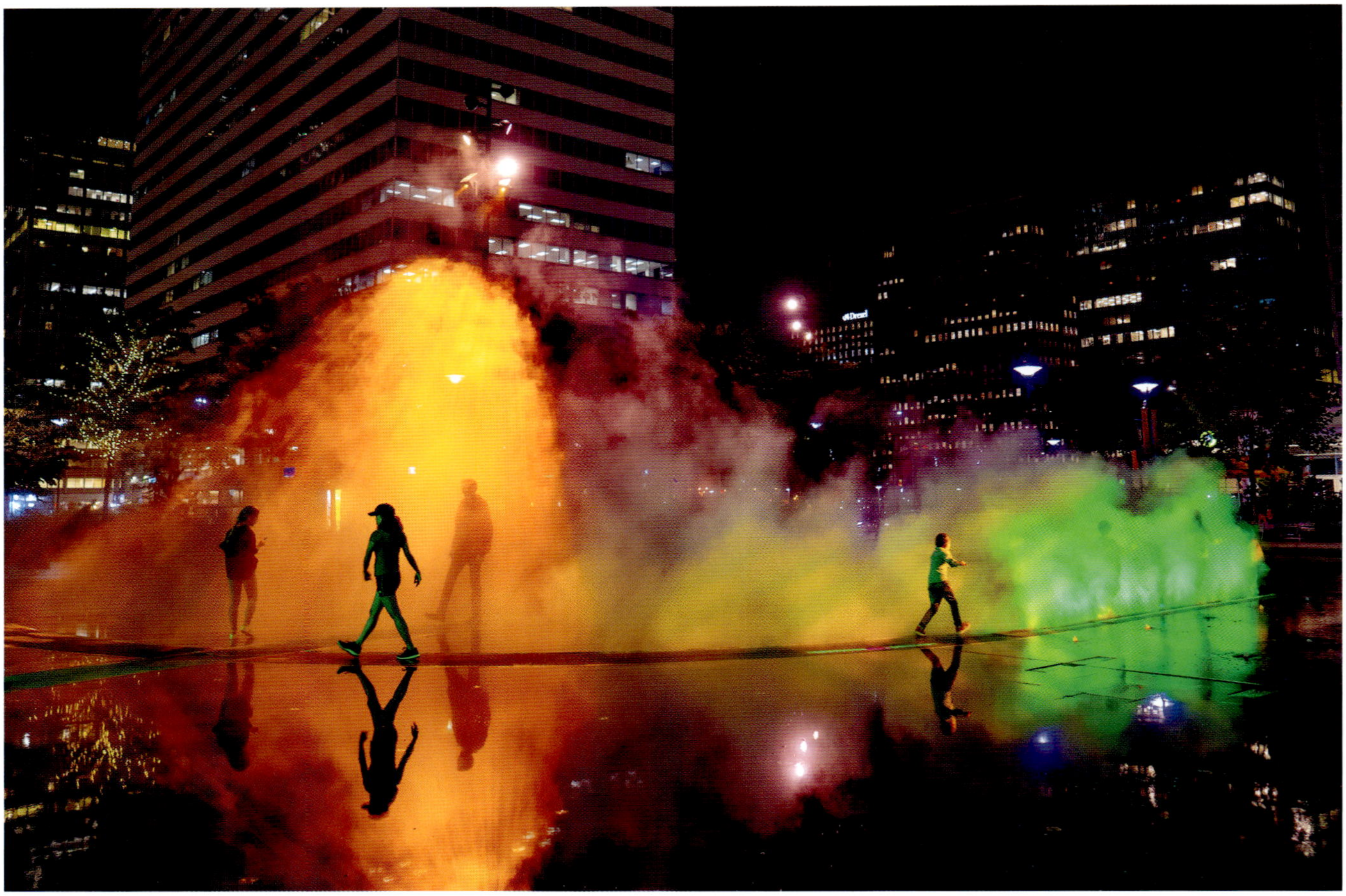

We Take Our Fun Very Seriously, Okay?

—

Laurie Olin and Jared Green in conversation

In an interview for the American Society of Landscape Architects, editor and writer Jared Green asked Janet Echelman to define her role as a visual artist working in the public sphere today, posing the question "Are you here to enliven dead places, create a new sense of place, or just get us to feel something new?"[1] While her public artworks do all of the above, Echelman noted that she often thinks of her work as "creating a sense of place... because many of these places felt anonymous before," underscoring the fact that she is often working as "part of a larger effort that involves a landscape architect, architect, and urbanist."[2]

Here Green interviews one of Echelman's long-standing collaborators, distinguished landscape architect Laurie Olin, who has guided many of studio OLIN's signature projects, including the Washington Monument grounds in DC, New York City's Bryant Park, and the J. Paul Getty Center in Los Angeles. Olin and Green's conversation is bookended by two of Echelman's projects with OLIN that demonstrate the vast temporal scale that Echelman often works within. The first is a nine-year effort to create a focal point for the redevelopment of Dilworth Park just outside Philadelphia City Hall with her public sculpture *Pulse* (2018), created with OLIN partner Susan Weiler. Embedding a 60-by-230-foot mechanical system in the park's 11,600-square-foot fountain, *Pulse* playfully emits 4-foot-tall curtains of atomized water whenever subways pass underneath. Colored LED lights correspond to the train lines that bring more than seventy thousand passengers to the site each day. The conversation closes with Olin sharing his insights into the material and philosophical aspects of *The Space Between Us* (2013), a sculpture built on Santa Monica State Beach that was up for only one evening, from dusk to dawn, in the fall of 2013.

Jared Green: How did you first encounter Janet Echelman's work?

Laurie Olin: At the San Francisco airport, her sculpture *Every Beating Second* (2011) seems like an invasion of some organic thing in a place that is one of people's least favorite in the world—the concourse of an airport. Her work occupies space in a way that engages people. When we see it, we immediately start wondering, "What is this? What is going on here?" The "what's going on here?" question is something artists have tried to make people ask throughout history—to make people more aware and pay attention. It's a wake-up call to be alive.

JG: Why is it important to integrate art like Echelman's into public spaces?

LO: To create something that wakes people up and calls attention to their surroundings and themselves and provides a sense of being alive is the point of her work. But it then goes on to stimulate other thoughts, whether they are representational or metaphysical, about things that are not present but rather have to do with ideas, imagination, memory, the past. Wherever they are, everyone brings along with them their own culture, memories, history, childhood. Any five people looking at a project of Echelman's will have many sets of associations—some of which would overlap, and some of which would be unique to that person's history of encountering the world. *Her* world is part of *the* world.

JG: Echelman has collaborated with [your Philadelphia-based landscape and architecture firm] OLIN twice, for *Pulse* (2018) in Philadelphia and *The Space Between Us* (2013) in Santa Monica, California—two distinct artworks and landscapes. *Pulse*, a LED- and mist-based artwork, follows the paths of Philadelphia subway and trolley lines converging below Dilworth Park, the central landscape surrounding City Hall, redesigned by OLIN and opened in 2014. Echelman's piece was completed later, in 2018, but made an immediate impact. According to

previous and opposite: *Pulse*, 2018, Philadelphia, Pennsylvania, opening of the Green Line phase

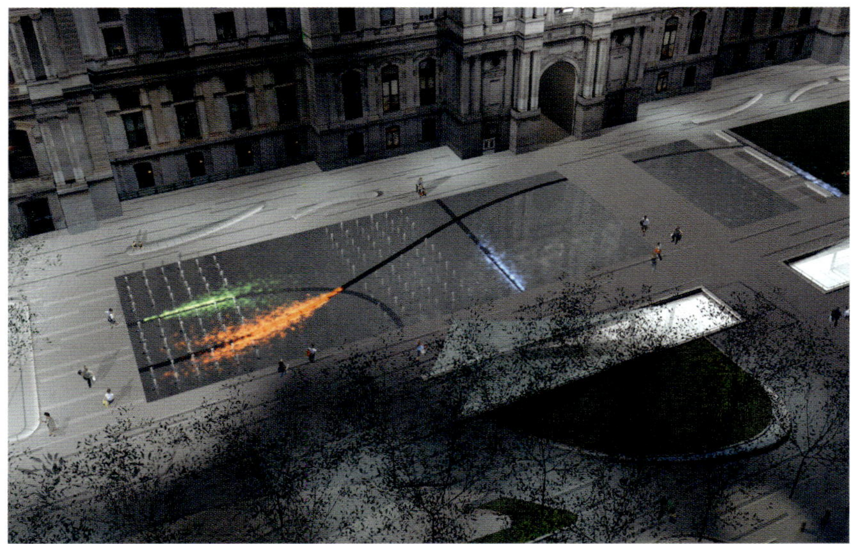

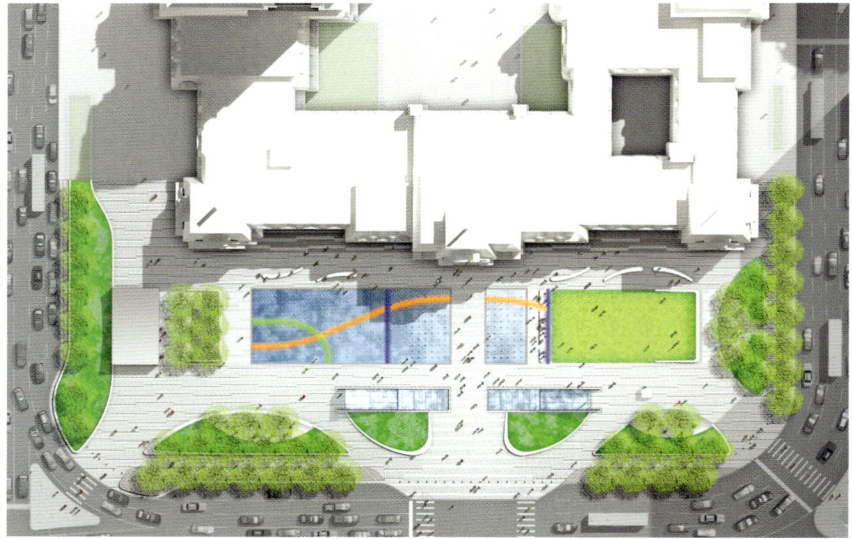

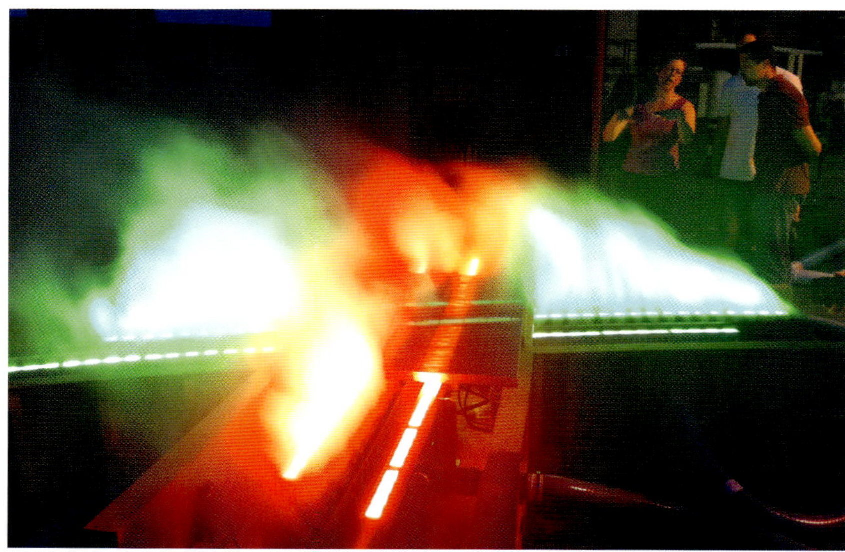

top and middle: Mist plan layout for *Pulse*, 2018, at Dilworth Plaza, Philadelphia, above the City Hall subway station at the intersection of the Market-Frankford elevated line (blue), Broad Street subway (orange), and the subway-surface trolley lines (green)
bottom: Echelman and the OLIN team review fog intersection prototype in 2013

the *Philadelphia Business Journal*, in 2018 the park received ten million visitors, an almost 20 percent increase from 2015, and thirty thousand people a day interacted with *Pulse*. Echelman described her vision for the piece, her first permanent artwork using cool mist and colored lights, echoing three train lines crossing under the park, as a living X-ray of the city's circulatory system. The vibrantly colored mist curtains evoke the steam rising from the city's first water pumping station, which was located on the site at the beginning of the nineteenth century, as well as the steam from the trains at the former Pennsylvania Station across the street, while also alluding to new technologies. How did OLIN work with the artist to make *Pulse* such a key part of the park?

LO: Dilworth Park is a deck over a public concourse that feeds three subway lines. One of them, the green line, is mostly a surface trolley, like in Boston, but then it goes underground in the center of the city. Then there is the orange line, a major north-south subway line, and a red line, an east-west subway line. All three meet at this one mixing bowl downstairs, underneath this plaza. My colleagues Susan Weiler and Richard Roark designed a fountain that could be programmed with different kinds of splashes and a very thin reflective scrim that can be turned off to do other things in the empty plaza—performances, dances, an ice rink. Susan very astutely asked Echelman to participate because her work so often engages people and increases their fascination. When Janet learned that these trains were traveling under Dilworth Park, she asked, "How could we show that aboveground?" She came up with the idea that as the trains move through underneath, you could know it up above. Then she thought of mist. And if you could color the mist, wouldn't that be interesting?

Janet wanted to represent the movement of the different lines—one green, one orange, one red—in the plaza, with mist coming up that would be the color of the relevant train line. Art can make you see something that isn't there. Art quite often evokes things from the past or something from somewhere else. Something that is ephemeral, and moves, can tell you about something else that is moving that you cannot see. Isn't that intriguing? And, of course, that's what intrigues people when they see it. They think, "What is this?"

With the micromist, you don't get wet. We all know that if you go out in a fog you end up feeling damp, but *Pulse* doesn't do that. The particles are so fine, they're more like dust, only they're made from water. As the green line comes in downstairs, a little bit of green mist comes up at one end of the plaza, and then it curves along,

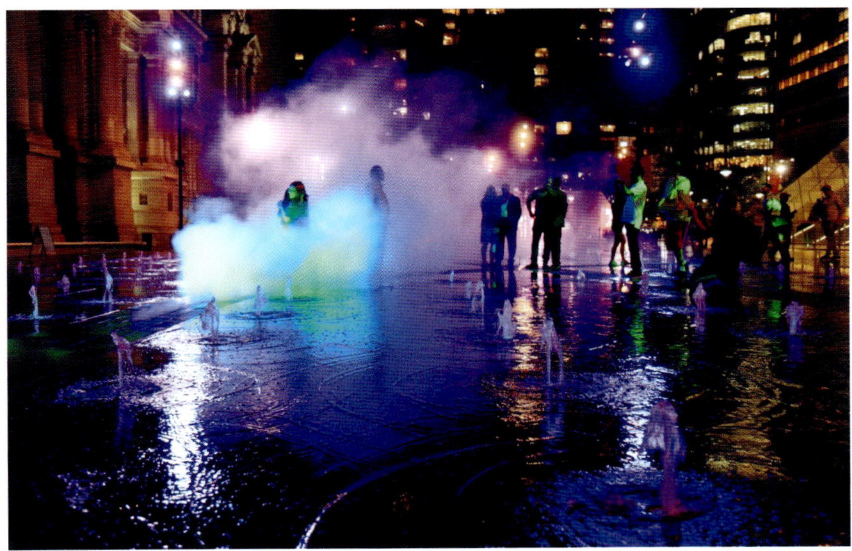

Opening of the Green Line phase of *Pulse*, 2018

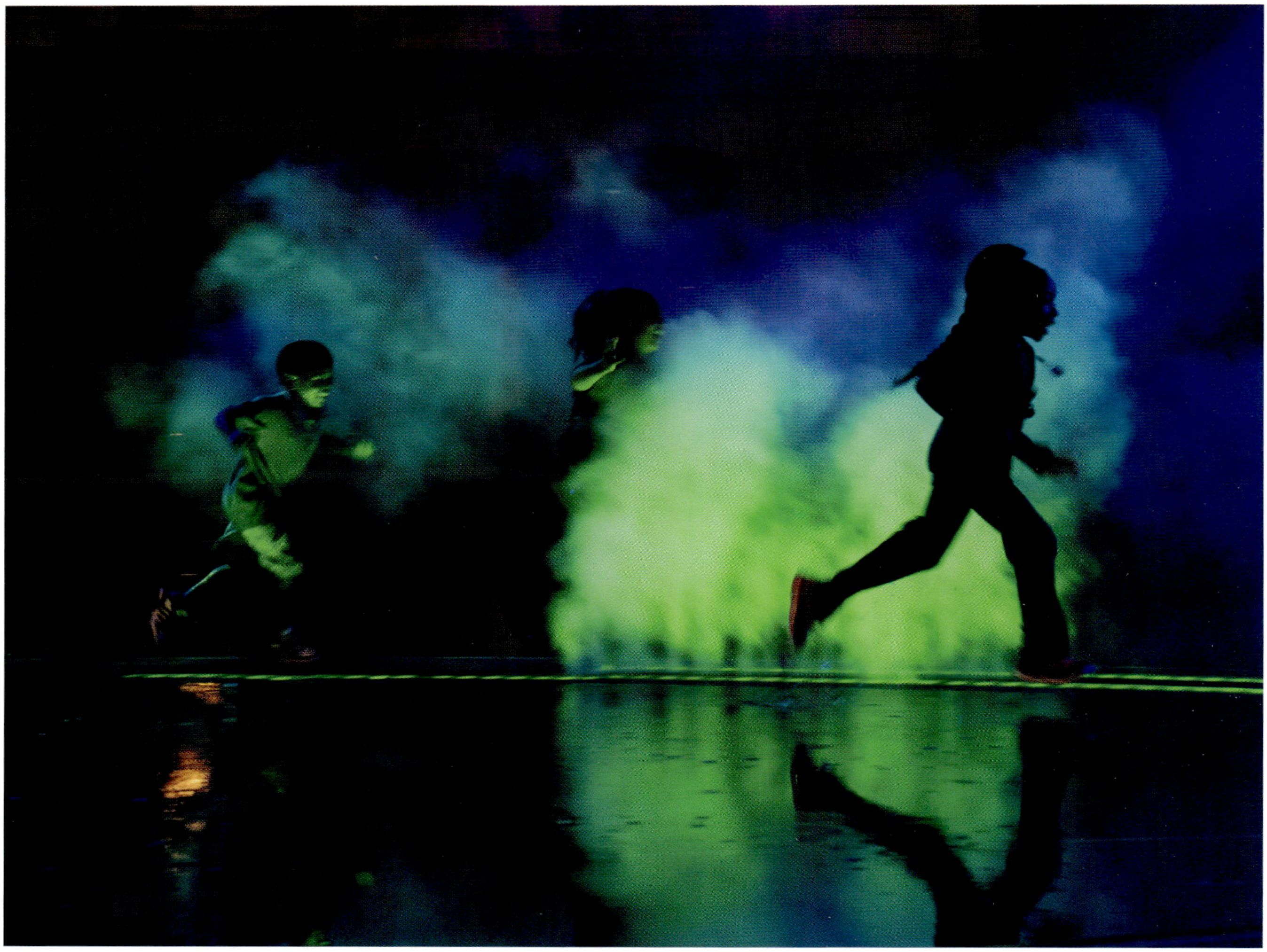

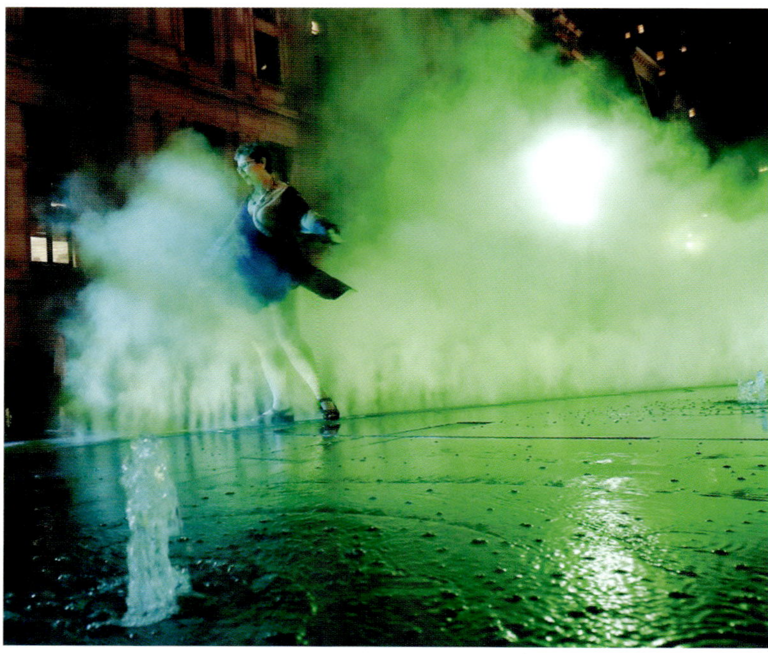

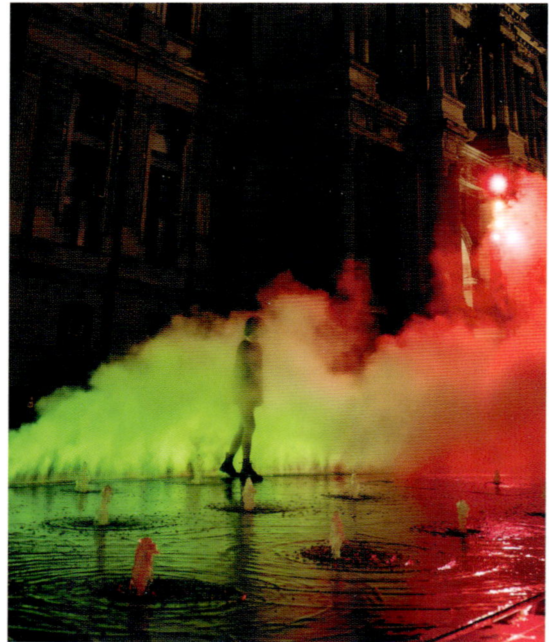

and disappears behind as it's rising. There is this moving curtain of mist, and then it all goes away, it doesn't make a noise. If you look away, it's gone. So this work also has a sense of anticipation and memory. You anticipate it, you remember it. You enjoy it when it's there, and it comes and goes. It's like a lot of things about life.

OLIN purposefully embedded *Pulse* in the park infrastructure so that it couldn't get scaled back later. The strategy OLIN and Echelman accomplished together ensured that the artistic vision would be realized in its totality. Is this a strategy for future public art—to make it infrastructure? As with fine art, our work as landscape architects is often mistakenly seen as being as an add-on instead of intrinsic and fundamental. But aspects of a project that have to do with quality of life should not be extra; they should be the point of the project. Art is not frosting. It's actually one of the principal productions of civilization. We take our fun very seriously, okay?

If you can conceive of a work of art that is part of the infrastructure so that you can't have the one without the other, I think that's great. I know what the effect of Echelman's work is, how important it is, and how devoted everyone on the OLIN team was to getting it done.

JG: In contrast to the permanent nature of *Pulse*, *The Space Between Us* in Santa Monica was a site-specific work for only one night—September 28, 2013. Created for the GLOW festival, which brought 150,000 people to Santa Monica State Beach, the artwork involved OLIN and Echelman carving out canyons in the sand that enhanced the experience of the illuminated net sculpture. What is the value of Echelman's temporary public art?

LO: You can be under it and be totally overwhelmed by it. Participate in it. Be caught in it without being actually being in it. One looks at this and wonders, "Why is this here?" Being at the ocean, the first thought is of a fishnet, the second perhaps of sails. Then there are clouds and waves. All the things one immediately thinks of with the ocean are in *The Space Between Us*. It moves in the breeze. With the light, it changes and shifts. People went up on those constructed dunes and down in the hollow. When you're down in the hollow, it's all around you and over you. It's like the aurora borealis. With temporary public art, you go to all that trouble and then it goes away. There's a poignancy to that, as there is a poignancy to life. But I think it's very worth doing, because it takes people out of themselves and shows them something they would never think of otherwise. They never saw it before, and they're not going to see it again. It's this moment that heightens life. It also tells people, "Artists do things that are different. Here's an artist who does something I could never have thought of. I've never seen anything like it." It opens people up to change in a positive way. Although the work is ephemeral, everyone who experienced it is different afterward, and that's the point. Art that is ephemeral has that quality of helping us think not only about the passage of time and our own mortality, but also about the environment, and about paying more attention.

In Echelman's case, we are always surprised by the work. Her work is never common because it is shape-shifting. That gives it more traction than things that are static because the world isn't static, the world is dynamic, and we're dynamic. The work is often made of fibrous materials. Even if she's using some plastic material, it's generally organic. Oil is from plants. Plastic is from plants. What are plants from? They are from the sun. There's energy in the work—first-, second-, third-, fourth-degree energy, which flows through the work like it flows through life and the Earth. A person who saw *The Space Between Us* would tell you it made them think, but also that it made them feel.

Laurie Olin is practice professor of landscape architecture at the University of Pennsylvania and founding partner of OLIN.

Jared Green is an author, landscape architecture critic, and journalist.

opposite: *Pulse*, 2018, opening of the Green Line phase

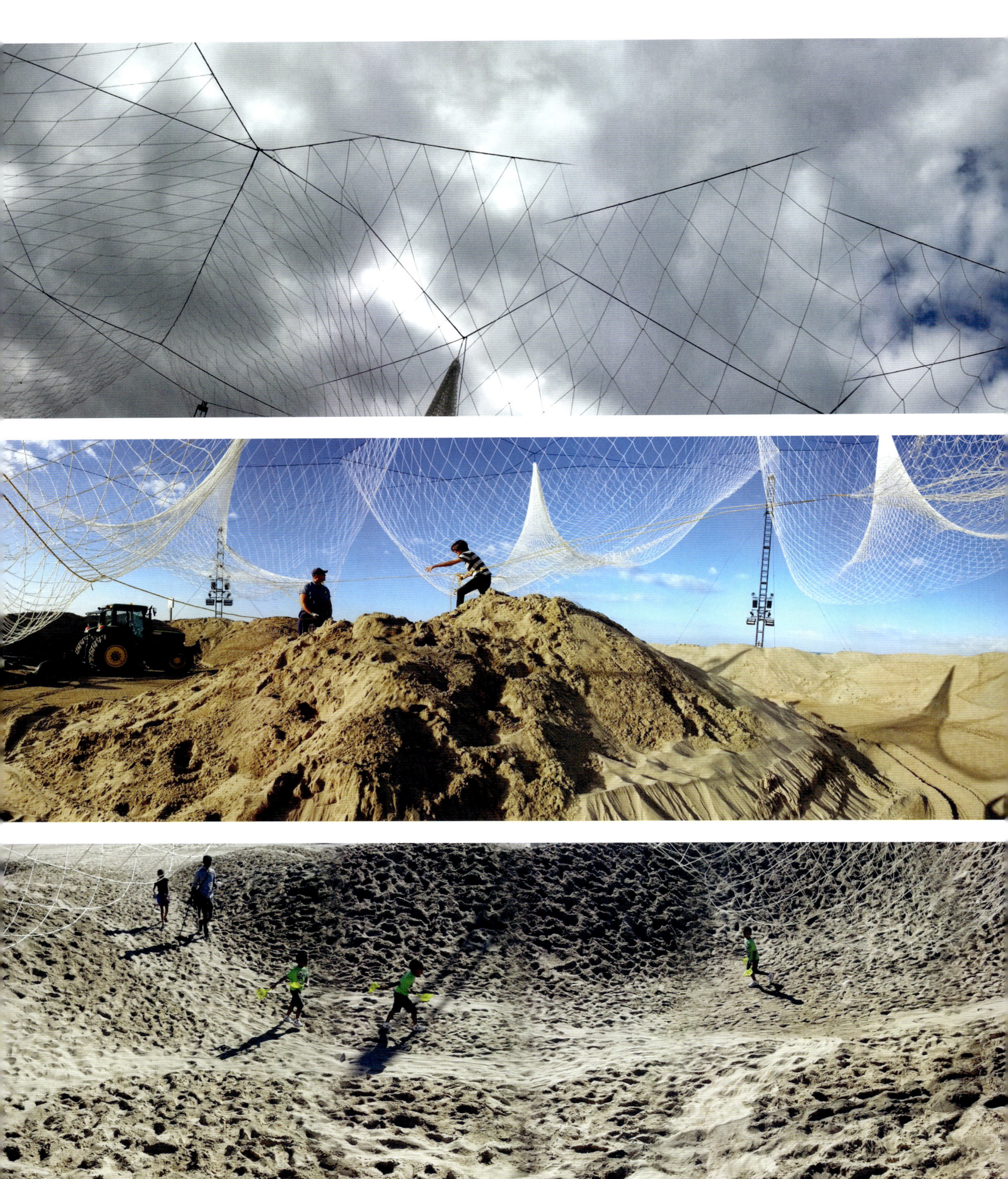

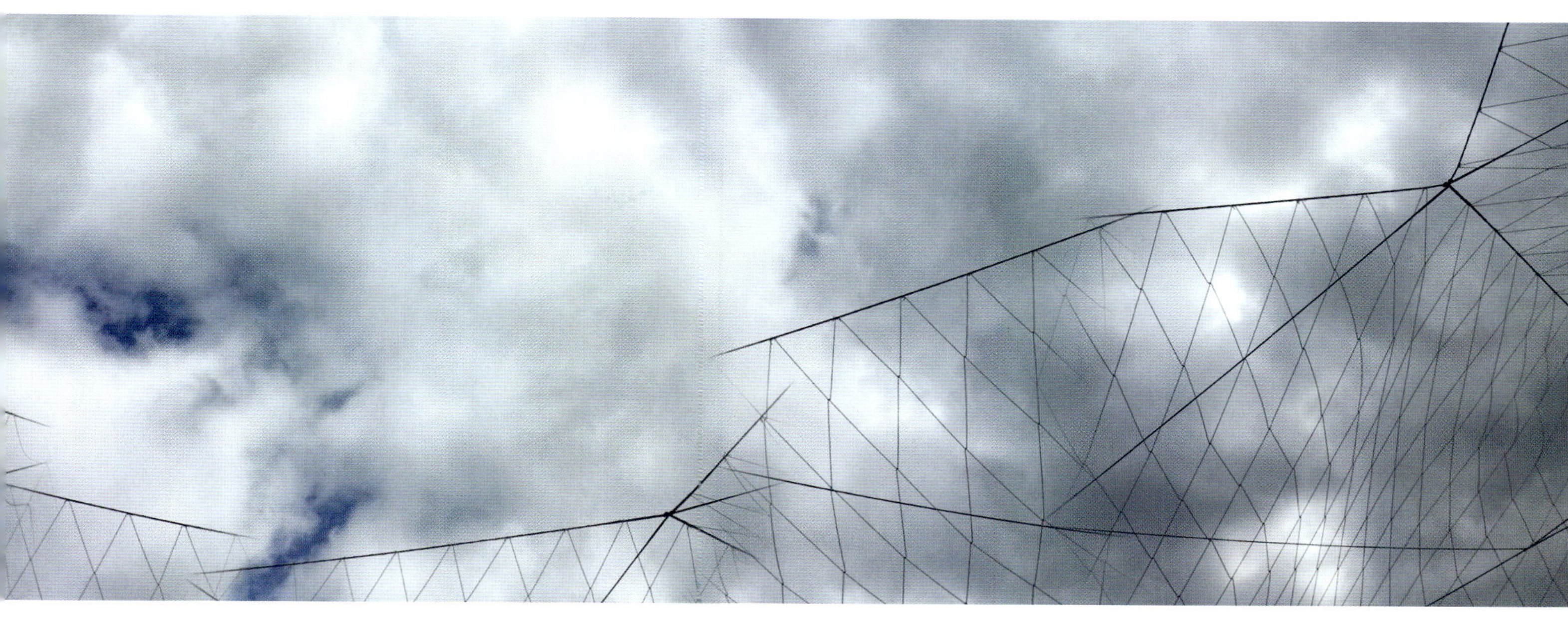

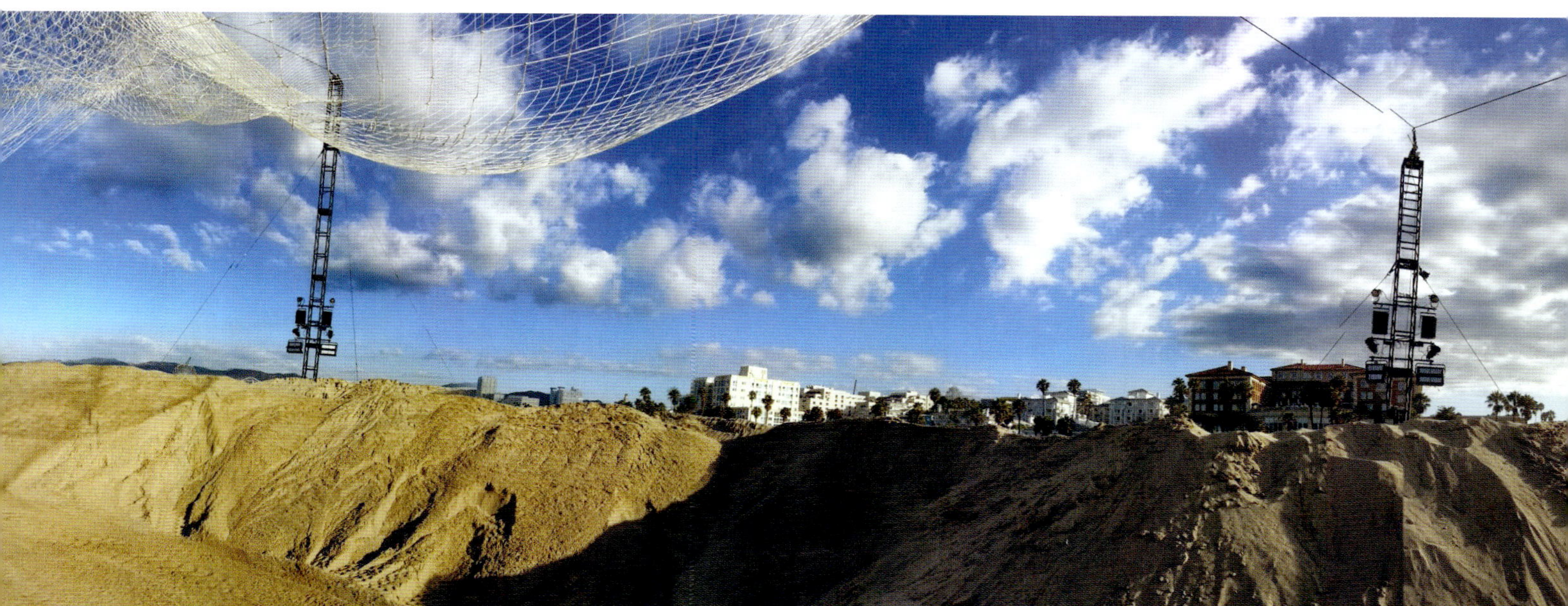

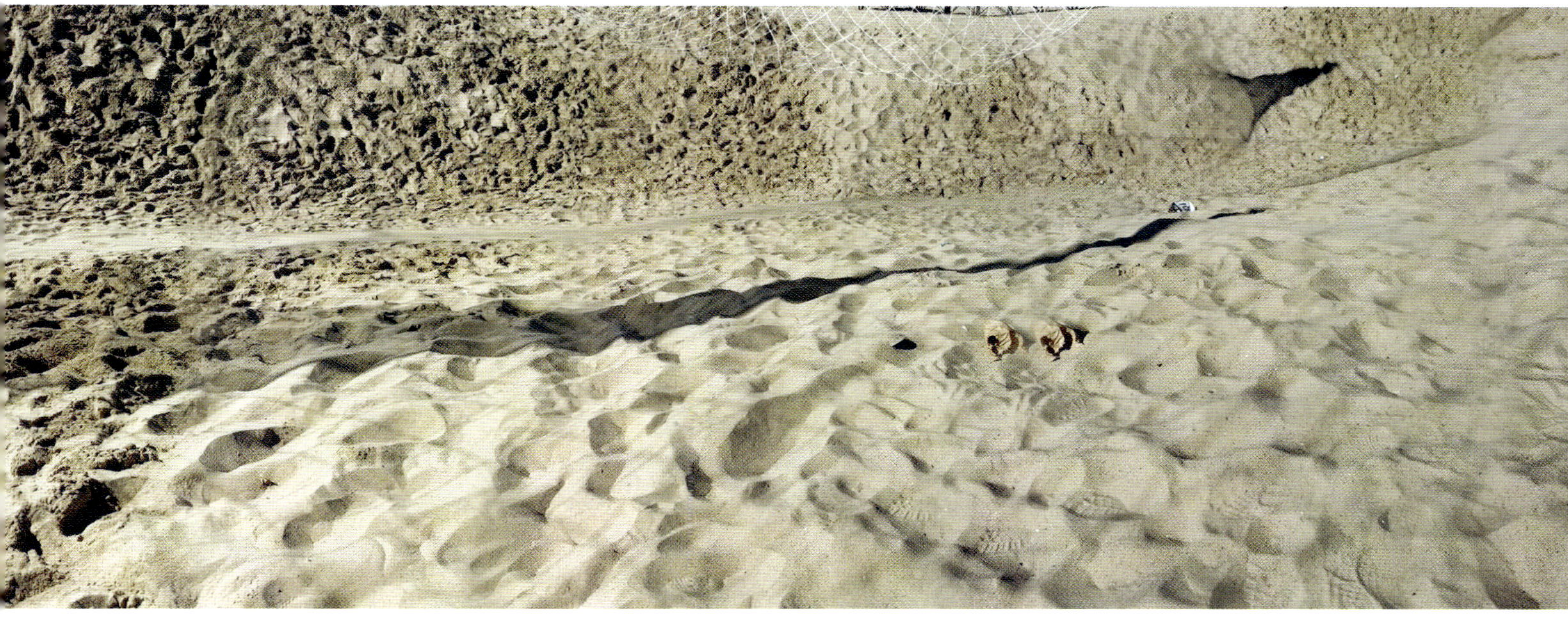

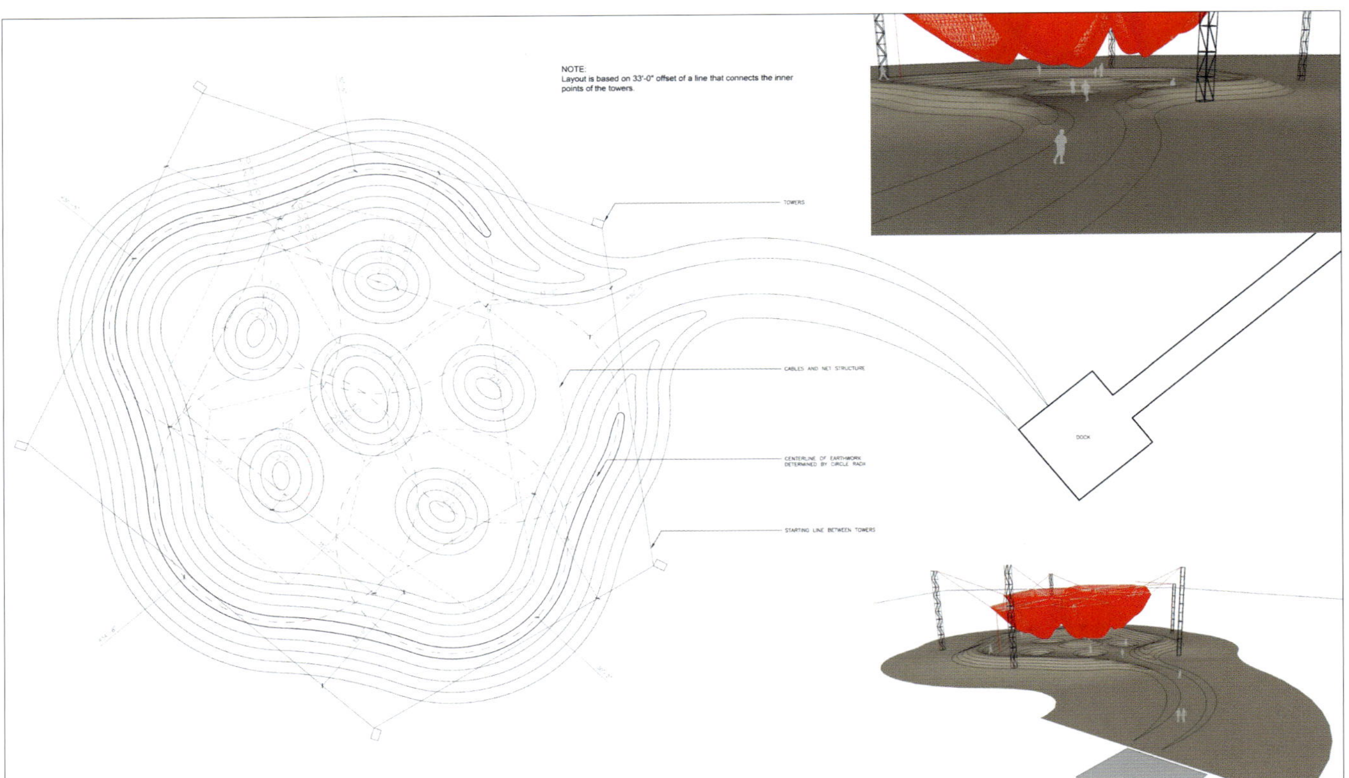

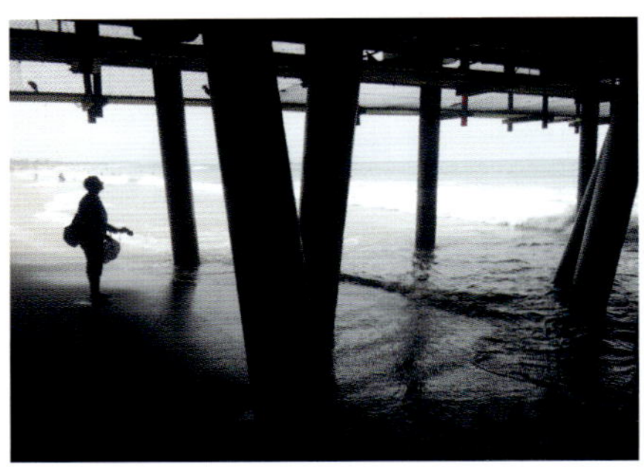

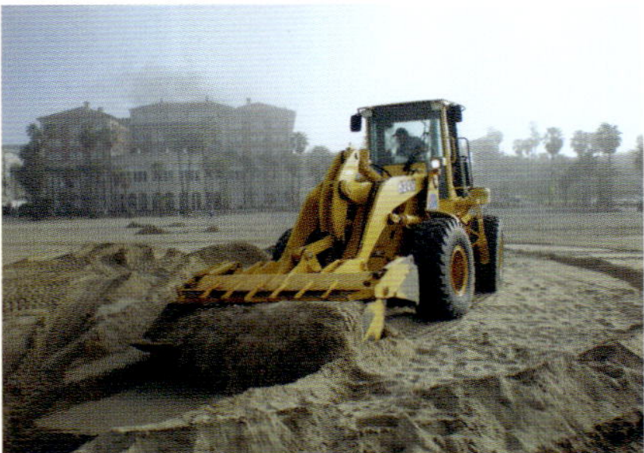

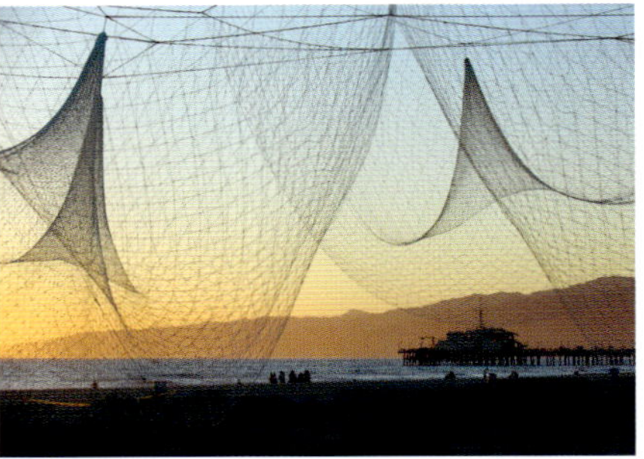

top: Landscape plan and perspective views created with Susan Weiler and Richard Roark of OLIN
bottom row: Sound collection beneath the Santa Monica Pier to develop the audio component for *The Space Between Us*, 2013, with composers Zach Alterman and Daniel Rome; Echelman directs bulldozer operators to implement sand design with the Santa Monica Department of Public Works and OLIN; *The Space Between Us*, 2013
opposite: In one night, an estimated 150,000 people visited *The Space Between Us*, 2013

previous: Echelman's panoramic photography before and after *The Space Between Us*, 2013, Santa Monica State Beach, California

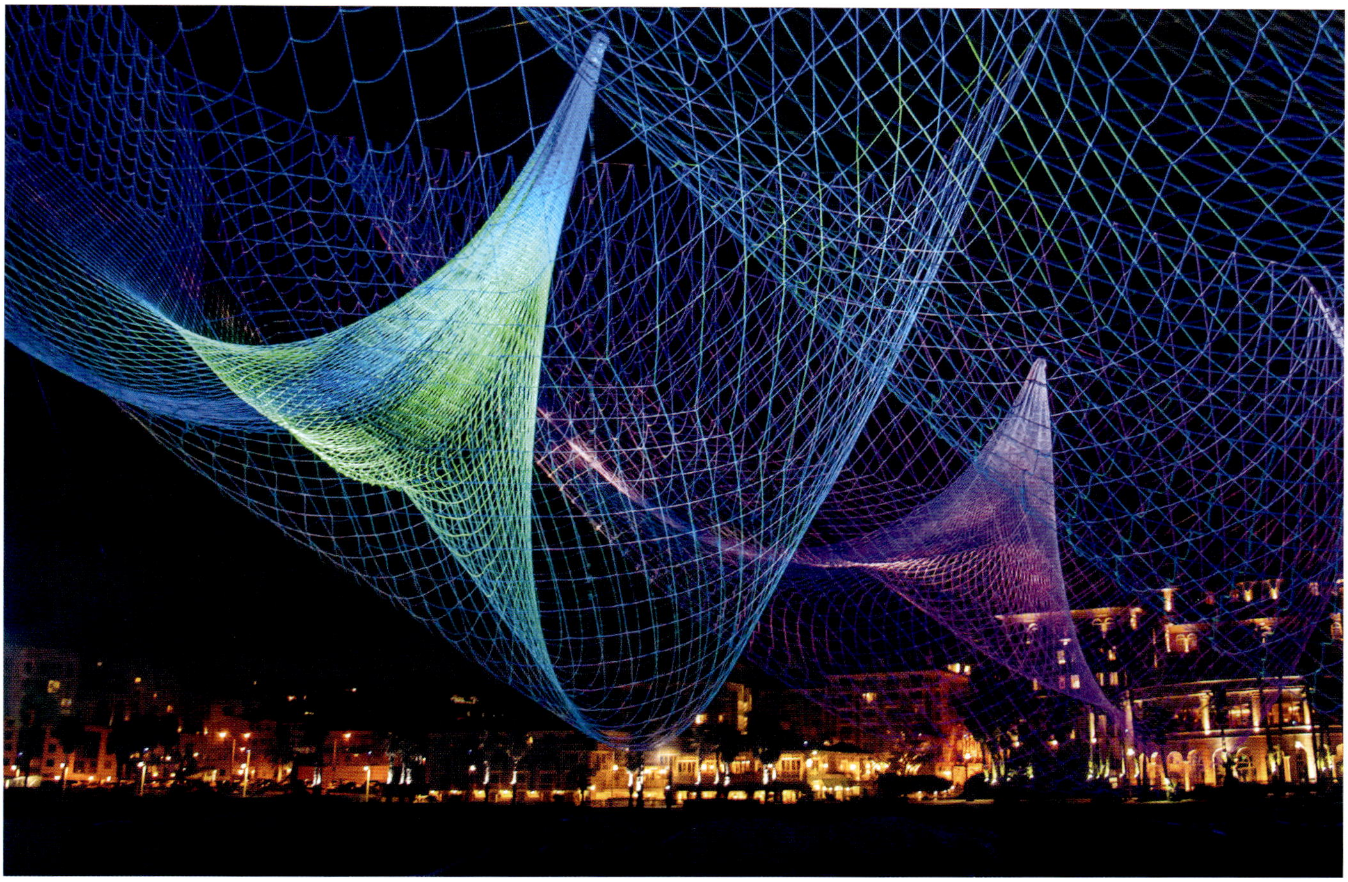

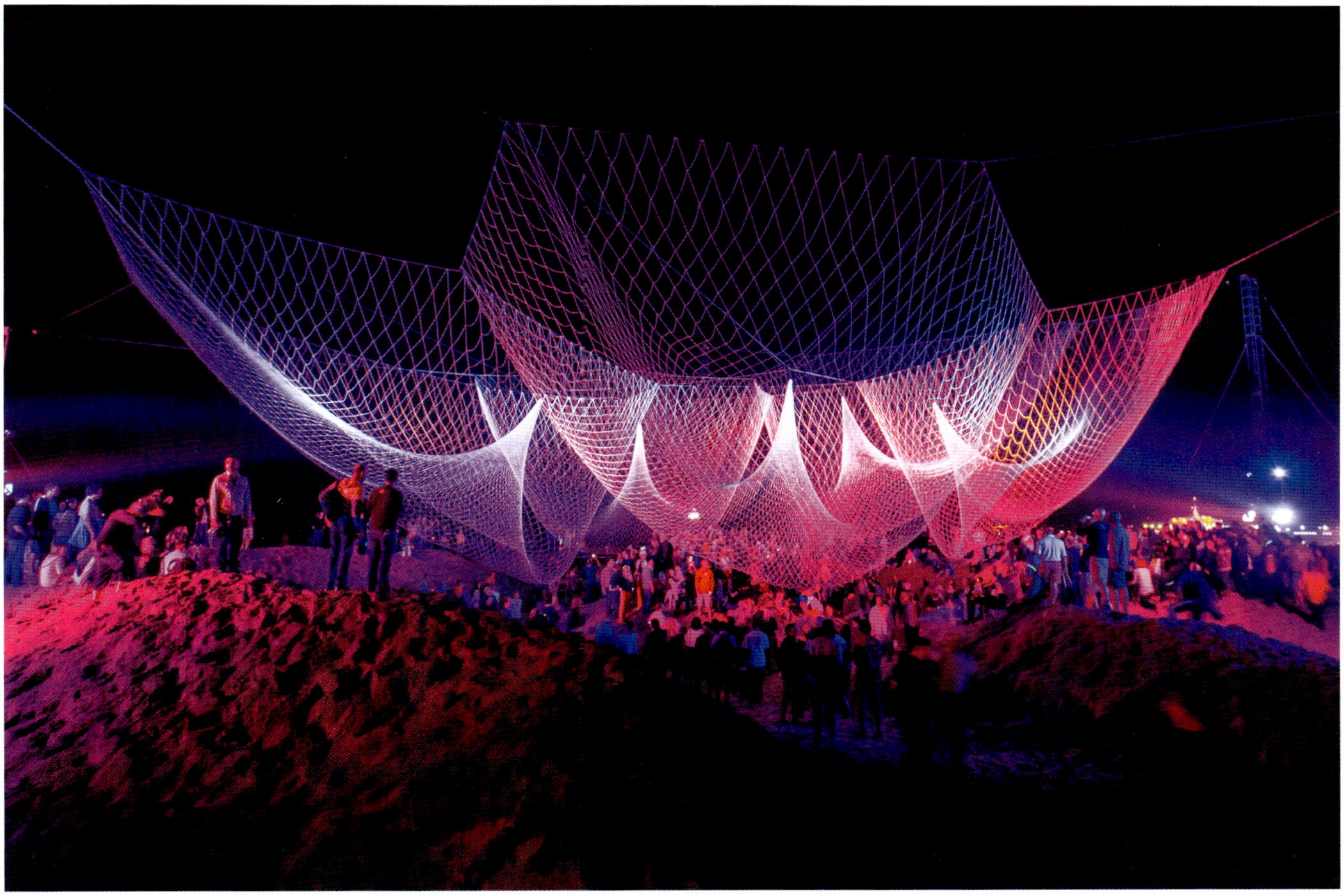

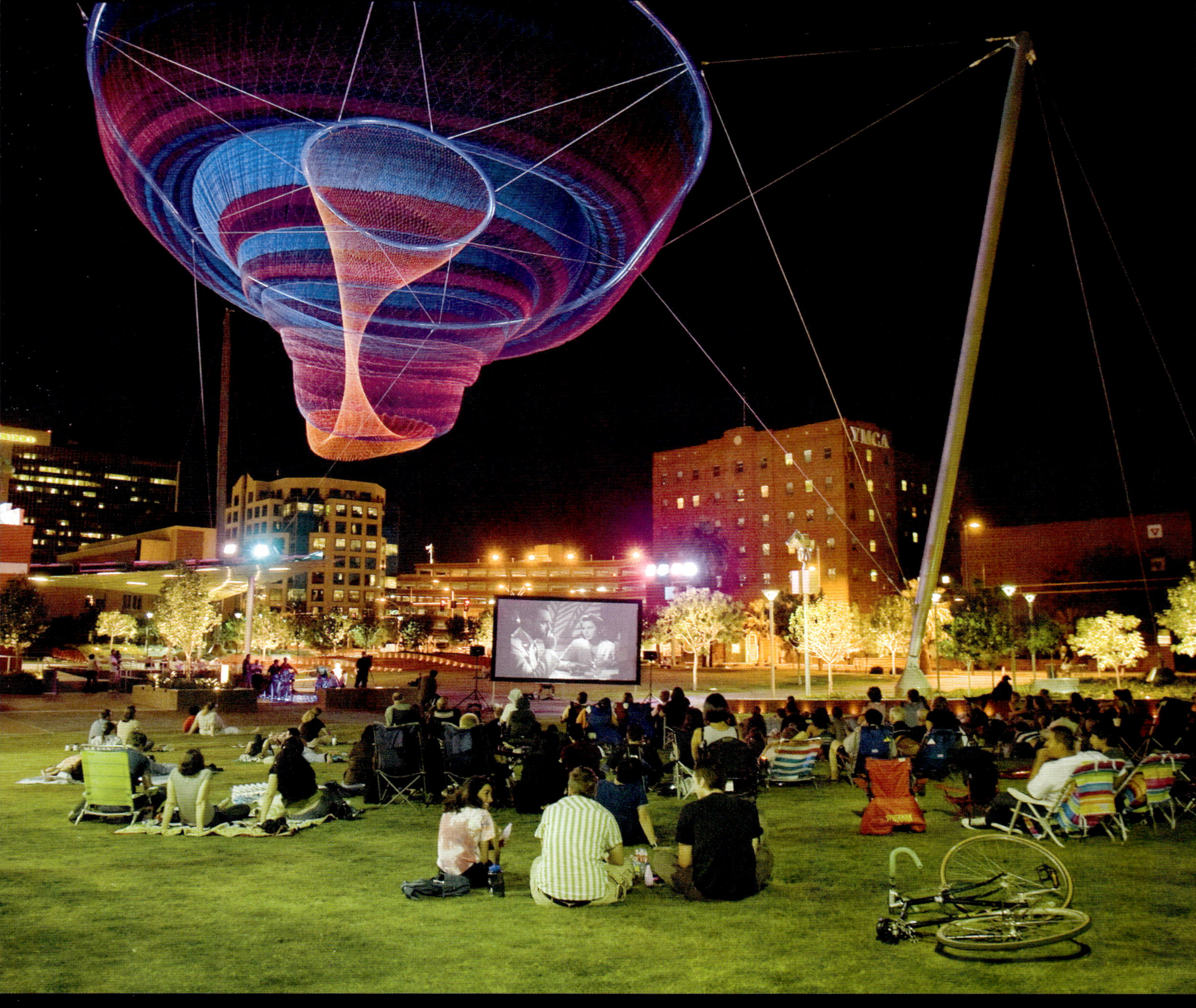

Her Secret Is Patience, 2009, Phoenix, Arizona

The Place Economy

—

Andrew Hoyne

Great public art creates audiences, drawing people to places and transforming perceptions. Throughout the twentieth century, public art emerged as an important tool for creating city and place identities. And while many of Janet Echelman's monumental sculptures are funded by governments and can be seen in this context, from *She Changes* (2005) in Porto, Portugal, to *Bending Arc* (2020) in St. Petersburg, Florida, to *Her Secret Is Patience* (2009) in Phoenix, Arizona, her works have also expanded and exceeded expectations for the power of public art to inspire change. Now, beyond government bodies and philanthropists, everyone from private developers to community groups is funding art in public places. Echelman's *Dream Catcher* (2017) on the Sunset Strip in West Hollywood, California, *Where We Met* (2016) in Greensboro, North Carolina, *Current* (2023) in Columbus, Ohio, and *Butterfly Rest Stop* (2024) in Frisco, Texas, are all privately funded artworks whose ownership resides in public collections with maintenance arranged by nonprofits.

Chicago's "Millennium Park effect" was studied by Americans for the Arts, which published a report estimating that the $475 million investment shared by public and private donors generated between $1.9 and $2.6 billion in its first decade. Another example is the City of New York's investment in Olafur Eliasson's monumental artwork *The New York City Waterfalls* (2008), which achieved an estimated economic impact of $69 million in under four months. Even back in 2008, more than 6,000 images were uploaded to Flickr and 250,000 videos to YouTube.

In the era of social media, "likable places" such as Echelman's works mentioned above are snapped on mobile phones by visitors and locals equally and have the potential to become popular and desirable hot spots, bringing increased visitation and at times providing a halo effect for an entire neighborhood. Architecture critic Oliver Wainwright of *The Guardian* summed up the situation in 2018, saying that "photogenic design" is now a primary concern driving developers and designers, sometimes attracting multimillion-pound budgets.[3]

The power of social media can be put to good use. As a visual marker, public art becomes the thing many places become famous for. And while it may sit comfortably on a place's marketing and advertising materials, its value exponentially increases when "the people" decide it's loved and tell the world about it. This is exemplified by *Her Secret Is Patience*. The project was initially canceled when the 2008 recession hit. But Phoenix's Downtown Community Alliance protested and called for a full city council review and public vote, which modeled how art can rally the public. As the artist explains: "I flew in and was taken to meet individually with each of the nine city council members. More than one hundred people registered to speak at that city council meeting, with only one opposed to the project. What made the difference was the breadth of support, especially that it included a coalition of downtown businesses. The *Arizona Republic* newspaper, which had run articles every day all week, printed the big headline 'Art Triumphs.' Years later, when I came to speak at an international conference of city managers that was held in Phoenix, I was surprised when the city manager who had originally tried to cancel the project introduced me by exclaiming that 'Paris has the Eiffel Tower, and we have *Her Secret Is Patience*, and I can no longer imagine our city without it.'"[4] *She Changes* now has its own dedicated Wikipedia page, and multiple images show up instantly upon typing the artwork's name into Google. While these facts may seem banal, they show that people around the world are hungry for and appreciative of this type of artwork; it is quite literally what they are looking for.

Destination marketing, precinct curation, and property development are competitive spaces. For property projects, an Instagrammable landmark becomes what my organization calls an Instaplace®. We will often specifically identify or create elements unique to a client's place vision that can then be leveraged as social media magnets, creating interest, setting the tone, changing perceptions, breaking news, telling stories, and attracting warm bodies. And if dwell time equates to spend time, then public art is a great investment. Echelman's work is a strong example of this philosophy in action. Over half a million photos of her work have been shared online by the media, visitors, architects, designers, other artists, and influential individuals such as Melinda Gates and Michelle Obama. Creating this digital dialogue is key to ensuring physical engagement and visitation.

Echelman's urban art commission featured on the dust jacket and inside our seven-hundred-page book *The Place Economy 3*, like all her works, was created with local stories in mind. For Tulsa, Oklahoma, she draws upon local legends of how the firewheel (also known as Indian blanket flower) got its colors to connect history to place. She continues to design ambitious projects for cities to transform and solidify urban identities across the globe, drawing from the cultural and ecological landscape specific to each region. In Germany, the city of Bonn commissioned her design that translates music into visual form to celebrate Beethoven's birthplace. In New York City, Echelman was commissioned by a private luxury brand to reimage the facade of its flagship Fifth Avenue building, and by the Seaport to enliven its historic waterfront. She also ambitiously cuts across the city's airspace, as in her design that connects the Whitney Museum of American Art to the High Line, a public park built on an elevated rail structure along Manhattan's West Side. For Venice, Italy, Echelman worked with the Peggy Guggenheim Museum to design a sculpture that could safely span the Grand Canal between historic buildings.

Echelman understands how public art can attract people, turn blighted areas into destinations, and enable businesses to flourish. This is what delivering exceptional value looks like. As people prefer to live, work, invest, and develop in culturally rich environments, art can generate significant financial returns while simultaneously expressing diversity, helping us understand our relationship to the places where we live and work, and creating a sense of community and belonging. The value of this seems endless.

Andrew Hoyne is a thought leader on place-making strategy and branding.

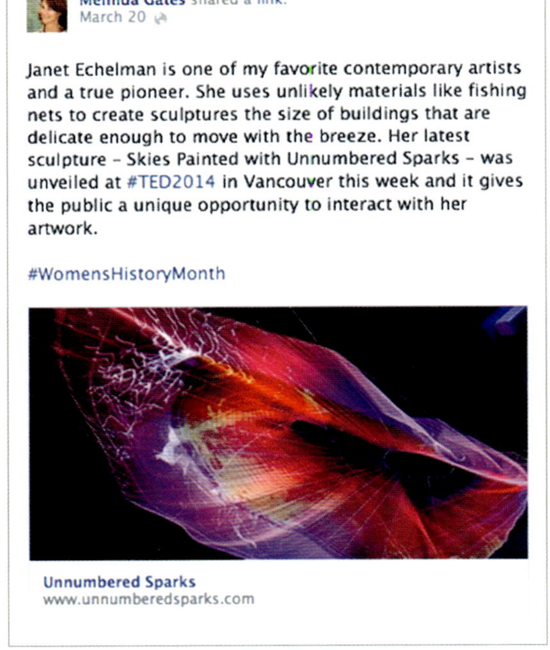

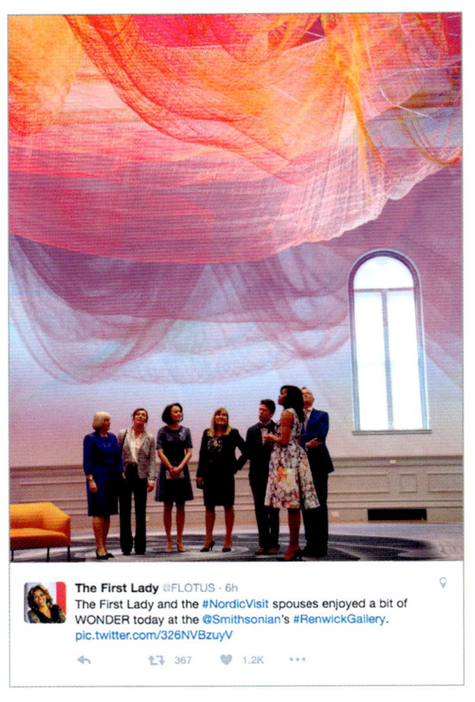

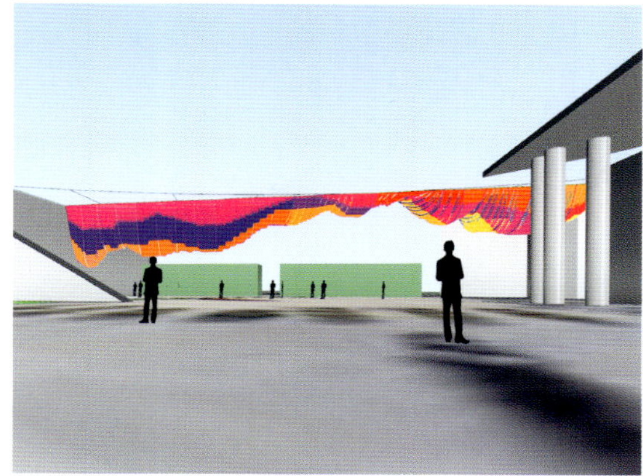

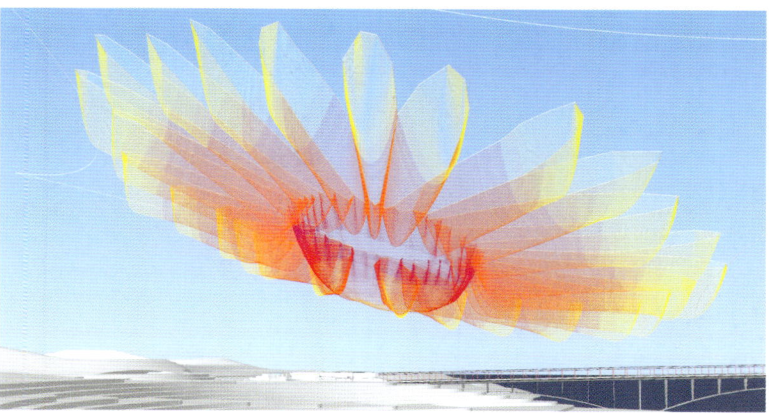

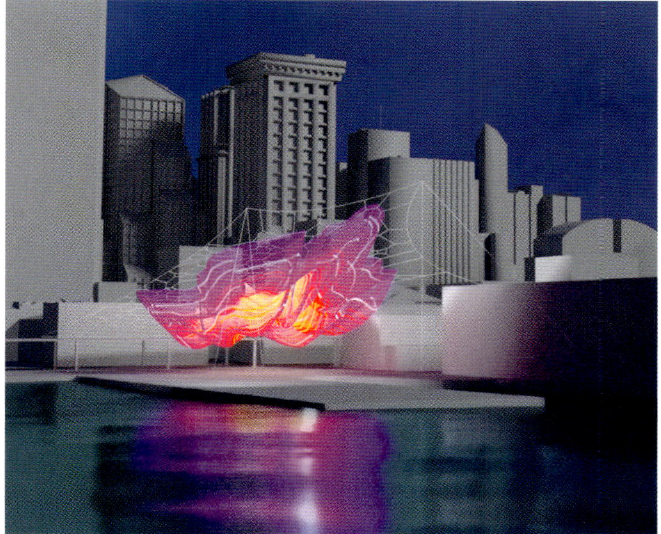

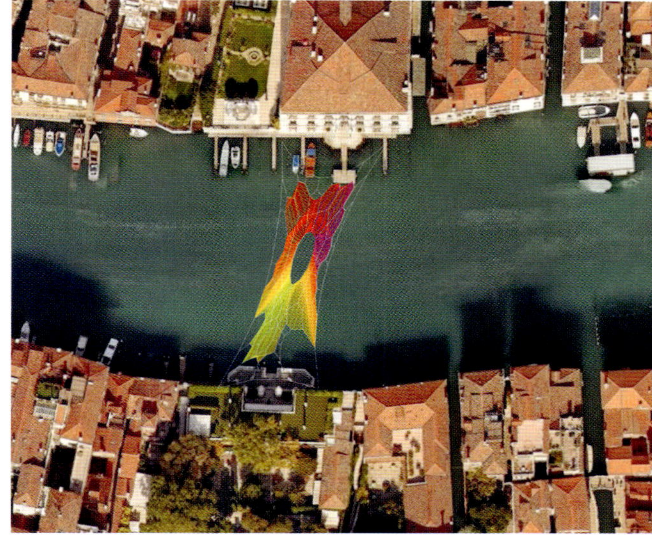

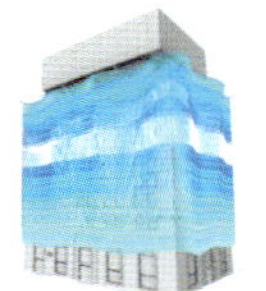

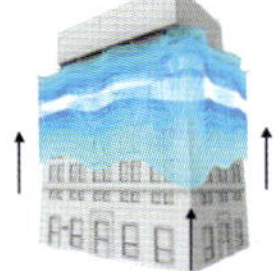

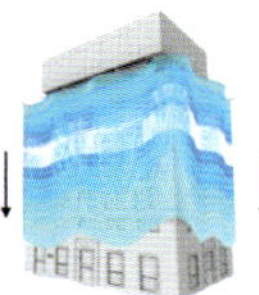

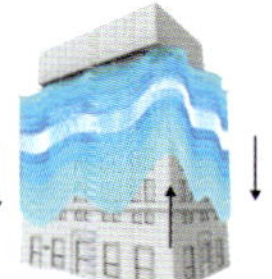

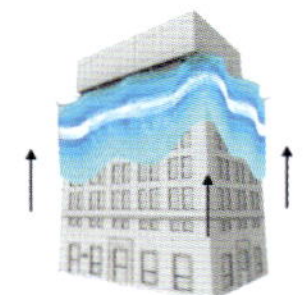

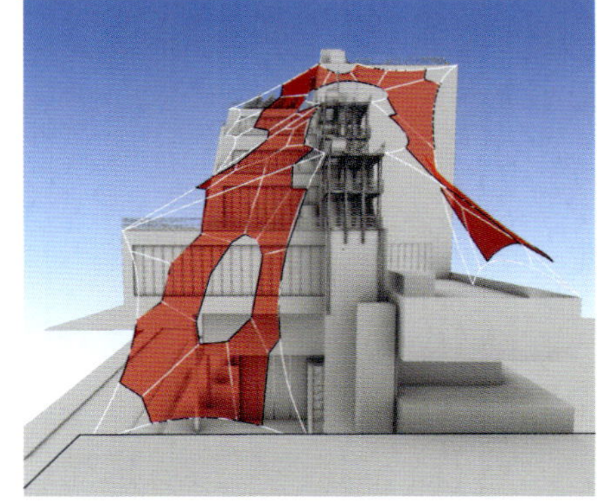

opposite, left: Melinda Gates posts Echelman's work on her social media to commemorate Women's History Month
opposite, right: First Lady Michelle Obama posts Echelman's work on her social media to highlight her introduction of the Nordic delegation to US art at the Smithsonian's Renwick Gallery
top row: Design visualizing Symphony No. 9 to celebrate Beethoven's 250th birthday celebration in 2020, stretching between the National and City Museums in Bonn, Germany; model for *Firewheel*, 2021, Tulsa, Oklahoma

middle row: Model for *Light Ship*, 2018, a design for New York City's Seaport at Pier 17; design for a sculpture suspended from the Peggy Guggenheim Collection building across the Grand Canal in Venice, 2017
bottom row: Design for a dynamic sculpture for an iconic flagship store in New York City, 2023; model for a sculpture connecting the Whitney Museum of American Art to the High Line, New York City, 2022

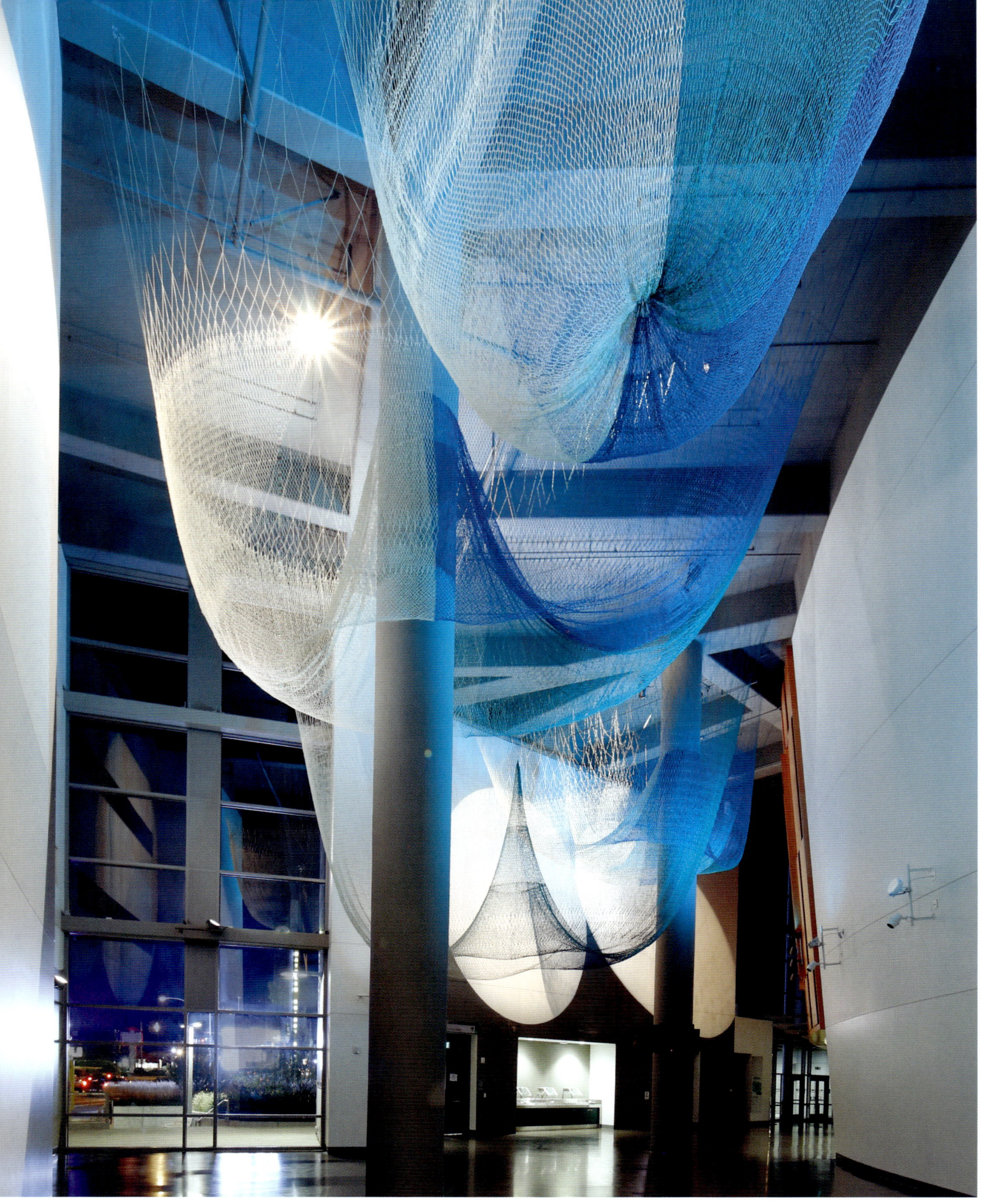

Allegory

—

Kathleen Dean Moore

What you first see as you enter *Allegory* (2014), sited in the northeast curve of Matthew Knight Arena at the University of Oregon in Eugene, are huge, circular nets billowing overhead. Green, white, blue—they encircle space the way a seine encircles herring, or a spiral galaxy encircles stars, or the sweeping arms of a giant Douglas fir gather the sky. But as you move through the hallway, the nets themselves seem to disappear, replaced by the shadows they throw onto the wall. Then the glimpse of the shadows fades, and again, there are the nets themselves wafting toward the ceiling high above.

Sunlit shadow fascinated Echelman from her very first public commissions (*She Changes* [2005], *Her Secret Is Patience* [2009]), and projected shadows later became a focal point in sites that offered surfaces on which she could project, from railroad passageways (*Tampa Line Drawing* [2007]) to museum walls (*Earthtime 1.8 Renwick* [2015]). "A sculpture should be thrilling to look at," Echelman says. "But a lasting sculpture has to be more than that. It has to hint at some connections that we don't entirely understand."[5] True to her vision, there is no point of view from which an observer can see all of a sculpture at once. While the nets and knots are three-dimensional, what you see on the wall is flat and devoid of color. The sculpture is designed to respond to and engage with its surroundings, acknowledging the importance of the spectator as a trigger for interactivity. Sensors near the artwork pick up the physical movements of viewers, activating specially programmed spotlights that cast shadow drawings onto surrounding walls. These shadows layer onto a silhouette wall painting that follows the parabolic curves of the suspended sculpture.

As she developed her idea for *Allegory*, Echelman took inspiration from the siting of the sculpture in a basketball arena. "People might think of the interconnectedness of the game," Echelman muses. "The trajectory of the basketball weaves nets that connect the five players on the floor, who are knitted into patterns of family and fans."[6] The sculpture refers also to the larger forested ecosystem surrounding the campus, its upsweeping nets inspiring, perhaps, thoughts on the interconnectedness of the ecosystems that sustain us, the great branching webs of life. The weekend before Echelman came to Eugene for the opening of *Allegory*, she visited H. J. Andrews Experimental Forest at the headwaters of the McKenzie River. On ropes, she ascended 130 feet up a five-hundred-year-old Douglas fir. There, in low evening light cast through the ancient, tangled, mist- and moss-shrouded boughs, she could see the shadows of the nets and knots of the forest ecosystem, draped over the encircling hills.

"When developing an idea," Echelman says, "I envision the ideal manifestation of the idea. I try to imagine my goal as a reality, and then work backward to figure out all the steps I need to make it so. We all have the potential to do that," she insists, "but it's a skill that takes practice."[7] So it's not only a sculpture that is taking shape in the university's arena, but a model for the dreams and aspirations of generations of young people who will envision an ideal and then work to make it real.

Kathleen Dean Moore is an author, environmental activist, and distinguished professor of philosophy emerita, Oregon State University.

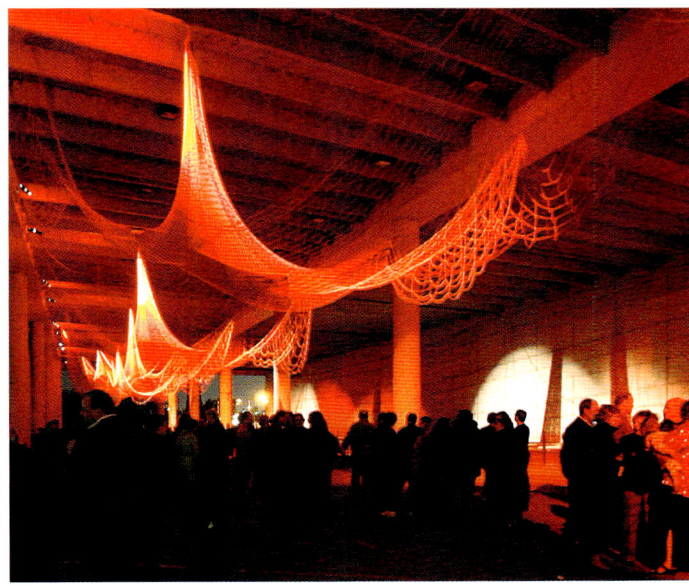

opposite: *Allegory*, 2014, Matthew Knight Arena, University of Oregon at Eugene
above: *Line Drawing*, 2006, Tampa, Florida

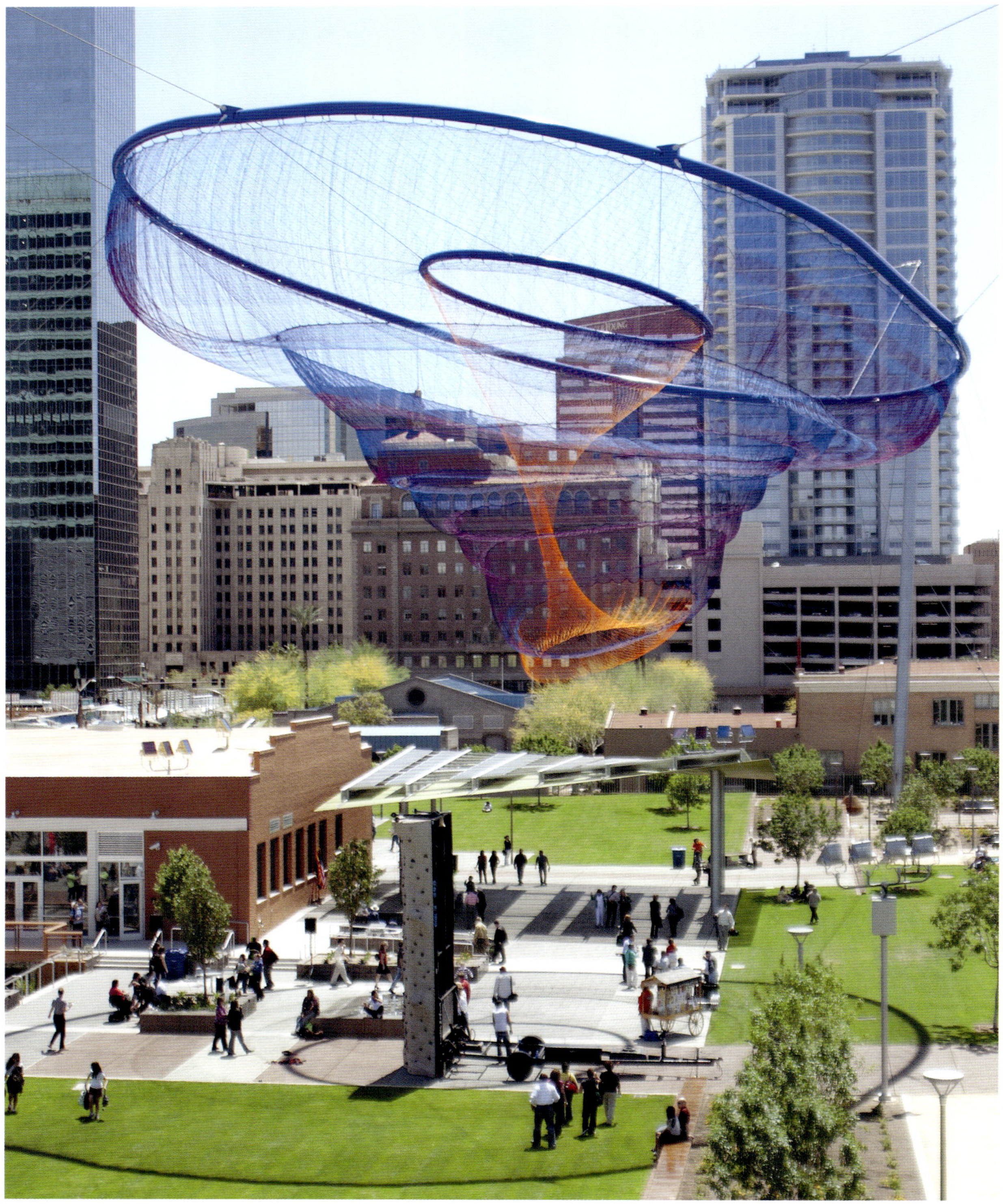

Her Secret Is Patience, 2009, Phoenix, Arizona

Transparency and Contradiction

—

Andrew Wasserman

Janet Echelman does not install objects; she makes places. Perhaps more accurately, she guides encounters with places. Rather than halting vision, Echelman's public projects heighten perceptions of built environments. Less filling than connecting spaces, her projects enhance rather than occlude. They frame urban forms, spied beyond the materials she introduces to a site. These materials—knotted, wound, and layered fiber networks hoisted overhead or curtains of steam rising from the ground—vacillate between substantial presence and evanescence. Audiences look through their materials to the physical and cultural landscapes surrounding them, landscapes themselves held between stability and flux.

Echelman's series of *Earthtime* sculptures (2010–) have mingled among the diverse centuries-spanning stuff of contemporary urban spaces, from Amsterdam's canal system to Madrid's Plaza Mayor, Montreal's Quartier des Spectacles, Munich's Odeonsplatz, and Santiago's Parque Forestal. Her projects also introduce references to the materials, economic systems, and civic engagements of their sites' longer histories. Inspired by Columbus's nineteenth-century electrified and illuminated arched trusses, *Current* (2023) floats above the so-called Arch City's downtown. Soaring over Greensboro's LeBauer Park, *Where We Met* (2016) references historical rail lines connecting regional textile mills. *Her Secret Is Patience* (2009) speaks to the pace of urban development in downtown Phoenix, as the park beneath the sculpture was formerly a notorious strip club and parking lots. Local lacework traditions and a maritime trade reliant on striped lighthouses guided the design of *She Changes* (2005), gently bobbing above a traffic circle along Porto's waterfront. *Pulse* (2018) periodically brings to the surface of Philadelphia's Dilworth Park a subterranean infrastructure born of nineteenth-, twentieth-, and twenty-first century debates over the locations and operations of public transit. Drawing forth these historical traces, Echelman's transparent sculptures make visible the layered temporalities that define urban places. In a pair of articles published the late 2000s, architectural historian and theorist Eve Blau proposed understanding transparency as a perceptual effect and a conceptual framework. Rather than making something insensible, transparency creates "a series of irreconcilable contradictions: between objective and subjective modes of cognition; between different systems of organization and structure, perception and knowledge, material and virtual presence; and the relationship between the architectural object and the equally dynamic and mutable physical and social environments in which it operates."[8] For Blau, transparency's capacious offerings exceed the domain of the architectural. They are found in a range of media, including still and moving-image experiments that decontextualize and recontextualize imagistic and material content, as well as sculptural installations made of intensely luminous technologies. They foster novel perceptual experiences, guiding viewers not just to see new things but to see in new ways. Transparency is a "function of projection beyond the object itself," which Blau clarified as "generating space beyond the object itself, which is experienced optically but which is immaterial." This condition of transparency "does not inhabit space, it does not contain space, it instead expresses space."[9]

The irreconcilable contradictions of transparency create openings rather than limitations. The goal is not to resolve these contradictions, but rather to engage them in order to construct new habits of encounter and expand the possible meanings places can yield. To gaze toward and navigate through Echelman's literally transparent and translucent public installations is to glimpse imbricated landscapes. In dialogue with Blau's call for artists, architects, and designers "to continuously engage and challenge proliferating technologies and the irreconcilable contradictions of the new environments they create,"[10] Echelman looks to transparency to express space as a condition of making places for others. Her works make audiences aware of the places through which they pass, or linger, whether once or again and again. Falling in and out of sight, Echelman's sculptures expand what can be known about and from places.

Andrew Wasserman is the author of The World Atlas of Public Art *and former co-chair of Public Art Dialogue.*

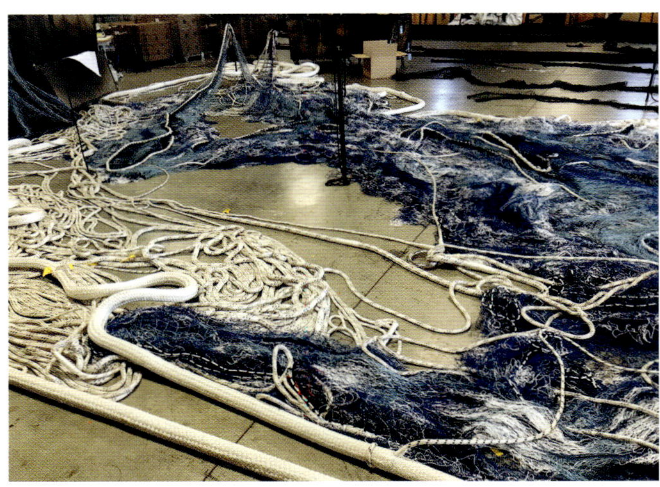

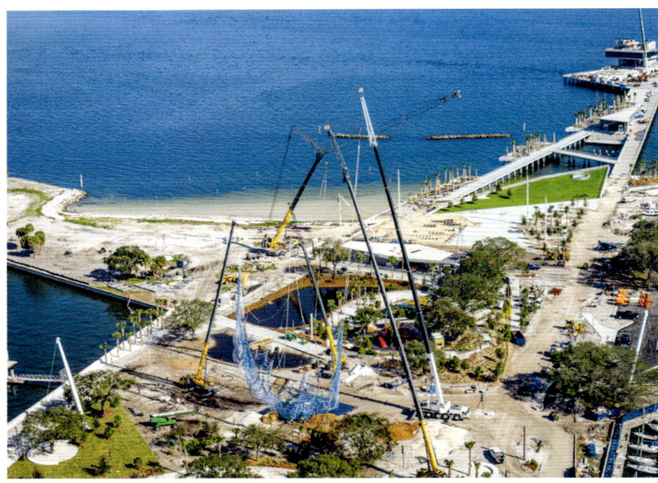

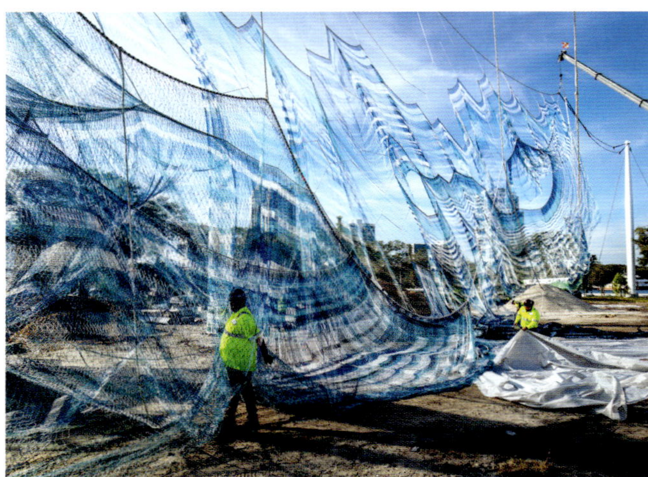

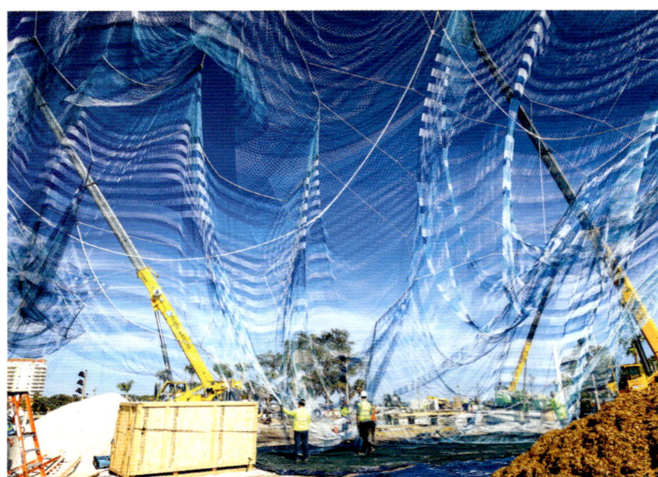

above: Fabrication and installation of *Bending Arc*, 2020, St. Petersburg, Florida

opposite: Aerial views of *Bending Arc*, 2020

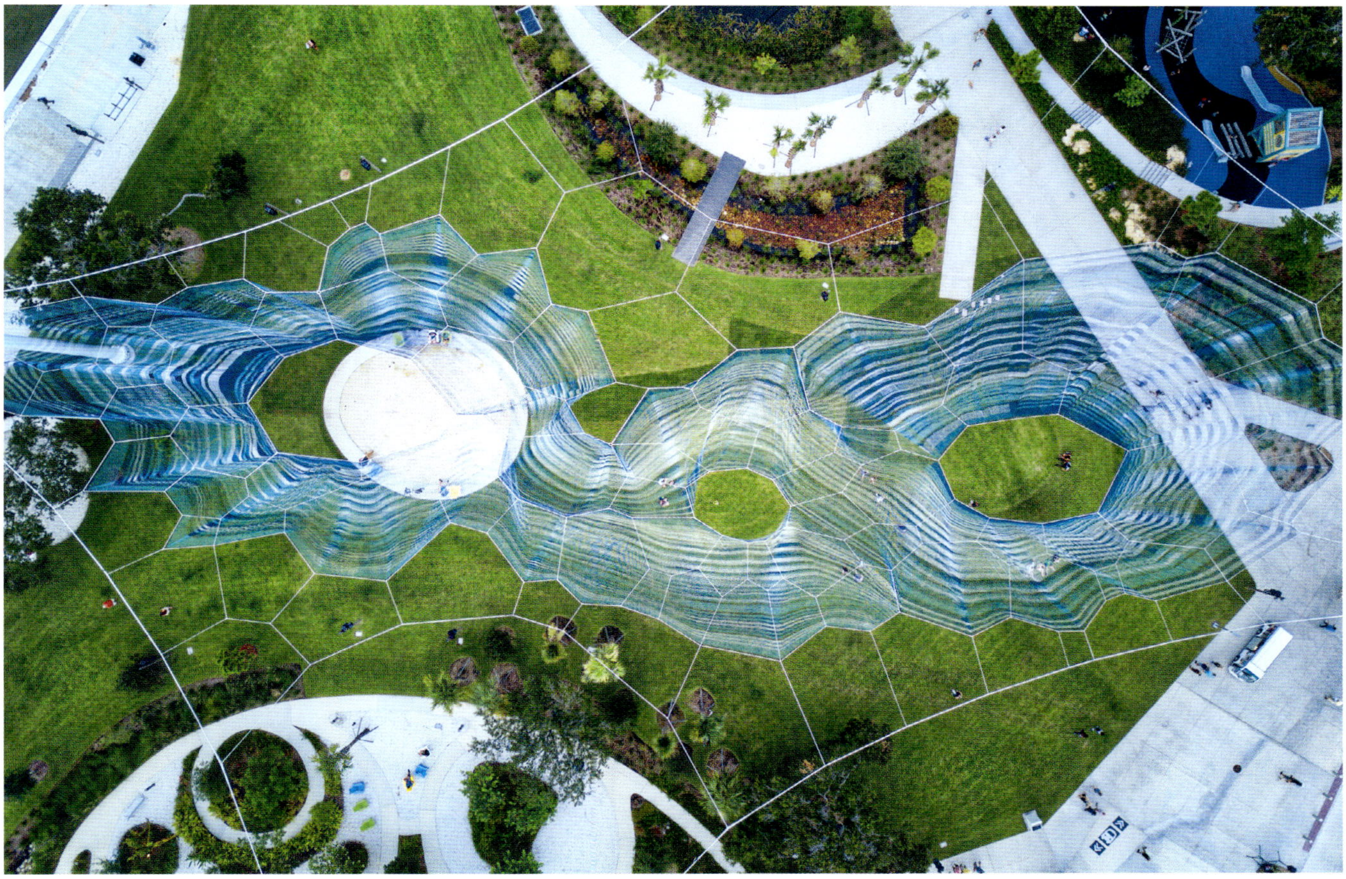

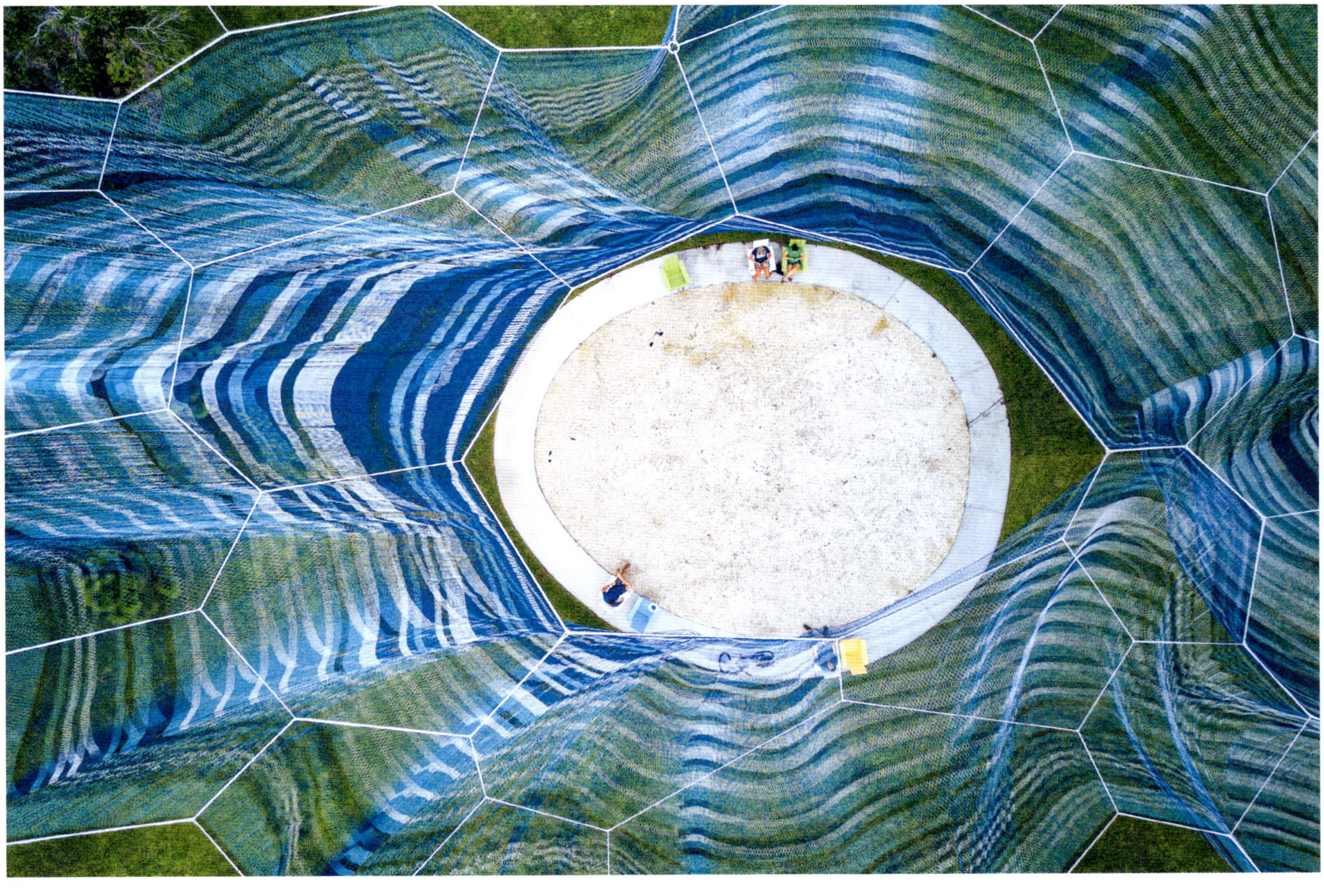

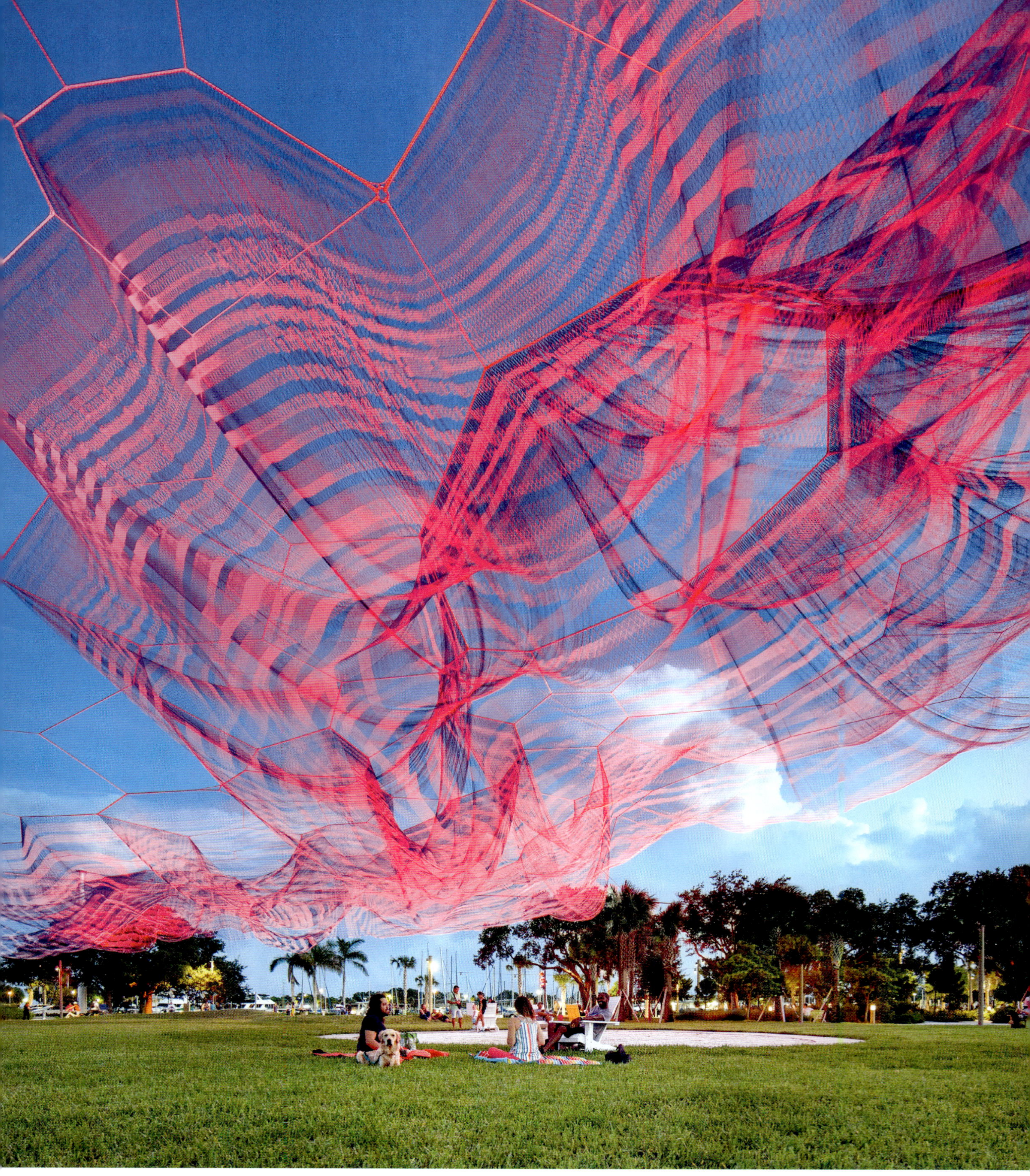

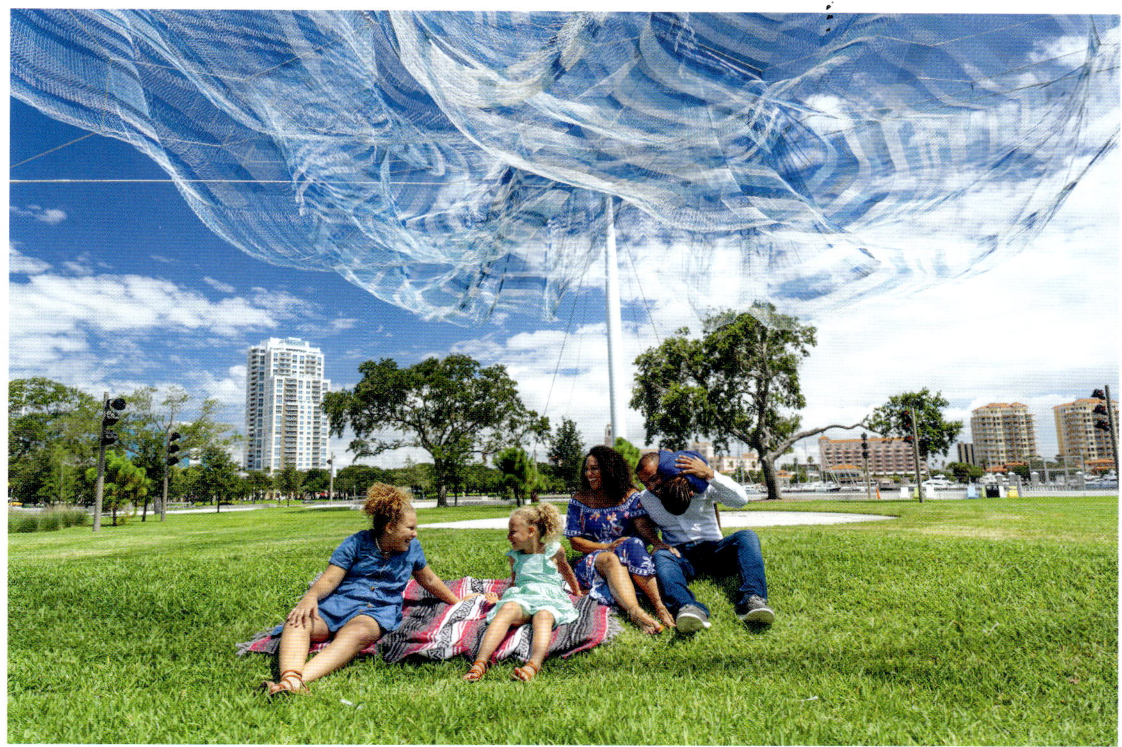

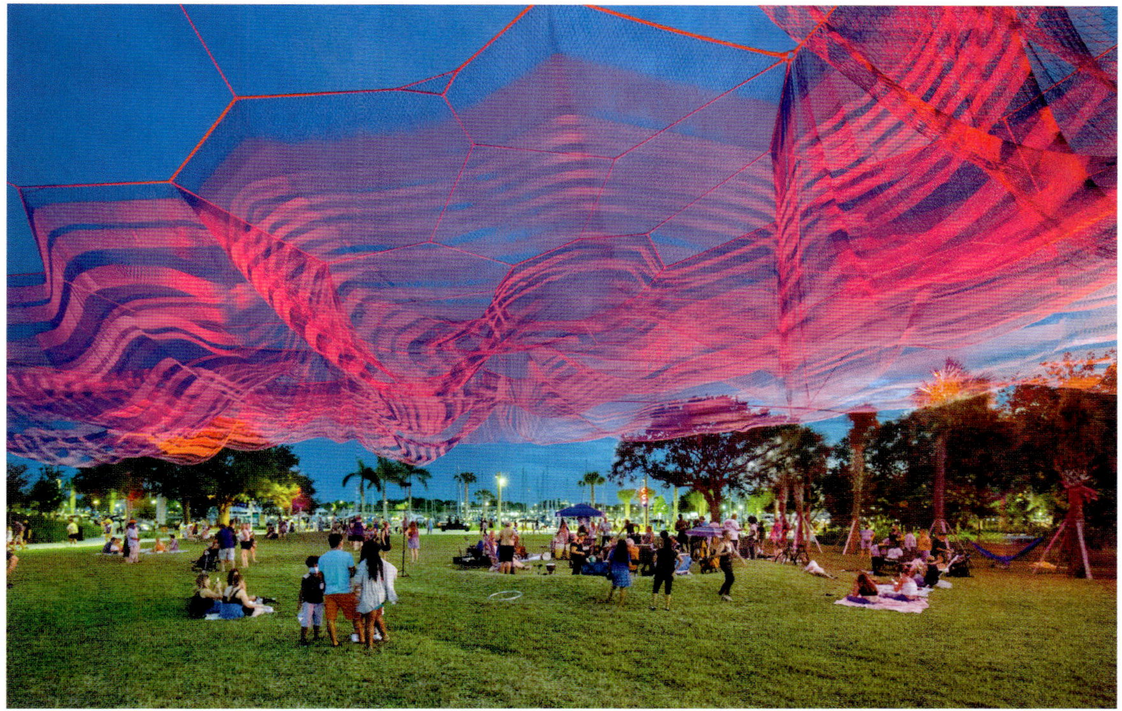

opposite and above: *Bending Arc*, 2020, is used by the public for both formal programs and informal gatherings, from picnics and yoga to pop-up weekly drumming circles

As If It Were Already Here

—

Sarah Williams Goldhagen

To paraphrase for a moment from the project description: *As If It Were Already Here* was a monumental aerial sculpture suspended over Boston's Rose Kennedy Greenway from May through October 2015 as the signature contemporary art installation in the Greenway Conservancy's Public Art Program. The artwork was awarded the 2022 Harleston Parker Medal, which recognizes "the most beautiful piece of architecture, building, monument, or structure" in the city of Boston. Established in 1921 and voted on annually by the Boston Society for Architecture, any project built within the past ten years is eligible. This was the first time in its 102-year history that the award was given to a work of fine art, and also the first time it was given to an ephemeral work. The sculpture spanned the void where an elevated highway once split downtown from the waterfront. Knitting together the urban fabric, it soared six hundred feet through the air above street traffic and the pedestrian park. The form echoed the history of its location. The three voids recalled the "tri-mountain," which was razed in the eighteenth century to create land in the harbor. The colored banding was a nod to the six traffic lanes that once overwhelmed the neighborhood, before the Big Dig buried them and enabled the space to be reclaimed for urban pedestrian life. The work invited one to linger, whether seen against the skyline from afar, or while lying down on the grassy knoll beneath. It embraced Boston as a city on foot, where past and present are interwoven, and took our gaze skyward to feel the vibrant pulse of now. It invited contemplation of a physical manifestation of interconnectedness—soft with hard, earth with sky, things we control with the forces beyond us.

As If It Were Already Here etched a latticed, transparent ceiling above our heads, prompting use as a "home base" on the serpentine mile-and-a-half-long greenway. This is why so many people who enjoyed it spoke of their decision to lie down under it to rest. The billowing nets violated our expectations of what a city can offer, and be. Buildings are inert, hard, planar, and usually monochromatic, yet here was an urban moment that unfolded over time in a soft, permeable, colorful experience of rapture.

As If It Were Already Here—and this is true of all Echelman's artworks—recruited and played on these human perceptual fundamentals to deliver a communal aesthetic experience of urban delight. Echelman's immense, colorful nets flow with the wind, shift in the light, and change colors over the course of the day. We cannot but look, and we cannot but keep looking, glancing up, checking. Within milliseconds, we apprehend the sculpture's basic pattern—fishing nets!—while the wind, the quivering, luminous colors, the surprise of seeing so fluid and immense a structure above supply the delight of predictable and unpredictable complexity.

Whatever else people are, we are evolutionarily evolved beings who relate to our surrounding environments in some established ways. First: humans are highly visual. A large percentage of our brain's real estate, upward of 40 percent or higher, is devoted to visual processing. Second: in inhabiting environments, humans, who spent millennia dominated by nature, its predators, and its opportunities, are exquisitely attuned to change and especially to motion (what's moving? is it safe?). Third: this attunement holds in the immediate moment, and continues to hold over time (that thing that was moving—it was safe then, but is it *still* safe?). Fourth: humans are innately attracted to bright colors (think: sunsets, berries, flowers). Colors strum on our emotions as the strings of a violin make music. Fifth: humans orient to their surroundings by establishing in their environments a home base, from which everything else becomes periphery. Sixth: the human visual system is a pattern-seeking machine. Identifying the patterns constituting an environment makes us feel safer. Seventh: as much as humans crave the predictability of patterns, we also loathe understimulation, so we are especially drawn to, and intrigued by, patterns that are visually complex. If those patterns change a lot while maintaining their basic comprehensible structure, so much the better.

Sarah Williams Goldhagen is an author, scholar, and former architecture critic for The New Republic.

opposite: *As If It Were Already Here*, 2015, Rose Kennedy Greenway, Boston, Massachusetts

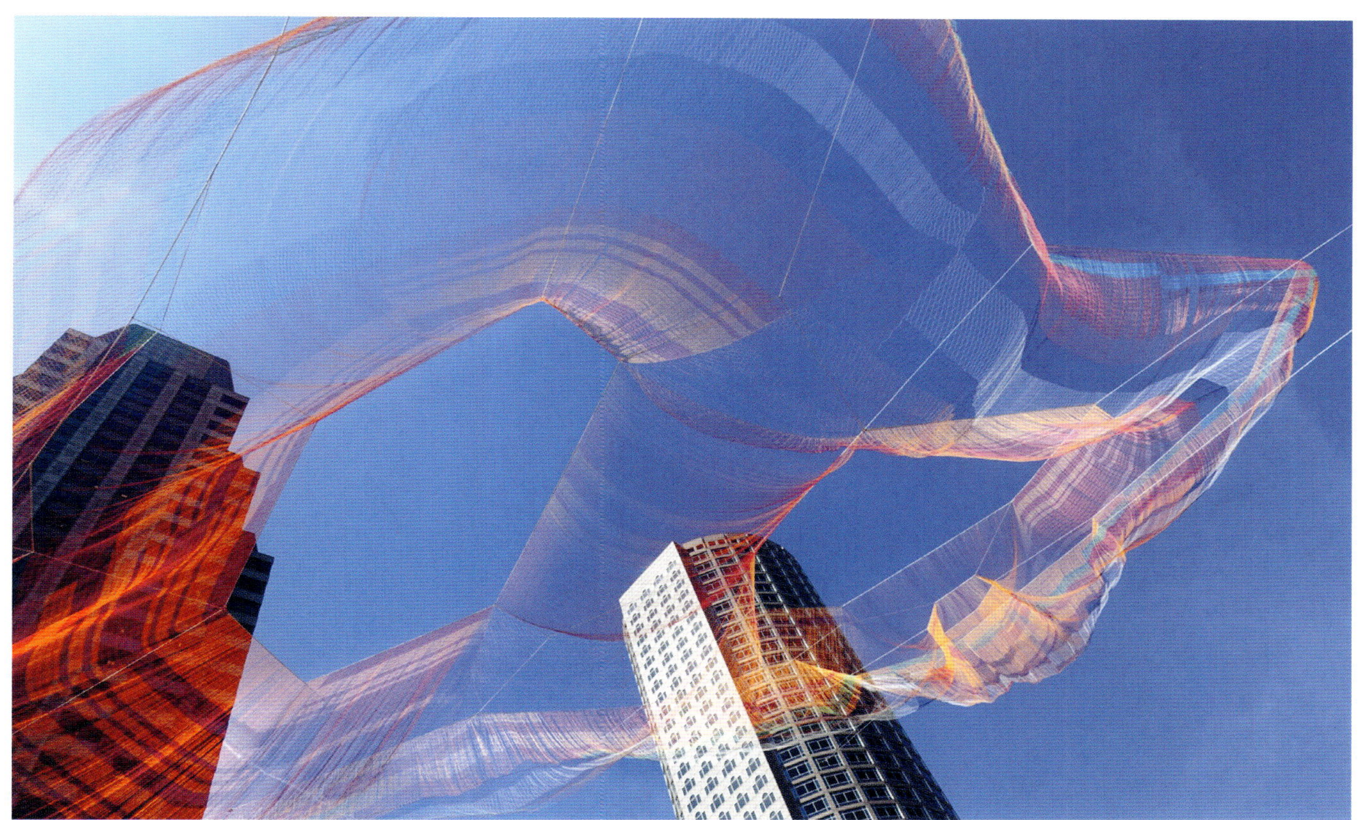

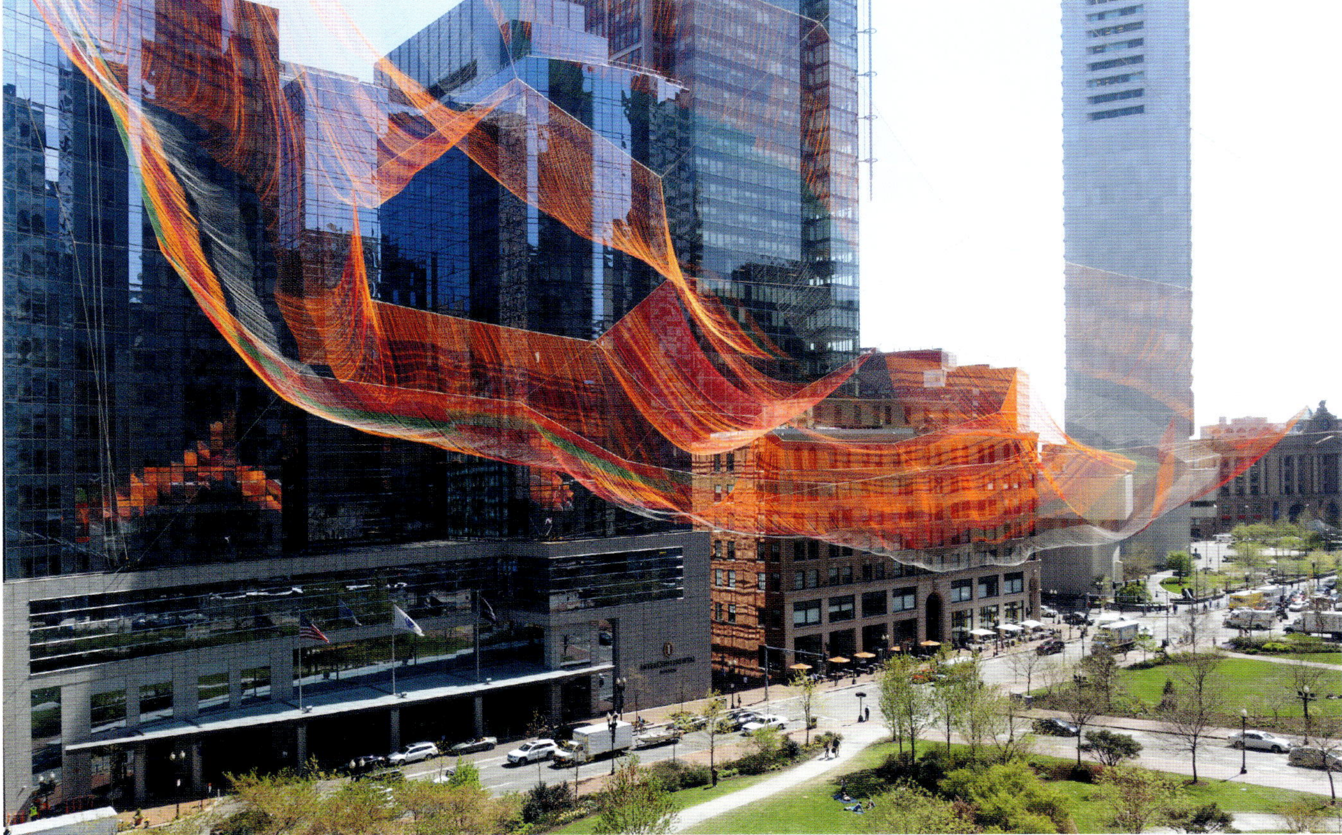

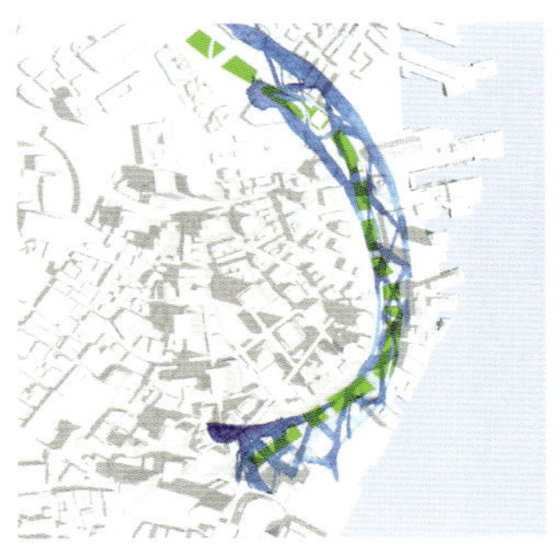

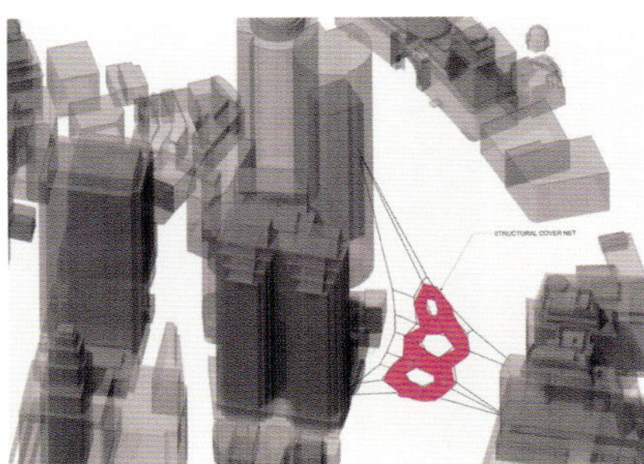

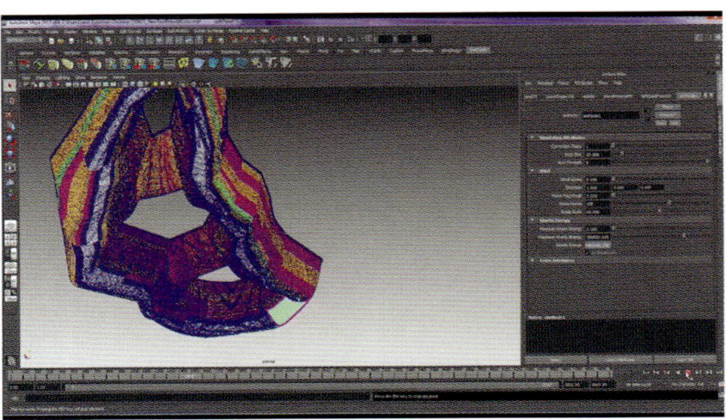

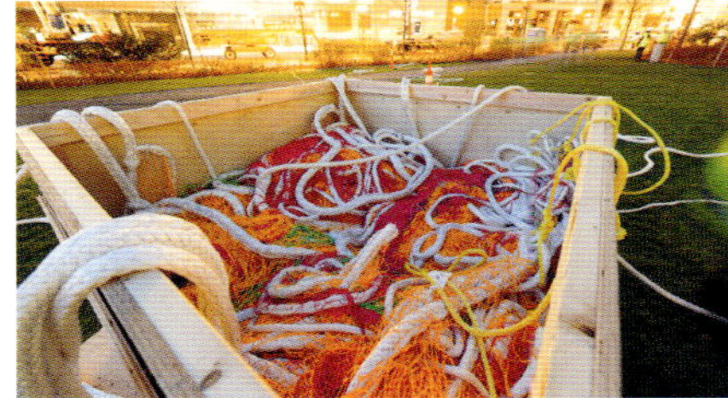

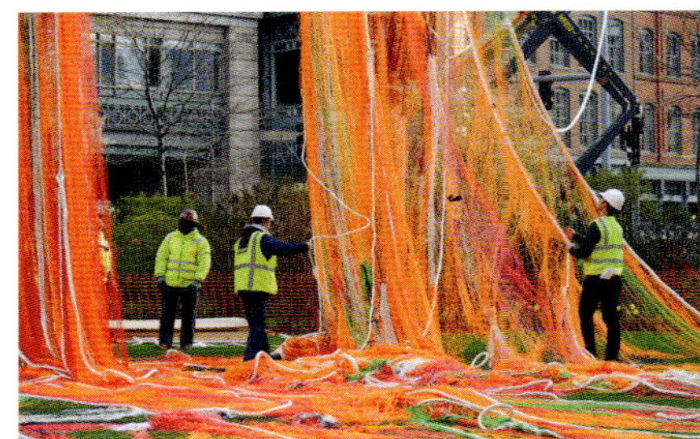

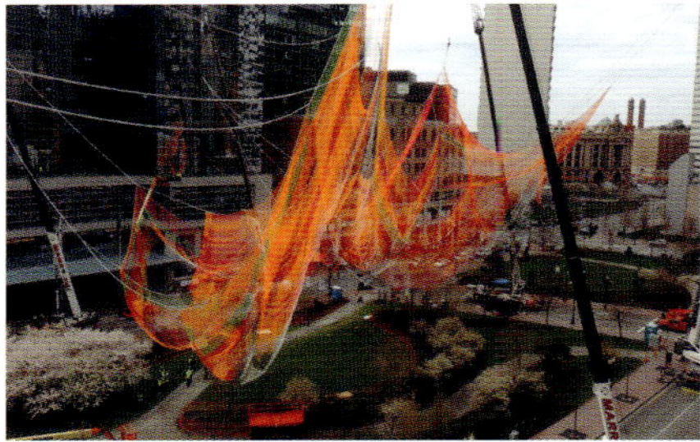

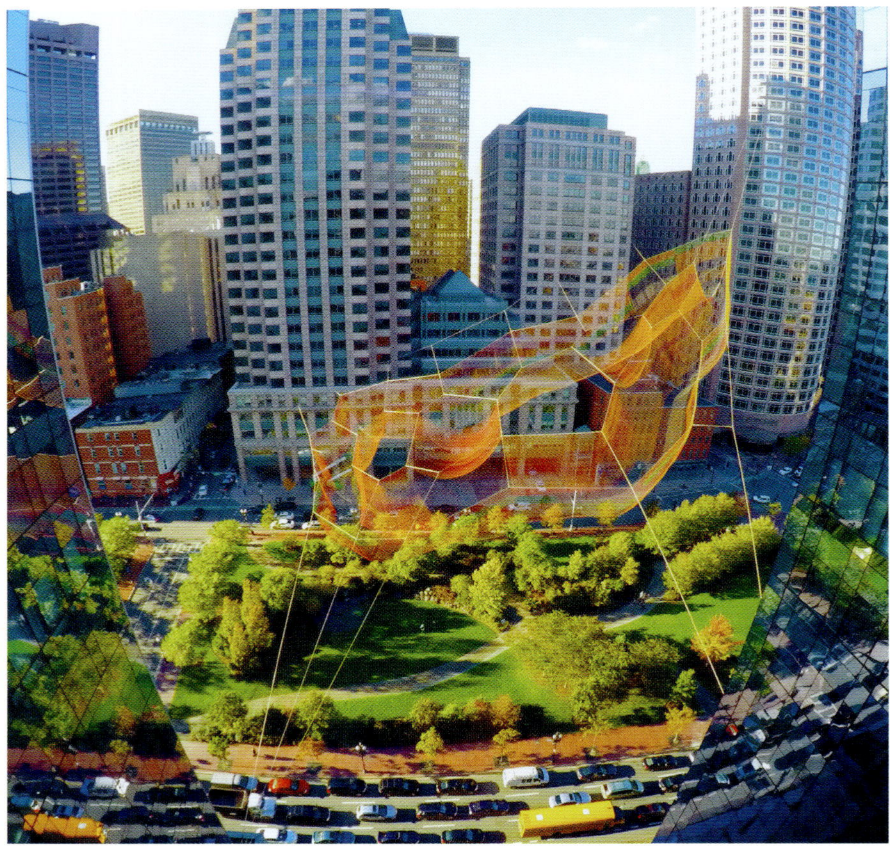

top row: Preliminary ink sketch; 3D urban model showing attachment points; 3D sculpture modeling and color bobbin patterning using the studio's JNET software
bottom left column: *As If It Were Already Here*, 2015, arrives in its wooden crate and is installed

above and opposite: *As If It Were Already Here*, 2015
overleaf: The I-90 entrance in downtown Boston was closed as seven cranes mobilized to install *As If It Were Already Here*, 2015.

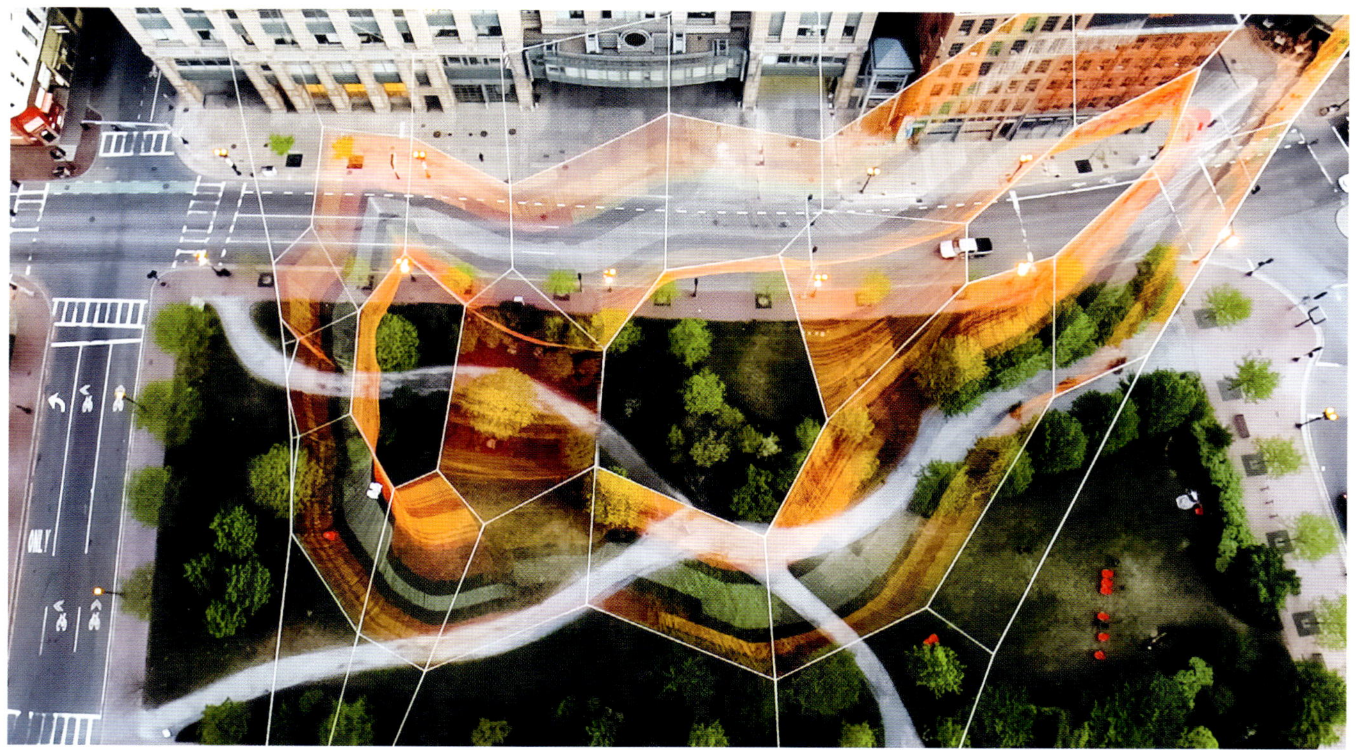

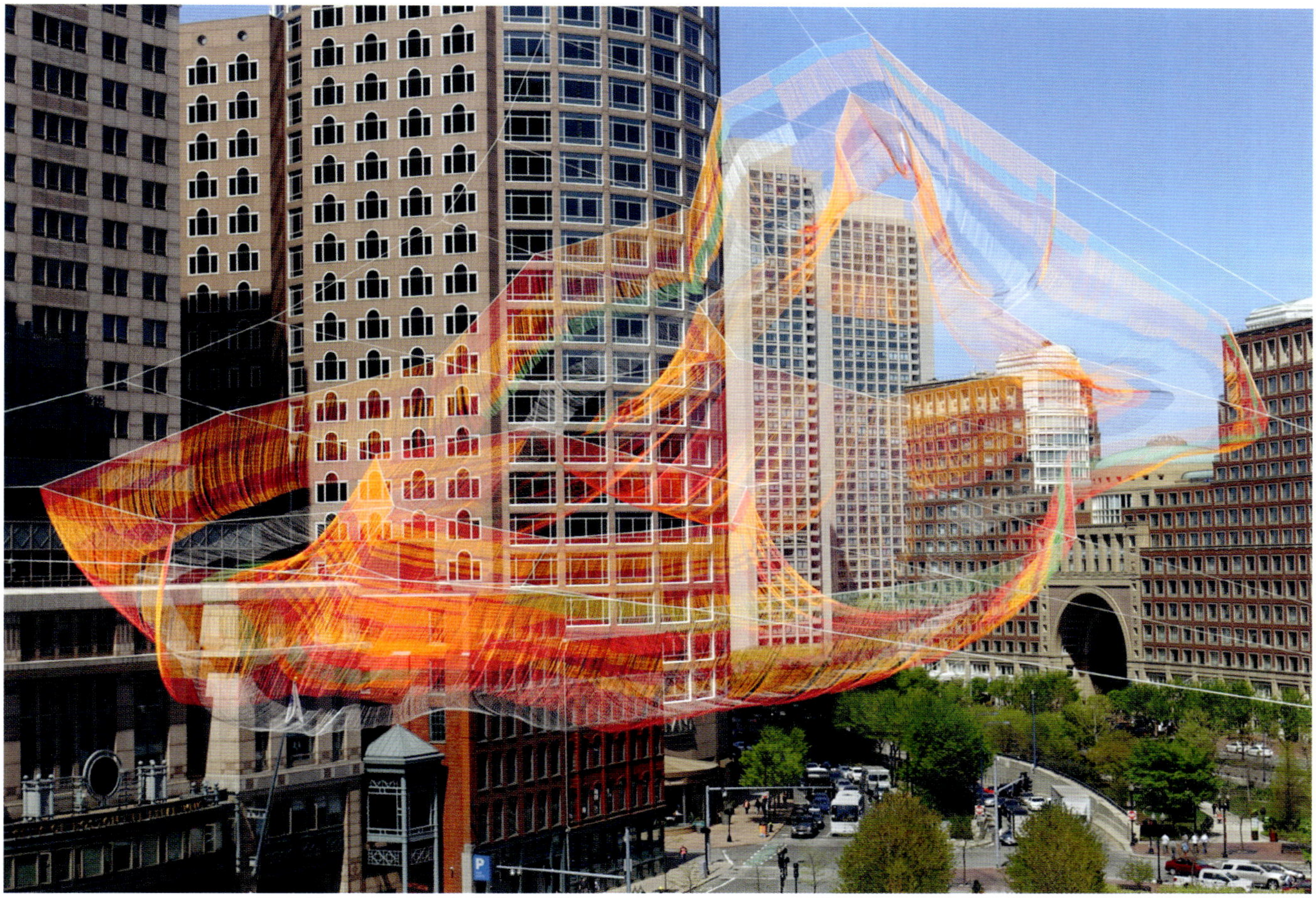

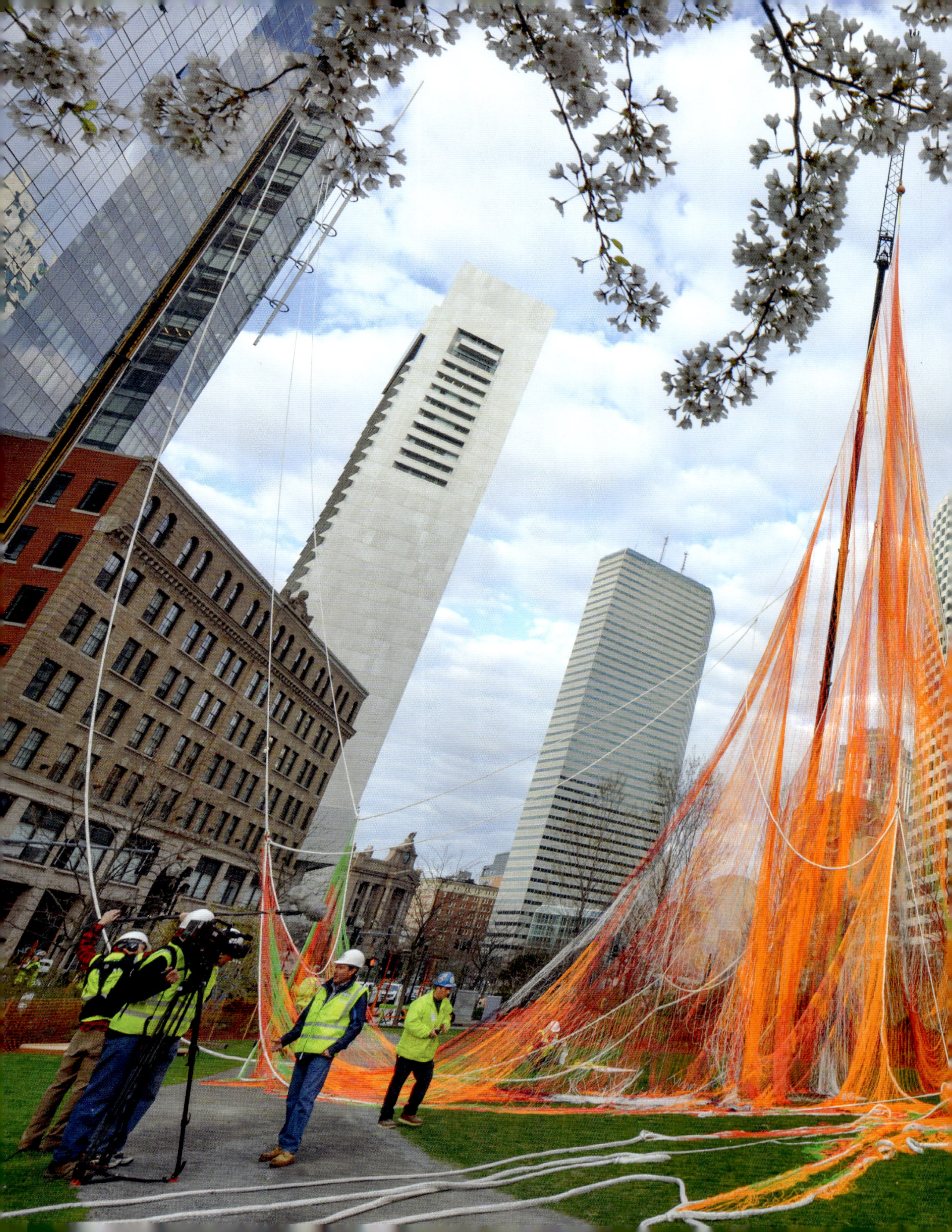

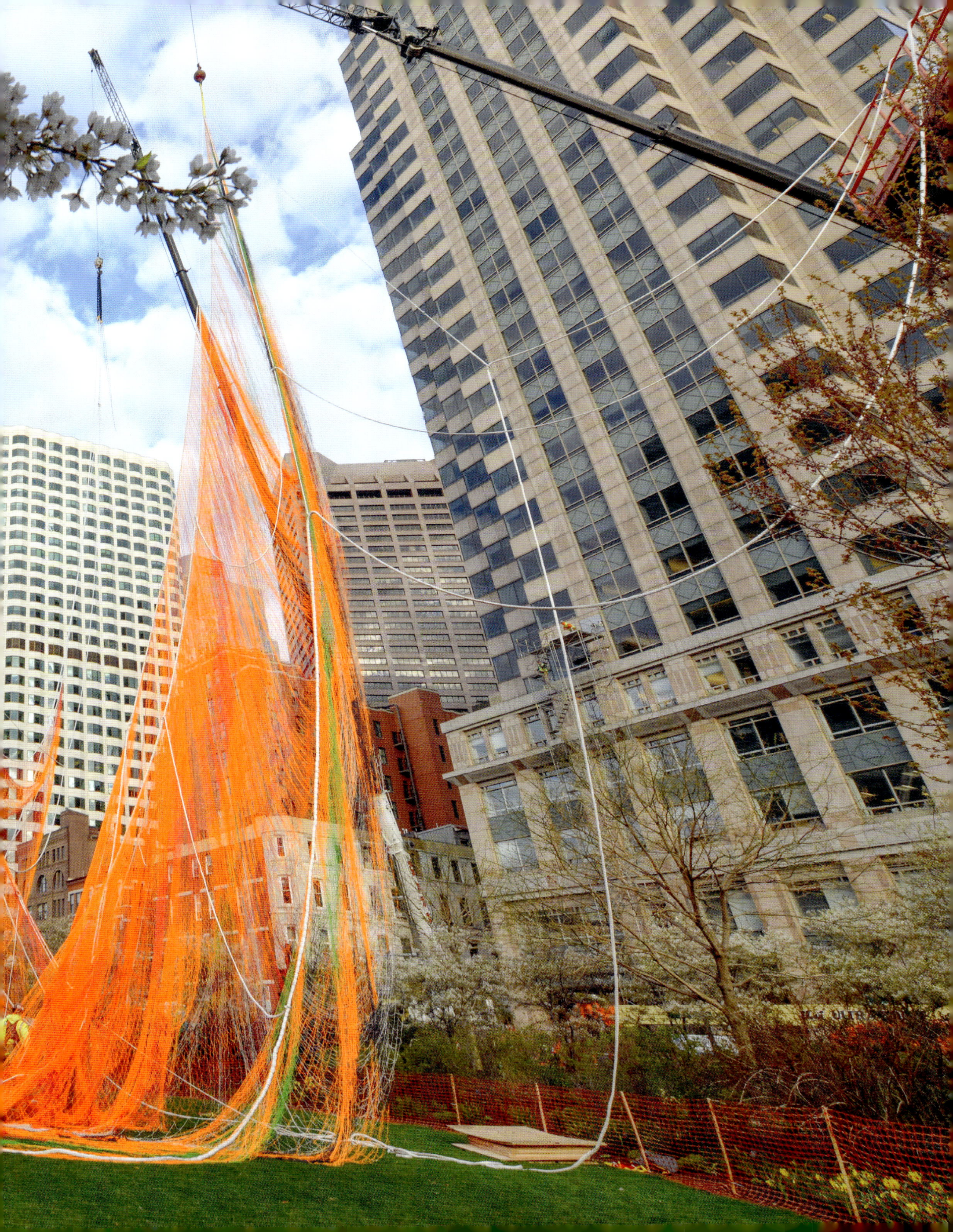

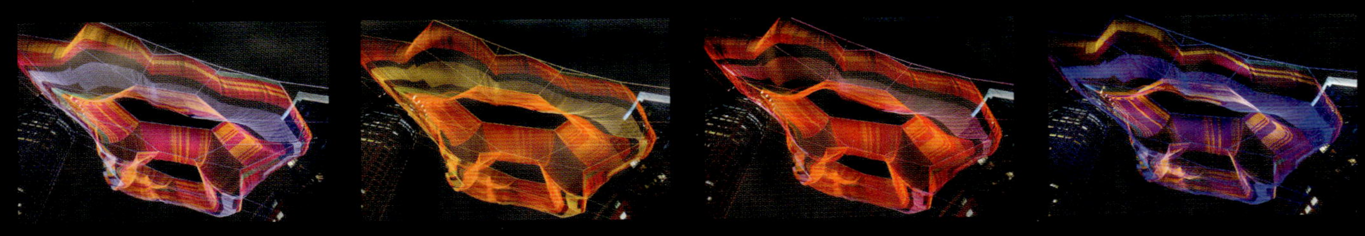

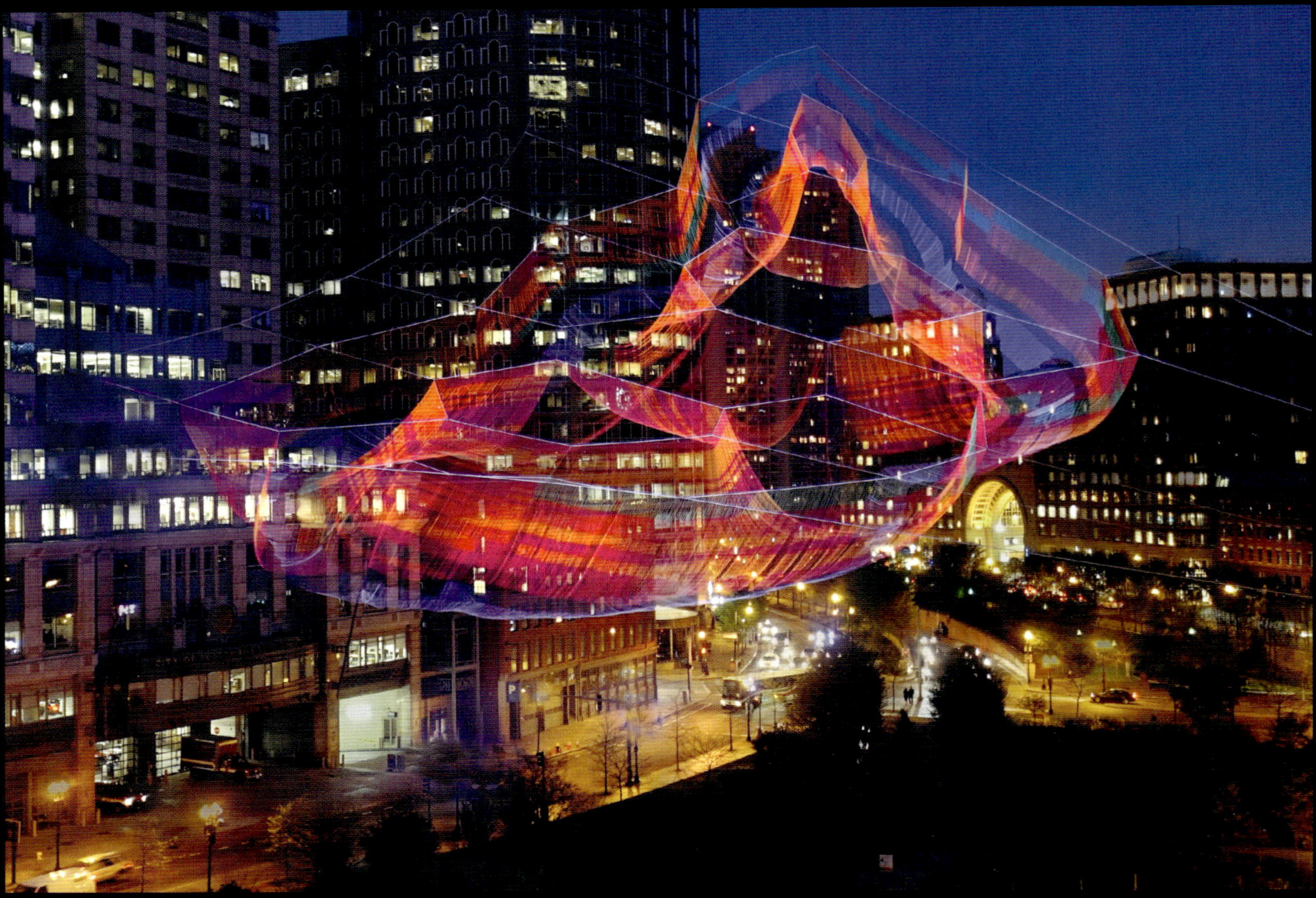

above and opposite, overleaf:
As If It Were Already Here, 2015

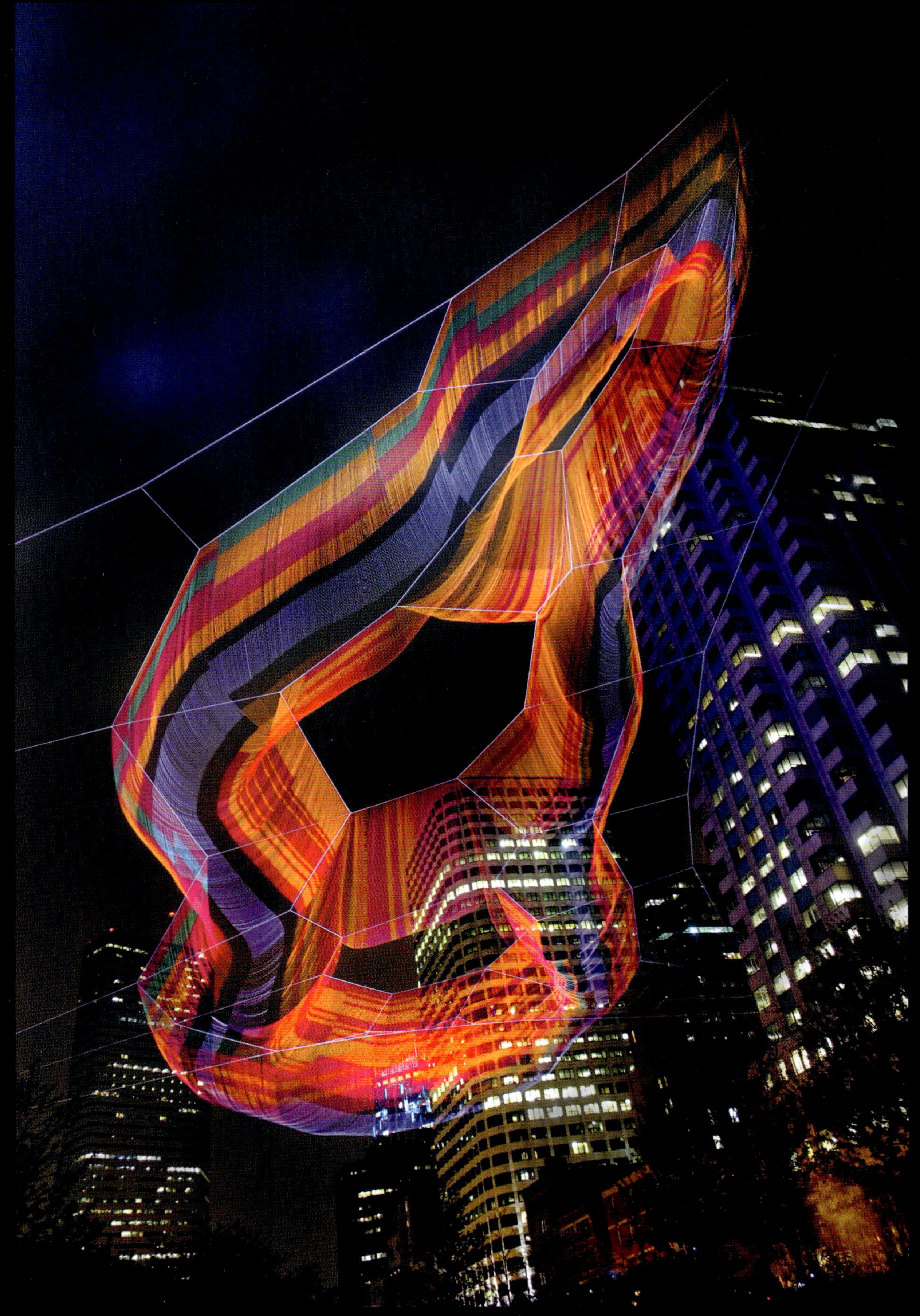

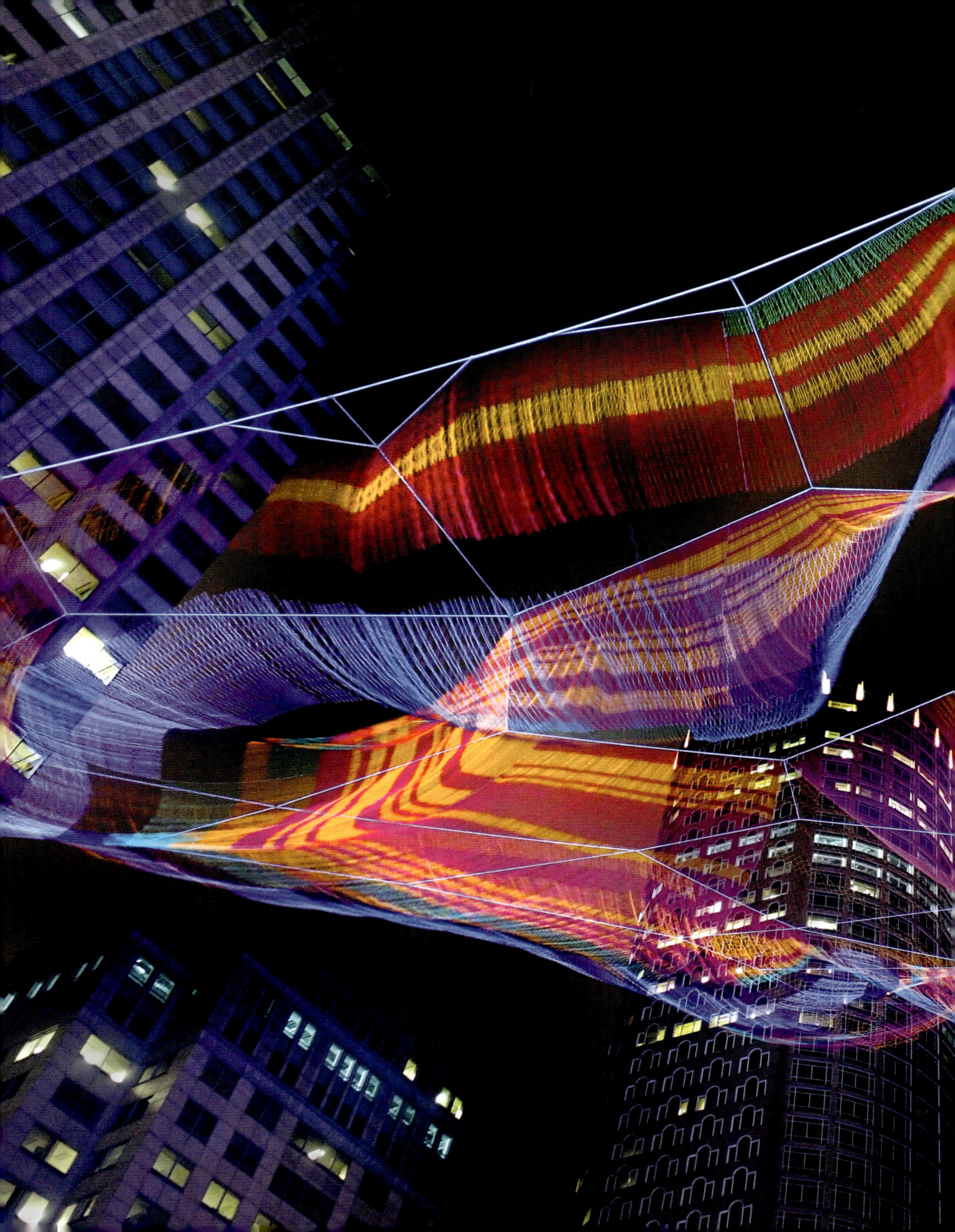

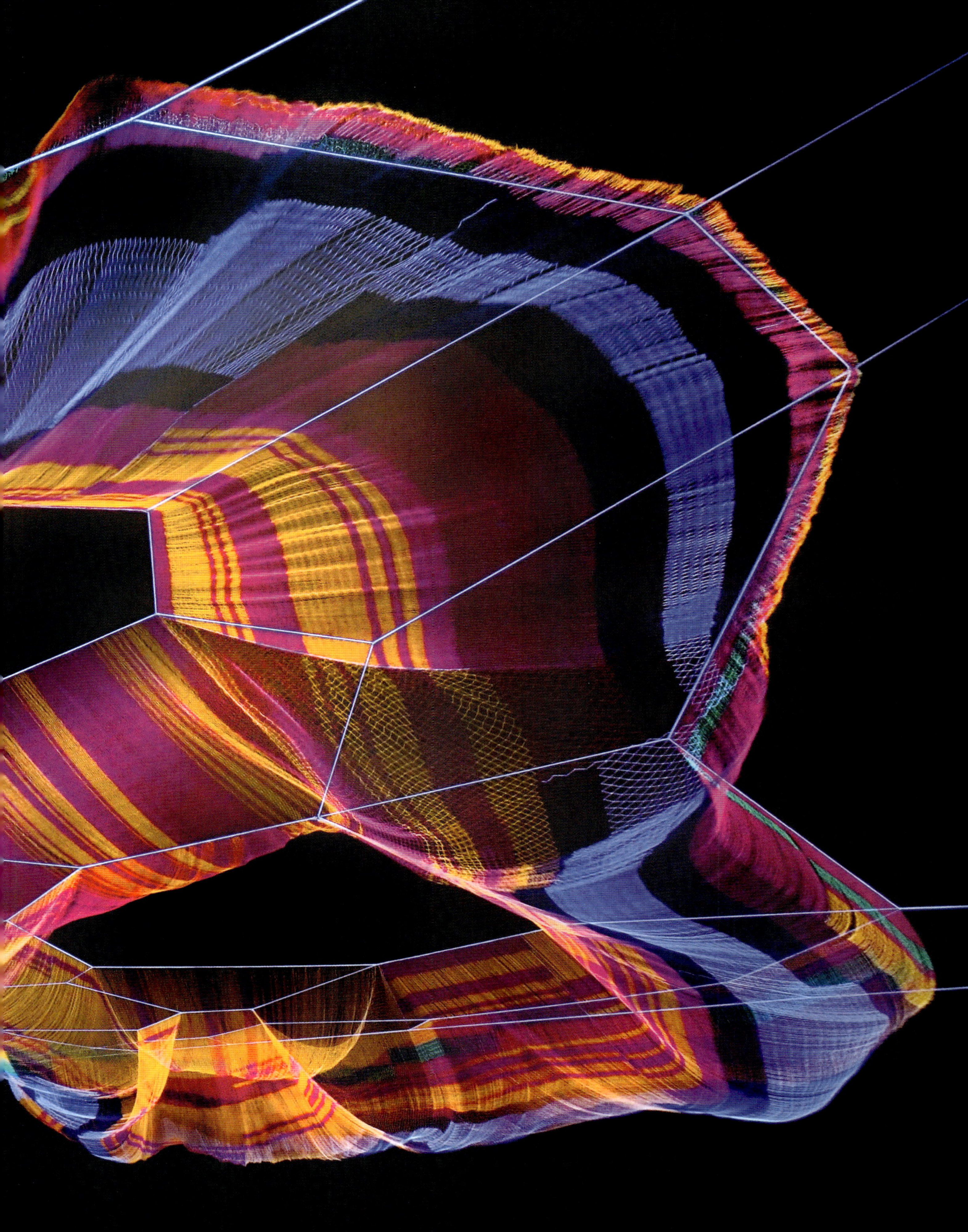

Sky Sculpture

—

Robert Pinsky

Restless at their plural knots
Anchored to towers higher
Than the hills long ago

Leveled to fill the harbor
These confluences of color
Ride the wind in a rope shape

Shifter that unlike windows
And more like trees or shadows
Does not bewilder the birds

Viewing this work of art was a bit like looking at the Grand Canyon or at the ocean: What you behold is something not entirely made by human means and imagination but also clearly made, in an exhilarating way, by the artist. That's how I remember my springtime visit to this festive work of public art, with a communal audience experiencing Janet Echelman's work in the ordinary, daily life of Boston. Seeing this work of art was like going outside. Each time you go outside, whatever you see is a little different, and ever-changing. In a particular way, nature is a co-artist on whatever day, at whatever moment, you happen to be looking at the capering, fluid forms and colors teasing at their high anchors. The changing light and the changing winds that move the material are part of the work. My memory of having seen the "sky sculpture" includes a civic pleasure in the way we viewers all enjoyed it together: a work not only of public but of civic art. It was fun to take the MFA students to see it. The young poets were awed and knocked out. Each one of them wrote something quite different. It was a happy day.

Robert Pinsky is a poet, critic, and three-term US poet laureate.

opposite: Visitors lie on the grass to look up at *As If It Were Already Here*, 2015, Rose Kennedy Greenway, Boston, Massachusetts

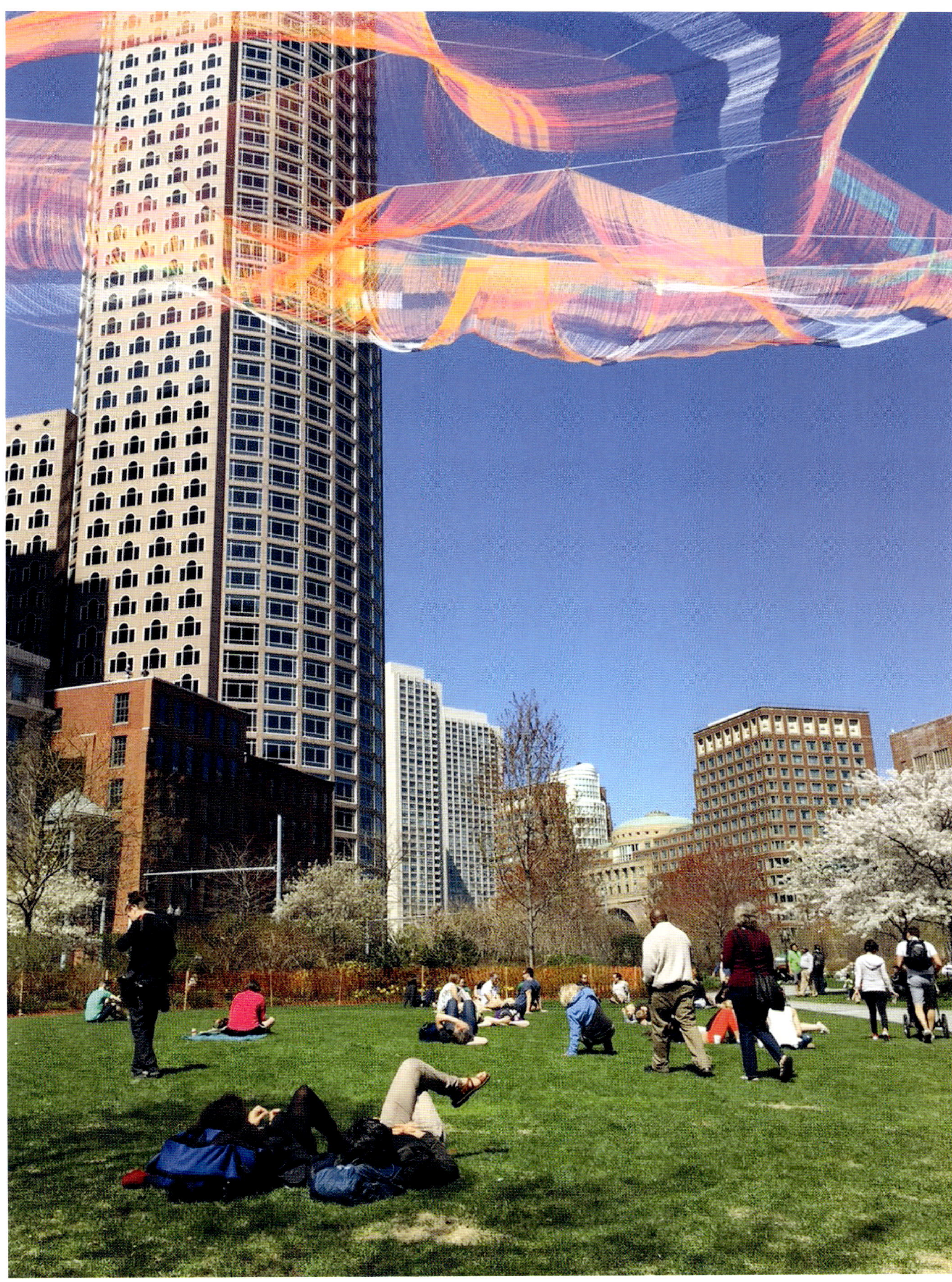

Four

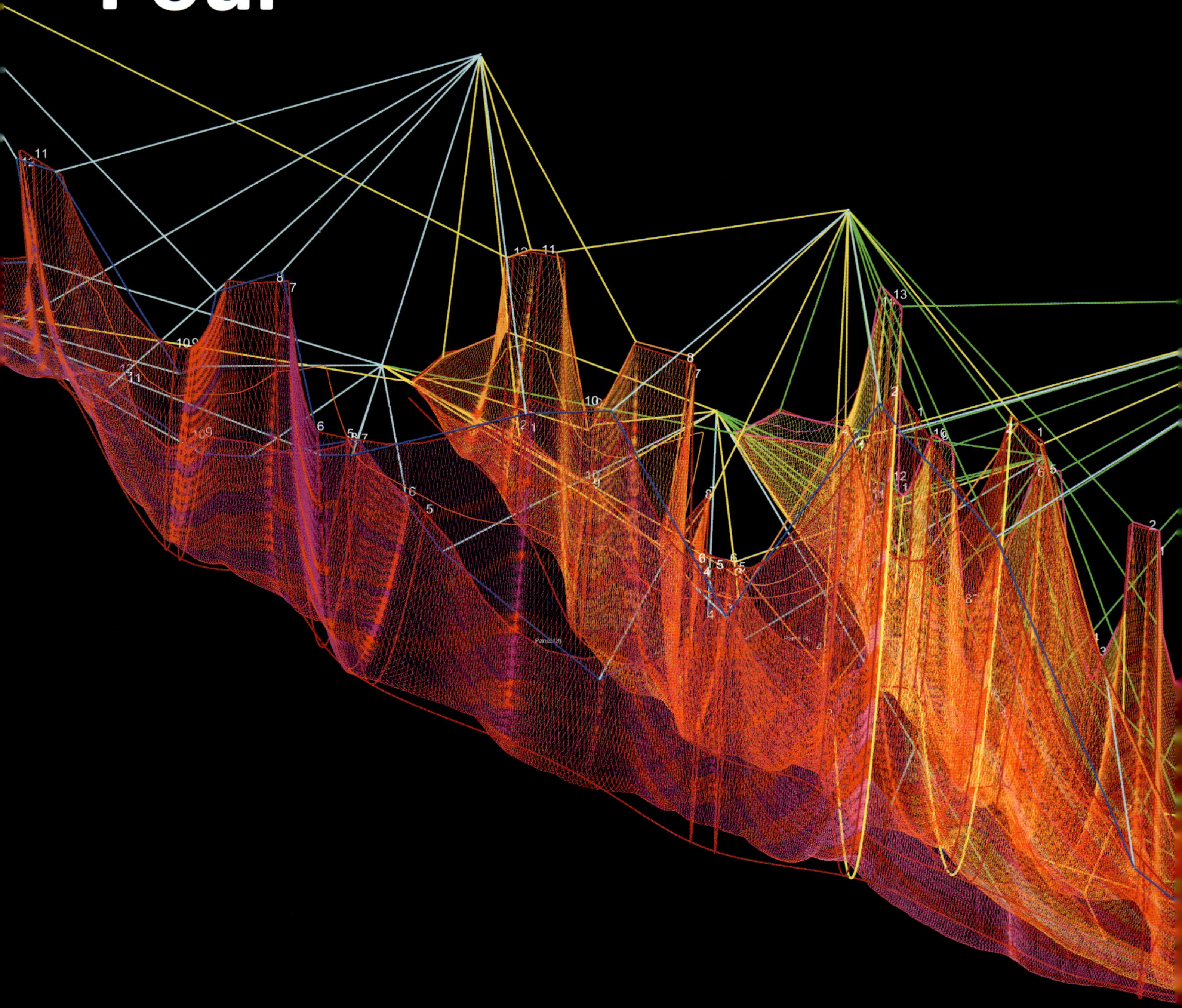

Soft Systems: Nets to Software

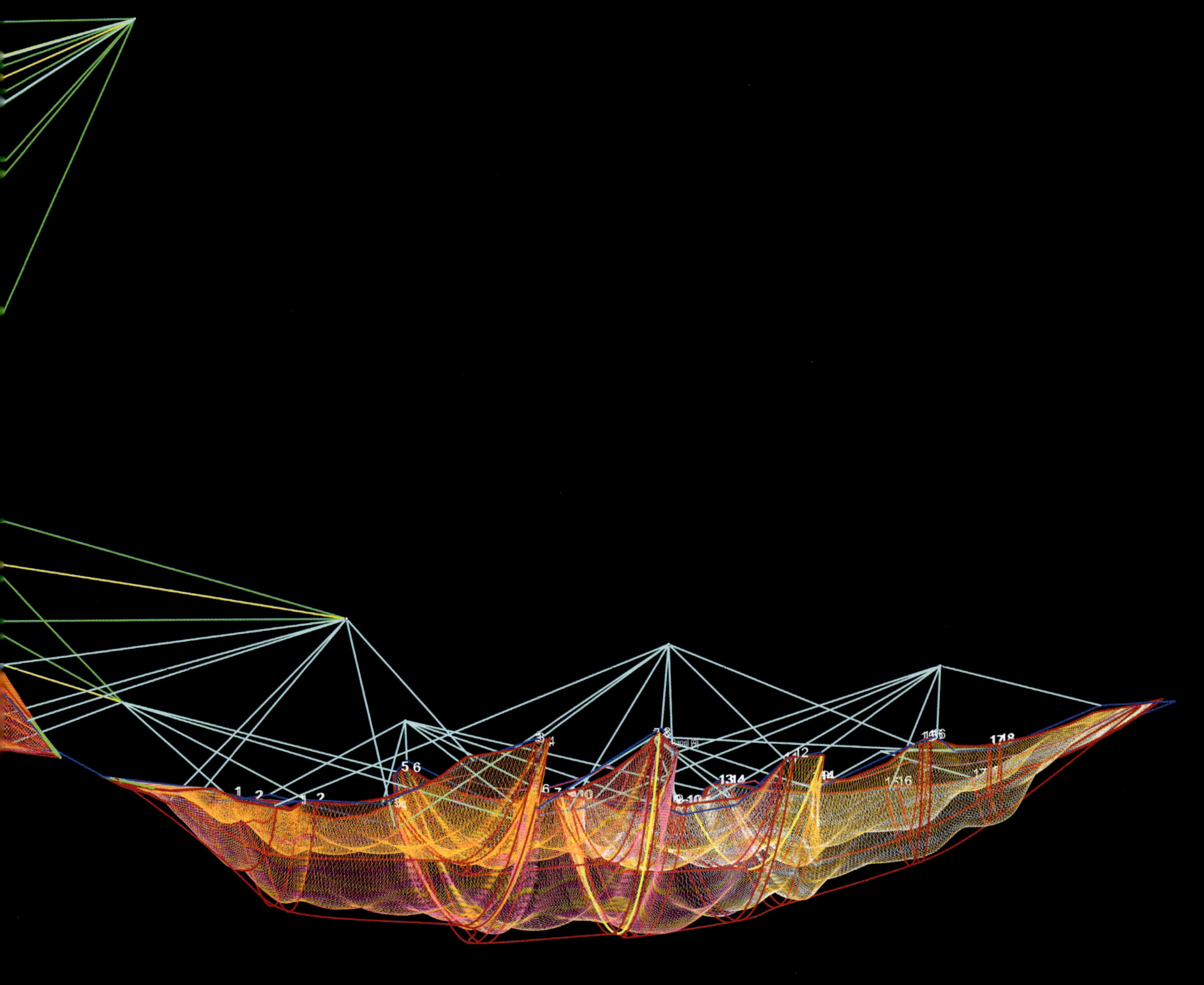

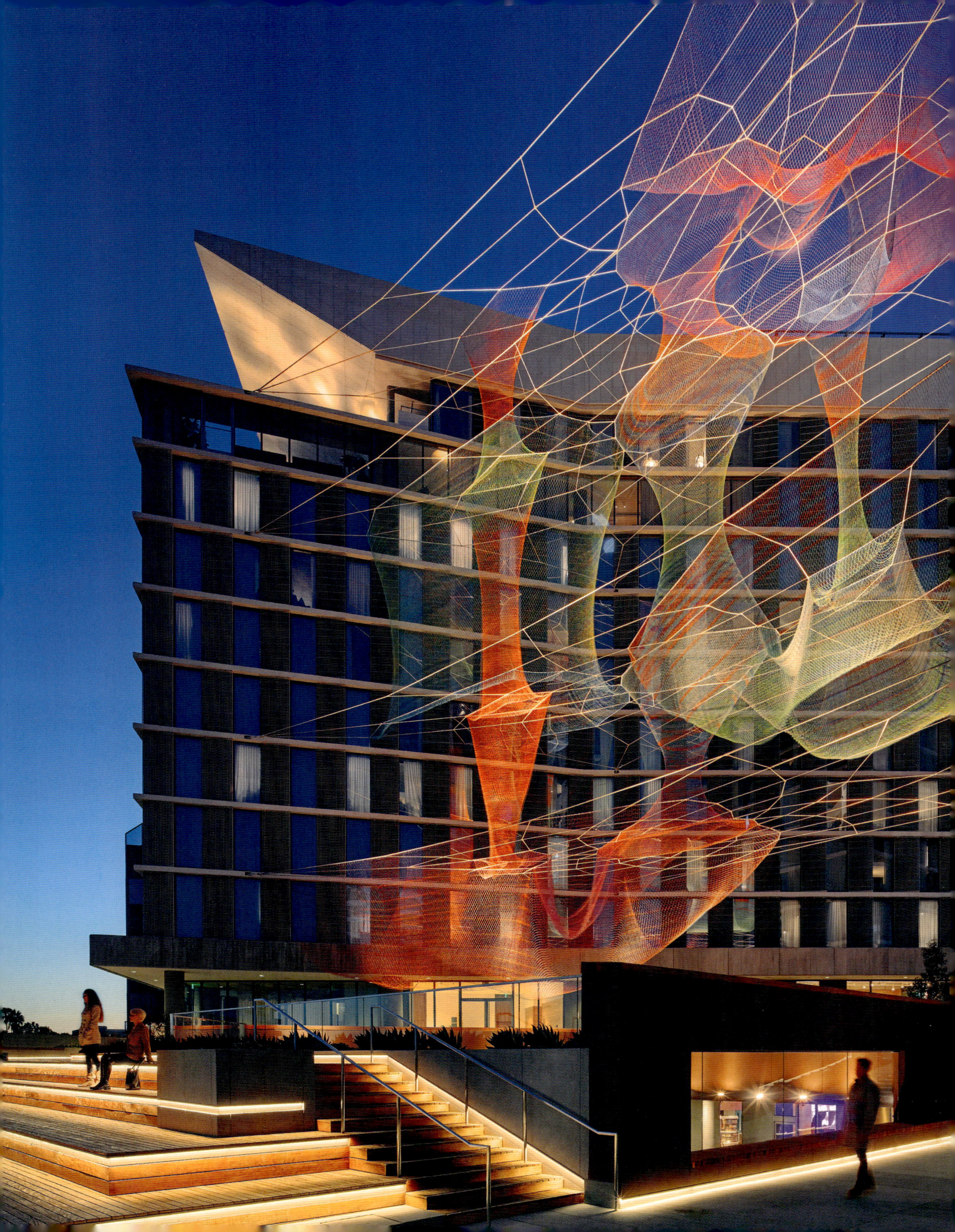

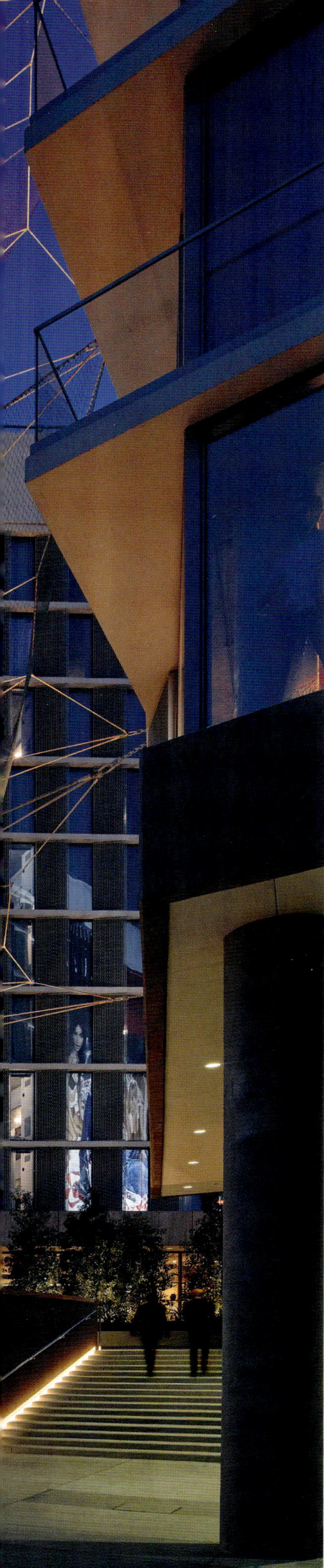

Tensile Truths

—

John Ochsendorf

Janet Echelman's art transforms public space and lifts the human spirit. The works' dynamic networks of color and form upend the familiar into the exotic and new. And while each person experiences art differently, this work has a particular resonance for engineers, since it exposes invisible forces for all to see.

Echelman's lightweight, often ephemeral constructions are the opposite of masonry monuments. Stone architectural heritage moves us in part because of a fundamental truth: stones work primarily in compression. By stacking stones, cultures have invented infinite compressive forms, from the gabled walls of Machu Picchu to the corbeled temples of Angkor Wat to the arched aqueducts of Rome. These networks of compressive forces are not always easy to visualize, but they are ever-present. Compressive forces dance dynamically inside stone architecture with each passing breeze. Such compressive forces are invisible, even in the skeletal flying buttresses of Gothic cathedrals.

Echelman's nets represent tensile truth. Cables do not lie. Her cable nets express the tensile forces within them like a massive spiderweb. A taut cable under tension follows the shape applied by the loads pulling on it, and a lightweight hanging string flutters in the breeze like a silk sheet on a taut clothesline. The engineered net in tension and the slack fishing net are equally inspiring. Together they alter our relationship with air and space and the invisible universe. The invisible forces can now be visualized.

John Ochsendorf is a historian of construction, structural designer, and professor of architecture and of civil and environmental engineering, MIT.

previous: 3D model utilizing the studio's Mango software for the MIT Museum exhibition
left: *Dream Catcher*, 2017, West Hollywood, California

Human History of Engineering Ropes and Nets

—

Sigrid Adriaenssens

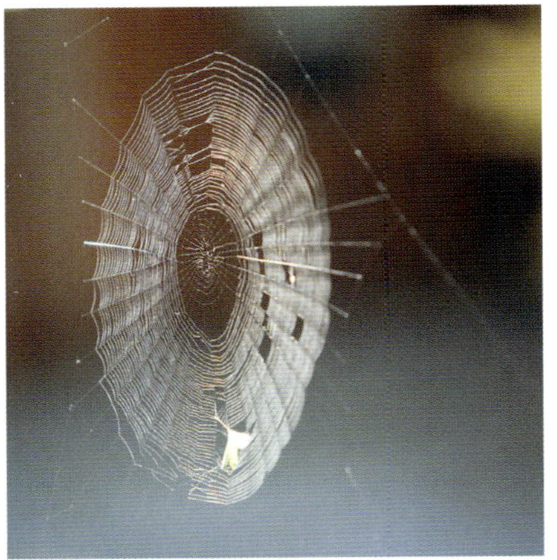
1

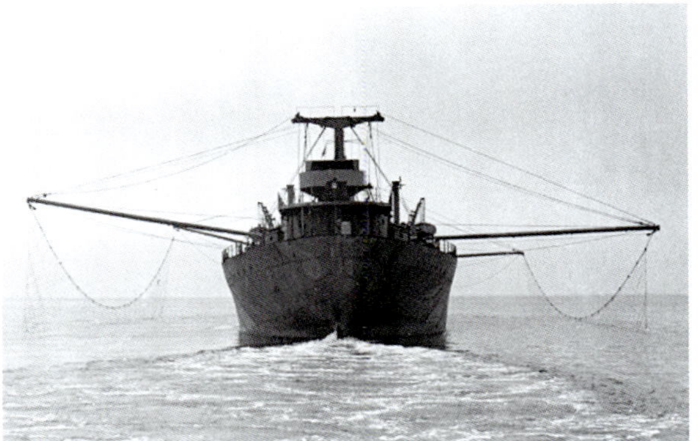
2

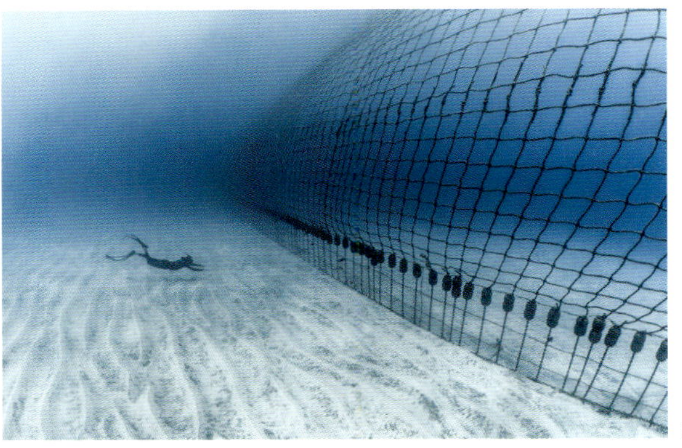
3

Fig. 1: In an orb web network, the spider determines the exact location of an insect caught on the spiraling twines by sensing vibrations of the radial twines.
Fig. 2: World War II ship with net deployed to intercept torpedoes
Fig. 3: Shark net barrier deployed in a wave-break zone

How can we understand the form and behavior of the nets that Janet Echelman designs and realizes? This is not a simple question. Engineers and mathematicians do not learn how nets deform and behave. Nets are quite different from conventional rigid structural systems such as reinforced beams and columns or truss systems. Forces, form, twine connectivity (that is, net topology), and net support conditions all have a say in the matter. In engineering terms, nets are highly nonlinear complex networks. This means that they undergo large displacements with time (for instance, they constantly change their form under wave loading); their changing behavior (output) is not proportional to the loads they are subjected to (inputs); and as twines form an interconnected network, a change in the behavior of one twine affects all the other twines in the net.

With this mechanical and geometric complexity also comes unique functionalities. For example, in a radial orb web (Fig. 1), the spider, positioned at the center, can determine the exact location of its trapped prey on the spiraling twines by sensing the vibrations in the main radial twines. Nets are ubiquitous in our lives, appearing in natural and engineered systems and cultural artifacts alike. Examples include entrapments to catch fish, insects, or torpedoes (Fig. 2); safety barriers to intercept sharks (Fig. 3), falling acrobats, skiers, or stones; tensioned string networks to propel balls; architectural cable net roofs to shield people from the elements; and nets to contain fruit, hair, or hot air.

The Interaction between Load and Net Form

Nets can be two- or three-dimensional. Their form depends on the forces applied to them as well as the support conditions and net topology. For example, in a net hammock, a 2D net, the form is continuously curved under the distributed loading of bodies. Yet it can take on a segmented shape (consisting of straight lines that connect through kinks) when a person sits in the middle of the hammock. Under its own weight only, a flexible net takes on the shape of a catenary (from the Latin *catina*, meaning chain) (Fig. 4a), a shape that is close to, but not exactly, a parabola.
A good example of a catenary shape is seen in the seaweed plantation net that carries its own weight and that of the seaweed (Fig. 4b). The Catalonian architect Antoni Gaudí used such a loaded net to determine the inverted shapes of some of his building designs, for example, the stone entrances to Palau Güell (Fig. 4c) or the columns in the Cripta de la Colònia Güell (Fig. 4d).

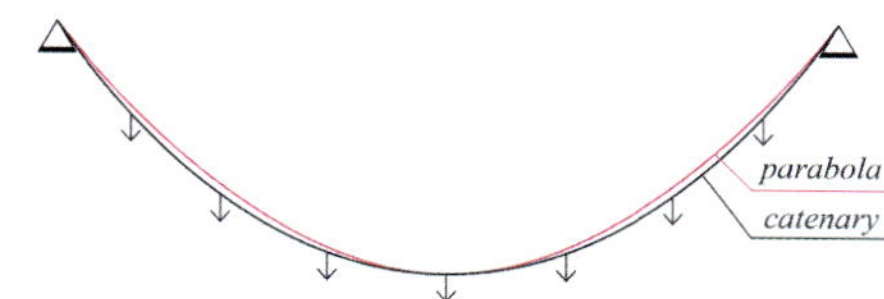

4a

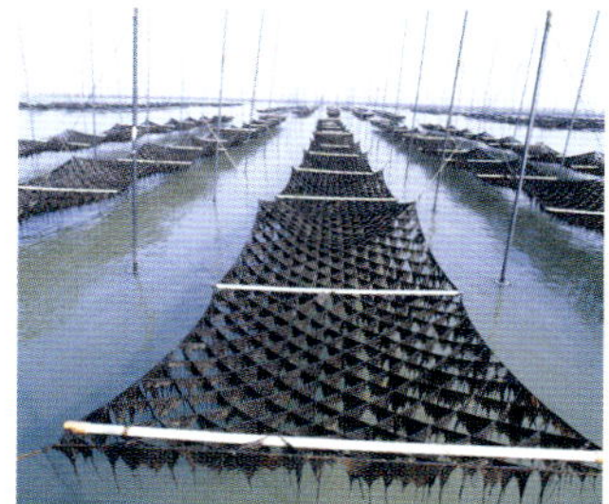

4b

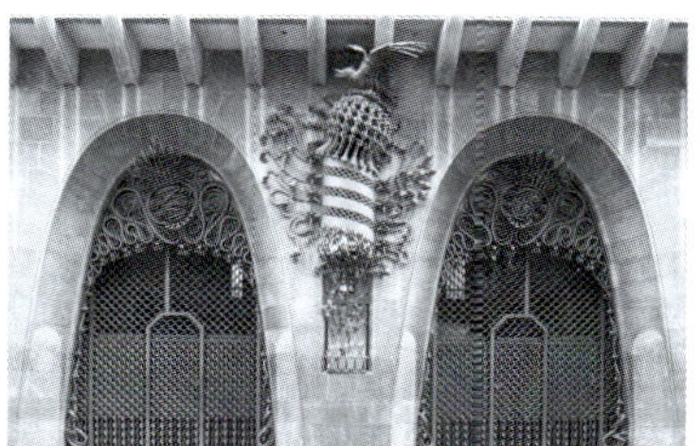

4c

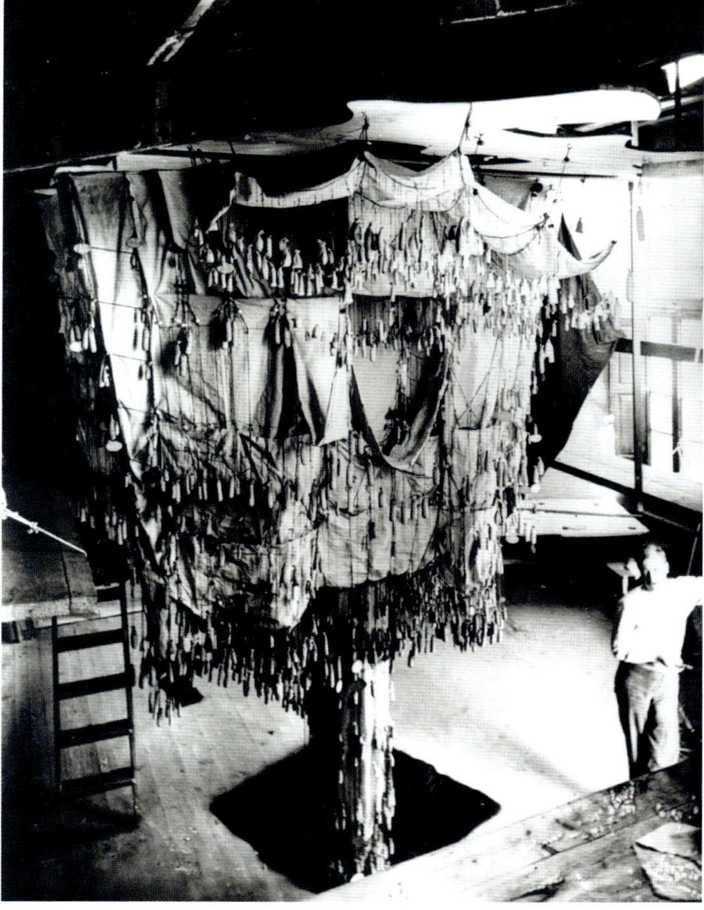

4d

Fig. 4a: A catenary shape under its self-weight; Fig. 4b: A seaweed plantation net hanging in a catenary form; Fig. 4c: Inverted catenary stone shapes at the entrance to Antoni Gaudí's Palau Güell; Fig. 4d: Reconstructed hanging model of the shape of the Cripta de la Colònia Güell in Antoni Gaudí's studio between 1898 and 1908

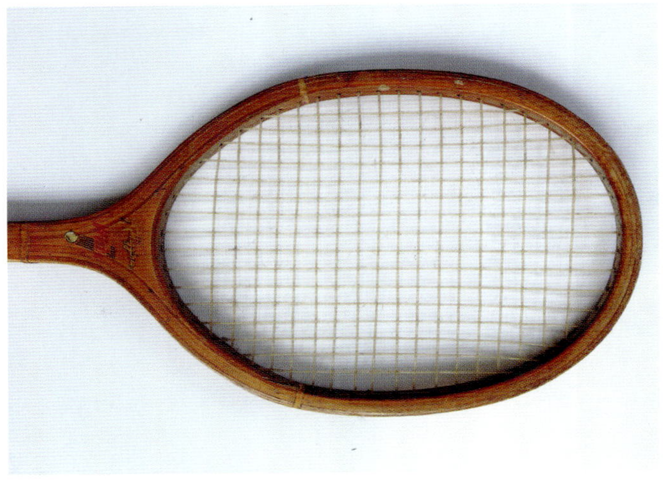

5a

A 2D net can be stiff or flexible. For example, a tennis racket string network is a stiff planar 2D net thanks to the tightening, or "pre-tensioning," of the strings. When hit by a ball, the network deforms relatively little (Fig. 5a). Such 2D pre- tensioned nets are a primary structure in Echelman's 2017 *Dream Catcher* installation in West Hollywood, California (Fig. 5b). In contrast, a flexible (non-pre-tensioned) 2D safety net barrier deforms largely when impacted by loading (Fig. 5c).

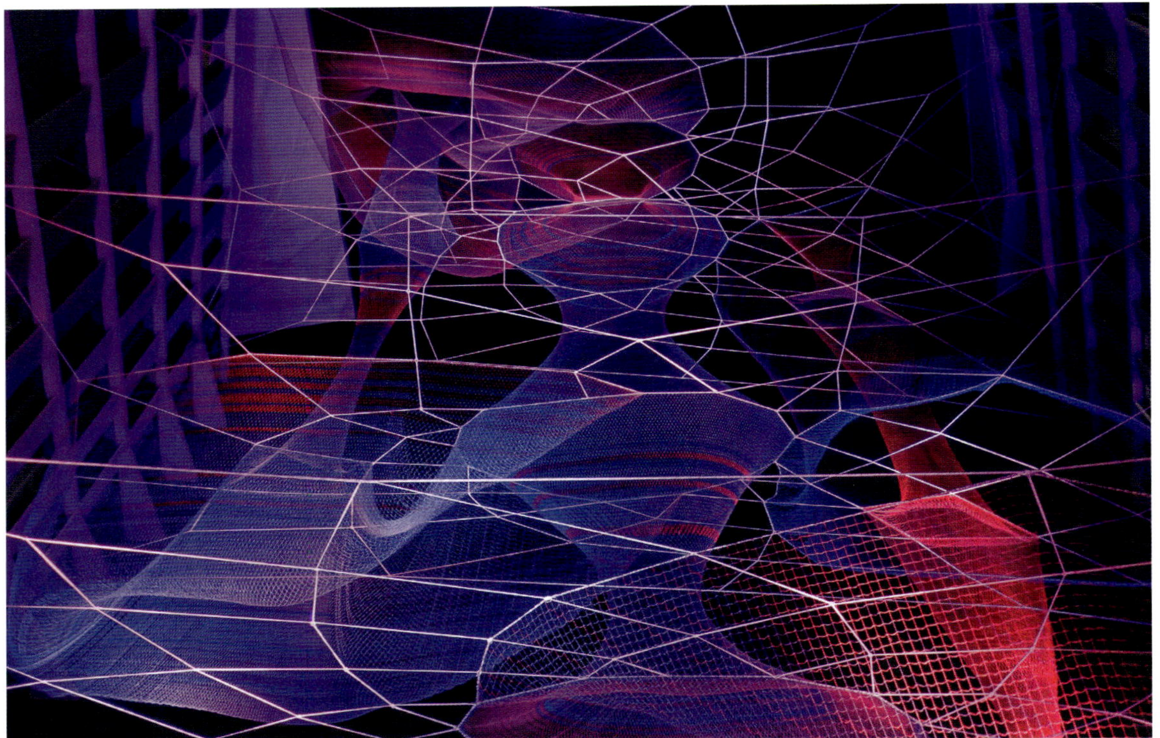

5b

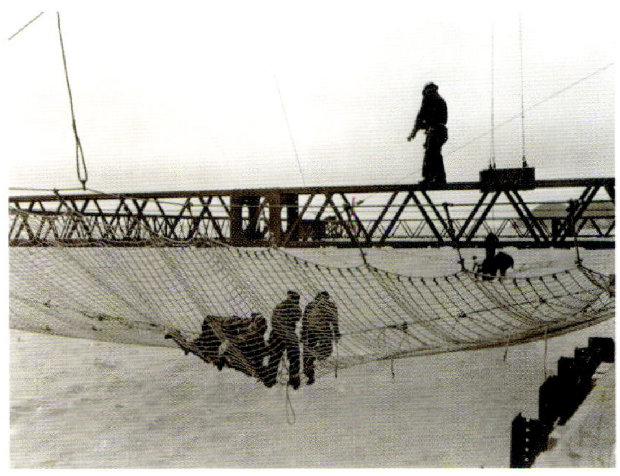

5c

Fig. 5a: Stiff pre-tensioned 2D net in a tennis racket
Fig. 5b: 2D primary structure in Echelman's *Dream Catcher*, 2017, West Hollywood, California
Fig. 5c: Flexible non-pre-tensioned net barrier during the construction of the Golden Gate Bridge in San Francisco, 1935

When a net is attached to four or more out-of-plane supports, a 3D net form arises. The flexible fishing net (Fig. 6a) is in tension under its own weight, yet it is not pre-tensioned. Such a net moves easily in the wind or when a ball hits it. This characteristic is desirable in many (but not all) of Echelman's sculptures, like *Earthtime 1.26 Sydney* (2011, Fig. 6b). The movement of this sculpture makes the wind flows visible and holds tranquil appeal for spectators. But such large movements would not be desirable for a roof, which should not change form under wind loading. To make the 1972 Munich Olympia-stadion cable-net roof stiff, the twines and cables needed to be tensioned using turnbuckles, like tightening the strings on a tennis racket or a guitar (Fig. 6c). To find the ideal shape and study the behavior of such cable-net roofs, Frei Otto and his collaborators used small-scale physical models like the one shown in Fig. 6d.

Another way of making a 3D flexible shape stiff is by using geometry rather than pre-tensioning. Such a geometry can either be syn-clastic (this is also called positive Gaussian

6a

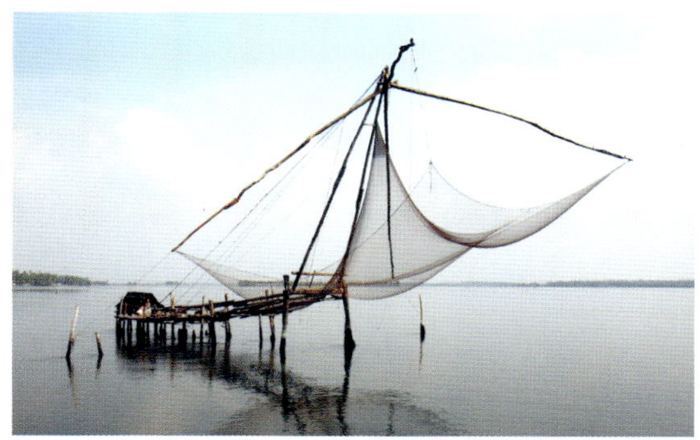

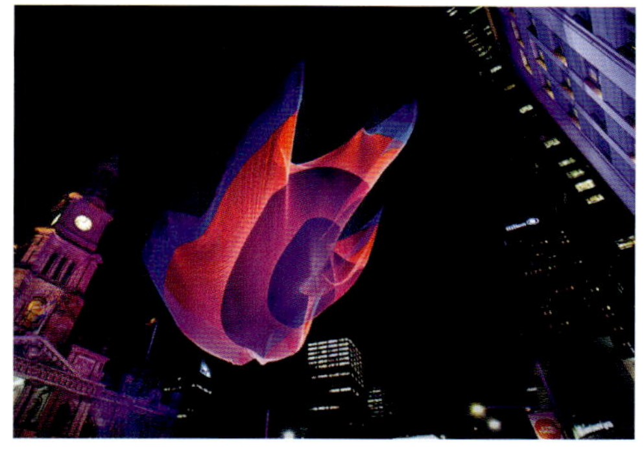

6b

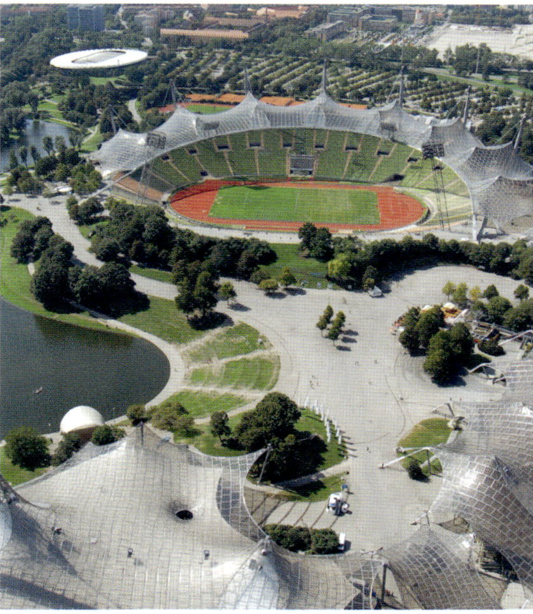

6c

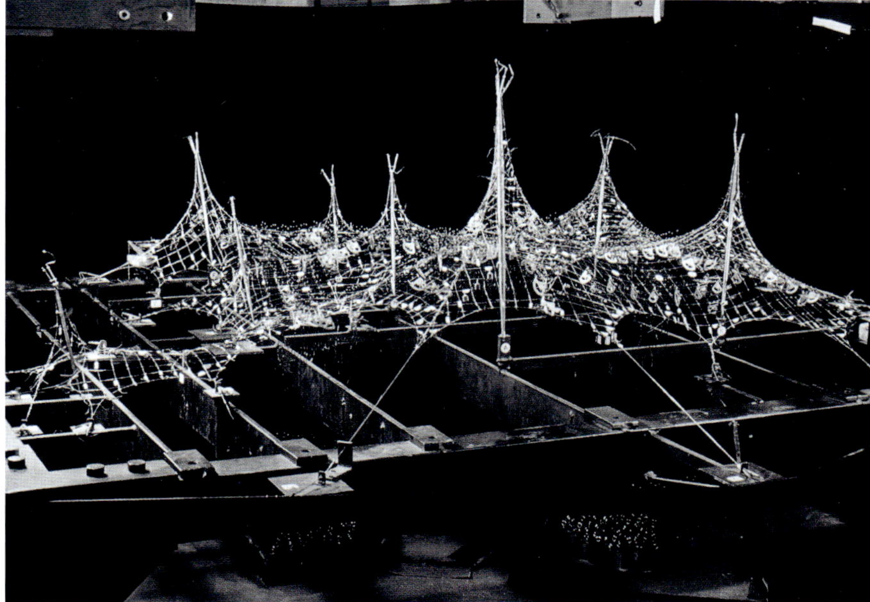

6d

Fig 6a: A Chinese fishing net under self-weight takes on a 3D flexible shape
Fig 6b: Echelman's *Earthtime 1.26 Sydney*, Australia, 2011, moves gently with the wind

Fig 6c: Munich's Olympiastadion's cable-net roof, a stiff pre-tensioned system
Fig 6d: scale model of a cable-net roof designed by Frei Otto and used to carry out structural analysis

curvature, like the curvature experience in an inflated balloon) or anticlastic (or negative Gaussian curvature, where the two main curvatures of the net oppose each other, as in a Pringles potato chip). To achieve stiff synclastic (or positive Gaussian) curvature in a net, the net could be filled with a solid, like oranges or hair (Fig. 7a) or a fluid, like gas in a balloon covered with a net (Fig. 7b). These loads shape, tension, and thus stiffen the net.

Three-dimensional net forms may achieve their stiff shape thanks not to a solid or a fluid, but to specific supports. The reason why certain anticlastic net forms are stiff can be understood from Fig. 8.

In an anticlastic net, any upward loading will be carried by the arching net strands (Fig. 9a), while the hanging net strands will go slack. Conversely, any downward loading will be carried by the hanging net strands (Fig. 9b) and the arching net strands will go slack. There is always a clear path for the forces to flow to the supports, and the net is always stressed and stiff. Interesting examples of stiff anticlastic nets include the smaller-scale catfish net (Fig. 9c) and Echelman's large-scale secondary nets in *Dream Catcher* (Fig. 9d).

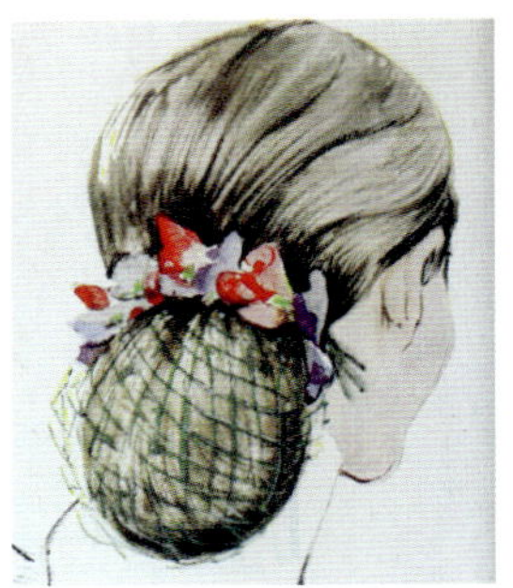

7a

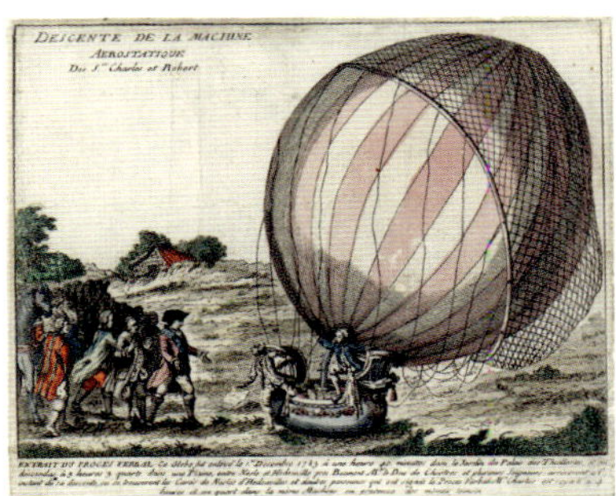

7b

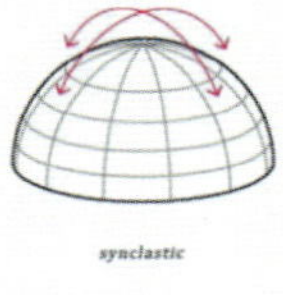

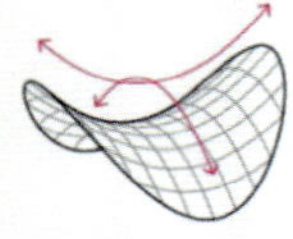

8

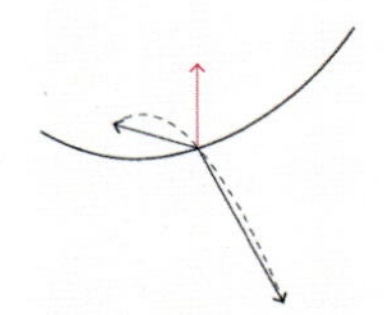

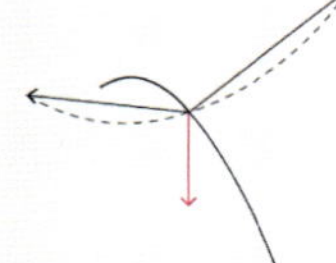

9a/9b

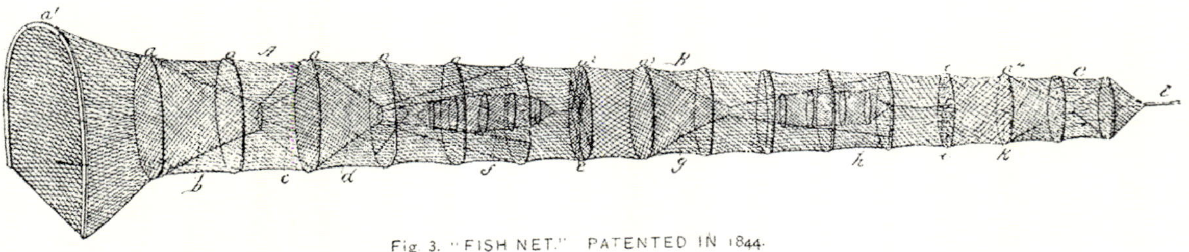

9c

Fig. 7a: 3D synclastic stiff net forms in a 1940s hairnet illustration
Fig. 7b: Net shaped by a balloon
Fig. 8: 3D net form, made stiff through synclastic or anticlastic geometry

Fig. 9a/9b: Net mechanics in an anticlastic geometry
Fig. 9c: Anticlastic stiff geometry in a hooped fish net
Fig. 9d, opposite: Anticlastic stiff geometry in *Dream Catcher*, 2017

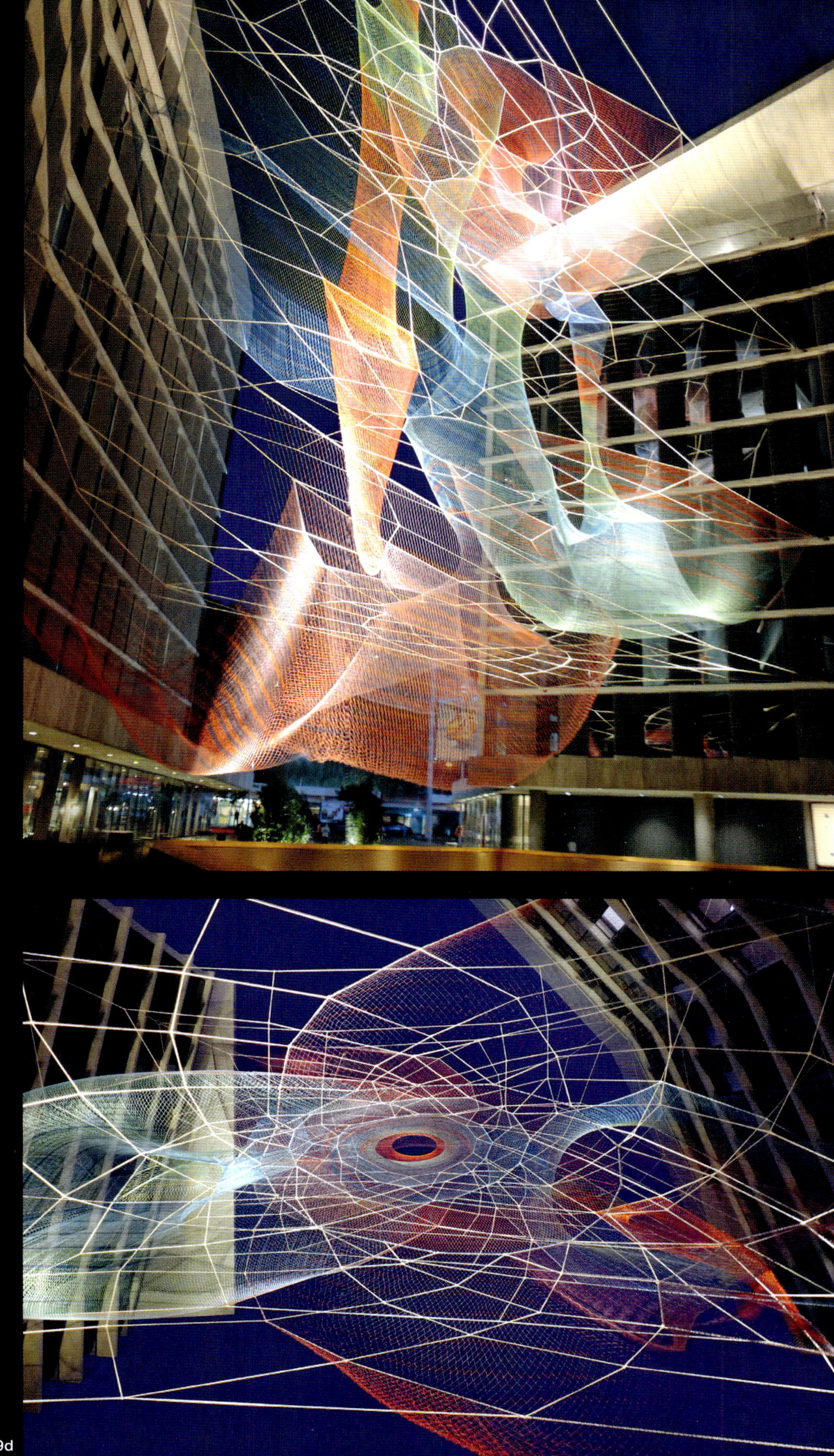

9d

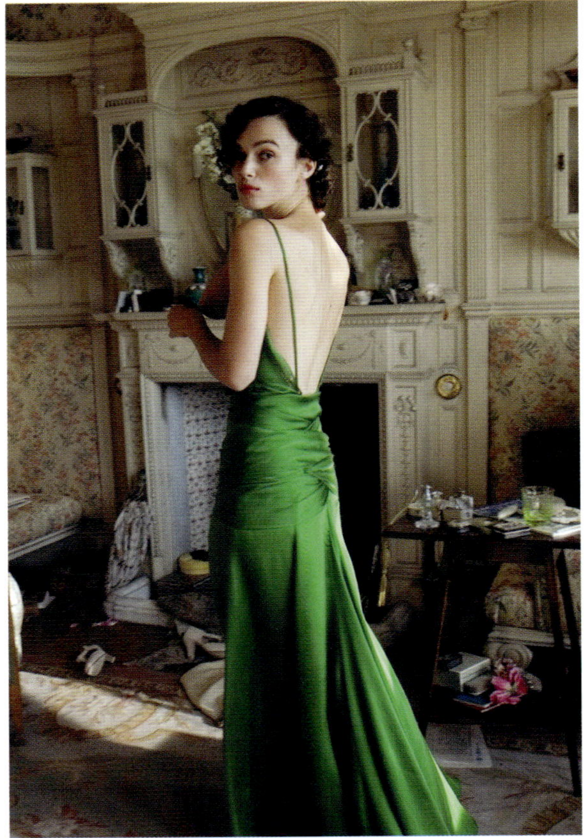

10a

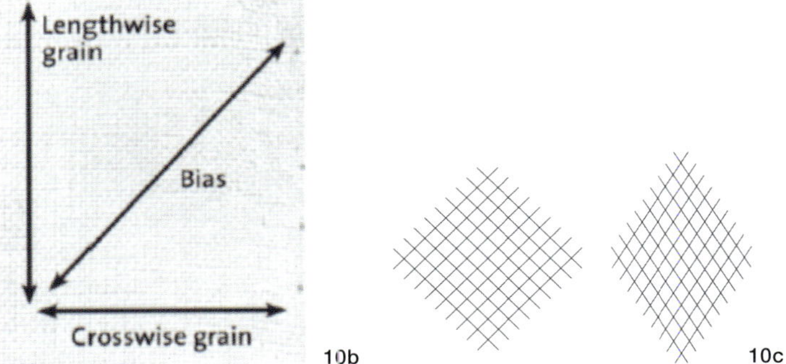

10b

10c

Fig. 10a: Keira Knightley in a curve-hugging bias-cut dress
Fig. 10b: Schematic illustrating bias and other grains
Fig. 10c: Large bias net deformations under self-weight

Importance of Twine Connectivity

In addition to the force, form, and support conditions, net topology (or twine connectivity) is key to the way a net behaves. This topology parameter is widely understood in the fashion world, where bias-cut dresses create a 1920s curve-hugging look. Recent examples include the iconic dresses worn by Pippa Middleton at the 2011 British royal wedding and by Keira Knightley in the seduction scene in the 2007 movie *Atonement* (Fig. 10a). This bias technique of orienting the twines (or threads in a fabric) at 45 degrees to the horizontal (Fig. 10b) takes advantage of the bias stretch or the large deformations that occur under the fabric or net's own weight and any imposed loading of wind, waves, or wearer. Figure 10c shows how a net with a bias mesh deforms largely under its own weight: it elongates in the longitudinal direction and contracts heavily in the transverse direction. In engineering terms, this means that this net has a high Poisson's ratio. In the fashion world, this greater stretch in the bias accentuates body lines and curves, and allows the fabric to drape softly. Echelman's sculptures, such as the 2014 Stuttgart Ballet nets (Fig. 10d), harness this inherent bias property to achieve nets that are expressive, with large deformations, and drape softly.

Echelman's net sculptures spatially evolve nonlinearly with time and dramatically change shape when interacting with external entities such as wind or human bodies. Their design and expression manifest a deep understanding and control of form and flow. By making changing equilibrium visible, they reveal great beauty.

Sigrid Adriaenssens is a professor of civil and environmental engineering, Princeton University.

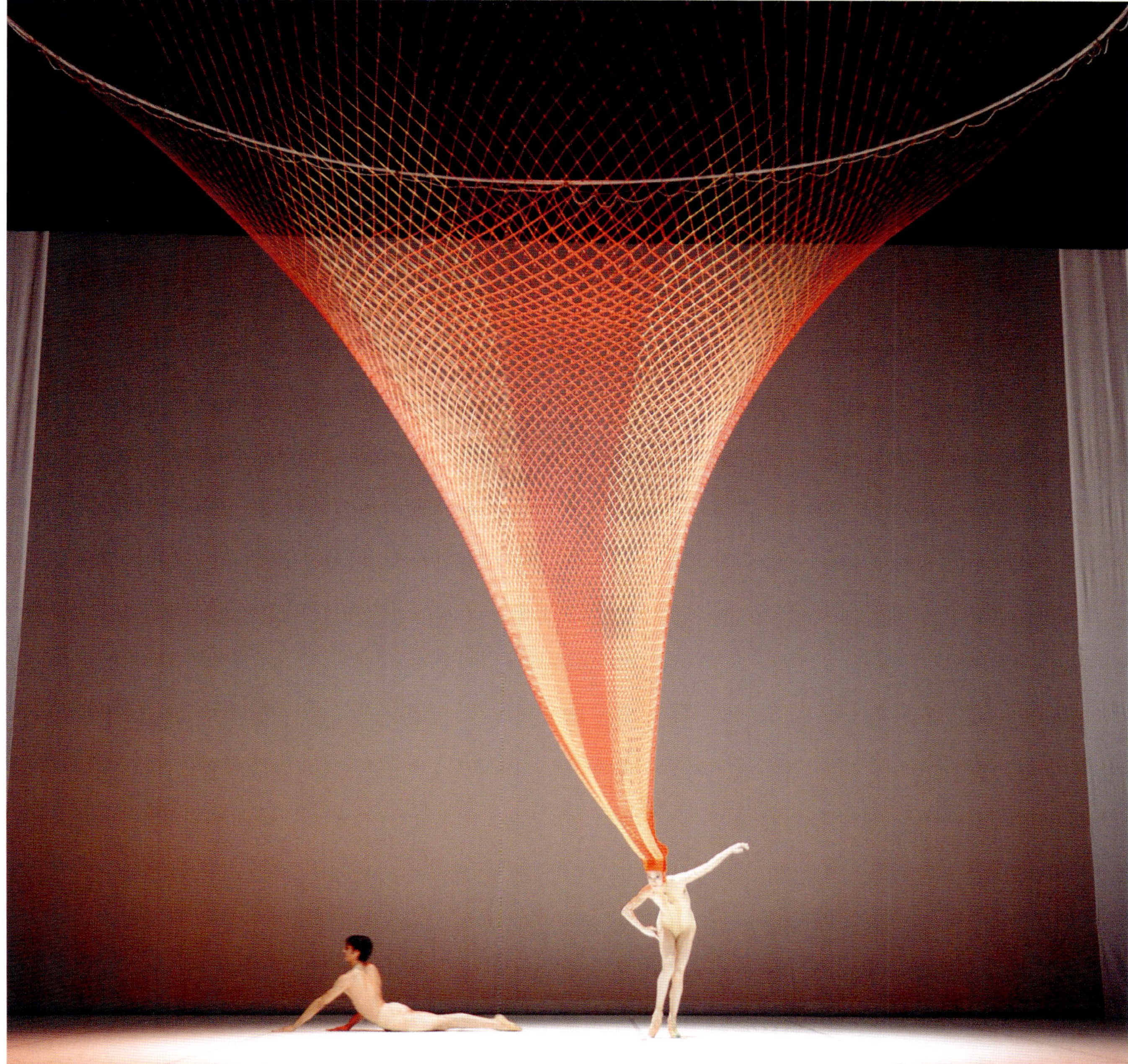

10d

Fig.10d: Net arranged on the bias in Echelman's 2014 Stuttgart Ballet collaboration

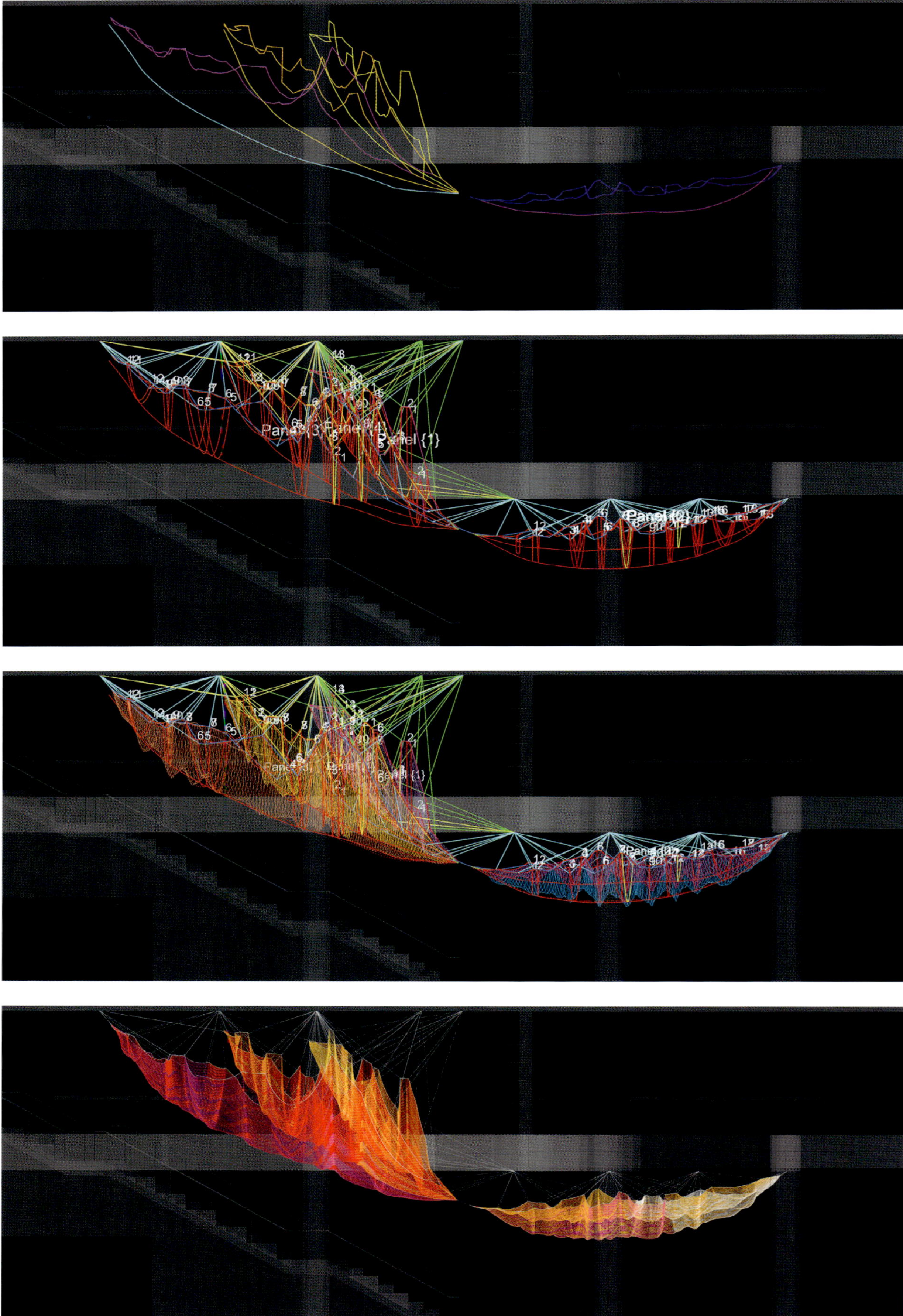
Panel {1}

Advancing Sculptural Form Finding through Computer Software in Studio Echelman

—

Caitlin Mueller, Adam Burke, and Andrew Sageman-Furnas

The soft tensile forms pioneered in Studio Echelman's work carry a paradox for simulation and design: their physical flexibility allows for extreme lightness, but also imposes rigid constraints on the shapes that can be manifested in the net-based material system. The nets embody forms dictated by a balance between gravity and the flow of forces through the structure and necessitate a process of form finding for design: the sculptural form cannot be arbitrarily shaped like clay. Throughout history, architects, engineers, and designers such as Antoni Gaudí, Frei Otto, and Heinz Isler used sophisticated physical form-finding models to generate expressive forms in tensile equilibrium. In contemporary times, computational form finding has become a powerful tool in both structural engineering and computer graphics, enabling artists and designers to achieve complex forms and intricate sculptures by simulating physical phenomena.

A variety of computational approaches for form finding used in engineering large-scale structures were developed in the twentieth century, including nonlinear finite element analysis and the force density method.[1] Although the results of these simulations can be quite precise, they are often very difficult to set up and can be extremely slow and computationally intensive. Computer graphics researchers have also developed a variety of advanced techniques for simulations of relevant flexible structures such as fiber, cloth, and nets. However, the simulations developed for computer graphics typically prioritize speed and visual accuracy over physical reality and don't consider constraints that might be required for physically fabricating a structure. In short, when Janet Echelman began to expand into larger-scale sculptural work, no off-the-shelf simulation tools existed that were fast, flexible, and accurate enough to support her studio's design processes. As a result, a key aspect of the studio's artistic production over its two-decade history has been a parallel effort in technological innovation, including bespoke computational modeling and software development.

These innovations have been uniquely empowered by Echelman's partnership with David Feldman. Feldman began his career as an early software developer at Apple, and later worked on the 3D computer graphics program Infini-D. Through these experiences, he developed a sophisticated expertise in both user-facing software tools and complex geometry representation and manipulation in computing environments. To his work with Studio Echelman he brought a keen understanding of the creative potential the right tools can unlock. His contributions to Echelman's large-scale structures began in 2001, when he offered to help calculate the amount of material required to fabricate *Target Swooping Down… Bullseye!* in Madrid. To do so, he wrote a custom computer program in C to model the sculpture in enough detail for an accurate estimate. This initial collaboration was small but set the stage for much more involved technical collaborations.

With *She Changes* (2005) in Porto, Portugal, Studio Echelman faced its first large-scale project requiring rigorous engineering validation. The studio was asked to prove that the sculpture could withstand high winds during a storm. This was a new challenge and required the engagement of a structural engineer. The skills needed to analyze a sculpture made of very open netting were extremely rare. After contacting several engineers, they finally found Peter Heppel, a specialist in high-performance sail design. His expertise was uniquely suited to evaluate the wind loads on a large textile sculpture. Echelman began a collaboration with Heppel, and together with Feldman they worked to find an analytical (mathematics-based) model for describing the shape of the sculpture with equations, allowing it to be visualized readily in computer code. But only a relatively limited palette of forms could be represented through a simple mathematical formula.

opposite: Process images utilizing Studio Echelman's Mango software for the MIT Museum exhibition

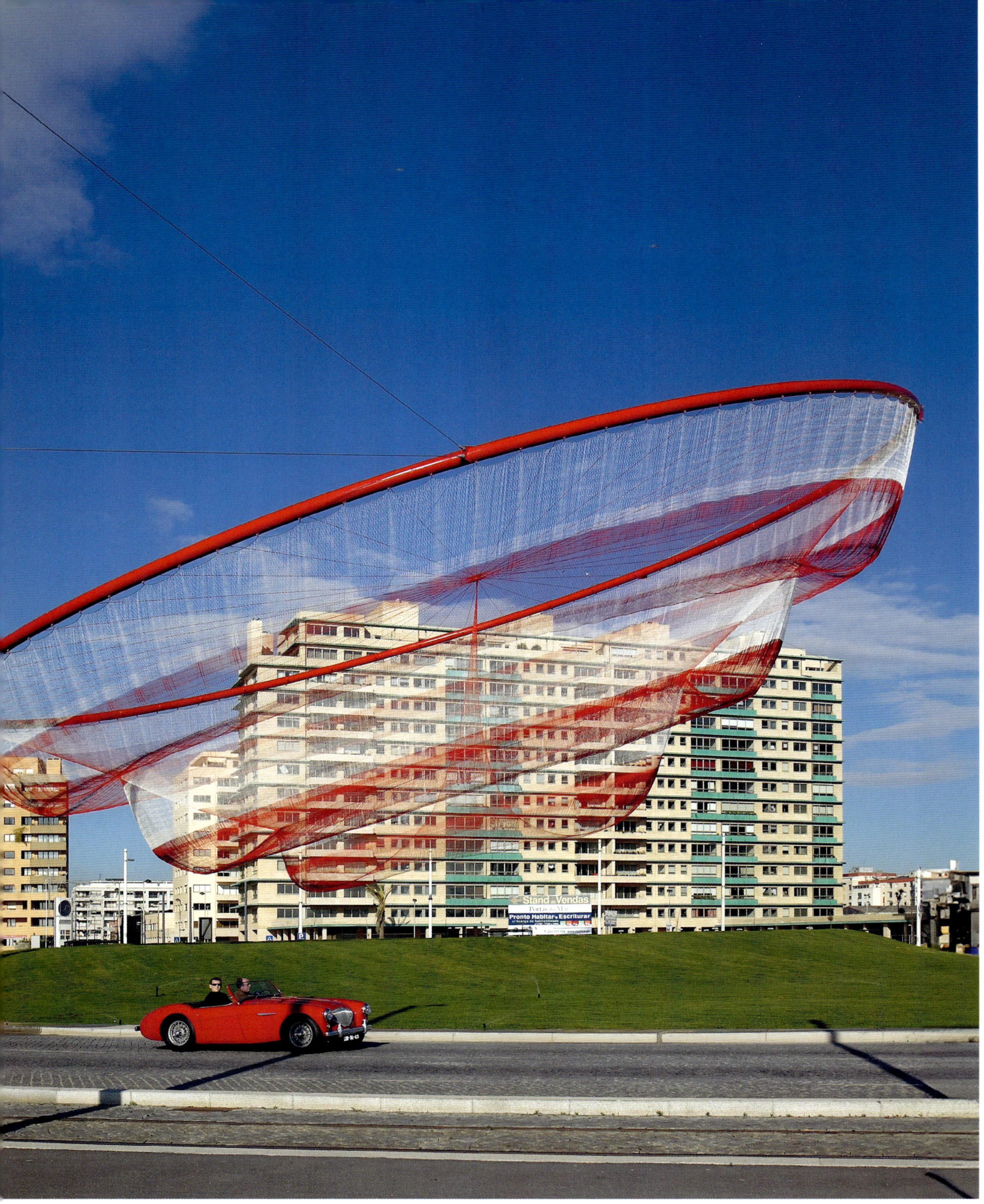
Stand de Vendas
Portas do Mar
Pronto Habitar e Escriturar
c/ licença de habitabilidade

To validate that the sculpture would be safe under wind loads, Heppel introduced to the studio's process digital simulation tools that could model more complex behaviors than can be understood with classical techniques. He had previously developed a software tool called Relax for simulating sails, and now used it to evaluate the sculpture's form. This successful collaboration led to the installation of Echelman's largest-yet sculpture and opened new avenues for the studio's artistic expression.

Advancements in computation led to further collaborations with structural engineers on projects like *Her Secret Is Patience* (2009) in Phoenix and *Water Sky Garden* (2009) in Richmond, British Columbia. For these projects, the studio collaborated with the engineering firm Buro Happold along with Heppel to design more complex draped forms. Buro Happold utilized their in-house simulation tool Tensys, which uses a process called dynamic relaxation, to form find these two pieces. The tools allowed the design work to take on more complex forms with intentional, organic asymmetry. While there were challenges with these early simulation tools in their speed and accuracy, they inspired the studio to pursue an increasingly digital design approach.

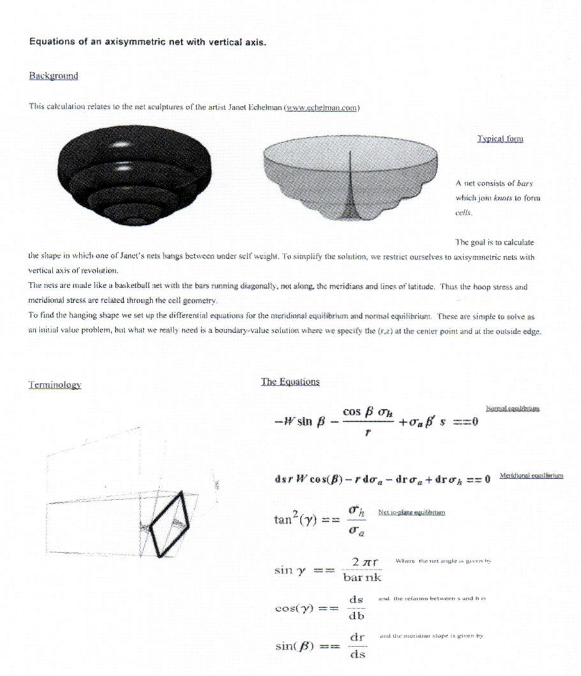

Equations of an axisymmetric net with vertical axis.

Background

This calculation relates to the net sculptures of the artist Janet Echelman (www.echelman.com)

Typical form

A net consists of *bars* which join *knots* to form *cells*.

The goal is to calculate the shape in which one of Janet's nets hangs between under self weight. To simplify the solution, we restrict ourselves to axisymmetric nets with vertical axis of revolution.

The nets are made like a basketball net with the bars running diagonally, not along, the meridians and lines of latitude. Thus the hoop stress and meridional stress are related through the cell geometry.

To find the hanging shape we set up the differential equations for the meridional equilibrium and normal equilibrium. These are simple to solve as an initial value problem, but what we really need is a boundary-value solution where we specify the (*r*,*z*) at the center point and at the outside edge.

Terminology

The Equations

$$-W \sin \beta - \frac{\cos \beta \, \sigma_h}{r} + \sigma_a \beta' \, s == 0$$ Normal equilibrium

$$ds\, r\, W \cos(\beta) - r\, d\sigma_a - dr\, \sigma_a + dr\, \sigma_h == 0$$ Meridional equilibrium

$$\tan^2(\gamma) == \frac{\sigma_h}{\sigma_a}$$ Net in-plane equilibrium

$$\sin \gamma == \frac{2 \pi r}{\text{bar nk}}$$ Where the net angle is given by

$$\cos(\gamma) == \frac{ds}{db}$$ and the relation between s and b is

$$\sin(\beta) == \frac{dr}{ds}$$ and the meridian slope is given by

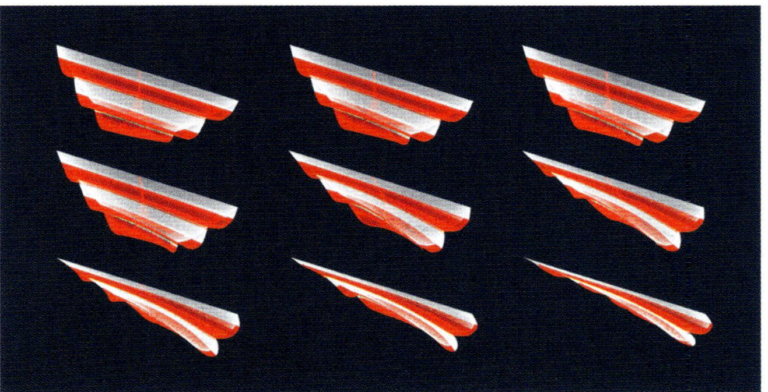

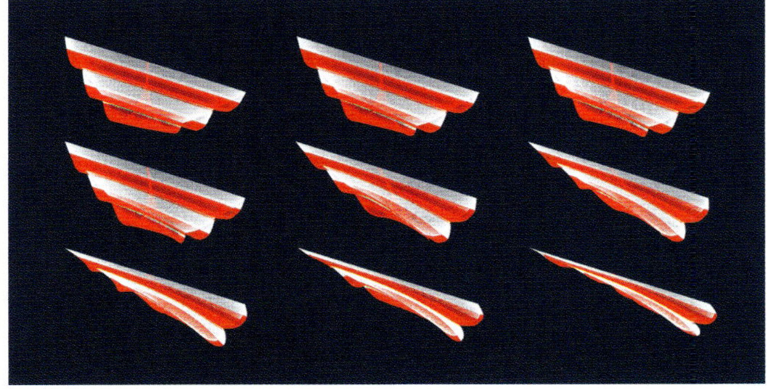

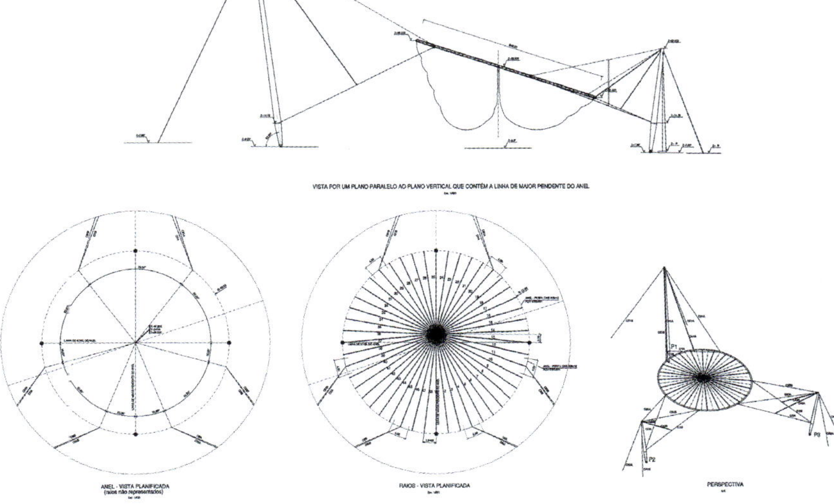

opposite: *She Changes*, 2005, Porto, Portugal
top: Mathematics by engineer Peter Heppel to calculate Echelman's net form for *She Changes*, 2005
middle: Wind deformation study
right: Plan and elevation drawings of steel cables and ring structure to suspend *She Changes*, 2005, with AFA Engineers, Portugal

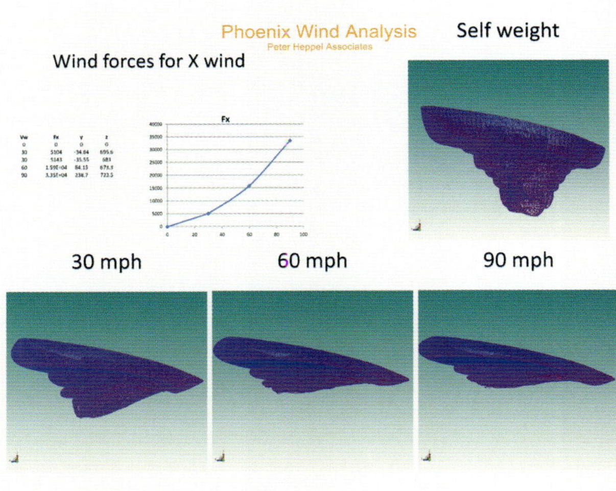

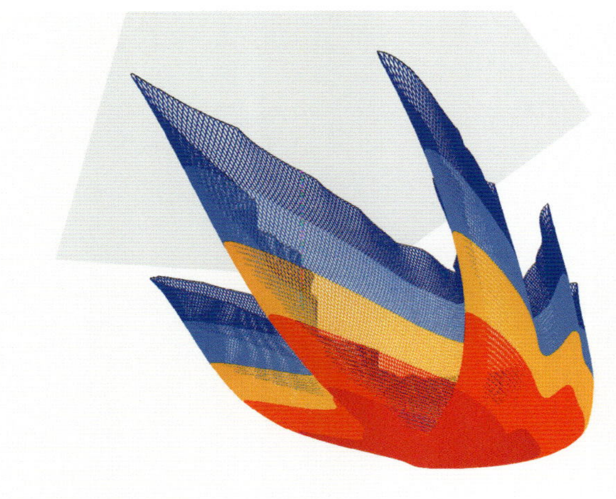

top: 3D model with wind analysis for *Her Secret Is Patience*, 2009, Phoenix, Arizona
bottom: Rendering of *Earthtime 1.26 Denver*, 2010, Colorado, using the studio's first software

From these experiences, Feldman saw the potential of software but also the limitations of the existing design process, which permitted only very few iterations of form finding carried out by specialized engineers, without much opportunity to iterate through designs or customize tools themselves. He suggested that the studio undertake the development of its own form-finding software. This was a radical approach to expanding an artistic process. Echelman was initially uncertain what could come of it, but trusted Feldman to explore this development. The earliest version of the in-house tool JNET was developed by Greg Pintilie, who was at that time a PhD candidate in MIT's Computer Science and Artificial Intelligence Laboratory. With guidance from Heppel and direction from Studio Echelman, he developed a small stand-alone application that would allow designers in the studio to generate form-found sculptures without needing to send a rough sketch to an engineer.

This tool was first employed for the early design studies of *Earthtime 1.26 Denver* (2010). This was Echelman's most complex form to date, with a highly articulated support boundary that slowly transitioned to a smooth circular bowl. During its development, a variety of physical models and hand drawings were used in conjunction with the computational tools to develop the sculpture.

The initial version of JNET allowed for rectangular net panel generation and a user interface for modifying panel parameters such as the number of meshes in each dimension and the lengths of the edges of the net diamond, as well as modifying the colors of different sections of twine. Once the panel parameters were established, a user of the tool could run a simulation to see the shape of the geometry under the weight of gravity. This version of the tool showed the power of bespoke interactive tools for the design of form-found sculptures. Its rapid development, however, introduced necessary simplifications, which restricted the design outcomes to a palette more limited than the capabilities of the expert fabricators. An opportunity arose to develop a more complex version of JNET when Echelman was commissioned to develop a sculpture for the 2014 TED conference in Vancouver.

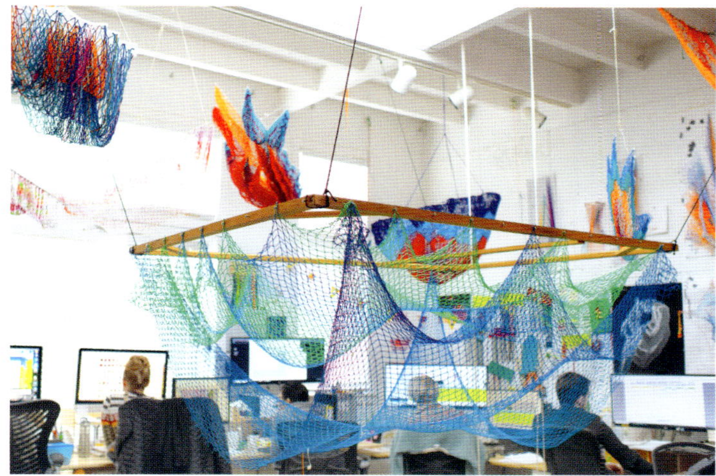

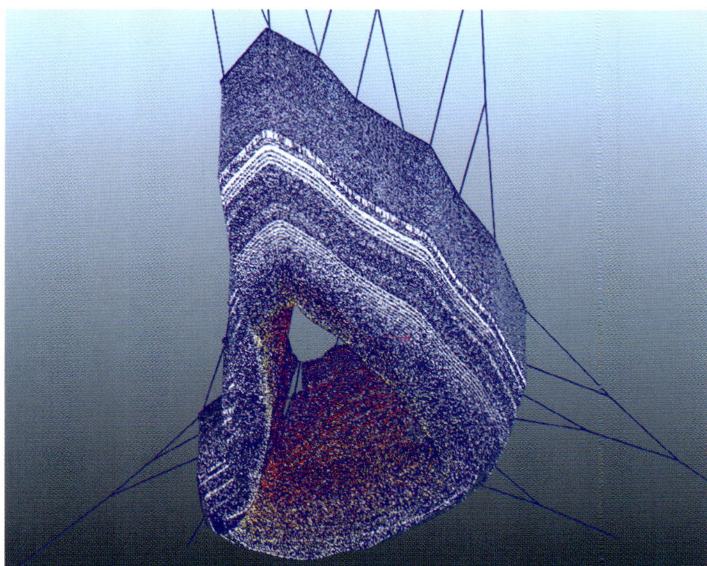

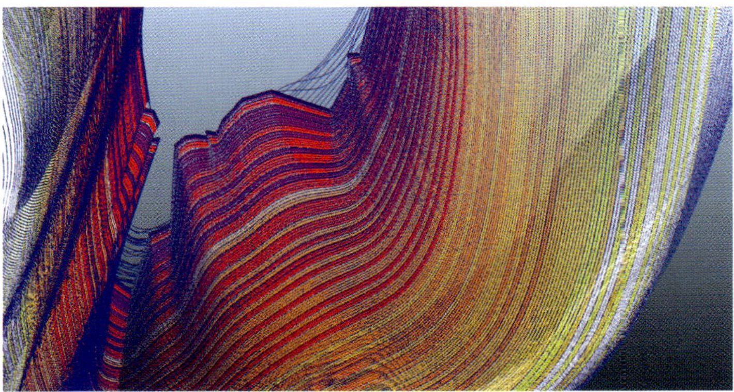

top: Studio Echelman, 2018
middle and bottom: 3D models using Studio Echelman's JNET software, for *Skies Painted with Unnumbered Sparks*, 2014, Vancouver, British Columbia

After her TED presentation in 2011, Echelman had met Jeff Kowalski, then CTO of Autodesk, and discussed some of the limitations of the existing version of JNET. From this conversation emerged a collaboration on a new version of JNET. The Autodesk collaboration, led by Peter Boyer, was envisioned to support the development of the sculpture *Skies Painted with Unnumbered Sparks* (2014) in Vancouver for the 2014 TED conference. The new version of JNET was developed as a plug-in for Maya and allowed the studio to explore more sophisticated design operations such as trimming of rectangular mesh panels, interactive coloration, and more complex panel connections.

After the success of the sculpture for TED, Feldman's vision for in-house computational form finding became a reality and a cornerstone of the studio's process, enabling other high-profile projects such as *Impatient Optimist* (2015) in Seattle and *As If It Were Already Here* (2015) in Boston. The studio's sculptural practice flourished, with JNET allowing for more precise and efficient design iterations. With JNET, sculptures could be generated with material cut away from certain panels and interactively colored to explore a variety of pattern options that were set up to mimic the fabrication constraints of the net material. JNET's application extended to numerous projects, including *Earthtime 1.8* (2016–ongoing); *Where We Met* (2016) in Greensboro, North Carolina; *Dream Catcher* (2017) in West Hollywood, California; *Earthtime Korea* (2020) in Gwanggyo, South Korea; and *Bending Arc* (2020) in St. Petersburg, Florida.

The versatility of JNET allowed Echelman to explore various sculptural forms and refine and realize her artistic visions on an unprecedented scale. Yet there remained some limitations in the types of sculptural forms that could be realized in JNET. Some of the studio's earliest designs developed using physical models were still impossible to represent accurately in the digital environment. As a result, Feldman envisioned a new tool, taking lessons from JNET, to continue to expand Echelman's sculptural vocabulary with increased flexibility and accuracy.

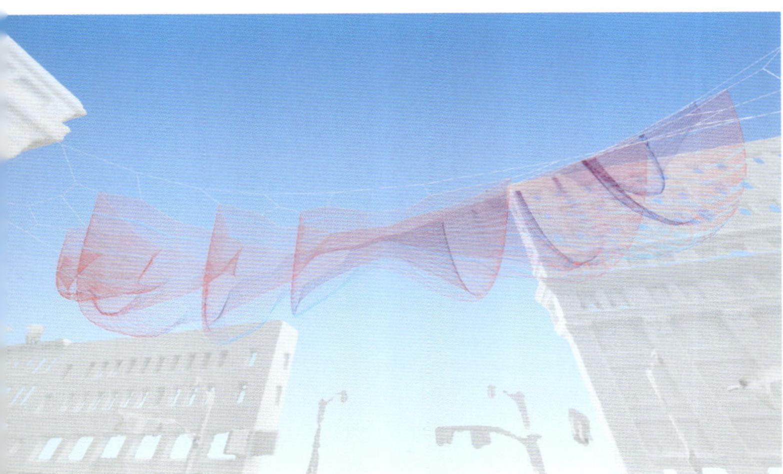

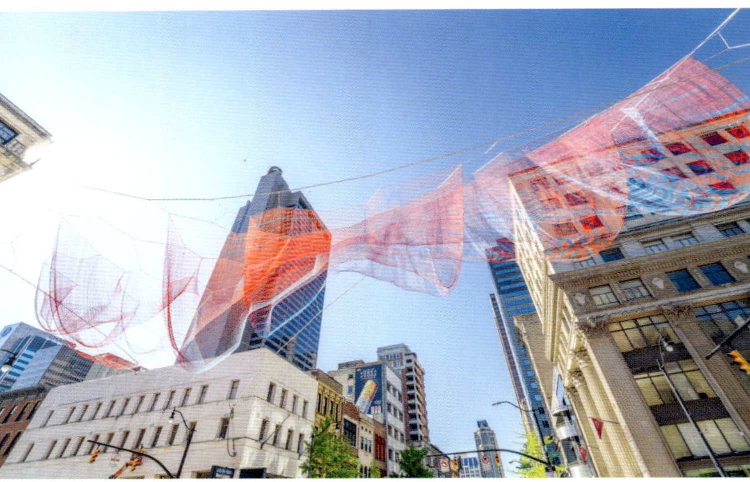

The development of an improved design and simulation tool began in 2019, led by mathematician Andy Sageman-Furnas in Berlin and computer graphics experts David Harmon in Virginia and Akash Garg in California, working with Feldman and studio designers Adam Burke, Daniel Smith, and Keith Hartwig.

The vision for the new tool was structured by four guiding principles: drapeability, expressibility, interoperability, and usability. From early 2019 to early 2020 the team focused solely on the aspect of drapeability, exploring a variety of simulation techniques from computer graphics with the aim of improving simulation speed and fidelity, while emphasizing a more fluid design process. Feldman coined the name Pineapple for the first iteration of the draping engine, as it was thorny to use but powerful on the inside. Throughout the first half of 2020 the focus shifted to a custom plug-in for Rhino/Grasshopper, named Avocado, to act as a user interface for the Pineapple draping engine. However, by the summer of 2020 it became increasingly clear that it was necessary to build a stand-alone tool that would allow all four guiding principles to be considered simultaneously.

The development of this stand-alone tool, Mango, began in fall 2020. David Feldman coined the new name as it represented the perfect combination of pineapple and avocado in fruit space. Building on Pineapple's drape engine and the lessons learned from Avocado, the exploration initially focused on expressibility and interoperability. This led to the development of a high-level sculpture description file that decoupled design elements such as support rails and panels and allowed for old and new design processes like trims, cinch ropes, and rail-sliding for increased expressibility. By having a high-level description of major components, a sculpture could be digitally specified using the same logic as the sculpture fabricators without having to think about low-level details such as knot-level descriptions of how panels should attach to one another. This high-level description file could then be compiled into a drapeable sculpture for design development. The sculpture description file was also designed to be human-readable and standardized, for increased interoperability between external programs and for robust archiving.

The ability to read and write the human-readable file format opened up new possibilities for sophisticated workflows and much greater control over the design variables. The first large-scale sculpture developed using Mango was *Current*, a permanent installation in Columbus,

above: Final design rendering using Studio Echelman's Mango software and comparison photo of *Current*, 2023, Columbus, Ohio

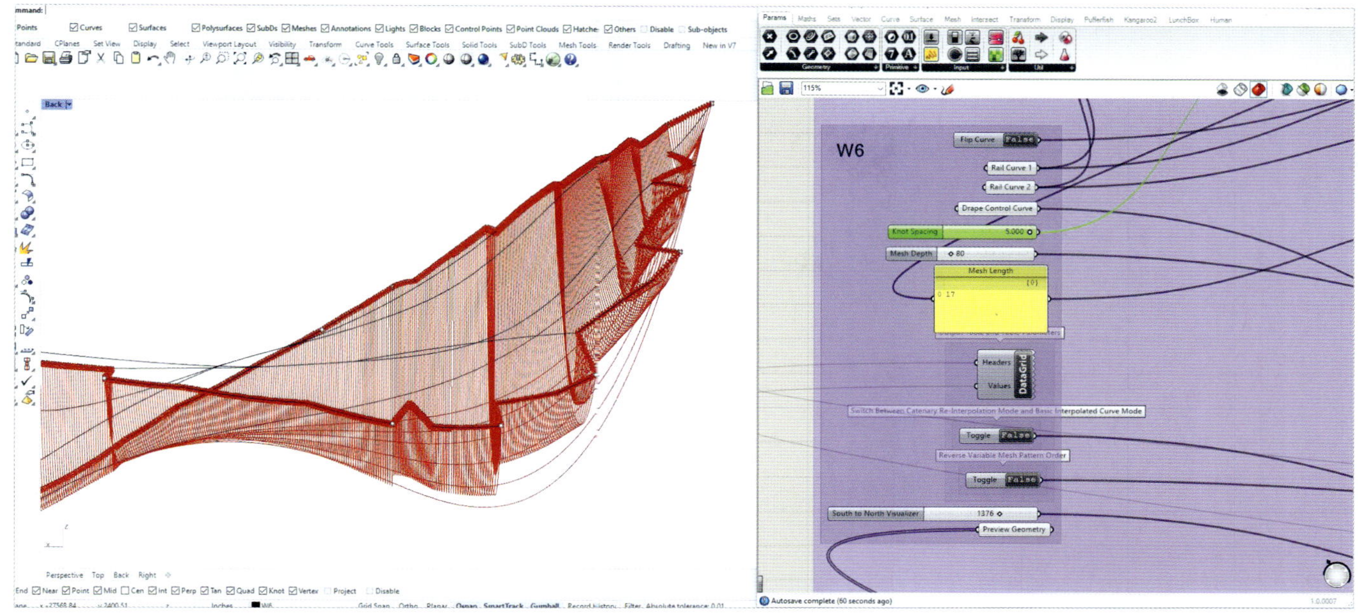

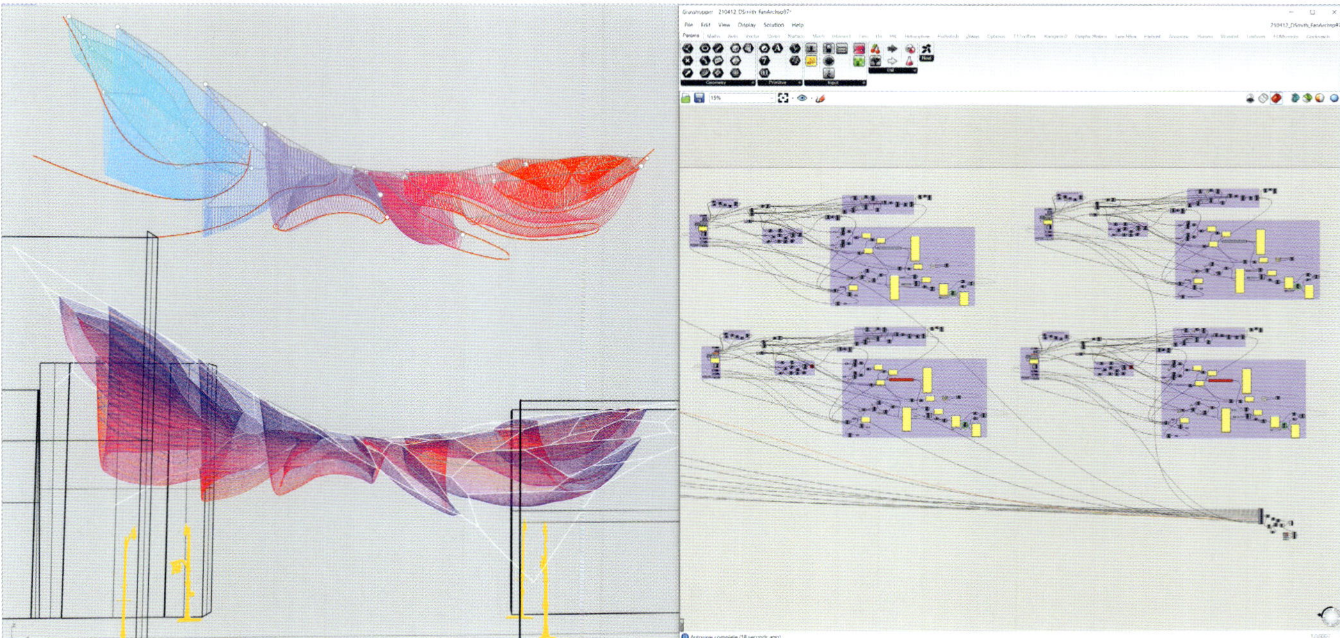

above: Interactive string model using Studio Echelman's custom software tools

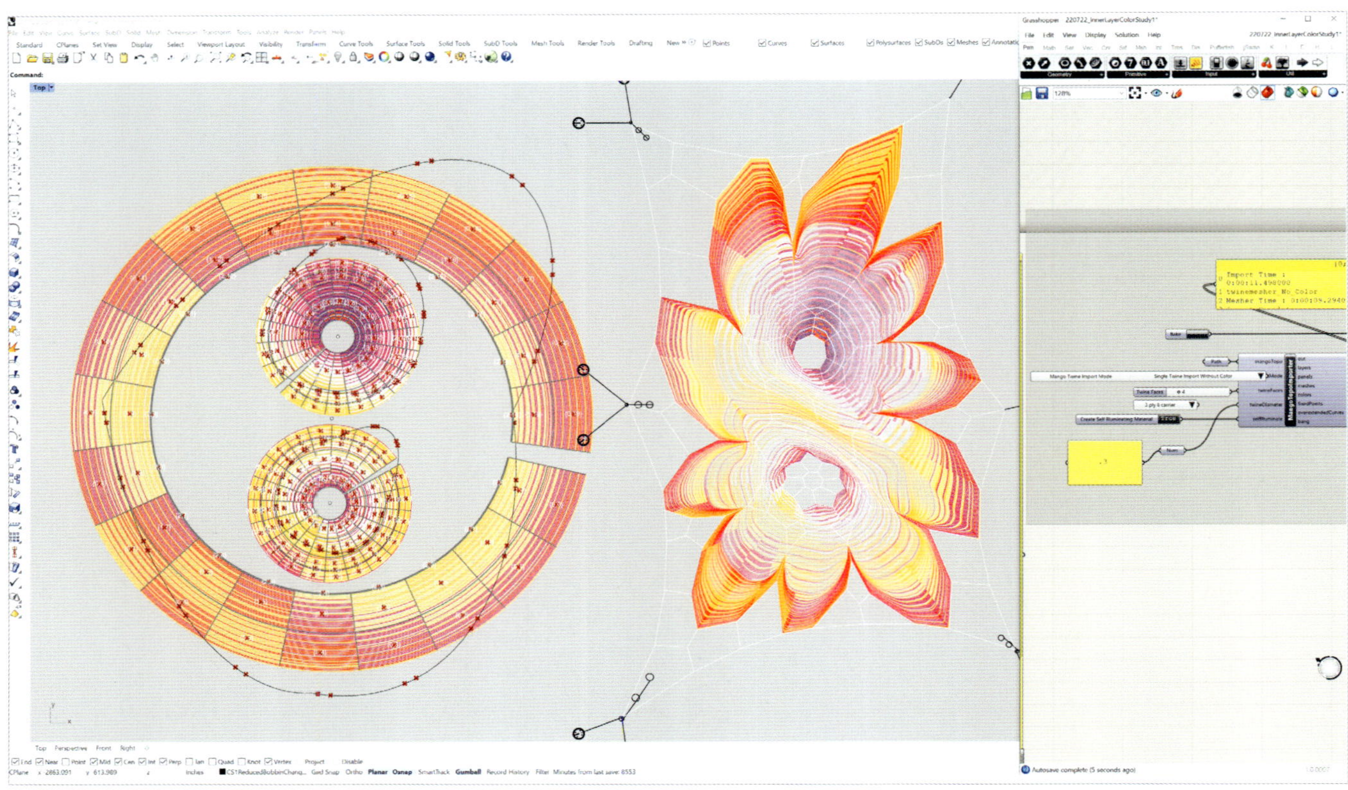

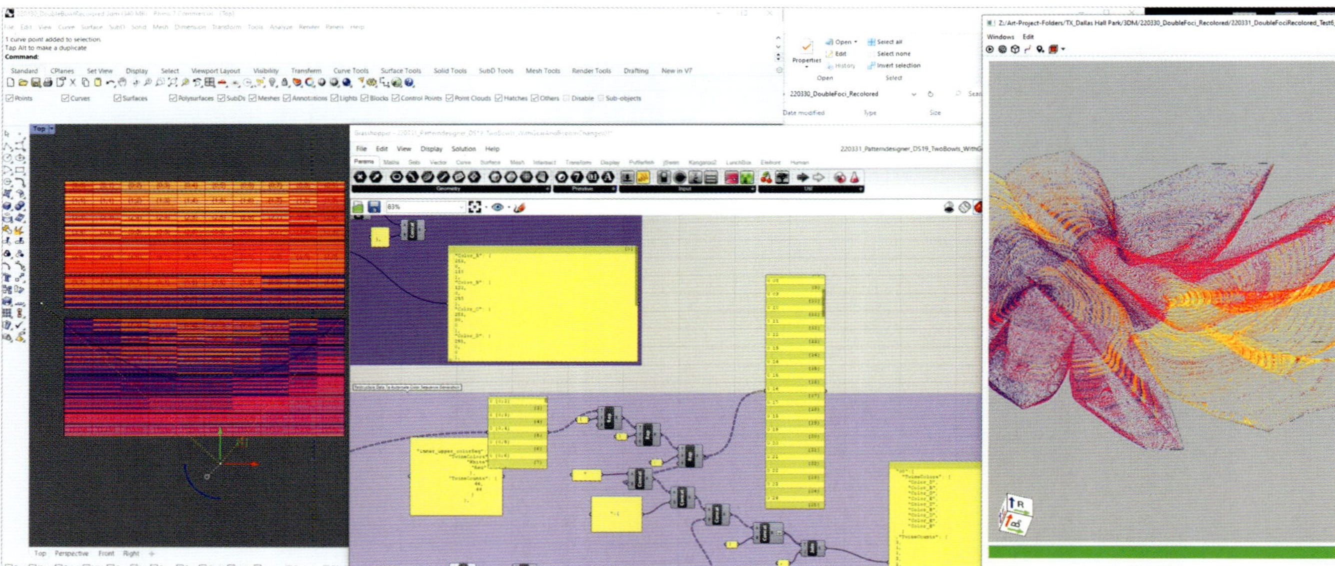

Interactive color mapping and looming model translated onto 3D geometry of *Butterfly Rest Stop*, 2024, using Studio Echelman's custom schematic pattern interface software, developed with Daniel Smith

opposite: *Butterfly Rest Stop*, 2024, Frisco, Texas

Ohio, installed in 2023. The development of *Current* began with the JNET software, but transitioned to Mango as new design methodologies were enabled by the faster, more flexible tool.

Mango allows for complex parametric definitions of sculpture variables and interoperability with other 3D design tools such as Rhino and Grasshopper. Here the smooth curves in *Current* are shaped and fine-tuned, and values for the simulation variables are generated.

Mango continues to evolve as Studio Echelman explores the expanded design space enabled by the tools. In particular, Mango allows for the exploration of quickly rehanging a soft net, resembling the original physical design process of sliding a soft net along its support structure and studying the resulting forms.

Butterfly Rest Stop, a piece for a park in Frisco, Texas, pushed the designers and software developers to consider much more deeply the nuances of connections between panels. The simultaneous development of software tools and sculptural design has resulted in mutual advancements, expanding the design space available to Studio Echelman and highlighting new frontiers in computational form finding.

Feldman's pioneering spirit and dedication to software development have been vital to Echelman's art studio. From early computations to the development of JNET and Mango, Feldman has helped Studio Echelman merge the realms of art and technology, redefining the boundaries of sculptural form finding. His contributions have left an indelible mark on Echelman's visionary artwork, inspiring future generations of artists to embrace innovation and push the boundaries of artistic expression. Through the innovative integration of art and technology, the studio's continued pursuit of sculptural innovation is a testament to Feldman's unique vision for productive collaboration among artists, engineers, mathematicians, and programmers.

Caitlin Mueller is an associate professor of civil and environmental engineering and of architecture, MIT.

Adam Burke is a visiting lecturer in design technology, Cornell University.

Andrew Sageman-Furnas is an assistant professor of mathematics, North Carolina State University.

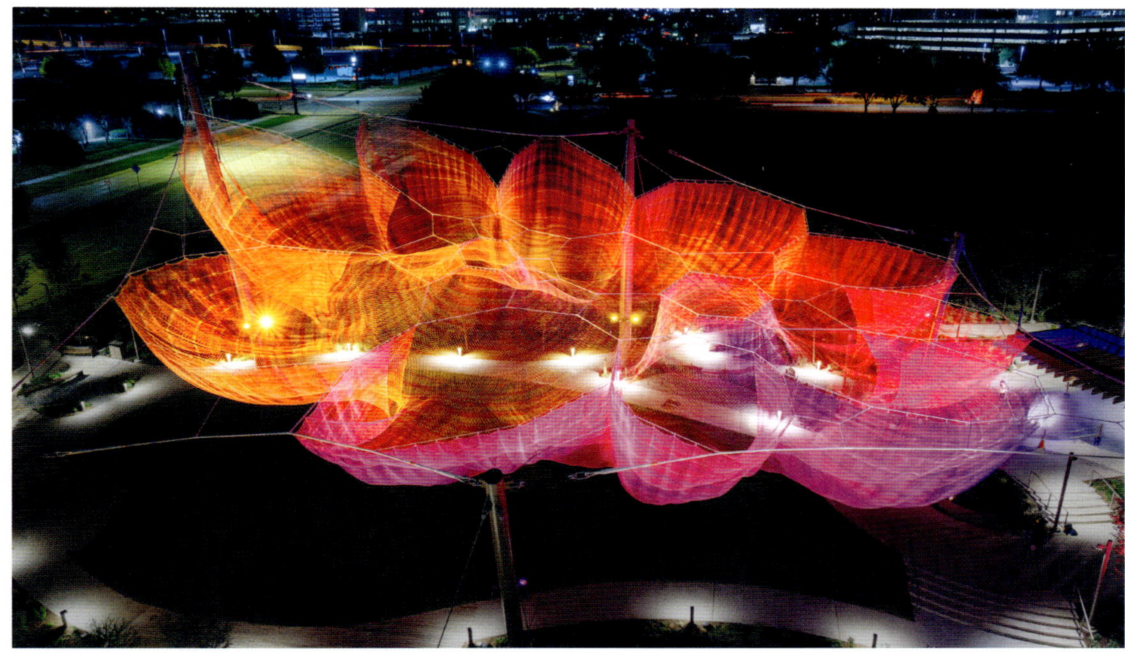

How Echelman's Sculpture Changed My Life

—

William F. Baker

When I first saw Janet Echelman's *Dream Catcher* (2017), I was awe-struck. My Skidmore, Owings & Merrill colleagues Alessandro Beghini and Nicole Wang had worked with Echelman on an art installation that spans two SOM-designed buildings in California, and Alessandro told me, "Bill, you have to see this." It was beautiful, elegant, and honest—everything that I value in art and architecture. It was pure art and pure structure; it was place making; it was architecture. It was Vitruvius's *firmitas*, *utilitas*, and *venustas*.

As I got to know Echelman and worked with her on later projects, I found her to be an artist who collaborates closely with engineers and mathematicians on form finding and the support of her nets. Her creative process is based on a total integration of aesthetics and technology. She looks to her collaborators for ideas that she can make into art. Through experimentation and exploration of solutions, she continually innovates and discovers new ideas and designs. Her interactions with engineers and mathematicians are inclusive and joyful.

Echelman, in collaboration with her in-house studio, engineers, and mathematicians, creates her designs and then oversees their fabrication and erection, a process in which David Feldman plays a critical role. She is involved in all aspects of her creations, from the color of the threads in the nets to the lighting designs to make those colors come to life to the final on-site execution. Her installations touch the environment lightly.

Dream Catcher epitomizes this, comprised as it is of several forms of nets, from stressed catenoids to hanging shapes, all supported by horizontal structural webs of ropes. Every element is in tension. The nature of ropes and nets is such that one cannot cheat. You have to work with nature to create your art, and, in the process, you get something that is totally honest. On a calm day, the geometry represents a natural shape that is the result of structural forces and gravity. When the wind blows, the shape changes to find a new geometry that is in dynamic equilibrium. The horizontal webs of ropes reference the geometry of Native American dream catchers while transforming their scale and impact as they stretch between the two buildings.

Beyond what you see, the installation represents the invisible, but equally real, world of equilibrium—a world where the forces in the ropes and nets combine with the forces of gravity and wind to form a three-dimensional geometrical world of lines of force and an invisible geometry of equilibrium. Just as the brilliant nineteenth-century physicist James Clerk Maxwell realized that a horizontal projection of a spiderweb is a projection of an invisible three-dimensional flat-faced polyhedron, *Dream Catcher* is a projection of amazing higher-order geometries. It has inspired engineering research into the geometry of equilibrium that has led to new fundamental knowledge.

Dream Catcher changed my life.

William F. Baker is a structural and civil engineering partner of Skidmore, Owings & Merrill, known for engineering the world's tallest building, the Burj Khalifa.

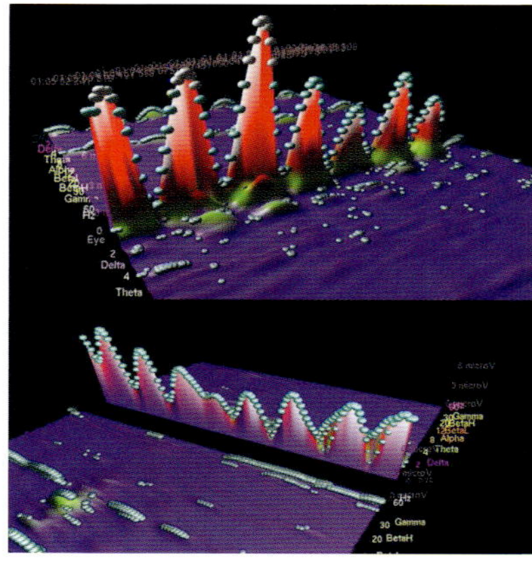

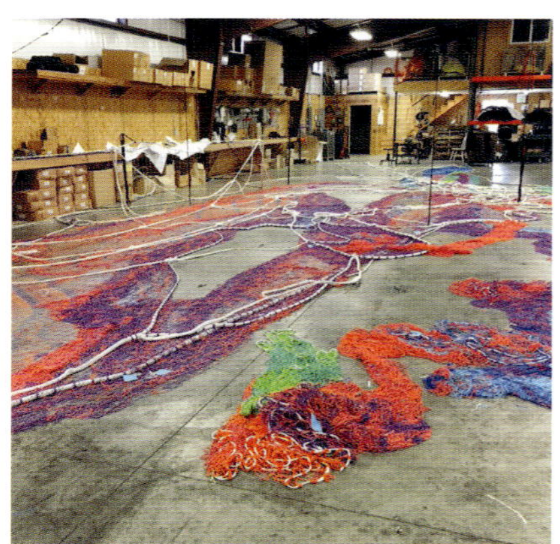

right: Data set of brain wave activity during periods of dreaming from which Echelman extrapolated the forms for *Dream Catcher*, 2017, West Hollywood, California
far right: Fabrication of *Dream Catcher*, 2017
opposite: *Dream Catcher*, 2017

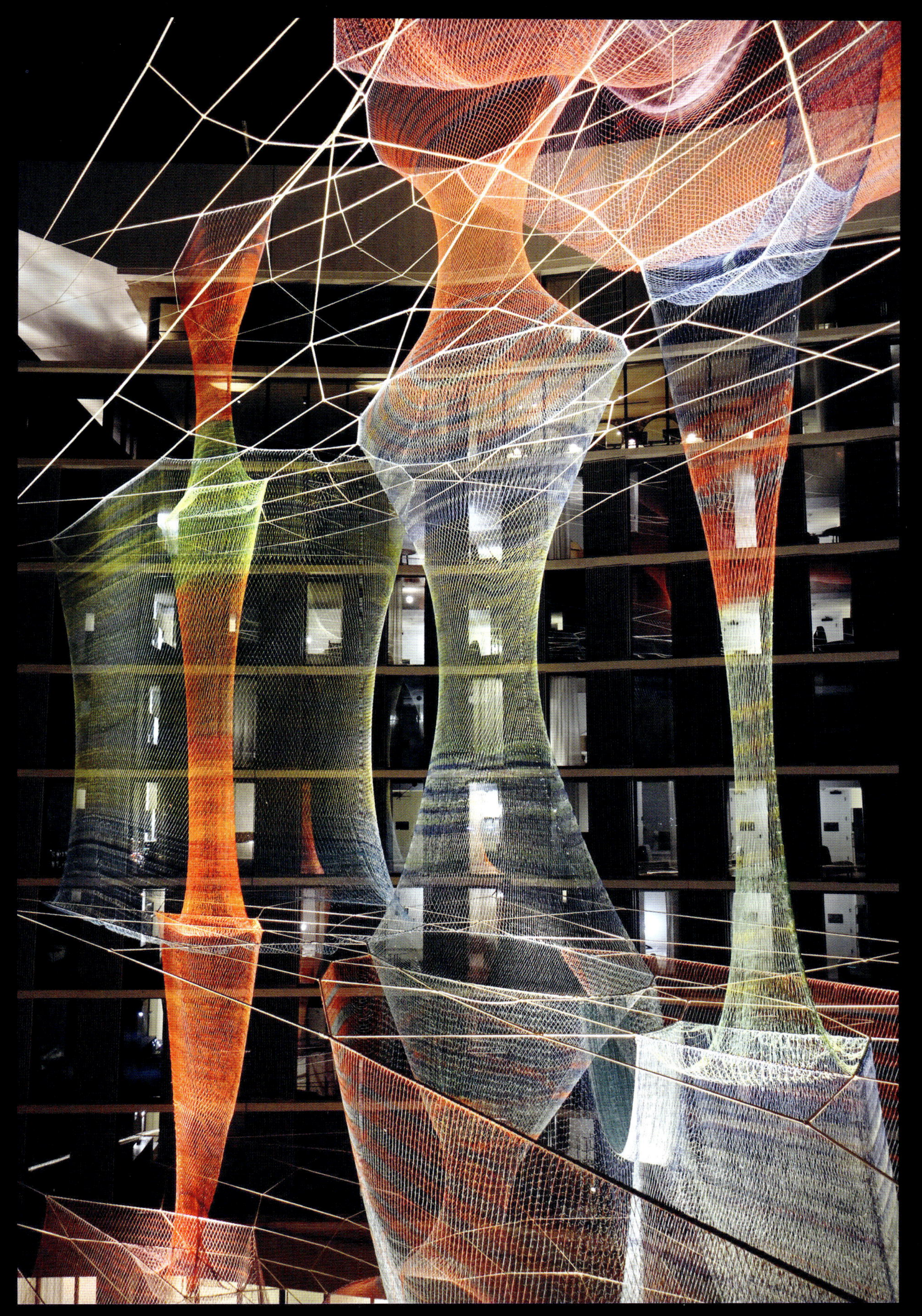

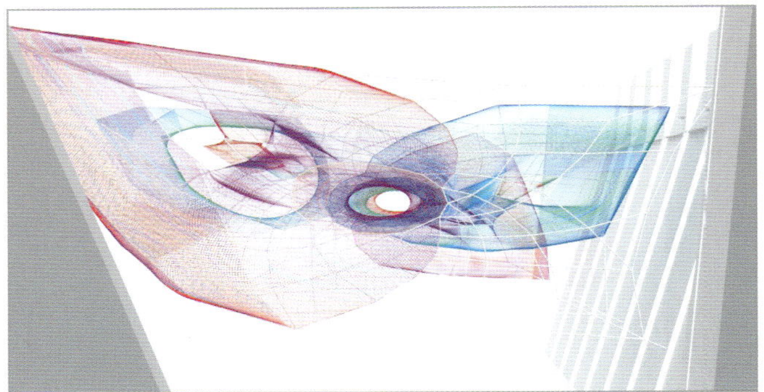

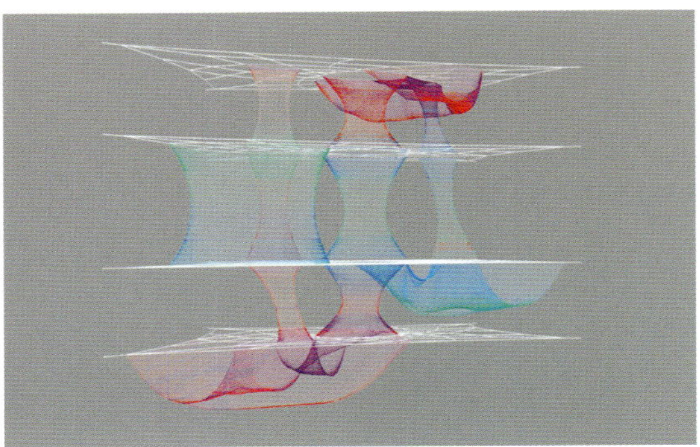

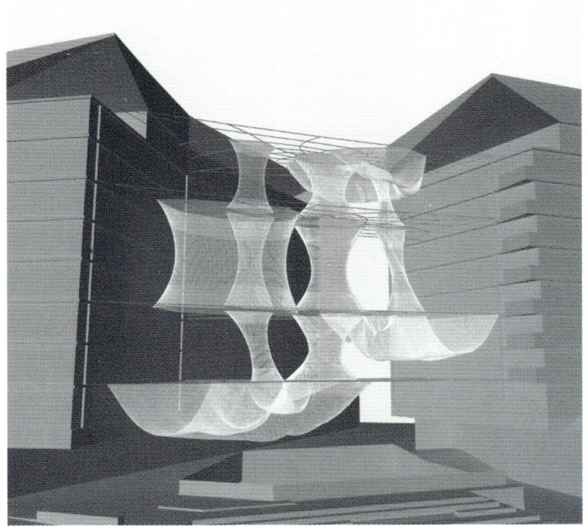

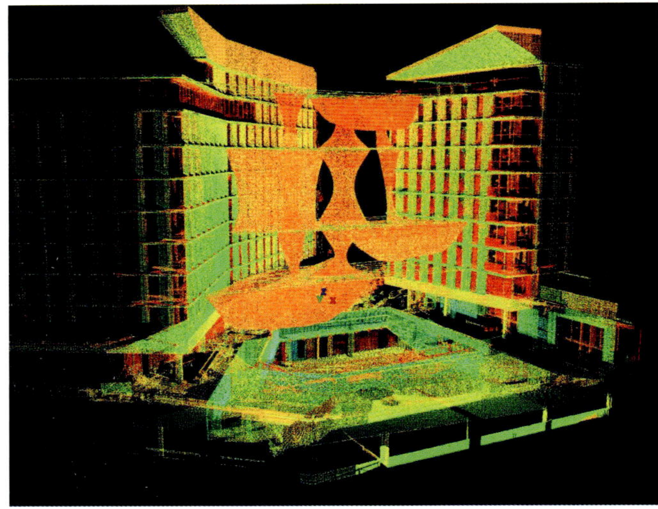

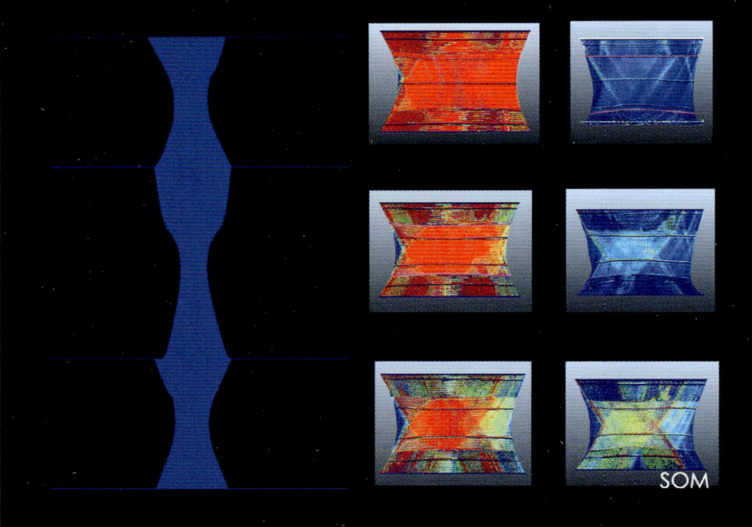

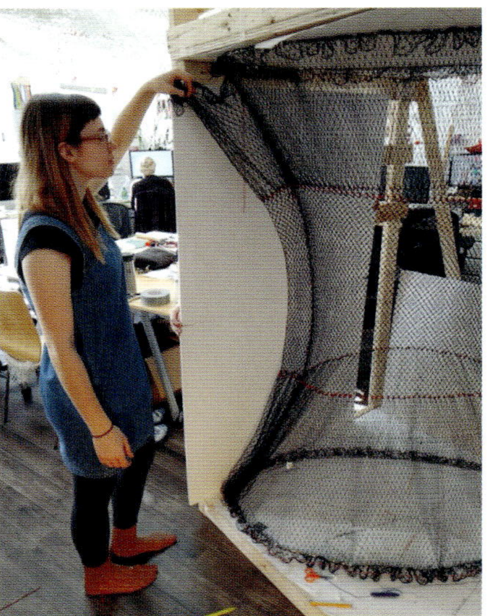

top row: Plan and elevation renderings using the studio's Mango software for *Dream Catcher*, 2017
middle row: Comparison study of the studio's Mango software rendering to the as-built sculpture captured using LiDAR scan
bottom left: Dynamic engineering stress analysis performed by SOM engineers Alessandro Beghini and Nicole Wang

bottom right: The studio builds physical scale models to test the accuracy of the geometry of the studio's JNET software
opposite and overleaf: *Dream Catcher*, 2017

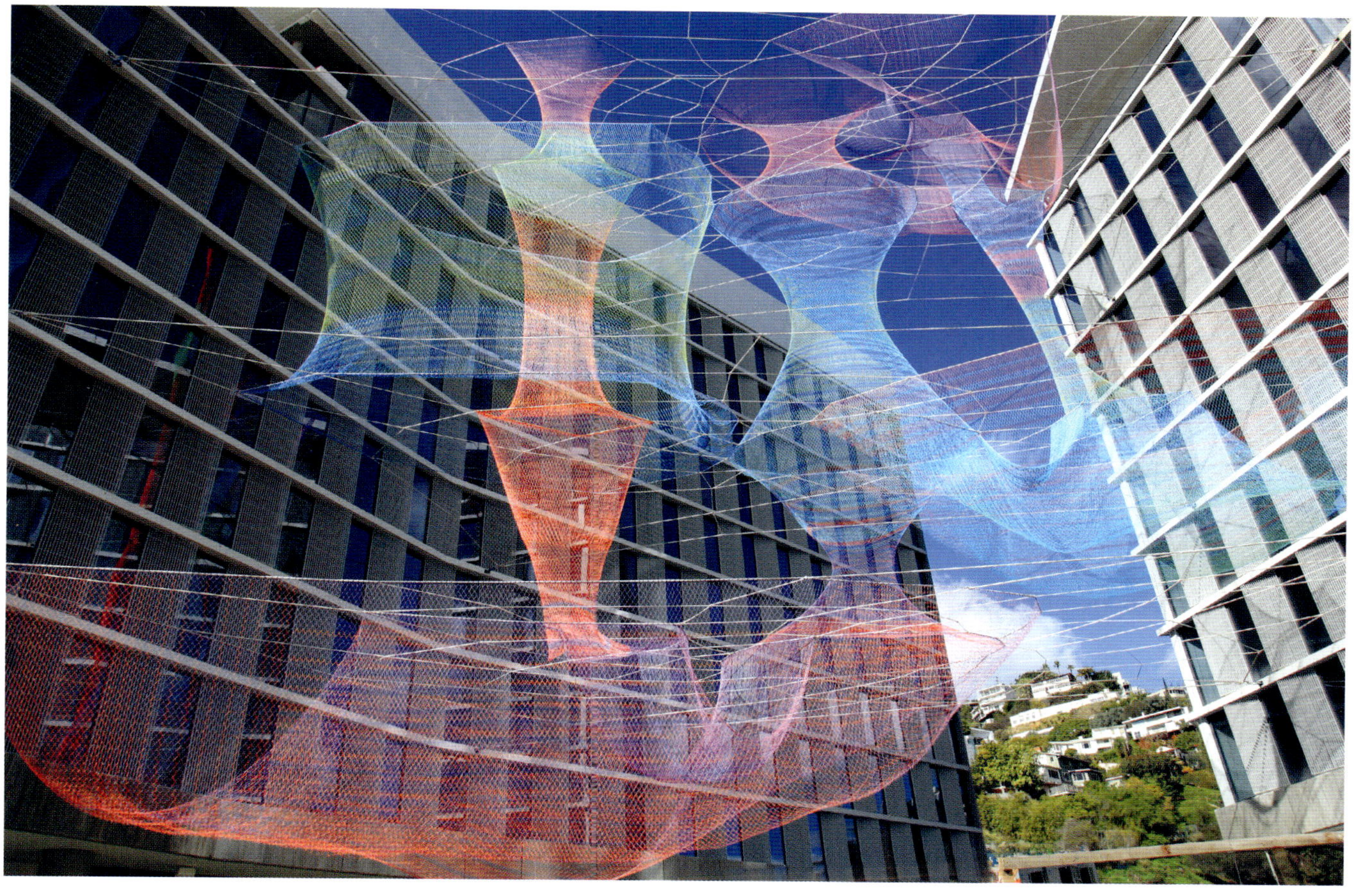

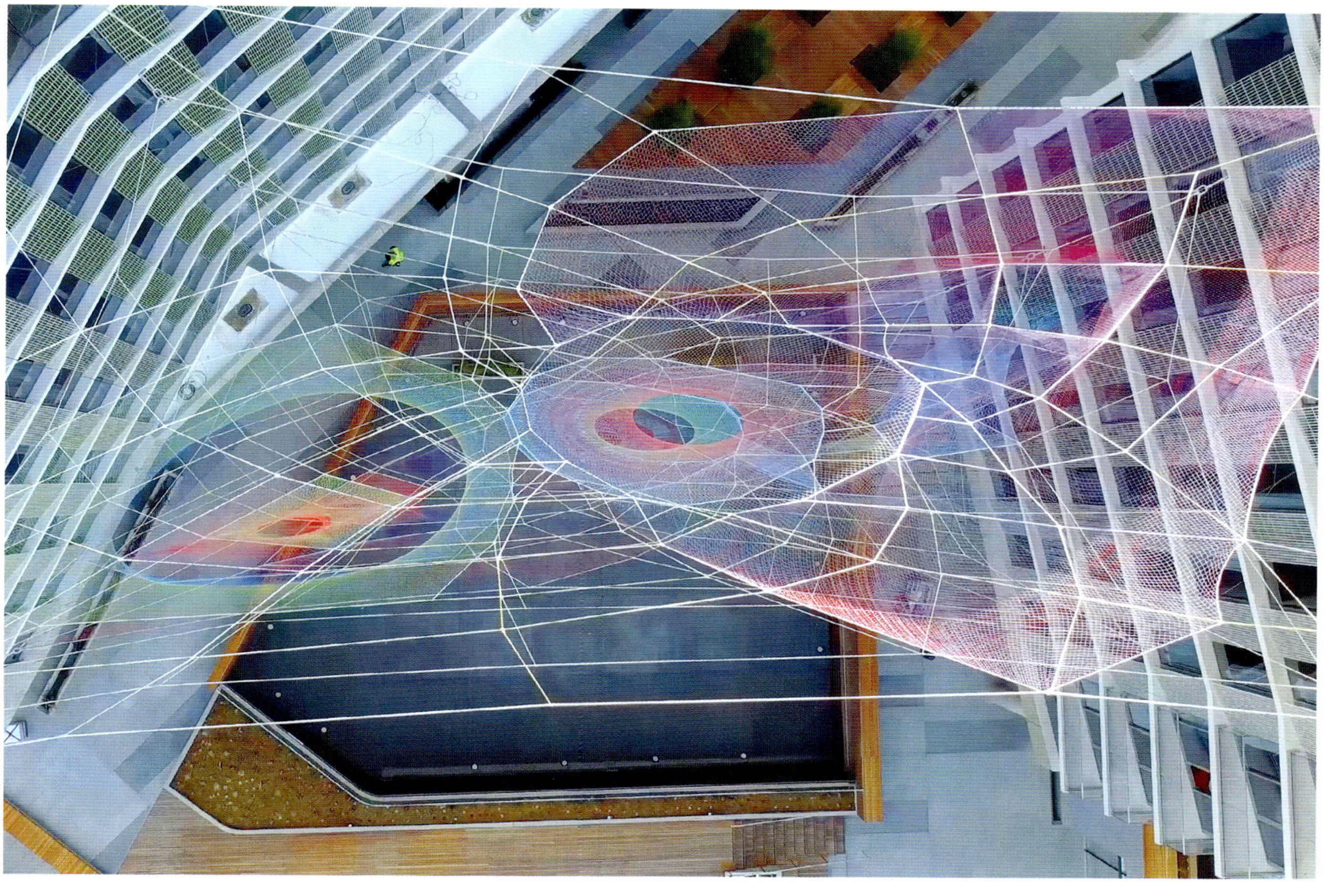

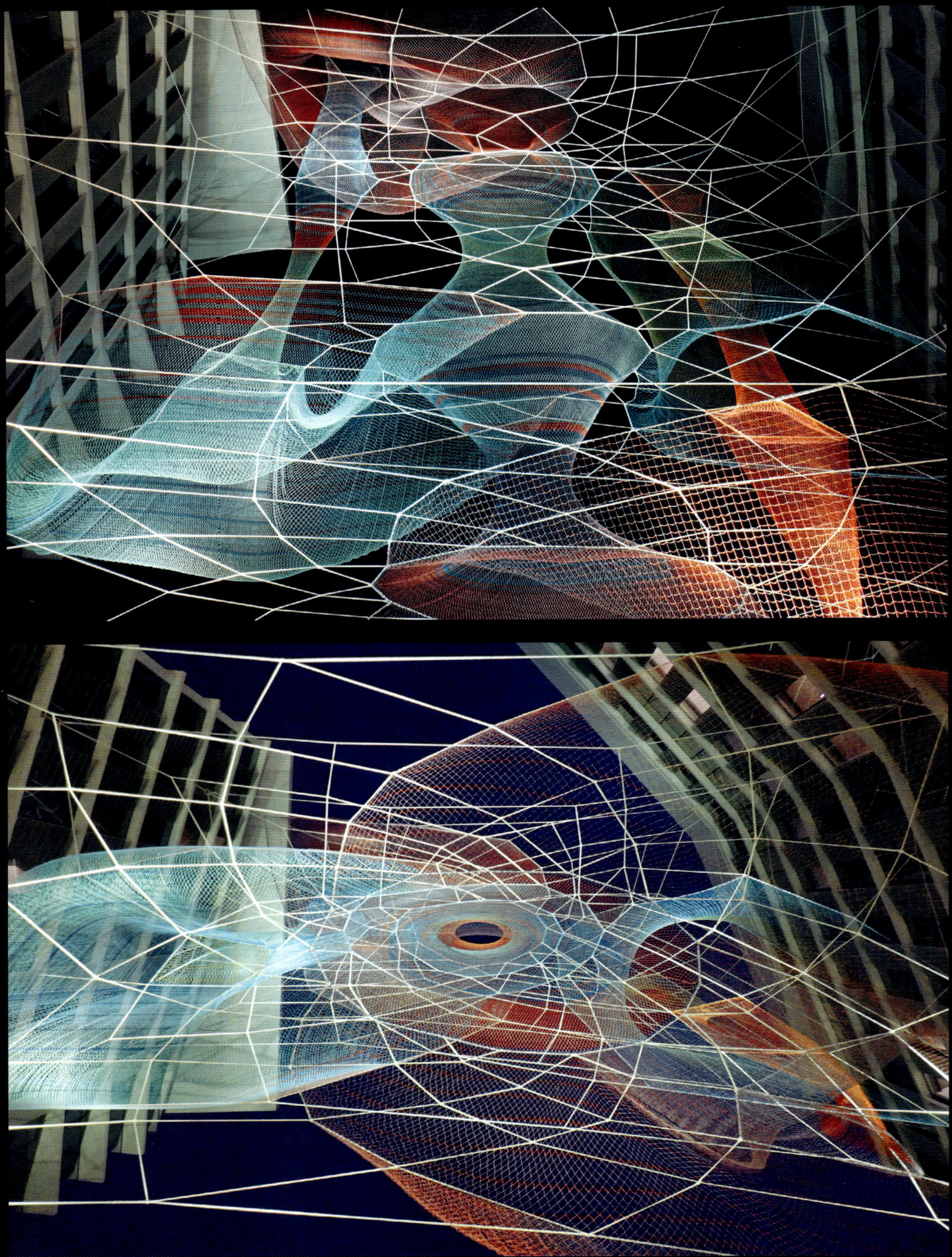

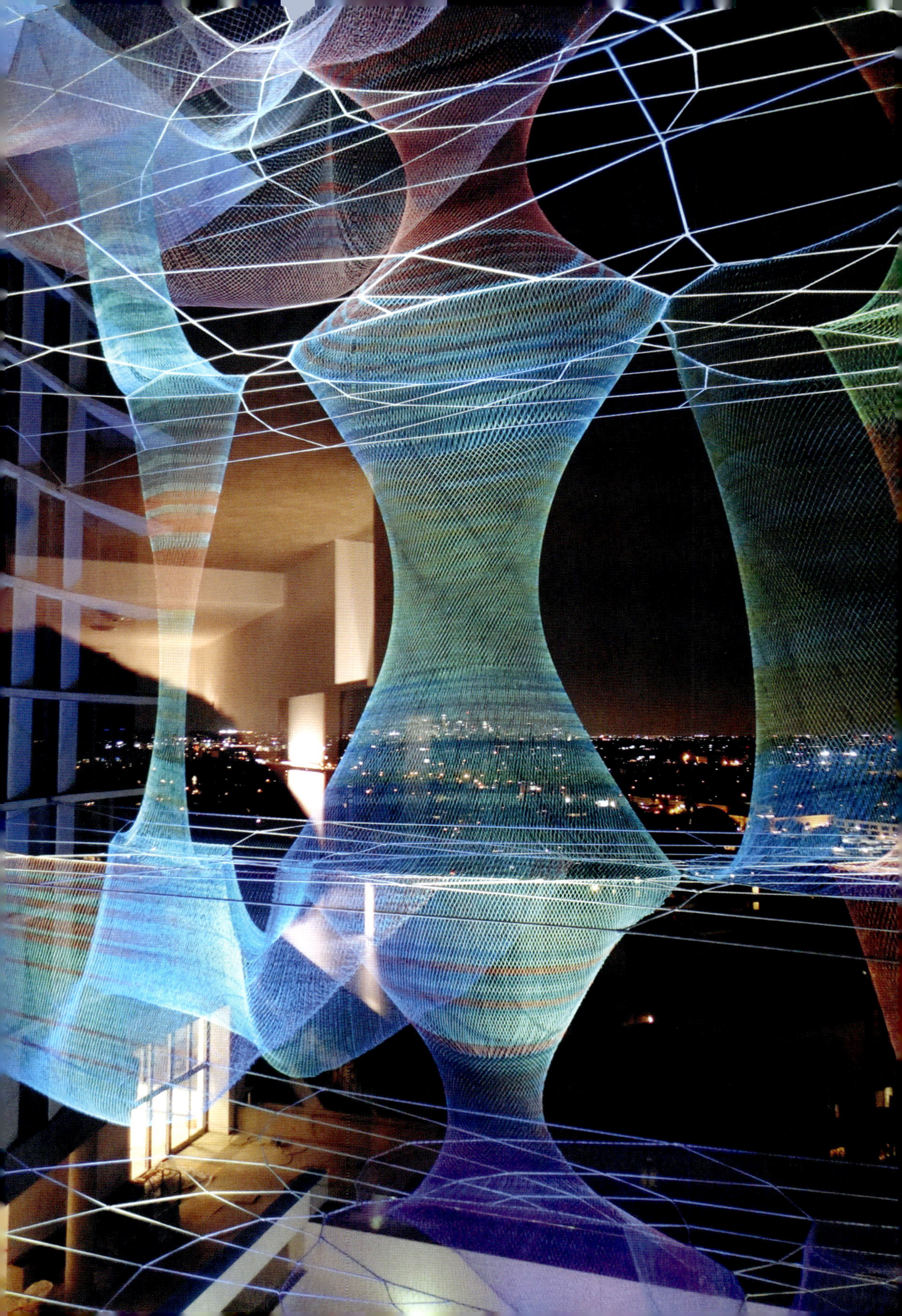

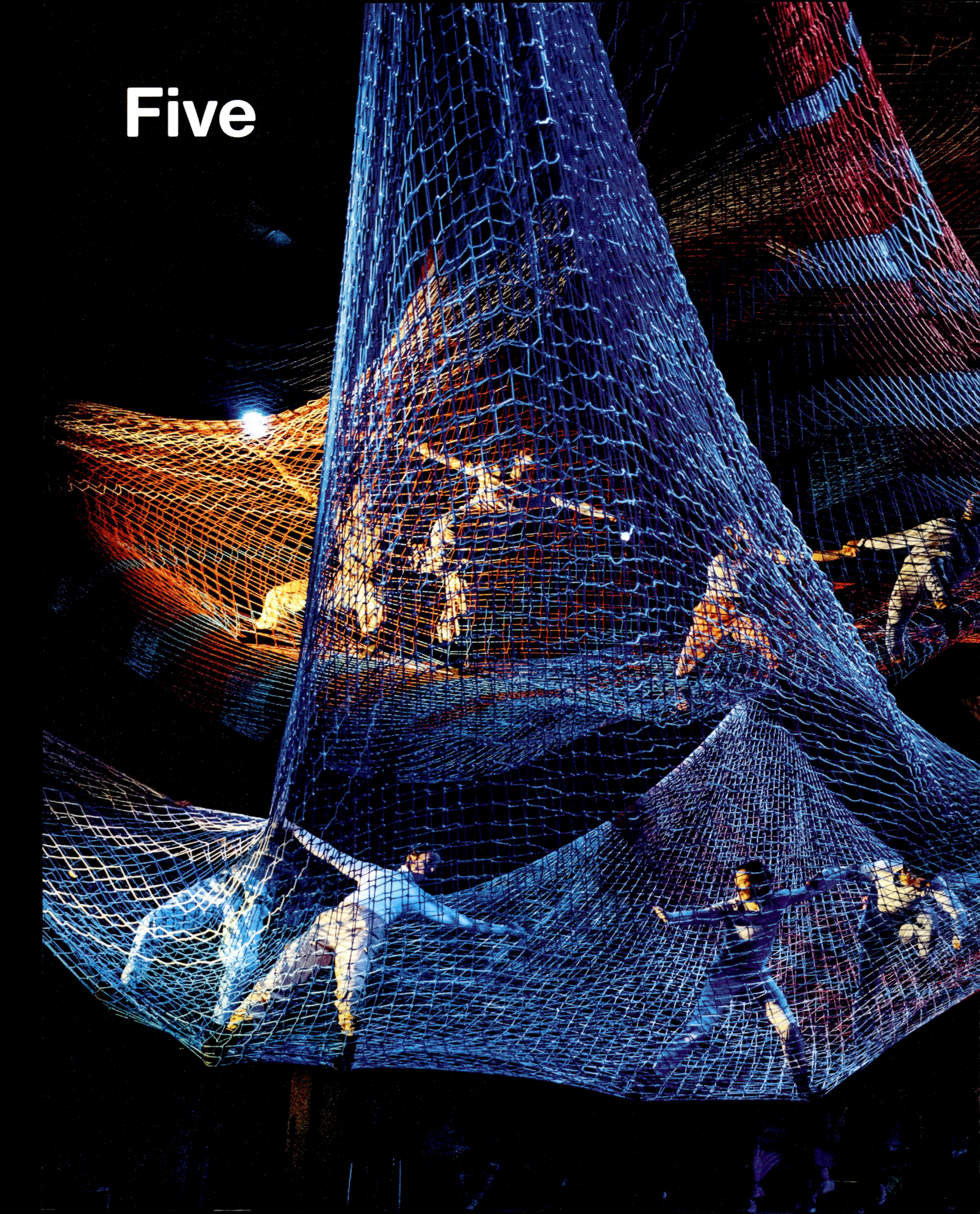

Five

Movement, Light, and Sound

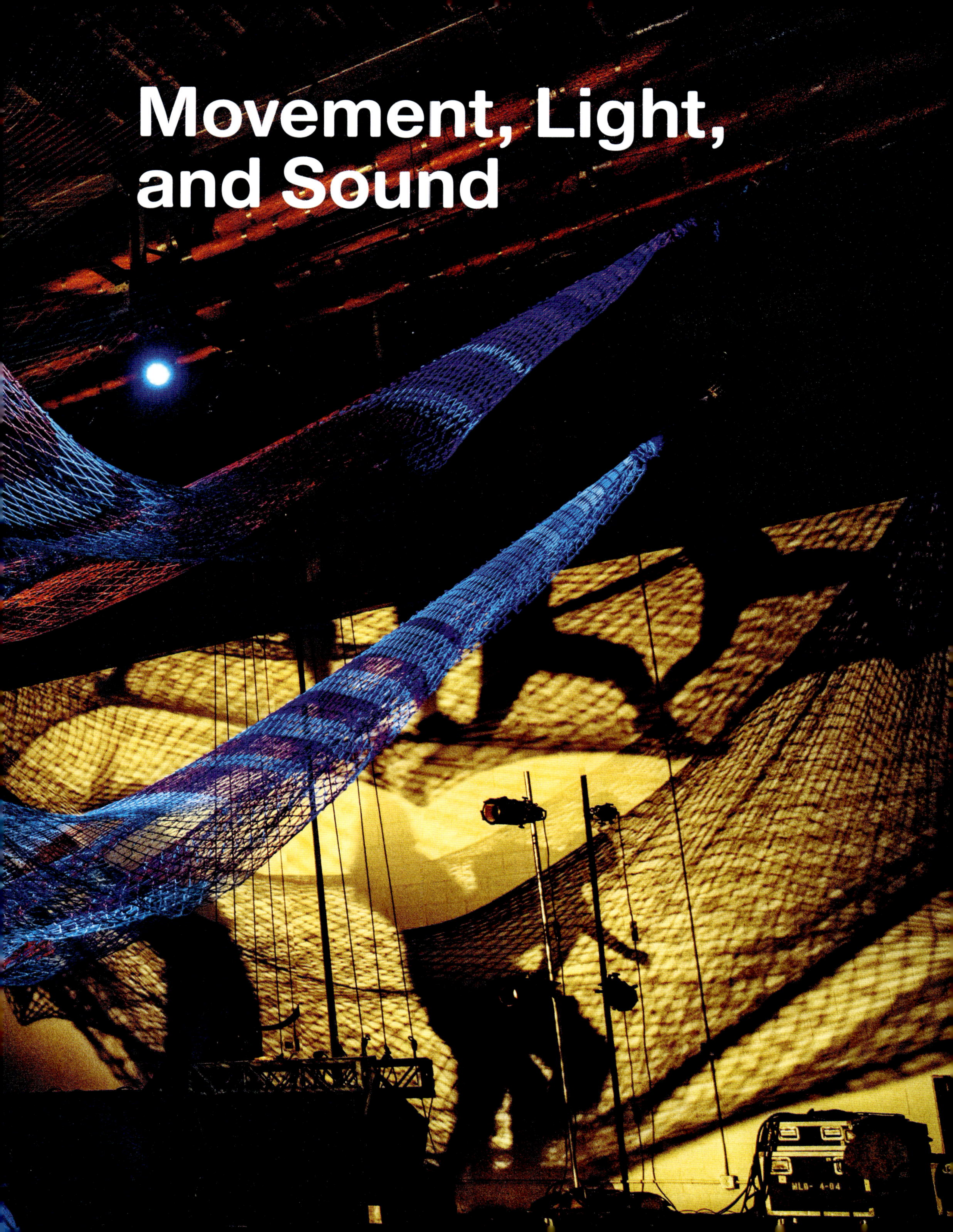

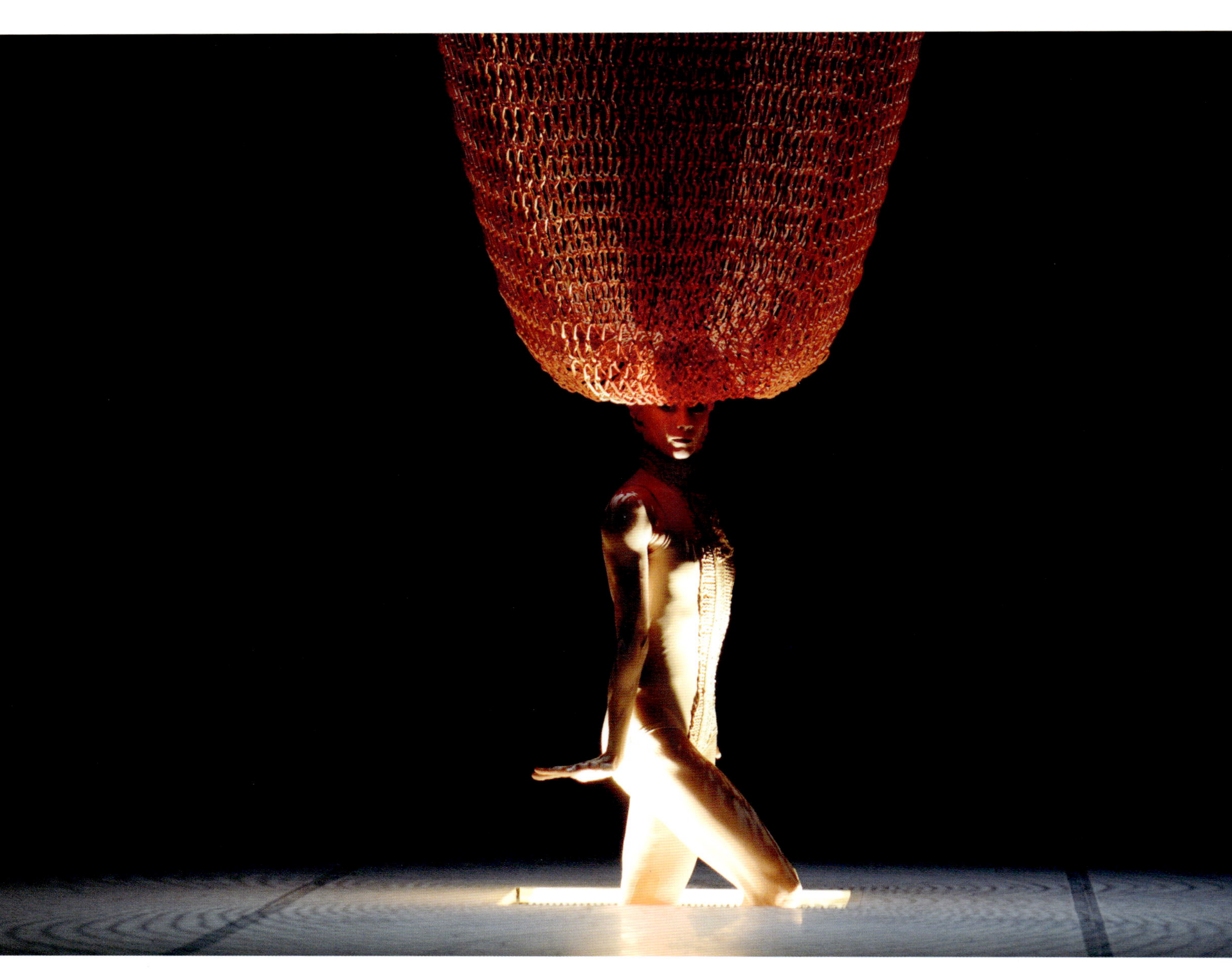

previous: *Noli Timere*, *Dance #1 (Everywhere the Edges)*, 2023, Montreal, Canada
above and opposite: *A. Memory*, 2014, Stuttgart Ballet, Germany

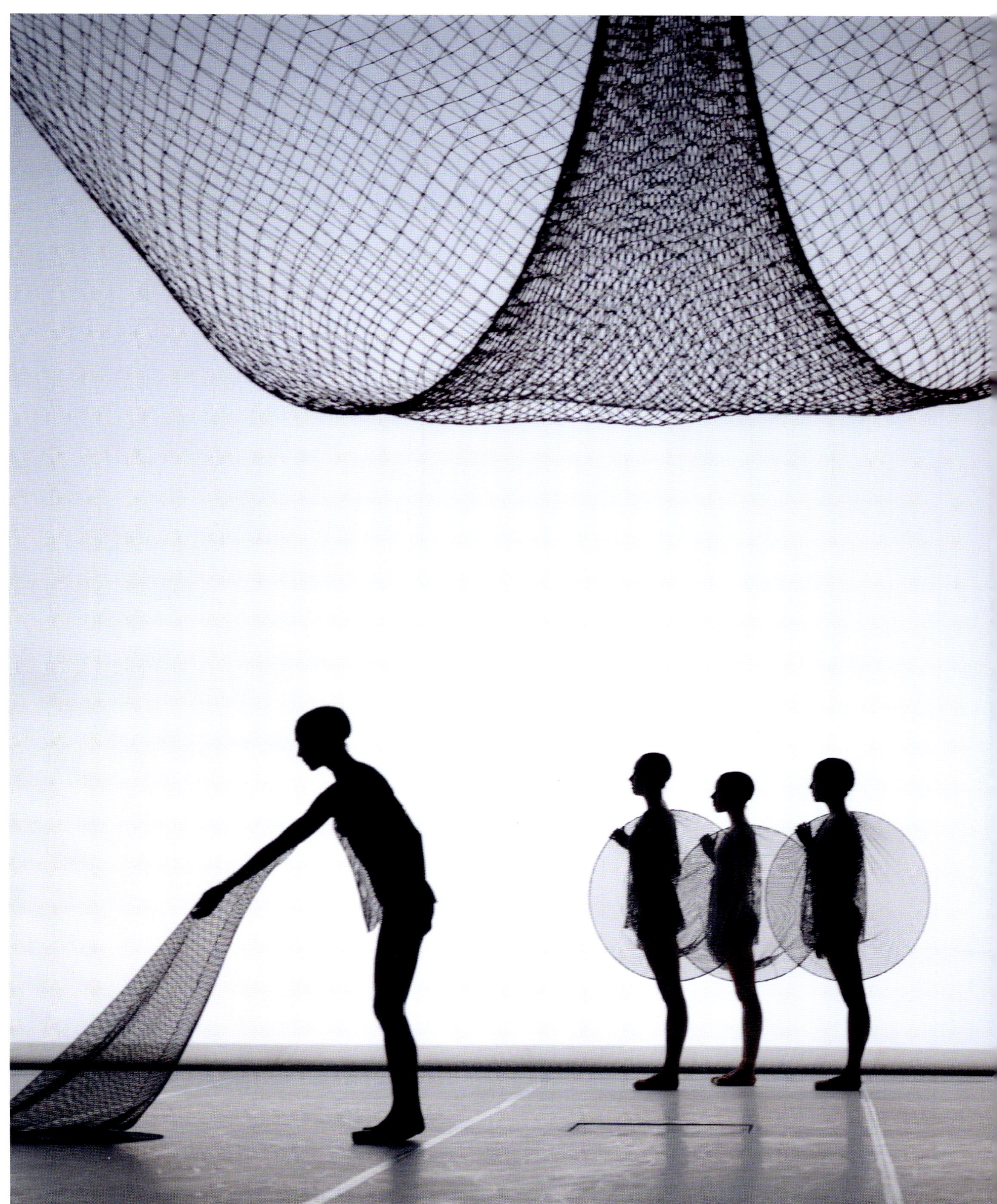

Entangled Bodies

—

Katy Dammers

Janet Echelman's sculptures have often been described with metaphors drawn from movement vocabulary, including Diana Lind's crafting of "choreography with wind" and "dancing whimsically in the air." But while these phrases evoke the mesmerizing gestures of Echelman's large-scale pieces, they fail to articulate how the sculptures manifest her long-term exploration of embodiment and encounter. From her early experiments in Bali in 1988 to her current collaboration with choreographer Rebecca Lazier, begun in 2018, Echelman has generated works whose porous, organic forms consider questions of corporeality, affect, and entanglement in an unstable world.

Throughout her practice, Echelman has interrogated the relationship between object and viewer, plumbing proprioceptive and limbic thinking to craft ephemeral, sensory experiences. The bulbous forms of her 1997 *Bell Bottom* series, inspired by South Indian fishing nets, made wind currents visible as they billowed in the air. One work, composed of a woven bottom like the hull of a boat with a single rudder and mesh sides drawing up like a voluminous sail, was suspended some twenty feet above the beach. As it bobbed and darted in the seaside breeze, it metamorphosed from an inflated form to a limp assortment of ropes as wind currents changed its volume, direction, and quality of movement. Describing these works as "embodied presences," in this series Echelman ruminated on how each piece, formed of a thin membrane, had infinite potential to change in response to its environment.

Further exploring the permeable nature of her sculpture's "skin," as Echelman describes it, her 1998 piece *Inside-Outside* invited people to interact with the piece, which was suspended from the ceiling of Harvard University's Fogg Art Museum, by standing underneath it and inserting their heads into its tall column knitted from steel wire encased in fabric. The work suggested both the ineffable strength of a tornado's vortex, sucking victims into its cyclone, and the vulnerability of a bodily orifice, particularly poignant amid the AIDS crisis. Whereas earlier works considered how elements could move through and animate sculpture, *Inside-Outside* reexamined boundaries as individuals were enveloped by its thin, translucent net. This intimate penetration reframed the sculpture as a somatic encounter between participant and artwork, activating the body as a sensing organism and resisting the hegemonic power of sight.

Moving from interaction to environment, Echelman then explored what it might mean to surround the visitor, bringing them into relationship with a habitat rather than a landscape to be visually manifested or traversed. *Red Spikes on 29th Street*, shown at Florence Lynch Gallery, New York, in 2000, presented cone-like pyramids as soft extensions of the exhibition's corpus that fluttered out the gallery windows like painted fingers, drawing attention to the thick volume of the room and the viewer inside of it. Following up on this cocoon-like sensation, Echelman's later outdoor public sculptures crafted kinesthetic environments that prioritize what she terms "an experiential interaction with the viewer." Her 2001 piece *Target Swooping Down...Bullseye!* threaded a sculptural membrane across the courtyard of the IFEMA national trade fair complex in Madrid, and its funnel-like shape of alternating red and white rings drew attention to the mass and volume of the previously evacuated oculus. Recalling the joy of creating forts as a child, Echelman's large-scale public works engender both awe at their fantastical forms and bright colors as well as a feeling of being held, primarily from their specific orientation to scale and siting. Speaking about the affect of large-scale works, Echelman notes, "I want people to feel protected, yet linked to open sky."[1] This sensation sought to bring people closer to one another, supporting them in an experience of collective wonder.

The somatic quality of Echelman's sculpture is in part thanks to her long-standing work with choreographers, which puts her practice in dialogue with moving bodies, from classically trained ballet dancers to circus performers and contemporary movement practitioners. In her first formal foray into collaboration with dance in 2014, Echelman crafted sculpture components for *A. Memory* with choreographer Katarzyna Kozielska for the Stuttgart Ballet. At its beginning, a red-and-orange woven mass emerges from the stage surface, its long polyester strands drawn upward to form a billowing pyramid, ultimately

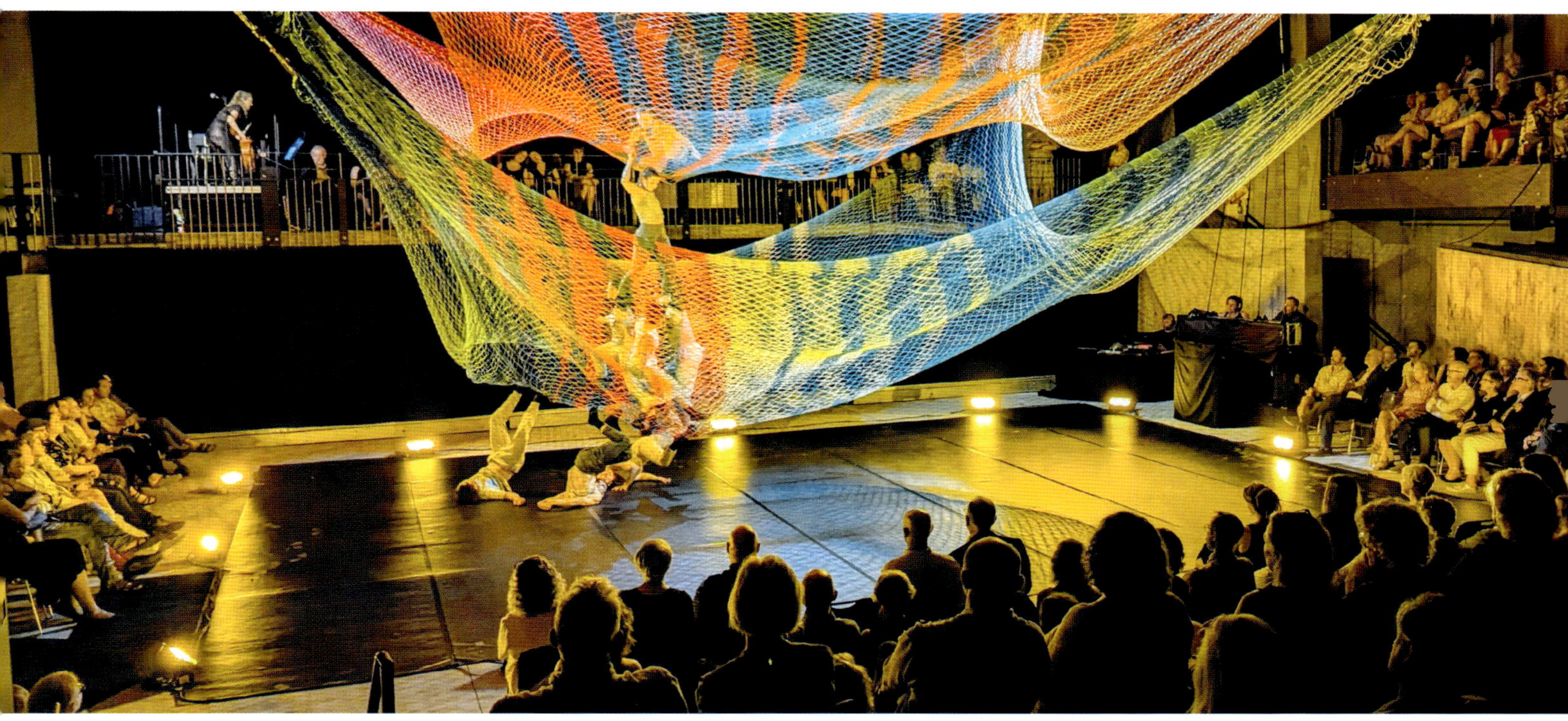

punctuated by a dancer en pointe, her head affixed to the bottom of its softly curved fibers. This dramatic opening to the formal, concert-length ballet demonstrates how Echelman's beguiling, mutating forms slip between protagonist, costume, set piece, and environment, mirroring the many ways her sculptures have functioned over her career. While inspired by her mentor Robert Rauschenberg's collaboration with choreographer Trisha Brown—in particular the piece *Set and Reset* (1983), for which Rauschenberg hung geometric screens for video projection and designed soft pleated costumes—Echelman moved beyond a traditional arrangement where a visual artist provides accompaniment through a fixed role to assert a multidimensional collaboration between sculpture and dance.

In her ongoing dance collaboration *Noli Timere* with choreographer Rebecca Lazier, Echelman is a creative partner in crafting an ecosystem that offers—in both its creative process and its performance—a model of entangled coexistence amid precarity. Lazier, a professor of practice in the dance program at Princeton University, is renowned for her thought-provoking interdisciplinary works that utilize movement as a research tool to examine the tension between improvisation and set directives, between individual agency and collective decision-making—all of which continue to be developed in *Noli Timere*. Echelman and Lazier began working together in 2018 to explore: How do we find a way to move through an unstable world? And how might we do so—alluding to the Latin title—without fear?

For the first time, Echelman is creating a net for dancers to move on, over, and through, partnering with the sculptural expanse in a complex choreography. A seemingly weightless entity that holds up to six dancers, the large forty-by-forty-foot net serves as a manifestation of our uncertain world as dancers carefully traverse its thin, uneven rope surface by balancing across the

above: *Noli Timere*, *Dance #2*, 2024, PS21, Chatham, New York

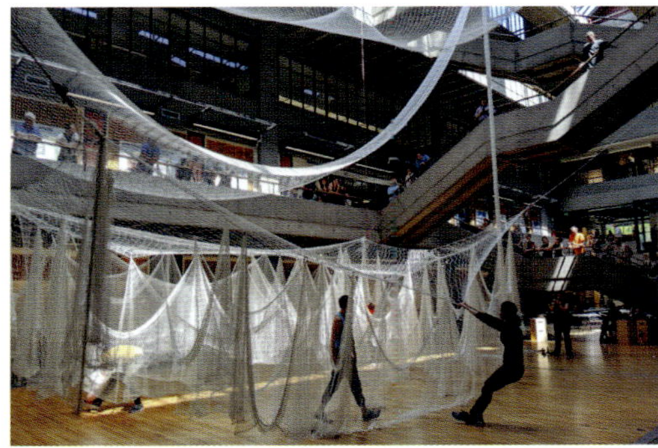

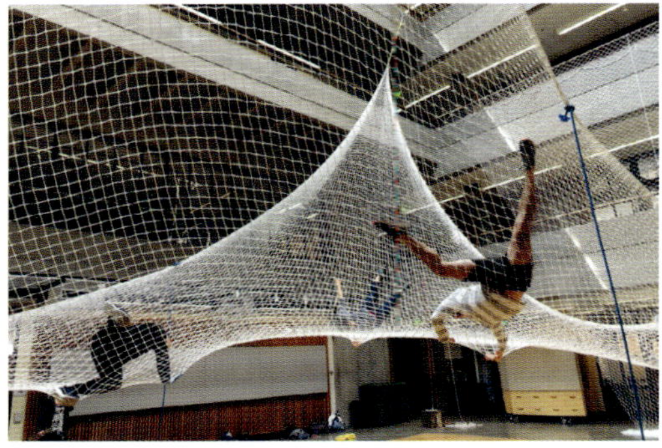

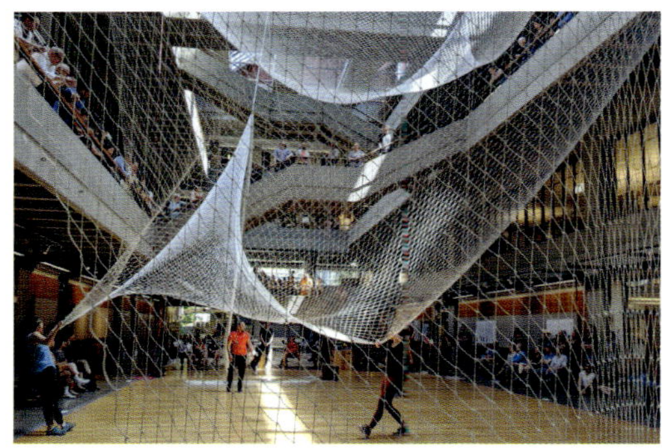

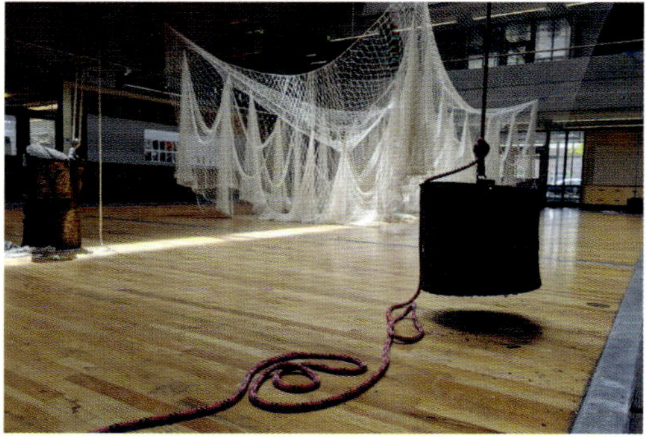

above: Dance-engineering workshop and performance in Gould Hall, University of Washington, Seattle, 2019
opposite: Premiere of *Noli Timere, Dance #3*, 2025, McCarter Theatre, Princeton, New Jersey

woven structure or climbing onto intersecting layers. Suspended up to twenty-five feet above the ground, the dancers' deft movements evoke both the shaky steps of a toddler and the virtuosic feats of circus performance, reveling in the incredible vulnerability and strength of the human body.

Echelman and Lazier have worked closely on the development of *Noli Timere*, enacting in their creative collaboration the same dynamic, intertwined, and flexible properties that they have sought to develop in the net itself. Their creative process defies a traditional hierarchy where a lead artist defines the terms of engagement, whether it be the sculptor fashioning an environment that a choreographer then works within, or a choreographer formulating a series of movements that an artist then sculpts a ground to support. Instead, Echelman and Lazier have worked in lockstep through a series of concentrated workshops, equally exploring various net structures and diverse movement vocabularies, then redrafting and fine-tuning together. Recalibration became even more central to their process as they shifted between in-person and remote work during the pandemic, adapted to various presentation possibilities—a theater, outdoors, a public atrium—as the work has evolved, and innovated to meet health and safety requirements for working at heights.

More than a precious ground, the net renders how a seemingly independent series of steps affects others, and how a seemingly fleeting feeling can have long-lasting impacts. As the dancers move, the net receives their weight and propulsion and reacts in kind, growing taut or rippling. This responsiveness shifts the net from a set piece to an activated collaborator with what Lazier calls "kinetic empathy." Rather than independent sculptural forms that are in relationship with dancers, as in *A. Memory*, Echelman describes the net in *Noli Timere* as itself "a dancer.[2] This distinction is crucial, and emphasizes the simultaneously receptive and responsive nature of the webbing in *Noli Timere*. Whereas the tubular arm extensions that the corps de ballet wear in *A. Memory* respond to their movements—expanding to the floor or contracting to rest on a shoulder as each dancer manipulates them—dancers in *Noli Timere* do not manipulate

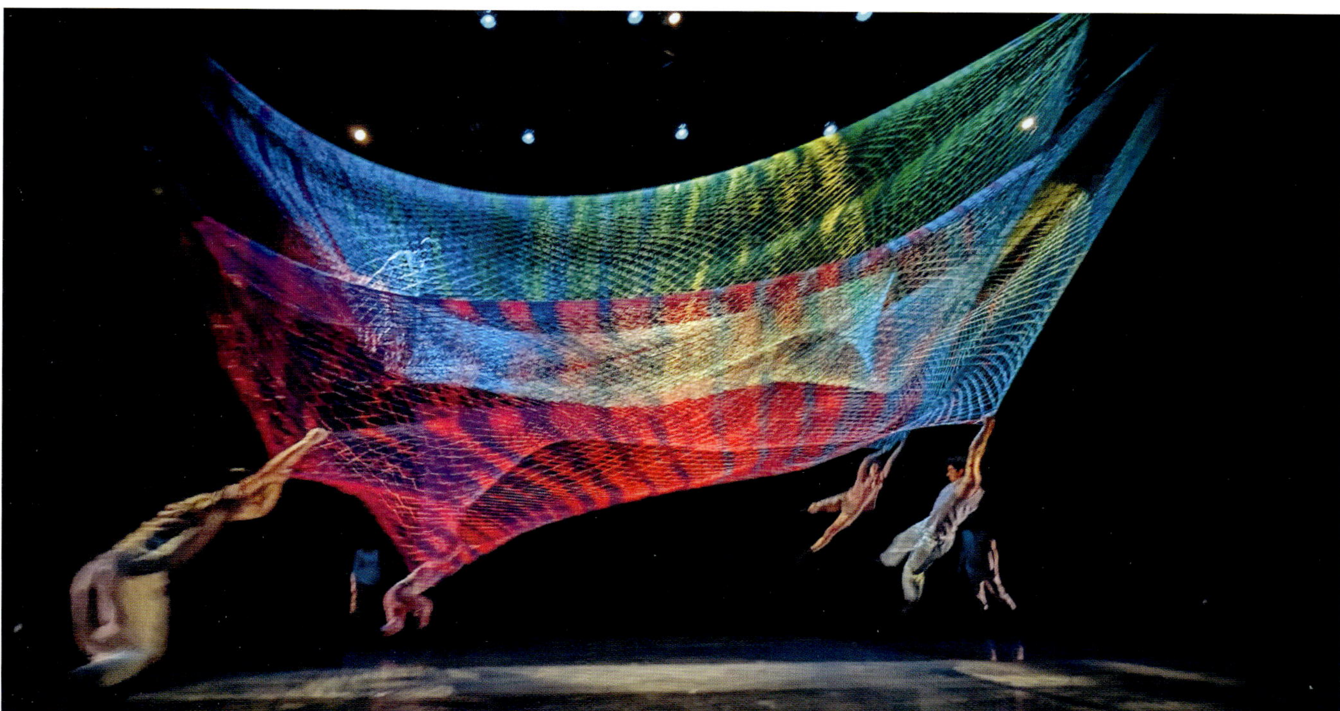

the net; they partner with it in a complex duet of action and reaction that quickly blurs with many layered inputs and feedbacks.

Ultimately, *Noli Timere* makes visible our precarious world of shifting relationships and highlights our symbiotic entanglement. Describing the piece as "watching a network," Lazier notes how it illustrates gathering power and oppositional vectors moving along the net and undulating into each dancer, like a storm brews along a coastline, churning water and gathering gales. This complex dynamism of forces recalls Karen Barad's term "intra-action," which replaces a staid "interaction" of two bodies in conflict with a fluid, exchanging system of energies.[3] Just as Echelman's early sculptures questioned the permeable boundaries of form, *Noli Timere* continues this exploration on a monumental scale as dancer and net evolve together. Whereas Lazier's previous choreography grappled with the binary between individual motivation and group collaboration, in this new work, that distinction is voided by an ever-present sympoiesis, or "making with," with the net. Numerous reverberating streams of energy across the net and the dancers make it futile to isolate action or reaction. Instead, the work embodies what Donna Haraway describes as "the tentacular [which are] also nets and networks. Tentacularity is life lived along lines—and such a wealth of lines—not at points, not in spheres."[4] The many interwoven vectors in *Noli Timere* recall our exquisite ecologies, where a change in one factor—be it habitat loss, illness, or global warming—has cascading effects across the world.

Calling herself a "designer of life," Echelman considers an expanded notion of embodiment for a more synergetic world. From her early sculptures to her recent work in dance, she has probed the boundaries of the body, delighting in its permeable nature to draw attention to its intertwined relationship with others and the environment. Moving from the theatricality of an encounter with form to recasting sculpture as an extension of the body and, later, an environment, Echelman has steadily decentralized the individual actor to craft an ecosystem of interrelated and entangled sensations.

Katy Dammers is deputy director and chief curator of performance, REDCAT, Los Angeles.

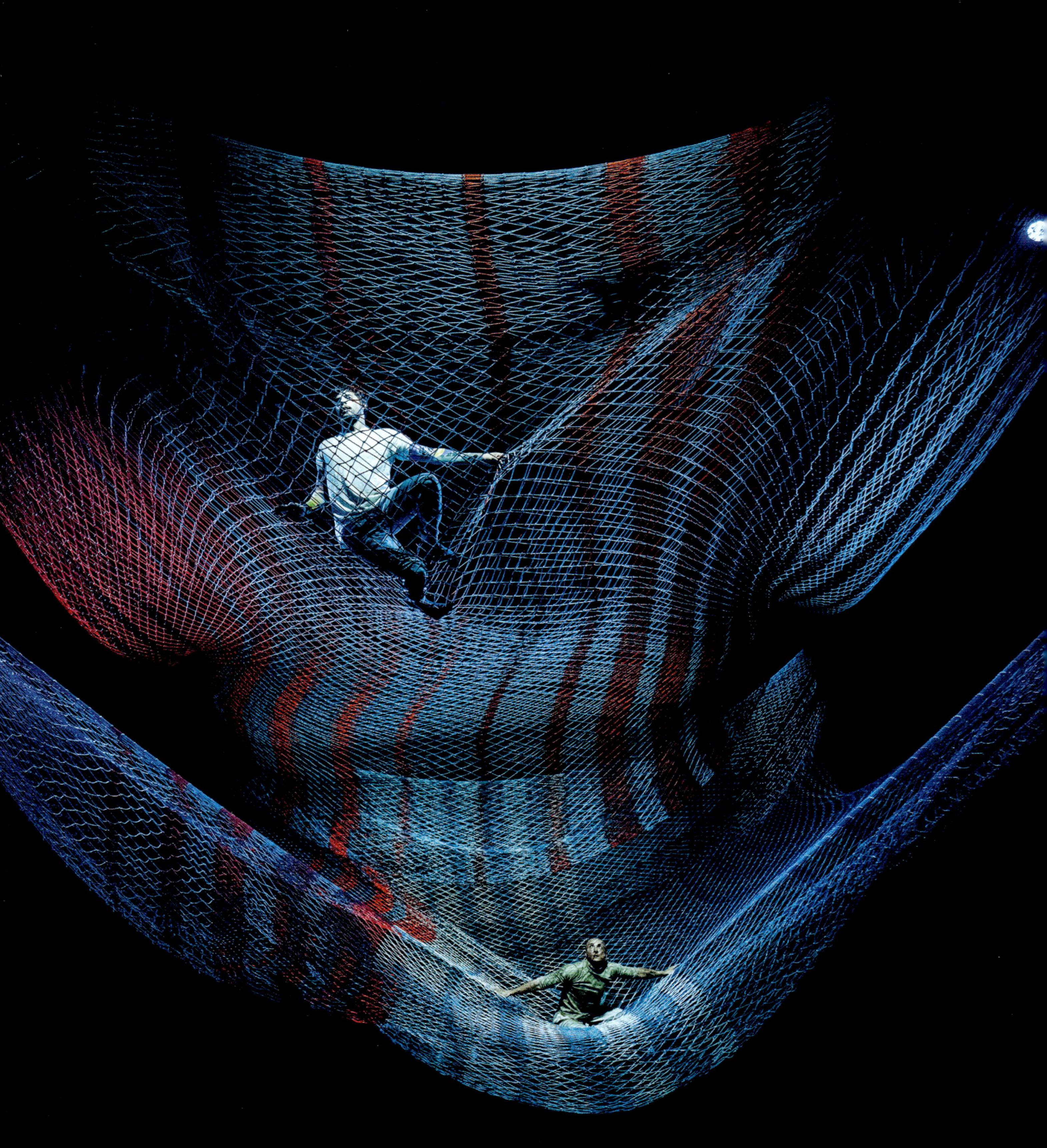

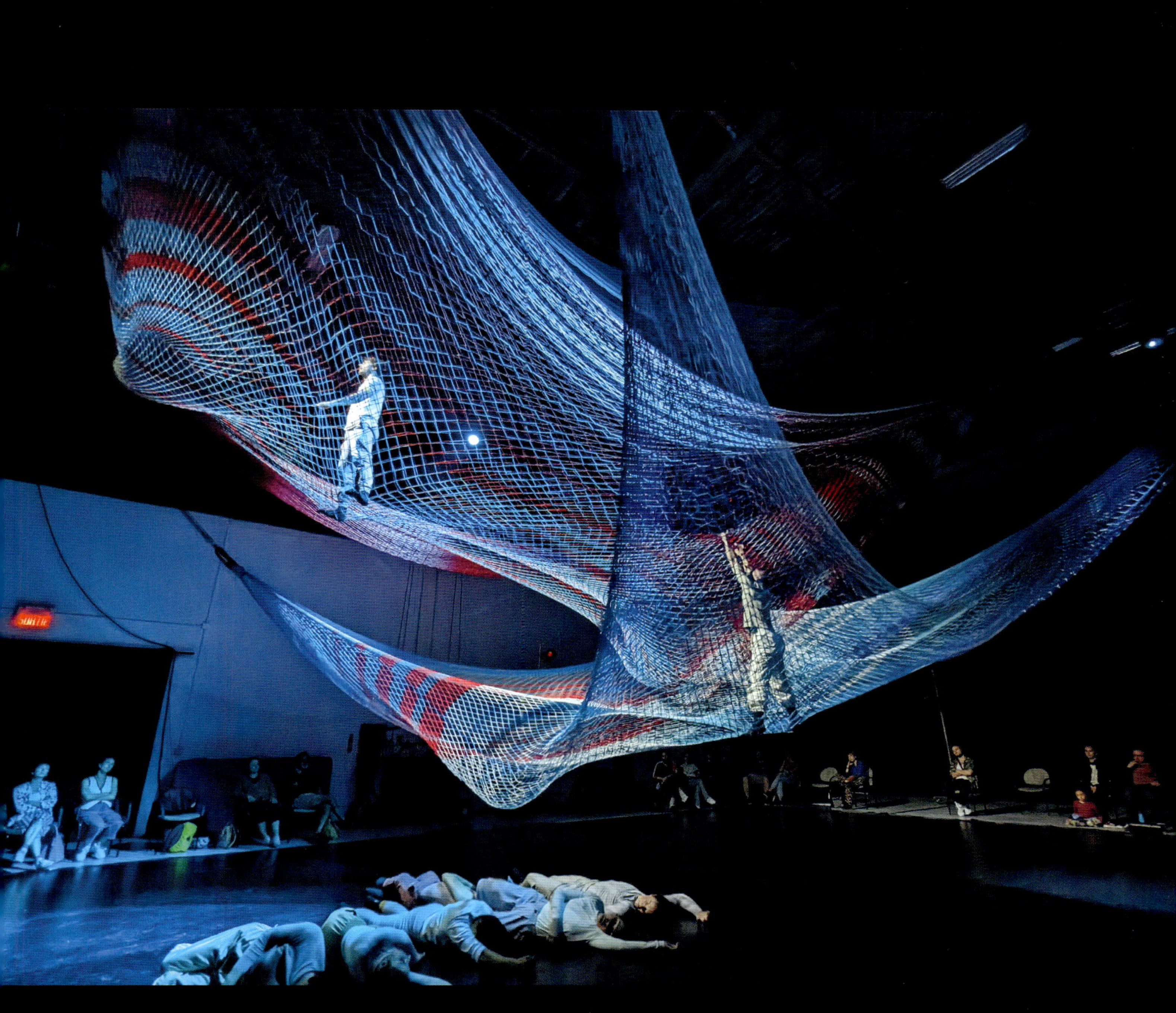

opposite and above: *Noli Timere*, *Dance #1 (Everywhere the Edges)*,
2023, Montreal, Canada

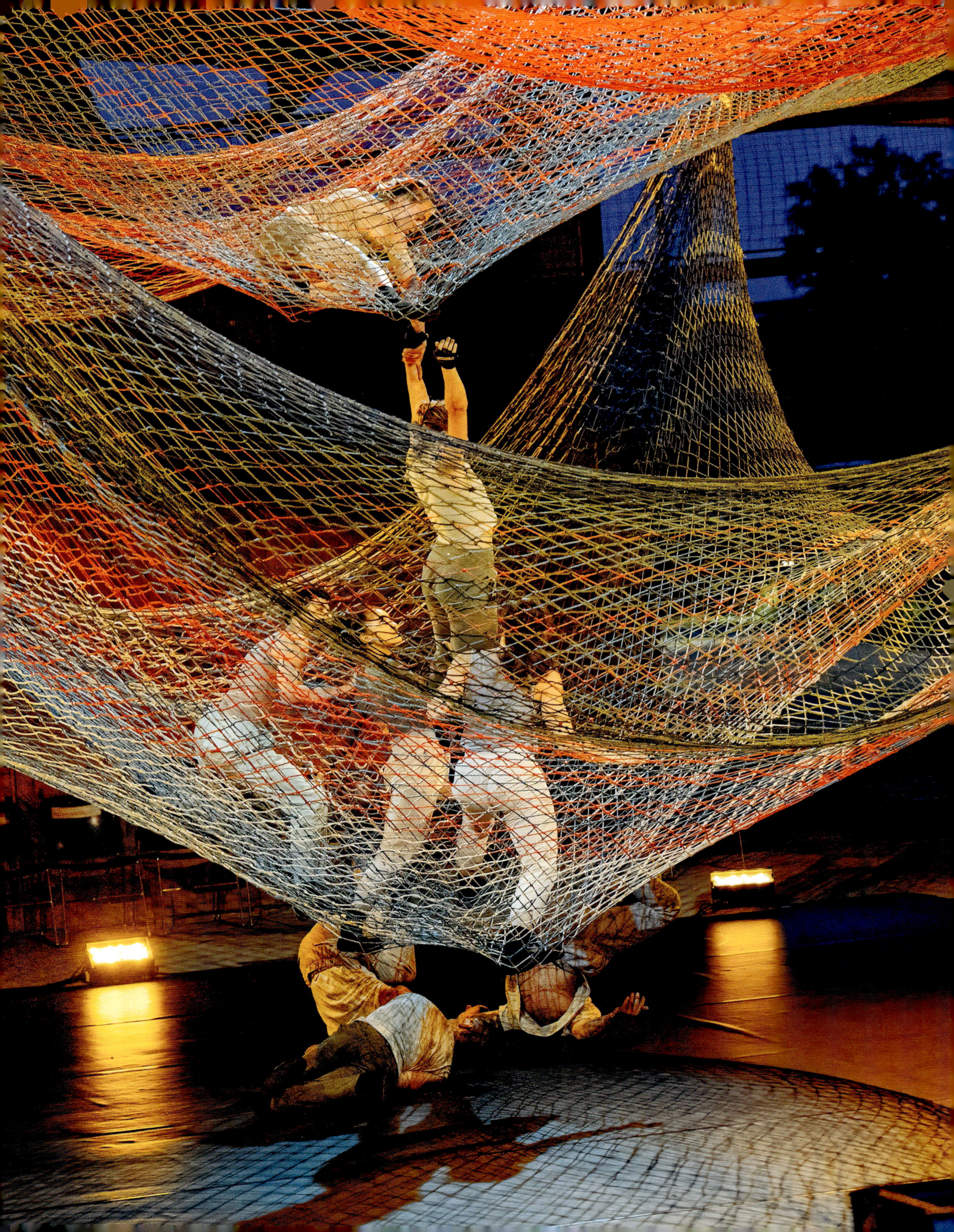

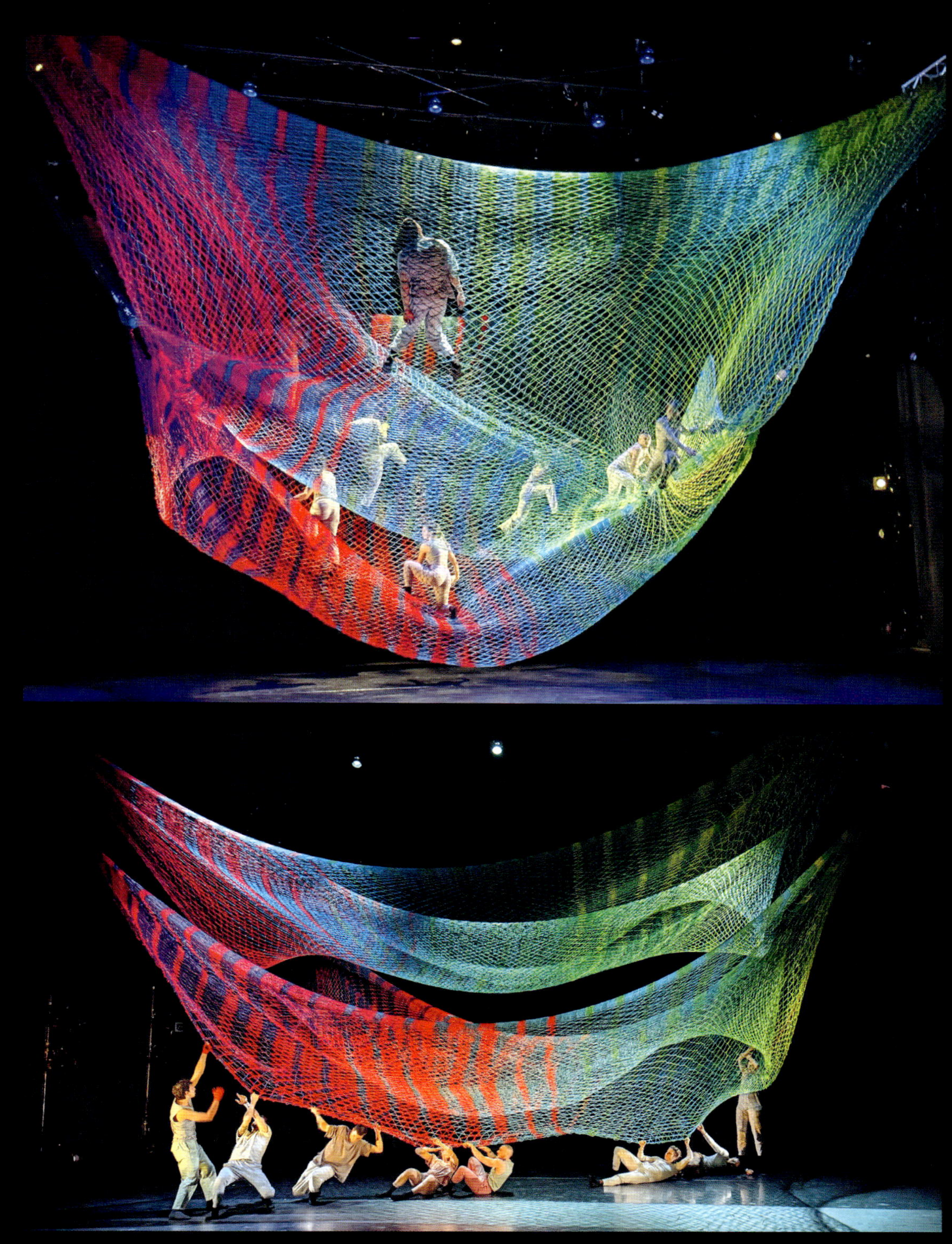

opposite: *Noli Timere, Dance #2*, 2024
above: Premiere of *Noli Timere, Dance #3*, 2025

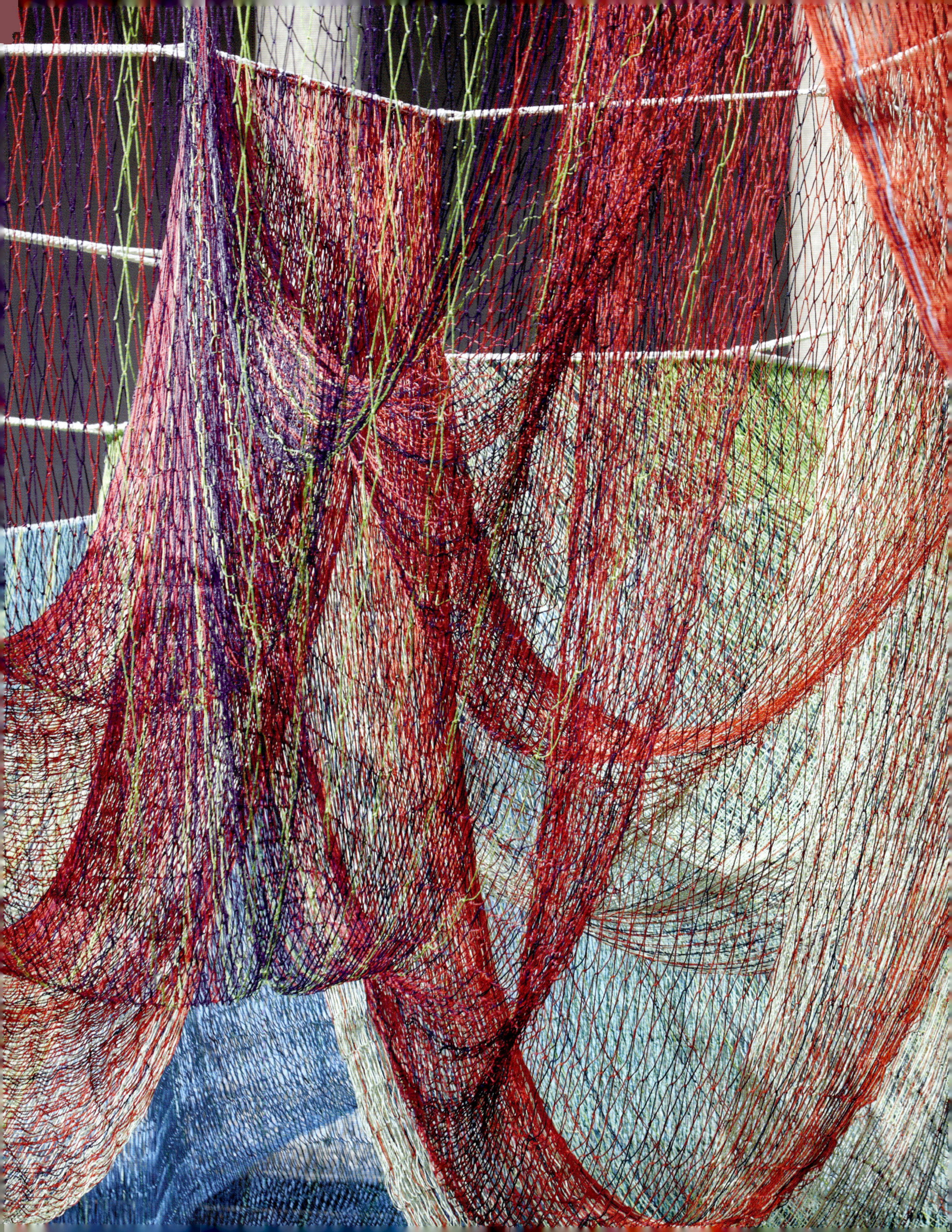

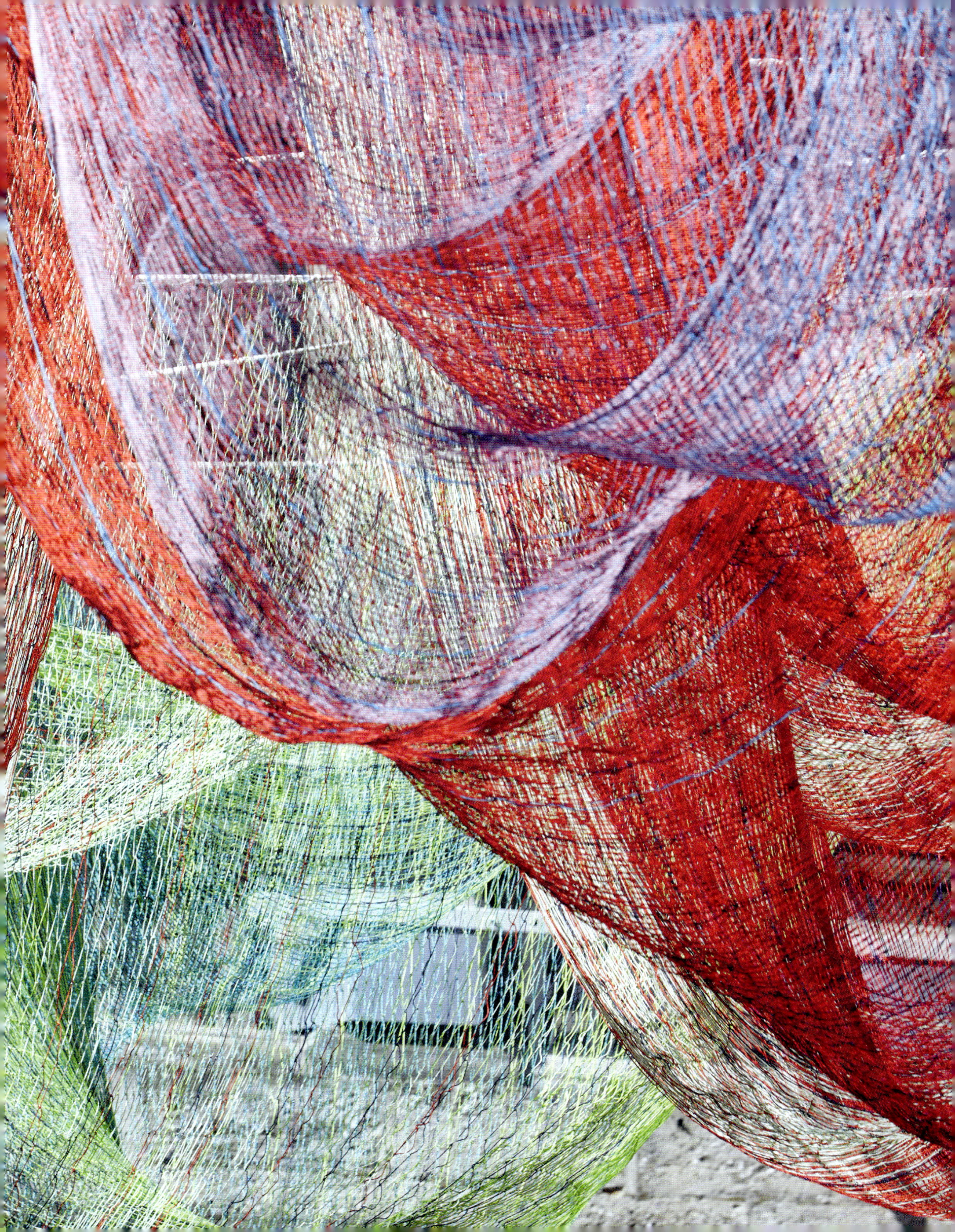

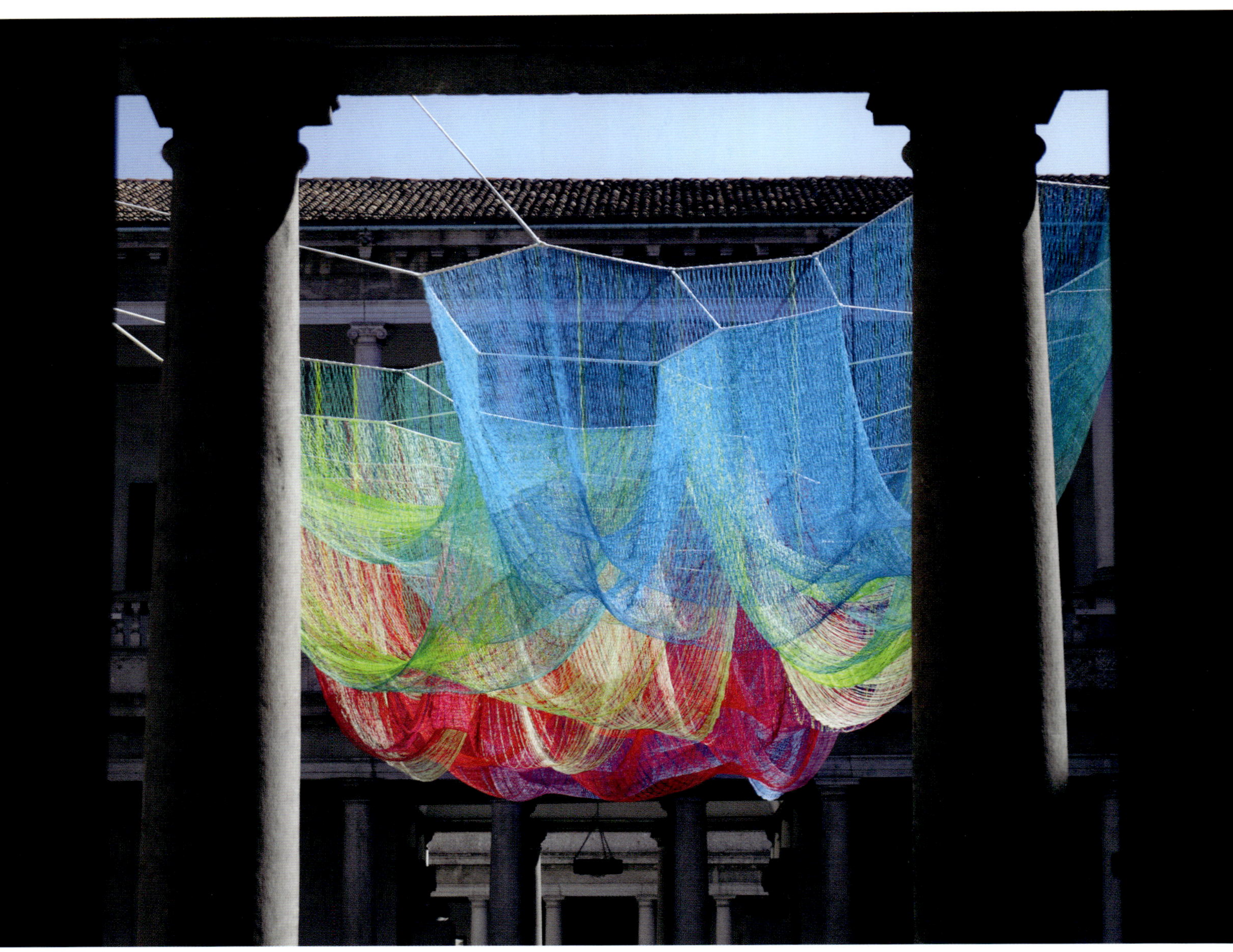

previous, above, opposite, and overleaf:
Noli Timere, *Sculpture #1*, 2023, Milan, Italy

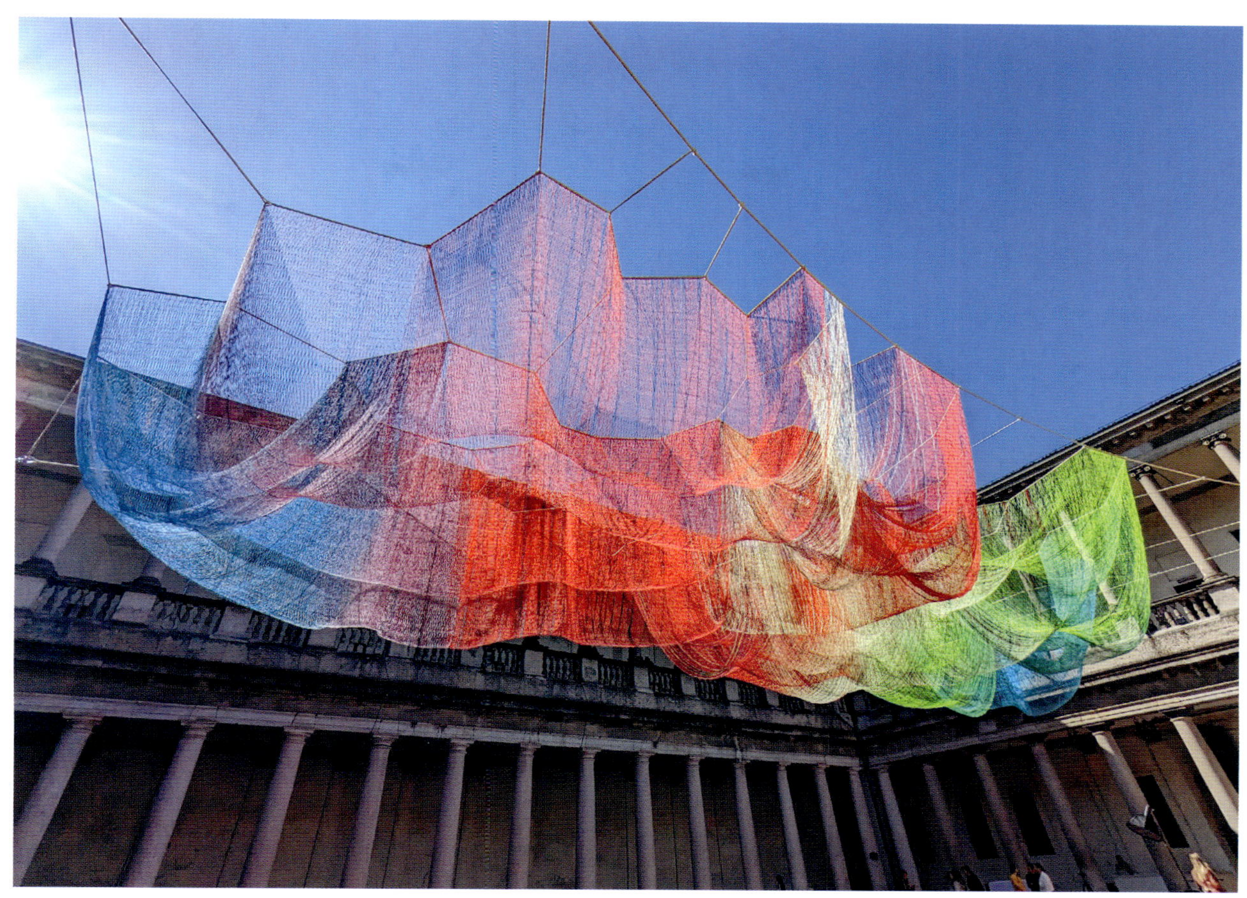

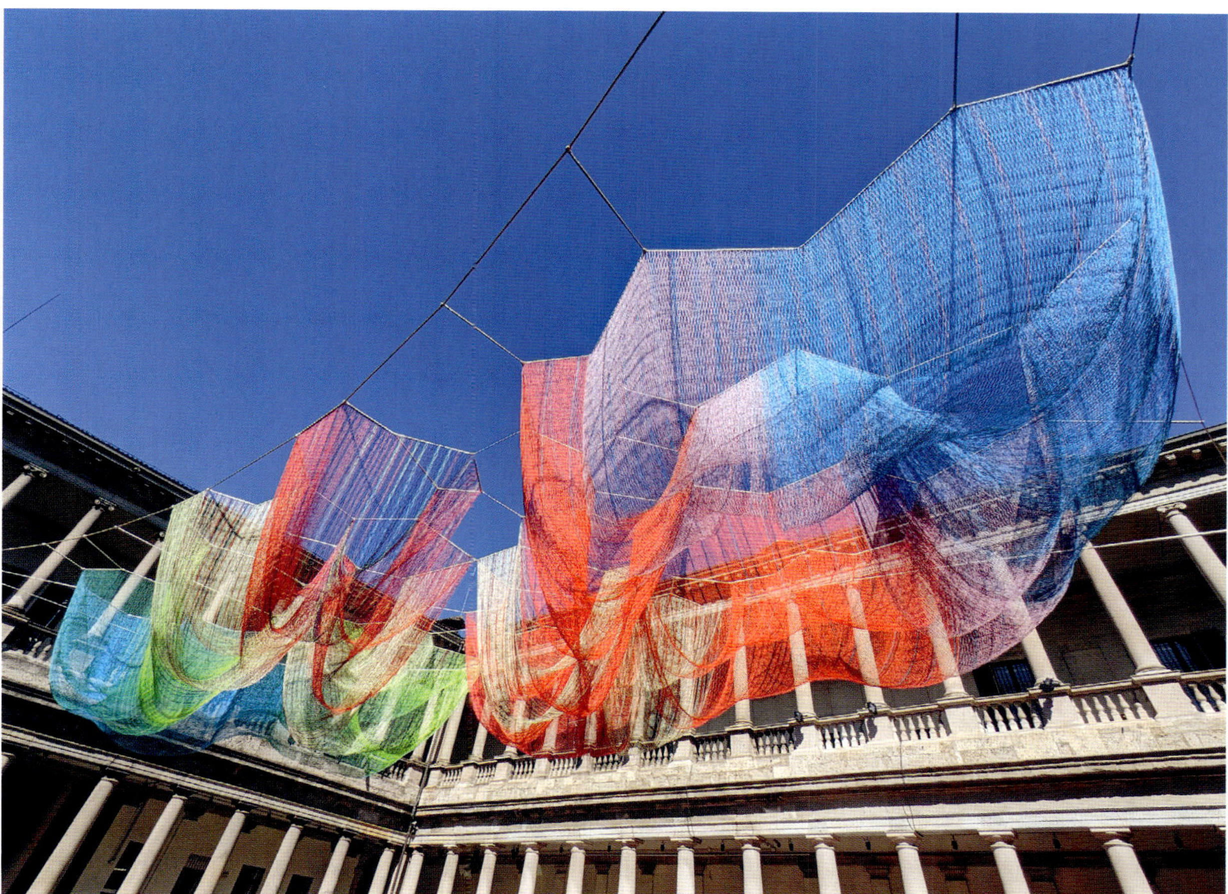

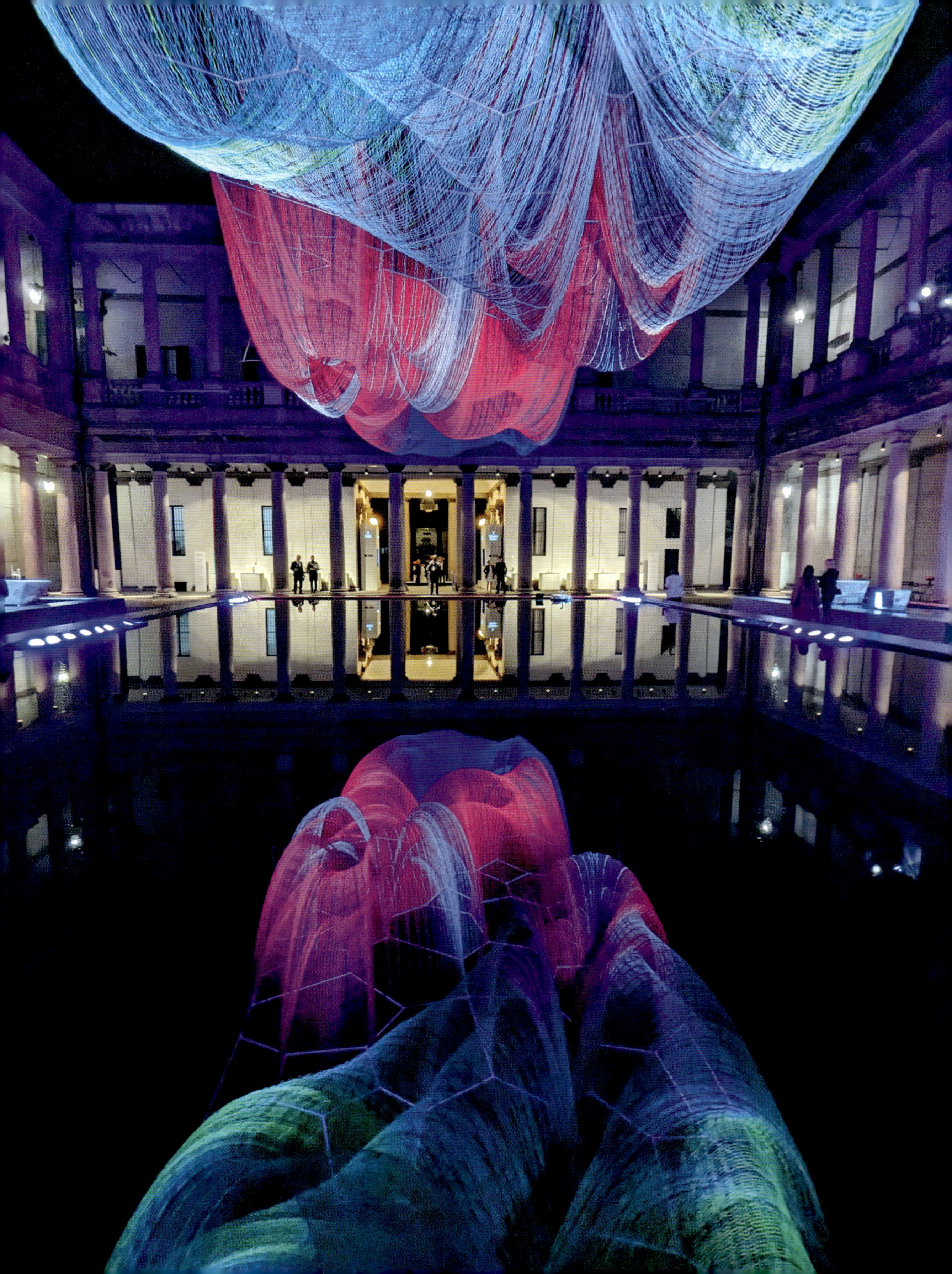

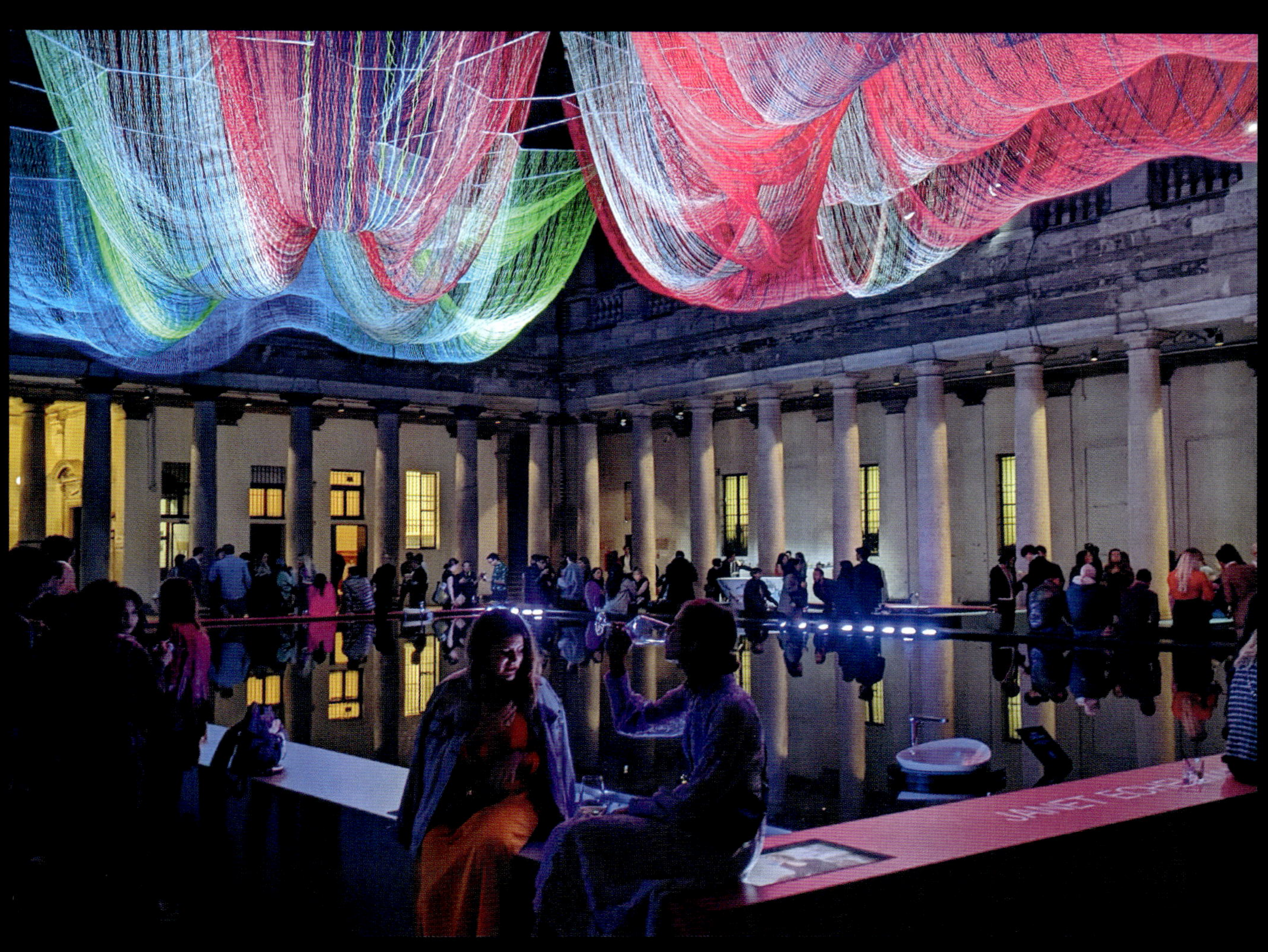
JANET

Embracing Light

—

Brian Stacy

Echelman's art practice embraces light as a key medium. Her sculptures are illuminated by complex LED luminaires and digital control systems that change color and intensity, sometimes customized to meet specific color demands by her astute creative eye. They are not only visually stunning, but also interactive and immersive, and invite viewers to experience a space and an environment in a new way.

Light is an artistic medium that adds a layer of complexity and dynamism to Echelman's sculptures and creates a sense of wonder and awe in viewers. The nighttime sculpture illuminations in particular transform public space and the human experience, creating a sense of connection and community. The nighttime illuminations also communicate a message and a vision, as the sculptures reflect the values and the goals of the organizations and the cities that host them.

A major moment in Echelman's artistic progression with lighting was her commission *Pulse* (2018) for Dilworth Park, in front of Philadelphia's City Hall. Movements of the city trains beneath the piece give purpose to choreographed light and fog to create a dynamic effect, reminiscent of the old trains that once ran nearby. Interactivity is achieved through a digital control system that integrates custom RGBW LED luminaires and a digital fog system triggered by the ever-changing movements of the underground train lines. This captures a playful side for the public by encouraging park-goers to interact with piece. During her creative explorations for the work, as Echelman searched for lighting that "felt like walking into a Rothko painting," we found we needed to create layerings of solid verticals of coloration on top of the background up-lighting from the trains to create three-dimensionality.

For her commission for the Bill & Melinda Gates Foundation in Seattle, Echelman began exploring the symbolism of optimism at the start of a new day with the creation of unique lighting scenes that utilize sunrise sky colors. A research-based approach into sky conditions and causation of sunrises provided the color palette for the lighting of *Impatient Optimist* (2015). We created a virtual time clock of scenes that are projected according to live data feeds of sunrise that change each day. As each of the foundation's offices wake up, from Addis Ababa to Beijing, the sculpture's lighting scheme utilizes LED lights to manifest the colors of that local sunrise.

Earthtime 1.8 Renwick, permanently installed at the Renwick Gallery of the Smithsonian American Art Museum in Washington, DC, uses color mixing theory to create a pulsing color and shadow effect. Evocative of the movement of the oceans and the Earth, this installation lets light take center stage. In addition to lighting the physical net sculpture, which is pulled high up into the vaulted ceiling, the four walls become active spaces for what Echelman calls "shadow murals" that create a total environment in the gallery. These lighting murals create a dynamic scene in which shadow and additive color mixing of light projects onto the sculpture, the walls, and viewers as well.

Lastly, Echelman's monumental exterior public work *Bending Arc* (2020) explored public history and the progression of civil rights at a historic site in the heart of St. Petersburg, Florida. Positive glow and coloration through subtle movements created dynamic nighttime place making on an urban scale. Using combined chip CMYK LEDs on a scale typically reserved for stadium events, the project was glistening and awe-inspiring for the public both near and afar. Whether they were approaching the pier park by ferry from Tampa or by automobile, bicycling along the coast, or right underneath it, sitting in Adirondack chairs or lying in the grass, nighttime visitors were mesmerized by the unfolding color movements.

Through my lens as a designer who creates story and expresses the nuance of three-dimensional form and environment through light, I have watched Echelman evolve in her embrace of light as an artistic medium. As lighting design has become an essential element of her art—enhancing the beauty, the meaning, and the interactivity of her sculptures—Echelman's work with the medium has become an inspiration to the global lighting community.

Brian Stacy is the global lighting design leader at Arup.

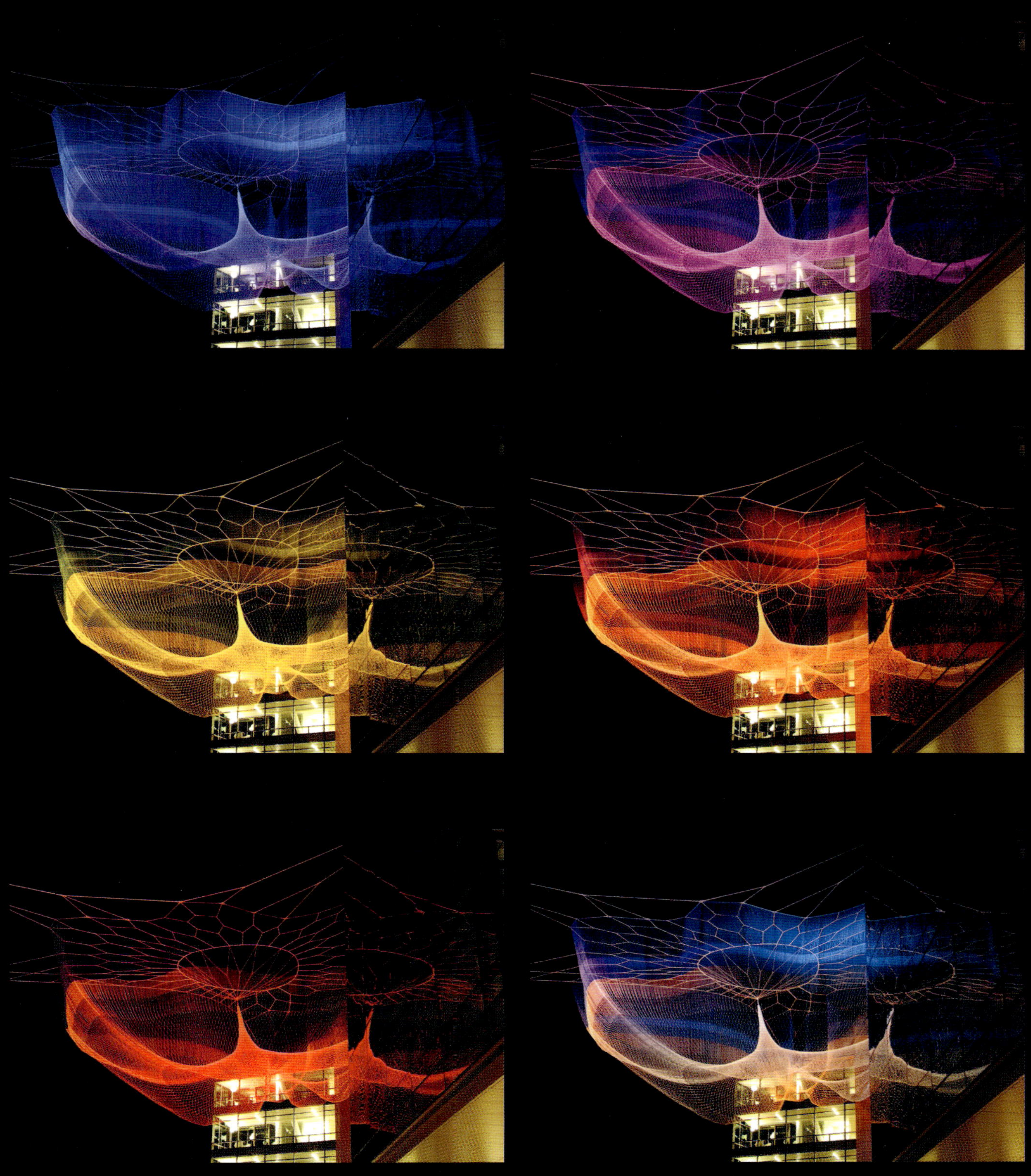

Testing the lighting color palette on-site at the Bill & Melinda Gates Foundation for *Impatient Optimist*, 2015, Seattle, Washington

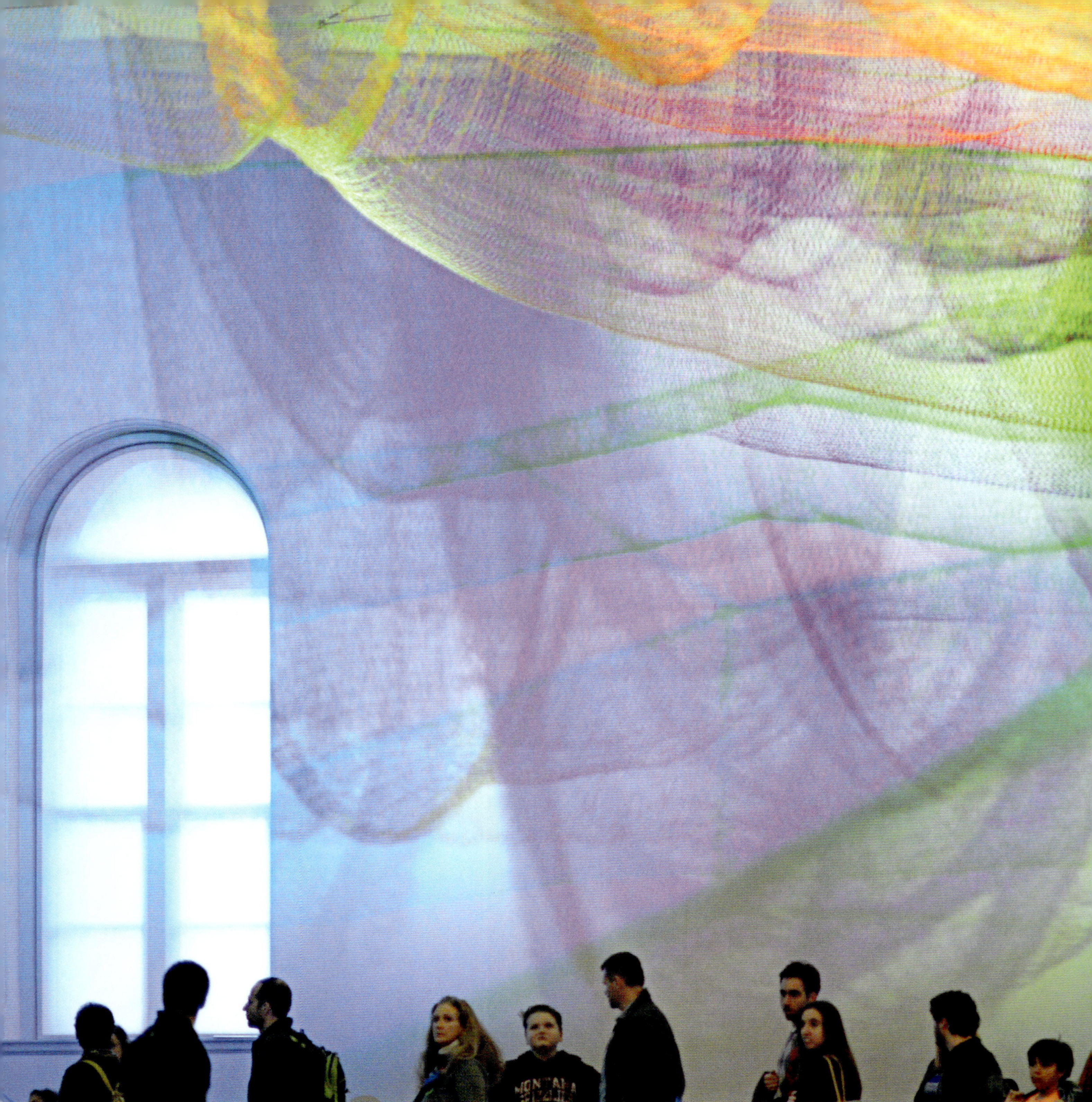

Projection of shadows utilizing a multilayered color palette for *Earthtime 1.8 Renwick*, 2015, in the Grand Salon of the Smithsonian American Art Museum, Washington, DC

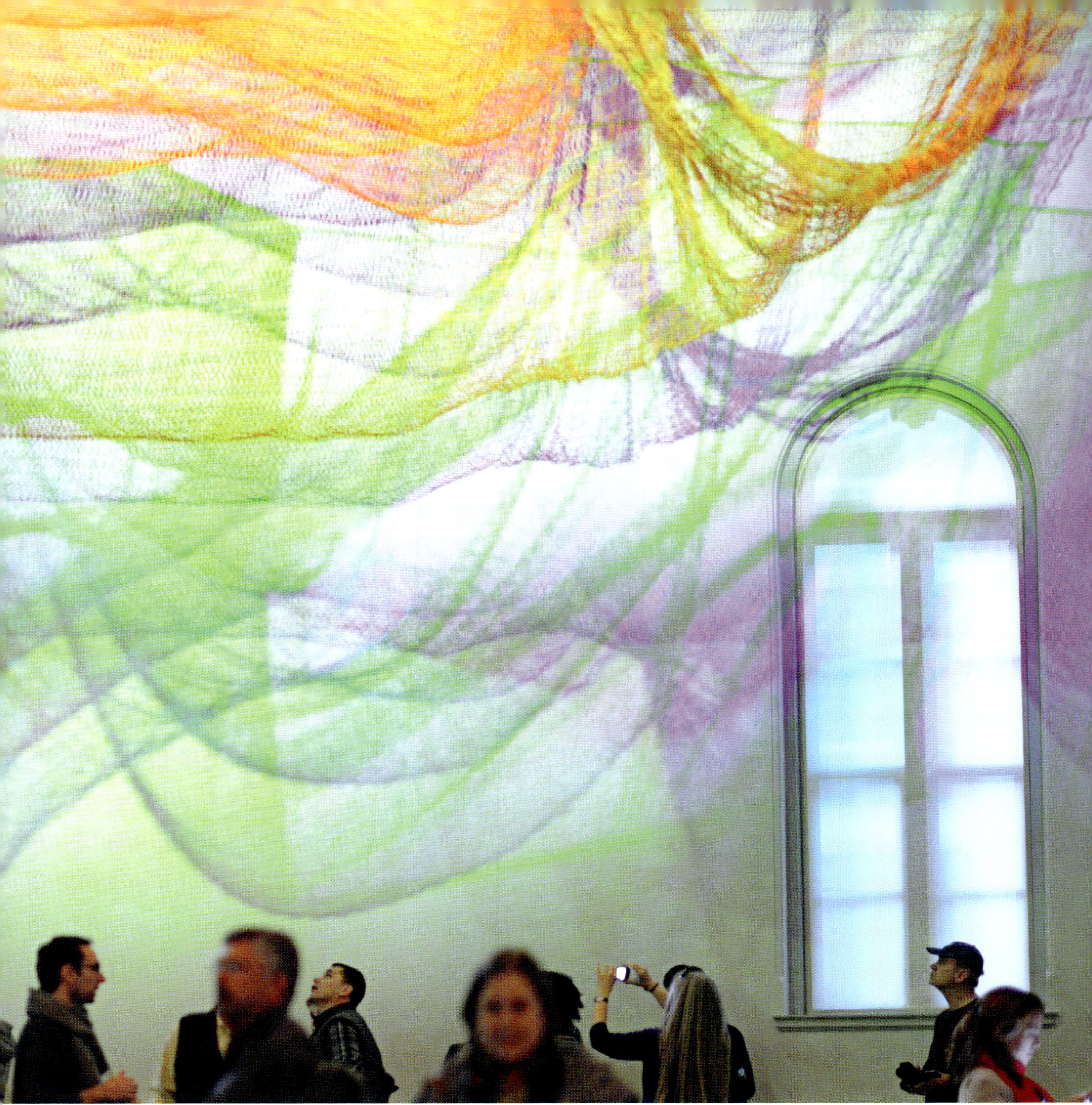

Interconnectedness Knotted into the Helsinki Biennial

—

Taru Tappola
and Kristiina Ljokkoi

Everything is connected, and therefore dependent on everything else. In our interconnected world, a ripple in one part may cause a storm in another. Every action—and inaction—reverberates. This is a basic fact and condition of the world and our existence. It was also the starting point in our curatorial concept for the first edition of the Helsinki Biennial 2021, *The Same Sea*. The artist whose practice most beautifully fit the concept, as the Finnish saying goes, "like a nose on the head," was Janet Echelman. *Earthtime 1.78 Helsinki*, like all the works in the *Earthtime* series, truly embodied interconnectedness and mutual dependency.

Echelman's aerial sculpture and light artwork took over Senate Square in the heart of Helsinki. Its mesmerizing presence became the apex of a new contemporary art event for four weeks in August 2021. Presenting artworks from forty-one artists and artist groups from Finland and around the world, the biennial took place mainly on the historical fortress island of Vallisaari, but also at mainland locations. Initiated by the city, it was organized and produced by HAM Helsinki Art Museum and curated by its senior curators Pirkko Siitari, head of exhibitions, and Taru Tappola, head of public art, in cooperation with the rest of the HAM curatorial team. Public art curator Kristiina Ljokkoi was responsible for the production of *Earthtime 1.78 Helsinki* and the coordination of the unique musical expansion for the work.

The title of the biennial, *The Same Sea*, was a metaphor for interconnectedness. We all breathe the same air, and we are all surrounded by one interconnected, large ocean whose water molecules never disappear completely, only move from one state to another. *The Same Sea* refers to aspects of life that are fundamentally shared, infinite, and collective, even if constantly changing and appearing in various forms. *The Same Sea* reminds us that we coexist on a planet where everything affects everything else and that our survival depends crucially on our environment and all others around us. This has become increasingly evident during the current ecological crisis and coronavirus pandemic.

The works in Echelman's *Earthtime* series are based on scientific data and meant to remind us of our complex interconnectedness with larger cycles of time and the systems of our physical world. The numbers in the titles refer to the number of microseconds by which the Earth's day was shortened due to a single physical event—a shifting of the tectonic plates—that caused an earthquake and tsunami, which in turn altered the speed of the Earth's rotation. In Echelman's work, the material meets the physical and the conceptual. Sea and air currents are simultaneously present. The work is woven like a fishing net. When a breeze hits one part of the netted structure, the entire work starts to sway.

Echelman's work was essential to the biennial because it widened the perspectives of interconnectedness and mutual dependencies to physics and planetary phenomena, such as tectonic and oceanic movements. Interconnectedness and mutual dependency could be explored from endless vantage points, but we especially concentrated on themes arising from the island of Vallisaari: time, transformation, change, borders and identities, connection and relationship with nature, empathy and community. Echelman's practice touches on almost all of these themes. The artist describes how her net sculptures were inspired by fishing nets historically made as a community effort. Their structure and movements can be understood as visualizations of empathy, since the movements of the parts and the whole follow and resonate with each other. The artwork combines ancient survival technology with science and modern nanotechnology, and it reminds us that regardless of our efforts to control our environment, we are subject to natural and planetary forces beyond human influence.

opposite: *Earthtime 1.78 Helsinki*, 2021, Senate Square, Finland

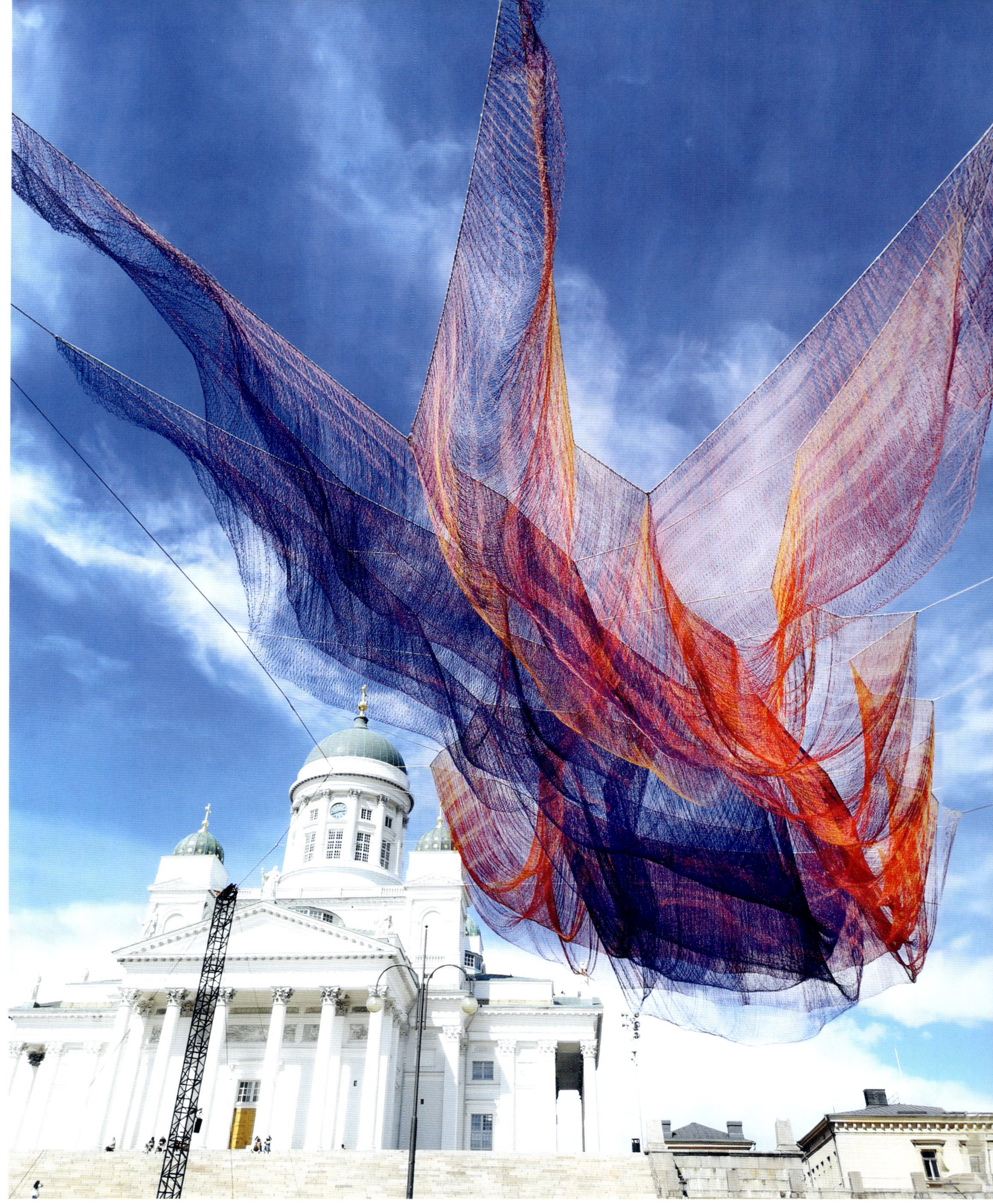

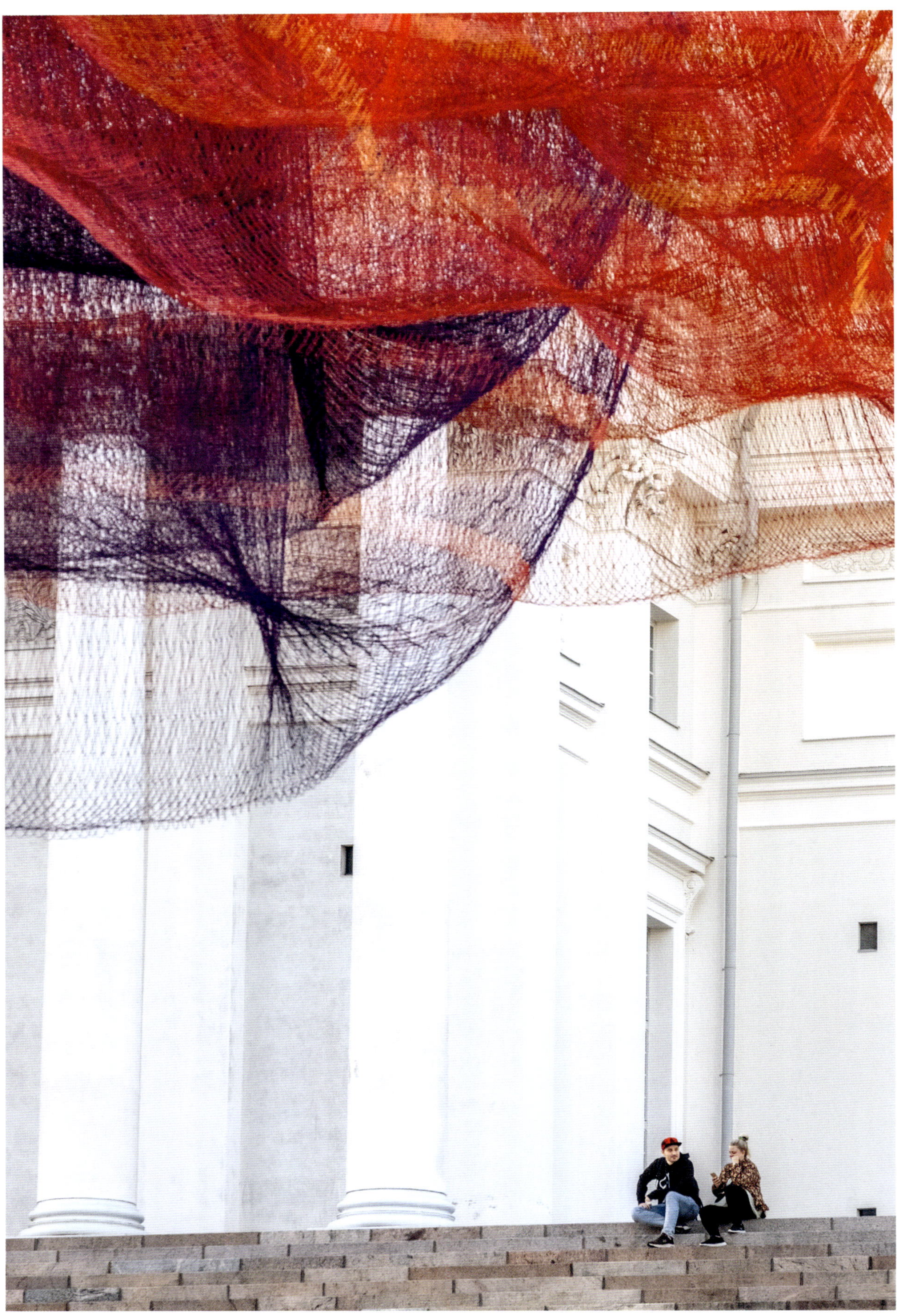

The sculpture refers to earthquakes causing tsunamis, and its form suggests the steepening of a wave as it approaches land: water and land form borders for each other. At the core of Echelman's practice is the problem of time. Her work makes us wonder about the concepts of time and change: What actually is time, and how do we define and measure it? It is both a cultural convention and an inevitable, uncontrollable fact, measured by the Earth's rotation. When an earthquake shifted the Earth and sped its daily rotation by 1.78 microseconds, what happened to our measurement of time?

Location Full of History

Technically too challenging to be installed on the island, *Earthtime 1.78 Helsinki* became the anchor of the biennial on the mainland. We found a perfect site for it in the heart of the capital, above the historic Senate Square. This unique spot manifested connections between government, religion, and science. Designed to impress, emulating St. Petersburg in its neoclassical style, the square is flanked with the pillars of the state—university, senate, and church—and, in a later addition, a bank and commercial buildings. The shoreline is not far from the square—only two hundred meters away—and is the jumping-off point to Vallisaari, the Helsinki Biennial's main venue, and further out to the rest of the world.

The fateful moments in our land's history are present in both Vallisaari and Senate Square. Paradoxically, Finland's separation from Sweden and transfer to Russian rule prepared our land to become independent. Russia fortified Vallisaari because it wanted to defend the island against Sweden, and the capital was changed from Turku to Helsinki, which was farther east. Senate Square was designed and built to improve the city's status, and so it has an important symbolic role in Finland's cultural and political history.

Senate Square was redesigned when Finland became an autonomous part of Russia in 1812 and the capital was moved to Helsinki. The new capital needed presentable state architecture, and the German architect Carl Ludvig Engel was invited to design and lead a monumental construction project. The design of the square and its surrounding buildings form a remarkably solid neoclassical entity. Engel's buildings are Helsinki Cathedral (1852) on the northern side, Government Palace (1822) on the eastern side, and the main building of the University of Helsinki (1832) and the National Library of Finland (1840) on the western side. Buildings on the southern side of the square remind us of the history of the previous period under Swedish rule, such as Sederholm House (1757), which is the oldest stone building in Helsinki. Senate Square and its surrounding buildings were preserved in 1952.

The statue of Emperor Alexander II in the center of the square, erected in 1894, expresses the governmental objectives once set in Senate Square. The monument, by artists Walter Runeberg and Johannes Takanen, portrays the Tsar of Russia and Grand Duke of Finland of the time. Its pedestal's symbolic figures represent Law (Lex), Light (Lux, meaning Science and Art), Peace (Pax), and Work (Labor). The figure symbolizing Law is the maiden of Finland wearing a bearskin. The memorial is typical of Runeberg's art in its idealistic Realism. As such, it is a representative example of nineteenth-century Finnish sculpture. When Russia tightened its grip on Finland at the end of the nineteenth century and began its attempts to Russify the country, the statue of the "good" emperor (one who had advanced Finland's autonomy) and events organized next to the statue acted as protests against the "bad" emperor's administration.

The building stock in Senate Square and on Vallisaari represents Finnish history first under Swedish and then Russian rule, and later from the time of independence. The history of Finland's government, religion, and science are highlighted in Senate Square, whereas the army's presence is more visible on Vallisaari. Senate Square is a fully human-made environment and unified in its architecture, whereas Vallisaari is rougher and has more versatile temporal layers. The country-like village community has given Vallisaari its unique nature. The community, with approximately three hundred residents at most, was formed by pilot and military families and their domestic animals, and they had their own school on the island. Since 1996, the island has not

opposite: *Earthtime 1.78 Helsinki*, 2021

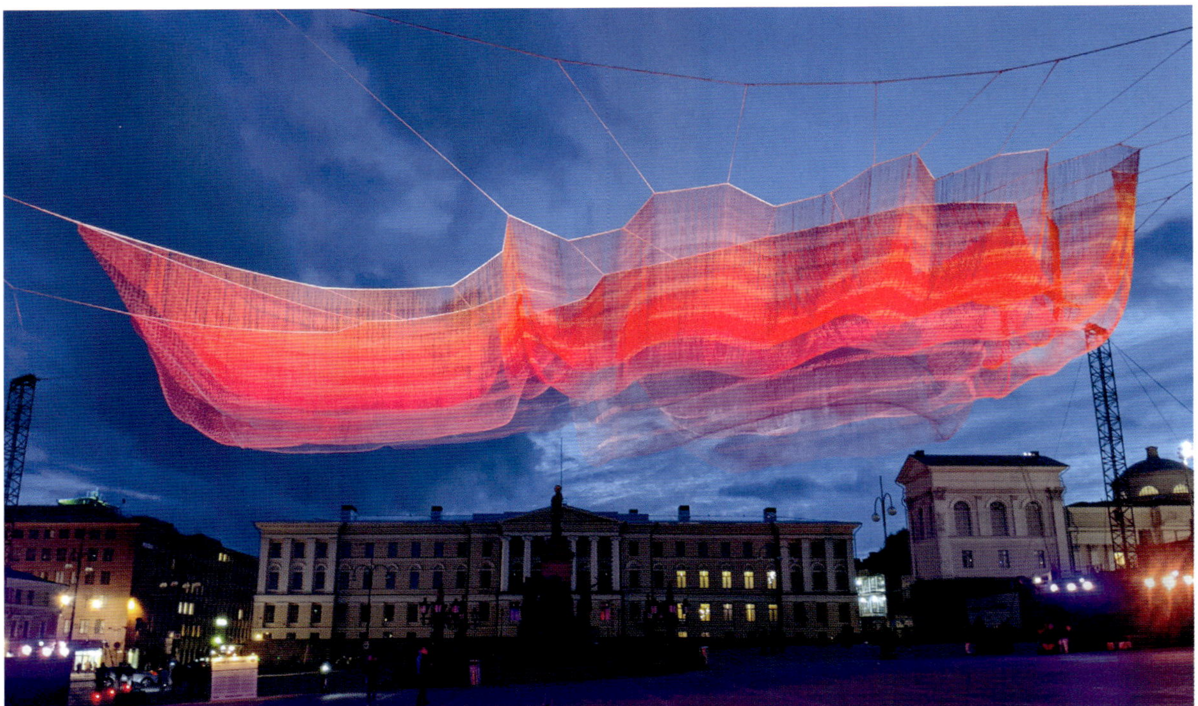

been populated by residents year-round, and the abundant flora and fauna have reclaimed it. The wildlife is a combination of endemic species and species brought by the Swedish and Russian armies, making the island one of the most diverse nature destinations in the metropolitan area. A few years ago, Vallisaari was partly opened to the public.

Echelman's artwork was an already-existing one, a loan from the artist. Installed in different environments, it absorbs the meanings and physical features of its surroundings. These become layers of the work, slightly changing the connotations of the physical object in each new location and giving it a special site-specificity. The position of *Earthtime 1.78 Helsinki* suggested a wave rushing inland from the direction of Vallisaari.

Aerial and Underwater Experience

For the biennial, Helsinki-based sound artist Tuomas Norvio was invited to create a site-specific sound installation, *Empathy for the Fish and Others*, which made the aerial and underwater realms part of the experience.

Norvio's installation combined wind data measured at Senate Square and an underwater soundscape simultaneously streamed with hydrophones from Vallisaari. The transformed live underwater soundscape, with all its snaps, splashes, hums, and frequencies of motor vehicles, alternated with the composed choir-like wind soundscape, both conducted using the live wind data. These two truly site-specific elements entwined the installation more deeply into Senate Square and Vallisaari, but also into global wind systems and worldwide ocean currents.

The sound installation was audible to visitors daily until ten o'clock in the evening via a public address system at Senate Square. After that, it could be heard via headphones connected to a mobile device. Day turning to night also influenced the visual experience. In August, summer folds into autumn, with the days growing shorter. During the first days of the *Earthtime 1.78 Helsinki* installation, the sun set around ten o'clock, whereas in its final days at the end of August, the darkness descended around half past eight. The darker the night, the brighter the artwork's lights appeared. The light

above: *Earthtime 1.78 Helsinki*, 2021

projection's colors faded from one shade to another, from warm to cold, highlighted against the darkening sky. Panu Pikkuaho from Sun Effects designed the lighting, which was likewise intertwined into the site-specific wind data; it was programmed with sensor-based reactivity to the data. The direction of the wind affected the light direction and intensity, making local winds visible in a delicate and subtle manner.

The sound installation lured people to linger under the work around sunset each day. The airspace was filled with the sound installation's underwater humming, the wind's choir, and the net flowing in the wind, magically gleaming with colors. Some stood, and some lay down on the pavement. All seemed to experience the same unhurried atmosphere—wind as movement and sound, and water as soundscape, power, and metaphor.

Collaboration under the Northern Sky

Implementing and engaging this site-specific, multimedia sound-and-light installation was possible due to close cooperation between Helsinki Biennial and Helsinki Festival. Helsinki Festival is the largest arts festival in the Nordic countries, held annually in late summer. The cooperation began soon after Echelman was invited. The original idea was to cooperate on a participatory, interactive application between work and audience, but these plans took an unexpected turn due to the COVID-19 pandemic. Helsinki Biennial and Helsinki Festival were both postponed a year, and plans had to be adjusted to fit the strict restrictions related to public events. The organizers did not want to give up on interactivity, and so the work was modified to fit existing circumstances. The interaction was changed so that it occurred between non-human agencies—the net, wind, underwater world, light, and sound—which would be intertwined in the installation experience.

Tuomas Norvio, saxophonist Tapani Rinne, and singer Hildá Länsman performed under *Earthtime 1.78 Helsinki* on the opening night, August 19, 2021, in a unique live concert combining sound and visual elements. The show was accompanied by a unique world of sounds and visuals driven by live wind data. Joonas Tikkanen from HUE Lighting Oy was responsible for the light projections during the concert. The visual design combined laser, hazer (a lighting enhancement made via a superfine water mist), and video projections that interacted with the wind data, live music, soundscape, and net structure. The lighting design acted as an expressive but also unifying factor between music, soundscape, and sculpture. Norvio's sound installation and the concert by Länsman, Norvio, and Rinne were a collaboration between Helsinki Biennial and Helsinki Festival.

Länsman is a Sámi singer whose music draws inspiration from the Sámi *joik* tradition, with a modern twist. Sámi territory includes the northern parts of Norway, Sweden, Finland, and Russia. A natural phenomenon recalling Echelman's moving and lighted netted artworks occurs in the same geographical region near the North Pole: the northern lights, or aurora borealis. Like Echelman's works, the northern lights are connected to cosmic cycles and events: the sun's activity and particles from the sun entering Earth's magnetic field. The resulting visual phenomenon is a majestic cosmic dance of waves and changing lights, such as represented in *Earthtime 1.78 Helsinki*.

While working on an earlier *Earthtime* piece, *Earthtime 1.26 Denver* (2010), Echelman described her process as bringing two parts of the brain—the neocortex and the limbic system—together, with one consciously processing the background data or the intellectual content and the other simply taking in the physical experience, the presence of the sculptural, moving form. The superpower of art is to appeal simultaneously to these two brain functions and modes of perception, interconnecting intellect and emotion, the physical and the metaphysical.

Taru Tappola is the head of public art, Helsinki Art Museum.

Kristiina Ljokkoi is curator of public art at the Helsinki Art Museum.

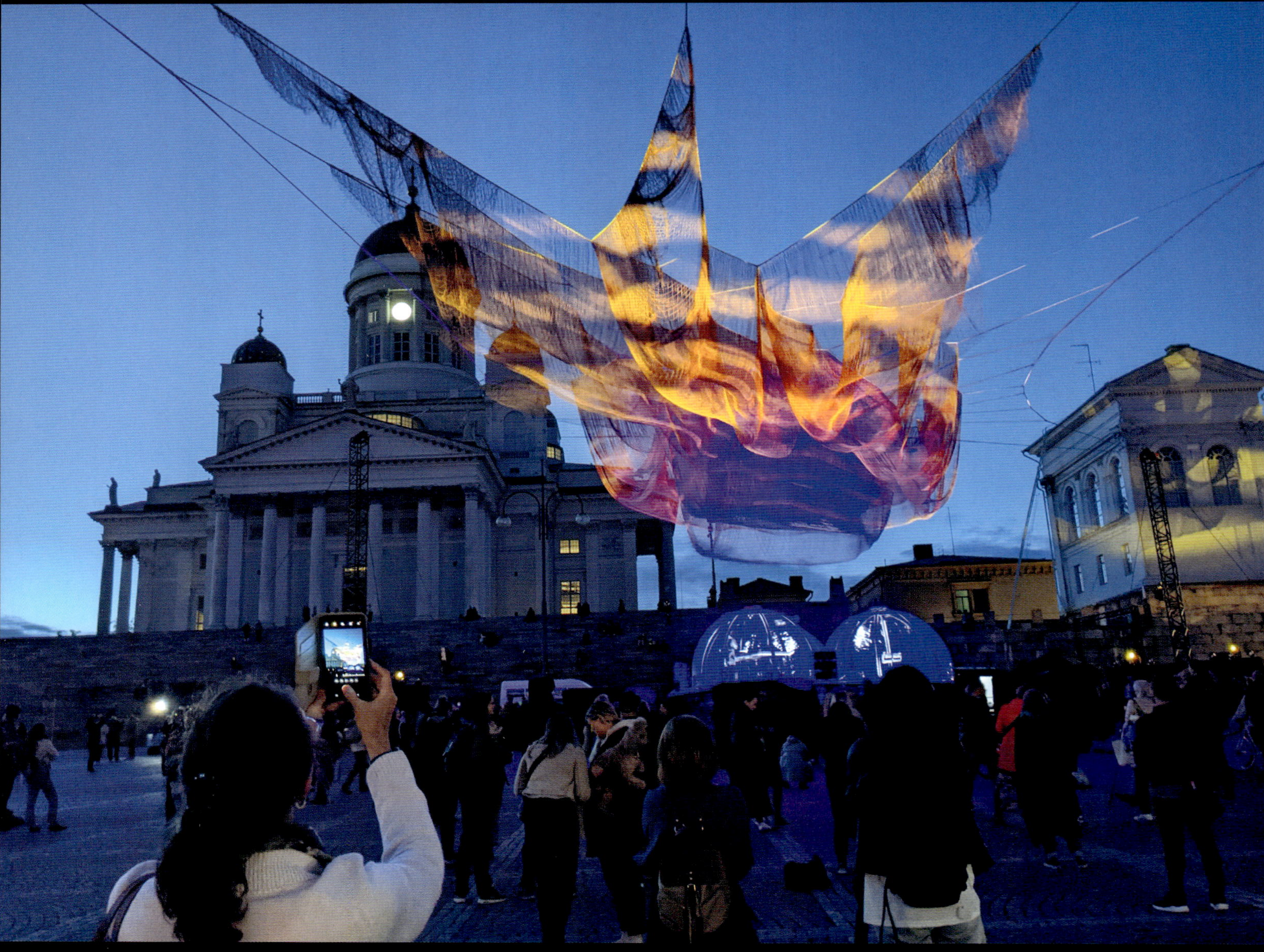

above and opposite: The opening night concert of the 2021 Helsinki Festival by Länsman, Norvio, and Rinne featured Sámi *joik* vocals and original live sound art developed with Echelman, which combined an underwater soundscape streamed from Vallisaari and wind data simultaneously measured at the Senate Square.

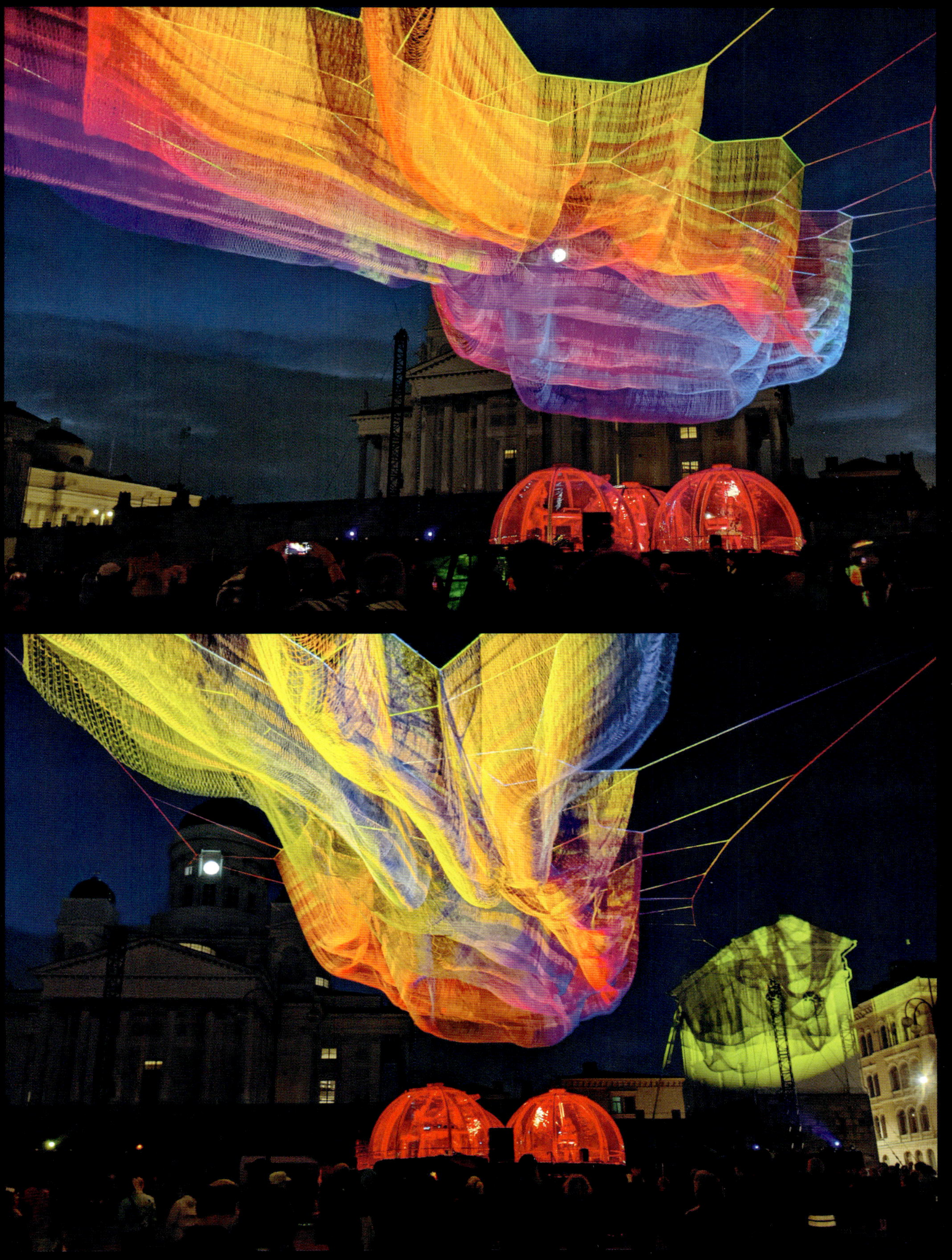

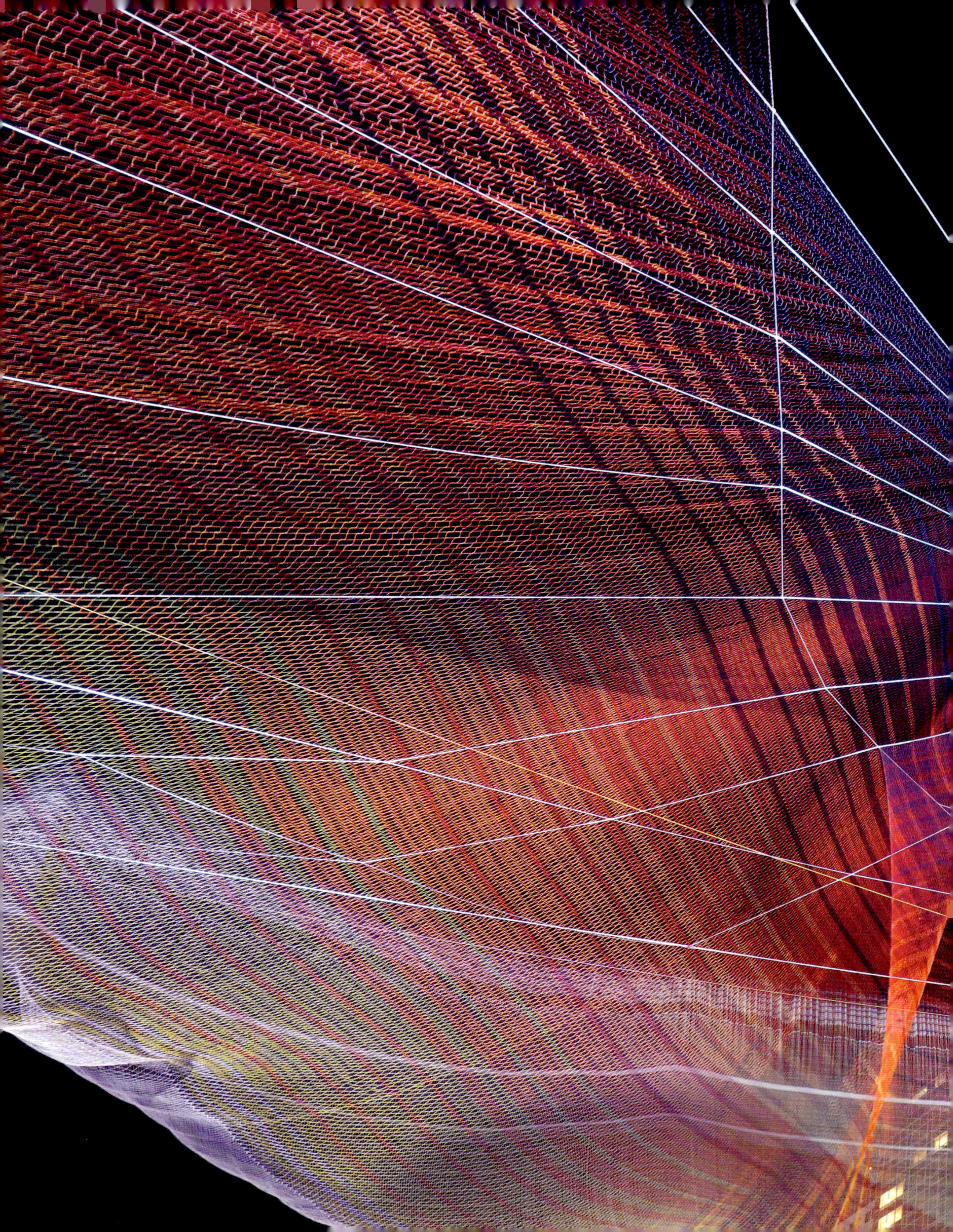

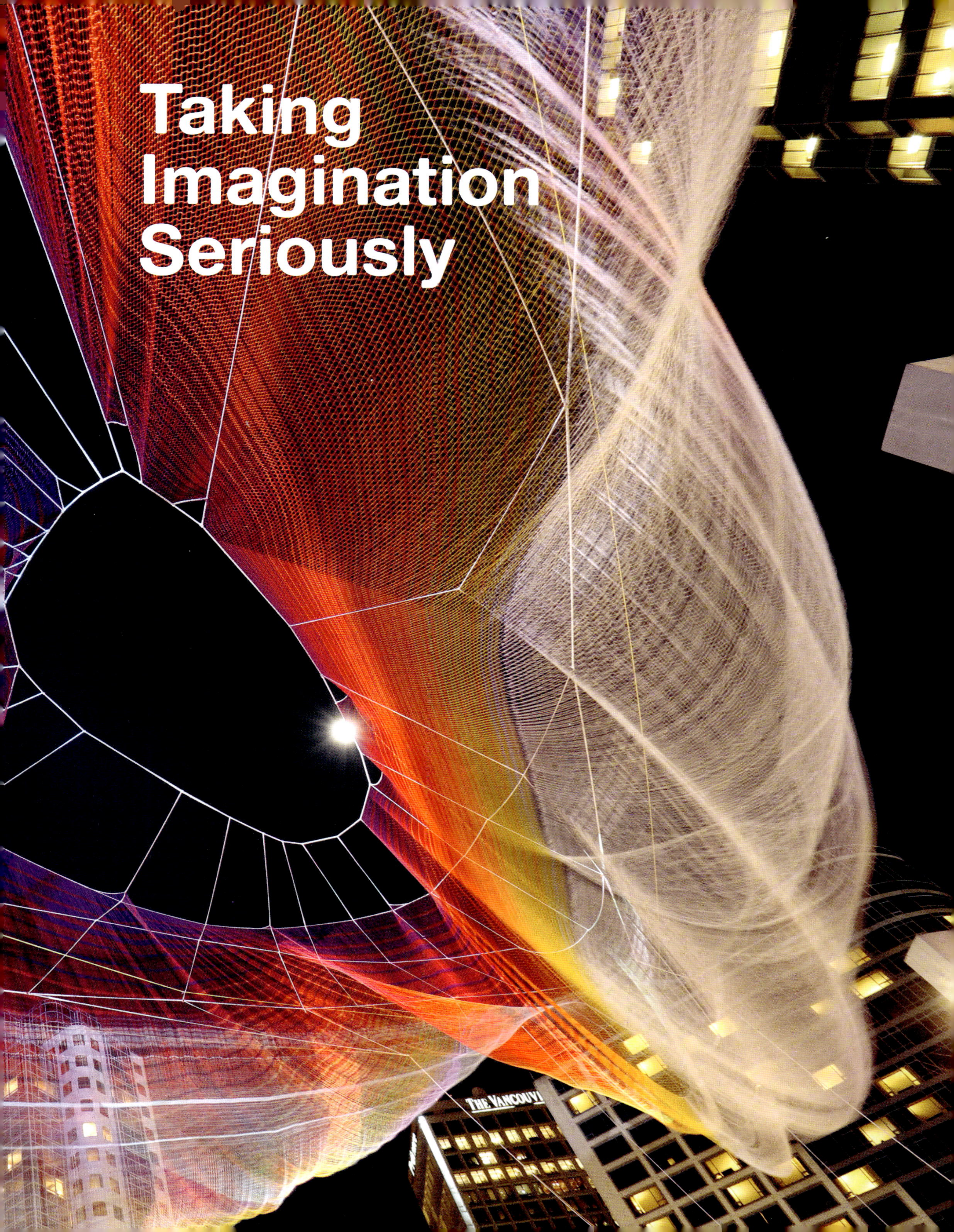

Taking Imagination Seriously

Janet Echelman's 2011 TED Talk

—

This story is about taking imagination seriously. Fourteen years ago, I first encountered this ordinary material, fishnet, used the same way for centuries. Today, I'm using it to create permanent, billowing, voluptuous forms the scale of hard-edged buildings in cities around the world. I was an unlikely person to be doing this. I never studied sculpture, engineering, or architecture. In fact, after college I applied to seven art schools and was rejected by all seven.

I went off on my own to become an artist, and I painted for ten years, when I was offered a Fulbright to India. Promising to give exhibitions of paintings, I shipped my paints and arrived in Mahabalipuram. The deadline for the show arrived—my paints didn't. I had to do something. This fishing village was famous for sculpture. So I tried bronze casting. But to make large forms was too heavy and expensive. I went for a walk on the beach, watching the fishermen bundle their nets into mounds on the sand. I'd seen it every day, but this time I saw it differently—a new approach to sculpture, a way to make volumetric form without heavy, solid materials.

My first satisfying sculpture was made in collaboration with these fishermen. It's a self-portrait titled *Wide Hips*. [*Laughter*] We hoisted them on poles to photograph. I discovered their soft surfaces revealed every ripple of wind in constantly changing patterns. I was mesmerized. I continued studying craft traditions and collaborating with artisans, next in Lithuania with lace makers. I liked the fine detail it gave my work, but I wanted to make them larger—to shift from being an object you look at to something you could get lost in.

Returning to India to work with those fishermen, we made a net of a million and a half hand-tied knots, installed briefly in Madrid. Thousands of people saw it, and one of them was the urbanist Manuel de Solà-Morales, who was redesigning the waterfront in Porto, Portugal. He asked if I could build this as a permanent piece for the city. I didn't know if I could do that and preserve my art. Durable, engineered, permanent—those are in opposition to idiosyncratic, delicate, and ephemeral.

For two years, I searched for a fiber that could survive ultraviolet rays, salt air, pollution,

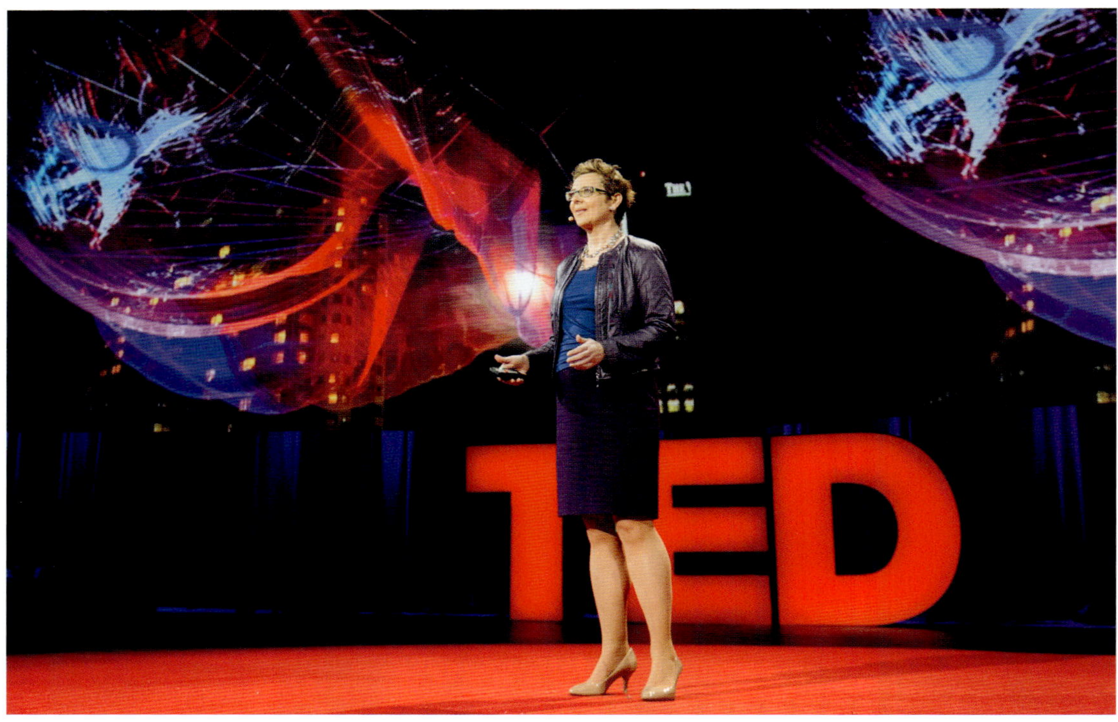

and at the same time remain soft enough to move fluidly in the wind. We needed something to hold the net up out there in the middle of the traffic circle. So we raised this forty-five-thousand-pound steel ring. We had to engineer it to move gracefully in an average breeze and survive in hurricane winds. But there was no engineering software to model something porous and moving. I found a brilliant aeronautical engineer who designs sails for America's Cup racing yachts named Peter Heppel. He helped me tackle the twin challenges of precise shape and gentle movement.

I couldn't build this the way I knew because hand-tied knots weren't going to withstand a hurricane. So I developed a relationship with an industrial fishnet factory, learned the variables of their machines, and figured out a way to make lace with them. There was no language to translate this ancient, idiosyncratic handcraft into something machine operators could produce. So we had to create one. Three years and two children later, we raised this fifty-thousand-square-foot lace net. It was hard to believe that what I had imagined was now built, permanent, and had lost nothing in translation.

This intersection had been bland and anonymous. Now it had a sense of place. I walked underneath it for the first time. As I watched the wind's choreography unfold, I felt sheltered and, at the same time, connected to limitless sky. My life was not going to be the same. I want to create these oases of sculpture in spaces of cities around the world. I'm going to share two directions that are new in my work.

Historic Philadelphia City Hall: its plaza, I felt, needed a material for sculpture that was lighter than netting. So we experimented with tiny atomized water particles to create a dry mist that is shaped by the wind, and in testing, discovered that it can be shaped by people who can interact and move through it without getting wet. I'm using this sculpture material to trace the paths of subway trains aboveground in real time—like an X-ray of the city's circulatory system unfolding.

Next challenge, the Biennial of the Americas in Denver asked, could I represent the thirty-five nations of the Western Hemisphere and their interconnectedness in a sculpture? [*Laughter*] I didn't know where to begin, but I said yes. I read about the recent earthquake in Chile and the tsunami that rippled across the entire Pacific Ocean. It shifted the Earth's tectonic plates, sped up the planet's rotation, and literally shortened the length of the day. So I contacted NOAA, and I asked if they'd share their data on the tsunami, and translated it into this. Its title, *1.26*, refers to the number of microseconds that the Earth's day was shortened.

I couldn't build this with a steel ring, the way I knew. Its shape was too complex now. So I replaced the metal armature with a soft, fine mesh of a fiber fifteen times stronger than steel. The sculpture could now be entirely soft, which made it so light it could tie into existing buildings, literally becoming part of the fabric of the city. There was no software that could extrude these complex net forms and model them with gravity. So we had to create it.

Then I got a call from New York City asking if I could adapt these concepts to Times Square or the High Line. This new soft structural method enables me to model and build these sculptures at the scale of skyscrapers. They don't have funding yet, but I dream now of bringing these to cities around the world where they're most needed.

Fourteen years ago, I searched for beauty in the traditional things, in craft forms. Now I combine them with high-tech materials and engineering to create voluptuous, billowing forms the scale of buildings. My artistic horizons continue to grow.

I'll leave you with this story. I got a call from a friend in Phoenix. An attorney in the office who'd never been interested in art, never visited the local art museum, dragged everyone she could from the building and got them outside to lie down underneath the sculpture. There they were in their business suits, lying in the grass, noticing the changing patterns of wind beside people they didn't know, sharing the rediscovery of wonder.

previous: *Skies Painted with Unnumbered Sparks*, 2014, Vancouver, Canada
opposite: Echelman presents on the TED Conference stage in Vancouver, 2014

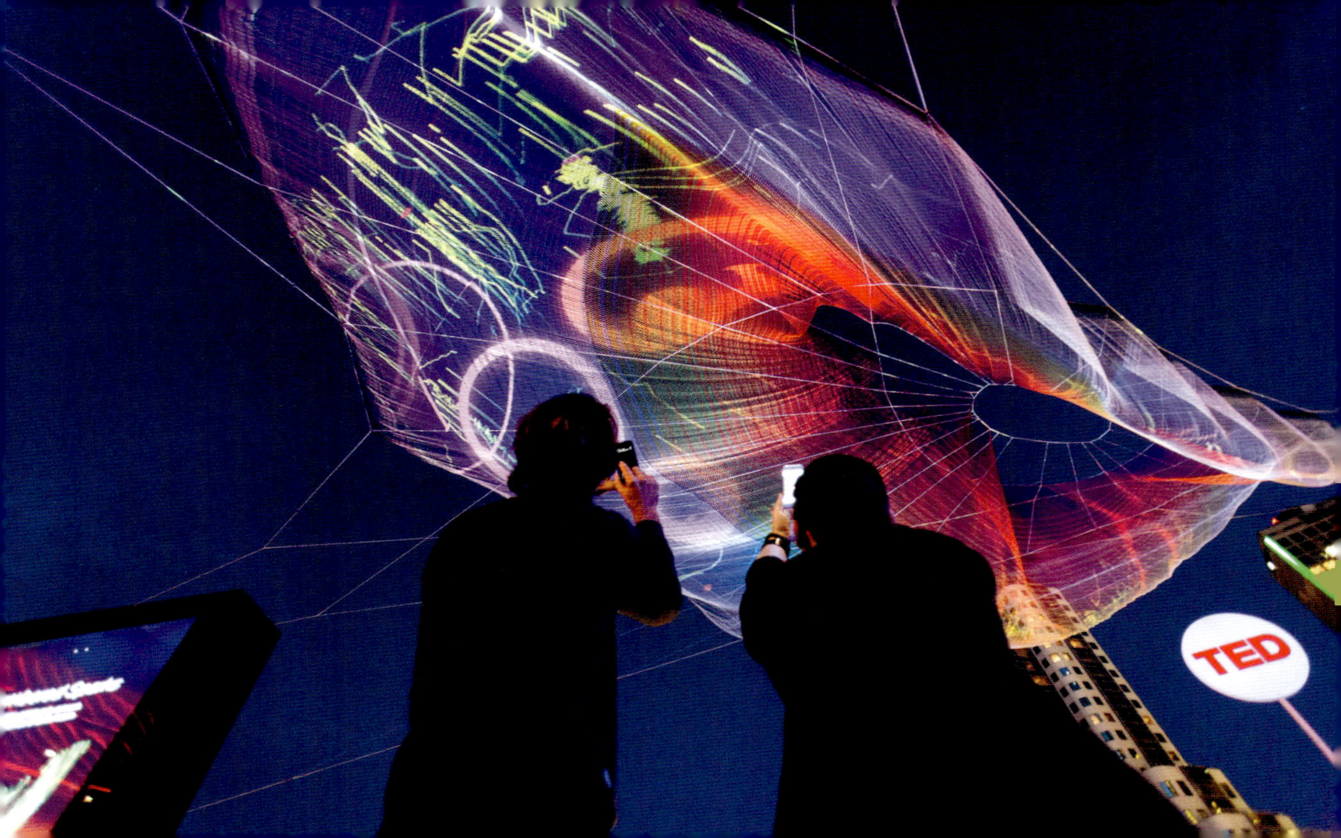
TED

Janet Echelman's 2014 TED Talk

I create voluptuous sculptures that make me feel protected, yet free to explore the world. Like being a toddler, one hand gingerly holding my mom's leg, her skirt billowing above, to feel a comfort that can't be described because it's preverbal.

I just found this photo on Flickr. This sculpture's been up ten years now, and only just discovered that people gather underneath it. What you can't see is there's no crosswalk. These people darted across a four-lane highway. I didn't expect this social element.

So I explored it with an installation in California. In one night, a hundred and fifty thousand people came, yet it was surprisingly contemplative. A post described it as "calm and quiet, almost reverent."

I began to think about the kinds of social spaces built in cities for millennia, like the Colosseum in Rome. Which I learned had a textile covering suspended from ropes, called a velarium. In addition to shielding spectators, I imagine it fostered a sense of togetherness.

Of course, they were watching violent spectacle, and here we are gathered to parlay ideas. So when TED asked me to create a sculpture for its thirtieth anniversary, I asked: What would a velarium for our time be? A gathering place, laced into the fabric of the city as a soft counterpoint to hard-edged buildings, in conversation with changing weather and light, to create intended space and the possibility for a shared moment with a neighbor you don't yet know.

I needed help to turn idea into reality.

Autodesk makes design tools and believed in this idea from the start. They built the tool I needed. It understands the constraints of my craft—drapes with gravity and movement in wind—so we can build at this scale and complexity.

On this stage in 2011, I met an inspiring digital artist, Aaron Koblin, a creative director at Google. He created this playful, interactive artwork that enables people to be co-creators as they paint the sculpture with light.

When I first set out, I was rejected by everyone. I quickly realized I'd have to define life as an artist on my own terms. I sculpt preverbal experience and share it directly in the midst of everyday life in the city. And now it's real, thanks to collaboration with engineers and designers, craftsmen and contributors. Together we present *Skies Painted with Unnumbered Sparks*.

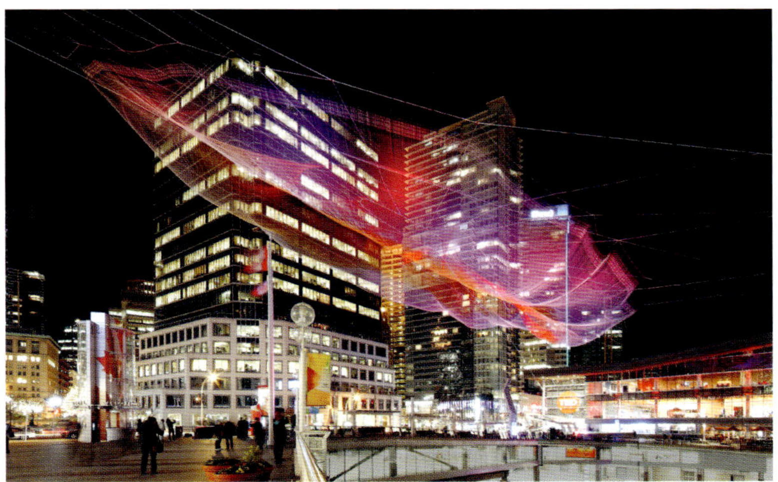

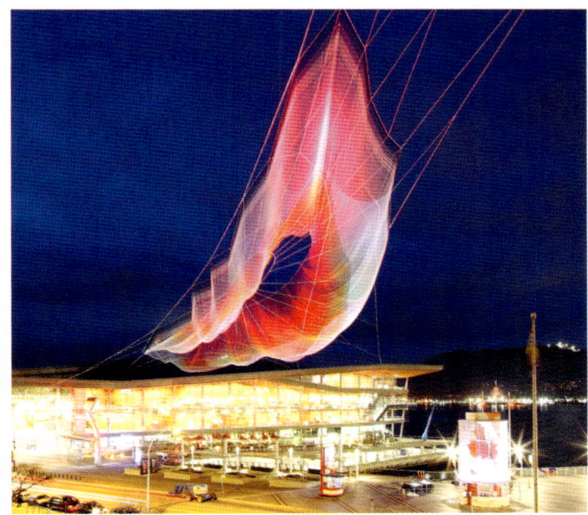

opposite and above: The public interacts with *Skies Painted with Unnumbered Sparks*, 2014, Vancouver, Canada, using a custom interface on their mobile phones (developed by the Google Data Arts team led by Aaron Koblin) to paint with projected light onto the surface of the sculpture.

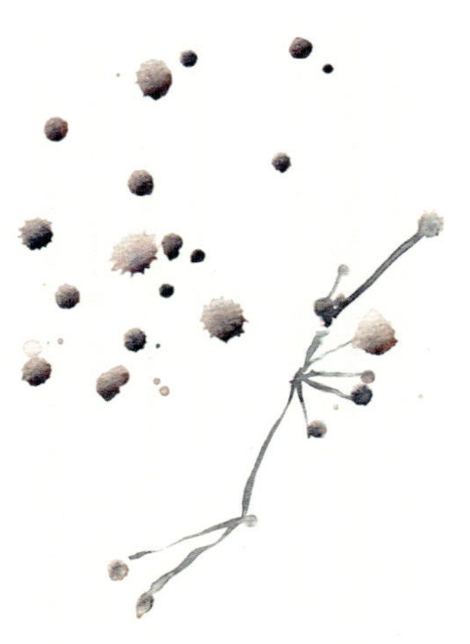

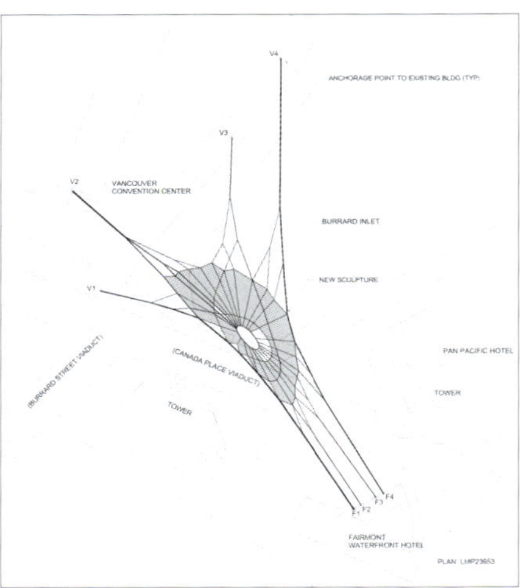

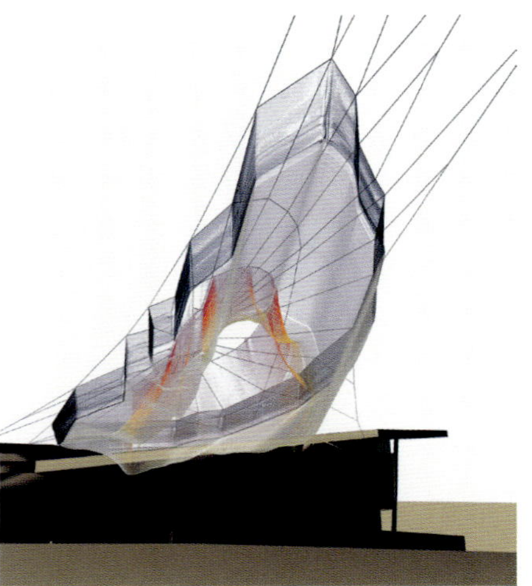

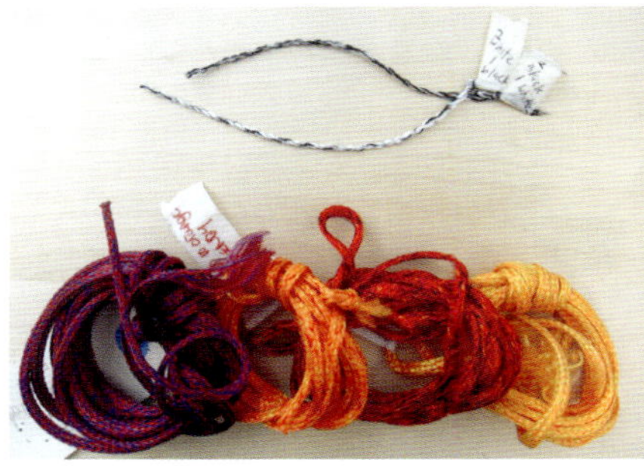

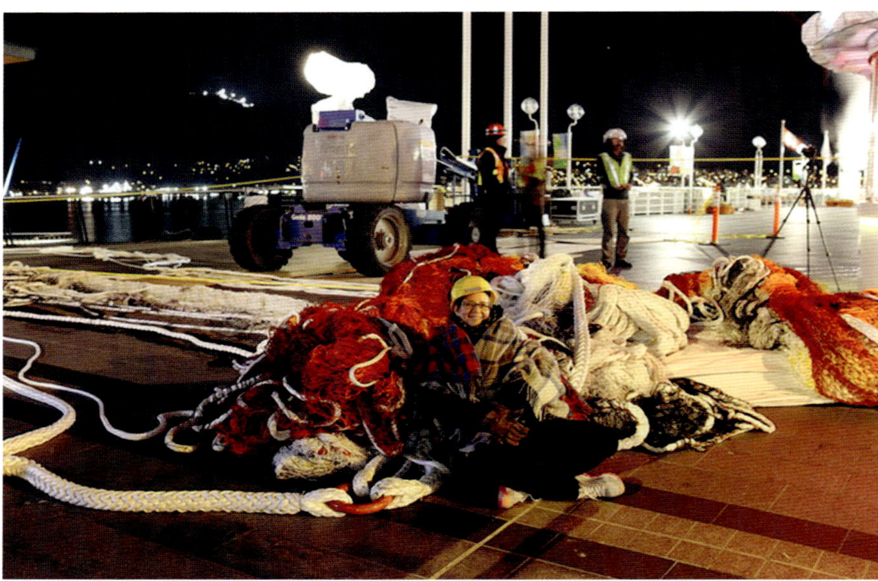

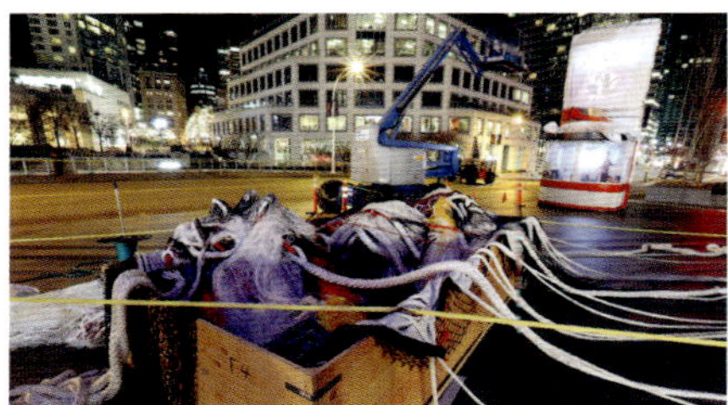

top row: Watercolor study and final plan view of the tensioned spliced-rope structure—the largest prestressed rope structure in human history; 3D model created with the studio's JNET software
middle left and bottom: Preliminary twine samples and the final fabricated sculpture during installation in Vancouver, 2014

opposite: *Skies Painted with Unnumbered Sparks*, 2014

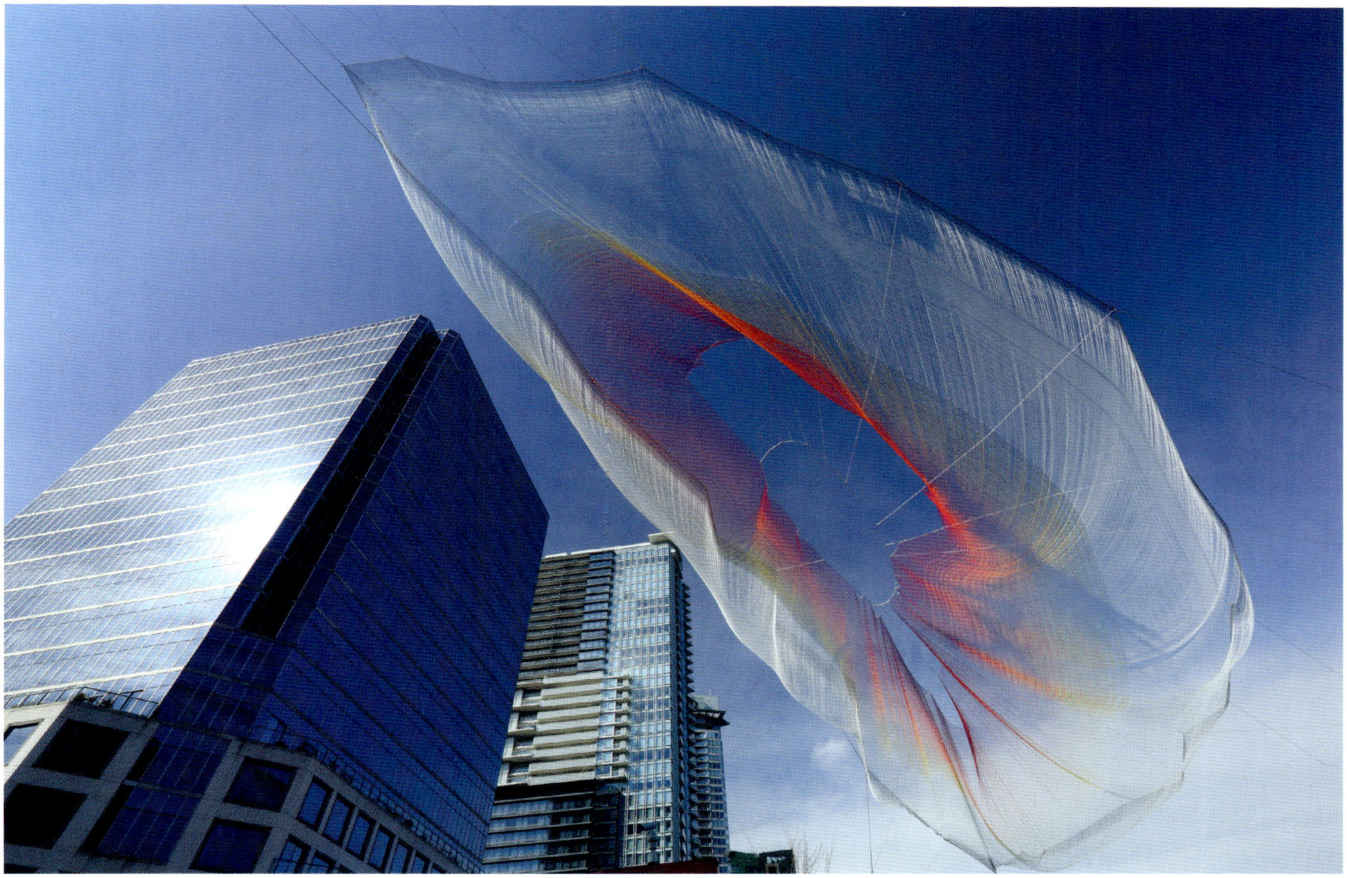

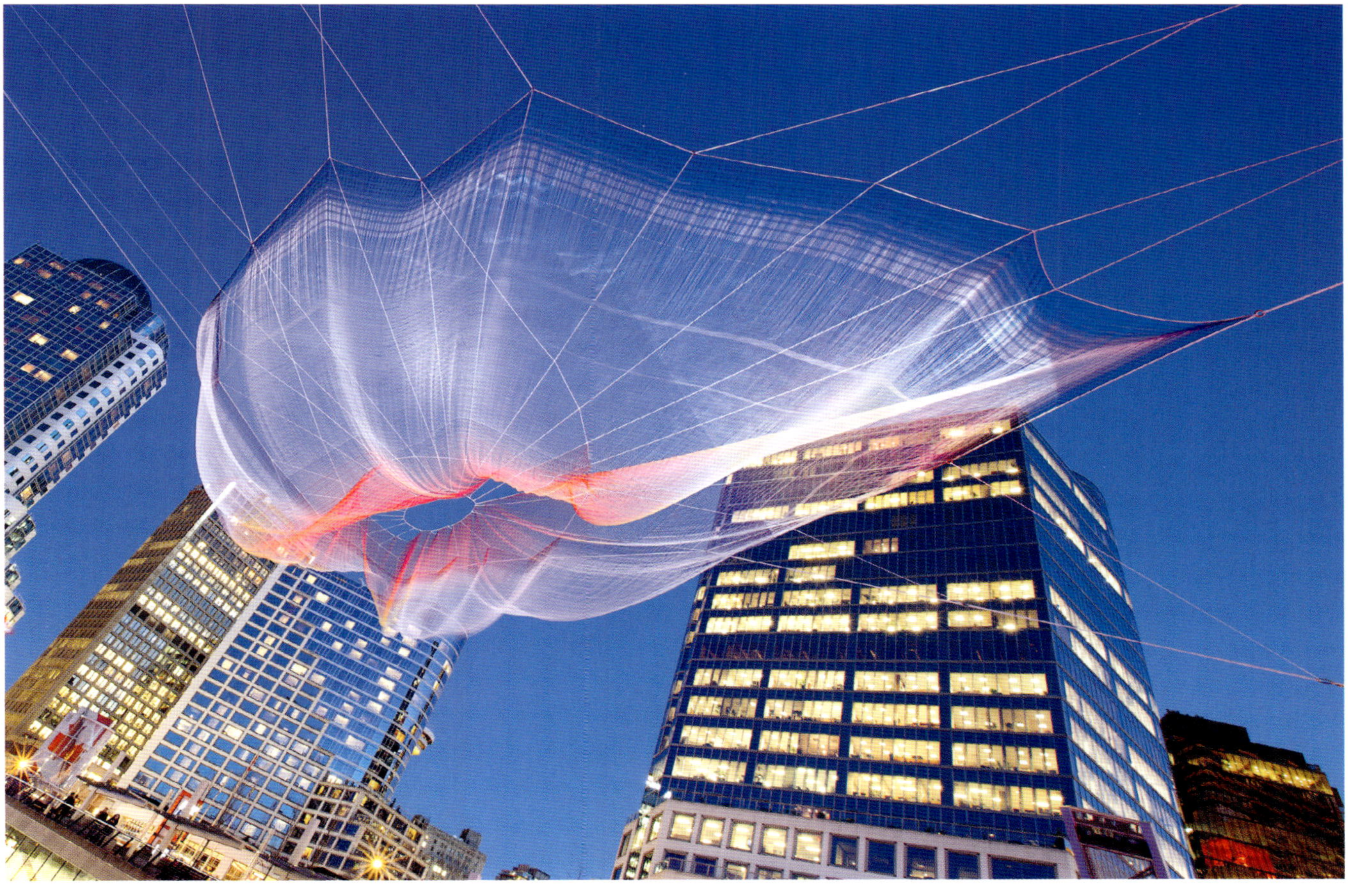

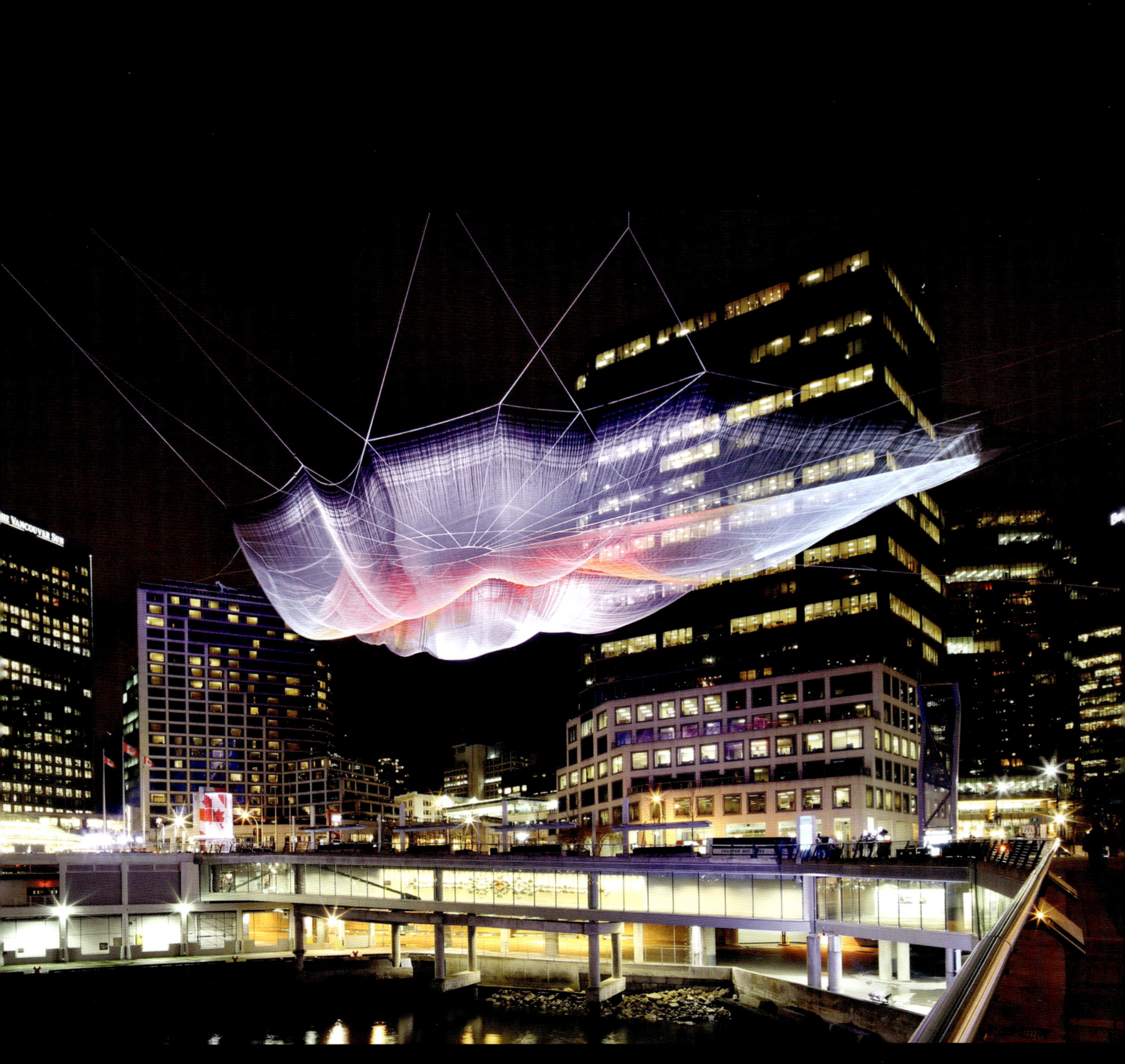

Skies Painted with Unnumbered Sparks, 2014

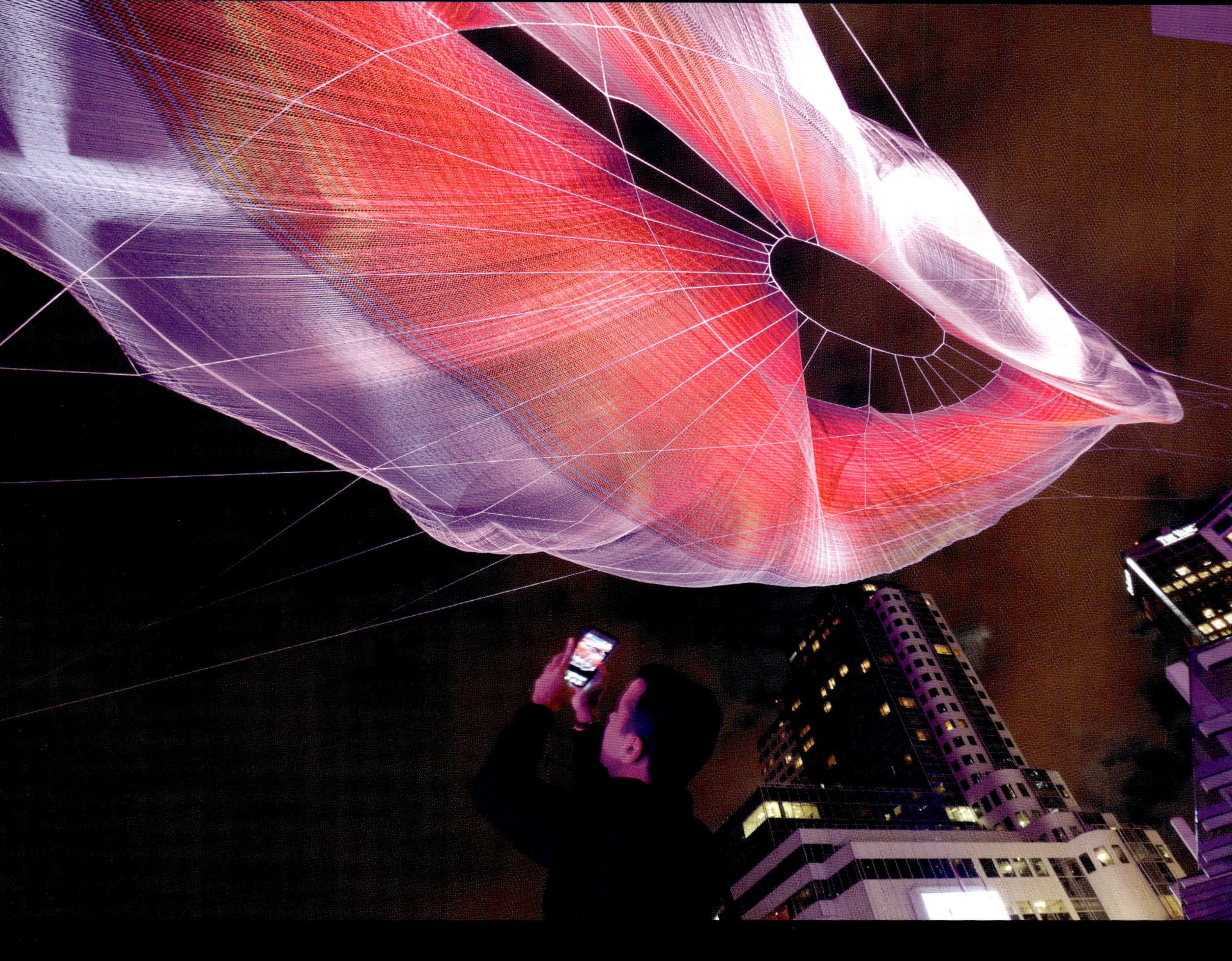

above: A custom smartphone interface enables members of the public to interact with *Skies Painted with Unnumbered Sparks*, 2014

overleaf: *Water Sky Garden*, 2009, in Richmond, Canada, legacy project created for the 2010 Vancouver Winter Olympics

Chronology

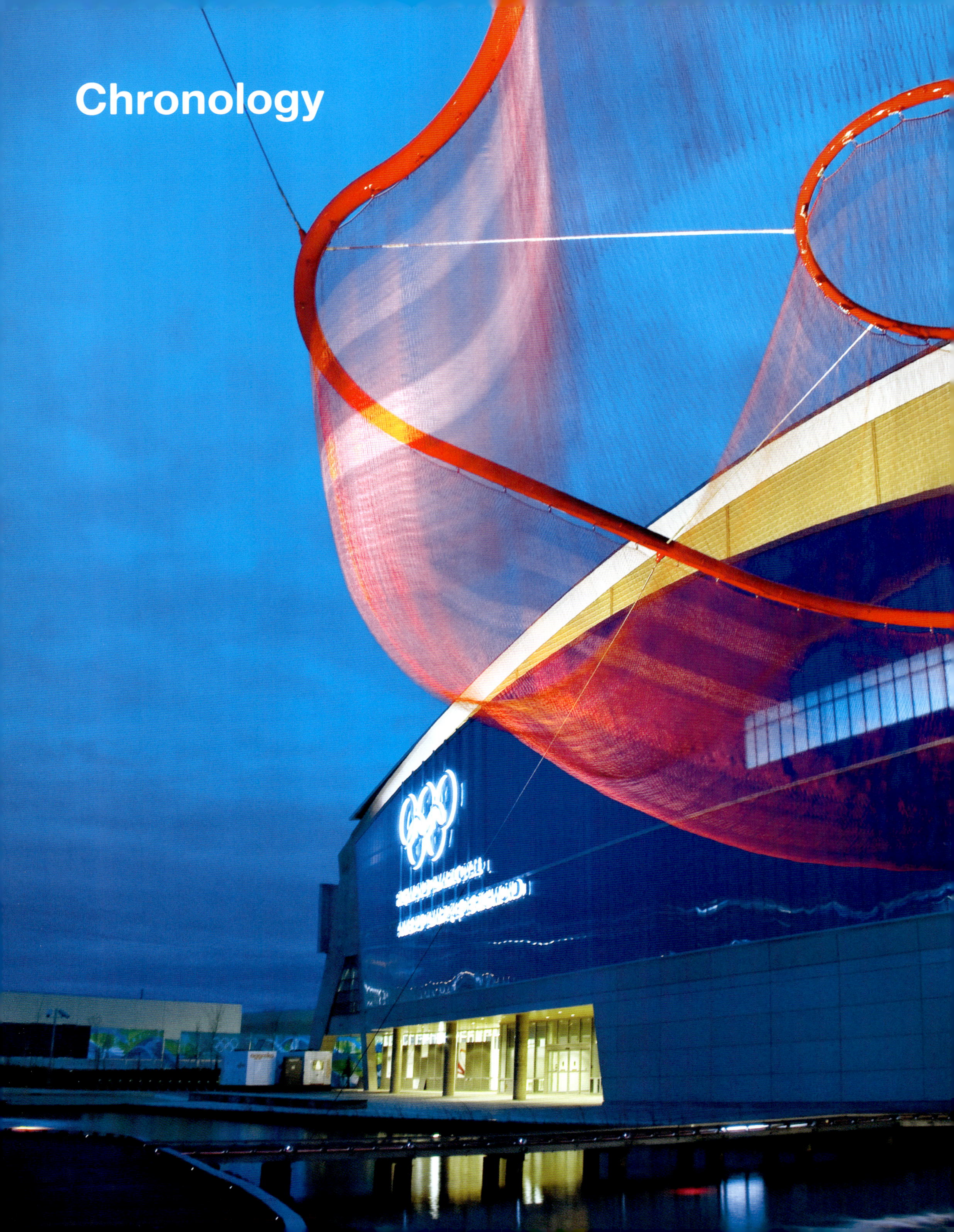

1966
Janet Sue Echelman is born in Tampa, Florida, to endocrinologist Gilbert Echelman and silversmith Anne Echelman.

1971
Echelman starts studying piano and music theory with Lucille Dvorak and begins assisting in her mother's art studio with sanding and buffing cast-silver craft objects.

1973
Echelman's mother gives classes in macramé knotting and brings along her seven-year-old daughter to teach knot making to participants.

1980–81
At fourteen, Echelman wins a concerto competition with the Florida Orchestra and performs Edvard Grieg's Piano Concerto in A Minor in four public concerts. She travels to New England to attend the Tanglewood Institute, a young artists' summer program affiliated with the Boston Symphony Orchestra. [**1**]

1983
Echelman enters Harvard College and enrolls in her first studio art course, "Drawing through Space," with Carole Bolsey, and gets a B-minus. She focuses on documentary filmmaking with Robb Moss, Alfred Guzzetti, and Ross McElwee.

1985
At Harvard, she declares a dual concentration in History and in Visual and Environmental Studies but departs for a yearlong program studying abroad with international anthropologists and filmmakers in Eastern Europe, Japan, India, and Indonesia. While researching ritual and cultural life in Bali, she learns to play *kanthilan*, traditional gamelan music accompanying ritual dance.

1986
Echelman returns to Harvard for her senior year and studies with evolutionary biologist Stephen Jay Gould, where she is exposed to the fossil record as an encyclopedia of the evolving design of life forms. She shoots and edits the 16mm film *Me Mom Nana*, which is selected for the Harvard Film Archive permanent collection. She receives a Rotary Foundation Ambassadorial Fellowship to study at the University of Hong Kong.

1987
The morning after graduation, Echelman departs for Eastern Europe to sing on tour with the Radcliffe Choral Society, then continues to Asia to begin her fellowship at the University of Hong Kong. She studies Chinese calligraphy and brush painting.

1988
Echelman's paintings are exhibited at the Hong Kong Foreign Correspondents' Club. This work leads to an invitation to present a solo exhibition at the University of Hong Kong's Art Department Gallery. She travels to Bali to create her first body of work combining batik-dyed canvases with painting.

—

Echelman moves to Bali with a total of three hundred dollars in her pocket. In Ubud she rents a bamboo-and-grass house overlooking rice fields and volcanoes.

—

Echelman learns to play the two-handed Balinese *gendèr*, a type of metallophone used in Balinese and Javanese gamelan music, and continues to play *kanthilan*. She is the only non-Balinese-born musician invited to perform regularly with her Ubud neighborhood gamelan orchestra for both temple ritual and ticketed performances. She makes charcoal gesture drawings of the performers behind the scenes.

—

Echelman apprentices with traditional textile artisans and begins making her first large canvases, dyed with a wax-resist batik method and printed with hand-carved stamps. [**2–5**]

1989
Robert Rauschenberg sees Echelman's batik paintings firsthand and asks to curate her first solo exhibition in the United States. He invites her to stay at his compound in Captiva, Florida, where he advises her and selects work for the exhibition space in Fort Myers (now known as the Bob Rauschenberg Gallery at FSW). He shares stories of his collaborations with Merce Cunningham and John Cage at Black Mountain College, and later with Trisha Brown in New York, and suggests leaving some of Echelman's batik canvases unstretched so they can move with the air currents. On opening night, Rauschenberg purchases a triptych for his personal collection (now in a private collection at Renzo Piano's House in the Rockies, Aspen).

1990
The Fung Ping Shan Museum at the University of Hong Kong presents Echelman's first solo museum exhibition, *Acrylic-Batik-Crayon Paintings: Works from Bali.*

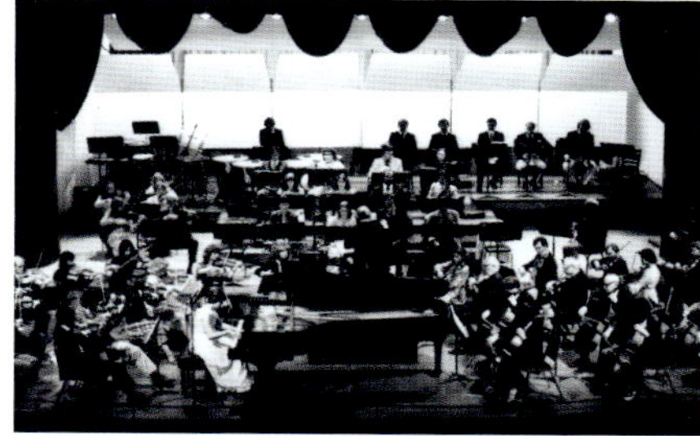
1

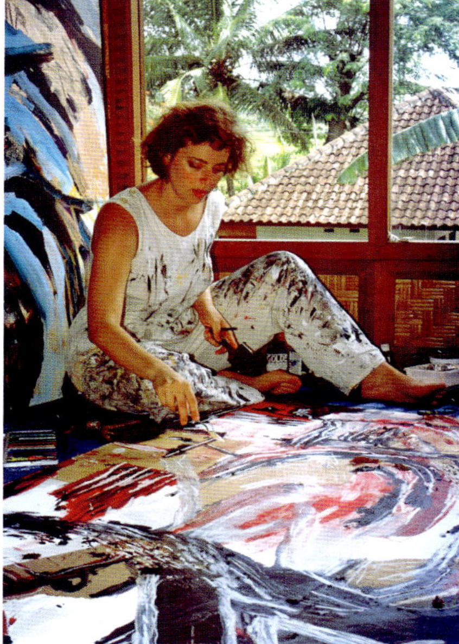
2

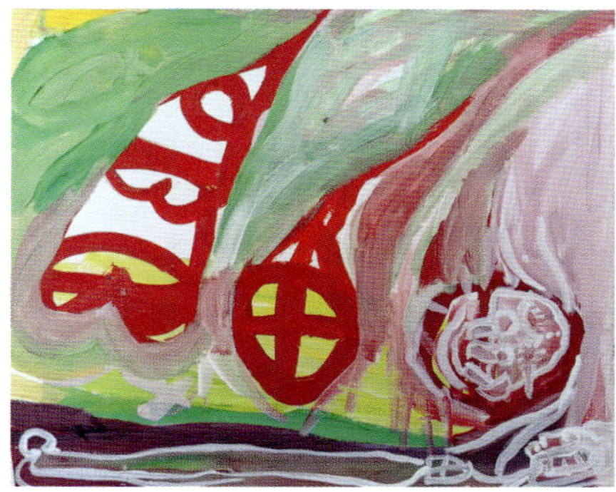
3

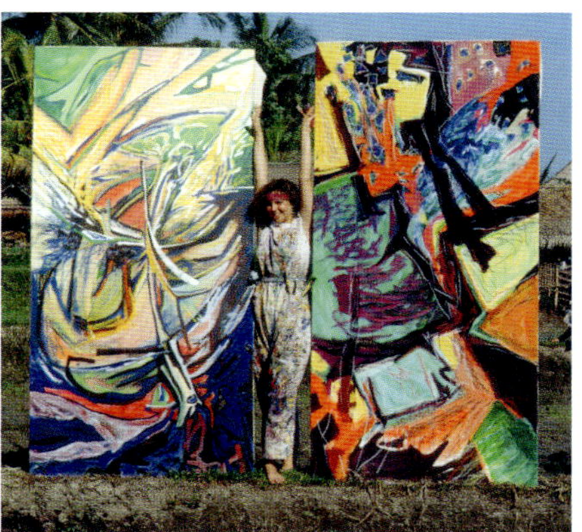
4

1991
Echelman begins creating original designs for ikat (a fabric in which the yarns have been tie-dyed before weaving), which she stretches, primes with clear rabbit-skin glue, and combines with vellum and paint.

1993
Echelman sublets her house in Bali while she installs the exhibition *Two Worlds, One Artist: Works from Indonesia and America* at the Jakarta Cultural Torch Museum, on view January 22–30. [**6**]

—

At the exhibition, she learns that her tenant in Bali left candles burning and her home of five years burned to the ground.

—

With her belongings gone, Echelman returns to the United States and completes two graduate programs simultaneously: in counseling psychology at Lesley University, and a low-residency MFA in painting at Milton Avery Graduate School of the Arts, Bard College.

—

Echelman opens her first US solo museum exhibition, *Janet Echelman: New Vision*, at the Tampa Museum of Art, on view November 14–January 9. [**7**]

1995
While working as an artist in residence at Harvard College, Echelman creates her first sculptural projects utilizing casting methods with alginate, wax, silicone rubber, and plaster. To make *Breastplates*, she installs plaster casts of male and female breasts on dessert plates in an active cafeteria. Some pieces are taken by students, who think they are meringues or ice cream molds. [**9**]

1996
With *Wax Gloves*, Echelman casts human hand gestures in white paraffin wax and combines them with architectural elements in the entry of Harvard's Sackler Museum. Included is her cast of Nobel laureate Seamus Heaney's "writing paw."

1997
In January, Echelman travels to India on a Fulbright senior research and lectureship to teach painting at the National Institute of Design. Her painting supplies never arrive. She travels to South India for the Fulbright conference in Mahabalipuram and learns the lost-wax method of bronze casting. She wants to bring her forms to larger scale but can't afford bronze casting. Echelman turns to local fishermen, who teach her to hand-knot fishnets. She drills holes in her cast bronze sculptures and begins extending the visual gestures by tying in hand-knotted net panels and fabric forms sewn from mosquito netting and used saris. [**8**]

1998
In January, Echelman returns to Tamil Nadu to create *Garden of Earthly Delights* with Hindu temple carvers in Coimbatore, who chisel solid brick forms to mirror a floating white netted form.

—

Echelman accepts an invitation to create a piece for the Open-Air Museum of the Centre of Europe Europos Parkas in Vilnius, Lithuania. She works with a local lace maker and discovers that the lace knots are the same as the knots the South Indian fishermen taught her. The newfound ability to add and drop knots creates opportunities for complex lace patterns and geometries. She constructs *Trying to Hide with Your Tail in the Air* for the museum's permanent collection.

—

Echelman travels to Almería, Spain, for the Valparaiso residency and creates earth drawings in the desert. She contrasts the cracked lines of the dry riverbeds with her drawn white lines created with a flour sifter. [**10**]

—

Echelman's first architectural collaboration, *Inside-Outside*, is attached to the skylight structure in the historic courtyard of Harvard University's Fogg Art Museum. The tall, hollow, layered sculpture is formed from steel and nylon nets and spirals downward from a forty-four-foot-high ceiling, meeting visitors at eye level and welcoming them inside. [**11**]

1999
The Pollock-Krasner Foundation awards Echelman a major grant. In the summer, she creates work in the landscape at Art Omi in Columbia County, New York.

—

Echelman marries computer scientist David Nathaniel Feldman

2000
Echelman opens her first solo exhibition in New York, on view June 7–14, at Florence Lynch Gallery in Chelsea, where she decides to install sculptures in the window openings that transgress into the public airspace of the street. The gallery is filled only with the color and pattern of the shadows cast by the exterior installations.

—

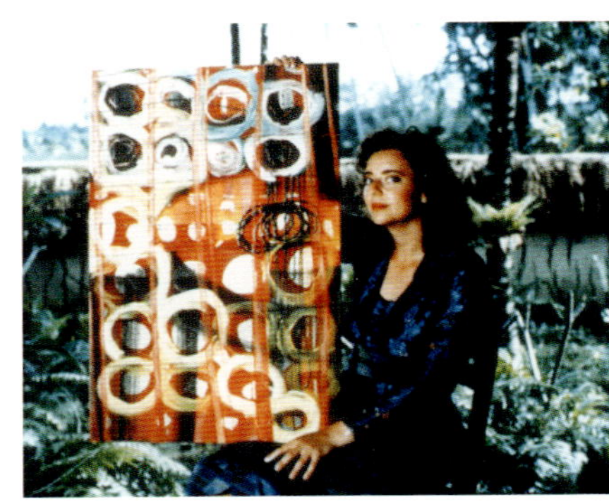
5

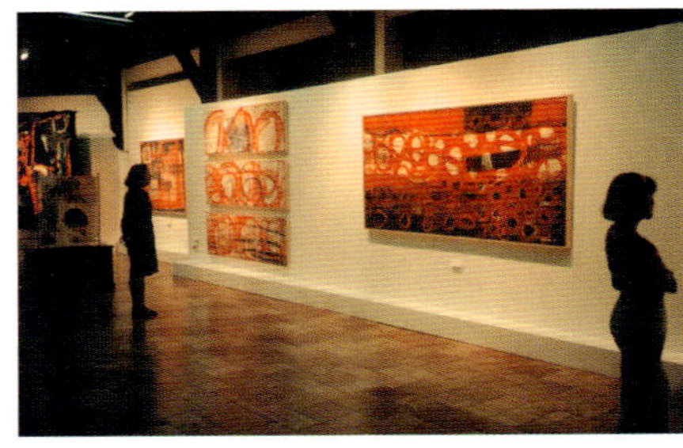
6

7

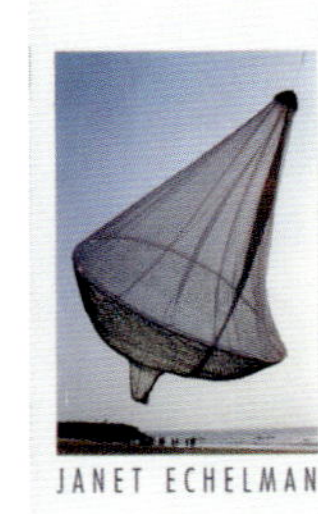

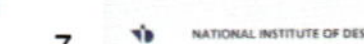

8

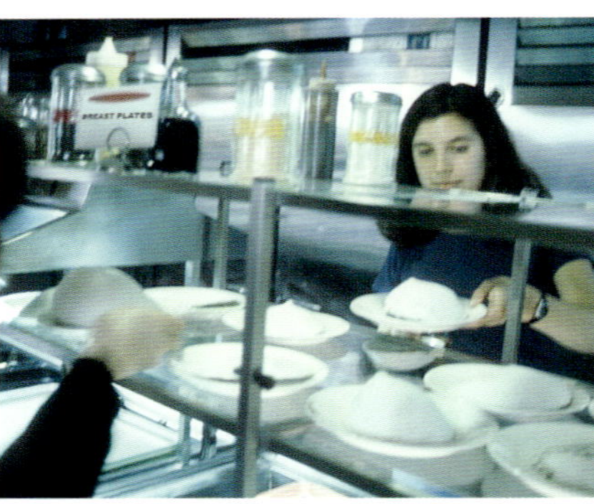
9

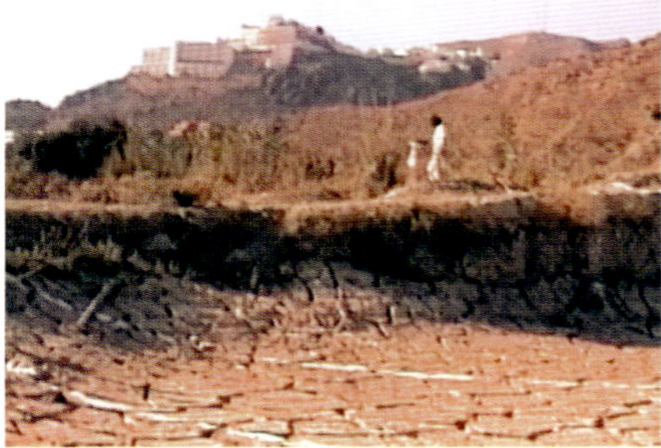
10

Echelman moves to New York and establishes her new art studio on West 97th Street.

—

A Japan Foundation artist fellowship enables Echelman to study Buddhist temple gardens and later create the installation *Kyoto Project* in the garden of Hōnen-in, a Buddhist monastery on the Philosopher's Path in Kyoto.

—

In October, Echelman installs *Roadside Shrine I: Cone Ridge*, temporarily clamped to the underside of an I-45 overpass in Houston. This is the first time the Texas Department of Transportation has allowed art to touch infrastructure.

2001

In January, Echelman returns to India to work with nine fishermen to create a sculpture composed of 1.56 million hand-tied knots. She installs *Floor Target*, a one-hundred-square-foot temporary installation on a warehouse floor in Coimbatore, then travels to Spain with the net in a large duffel bag. She installs *Target Swooping Down... Bullseye!* in Madrid at the international art fair ARCO, on view February 8–13. Her first exterior installation and the fair's centerpiece, the net is laced into the building's roof deck railing and spans the circular courtyard of the IFEMA trade fair complex. In less than one week, more than one hundred thousand people come through—including Manuel de Solà-Morales, the architect redesigning the waterfront of Porto, Portugal, who invites Echelman to Portugal to create her first monumental permanent piece, *She Changes*. [**12–13**]

—

For the Porto commission, Echelman seeks out Peter Heppel, known for engineering America's Cup racing sails, tensile fabric airlocks for NASA, and the Glasgow Tower (which rotates in the wind), and they begin a nearly decade-long collaboration. They work with computer scientist David Feldman to develop physical models and the first computer software tools to model Echelman's proposed design, which she had aesthetically visualized with Columbia architecture student Philip Speranza using Maya, a 3D computer graphics application frequently used in the film industry She explores material science and begins using UV-resistant PTFE architectural fiber. Using Heppel's Relax software, made for the sailing industry, Echelman designs aero-elastic sculptures able to withstand strong winds and harsh environments. Aware that hand-tied knots aren't sturdy enough for permanent installations, she finds an industrial net manufacturer in Washington's Puget Sound region and learns the variables of machine looming.

—

In March, the Madrid sculptural net, now retitled *Target Swooping II*, is reinstalled above the fifteenth-century carved stone courtyard of Casa del Cordón in Burgos, Spain.

2002

In January, *Target Swooping III* is unveiled at Florence Lynch Gallery, New York.

—

In February, Florence Lynch Gallery installs *Roadside Shrine II* under Piers 88 and 90 for the Armory Show in New York.

—

In December, *Target Swooping IV* premieres at the inaugural Art Basel Miami, in the courtyard of the Bass Museum of Art, Miami Beach. [**14**]

2003

In July, Echelman forms a team with architect Jeanne Gang and Thornton Tomasetti engineers to create a design for the 9/11 Memorial competition sponsored by the city of Hoboken, New Jersey (which lost fifty-six citizens in the terrorist attack). They are announced the winners, but a city budget crisis stalls issuance of the bond for construction. [**15**]

2004

In February, *Target Swooping V* debuts during Art Rotterdam, attached between the cruise terminal and the port.

—

New York gallerist Florence Lynch invites Echelman to exhibit in the gallery and simultaneously create an installation using projection in Venice, which is included in *Venice Biennale—Fifty Plus*.

—

In December in Porto, Echelman installs *She Changes*, which is declared the "largest piece of lace in the history of the world" by David Revere McFadden, chief curator at New York's Museum of Arts and Design. Her first permanent monumental sculpture, it is suspended above a highway roundabout with three masts stretching up to 165 feet supporting a twenty-ton steel frame. Inspired by traditional local lace making and fishing traps, its red-and-white woven striped netting also references nearby smokestacks and lighthouses. *She Changes* becomes a symbol of the city, and a thumbnail image of it represents the country of Portugal on Google Earth.

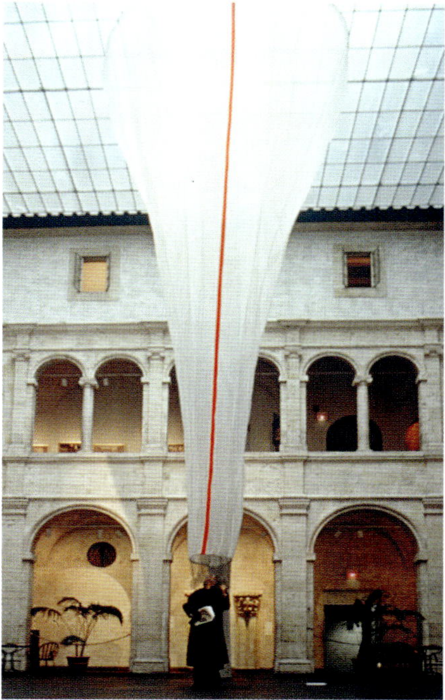
11

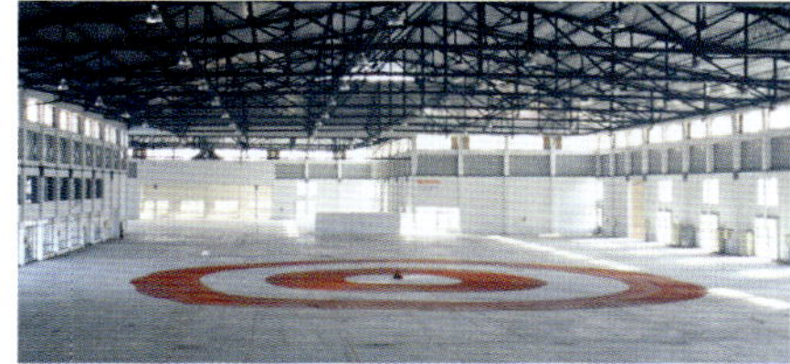
12

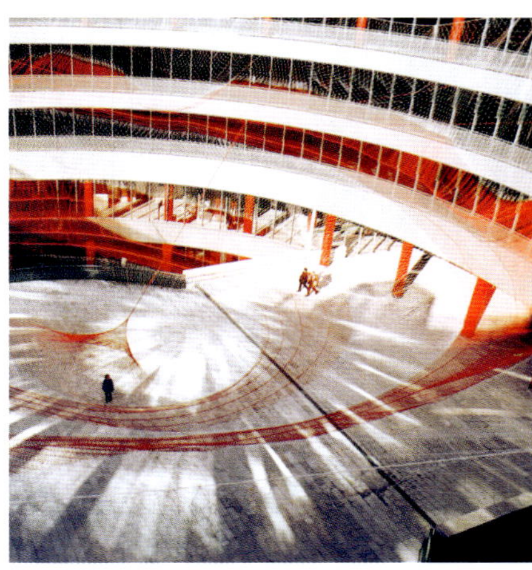
13

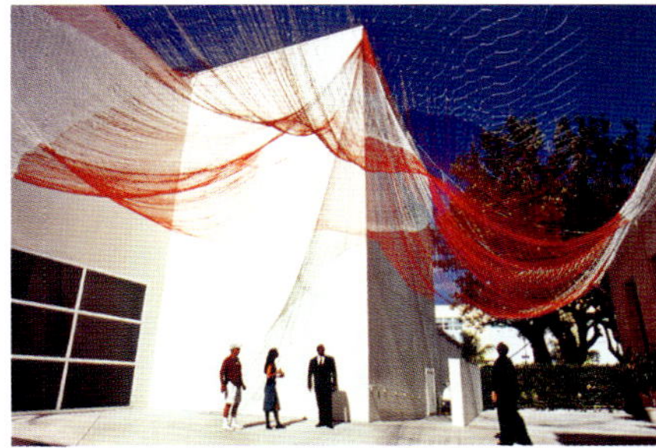
14

Public Art Network recognizes it as one of "the most compelling public artworks of the year." [16]

2006

Echelman begins the Aspen Institute's Henry Crown Fellowship, studying original texts from ancient times to the present.

2007

In January, the Museum of Arts and Design in New York commissions Echelman to make a new work for the exhibition *Radical Lace & Subversive Knitting*. She creates *Expanding Club*, a variable-mesh netted sculpture loomed with colored twine representing the flags of countries that have tested nuclear weapons, arranged in chronological order of the detonations. [17]

—

Echelman begins a Loeb Fellowship at Harvard Graduate School of Design.

2009

In February, Echelman installs the permanent *Water Sky Garden* in advance of the 2010 Winter Olympics at the Richmond Olympic Oval speed-skating venue near Vancouver, British Columbia. It consists of two colossal steel-framed netted sculptures and Echelman's designs for red wooden walkways meandering between her curving water features, which process runoff water from the venue's five-acre roof. [18]

—

In April, Echelman debuts *Her Secret Is Patience*, a permanent installation in Civic Space Park in downtown Phoenix. She collaborates with a roller-coaster manufacturer to bend steel framing, with net fabricators to hand splice each mesh joint (as every edge of the internal structural net is a different length), and with a lighting designer to create palettes of colored illumination that gradually unfold over 365 days. (Public protest had spurred the Phoenix City Council to reinstate the project after they attempted to cancel it during the 2007 recession.)

2010

Echelman creates the Planned Parenthood Margaret Sanger Award by casting glass in a form that simultaneously references a Greek amphora and fallopian tubes.

—

Because Echelman's search for immersive art experiences has been leading her to design at architectural scale, and there is no commercially available software capable of modeling designs that are that large, dynamically moving, and porous, Echelman and David Feldman interview computer scientists at MIT to develop her own proprietary software.

—

In February, the city of Denver asks Echelman to create a sculpture representing "the interconnectedness of nations" to commemorate their hosting the Biennial of the Americas. She begins exploring imagery of scientific data sets reflecting interconnected processes of the natural world, specifically NASA and NOAA data reflecting the impact of the 2010 Chilean earthquake on Earth's systems and the resulting 1.26-microsecond shortening of the day. Using analog methods, Echelman and her colleagues create small-scale models in her studio, then grid up a full-scale template by taping together blue plastic tarps on an empty hockey rink floor. Simultaneously they test their first custom software tool and compare it with the physical models. To create the grid, Echelman begins working with ultra-high-molecular-weight-polyethylene (UHMWPE) fiber, which offers more than fifteen times the strength of steel by weight. By pulling an X-Y axis grid of these fibers into tension, she creates a tensile structural layer for the first time, which enables her to completely eliminate the heavy steel armatures of prior works. This structural "top net" is hand tied to each loomed net panel, and each panel is cut by hand to create the volumetric form. The result is a completely soft urban sculpture, monumental yet light enough to attach to existing buildings. This is the breakthrough that allows Echelman's work to travel worldwide.

—

In July, *Earthtime 1.26 Denver*, the first sculpture in the *Earthtime* series, is suspended between the roof of the Denver Art Museum and Civic Center Park.

—

In August, Echelman visits Paris and develops the *Marianne's Breast* installation proposal for the Louvre's glass pyramid. It is inspired by Eugène Delacroix's *Liberty Leading the People* (1830) in consultation with the FIAC art fair and Louvre staff. [19]

—

In November, Echelman begins an appointment as the 2010 Resident of the American Academy in Rome in Visual Arts. She researches the monumental textile velarium that was suspended above the Roman Colosseum in ancient times.

2011

In March, Echelman presents her first TED talk in Long Beach, California. "Taking

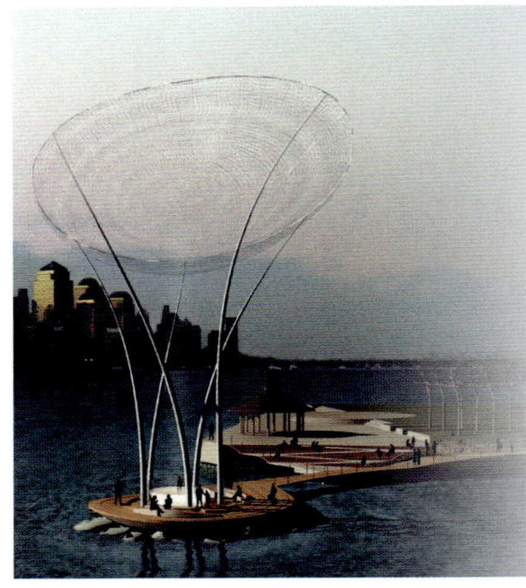

15

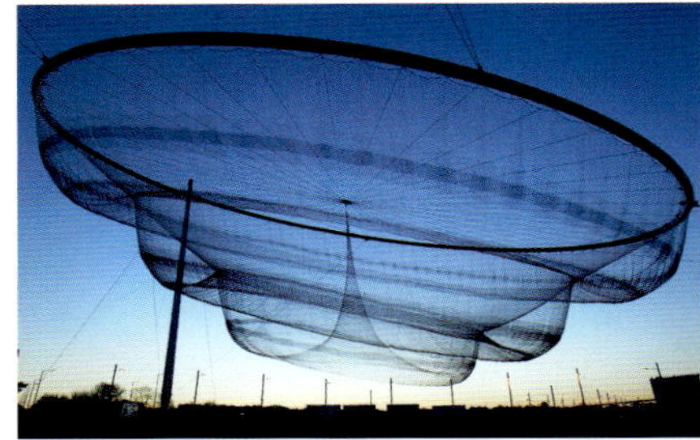

16

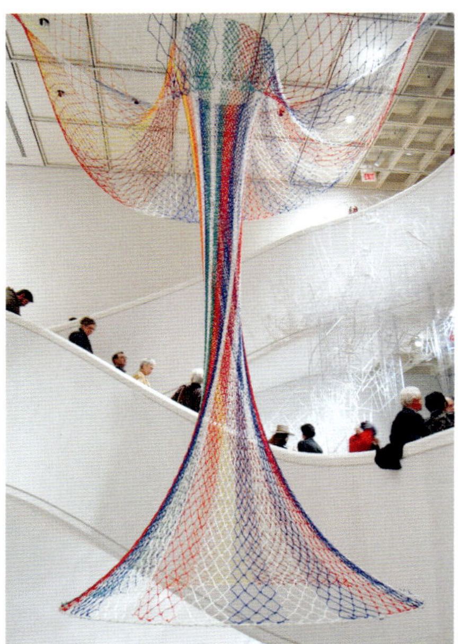

17

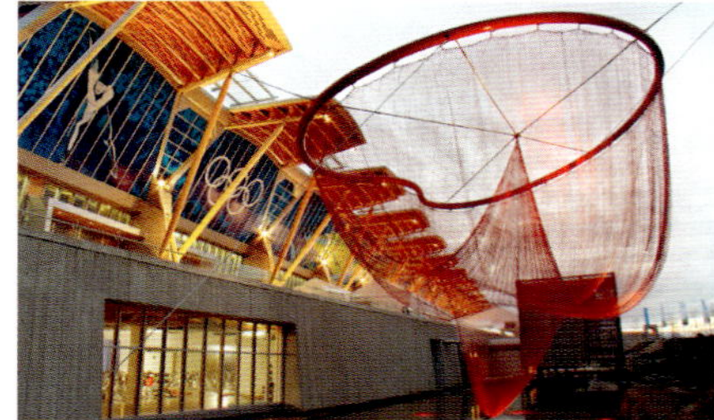

18

Imagination Seriously" has since been translated into thirty-five languages and viewed by more than two million people worldwide. Afterward, Echelman and Feldman meet the CEO and CTO of Autodesk, who offer to assist with her art's computational needs. Feldman guides the collaboration, which in the coming years leads to the Autodesk team meeting biweekly at Echelman's studio to develop custom software to enable modeling of soft-body forms as they seek more accurate simulations of net geometries and draping with gravity. **[20]**

—

At the TED conference, Al Gore meets Echelman and later visits her studio to discuss how to communicate environmental data via public art. **[21]**

—

In April, *Every Beating Second*, commissioned by the San Francisco Arts Commission, premieres in the newly renovated Terminal 2 at San Francisco International Airport. Echelman cuts three round skylights into the ceiling and suspends from them translucent colored netting. She shapes patterns into the terrazzo floors corresponding to the overhead sculptural forms, and choreographs fans to create airflow that animates the work.

—

Echelman receives a John Simon Guggenheim Memorial Foundation fellowship.

—

In November, the second iteration of the *Earthtime 1.26* series travels to its second continent, Australia. Suspended from the historic Sydney Town Hall as part of the Powerhouse Museum's *Love Lace* exhibition, *Earthtime 1.26 Sydney* hovers over the busiest traffic intersection on the continent.

2012

Echelman's collaboration with Autodesk intensifies as they begin to develop custom software specifically for the netted sculptures. Feldman and Autodesk CTO Jeff Kowalski hatch a plan to create a Maya 3D software plug-in. Kowalski assigns a summer intern, Peter Boyer, to create software capable of modeling net densities and shape at scale while simulating effects of gravity, which they dub JNET. Visually expressive wind simulations are now possible, but because Maya is geared more to film animation than to construction, accurate wind modeling must still be done independently by licensed engineers.

—

Echelman creates props for M. Night Shyamalan's movie *After Earth*, starring Will Smith.

—

In May, Echelman visits Nike headquarters in Oregon to deliver a lecture and discuss innovations in custom knitting with the team developing the first Flyknit material.

—

In August, *Architectural Digest* selects Echelman as a 2012 Innovator, describing her sculpture as "changing the very essence of urban spaces." **[22]**

—

In December, *Earthtime 1.26* travels to its third continent to make its European debut as the signature project of the inaugural Amsterdam Light Festival. *Earthtime 1.26 Amsterdam* straddles the Amstel river, attaching to City Hall, the Muziektheater, and platforms floating on the river. Echelman invites Rogier van der Heide, chief design officer of Philips Lighting, to collaborate. They develop an innovative lighting technique they dub "color laundering": focusing a light of the complementary color of the sculpture's physical color to "wash out" that color; this is used as a contrast to the bright pop of color that occurs when the light hues match the physical color of the sculpture.

—

In December, Echelman begins a bird safety collaboration with Bioengineering Group, whose founder, Dr. Wendi Goldsmith, articulates that Echelman's thick cords and wide mesh openings are highly visible to wildlife and pose neither an attraction nor an entrapment danger to birds or bats.

2013

In August, *O, The Oprah Magazine*, ranks Echelman's work number one on its "List of 50 Things That Make You Say Wow!" **[23]**

—

Poet Seamus Heaney, Echelman's collaborator from *Wax Gloves*, dies in August. She sees his last words, "*Noli timere*," painted in translation ("Don't be afraid") on a Dublin building and begins conceptualizing her *Noli Timere* sculpture and dance series. **[24]**

—

In September, *The Space Between Us* premieres at GLOW, an all-night art event on Santa Monica State Beach in California. From dusk to dawn, this temporary site-specific sand-and-net installation transforms the beach and includes a custom audio component that syncs with lighting colors. One hundred and fifty thousand people attend and reshape the sand beneath the aerial sculpture.

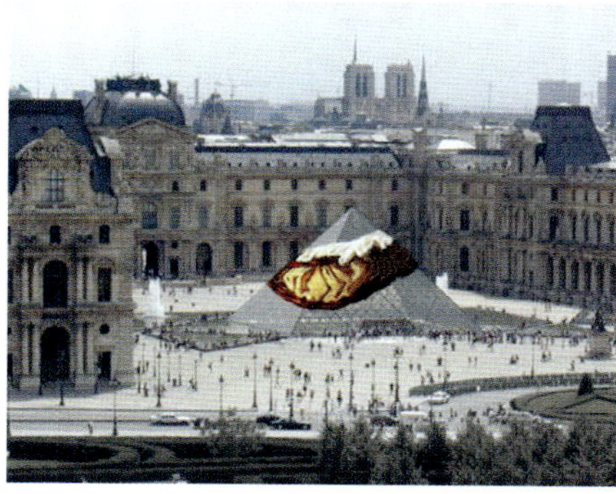

19

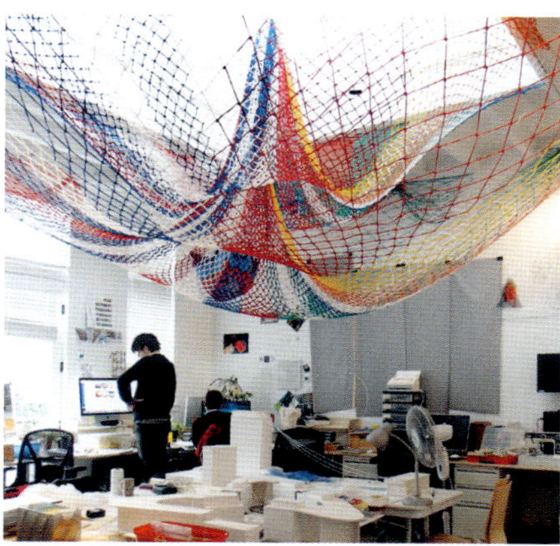

20

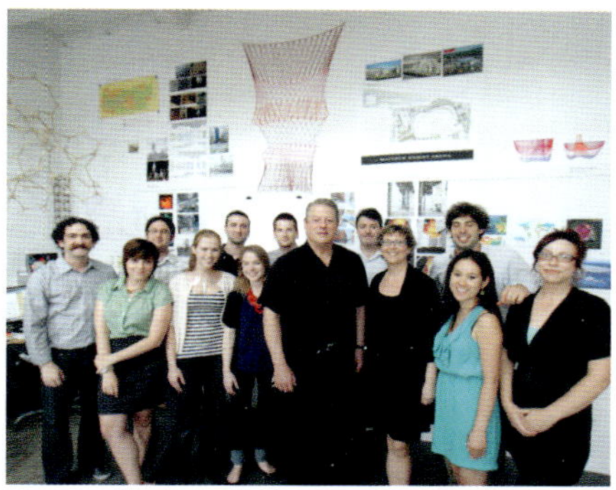

21

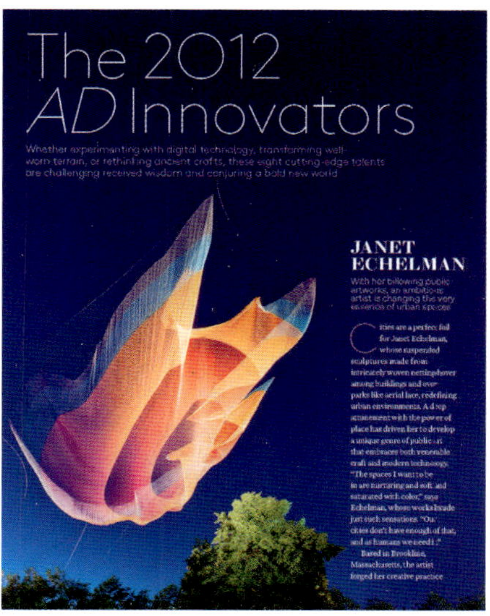

The 2012
AD Innovators

Whether experimenting with digital technology, transforming well-worn terrain, or rethinking ancient crafts, these eight cutting-edge talents are challenging received wisdom and conjuring a bold new world

JANET ECHELMAN

With her billowing public artworks, an ambitious artist is changing the very essence of urban spaces

Cities are a perfect foil for Janet Echelman, whose suspended sculptures made from intricately woven netting hover among buildings and over parks like aerial lace, redefining urban environments. A deep attunement with the power of place has driven her to develop a unique genre of public art that embraces both venerable craft and modern technology. "The spaces I want to be in are nurturing and soft and saturated with color," says Echelman, whose works exude just such sensations. "Our cities don't have enough of that, and as humans we need it."

Based in Brookline, Massachusetts, the artist forged her creative practice

22

2014

Allegory, a permanent fiber sculpture with projected shadow drawings, is installed in Matthew Knight Arena at the University of Oregon in Eugene.

—

In March, after three years of planning, Echelman installs her most technologically challenging project yet in Vancouver for the TED conference's thirtieth anniversary. *Skies Painted with Unnumbered Sparks* spans 745 feet over a harbor, major roadway, and pedestrian traffic, attaching the top of the twenty-four-story Fairmont Hotel to the roof of the Vancouver Convention Centre. Arup engineers announce that it is the largest prestressed rope structure in human history. It requires multiple federal, provincial, and municipal permits as well as Canadian aviation approvals. Digital artist Aaron Koblin and the Google Data Arts Team partner with Echelman to create a social interface for the artwork that is fully interactive through smartphones without requiring a special app. Seventy-five earlier TED speakers are invited to return for this occasion, and Echelman delivers her second TED main stage talk.

—

Earthtime 1.26 debuts on its fourth continent, at the i Light Singapore festival, as *Earthtime 1.26 Singapore*.

—

In May, Echelman collaborates with Stuttgart Ballet choreographer Katarzyna Kozielska to create *A. Memory*, showcasing Echelman's first sculptural "body extensions" and set design. All performances are sold out.

—

In October, architect Daniel Libeskind presents Echelman with the Smithsonian American Ingenuity Award in Visual Arts during a ceremony celebrating "the greatest innovators in America today" at the National Portrait Gallery in Washington, DC. **[25]**

—

The first phase of *Pulse*, Echelman's artwork for Philadelphia's Dilworth Park in front of City Hall, premieres.

—

Teaming up with the Coral Restoration Foundation and marine ecologist Joanie Kleypas, Echelman develops her first design to build underwater sculpture that grows coral. The project continues to seek sponsorship. **[26]**

2015

In February, the permanent aerial sculpture *Impatient Optimist* is unveiled at the Bill & Melinda Gates Foundation headquarters in Seattle.

—

In May, *As If It Were Already Here* debuts, spanning the Rose Kennedy Greenway in Boston. The installation attaches to three privately owned buildings, soaring six hundred feet through the air above street traffic and a pedestrian park. Advanced computational design and new looming techniques allow for variations in color, bobbin by bobbin, to generate a fine-patterned, multihued work. **[27, 28]**

—

In October, *Earthtime 1.26 Prague* is installed in front of the Rudolfinum, home to the Czech Philharmonic, along the bank of the Vltava river during the Signal Festival.

—

Also in October, *Earthtime 1.26 Montreal* premieres in the city's downtown Quartier des Spectacles. It will be reinstalled in 2016 and 2017.

—

In November, The Shard, London's tallest building, announces Echelman the winner of its art commission. Simultaneously in England, *Earthtime 1.26 Durham* is unveiled above the River Wear during Lumiere Durham.

—

Also in November, *Earthtime 1.8 Renwick* opens in Washington DC. Commissioned by the Smithsonian American Art Museum to transform the Renwick Gallery after renovation, Echelman for the first time creates pictorial carpeting below that references the topographic lines of the 3D form above. The museum acquires it for its permanent collection.

2016

In January, *Earthtime 1.8 London* debuts during Lumiere London, floating 180 feet above Oxford Circus, the busiest pedestrian area in the city. At the instigation of cultural entrepreneur Helen Marriage, London shuts down all vehicular traffic on Oxford and Regent Streets for four nights and makes the Oxford Circus Underground station exit-only to avoid trampling. Despite the winter cold, pedestrians begin lying down on the asphalt to gaze up at the sculpture and watch it change with wind patterns and projected lighting colors that they influence via their smartphones.

—

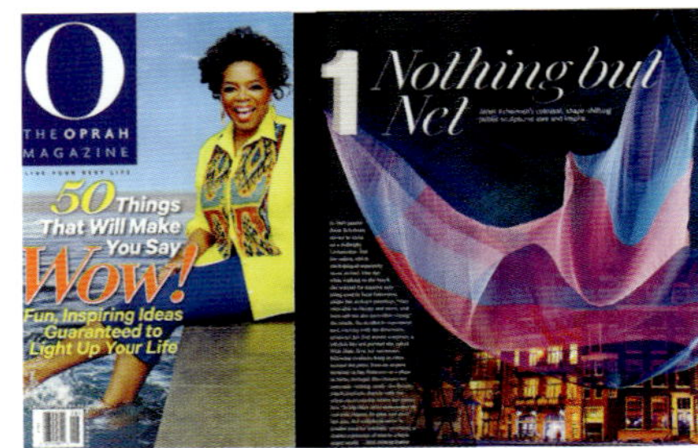

23

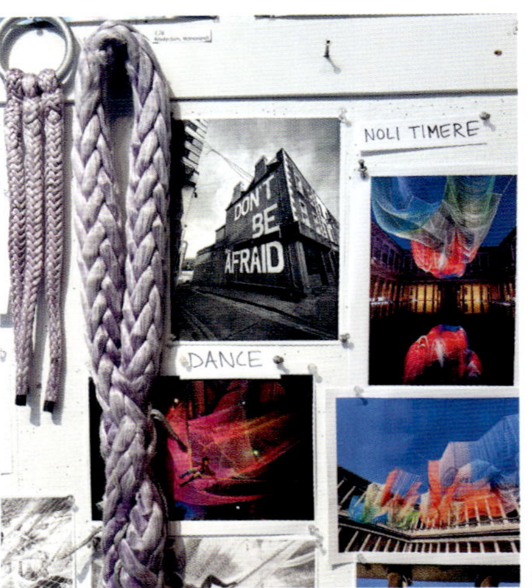

24

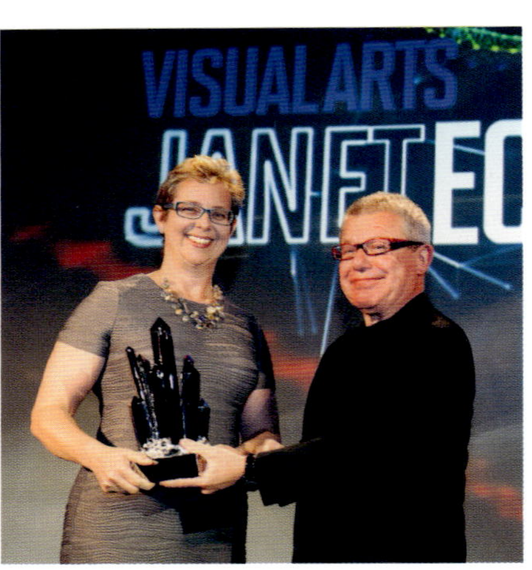

25

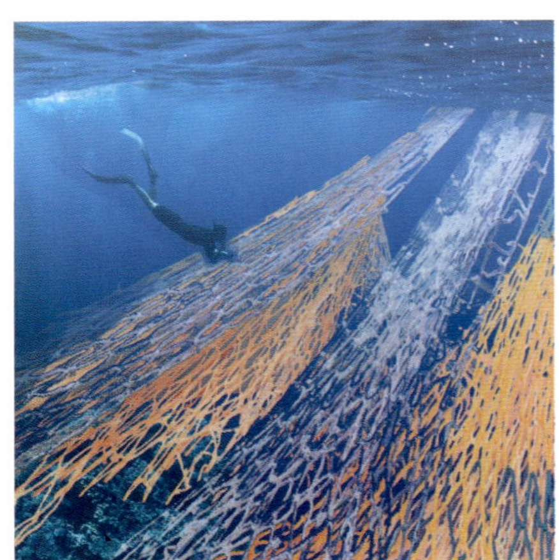
26

In May, Echelman receives an honorary Doctor of Fine Arts degree from Tufts University.

—

In July, *Where We Met*, a permanent aerial fiber sculpture inspired by textile history and its interconnection with railroad lines, opens in LeBauer Park, Greensboro, North Carolina.

—

Possible Futures of a Line, Traveling through Space and Time, Echelman's first traveling artwork that pairs suspended fiber sculpture with bespoke topographic carpet, premieres in October in Como, Italy. In 2017 it will appear in Paris in February, then continue on to the Cheongju Craft Biennale, South Korea, in September. [**29**]

—

In November, *Earthtime 1.26 Santiago* at the Museo Nacional de Bellas Artes in Santiago, Chile, and *Earthtime 1.8 San Diego* at Embarcadero Marina Park South, California, premiere.

—

In December, Echelman receives the United States Artists Fellowship.

2017

The permanent artwork *Dream Catcher* is installed on Los Angeles's Sunset Strip, suspended between the towers of the 1 Hotel West Hollywood. Inspiration for the piece comes from the idea of pursuing one's dreams in Hollywood, and representations of brain wave data mapped during dreaming. The hotel and the artwork are engineered by Skidmore, Owings & Merrill (SOM), which marks the beginning of a long collaboration between Echelman and SOM. To make the anchor hardware visually seamless, the team embedded it into each of the concrete slabs as it was being poured.

—

Echelman begins an appointment as a visiting professor at the Massachusetts Institute of Technology (MIT) in the Department of Architecture. In January, she is invited to be an artist in residence at Philip Johnson's Glass House and simultaneously begins co-teaching an MIT studio called "Soft Structure Meets the Glass House" with Professor Caitlin Mueller and David Feldman. [**30**]

—

In April, *Target Swooping Austria* is on view during the Klanglicht light festival in Graz, Austria. It is a new installation utilizing the 1.6 million hand-knotted net component that first premiered in 2001 in Madrid, then traveled to Burgos, New York, Miami, and Rotterdam.

—

In May, Echelman is selected for the major art commission at the new St. Pete Pier in Florida. She begins collaboration with the Florida Fish and Wildlife Conservation Commission, whose shorebird biologists publicly support the sculpture's design, noting that its "movement, color, wide net mesh openings, and thick guide lines" suffice to minimize any risk of bird entanglement.

—

In September, Echelman prepares to install *Earthtime 1.8 Mexico City* in the Zócalo, the city's main square. The major earthquake on September 19 causes a relocation to the Centro Cultural del México Contemporáneo for Filux, an international festival of lights, which opens in November.

—

In December, two *Earthtime* works debut in China: *Earthtime 1.26 Shanghai* during the Lumières Shanghai festival, and *Earthtime 1.8 Beijing* at the Solana Light Festival.

2018

In February, *Earthtime 1.78 Madrid* is installed in the Plaza Mayor to commemorate its four hundredth anniversary. The colors of fire are integrated into the twines to recall fire in multiple centuries of the plaza's history, from public burnings during the Spanish Inquisition to the Spanish Civil War to its current transformation into a flame of learning and cultural openness.

—

In April, *Earthtime 1.78 Dubai* makes its debut, acting as a soft counterpoint to the Burj Khalifa, the world's tallest building, both engineered by SOM.

—

In August, Echelman creates her first energy-generating sculpture, incorporating photovoltaic tiles that power its illumination at night, as part of the workshop "Organic Solar Futures: Investigating Art + Energy Technologies" with landscape architect Trevor Lee at the Domaine de Boisbuchet, Lessac, France.

—

In September, Echelman's first water-based sculpture, *Pulse*, opens in downtown Philadelphia after seven years of collaboration with OLIN and Center City District. Using curtains of mist and colored light, this permanent installation traces active subway paths and trolley lines in real time as they converge beneath Dilworth Park.

—

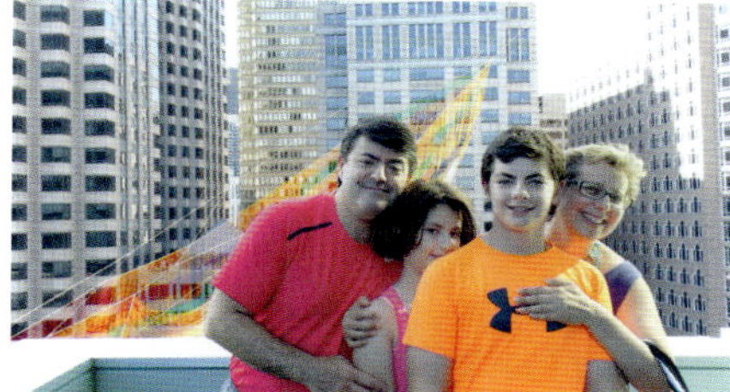

27

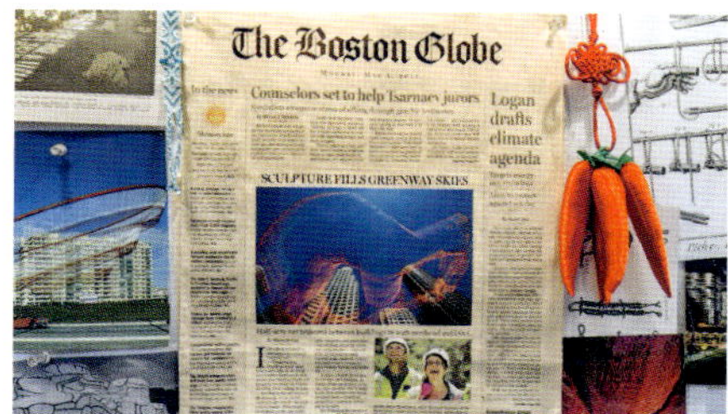

28

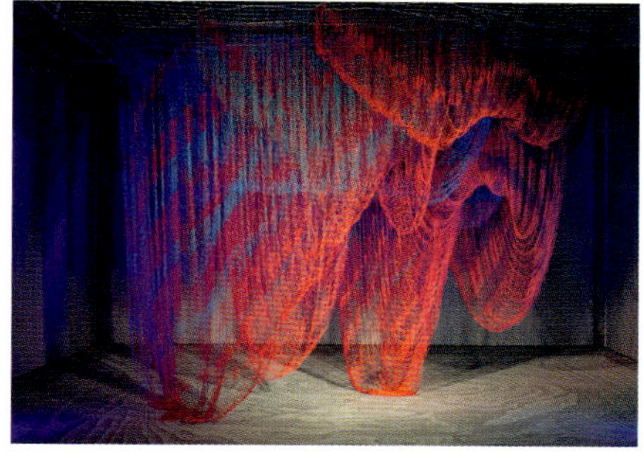

29

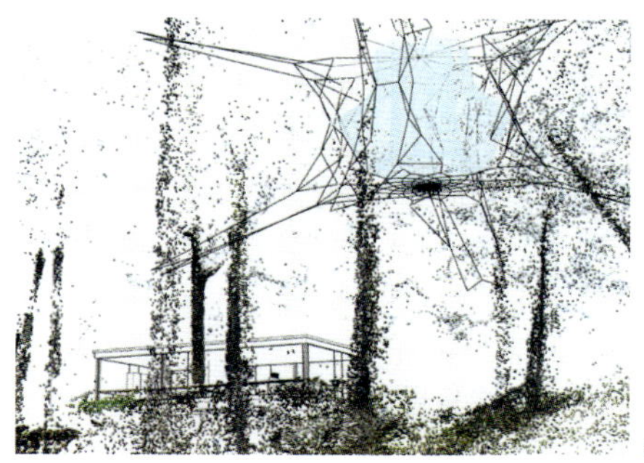

30

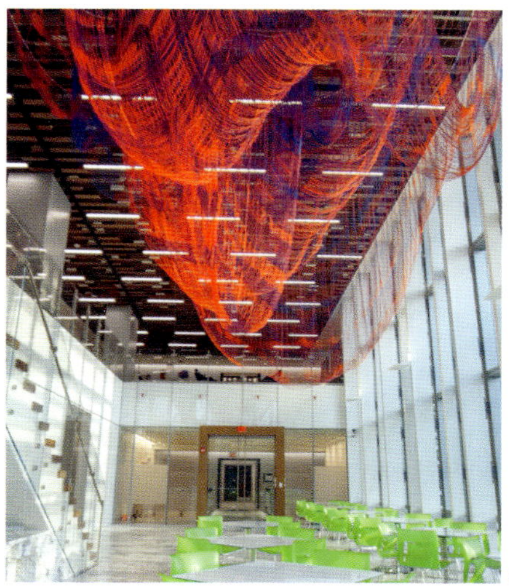

31

In November, Echelman's permanent commission for the US Embassy in Jakarta premieres. *Possible Futures of a Line, Traveling through Space and Time* is a permanent adaptation of Echelman's previous traveling work, which invites visitors into its soft folds and ethereal masses as it transforms with colored light. [**31**]

2019

Echelman begins a visiting lectureship at Princeton University's Lewis Center for the Arts.

—

In March, for Art Basel Hong Kong, curator Isolde Brielmaier teams up with curator and cultural consultant Bettina Prentice to launch the Peninsula Hotel's global art program, Art in Resonance, with Echelman's *Earthtime 1.26 Hong Kong*, spanning 160 feet and lacing directly into the Peninsula Hotel's historic architecture. The New York Peninsula Hotel joins in promoting the project. [**32**]

—

From April through June, Echelman and choreographer Rebecca Lazier join engineer Sigrid Adriaenssens's workshop with Tyler Sprague at the University of Washington, where they develop and present a public performance of professional dancers within net sculptures that span multiple floors of the interior courtyard of the Architecture building.

—

In May, Echelman is elected to serve on Harvard University's Board of Overseers. She is the first professional visual artist elected in the board's 377-year history.

—

In the summer, for the Green Box Arts Festival in Colorado, a lake is drained to install *Earthtime 1.8 Green Mountain Falls*, which features reflections below after the lake is refilled. *Earthtime 1.78 Beverly Hills* is installed over Santa Monica Boulevard.

—

The Smithsonian American Art Museum nominates Echelman to represent the United States in the national pavilion at the Venice Biennale, paired with a corollary work bridging the Grand Canal from the roof of the Peggy Guggenheim Collection building. She receives a support letter from Guggenheim Museums and Foundation director Richard Armstrong, but the Smithsonian's proposal is not selected. [**33**]

—

In September, Echelman and Feldman present their research at the SOM Forum in Chicago alongside international architecture and engineering luminaries. [**34**]

—

Echelman collaborates with Eindhoven University of Technology and SOM to propose an ice sculpture for the 2022 Winter Olympics in Beijing. Her vision involves using engineered molds, spraying structures with ice, and sculpting with snow. [**35**]

2020

In January, Echelman commutes weekly to Princeton to jointly teach the Princeton Atelier course "The Understor(e)y: Suspension, Movement, Space" with Lazier and Adriaenssens. The course is cut short by the start of COVID-19 epidemic in March.

—

In July, *Bending Arc*, Echelman's largest permanent sculpture to date—composed of three arc-like parasols laced together, 5,330 pounds of netting, 1,662,528 knots, and 180 miles of twine—is installed at the new St. Pete Pier in Florida. It was once the site of "swim-ins," where local Black citizens challenged racial barriers, ultimately leading to the 1957 US Supreme Court ruling that integrated all municipal beaches and pools across the nation. Its title references the words of civil rights activist Martin Luther King Jr.: "The arc of the moral universe is long, but it bends toward justice." [**36**]

—

In September, *Earthtime 1.26 Korea*, situated near Gwanggyo Lake Park, South Korea, becomes the first permanent iteration of Echelman's *Earthtime 1.26* series. It is juxtaposed with a twenty-three-foot figurative KAWS sculpture. [**37**]

2021

In Munich, a major transformation of the aerial and ground planes of the history-laden Odeonsplatz showcases *Earthtime 1.26 Munich*, complete with a green-roofed amphitheater underneath the sculpture for nightly live music performances.

—

In Finland, *Earthtime 1.78 Helsinki* premieres at Senate Square. At the unveiling, which coincides with the Helsinki Biennial and the Helsinki Festival, a performance of original music utilizing wind instruments and a Sámi vocalist takes place underneath the sculpture. For the remainder of the Helsinki Biennial, sound and light for the installation are generated based on live

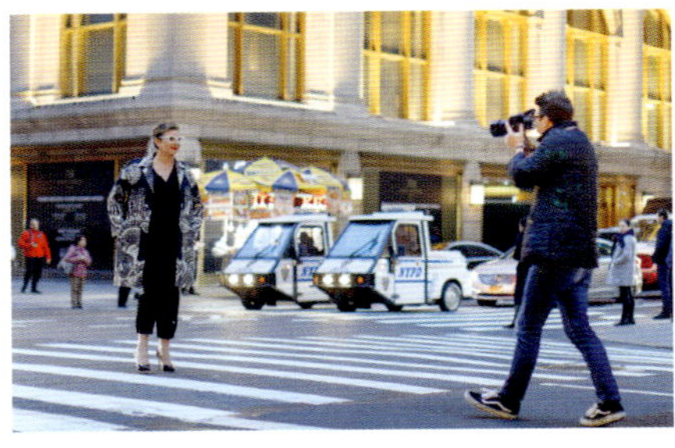

32

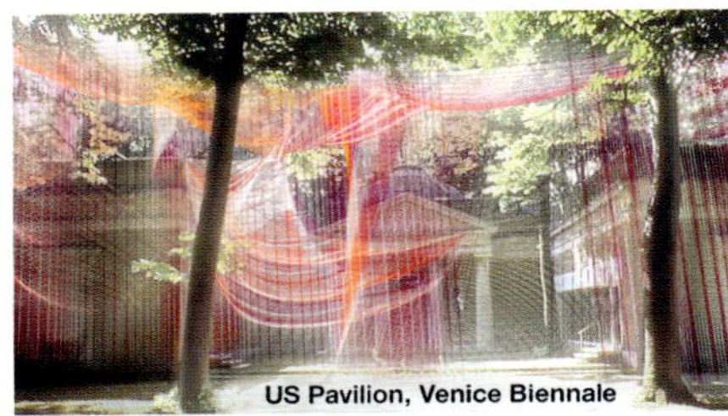

US Pavilion, Venice Biennale

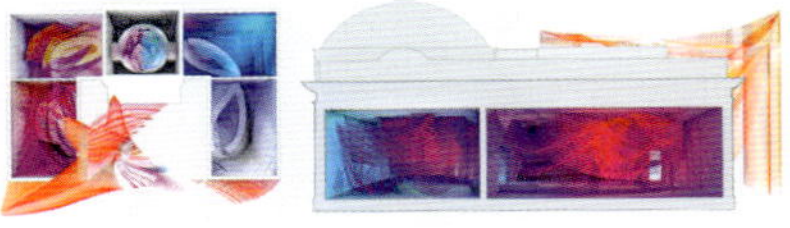

33

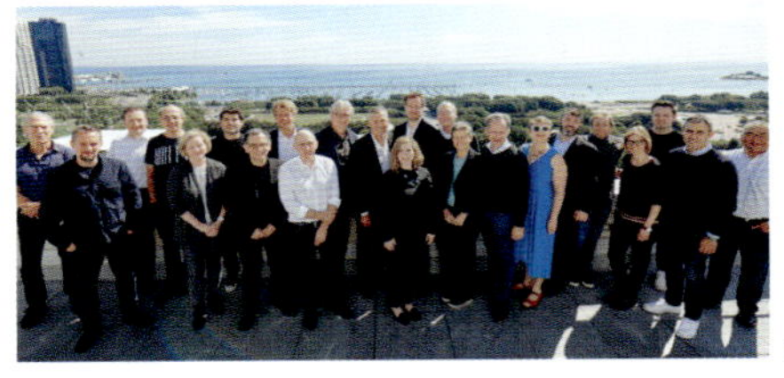

34

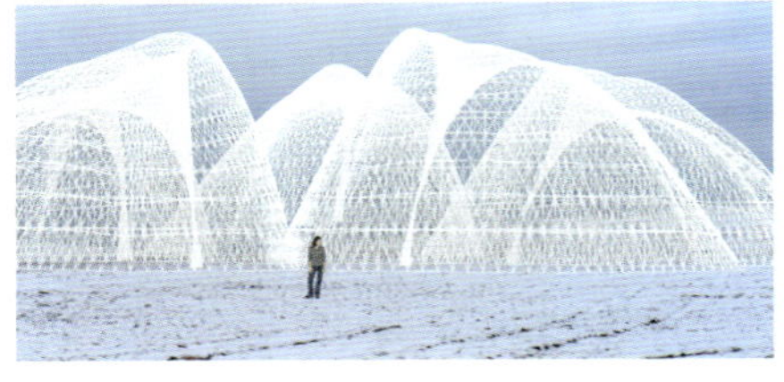

35

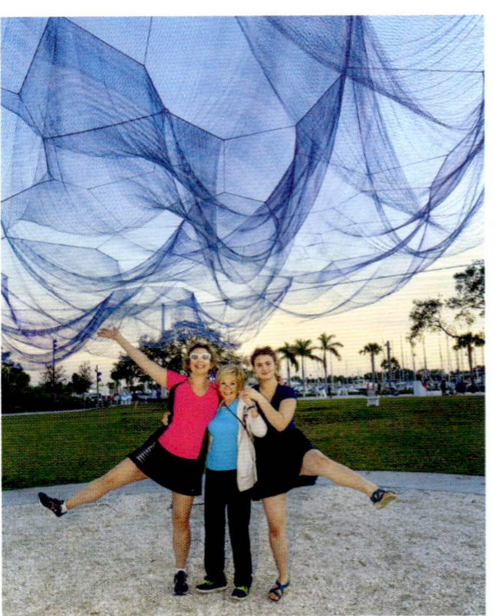

36

data feeds drawn from an underwater sound sensor in the adjacent Gulf of Finland and a wind sensor atop the structural tower.

—

Earthtime 1.78 Vienna premieres after four years of work devoted to sensitively connecting the piece with the historically protected MuseumsQuartier architecture: roof tiles are removed and simple ballast weights are placed on the historic floorboards without creating any permanent change. The Vienna Symphony performs a major concert underneath the sculpture.

—

US record producer and rapper Swizz Beatz presents *Earthtime 1.26 Jeddah* on the Jeddah Corniche to coincide with the inaugural Saudi Arabian Grand Prix.

—

Further iterations of *Earthtime* include *Earthtime 1.78 Borås*, Sweden, and *Earthtime 1.8 Perth*, Australia.

2022

Starting in February, Echelman's interior work *Study (Butterfly Rest Stop 1/9 Scale)* premieres in the group exhibition *CRAZY: Madness in Contemporary Art*, curated by Danilo Eccher, in the historic Chiostro del Bramante, Rome.

—

In June, Adrianenssens and Lazier invite Echelman, engineer Bill Baker, and mathematician Andy Sageman-Furnas to Princeton University for a dance-engineering research workshop involving Echelman's net sculptures. [**38**]

—

In September, *Earthtime 1.78 Milan* is presented in the city's Piazza Gae Aulenti and *Earthtime 1.26 Milan* is installed in Biblioteca degli Alberi park.

—

In October, Echelman installs her first architecturally integrated residential project, *Enfold*, a permanent commission for Hill House Montecito in California.

—

MIT's Center for Art, Science & Technology appoints Echelman as Mellon Distinguished Visiting Artist and Feldman as Distinguished Visiting Technologist for the coming academic year. Echelman begins collaborating with professor Caitlin Mueller and graduate student Adam Burke to create new computational software to design structural top-net layers in real time. [**39**]

2023

Studio Echelman develops inverse form-finding software tools that enable nets to be precisely shaped by varying the lengths of each mesh as they are loomed rather than through cutting with shears. This increases aesthetic control of the form while strengthening the structure and reducing waste.

—

In January, the Boston Society for Architecture awards Echelman the Harleston Parker Medal for *As If It Were Already Here* (2015), recognizing "the most beautiful piece of architecture, building, monument or structure" in the city. It is the first time in its 102-year history that the award has been given to an artist or to an ephemeral work. Previous winners include Le Corbusier, I. M. Pei, Frank Gehry, and Renzo Piano.

—

In April, Echelman premieres *Noli Timere, Sculpture #1*, over a reflection pond created for her installation in the Palazzo del Senato during Milan Design Week, the largest annual design event in the world. Presented by Studio Kohler, it is her first work exploring the topic of love. [**40**]

—

In June, *Current* premieres in downtown Columbus, Ohio. Stretching 229 feet across Gay and High Streets, the work incorporates 78 miles of twine woven with more than 500,000 knots. New fabrication techniques allow variable-mesh articulated shaping during looming to reduce seams and cuts. Donated by Jeffrey Edwards to the Columbus Museum of Art's permanent collection, the work represents the largest private contribution to public art in the city's history.

—

In July, Echelman is awarded the inaugural Isler Prize by the International Association for Shell and Spatial Structures, recognizing work that embodies exploration, realization, discovery, and innovation; playfulness and inclusivity; and sustainability and low environmental impact.

—

Also in July, Echelman is included in the list of "100 Most Influential Urbanists, Past and Present" published by Planetizen. The list also includes Jane Jacobs, W. E. B. Du Bois, Thomas Jefferson, Rosa Parks, Jimmy Carter, Frederick Law Olmsted, Buckminster Fuller, and Theaster Gates.

—

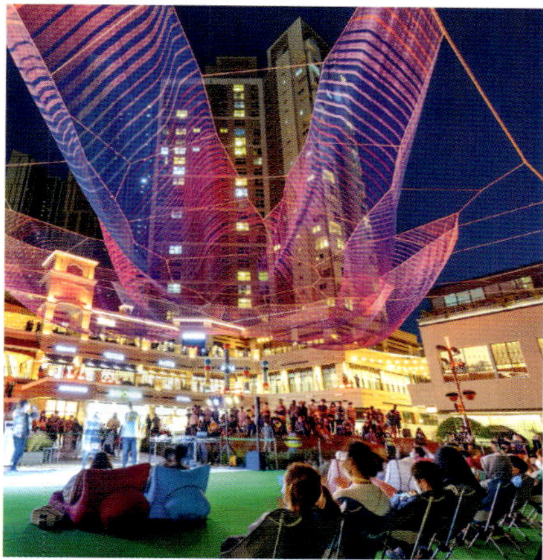

37

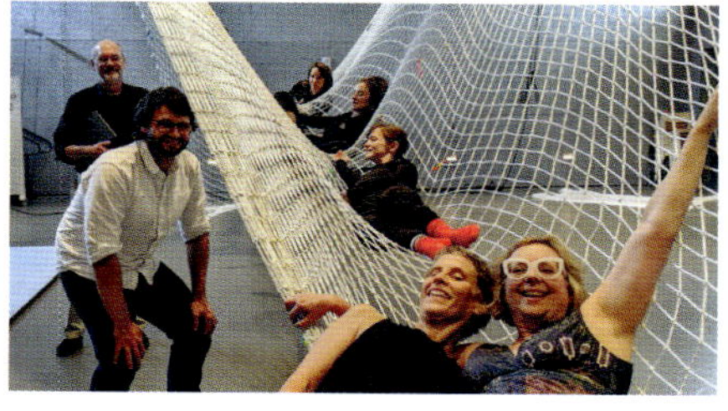

38

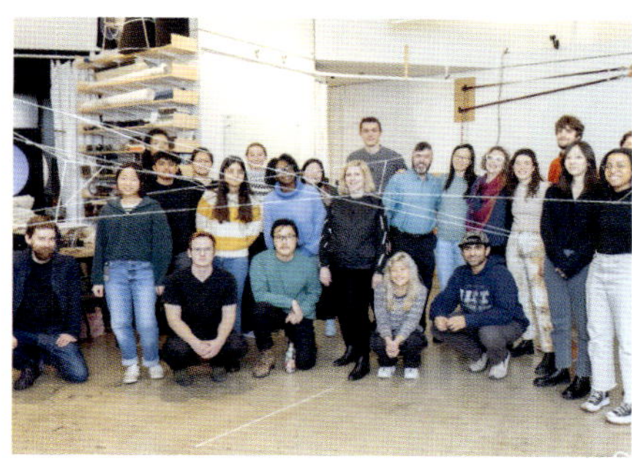

39

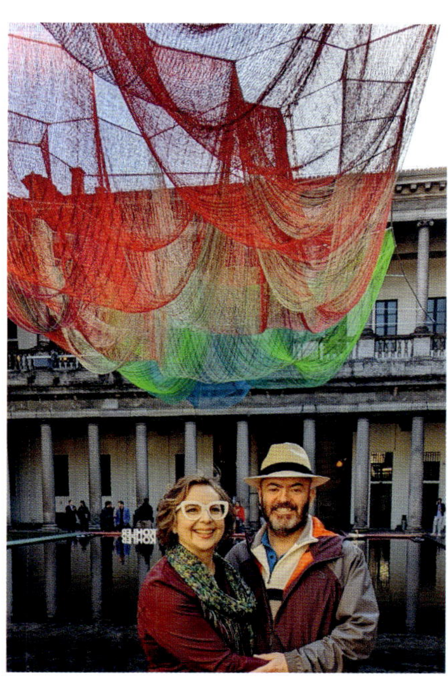

40

In August, *Noli Timere, Dance #1 (Everywhere the Edges)*, debuts in Montreal. A work in progress involving a voluminous net installation in combination with off-ground dance by six multinational performers, it synthesizes sculpture, dance, fiber art, avant-garde circus, music, engineering, and social practice while pushing boundaries of multidisciplinary artistic performance.

—

Echelman is reappointed Mellon Distinguished Visiting Artist at MIT for 2023–24 and is commissioned for a major installation at the MIT Museum in 2025.

—

In October, David Feldman, the studio's chief technologist who played a pioneering role in many of its advances in design engineering, software development, and computational tools, dies of glioblastoma.

—

In December, Echelman premieres *Earthtime 1.26 Wadi Namar* for the Noor Riyadh festival in Saudi Arabia, under the curatorial direction of Jérôme Sans and Pedro Alonzo.

2024

The Broad Institute of MIT and Harvard commissions Echelman to design her first permanent work spanning interior and exterior architectural spaces. Since 2014, Echelman and Feldman had met with Broad Institute researchers to develop ideas for the project. In the last years of Feldman's life, he participated in a Harvard clinical trial for personalized cancer vaccines, which utilized the Broad Institute for his genomic analysis. In the final design, Echelman weaves the patterns of her late husband's genomic sequence into the colors of each loomed panel. [**41**]

—

In June, *Noli Timere, Dance #2*, premieres at PS21 in Chatham, New York.

—

In October, Echelman unveils the 186-foot *Butterfly Rest Stop* to anchor the new Kaleidoscope Park in Frisco, Texas, along the monarch butterfly's migration path. Curated by Virginia Shore, Echelman's aerial sculpture is inspired by the form, pattern, and color of the native milkweed flowers that sustain the monarch throughout its migration. It is her first artwork utilizing plants as an art material: it contains 3,384 pollinator-sustaining plants in addition to 89 miles of twine. [**42, 43**]

2025

In February, *Noli Timere, Dance #3*, premieres at the McCarter Theater at Princeton University. A five-year collaboration between Lazier and Echelman, the aerial performance features eight multidisciplinary performers dancing up to twenty-five feet in the air within a voluminous, custom-designed net sculpture, and an original score by Jorane. It explores the delicate interconnectedness and fragility of our world, offering a profound commentary on navigating our unstable ecosystem through art and advanced engineering.

—

In July, Echelman travels to Lake Como, Italy, for the Bellagio Center Residency Program of the Rockefeller Foundation, then continues to England to design work for the London Transport Museum.

—

Echelman develops prototypes and prepares for the September premiere of a sculpture installation and related exhibition at the new MIT Museum. Filling the multi-story entry and visible through its glass curtain walls to the public at the busy Kendall Square subway stop, the installation engages with the history of the Earth's climate from the last ice age to the present and then envisions multiple futures. The exhibition includes video of Echelman's dance collaborations and an interactive component showcasing original computational design tools developed at MIT that enabled the innovations of the work. [**44**]

—

In November, Sarasota Art Museum in Florida premieres the traveling exhibition *Radical Softness*, the first mid-career retrospective to include Echelman's paintings and sculpture.

2026

Echelman finalizes design for *Intracoastal*, a permanent sculpture to suspend between four buildings in Delray Beach near the Intracoastal Waterway, which flows from Florida to Massachusetts. [**45**]

compiled by Amy Damutz

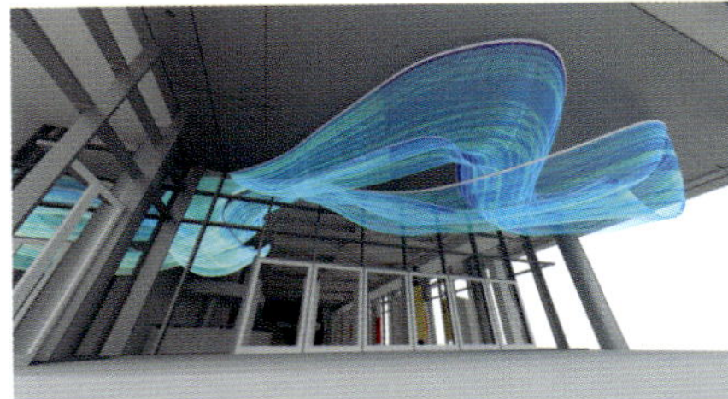

41

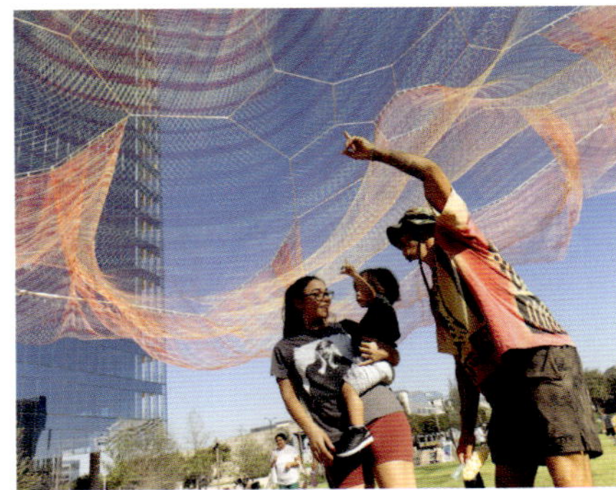

42

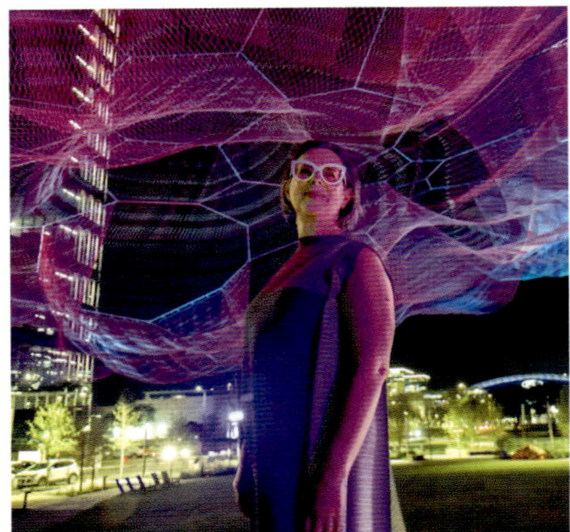

43

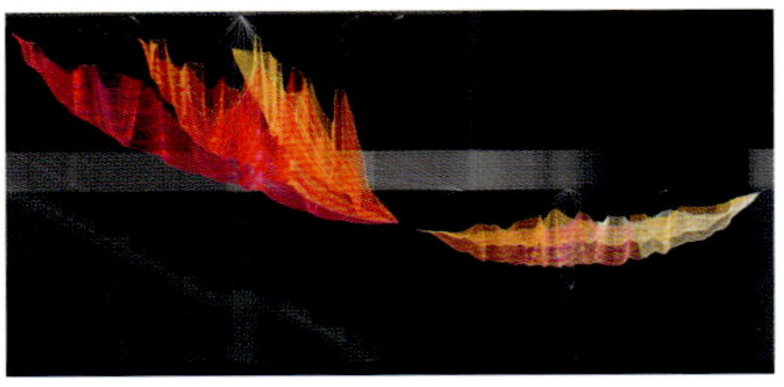

44

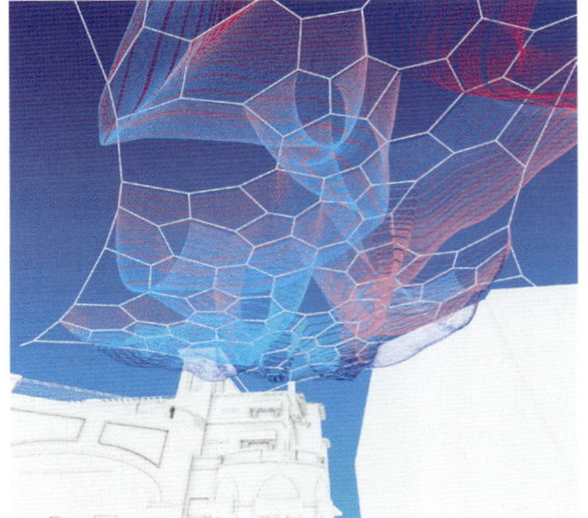

45

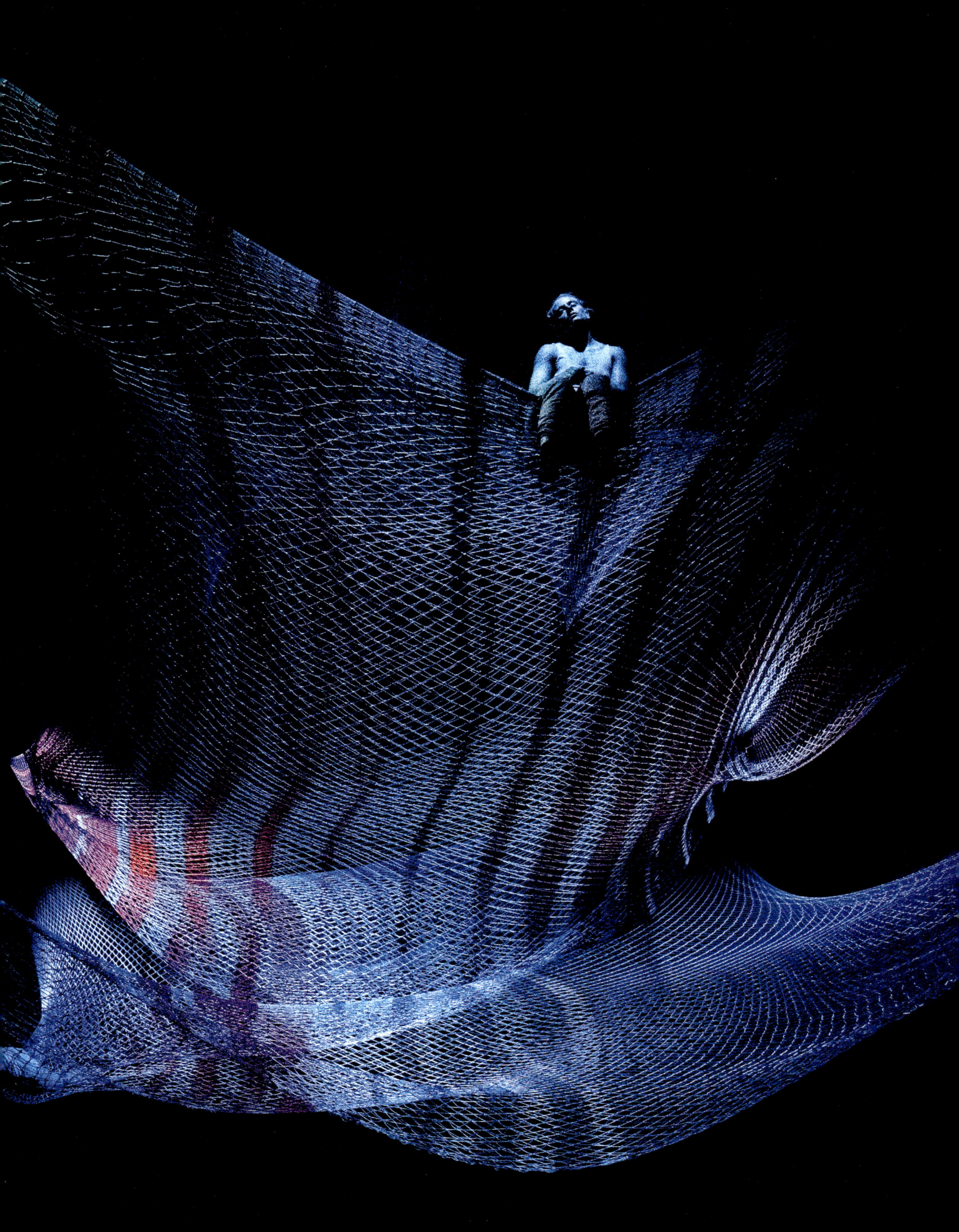

Chronological Sculpture Index

—

Dimensions: overall length × width × height above ground

Earthtime 1.26 Denver, 2010
Denver Art Museum, CO; Spectra fiber, knotted and braided high-tenacity polyester, LED lighting, roadway, and sky; 130 × 140 × 135 ft.
Pages 23, 101, 214, 271

Earthtime 1.26 Sydney, 2011
Sydney Town Hall over George Street, Australia; Spectra fiber, knotted and braided high-tenacity polyester, programmed LED lighting, DMX controller, and sky; 170 × 140 × 60 ft.
Pages 104, 205

Every Beating Second, 2011
Terminal 2, San Francisco International Airport, CA; powder-coated steel, fiber, skylights, terrazzo floor, programmed airflow, and LED lighting; net 1: 33 × 39 × 19 ft.; net 2: 30 × 35 × 22 ft.; net 3: 18 × 18 × 19 ft.; overall: 177 × 39 × 22 ft.
Page 15

Earthtime 1.26 Amsterdam, 2012
Suspended over the Amstel river and attached to City Hall and the Muziektheater, Netherlands; Spectra fiber, knotted and braided high-tenacity polyester, programmed LED lighting, DMX controller, and sky; 230 × 140 × 30 ft.
Pages 105, 272

The Space Between Us, 2013
Santa Monica State Beach, CA; sculpted sand, spliced and braided high-tenacity polyester, knotted and twisted high-tenacity nylon, steel trusses, programmed LED lighting and sound, DMX controller, and sky; 220 × 170 × 60 ft.
Pages 170–71, 172, 173

Allegory, 2014
Matthew Knight Arena, University of Oregon, Eugene; braided polyester with hand-knotted lace patterning, metal halide lighting, and motion sensors; 82 × 34 × 30 ft.
Page 178

A. Memory, 2014
Collaboration with the Stuttgart Ballet, Germany; knotted and braided high-tenacity polyester and lighting attached to ballet dancers' bodies; variable dimensions
Pages 209, 228, 229

Earthtime 1.26 Singapore, 2014
The Float at Marina Bay, Singapore; Spectra fiber, knotted and braided high-tenacity polyester, programmed LED lighting, DMX controller, artificial turf, and sky; 285 × 200 × 80 ft.
Page 98

Skies Painted with Unnumbered Sparks, 2014
Waterfront of Vancouver, Canada; hand-spliced braided Spectra fiber, knotted and twisted high-tenacity nylon, braided high-tenacity polyester, mobile phone interface, Wi-Fi, interactive computer programming, projectors, LED lighting, DMX controller, and sky; 745 × 475 × 175 ft.
Pages 61, 176, 215, 256–57, 260, 261, 262, 263, 264, 265

As If It Were Already Here, 2015
Rose Kennedy Greenway, Boston, MA; spliced braided UHMWPE (ultra-high-molecular-weight polyethylene), braided high-tenacity polyester, programmed LED lighting, DMX controller, architecture, and sky; 600 × 360 × 300 ft.
Pages 17, 20, 187, 188, 189, 190–91, 192, 193, 194–95, 197, 273

Earthtime 1.26 Durham, 2015
Suspended above the River Wear, Durham, UK; Spectra fiber, knotted and braided high-tenacity polyester, programmed LED lighting, DMX controller, and sky; 240 × 90 × 46 ft.
Page 98

Earthtime 1.26 Prague, 2015
Jan Palach Square at Rudolfinum, Czech Republic; Spectra fiber, knotted and braided high-tenacity polyester, programmed LED lighting, DMX controller, and sky; 250 × 150 × 50 ft.
Page 103

Earthtime 1.8 Renwick, 2015
Renwick Gallery, Smithsonian American Art Museum, Washington, DC; hand-spliced UHMWPE, knotted and braided high-tenacity polyester, programmed LED lighting, DMX controller, injection-dyed carpet made from recycled netting, and sewn textile filled with closed-cell beads on floor; 100 × 40 × 40 ft.
Pages 19, 114, 115, 116, 117, 118–19, 120, 121, 122–23, 176, 246–47

Impatient Optimist, 2015
Bill & Melinda Gates Foundation, Seattle, WA; hand-spliced UHMWPE, knotted and braided PTFE, high-tenacity nylon, high-tenacity polyester, programmed LED lighting, DMX controller, architecture, and sky; 300 × 175 × 55 ft.
Pages 152, 153, 154, 155, 156, 157, 158, 159, 160, 161, 245

Earthtime 1.26 Montreal, 2015–17
Quartier des Spectacles, Montreal, Canada; Spectra fiber, knotted and braided high-tenacity polyester, programmed LED lighting, DMX controller, and sky; 417 × 165 × 110 ft.
Page 99

Earthtime 1.26 Chile, 2016
Museo Nacional de Bellas Artes, Santiago, Chile; Spectra fiber, knotted and braided high-tenacity polyester, programmed LED lighting, DMX controller, and sky; 235 × 167 ft. × variable height
Page 102

Earthtime 1.8 London, 2016
Oxford Circus, UK; hand-spliced UHMWPE, knotted and braided high-tenacity nylon, steel trusses, Wi-Fi and interactive computer programming, mobile phone interface, projectors, LED lighting, DMX controller, and sky; 180 × 180 × 70 ft.
Pages 19, 92–93, 124, 125, 126–27, 128–29, 130, 132, 133, 134–35

Earthtime 1.8 San Diego, 2016
Embarcadero Marina Park South, CA; hand-spliced UHMWPE, knotted and braided high-tenacity nylon, steel trusses, concrete ballast, programmed LED lights, and sky; 185 × 185 × 50 ft.
Page 137

Possible Futures of a Line, Traveling Through Space and Time, 2016
Church of San Francesco, Como, Italy; knotted and braided polyester, injection-dyed carpet made from recycled netting, and programmed LED lighting; 18 × 18 × 16 ft.

Where We Met, 2016
LeBauer Park, Greensboro, NC; hand-spliced braided UHMWPE, knotted and braided high-tenacity nylon and polyester, steel pylons embedded with winch system, fixed LED lighting, and sky; 200 × 130 × 58 ft.
Pages 25, 26–27

Dream Catcher, 2017
Sunset Boulevard at La Cienega Boulevard, West Hollywood, CA; hand-spliced and braided UHMWPE, PTFE, programmed LED lighting, DMX controller, steel hardware embedded in concrete floor slabs, and sky; 47 × 110 × 110 ft.
Pages 200–1, 204, 207, 220, 221, 222, 223, 224, 225

Earthtime 1.26 Shanghai, 2017
The Hub, Hongqiao district, Shanghai, China; Spectra fiber, knotted and braided high-tenacity polyester, programmed LED lighting, DMX controller, and sky; 221 × 162 × 59 ft.
Page 103

Earthtime 1.8 Beijing, 2017
Solana Light Festival, Beijing, China; hand-spliced UHMWPE, knotted and braided high-tenacity nylon, steel trusses, programmed LED lighting, DMX controller, and sky; 150 × 131 × 55 ft.
Page 138

Earthtime 1.8 Mexico City, 2017
Centro Cultural del México Contemporáneo, Mexico; hand-spliced UHMWPE, knotted and braided high-tenacity nylon, steel trusses, programmed LED lighting, DMX controller, and sky; 100 × 45 × 36 ft.
Page 138

Possible Futures of a Line, Traveling through Space and Time, 2017
Cheongju Craft Biennale, South Korea; knotted and braided polyester, injection-dyed carpet made from recycled netting, and programmed LED lighting; variable dimensions
Page 273

Target Swooping Austria, 2017
Freiheitsplatz, Graz, Austria; hand-knotted and braided high-tenacity nylon, steel trusses, crane, programmed LED lighting, and DMX controller; 140 × 130 × 213 ft.

Earthtime 1.78 Dubai, 2018
Dubai Fountain, UAE; hand-spliced UHMWPE, knotted and braided high-tenacity nylon, steel trusses, programmed LED lighting, DMX controller, water, and sky; 145 × 115 ft. × variable height
Page 148

Earthtime 1.78 Madrid, 2018
Plaza Mayor, Spain; hand-spliced UHMWPE, knotted and braided high-tenacity nylon, steel trusses, programmed LED lighting, DMX controller, historic architecture, and sky; 145 × 115 ft. × variable height
Pages 140, 141, 142, 143

Possible Futures of a Line, Traveling through Space and Time, 2018
US Embassy, Jakarta, Indonesia; knotted and braided polyester and steel armature; variable dimensions
Page 273

Pulse, 2018
Dilworth Plaza, Philadelphia; atomized water particles, air handlers, bronze grating, programmed LED lighting, DMX controller, and sensors; 60 × 230 × 5 ft.
Pages 162–63, 164, 166, 167, 168

Earthtime 1.26 Hong Kong, 2019
Peninsula Hotel, Hong Kong, China; hand-spliced UHMWPE, knotted and braided high-tenacity nylon, steel trusses, programmed LED lighting, DMX controller, and historic architecture; 157 × 109 × 130 ft.
Pages 94, 95, 96, 97

Earthtime 1.78 Beverly Hills, 2019
Suspended over Santa Monica Boulevard, Beverly Hills, CA; hand-spliced UHMWPE, knotted and braided high-tenacity nylon, steel trusses, programmed LED lighting, DMX controller, roadway, and sky; 145 × 115 ft. × variable height
Pages 4–5, 149

Earthtime 1.8 Green Mountain Falls, 2019
Gazebo Lake, Green Mountain Falls, CO; hand-spliced UHMWPE, knotted and braided high-tenacity nylon, steel, programmed LED lighting, DMX controller, water , and sky; 145 × 115 ft. × variable height
Page 136

Bending Arc, 2020
St. Pete Pier, St. Petersburg, FL; hand-spliced braided UHMWPE, knotted and braided PTFE, steel masts, concrete foundations, programmed LED lighting, DMX controller, and sky; 424 × 374 × 72 ft.
Pages 2–3, 12–13, 16, 182, 183, 184, 185, 274

Earthtime Korea, 2020
Alleyway Gwanggyo, South Korea; hand-spliced braided UHMWPE, knotted and braided PTFE, steel, programmed LED lighting, DMX controller, architecture, and sky; 172 × 159 × 48 ft.
Pages 100, 275

Without Beginning Middle or End, 2020
Private collection, Karuna Sindhu, Mumbai, India; hand-spliced UHMWPE, knotted and braided high-tenacity nylon, carbon fiber armature, programmed LED lighting, DMX controller, and architecture; 50 × 43 × 14 ft.
Pages 30–31, 43, 44, 45, 46, 47, 48, 49, 50–51

Earthtime 1.26 Jeddah, 2021
Jeddah Corniche, Saudi Arabia; hand-spliced knotted UHMWPE, knotted and braided high-tenacity nylon and polyester, steel masts, concrete foundations, programmed LED lighting, DMX controller, and sky; 117 × 102 × 50 ft.
Page 10

Earthtime 1.26 Munich, 2021
Odeonsplatz, Germany; hand-spliced knotted UHMWPE, knotted and braided high-tenacity nylon, steel trusses and ballast, programmed LED lighting, and DMX controller, above temporary green-roofed amphitheater; 113 × 68 × 52 ft.
Pages 106, 107, 108–9, 110, 111, 112, 113

Earthtime 1.78 Borås, 2021
Stora Torget Plaza, Sweden; hand-spliced braided UHMWPE, knotted and braided high-tenacity nylon, steel trusses, programmed LED lighting, DMX controller, historic architecture, and sky; 145 × 115 ft. × variable height
Pages 150, 151

Earthtime 1.78 Helsinki, 2021
Senate Square, Finland; hand-spliced braided UHMWPE, knotted and braided high-tenacity nylon, steel trusses, wind sensor, underwater microphones, speakers, responsive LED lighting, DMX controller, and sky; 209 × 180 × 55 ft.
Pages 249, 250, 252, 254, 255

Earthtime 1.78 Vienna, 2021
MuseumsQuartier, Vienna; hand-spliced braided UHMWPE, knotted and braided high-tenacity nylon, cables piercing terracotta roof tiles in historic architecture with temporary ballast, steel truss, programmed LED lighting, DMX controller, and sky; 220 × 330 × 60 ft.
Pages 144, 145, 146, 147

Earthtime 1.8 Perth, 2021
Supreme Court Gardens, Australia; hand-spliced braided UHMWPE, knotted and braided high-tenacity nylon, programmed LED lighting, DMX controller, steel trusses, park, and sky; 248 × 172 × 49 ft.
Page 139

Earthtime 1.26 Milan, 2022
Biblioteca degli Alberi park, Milan; hand-spliced UHMWPE, knotted and braided high-tenacity nylon and polyester, programmed LED lighting, DMX controller, park, and sky; 142 × 90 × 39 ft.
Page 100

Earthtime 1.78 Milan, 2022
Piazza Gae Aulenti, Milan; hand-spliced UHMWPE, knotted and braided high-tenacity nylon and polyester, programmed LED lighting, DMX controller, architecture, reflection pool, and sky; 145 × 115 × 37 ft.
Page 149

Enfold, 2022
Private collection, Hill House Montecito, CA; knotted and braided high-tenacity nylon, welded stainless steel armature, shaped architectural acoustic panel, programmed LED lighting, and DMX controller; 53 × 41 × 17 ft.
Pages 72, 73, 74, 75, 76, 77, 78–79, back cover

Study (Butterfly Rest Stop 1/9 scale), 2022
Chiostro del Bramante, Rome, Italy; hand-spliced braided UHMWPE, knotted and braided high-tenacity nylon, programmed LED lighting, DMX controller, and historic architecture; 24 × 13 × 13 ft.
Page 54

Current, 2023
Gay Street and High Street, Columbus, OH; hand-spliced UHMWPE, knotted and braided high-tenacity nylon and polyester, programmed LED lighting, DMX controller, historic architecture, roadway, and sky; 229 × 88 × 147 ft.
Front cover, pages 80, 81, 82, 83, 84, 85, 86, 87, 88–89, 216, 217

Earthtime 1.26 Wadi Namar, 2023
Riyadh, Saudi Arabia; hand-spliced UHMWPE, knotted and braided high-tenacity nylon and polyester, programmed LED lighting, DMX controller, steel trusses, Arabic *majlis* sofas, desert wadi, and sky; 88 × 42 × 29 ft.
Page 91

Noli Timere, Dance #1 (Everywhere the Edges), 2023
Montreal, Canada; knotted and braided high-tenacity nylon and polyester, programmed LED lighting and sound, with eight dancers; 35 × 35 × minimum height 24 ft.
Pages 226–27, 234, 235, 277

Noli Timere, Sculpture #1, 2023
Palazzo del Senato, Milan, Italy; hand-spliced UHMWPE, knotted and braided high-tenacity nylon and polyester, programmed LED lighting, DMX controller, historic architecture, custom-built reflection pool; 88 × 42 × 29 ft.
Pages 6, 238–43, 272, 275, 286

Butterfly Rest Stop, 2024
Kaleidoscope Park, Frisco, TX; hand-spliced UHMWPE, knotted and braided high-tenacity nylon and polyester, steel masts, six 40-cubic-foot concrete foundations, programmed LED lighting, DMX controller, 3,384 pollinator-supporting plants, and sky; 190 × 126 × 66 ft.
Pages 18, 29, 53, 55, 56, 57, 58–59, 218, 219, 276

Noli Timere, Dance #2, 2024
PS21, Chatham, NY; knotted and braided high-tenacity nylon and polyester, programmed LED lighting, and live original music with eight dancers; 35 × 35 × minimum height 24 ft.
Pages 231, 236

MIT Museum Installation, 2025
Cambridge, MA; hand-spliced knotted and braided high-tenacity polyester, programmed LED lighting, DMX controller, dancers, and video; 67 × 24 × variable height up to 35 ft.
Pages 198–99, 210, 276

Noli Timere, Dance #3, 2025
McCarter Theatre, Princeton, NJ; braided fiber, programmed LED lighting, and live original music with eight dancers; 30 × 40 × minimum height 24 ft.
Pages 233, 237

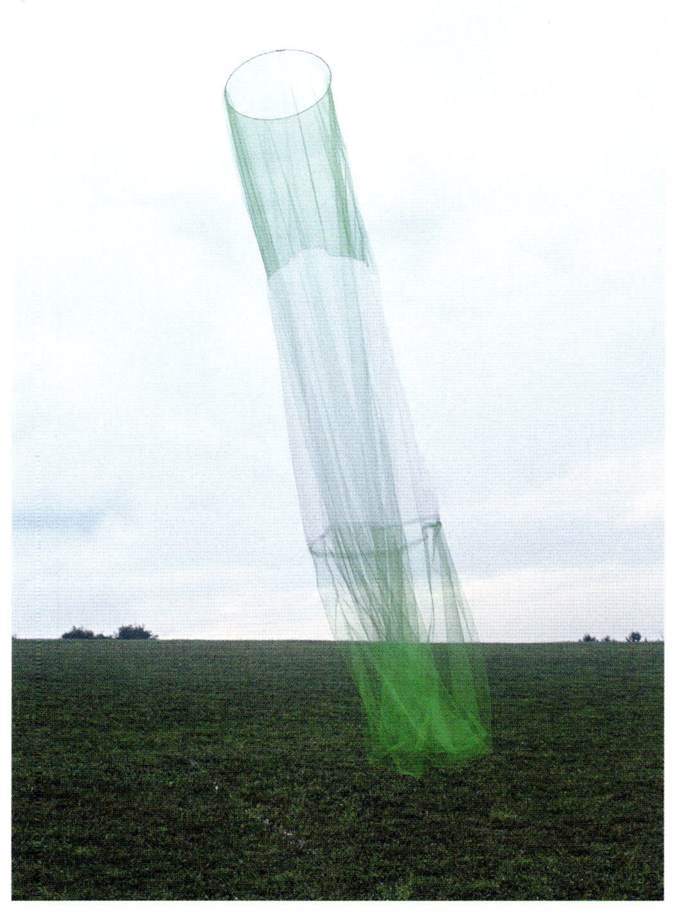

Green Torus with Modesty Panel, Art Omi, Ghent, New York

Artist's Acknowledgments

—

Like the sculptures found in these pages, I find myself enmeshed in a web of creative collaborators. I owe everything to them. Removing even a single knot or length of fiber would irreparably change me, the artwork, and this book. We have all shown up to work together with curiosity and vulnerability. My collaborators are part of an intricately interwoven fabric: Their openness emerges in the capacious pages and spaces we've created, and their generosity ripples through the soft folds of the printed and knotted surfaces. Creating this book and each of the works within it has felt like an act of love.

I want to express my deepest appreciation:

To the brilliant contemporary art historian Gloria Sutton, who brought immeasurable expertise, creative thinking, and energy to this book project, transforming and expanding it to include voices from multiple disciplines and cultural contexts, and to each of the thirty contributing authors for their inspiring ideas and hard work on the texts that compose this book: Swizz, Michelle, Nancy, Danilo, Jenni, Ann, Jérôme, Isolde, Amy, Nora, Gus, Melinda, Laurie, Jared, Andrew, Kathleen, Andrew, Sarah, Robert, Sigrid, John, Caitlin, Adam, Andy, Bill, Katy, Brian, Taru, and Kristiina. At Princeton Architectural Press, the visionary editor Jennifer Thompson first imagined how my artwork could be translated into book form five years ago and stalwartly led to its realization with the tireless efforts of managing editor Sara Stemen and design director Paul Wagner.

To each member of my Echelman and Feldman family, but most especially to my children, Sam and Lilly, who ground me and at the same time keep me on my toes, and to their dad, my beloved late husband David Feldman, an unabashedly curious polymath who approached the last twenty-five years of art-making hurdles as opportunities for discovery, transforming everything shared in this book into an insanely fun adventure. Long ago, David articulated his professional goal: He said that he wanted to be successful enough to retire early and to travel the world as a "sculptor's assistant," and just last year in the hospital, he said, "I understand it now. My project is loving you." He achieved all his goals in too short a time, and his imprint is forever part of every artwork I make.

To the pivotal role of my late mother. After college, when I wrote to each of my parents declaring my dream to become an artist, my father asked if any of my professors had said I had talent and should pursue this. My answer was no on all counts. My mom's response was no Pollyanna cliché that I could become anything I dreamed. Instead, she wrote that to be an artist was a "worthy goal," that I would have to work very hard, recommending I "go make ninety-nine paintings." Looking back, I now recognize this implied that the first ninety-eight works could be bad, thus giving me the precious gift of permission to experiment and fail maddeningly with a long runway. When I shook the envelope, a check for $199 with memo "Buy plenty of paint" tumbled out. That practical help was the seed money for my first exhibition, which led to an entire career.

To my friends, who during this book's creation held my hand and held me accountable, without whom I could not have gone through a pandemic and the terminal illness of a spouse to reach this day, with special thanks to Tina and Jennifer, who organized meal trains, and all those who dropped meals on my porch; to Shellee, Meredith, Sonal, Barbara, Kamal, Wendi, Laura, Mike, David, Dennis, Damian, Paul, Konstantine, Tom, Janet, Philip, Marsha, Lisa, Adam, Don, Lucy, Gordon, Megan, Diane, Beth, Ellen, Kim, Pam, Ruth, Rob, Deborah, Jessica, Katie, Emily, Liane, Anita, Jennie, Sarah, Betsy, Tina, Maria, Amy, Mary, Rebecca, Margaret, Vivian, Sylvia, Sally, Linda, Elizabeth, Larry, Andrea, Susan, Maryanne, Cheryl, Maryana, Phyllis, Kate, Bryan, Deven, Tonya, Keith, Ben, and all my sisters and brothers of the Henry Crown Fellowship, the Council on an Uncertain Future, IHP, Book Group, Breakfast Group, Rav Claudia and TBZ Brookline, the Public Art Network Council, and my compatriots from the Harvard Board of Overseers.

One cannot make good art without great clients, supporters, and mentors who lead the way, so I want to express my gratitude to the following:

To visionary individuals like Melinda French Gates, Lynda Weinman and Bruce Heavin, Dr. Swati and Ajay Piramal, Margot and Tom Pritzker, Craig Hall, Jeff Edwards, Adele Armfield, Susan Smith and Debra Smith Knez, Carolyn and Peter Lynch, Dr. Todd Golub, Rajshree Pathy, Carl Bass, Jeff Kowalski, Rick Rundell, Juan Enriquez, and Chris Anderson.

To private-sector leaders including the inspired teams from the TED conference, Autodesk, Google, the Hall Group, Edwards Companies, Kohler Co., Alleyway South Korea, CIM and 1 Hotel West Hollywood, Emaar Properties, Autodesk, Honeywell, Mercedes-Benz, and the Peninsula Hotels teams.

To nonprofit leadership from the Smithsonian American Art Museum, the Bill & Melinda Gates Foundation team, the MIT Museum and the Center for Art, Science & Technology, the Harvard Art Museums and the Office for the Arts, the Museum of Arts and Design New York, the Broad Institute team, the Community Foundation of Greater Greensboro, the Armfield Foundation team, the Smith Family Foundation, the Lynch Foundation, the SOM Foundation, the Philadelphia Center City District, Helen Marriage and the Artichoke London team, the Boston Rose Kennedy Greenway Conservancy, the National Endowment for the Arts, the Knight Foundation, the Mellon Foundation, the William Penn Foundation, the Pollock-Krasner Foundation, ArtPlace America, the Bogliasco Foundation, Art Omi, the Japan Foundation, the Fulbright Foreign Scholarship Board, the Rotary Foundation, United States Artists, and the John Simon Guggenheim Memorial Foundation.

To government leadership and arts councils in the cities who commissioned permanent sculptures, including Frisco, Texas; Columbus, Ohio; St. Petersburg, Florida; Philadelphia and Center City District, Pennsylvania; West Hollywood, California; Eugene and the University of Oregon; San Francisco, California; Vancouver and Richmond, Canada, and the Vancouver Winter Olympics; Phoenix, Arizona; and Matosinhos and Porto, Portugal.

To all the curators and teams who hosted exhibitions and temporary installations, from Milan, Italy; Vienna, Austria; Helsinki, Finland; Borås, Sweden; Jeddah and Riyadh, Saudi Arabia; Perth, Australia; Geneva, Switzerland; Munich, Germany; Santa Monica, Beverly Hills, and San Diego, California; Green Mountain Falls, Colorado; Xian, China; Madrid, Spain; Dubai, United Arab Emirates; Hong Kong, China; Beijing, China; Mexico City, Mexico; Shanghai, China; Cheongju, South Korea; London, England; Santiago, Chile; Durham, England; Prague, Czech Republic; Como, Italy; Montreal, Canada; Vancouver, Canada; Boston, Massachusetts; Stuttgart, Germany; Singapore, Amsterdam, Netherlands; Sydney, Australia; and Denver, Colorado, with special thanks to Marc Pally, Penny Bach, Richard Andrews, Virginia Shore, Meagan Atiyeh, Cheryl Stewart, Umbereen Inayet, Pedro Alonzo, Bettina Prentice, Isolde Brielmeier, and Nicholas Bell.

To my teachers, on whose shoulders I stand, from mentor and curator of my first exhibition, Robert Rauschenberg, to my first New York City gallerist, Florence Lynch; to my music teachers, who taught me how to take things apart in order to put them back together; to artists Jim Rosenquist, for my first big roll of canvas, Mia Westerlund Roosen, for introducing me to the secret that painters could become sculptors, Carole Bolsey, Ross McElwee, Robb Moss and all my teachers and peers in college and grad school, the Loeb Fellowship, the Aspen Institute, the Bellagio Center, and the American Academy in Rome; to the skilled artisans who patiently tutored me from the National Institute of Design in India to the lace workshops in Lithuania and the industrial twine-braiding and net-looming factories in Puget Sound; and, more recently, to the pivotal colleagues who have been teaching me through our collaboration: to choreographers Rebecca Lazier and Katarzyna Kozielska and their dancers; to the extraordinary fiber craftsmen John Neal, Steve Gregory, Chris Dunn, Cheryl Luna, Les Powers, Robin Ritz, Dylan Nunn, and the late Jack Pace; to the brilliant attorneys Jeff Becker, Catherine Redmond, Julie Taylor, and Jay Wickersham, insurance agent Chris Poole, and accountant Bill Moore; to my dazzling collaborators in engineering, architecture, illumination, and landscape architecture, including Clayton Binkley, Caitlin Mueller, Bill Baker, Alessandro Beghini, Nicole Wang, Sigrid Adriaenssens, Patrick McCafferty, Brian Stacy, Robin Donaldson, Ibone Santiago, Aaron Koblin, Elia Kirby, Nate Sills, Tom McClain, Susan Weiler, Richard Roark, Laurie Olin, Chip Trageser, Jim Burnett, Peter Heppel, Jeanne Gang, Mark Schendel, Aine Brazil, Joost Bakker, Christopher Phillips, James Brown, and Walter Berry; to computer scientists and mathematicians Andy Sageman-Furnas, David Harmon, Akash Garg, and Peter Boyer; and to my current colleagues at Studio Echelman, Daniel Alexander Smith, Adam Burke, Keith Hartwig, Danielle Efrat, Eleanor Reyelt, and the indomitable Melissa Henry, who for fifteen years has expertly managed all of us (and this book) with her deep intellect and kindness. And I can never forget those who managed and contributed significantly to the studio in our early years, including Melanie Peterson, Becky Borlan, Rachel Newson, Drew Raines, Daniel Zeese, Jamie Li, Cameron Chateauneuf, Mieke Prins, Lucca Townsend, Yan Yan Mao, Mark Drummond Davis, and Philip Speranza.

To every single person who has contributed to my artworks. You know who you are, and you can find your name acknowledged at echelman.com.

And finally, to you, dear readers, and to each person who goes underneath the sculptures to experience them first-hand: You create your own narratives, interpretations, and photos, and sometimes even share them. You complete the art. Your actions are an integral part, and like the fibers in my twines, you and I will be forever braided together in the larger intertwining network of art and life.

Contributors

—

Nancy Adajania is a Mumbai-based cultural theorist and curator. She was joint artistic director of the 9th Gwangju Biennale and has curated major research-based exhibitions such as *Counter-Canon Counter-Culture: Alternative Histories of Indian Art*, Serendipity Arts Festival, Goa, India.

Sigrid Adriaenssens is a structural engineer and designer studying spatial structures and their behavior across a wide range of scales and materials. Professor of civil and environmental engineering at Princeton University, she directs the Form Finding Lab and teaches courses in structural engineering and the integration of engineering and the arts.

Nora Atkinson is executive director of the Museum of Craft and Design in San Francisco. Prior to that, she spent nearly ten years at the Renwick Gallery of the Smithsonian American Art as the Fleur and Charles Bresler Curator-in-Charge.

William F. Baker is one of the world's leading structural engineers, having designed innovative structures that range in scale from pedestrian bridges to the world's tallest human-made structure, the Burj Khalifa in Dubai. Widely recognized for his collaborations with renowned artists, Baker is the structural and civil engineering partner of Skidmore, Owings & Merrill. He is a fellow of the American Society of Civil Engineers and the Institution of Structural Engineers and was awarded the Fazlur Rahman Khan medal.

Isolde Brielmaier is deputy director of the New Museum, New York; guest curator at the International Center for Photography, New York; and an associate professor of critical studies in the Department of Photography, Imaging and Emerging Media at New York University's Tisch School of the Arts.

Adam Burke, a computational designer at Studio Echelman, specializes in the development of computational techniques for the design of tensile structures. He is a visiting lecturer in design technology at Cornell University, and received a master of science in Architecture Studies from MIT and a bachelor of architecture from Virginia Tech.

Gus Casely-Hayford is the director of V&A East in London and was formerly the director of the Smithsonian National Museum of African Art in Washington, DC. A British cultural historian with Ghanaian roots, he was appointed an officer of the Order of the British Empire (OBE) for his services to arts and culture.

Katy Dammers is the deputy director and chief curator of performance at REDCAT, Los Angeles. She is a writing fellow at the National Center for Choreography, and her essays about dance have been published in *The Brooklyn Rail*, *Movement Research Performance Journal*, *In Dance*, *On the Boards*, and other publications. She previously served as producing director for Lower Manhattan Cultural Council's River to River Festival and producer at Jacob's Pillow Dance Festival. She holds a master of fine arts in Curating from Goldsmiths, University of London, and a bachelor of arts in Art and Archaeology from Princeton University.

Amy Damutz is an independent scholar of public art focused on visual culture and social engagement within the urban landscape. She received a master's degree in Art and Society from the Department of Media and Culture Studies at Utrecht University and a bachelor of arts in Cultural Anthropology from Brown University.

Kasseem Daoud Dean, known professionally as **Swizz Beatz**, is a Grammy-winning producer, rapper, songwriter, and DJ. With his wife, Alicia Keys, Dean founded the Dean Collection, a contemporary family collection and cultural platform that organizes artist support initiatives such as the No Commission art and music festival and TDC 20, both designed to fund artists' practices and projects. Dean sits on the boards of trustees for the Brooklyn Museum and the Serpentine Americas Foundation, London, and is an executive board member of the electronics company Monster.

Danilo Eccher is an international curator and critic and one of Italy's leading contemporary art museum directors. He directed the GAM Galleria Civica d'Arte Moderna e Contemporanea in Turin, the MACRO Museo de Arte Contemporáneo de Roma, and GAM Galleria d'Arte Moderna, Bologna.

Melinda Gates is a philanthropist, businesswoman, and global advocate for women and girls. As co-chair of the Bill & Melinda Gates Foundation, she has been shaping the organization's strategies and overall direction and working with grantees and partners to further the foundation's goal of improving equity in the United States and around the world. In 2015 she founded Pivotal Ventures, a company working to accelerate the pace of social progress in the United States.

Sarah Williams Goldhagen is an author, scholar, and advocate for science-informed, human-centered design. She is widely known for her work as the architecture critic for *The New Republic*. Her book *Welcome to Your World: How the Built Environment Shapes Our Lives* (HarperCollins, 2017) won a Nautilus Book Award. Goldhagen currently sits on the board of the Academy of Neuroscience for Architecture and the advisory committee of the Johns Hopkins International Arts + Mind Lab and previously served as assistant professor in History and Theory at the Harvard Graduate School of Design.

Jared Green, an urban design and landscape architecture critic and journalist, is the author of *Good Energy: Renewable Power and the Design of Everyday Life* (Princeton Architectural Press, 2021) and editor of *Designed for the Future: 80 Practical Ideas for a Sustainable World* (Princeton Architectural Press, 2015).

Ann Hamilton is a visual artist internationally acclaimed for her large-scale multimedia installations, public projects, and performance collaborations. Hamilton has been the recipient of the National Medal of Arts, the Heinz Award, the MacArthur Fellowship, the United States Artists Fellowship, the NEA Visual Arts Fellowship, the Louis Comfort Tiffany Foundation Award, the Skowhegan Medal for Sculpture, and the Guggenheim Memorial Fellowship. She represented the United States in the 48th Venice Biennale and the 21st Bienal de São Paulo.

Andrew Hoyne is a thought leader on place-making strategy. Founding principal of Hoyne, Australia's largest place and property marketing agency, he produces *The Place Economy*, a significant series of resource books that looks at best practices for place making around the world.

Michelle Lim is a curator and writer based in New York and Singapore and an assistant professor in Design and Media at NTU School of Art, Design and Media, Singapore. She holds a PhD in art history from Princeton University and was a curatorial fellow in the Whitney Independent Study Program. She coedited *American Art in Asia: Artistic Praxis and Theoretical Divergence* (Routledge, 2022). She has worked on research and curatorial projects for the Asia Society Museum in New York, the Whitney Museum of American Art, Princeton University Art Museum, Singapore Art Museum, and the National Museum of Singapore.

Kristiina Ljokkoi is a curator of public art at HAM Helsinki Art Museum. She holds a master of fine arts in sculpture from the Academy of Fine Arts, Helsinki, and a master of arts from Aalto University's School of Arts, Design and Architecture.

Kathleen Dean Moore is Distinguished Professor of Philosophy Emerita at Oregon State University, where she directs the Spring Creek Project for Ideas, Nature, and the Written Word. An environmental philosopher and author of multiple books, she coedited the award-winning volume *Moral Ground: Ethical Action for a Planet in Peril* (Trinity University Press, 2010).

Caitlin Mueller, associate professor at MIT, directs the Digital Structures research group and teaches courses in structures and computational design in the Department of Architecture and the Department of Civil and Environmental Engineering. Mueller was awarded the ACADIA Innovative Research Award of Excellence by the Association for Computer Aided Design in Architecture in 2021.

John Ochsendorf, professor of architecture and of civil and environmental engineering at MIT, is widely known for his research on ancient structures and building methods for the benefit of modern construction. Recipient of the Rome Prize and the MacArthur Fellowship, he also served as director of the American Academy in Rome from 2017 to 2020 and has been founding director of MIT's Morningside Academy for Design since 2022. He and his students have contributed to numerous design projects, including the Mapungubwe Interpretive Centre and the 15th Venice Biennale of Architecture.

Laurie Olin is a leading American landscape architect and recipient of the National Medal of Arts. A fellow of the American Academy of Arts and Letters and the American Society of Landscape Architects and founding partner of OLIN, he guided many of its signature projects, including the Washington Monument Grounds in Washington, DC, and the Getty Center in Los Angeles. Other OLIN projects include the award-winning Barnes Foundation in Philadelphia and Apple Park in Cupertino, California. He is an emeritus professor of landscape architecture at the University of Pennsylvania and former chair of the Department of Landscape Architecture at Harvard University.

Robert Pinsky is the first United States Poet Laureate to serve three terms. A professor of English and creative writing at Boston University, Pinsky is the Pulitzer Prize–nominated author of ten books of poetry. He has also published five books of essays and a biography of King David, judged a metaphor contest on *The Colbert Report*, translated Dante's *Inferno*, penned a libretto, released two jazz/poetry albums, written a computer game, and performed with Bruce Springsteen. He earned his PhD in philosophy in 1966 from Stanford University, where he was a Wallace Stegner Fellow in creative writing.

Andrew Sageman-Furnas is an assistant professor in the Department of Mathematics at North Carolina State University. His areas of expertise include discrete differential geometry/topology, discrete integrable systems, mechanics of textiles/polymer networks, and computational fabrication, and he explores the fundamental question "What does it mean for a discrete geometry to be curved?" He received his PhD in mathematical sciences from the University of Göttingen.

Jérôme Sans, cofounder and former director of Palais de Tokyo in Paris, curated the 5th Taipei Biennale; the 8th Lyon Biennale; Li Qing at the Prada Rong Zhai Foundation, Shanghai; and Noor Riyadh 2024. Sans served as the creative director and editor in chief of the French cultural magazine *L'Officiel Art*.

Jenni Sorkin professor of the history of art and architecture at the University of California, Santa Barbara, is widely known for her writing in art criticism and for highlighting work by feminist artists and artists working in fiber and associated crafts. She co-curated the inaugural exhibition at Hauser Wirth & Schimmel in Los Angeles, *Revolution in the Making: Abstract Sculpture by Women Artists, 1947–2016*. She is the author of *Live Form: Women, Ceramics and Community* (University of Chicago Press, 2016) and *Art in California* (Thames & Hudson, 2021).

Brian Stacy, an Arup Fellow and Research Leader, directs Arup's lighting group across ninety offices in thirty-five countries. His award-winning designs integrate daylighting and electric lighting within the fabric of the built environment. He is also known for his pioneering work on media-architecture and fusing digital light and media art in built space.

Gloria Sutton is an associate professor of contemporary art history and new media at Northeastern University and a research affiliate in the Art, Culture, and Technology program at MIT. Her scholarship analyzes the ways durational media have shaped the reception of visual art since the 1960s. Sutton is the author of *The Experience Machine: Stan VanDerBeek's Movie Drome and Expanded Cinema* (MIT, 2015), and her scholarship has appeared in *Afterimage, Art Bulletin, Art in America, Rhizome,* and *Voices of Contemporary Art.* She received her doctorate from the University of California Los Angeles and her research has been supported by the Getty Research Institute, the Terra Foundation, and the Andy Warhol Foundation.

Taru Tappola is an art historian and head of public art at HAM Helsinki Art Museum, leading a team that curates and commissions public artworks for the city. With Pirkko Siitari, she co-curated the inaugural edition of the Helsinki Biennial.

Andrew Wasserman is an art and architectural historian and a former co-chair of Public Art Dialogue. He is the author of *The World Atlas of Public Art* (Yale University Press, 2024), and his writing has appeared in *American Art*, *The Art Bulletin*, *Art Journal*, and the *Journal of Urban History*. He is currently an assistant professor of art and design at Missouri State University.

Notes

Introduction

1 Unless otherwise noted, Janet Echelman's quotes throughout this introduction are from interviews with Gloria Sutton, 2021–2023.
2 Alessandro Beghini, lecture presented at "Building Technology: The Computational Design, Engineering, and Fabrication of Large Scale Sculptural Rope Networks," MIT Center for Art, Science & Technology, Cambridge, MA, January 26, 2023.
3 Mieke Bal, *Endless Andness: The Politics of Abstraction According to Ann Veronica Janssens* (Bloomsbury Academic, 2013), 71.
4 Anni Albers, "The Pliable Plane: Textiles in Architecture," *Perspecta: The Yale Architectural Journal* 4 (1957), abridged and reprinted as "Fabric: The Pliable Plane," *Craft Horizons* 18 (July–August 1958): 15–17.
5 Janet Echelman, email to Gloria Sutton, February 2, 2024.

One — Tracing Lines through Global Art History

1 Janet Echelman's quotes throughout this section are from a January 2023 email exchange with Michelle Lim.
2 Janet Echelman, interview with Nancy Adajania, 2022.

Two — Public Interfacing

1 Janet Echelman, interviews with Amy Damutz, 2021–23.
2 Quoted in Karen Patterson and Lenore Tawney, *Lenore Tawney: Mirror of the Universe* (John Michael Kohler Arts Center, 2019).

Three — Animating Architecture and Landscape

1 Jared Green, "Interview with Janet Echelman," *American Society of Landscape Architects News*, October 2014, https://www.asla.org/ContentDetail.aspx?id=44928.
2 Green, "Interview with Janet Echelman."
3 Oliver Wainwright, "Snapping Point: How the World's Leading Architects Fell under the Instagram Spell," *The Guardian*, November 23, 2018, https://www.theguardian.com/artanddesign/2018/nov/23/snapping-point-how-the-worlds-leading-architects-fell-under-the-instagram-spell.
4 Janet Echelman, interview by Andrew Hoyne, 2023.
5 Kathleen Dean Moore, "Nothing but Net," *Oregon Quarterly* 94, no. 3 (Spring 2015): 18, https://issuu.com/uomarketing-communications/docs/oregon_quarterly_spring_2015.
6 Moore, "Nothing but Net," 19.
7 Moore, "Nothing but Net," 19. See also Janet Echelman, "Imagination Becomes Reality," *Huffington Post*, December 13, 2012, https://www.huffpost.com/entry/imagination-becomes-reality_b_2296215.
8 Eve Blau, "Transparency and the Irreconcilable Contradictions of Modernity," *Praxis: Journal of Writing + Building* 9 (2007): 50.
9 Blau, "Transparency and the Irreconcilable Contradictions of Modernity," 55; Eve Blau, "Tensions in Transparency: Between Information and Experience: The Dialectical Logic of SANAA's Architecture," *Harvard Design Magazine* 29 (Fall/Winter 2008–9): 33.
10 Blau, "Transparency and the Irreconcilable Contradictions of Modernity," 59.

Four — Soft Systems: Nets to Software

1 See D. Veenendaal and P. Block, "An Overview and Comparison of Structural Form Finding Methods for General Networks," *International Journal of Solids and Structures* 49, no. 26 (December 2012): 3741–53, 10.1016/j.ijsolstr.2012.08.008.

Five — Movement, Light, and Sound

1 Janet Echelman, interview with Katy Dammers, 2022.
2 Echelman, interview with Katy Dammers, 2022.
3 Karen Barad, *Meeting the Universe Halfway: Quantum Physics and the Entanglement of Matter and Meaning* (Duke University Press, 2007), 141.
4 Donna Haraway, "Tentacular Thinking: Anthropocene, Capitalocene, Chthulucene," *e-flux Journal*, no. 75 (September 2016): https://www.e-flux.com/journal/75/67125/tentacular-thinking-anthropocene-capitalocene-chthulucene/.

Chronology

Janet Echelman's quotes throughout this chronology are from interviews with Amy Damutz, 2021–2023.

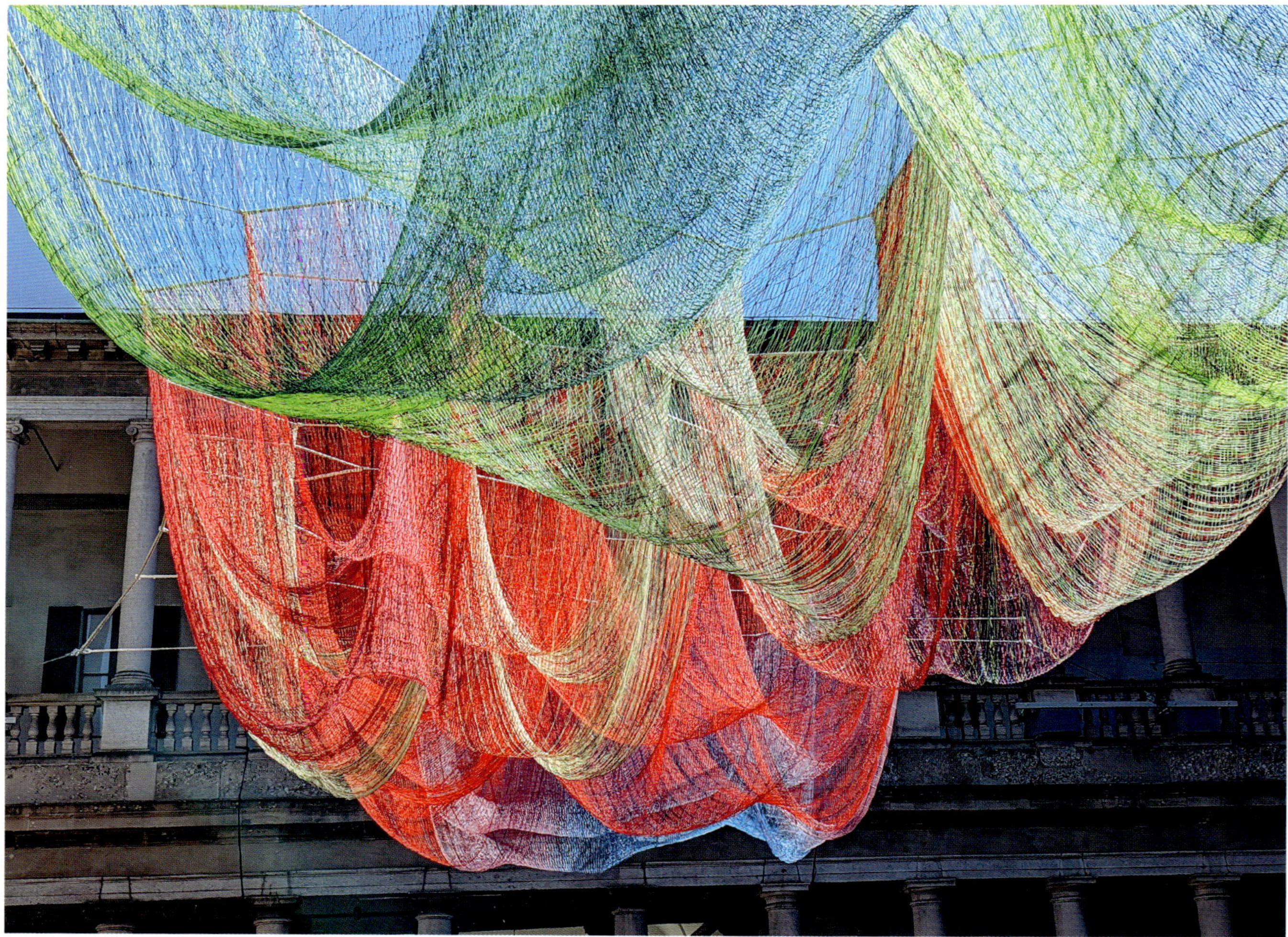

Image Credits

In order of appearance

Front cover: Amy Martz, courtesy Majeed Foundation
Back cover: Joe Fletcher
2–3: Amy Martz, courtesy Majeed Foundation
4–5: Beverly Hills Conference & Visitors Bureau
6: Kohler Co.
8–9: Bruce Petschek
10: Andrew Williamson
11: David Feldman
12–13: Amy Martz, courtesy Majeed Foundation
15 top: Bruce Damonte
15 bottom: João Ferrand
16: Amy Martz, courtesy Majeed Foundation
17 top: *Tampa Bay Times*, 1958
17 middle: Melissa Henry
17 bottom: Otis House
18 top: Bruce Petschek
18 bottom: Nicole Wang
19 top left: Rick Beuttner
19 top right: Angus McIntyre
19 middle top: © The Estate of Eva Hesse, courtesy Hauser & Wirth
19 middle bottom: John A. Ferrari, © The Estate of Eva Hesse, courtesy Hauser & Wirth
19 bottom: Ema Peter
20 top: Studio Echelman
20 bottom left: © The Josef and Anni Albers Foundation / Artists Rights Society (ARS), New York; photo: President and Fellows of Harvard College, BR48.47
20 bottom right: digital model: Studio Echelman; photograph: Melissa Henry
22 top: Jean-Léon Gérôme
22 middle top: U.D.F., Paris
22 bottom: *Jewish Encyclopedia* (1901–1906)
23 top: NOAA
23 bottom: Janet Echelman
25 top: Studio Echelman
25 bottom left: Cecelia Thompson
25 bottom right: Scott Hoffmann
26–27: Joshua Spitzig
29: Payne Wingate and Eric Gavin
30–31: Deepshikha Jain
32 bottom right: Van Gogh Museum, Amsterdam
33 top left: Mary Beth Camp
33 top right: Janet Echelman
34 middle, bottom: Janet Echelman
41 all but bottom left: Janet Echelman
41 bottom left: courtesy Wally and Duke Wright, The Not So Innocents Abroad (thenotsoinnocentsabroad.com)
42: Gianfranco Gorgoni, courtesy Suhrid Sarabhai, courtesy Robert Rauschenberg Foundation Archives, New York
43 top and middle rows: Janet Echelman
43 bottom left: John Emslie, published by James Reynolds
43 bottom right: Studio Echelman
44: Studio Echelman
45 top left, bottom: John Neal
45 top right: Studio Echelman
46–47: Arjun Dogra
48–51: Deepshikha Jain
52 middle left: Daderot, public domain, via Wikimedia Commons
52 middle right: Anónimo Colectivo
52 bottom right: Flickr, jpellgen (@1105_jp)
53: Studio Echelman
54 top: Studio Echelman
54 bottom: Giovanni DeAngelis
55 top: Janet Echelman
55 bottom left: Payne Wingate and Eric Gavin
55 bottom right: Andy Lang
56: Joseph Haubert
57: Andy Lang
58–59: Janet Echelman
60: João Ferrand
61: Clayton Binkley
62: Janet Echelman
63 left: Janet Echelman
63 right: Ilona Gaynor
64–65: Janet Echelman
66: Benutzer: Wolpertinger on WP de, public domain, via Wikimedia Commons
67 top right: Janet Echelman
67 middle right: David Feldman
67 bottom row: João Ferrand
68 top: Enrique Diaz
68 bottom: João Ferrand
69 left: Artwork © 2024 Ruth Asawa Lanier, Inc./Artists Rights Society (ARS), New York. Courtesy David Zwirner
69 right: © Fundación Gego, all rights reserved
71 top: Rep (Boulogne-Billancourt, Hauts-de-Seine), courtesy National Library of France
72–73: Joe Fletcher
74 top, bottom right: Joe Fletcher
74 bottom left: Janet Echelman
75: Studio Echelman
76 top left: Bruce Heavin
76 top right: Joe Fletcher
76 bottom: Janet Echelman
77: Janet Echelman
78–79: Joe Fletcher
80: Mike Cairns
81: Infinite Impact
82–83: Studio Echelman
84–86: Infinite Impact
87: Ryan Ransom
88–89: Infinite Impact
90 top left: John McGrall, courtesy Agnes Denes and Leslie Tonkonow Artworks + Projects
90 middle left: The Estate of Ana Mendieta
90 middle right: Retis, CC BY 2.0
90 bottom: Colleen Chartier
91: Janet Echelman
92–93: Ema Peter
94: Simon J Nicol
95 bottom: Janet Echelman
96 middle left: Rogier van der Heide (2019)
96 middle right, right: Janet Echelman
97: Nicki Houghton
98 top: URA Singapore
98 bottom: Melissa Henry
99: Martine Doyon
100 top: Alleyway Gwanggyo
100 bottom: Janet Echelman
101: Peter Vanderwarker
102: Mark Davis
103 top: Janet Echelman
103 bottom: Kaleidoscale Marcom
104: Marinco Kojdanovski
105: Ben Visbeek
106 top: Alkan Yilmaz
106 bottom: Roser Brothers
107 left: formTL Berlin
107 right: Bundesarchiv, Bild 119-1426 / CC BY-SA 3.0, CC BY-SA 3.0 DE
108–9: Roser Brothers
110: Jan Saurer
111 top, middle: Roser Brothers
111 bottom: Antonia Eisert
112–13: Andreas Keller
114: White House official photo
115: Julie Nyman
116 top: NOAA
116 middle left, bottom row: Studio Echelman
116 middle right: Studio Echelman and Ege Carpets
117: Studio Echelman
118–20: Smithsonian Institution
121: Bruce Petschek
122–23: Smithsonian Institution
124–29: Ema Peter
130 top: Janet Echelman
130 bottom row: Ema Peter
132–35: Ema Peter
136: Thomas Kimmell
137: Ania Bui
138 top: City of Perth, Australia
138 bottom: Solana Light Festival
139: Gabriel Berber
140–41: João Ferrand
142: Studio Echelman
143: João Ferrand
144–45: Vienna City Copter Cam
146: Camila Vieira
147 top: Vienna City Copter Cam
147 bottom: Lorenz Seidler
148: Verko Ignjatovic
149 top: Sky Italia
149 bottom: Janet Echelman
150: Hendrik Zeitler
151: Jessica Rundgren
152: Ema Peter
153: John Sage
154–55: Sean Airhart
156 top row, middle: Studio Echelman
156 bottom: Clayton Binkley, Arup Engineers
157: Janet Echelman
158–60: Ema Peter
161: Sean Airhart
162–63: Jeff Fusco
164 top: Melvin Epps
164 bottom: Jeff Fusco
166 top, middle: OLIN
166 bottom: Koolfog
167: Sahar Coston-Hardy
168: Sean O'Neill
170–71: Janet Echelman
172 top: Studio Echelman and OLIN
172 bottom row left, middle: Daniel Zeese
172 bottom right: Andrew K. Sachs
173 top: Rob Reid
173 bottom: William Short Photography
174: Jill Richards
177: Studio Echelman
178: Ema Peter
179: Janet Echelman
180: David Feldman
182 top left: Clayton Binkley
182 top right: Julie Palermo
182 bottom row: Ian Foe
183: Brian Adams
184: Amy Martz, courtesy Majeed Foundation
185 top: Visit St. Pete–Clearwater
185 bottom: Amy Martz, courtesy Majeed Foundation
187: Melissa Henry
188 top left: Janet Echelman
188 top middle, top right: Studio Echelman
188 left column: Peter Vanderwarker
188 bottom right: Bruce Petschek
189 top: Above Summit
189 bottom: Melissa Henry

189 bottom: Melissa Henry
190–91: Peter Vanderwarker
192–95: Melissa Henry
197: Julie Burns Campbell
198–99: Studio Echelman
200–1: Benny Chan
202 top: Curt Smith
202 middle: Royal Navy official photographer, public domain, via Wikimedia Commons
203 top: Sigrid Adriaenssens
202 bottom: Form Finding Lab
203 middle left: Marutoku Nori
203 middle right: Thomas Ledl, CC BY-SA 4.0
203 bottom: Desconegut - AA.VV., Gaudí 2002, Miscel·lània, Ed. Planeta, Barcelona (2002)
204 top: Christopher Sessums
204 middle: Janet Echelman
204 bottom: San Francisco History Center, San Francisco Public Library
205 top left: Hans A. Rosbach, CC BY-SA 3.0
205 top right: Janet Echelman
205 bottom left: Thomas Taylor
205 bottom right: saai | Archiv für Architektur und Ingenieurbau, Karlsruher Institut für Technologie, Werkarchiv Frei Otto
206 top: *Ladies' Home Journal* (1889), 463
206 middle top: Library of Congress Online Catalog (1,594,946)
206 middle, middle bottom: Sigrid Adriaenssens
206 bottom: Hugh McCormick Smith
207: Janet Echelman
208 top: Laura Loveday
208 bottom row: Sigrid Adriaenssens
209: Stuttgart Ballet
210: Studio Echelman
212: João Ferrand
213 top, middle: Peter Heppel Associates
213 bottom: AFA Engineers, Portugal
214 top: Peter Heppel Associates
214 bottom: Studio Echelman
215 top: Bruce Petschek
215 middle, bottom: Studio Echelman
216 left: Studio Echelman
216 right: Infinite Impact
217: Studio Echelman: Adam Burke and Daniel Smith
218: Studio Echelman: Daniel Smith
219: Janet Echelman
220 left: Luciana Haill
220 right: Nicole Wang
221: Janet Echelman
222 top row, middle left, bottom right: Studio Echelman
222 middle right: David Evans and Associates
222 bottom left: Alessandro Beghini and Nicole Wang, SOM
223 top: Nicole Wang
223 bottom: Arts Advance
224–25: Janet Echelman
226–27: Marie-Andrée Lemire
228–29: Stuttgart Ballet
231: Marie-Andrée Lemire
232: Janet Echelman
233: Janet Echelman
234–35: Marie-Andrée Lemire
236: Steven Taylor
237: Janet Echelman
238–40: Kohler Co.
241–43: Janet Echelman
245: Ema Peter
246–47: Bruce Petschek
249: Juho Ruohola
250: Tim Bird
252: Janet Echelman
254–55: Janet Echelman
256–57: Ema Peter
258: James Duncan Davidson
260: Bret Hartman
261: Ema Peter
262 top left: Janet Echelman
262 top middle: Arup Engineers
262 top right, middle left: Studio Echelman
262 bottom left, bottom right: Ema Peter
263–65: Ema Peter
266: Christina Lazar-Schuler
267, fig. 3: Janet Echelman
268, fig. 5: Mary Beth Camp
268, figs. 6, 9: Janet Echelman
268, fig. 7: Janet Echelman, Tampa Museum of Art
268, fig. 8: Janet Echelman, National Institute of Design
269, figs. 11, 13: Bruce Petschek
269, figs. 12, 14: Janet Echelman
270, fig. 15: Studio Echelman
270, fig. 16: João Ferrand
270, fig. 17: Museum of Arts and Design, New York
270, fig. 18: Christina Lazar-Schuler
271, fig. 19: Studio Echelman
271, figs. 20, 21: Bruce Petschek
271, fig. 22: *Architectural Digest*
272, fig. 23: *O, The Oprah Magazine*
272, figs. 24, 26: Studio Echelman
272, fig. 25: Richard Greenhouse
273, fig. 27: Bruce Petschek
273, fig. 28: Studio Echelman
273, fig. 29: Cheongju Craft Biennale
273, fig. 30: courtesy Caitlin Mueller
273, fig. 31: Claire D'Alba
274, fig. 32: Matthew Echelman
274, figs. 33, 35: Studio Echelman
274, fig. 34: SOM Foundation
274, fig. 36: Amy Martz
275, fig. 37: Alleyway Gwanggyo
275, fig. 38: Sigrid Adriaenssens
275, fig. 39: MIT
275, fig. 40: Lillian Echelman Feldman
276, figs. 41, 44, 45: Studio Echelman
276, figs. 42, 43: Kim Leeson
277: Marie-Andrée Lemire
285: Janet Echelman
286: Janet Echelman

Published by
Princeton Architectural Press
A division of Chronicle Books LLC
70 West 36th Street
New York, NY 10018
papress.com

Printed and bound in China
28 27 26 25   4 3 2 1 First edition

Editor: Jennifer N. Thompson
Image sequencing and cover design: Studio Echelman
Designer: PA Press

Library of Congress Cataloging-in-Publication Data
Names: Sutton, Gloria, editor.
Title: Radical softness : the responsive art of Janet Echelman / edited by Gloria Sutton.
Description: First edition. | New York : Princeton Architectural Press, [2025] | Includes bibliographical references and index. | Summary: "A visual compendium of Janet Echelman's artistic oeuvre, including detailed project documentation, archival source materials, and an illustrated chronology"—Provided by publisher.
Identifiers: LCCN 2024036119 | ISBN 9781797228679 (hardcover) | ISBN 9781797228686 (ebook)
Subjects: LCSH: Echelman, Janet, 1966—Criticism and interpretation.
Classification: LCC N6537.E375 R33 2025 | DDC 730.92—dc23/eng/20240821
LC record available at https://lccn.loc.gov/2024036119

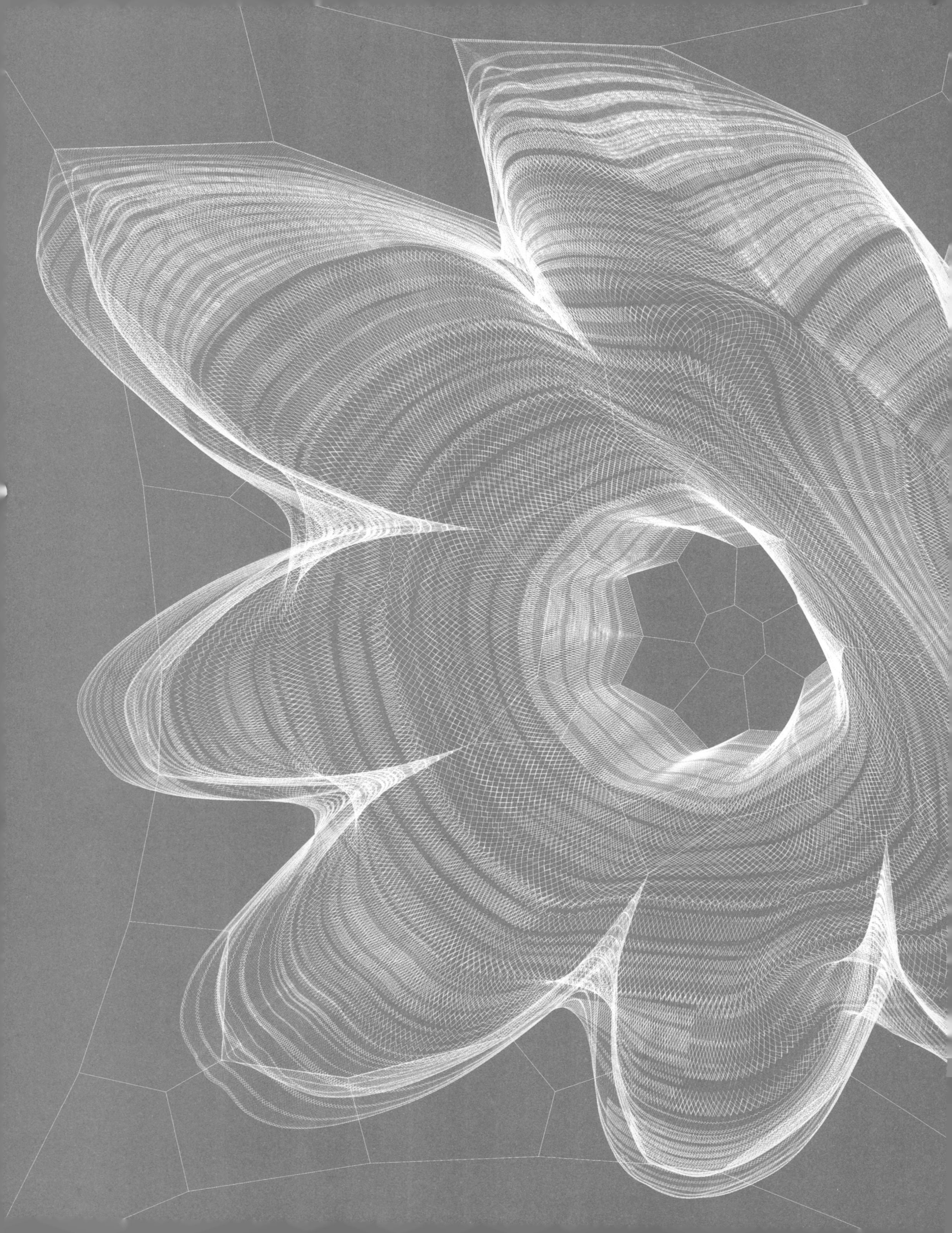